# NAZISM 1919–1945

## VOLUME 4
## THE GERMAN HOME FRONT IN WORLD WAR II

**EXETER STUDIES IN HISTORY**

*General Editors:* Jonathan Barry, Tim Rees and T.P. Wiseman

Also by Jeremy Noakes
and published by University of Exeter Press

*Nazism 1919–1945*, Volume 1: *The Rise to Power 1919–1934*
*Nazism 1919–1945*, Volume 2: *State, Economy and Society 1933–1939*
*Nazism 1919–1945*, Volume 3: *Foreign Policy, War and Racial Extermination*

*The Civilian in War:*
*The Home Front in Europe, Japan and the USA in World War II*

*Government, Party and People in Nazi Germany*

*Intelligence and International Relations 1900–1945*
(edited with Christopher Andrew)

# NAZISM 1919–1945

## VOLUME 4
## THE GERMAN HOME FRONT
## IN WORLD WAR II
A Documentary Reader

EDITED BY
JEREMY NOAKES

UNIVERSITY
*of*
EXETER
PRESS

First published in 1998 by
University of Exeter Press
Reed Hall, Streatham Drive
Exeter, Devon EX4 4QR
UK

**British Library Cataloguing in Publication Data**
A catalogue record of this book is available
from the British Library


ISBN 0 85989 311 1

Typeset in Times New Roman
by Exe Valley Dataset Ltd, Exeter

Printed in Great Britain
by Short Run Press Ltd, Exeter

# Contents

## Editorial Note

*The German Home Front in World War II* is Volume 4 in the series *Nazism 1919–1945: A Documentary Reader*. To maintain continuity with the previous three volumes, the chapter and document numbering follows on from Volume 3. All editorial comments within documents are placed in square brackets.

The reader will find a more detailed description of the chapter contents to this volume on pp. vi–viii.

# Chapter Outline

# *Preface*

This final volume of a four-volume edition of documents covering the history of Nazism and the 'Third Reich' bears very little resemblance to the relevant chapters of the volume *Documents on Nazism 1919–1945* (London: Cape, 1974) from which this edition originated. In this new volume I have tried to provide as comprehensive a coverage of wartime Germany as possible. However, this ambition has been made more difficult by the relative paucity of research on the subject. For, while the Resistance has been very thoroughly explored and documented, many other aspects of the German Home Front have been relatively neglected. For example, there is still no major study of the effects of the Allied air raids on the German population and the regime's response to them. This has meant that, even more than in the previous volumes, many of the topics covered have required extensive archival research, with the result that many of the documents in this volume have never been published before. At the same time, in certain areas I have benefited very greatly from the work of other scholars and have tried to acknowledge my intellectual debts in footnotes where I felt it appropriate.

Some of the most stimulating research on the Home Front has focused on the question of how far the war influenced social and economic change in Germany by looking forward into the post-war period. My approach has been simply to document politics and life in wartime Germany. In the process I have tried to illuminate the nature of Nazism and the regime it established in the context of a war to which it had been geared from the start. War was an environment in which it felt most at home and in which its essential features became most clearly exposed; the most extreme manifestations of this have already been dealt with in Volume 3.

I am very grateful to Dr Neil Gregor for taking on the laborious task of reading and commenting on the entire manuscript, to Professor Ian Kershaw for reading a substantial chunk of it and to Professor David

Welch for reading the chapter on propaganda. Needless to say I remain responsible for any errors.

I am also most grateful to Simon Baker, Anna Henderson and Richard Willis of the University of Exeter Press for putting up with what must have appeared as my insatiable demands in a particularly complex publishing process and to Jeffrey Meriwether for indexing the book.

JEREMY NOAKES
Exeter, January 1998

# ACKNOWLEDGEMENTS

I am very grateful to the following for permission to reprint excerpts from works for which they hold the copyright:

**Doubleday** (a division of Bantam Doubleday Dell Publishing Group, Inc., New York), for *The Goebbels Diaries: 1942–1943, by Goebbels,* copyright 1948 The Fireside Press, Inc.

**Leicester University Press** (an imprint of Cassell, London), for *Hidden Holocaust? Gay and Lesbian Persecution in Germany 1933–1945* by Günter Grau (1995).

**Oxford University Press** for *A German of the Resistance: The Last Letters of Count Helmut James von Moltke* (1947) and *Rituals of Retribution: Capital Punishment in Germany 1600–1987* by Richard J. Evans (1996).

**Peter Owen Ltd,** London, for *On the Other Side: To My Children from Germany 1940–45* by Mathilde Wolf-Mönckeberg (1979).

**Westview Press** (a division of HarperCollins Publishers, Boulder, Colorado), for a short extract from *The Buchenwald Report* by David Hackett (1997).

**Weidenfeld and Nicholson,** London, for *The Bormann Letters*, edited by H.R. Trevor-Roper (1954).

I am also grateful to Professor Geoffrey Pridham for the use of documents 1340, 1344, 1345 and 1363 from his section 'Opposition' in the original, jointly edited volume.

# *Abbreviations*

| | |
|---|---|
| ANSt | Arbeitsgemeinschaft nationalsozialistischer Studentinnen |
| AWI | Arbeitswissenschaftliches Institut |
| BAB | Bundesarchiv Berlin |
| BA/MA | Bundesarchiv/Militärarchiv |
| BdM | Bund deutscher Mädel |
| BU | Bleib übrig |
| DAF | Deutsche Arbeitsfront |
| DEST | Deutsche Erd-und Steinwerke GmbH |
| DGT | Deutscher Gemeindetag |
| DJ | Deutsches Jungvolk |
| DNB | Deutsches Nachrichtenbüro |
| DWB | Deutsche Wirtschaftsbetriebe |
| DFW | Deutsches Frauenwerk |
| FHQ | Führerhauptquartier |
| GBK | Generalbevollmächtigter für die Kriegswirtschaft |
| GBV | Generalbevollmächtigter für die Reichsverwaltung |
| GBW | Generalbevollmächtigter für die Wirtschaft |
| GPU | Soviet Secret Police |
| HJ | Hitlerjugend |
| HStAS | Hauptstaatsarchiv Stuttgart |
| HStW | Hauptstaatsarchiv Wiesbaden |
| HWaA | Heereswaffenamt |
| IMT | International Military Tribunal |
| IWM | Imperial War Museum |
| JM | Jungmädel |
| JV | Jungvolk |
| KdF | Kraft durch Freude |
| KLV | Kinderlandverschickung |
| KPD | Kommunistische Partei Deutschlands |
| KZ | Konzentrationslager |
| LAB | Landesarchiv Berlin |
| Lebed | Gesellschaft für Textil und Lederverarbeitung |
| LSO | Leitsätze für die Selbstkostenabrechnung bei öffentlichen Aufträgen |

| | |
|---|---|
| ND | Nuremburg Document |
| NS/n.s. | nationalsozialistische |
| NSDAP | Nationalsozialistische Deutsche Arbeiterpartei |
| NSF | Nationalsozialistische Fraunschaft |
| NSFK | Nationalsozialistische Fliegerkorps |
| NSKK | Nationalsozialistische Kraftfahrerkorps |
| NSKOV | Nationalsozialistiche Kriegsopferversorgung |
| NSLB | Nationalsozialistische Lehrerbund |
| NSV | Nationalsozialistische Volkswohlfahrt |
| OKH | Oberkommando des Heeres |
| OKW | Oberkommando der Wehrmacht |
| OT | Organisation Todt |
| PO | Politische Organisation [of the NSDAP] |
| R&S | Rasse und Siedlung |
| RAD | Reichsarbeitsdienst |
| RAM | Reichsarbeitsministerium |
| RFSS | Reichsführer SS |
| RGBl | Reichsgesetzblatt |
| RJM | Reichsflustizministerium |
| RSHA | Reichssicherheitshauptamt |
| ROL | Reichsorganisationsleitung [of the NSDAP] |
| RVK | Reichsverteidigungskommissar |
| SA | Sturmabteilung |
| StAB | Staatsarchiv Bamberg |
| StAL | Staatsarchiv Ludwigsburg |
| SD | Sicherheitsdienst |
| SHD | Sicherheits-und Hilfsdienst |
| SPD | Sozialdemokratische Partei Deutschlands |
| SS | Schutzstaffel |
| UK | unabkömmlich |
| WaA | Waffenamt [see HwaA] |
| WHW | Winterhilfswerk |
| (W)WiRüA | Wirtschafts-und Rüstungsamt [of OKW] |
| WVHA | Wirtschafts-und Verwaltungshauptamt [of the SS] |

# CHAPTER 40

# *Government*

## (i) Introduction

Between 1933 and 1939, the Nazi state had been marked by a number of trends which were to accelerate during the course of the war. First, there occurred a fragmentation of government which resulted from Hitler's tendency to create new offices and agencies without establishing clear lines of demarcation of responsibility with existing government departments. The result was a continual struggle for dominance over spheres of responsibility. These struggles were sustained and exacerbated by two other pre-war trends. There was an increasing tendency for power to reside in individuals rather than in formally established offices. This was a reflection of Hitler's charismatic style of leadership in which power and authority were concentrated in the leader or Führer and were then delegated by him to individual followers who regarded themselves as his personal delegates rather than members of a corporate government whose powers and responsibilities were defined by law and by established and codified bureaucratic procedure.

Furthermore, the pre-war period was marked by Hitler's increasing unwillingness to become involved in regular government activity. He preferred to leave it to his subordinates to fight among themselves, intervening only occasionally when he felt an important issue was at stake and even then not always decisively. This behaviour was in part a reflection of Hitler's own personality, his distaste for regular office work. But it was also a product of his characteristic form of rule in that he was concerned not to weaken his charisma, the special 'magic' of his authority, by becoming too closely associated with particular decisions or policies which might prove unpopular, controversial or ineffective. He also wished to avoid engaging in discussions or debates with his subordinates in which he might find his arguments being openly challenged or contradicted. It was for this reason that he had allowed the cabinet to lapse by 1938. For while he was occasionally prepared to consider counter-arguments in private, he was determined to avoid any possibility of individual or corporate challenge to his authority. He was acutely aware of the need to preserve the image of the godlike Führer standing above mundane politics.

Finally, the pre-war period was marked by a permanent state of tension and conflict between the various Nazi agencies and those of the state. The most striking example of this was the way in which the SS had taken over control of the police from the Interior Ministry, culminating in the appointment of its leader, Heinrich Himmler, as Chief of the German Police in 1936. However, in virtually every sphere—in national, regional and local government, in labour, welfare, youth policies etc.— Nazi agencies were endeavouring to establish control over policy, leaving the state authorities as mere administrative lackeys of the Nazi movement. At the same time, the Nazi movement was by no means united and its various agencies—the Political Organisation (PO), the SS, the Labour Front (DAF), the welfare organization (NSV), Hitler Youth etc.—vied with each other for power and responsibilities. The war was greatly to accelerate these trends.

## (ii) Preparations for War[1]

The First World War had shown that to wage war successfully it was vital fully to mobilize a nation's economic and social resources and, by 1939, Germany was far better prepared for war than it had been in 1914. However, this success had been achieved in spite rather than because of the existing structures of government of the Third Reich. The years 1933–9 had seen a series of largely unsuccessful attempts to establish institutional mechanisms for coordinating the mobilization of the civilian sector for war. Initially, the War Ministry was responsible for the supervision of civilian war preparations. However, on 21 May 1935, a secret Reich Defence Law appointed the acting Reich Economics Minister and President of the Reichsbank, Hjalmar Schacht, as Plenipotentiary for the War Economy (GBK). But the objective behind this law, namely to institute effective coordination in the economic field, was vitiated by a number of factors.

In the first place, the creation of the Four-Year Plan organization under Hermann Göring in October 1936 initiated a rivalry between it and the Economics Ministry, which continued even after the resignation

---

[1] For more on this see below, pp. 185ff.

of Schacht in November 1937 and his replacement by the more pliable Walther Funk. Secondly, further conflict and confusion was caused by the decision to divide the responsibility for economic mobilization between the GBK, who was made responsible for those firms vital to the war effort and for sustaining civilian existence (*c.*25,000), and the Wehrmacht, which retained responsibility for the armaments plants as such (*c.*2,800, by 1940 5,425). In the event, on the one hand, the GBK lacked the resources or the commitment to carry out his responsibilities effectively, whereas, on the other, rivalry between the GBK and the Wehrmacht hampered the gearing of the economy to war. While Hermann Göring, the head of the Four-Year Plan, and Walther Funk, the Economics Minister, managed to cooperate in resisting attempts by the Wehrmacht to extend its control, the division of responsibilities between Göring and Funk remained unclear and the key question of who was to have overall authority to establish priorities in the use of resources remained unresolved.

On 4 September 1938, a renewed attempt was made to coordinate the economic preparations for war by issuing a second Reich Defence Law, which established a new Reich Defence Council and a Reich Defence Committee. It also appointed the Reich Interior Minister, Wilhelm Frick as General Plenipotentiary for the Administration (GBV) in a further attempt at more effective government coordination. The initiative came from General Keitel, head of the new Wehrmacht High Command (OKW). Following the establishment of OKW after the Blomberg–Fritsch crisis of February 1938, Keitel pressed for a reformulation of the Reich Defence Law of 1935 both to reflect the new situation and to improve the coordination of the various agencies involved in the war preparations.[2] However, like its predecessor of 1935, this attempt at co-ordination proved largely abortive and for similar reasons.

Firstly, it did not reflect the real balance of power within the economic sphere of government. For, although Funk, as Reich Economics Minister, was confirmed as Plenipotentiary for the Economy (GBW), in practice, Göring as Plenipotentiary for the Four-Year Plan carried far more weight and could already issue instructions to Government departments in the areas covered by the Four-Year Plan. At the first meeting of the new Reich Defence Council on 18 November 1938 Göring announced that it was his responsibility to ensure the integration of the civilian economy into the preparations for war.

Secondly, the division remained between the armaments sector of industry, for which the Wehrmacht Economics Office was responsible,

---

[2] On the Blomberg–Fritsch crisis and the creation of OKW, see Vol. 3, doc. 509.

on the one hand, and the rest of the economy vital to the war effort, on the other. In fact, the Reich Defence Council met only twice and then in formal sessions to hear speeches by Göring and the Reich Interior Minister, Wilhelm Frick. As with its predecessor, the 1938 Reich Defence Law did provide a legal framework for meetings of lower-level officials from the various government departments involved. Nevertheless, the key problem of a lack of coordination between competing centres of authority remained. And the position was made worse by the fact that there was competition not only *between* the Wehrmacht and the civilian authorities, but also *within* each of the two spheres. Within the Wehrmacht competition occurred between the Wehrmacht Economics and Armaments Office and the three armed forces, and also between the three armed forces themselves; within the civilian sector it occurred between the office of the Four-Year Plan and the office of the GBW. With the decline of the cabinet during the 1930s leading to its final demise in 1938 and with the failure of the Reich Defence Council, there was no coordinating body to mediate and reconcile the conflicting priorities. Moreover, far from resolving issues and setting clear priorities through dictatorial intervention, Hitler simply added to the problems by urging each of the commanders of the armed services to expand his forces faster and further, threatening to remove responsibilities from those who failed to meet increasingly unrealistic targets. As a result, German mobilization for war became a struggle for the available resources of raw materials, plant capacity and manpower.

### (iii)  The Ministerial Council for the Defence of the Reich

On the eve of war, this situation prompted Göring to press for the creation of a body with greater powers and in which his own position would be strengthened. Hitler, who was anxious to free himself as far as possible from the burdens of routine domestic government in order to focus his energies on the conduct of the war, was happy to hand over the coordinating role in domestic affairs to Göring, from whom he could anticipate a combination of ruthlessness and drive. On 30 August 1939 Hitler signed the following Decree concerning the Creation of a Ministerial Council for the Defence of the Reich, which, despite its importance, had typically been formulated by Hans-Heinrich Lammers, the head of the Reich Chancellery, at the last moment and without any consultation with the Government departments affected by it:

**919**    During the period of current international tension I decree the following for the coordination of the administration and the economy.

I. (1) A 'Ministerial Council for the Defence of the Reich' drawn from the Reich Defence Council is to be established as a permanent committee.
(2) The following will be permanent members of the Ministerial Council for the Defence of the Reich:

Field Marshal Göring as Chairman
The Führer's Deputy [Hess]
The Plenipotentiary for the Reich Administration (GBV) [Frick]
The Plenipotentiary for the Economy (GBW) [Funk]
The Reich Minister and Head of the Reich Chancellery [Lammers]
The Head of the High Command of the Wehrmacht [Keitel]

(3) The Chairman can coopt other members of the Reich Defence Council as well as other persons.

II. The Ministerial Council for the Defence of the Reich can issue decrees with the force of law in the event that I do not order the passage of a law by the Reich Government or the Reichstag.

III. The powers of Field-Marshal Göring deriving from the Decree to Implement the Four-Year Plan of 18 October 1936 remain intact, in particular his right to issue directives.

IV. The Reich Minister and Head of the Reich Chancellery is responsible for the administrative arrangements of the Ministerial Council for the Defence of the Reich.

V. I will determine the moment when this decree becomes ineffective.

————

This decree marked a significant increase in Göring's authority. Whereas he had only been deputy (to Hitler) head of the Reich Defence Council, he was head of the new Ministerial Council. Secondly, his authority was now extended beyond the economy to the civil administration. Under Article III the powers of the Council were potentially far-reaching. However, Hitler had built in a number of safeguards to ensure that the new body did not exceed its responsibilities (II, V). Moreover, the fact that Lammers handled the day-to-day business of the Council ensured that Hitler was kept informed of what was going on. Indeed, Lammers sought his approval for all decrees issued by the Council. And, on occasion, Hitler exercised his power of veto, notably in connection with a tax proposal from the Finance Ministry which had already been approved by the Council after much discussion.

Apart from Göring and the two General Plenipotentiaries, with one exception (the Reich Agriculture Minister, Darré) the first session of the Council was attended exclusively by state secretaries. This shows that it was not intended to be a proper War Cabinet, but rather a body dealing primarily with economic and administrative matters connected with the war. In fact, however, pressure soon built up from those ministers and other leading figures who were not members of the Council to be invited to its meetings. The following document—a minute by Friedrich Kritzinger, the State Secretary of the Reich Chancellery, for Lammers—is an illustration of this development and of the problematic character of this new body:

### 920 *Minute*
*Berlin, 11.10.39*

*Reichshauptsamtsleiter* Mahrenbach (DAF) raised the following point on the telephone today:

Dr Ley had heard that there was going to be a session of the Ministerial Council for the Defence of the Reich during the next few days at which the question of food supplies was going to be discussed. Dr Ley requested an invitation to this session. I replied to Herr Mahrenbach that I knew nothing of such a session of the Ministerial Council. Field-Marshal Göring held frequent meetings with smaller groups. The invitations to these meetings were not issued by us. I suggested that he should get in touch with Herr Gritzbach[3] concerning the matter. Herr Mahrenbach said that he intended to do that and remarked that Dr Ley was anxious to be invited to the sessions of the Ministerial Council not only in connection with this case but generally. I replied that up to now Field-Marshal Göring has personally decided who should be invited to each particular session. I could not, therefore, issue an invitation from here on my own initiative. However, if I was instructed to issue invitations to a session I would pass on Dr Ley's request.

The effect of this was to nullify the original object of the creation of the Ministerial Council, namely to simplify and speed up the process of legislation by reducing the numbers of those involved. Moreover, the Council itself had expanded in terms of both numbers and the political weight of those attending. The session on 15 November was attended by over thirty people including Goebbels, Himmler, Ley, Darré, the Finance Minister Schwerin von Krosigk, and Bouhler, the head of Hitler's personal Chancellery. And although its business remained overwhelmingly focused on domestic matters, it was beginning to look like a real cabinet.

This session of the Council proved to be the last. A further one planned for 1 February 1940 was cancelled at short notice. The effective winding up of the Ministerial Council for the Defence of the Reich as a forum for discussion and decision-making was probably due to Hitler's intervention, reflecting his concern that it should not become a sub-

---

[3] Erich Gritzbach, a senior aide of Göring's.

stitute cabinet under Göring's control. However, Göring himself also appears to have lost interest in it after he acquired the right to append his signature to all Government and Reichstag laws directly after Hitler's, thereby documenting his position as second man in the state.

Meanwhile, Göring had also acted to strengthen his position within the economy. On 7 December 1939 he had issued an unpublished decree which transferred the GBW's function of directing the War Economy to himself as Plenipotentiary for the Four-Year Plan. Although Funk retained the title of GBW, in fact his role was now restricted to the conventional activities of Economics Minister and President of the Reichsbank. The State Secretaries within the various Government departments most involved in the War Economy—Friedrich Syrup (Labour), Friedrich Landfried (Economics), Wilhelm Kleinmann (Transport), together with Paul (Pilli) Körner and Werner Neumann from the Four-Year Plan office, now formed a kind of ad hoc and informal cabinet committee under the auspices of Göring's Four-Year Plan organization.

The title of Ministerial Council for the Defence of the Reich continued to be used as the authority for various decrees primarily affecting economic and administrative matters, which were dealt with through the normal 'circulation process'.[4] Also the OKW, the GBV and the GBW (with Göring rather than Funk taking the decisions) continued to work together on matters of mutual concern, issuing decrees in these spheres and forming a so-called Group of Three (*Dreierkollegium*).

## (iv) Hitler's Rule

The lesson of the experience of the two Reich Defence Laws and the creation of the Ministerial Council for the Defence of the Reich was that attempts to introduce effective institutional mechanisms for the rationalization and coordination of legislation and administration faced insuperable obstacles under the political system of the Third Reich. These obstacles derived above all from the fact that it was a Führer state in which the Führer insisted on retaining his right to act as the sole effective coordinating instance and acted to prevent the emergence of alternative centres or thwarted them if they threatened to become too powerful. At the same time, however, through his very mode of government he was incapable of performing the coordinating role effectively himself. During the first two and a half years of the war, Lammers made

---

[4] See Vol. 2, doc. 146.

repeated attempts to reactivate the cabinet, but they were all frustrated by Hitler, as Lammers informed Allied interrogators after the war:

**921**   The last session of the Reich Cabinet was in November 1937. However, in 1938, at the beginning of February, there was a so-called ministerial meeting for the purpose of receiving information, at which the Führer announced the changes in the Reich Government which had been made at that time with Herr von Blomberg and Herr von Neurath. The last Cabinet meeting at which serious discussion occurred, in fact concerning the draft Penal Code, took place in November 1937 . . .

From then on, I made repeated attempts to bring about a concentration of the Reich Cabinet or, to put it another way, to reactivate it. The Führer consistently declined to do so. I prepared a draft [in January 1942], in fact a draft edict, according to which the ministers should at least meet together for discussions once or twice a month under the chairmanship of Reich Marshal Göring, or, if he was unable to attend, then formally under my direction. And the ministers should come together in these sessions and there should be informative talks. But the Führer rejected that idea. However, the ministers certainly felt a pressing desire to meet together. My further suggestion was that the ministers should meet once or twice a month socially for a beer evening so that we could come together and have a heart to heart. But the Führer replied to me: 'Herr Lammers that is not up to you, it is up to me. I'll do it the next time I come to Berlin . . .'.

The ministers were basically nothing more than the most senior administrative bosses of their departments and they could no longer act as political ministers in the Reich Cabinet of the Reich Government . . . no more meetings took place; discussions were even forbidden.

With regard to my attempts to reactivate the Reich Government by holding various sessions, the Führer told me that they should not take place; a mood might be created which he would find unpleasant. He did not use the words 'defeatists' club' to me. But I heard from Reichsleiter Bormann that he said that the ministers should not come together; it might turn into a defeatists' club.

The problem was that Hitler himself was not prepared to fill the vaccuum left by the lack of any coordinating body. While it is true that, during the war years, Hitler was primarily preoccupied with the day-to-day conduct of military operations, it was not the case, as has sometimes been suggested, that he opted out of the domestic side of the war and handed the home front over to Bormann, Goebbels, Speer and Himmler. In the most substantial study of the German government in wartime Dieter Rebentisch concluded that: 'contrary to other historical interpretations, Hitler did in fact determine the main lines of policy in the sense that the most important departmental matters remained within the context laid down by Hitler and changes of course against his explicitly expressed wish and without his specific agreement were out of the question.[5] In particular, Hitler maintained a close personal supervision of armaments policy and matters affecting morale, including propaganda, the allocation of food supplies, wages, prices, taxation and female labour. The following unpublished Führer Edict to Secure Price Stability, dated 14 March 1942, is a case in point:

**922** Price stability is the basis of a stable currency and one of the most important prerequisites for securing armaments production and the nation's fighting ability.

I therefore decree that the strictest criteria are to be laid down for the granting of price increases and that my decision should be sought before any price increases of fundamental importance. The following procedure is to be carried out:

Requests for price increases are to be put to the Delegate for the Four-Year Plan [Göring] by the Reich Price Commissioner [Popitz]. If he [Göring] does not reject such an application himself, it must be sent to me for a decision and this must be done via the Reich Minister and head of the Reich Chancellery [Lammers].

However, as Rebentisch himself admits, Hitler's decisions were frequently arbitrary, contradictory and followed no coherent plan reflecting his style of autocratic government. An interesting description of Hitler's style of government was provided by Hitler's press chief, Otto Dietrich in his post-war memoirs. Dietrich was a member of Hitler's immediate entourage:

**923** Hitler had a bohemian nature. He was very much a man of moods, who allowed himself to be governed almost entirely by emotional considerations. He did not believe in regular work and office hours. He said: 'a single brilliant idea is worth more than a whole life of conscientious office work'. The only occasions which were carried out punctually were diplomatic receptions which were arranged by the chief of protocol. Most other visitors, whether or not they had been summoned or had come to discuss the tasks assigned to them, had to wait for hours in the anterooms, adjutants' rooms or other quarters until they were admitted or sent away again to await a later appointment. Ministers and high-ranking officials were often not received for weeks and months on end despite every conceivable attempt. His adjutants had strict orders not to admit anybody without his express permission. If Hitler did not want to see someone then that person would not succeed in gaining admittance for years on end.

Apart from that, Hitler was far from being shy of people. Hitler could not bear to be alone. It was striking what lengths he went to avoid it. It often seemed to me as if he was frightened of his own company. Thus, he regularly only went to bed around 3 or 4 o'clock or even later and expected his guests to remain

---

[5] See D. Rebentisch, *Führerstaat und Verwaltung im Zweiten Weltkrieg* (Stuttgart 1989), pp. 403–04. This chapter owes much to this book.

until he had departed. He said that it was impossible for him to sleep before dawn.

Since Hitler literally turned night into day, he could not get up before midday. He normally did not leave his bedroom before 12 o'clock, often later. He used to have a rushed breakfast—usually a glass of milk or a cup of tea and a rusk, for he knew that by this time a lot of things were awaiting him. As a result of this schedule of "the boss", the machinery of authoritarian government was regularly at a standstill in the mornings. If anybody has any idea of just how important the late morning is for work in central government and military headquarters, they will know what hold-ups and missed deadlines could be involved . . . The fact, for example, that the daily OKW report was often given out so late that it missed the 2 o'clock news on the radio and thus failed to appear in the afternoon papers was entirely due to the fact that Hitler insisted on seeing and correcting this report, which the head of OKW had already received by 1 o'clock, before it went out, with the result that its publication was delayed because he had not emerged from his rooms in time.

Hitler spoke first to his adjutants, who were normally waiting in the corridor outside his door or in the anteroom with the most urgent business. They acquainted him with the most important matters and received his instructions on whom he wished to see during the course of the day. Hitler himself determined whom he wished to see and whose request to be seen should be rejected or postponed. Hitler did not have any special time for receiving visitors during the day. Everything depended on his state of mind, his moods and his personal attitude for which he did not give any explanations. Then, as a rule, when he was in Berlin in peacetime, he received the Chief of the Reich Chancellery, although not at a fixed time, while, during the war, the military conference with OKW took place in his field headquarters. Since his interminable disquisitions covered every conceivable subject, these conferences went on for several hours so that lunch began between 2 and 4 o'clock. When in Berlin, Hitler had lunch in his apartment together with his closest associates and invited guests; in his military headquarters he had it in the mess with the members of OKW.

Since Hitler often spoke for a long time at table, lunch varied in length, although in view of the simplicity of the menu it should have been over in half an hour. Often Hitler only got up from the table after two hours and, since the same thing happened at dinner, it was almost unbearable for the participants, since they still had their work to do. During the last years of the war Hitler introduced a second daily conference, which took place in the evening. However, in view of the shift in the time produced by his way of life, it usually only began in the night and, as the days went by, it got later and later. In the first six months of the war it was scheduled by Hitler to begin at 1 o'clock in the morning. Afterwards, Hitler did not retire but invited his closest associates, including his secretaries, into his sitting room as, in effect, his private guests. In his special train these tea sessions, which invariably took place, were held in the small salon next to his sleeping compartment. On the Obersalzberg the nightly sessions round the hearth fulfilled the same function of avoiding his having to be alone before he fell asleep.

Hitler did not give his official orders in a written form, which was officially recorded, but orally and spontaneously to those who happened to be standing near him, with the instruction to pass them on to the appropriate authorities either personally or by telephone. He did not give these instructions at particular times but in the course of the whole day as they occurred to him through his own thoughts or prompted by conversation. This practice of giving orders did not exactly produce clarity and precision. Military and other agencies, which were used to receiving signed orders, got into difficulties, as instructions given off the cuff by Hitler in a conversation were not recognized as such and so were not acted upon.

It frequently happened that visitors who had come to see Hitler for some reason which had nothing to do with politics, but which he found stimulating, then exploited his good mood or a favourable opportunity and were able to take him on one side and get him to promise something or accept something, which they then announced off their own bat as a 'Führer order' and which then caused confusion because it totally contradicted another 'Führer order'. In the course of time such incidents produced so many complaints and difficultuies for Hitler himself that he gave instructions through the head of the Reich Chancellery that in future departmental heads should only request orders if they had already reached agreement with those who would be adversely affected by these orders. In view of Hitler's policy of dual appointments to almost all departments, such an agreement between two rivals about their responsibilities for one and the same sphere of operation was of course impossible, so that while this Solomonic judgment reduced some of the problems for him, as far as the matter itself was concerned, it simply increased the difficulties and confusion even more.

The result of this style of government was that Hitler would often issue orders on minor matters, which happened to have been brought to his attention by his entourage and which provoked an outburst and an off-the-cuff decision, while major matters were left unresolved for long periods. The following are some examples of such 'Führer orders'.

**924**    *(a) The Führer and Supreme Commander of the Wehrmacht*
*Berlin, 12.10.40*

SECRET

I order that as far as possible the inmates of concentration camps, and convicts of all kinds should be used for the removal of bombs (duds, delayed action bombs) in so far as danger is involved for the clearance gangs. Prisoners of war and prisoners who are members of the Wehrmacht should not be used.

[signed] ADOLF HITLER

*(b)  Lammers to the Reich Master of the Hunt [Göring]*     *9.9.42*

In response to the report in the *Neue I.Z* [a newspaper] No. 35 of 1 September 1942, of which I enclose a copy, the Führer has expressed the wish that the current restrictions on the hunting of wild rabbits should be reduced in order to prevent the rabbit plague from getting out of hand. In particular, the Führer has criticized the licensing procedure for the use of firearms and the ban on the use of traps and poison. I request you to issue the necessary regulations to implement the Führer's instructions.

*(c)  The Secretary of the Führer Reichsleiter Martin Bormann*     *7.5.43*

Dear Dr Lammers,
For your information may I draw your attention to the following:
The Master of the Reich Guild of Hairdressers had instructed that hair could only be permed if it did not exceed 7 cm in length on the neck. In addition, he instructed that only grey hair could be dyed.
On the instructions of the Führer I have informed the Reich Economics Minister that both restrictions are to be abolished forthwith.

Heil Hitler!
Your obedient servant
BORMANN

[The restrictions on hairdressing had represented the outcome of a long and time-consuming debate within the administration about how to reduce the resources devoted to hairdressing in the interests of the war effort. This was one of numerous similar responses to Hitler's mobilization decree of 13 January 1943. In his post-war memoirs the Hitler Youth leader and Gauleiter of Vienna, Balder von Schirach, claimed that Hitler was prompted by his mistress, Eva Braun, to veto the measure, although no doubt his sensitivity to the morale of German women was decisive.]

*(d)  Bormann to Speer*     *1.3.44*

Dear party comrade Speer,
This evening, the Führer instructed me to inform you that he is extremely annoyed that the construction of bunkers for the foreign embassies has been halted. Orders from the Führer must be carried out by every German and it is by no means permitted for them to be suspended or blocked. Evidently, a number of your colleagues are unaware of this and, therefore, they must be enlightend by you once again on this basic point. If the Führer receives another piece of information such as is contained in the enclosed, he will immediately have the officials responsible arrested for contravening an order from the Führer and consigned to a concentration camp.

# Access of the most important leaders to the Führer

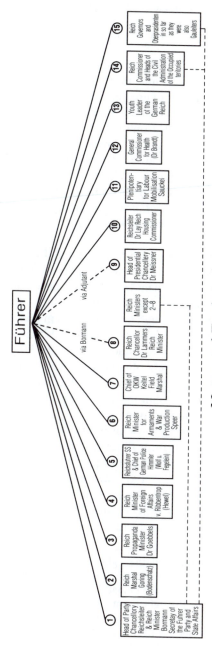

## Notes and Explanations

The paths from the Führer to the above were various and not governed by any rules. Names in brackets refer to permanent liason men with the Führer.

1:  Access to the Führer at all times

8 & 9:  Access to the Führer only at long intervals, often over several weeks, in the case of
9: via the Adjutants' Office
8: via Bormann

8:  Only a coordinating agency without powers of instruction or other authority over the Reich departments.

1–7;  } Possibility of direct access to
10–15:  } the Führer, usually at any time

7, 2,  } Continual, or at least frequent,
4, 6:  } participation in the daily military conferences with the Führer. Therefore possibility of bringing up other matters.

2–6;  } In matters of lesser import-
10–13:  } ance also path via 8 or 1

14–15:  In so far as they did not approach the Führer direct-ly, they preferred the path via 1 rather than 8 and particularly in the most important matters since Bormann had daily access to the Führer.

The Führer requests that you immediately order the continuation of the construction of the bunkers and confirm this in writing. The Führer expressly instructed me to pass on his orders to you verbatim.

Only a few major figures were able to secure more or less regular access to Hitler. After the war Lammers drew a sketch (doc. 925) to illustrate this. Since even major figures could not be sure of seeing Hitler, some ministers adopted the practice of sending Hitler briefing papers. From the beginning of 1942 onwards, Goebbels developed this into a regular procedure, sending Hitler almost 500 hundred so-called *Führerinformationen* by the end of the war. His example was followed by the state secretary and acting Minister of Justice, Franz Schlegelberger, who tried to enhance the reputation of his ministry in Hitler's eyes by sending him some 191 *Führerinformationen*, containing court judgments and other relevant material designed to deflect Hitler's deep hostility to the judicial process.

Unfortunately, however, this proved a forlorn hope. Indeed, in April 1942, Hitler's hostility to all legal and bureaucratic procedures prompted him to demand an official endorsement by the Reichstag of his absolute authority free from any restrictions, a position which was already implicit in his role as Führer. Although his action was in direct response to a particular criminal case, in which an offender had been given what he regarded as too lenient a sentence, in fact it reflected a long-standing aspiration for which the case merely offered the pretext. Hitler's move appears to have expressed a desire to radicalize the war effort in the aftermath of the crisis on the Russian front during the previous winter. However, instead of mass mobilization, Hitler began in a paranoid fashion to seek scapegoats among those in positions of authority who were alleged to be failing in their duty. Goebbels encouraged him in the view that the conservative bureaucracy, and particularly the judiciary, were putting obstacles in the way of the war effort because of their determination to stick to the rules. On 26 April 1942, Hitler made a major speech to the Reichstag in which he issued his request, justifying it through a populist attack on the bureaucratic establishment:

**926** ... You, my old comrades in the fight, will not doubt that I am determined to do everything necessary to carry out these tasks. But, to enable me to achieve this, I have several demands to make:

I expect the nation to give me the right to intervene immediately and to take the requisite action whenever people fail to obey orders absolutely or to act in the service of the great task in which our very existence is at stake. The people at the front and those at home, our transport system, administration, and system of justice must be governed by one thought alone—victory. At this moment, nobody may appeal to established rights; he must realize that today there are only duties.

I ask the German Reichstag, therefore, for explicit confirmation that I have the right to remind everyone of his duties, to cashier him or to remove him from his office or job, whoever he may be and whatever rights he may have, if, in my opinion, he is not conscientiously carrying out his duties.

This is particularly important, because among the millions of decent people there are only a few individual exceptions. And more important than any rights, and that includes the rights of these exceptions, is the fact that today there is one single common duty.

I am not interested, therefore, in the question of whether or not leave can be given to officials or employees at the present critical time, and I refuse to allow any leave which cannot be taken now to be credited for a future occasion.

If anyone has the right to ask for leave it is, in the first place, our front-line troops, and secondly, the workers who are working for the front. And since I have not been able to grant leave to the Eastern front for months, I do not want anybody in some office at home to talk about a so-called 'justified claim' for leave.

Similarly, I expect those engaged in the administration of German justice to understand that they are there for the nation and not vice versa. This means that the world, which also includes Germany, must not be allowed to fall to pieces for the preservation of some legal formula. Germany must live, whatever any formal interpretation of the law may have to say about it. I do not understand, just to cite one example, why a criminal, who gets married in 1937 and then ill-treats his wife until she has a nervous breakdown and dies as the result of a final beating up, should be condemned to five years' hard labour at a moment when tens of thousands of brave German men have to die to save their wives and children. From now on, I shall intervene in such cases and dismiss judges who clearly do not recognize the needs of the moment.[6]

What the German soldier, the German worker, the farmer, the women in town and country, the millions of our middle classes achieve and sacrifice, all with one thought of victory, demands a like-minded attitude on the part of those who have been appointed by the people themselves to look after their interests; at this time there are no sacrosanct bodies with established rights. We are all simply obedient servants of the interests of our people . . .

The fact that fate has selected me to lead the German people at such a great time is my sole reason for pride. I wish to link my name and my life with its fate. The only request I have to make of the Almighty is that he should continue to bless us in the future as in the past and let me live long enough as, in His eyes, is necessary to lead the fateful struggle of the German people. For there is no greater fame than the honour of leading a nation in difficult times and of bearing the responsibility for it. And I cannot feel any greater happiness than the awareness that this nation is my German people.

---

[6] This was a distorted account of the so-called "Schliff case".

[Göring, as President of the Reichstag, then read out the formula which Hitler had devised in consulation with Lammers, and which was unanimously approved:]

*Göring*: The nation knows the wisdom, the justness, the goodness and the greatness, and above all the genius of the Führer and, because it is convinced of it, it also feels a duty to do everything to support the Führer. And so I now request the men of the Reichstag, as the deputies of this nation, to confirm to me the following statement:

There can be no doubt that at the present stage in the war, in which the German nation is engaged in a life and death struggle, the Führer must possess the right which he claims to do everything that serves to bring about victory. Therefore, without being bound by existing regulations, in his capacity as Leader of the nation, Supreme Commander of the Armed Forces, Head of the Government, and Supreme Chief of the Executive, as Chief Justice and Leader of the Party, the Führer must be in a position to compel, with all the means at his disposal, every German, if necessary, whether he be common soldier or officer, high- or low-ranking official or judge, leading or subordinate official of the Party, worker or employee, to fulfil his duties. In the event of violation of these duties, the Führer is entitled, regardless of so-called established rights, to punish and remove the offender from his post, rank and position, without using the prescribed procedures.

Hitler was acutely aware of the symbolic significance of titles and thus ensured that his new status was reflected in his formal title. Until the law of 1 August 1934, merging the offices of Reich Chancellor and Reich President, Hitler's official title had been 'Reich Chancellor'. After 1 August, it was 'Führer and Reich Chancellor'. However, on 17 May 1939 instructions went out that in internal government communications and in communications with the press he should from then onwards be referred to simply as 'the Führer'. In the case of laws, however, his title should remain 'Führer and Reich Chancellor'. However, on 1 May 1942, a week after Hitler's Reichstag speech, Field Marshal Keitel, head of OKW, issued the following instructions:

**927**  The Führer wishes that the unity of the nation's and the Wehrmacht's leadership embodied in his person should also find formal expression in his personal decrees and decisions. In future therefore:

(1) In connection with expressions of the Führer's wishes and his decisions the suffixes 'and Supreme Commander of the Wehrmacht' as well as 'and Reich Chancellor' will be removed. The official title is 'the Führer' . . .

On 26 June 1943, Lammers issued the following instruction to the 'Supreme Reich authorities':

**928** The Führer wishes that in future in internal German discourse and also in laws, edicts and decrees he will be referred to exclusively as 'the Führer'. The Führer himself will sign laws, edicts, and decrees solely in this form and not as often was the case hitherto as 'the Führer and Reich Chancellor'.

It was as if the more Hitler felt that his project was becoming unstuck the more he felt the need publicly and formally to assert his leadership.

Hitler's increasing preoccupation with running the military side of the war and the fact that he spent more and more time at his military headquarters in East Prussia strengthened the position of those who had the greatest access to him. As far as the government departments were concerned, it strengthened the position of the Reich Chancellery. For, while some ministers appointed a liaison officer to Hitler's headquarters—for example, Göring had General Bodenschatz and Ribbentrop Walther Hewel—most were now even more dependent on the Reich Chancellery to gain access to Hitler. But, in the event, it was not Lammers but rather the head of the Staff of the Führer's Deputy for Party Affairs (Rudolf Hess), Martin Bormann, who was to benefit most from this development. However, Bormann's rise also owed much to an unexpected event which occurred in the spring of 1941.

## (v) The Rise of Bormann

*(a) The renaming of the staff of the Führer's Deputy as the Party Chancellery and the appointment of Martin Bormann to head it*

On 12 May 1941 the Nazi Party's official newspaper, the *Völkischer Beobachter*, made the following announcement:

**929** Party Comrade Hess had been strictly forbidden by the Führer from continuing his flying activities on account of a progressive illness which had been developing for years. However, in contravention of this order, he recently succeeded once more in acquiring an aircraft.

On Saturday, 10 May, around 1800 hours, Party Comrade Hess set out once more on a flight from Augsburg from which, up to the present moment, he has not yet returned. A letter which he left behind gives rise to the fear that Party Comrade Hess became the victim of insanity.

The Führer gave immediate orders for the arrest of Party Comrade Hess' adjutants, who alone knew of this flight and, contrary to the Führer's ban, did nothing to prevent it or report it at once.

In these circumstances the National Socialist movement must regrettably assume that Party Comrade Hess has crashed somewhere in the course of his flight and been killed.

In fact of course Hess had landed by parachute in Scotland. The departure of the Führer's Deputy for Party Affairs obliged Hitler to replace him in some form. Significantly, he did so not by simply appointing a new Führer's Deputy—he was clearly no longer happy with the idea of having a deputy—but instead by abolishing that title and renaming the office attached to it. On 12 May he issued the following order:

**930**    The Staff of the Führer's Deputy will henceforth carry the title 'the Party Chancellery'. It will be subordinate to me personally. Its head will be, as hitherto, Reichsleiter Martin Bormann.

Bormann had indeed been head of the Staff of the Führer's Deputy and the driving force behind it.

On 29 May 1941 Hitler issued the following order which, in effect, transferred to Bormann the powers which Hess had previously exercised as the Führer's Deputy for Party Affairs:

**931**    Through an order of 12 May I have given instructions for the sphere of the NSDAP that the Staff of the Führer's Deputy should in future carry the title the Party Chancellery and should be directly subordinate to me. Following on from this, in order to ensure the closest cooperation between the Party Chancellery and the Supreme Reich authorities, I hereby give instructions that:

The head of the Party Chancellery, Martin Bormann, has the authority of a Reich Minister; he is a member of the Reich Government and of the Ministerial Council for the Defence of the Reich.

Where in laws, decrees, edicts, instructions and other orders the 'Führer's Deputy' is referred to, he is to be replaced by the head of the Party Chancellery.

The requisite regulations for the implementation and supplementation of this edict will be issued by the Reich Minister and head of the Reich Chancellery in consultation with the head of the Party Chancellery.

Dr Klopfer of Department III of the Party Chancellery and Friedrich Kritzinger of the Reich Chancellery now entered into extensive consultations over the drafting of a decree which would define the powers of the new Party Chancellery.

### (b) Bormann's strategy for the Party Chancellery

Bormann's strategy as head of the Party Chancellery was, in the first place, to extend the Party's power at the expense of the state authorities and, in particular, to establish for the Party Chancellery a dominant position vis-à-vis the Government departments in the sense of acquiring the decisive influence over major policy issues. Working on the assumption that politics and administration could be conveniently separated, he envisaged the Party as the representative of the nation, determining policy while the civil service was reduced to the role of merely administering that policy. It was a division of labour not unlike that between the Communist Party and the Government offices in the Soviet Union. But, in order to achieve this goal, he needed to turn the Party into an effective political machine under the control of the Party Chancellery.

At this point, however, the Party Chancellery was faced with two different developments. In the first place, it was confronted with elements within the state who resented Party interference in their sphere of operations. Secondly, it was faced with a continuing challenge from elements within the Party who resisted the claim of the Party Chancellery to act as the coordinating agency for the Party vis-à-vis the state. Bormann's anxiety about these matters emerged in an undated minute which he wrote for the heads of Department II (Party), Helmut Friedrichs, and Department III (State), Gerhard Klopfer, of the Party Chancellery about a conversation with Göring:

**932**    *Minute for Party Comrade Klopfer and Party Comrade Friedrichs*

The Reich Marshal is at Obersalzberg at the moment. I asked him through General Bodenschatz for an interview which took place today. I spent an hour and a half in Göring's country house. First the Reich Marshal talked for some time about the construction work which I have carried out at Obersalzberg and then about political problems.

The Reich Marshal emphasized at various points that a number of people (Dr Frick etc.) thought that they could exclude the Party. Naturally, he, the Reich Marshal, did not go along with this. Rather, he too wanted the participation of the Party in laws and decrees to continue to the same extent as hitherto. The Reich Marshal was aware, for example, that in the case of the vetting of personnel, the awarding of the Cross for Distinguished War Service etc. some people wanted to exclude the participation of the Party on the grounds that the Gauleiters were after all simultaneously Reich Governors.

On my part, I informed the Reich Marshal that various *Reichsleiter* [of the NSDAP] wanted to take on responsibility for the participation of the Party in laws, decrees etc. for their particular spheres of operation themselves. The Reich Marshal rejected these ambitions as completely unviable. He too thought that the Party Chancellery, as the central agency, must continue to deal with these matters in the same way as before.

Bormann was anxious to use the opportunity presented by Hess' flight to Scotland to deal with both these challenges.

*(c) The attempt to assert the Party Chancellery's control over the state apparatus*[7]

In the first place, Bormann aimed to extend the powers of the Party Chancellery, which already covered the right to participate in the drafting of Government laws and decrees, to include the right to be involved in the drafting of the supplementary decrees issued to implement those laws and decrees.[8] These regulations played a crucial role in how the legislation was actually enforced. The first draft from the Party Chancellery of the proposed decree regulating its role included a statement to this effect.

The Reich Chancellery fully accepted the Party Chancellery's right to be involved in the drafting of Reich laws and decrees. However, it objected to the extension of this right to cover supplementary decrees on the grounds that it represented a further increase in the power of the Party at the expense of the state, but also because it would delay urgently needed measures. Dr Klopfer appeared willing to drop the move. Bormann, however, insisted on pressing the point. Cleverly, however, he did not adopt a frontal attack but rather endeavoured to win the support of the Reich Chancellery by pointing out the valuable service performed by the Party Chancellery in coordinating the response of the Party to legislation, and by emphasizing the dangerous development which was taking place in the legislative process, a view which he knew the Reich Chancellery shared. He also suggested that the Reich Chancellery should take on a new role in resisting it by vetting all ministerial decrees. The following letter to Lammers, the head of the Reich Chancellery, dated 19 November 1941, is an exceptionally illuminating example of Bormann's approach:

**933** Dear Dr Lammers,

With reference to the discussions between my desk officer, *Ministerialdirektor* Dr Klopfer, and *Ministerialdirektor* Kritzinger, I enclose a draft Decree for the Implementation of the Führer's Edict Concerning the Position of the Head of the Party Chancellery of 29 May 1941. The draft contains a summary of a number of decrees which the Führer issued for the Führer's Deputy and which, in accordance with the Führer's edict of 29 May 1941, are also to be applied to the head of the Party Chancellery. It is very difficult for those involved to keep abreast of the Führer's orders, which he issued on different occasions and which are scattered in several edicts and circulars. It thus appears necessary to summarize them once more. In my view we should utilize the possibility envisaged

---

[7] For Bormann's attempt to control the Party see below, pp. 69ff.
[8] See Vol. 2, doc. 161.

in the Führer's edict of 29 May 1941 of regulating such questions in the form of a supplementary decree which would be issued by the Reich Minister and head of the Reich Chancellery in agreement with the head of the Party Chancellery.

The objection has been made that legislation suffers an unfortunate delay as a result of the involvement of the Party Chancellery. This assertion may be just as validly made in the case of the involvement of any other Reich Minister. The task of the Party Chancellery is not to replicate the work of the ministries or even subject it to appraisal on technical or legal grounds. My office would not be in a position to do this on practical grounds alone. For I have given instructions that the number of its personnel should be kept small and they would not be in a position to carry out even a small part of the work of the ministries, each of which contains many times the number of desk officers in my office.

But, on practical grounds as well, participation in legislation along those lines would be completely worthless. It would indeed represent a completely superfluous complication of legislation. The expertise of the colleagues in my office would be insufficient to warrant an intervention by the Party Chancellery. The ministries could utilize it directly by employing them themselves.

The intervention of the Party Chancellery rests far more on the recognition that, in dealing with the most vital tasks of the state, it is necessary at some point to involve the nation under National Socialist leadership, which after all is going to feel the effects of all state measures and, in particular, its legislation.

If one was to leave the fulfilment of those tasks to the state alone, the Reich legislation, in particular, would have to depend on the reports of the officials in its subordinate agencies. However, their task is to implement the laws and not to act as agents of the nation representing its wishes and suggestions to the state authorities. It would be inevitable that sooner or later the work and form of the state would ossify and the nation, which is permanently growing and developing, would seek alternative opportunities to secure expression for the requirements of its development in the shaping and work of the state.

This development could not be prevented by an evaluation of individual complaints by complainants and malcontents sent to high offices of state. It would be a misrepresentation of the attitude and value of the nation if one were to regard malcontents and complainants as its competent spokesmen. Nor can anonymous reports on the mood of the people on their own convey an accurate picture of the true wishes of the people.

The competent spokesmen of the nation in our state, which is under National Socialist leadership, are the political cadres [*Hoheitsträger*] appointed by the Führer—the Gauleiters and district leaders [*Kreisleiter*], as well as the heads of the various specialist offices of the NSDAP. [Minute by Lammers: Correct!] It is only through the articulation of their opinions that the nation under National Socialist leadership can participate in the tasks of the state.

A direct communication between these numerous Party offices and the Reich ministries cannot lead to any satisfactory results. Almost all laws affect several spheres of life, which are often in conflict with one another. From a practical point of view, the officials employed in the individual ministries would simply not be in a position to give a hearing to all the relevant Party agencies and, at the same time, to find out what was the view of the Party in a way which would do justice to all the interests involved. They might even run the risk of being accused of adopting a non-National Socialist attitude if they felt themselves obliged not to take full account of the wishes of one or other of the Party agencies.

Thus, it is probable that all the ministries have been relieved that my office has taken on the thankless task of reconciling these often opposing opinions and then presenting the ministries with a uniform opinion which is binding on the whole Party [Minute by Lammers: Correct!]

It is after all easier to put up with the delay in a law caused by this, than if—as has repeatedly happened recently—a law, which has come about without the participation of the Party, has had subsequently to be altered or even not be put into effect, following the intervention of a Gauleiter, because it has not taken account of the practical necessities of life. It is not difficult to calculate the extent to which the authority of the Reich Government must suffer as a result of this.

I regard such events all the more seriously since recently, in the case of Reich laws which have been issued in the form of decrees, there has been an increasing tendency for those ministers who, in accordance with binding regulations, should have participated, were not in fact involved in the legislative process. In individual cases, those ministries which were not involved instructed their subordinate agencies to act as if the law did not exist, while in other cases the law was not implemented.

I keep receiving complaints from Gauleiters to the effect that they are no longer in a position to know what the Reich Government wishes to have recognized as valid law. They increasingly find themselves in the position of having to decide on the basis of their own judgment whether a Reich law, which has been properly proclaimed, should still be implemented or not.

If the legislation of the Reich is not to suffer a general dissolution and devaluation in the foreseeable future then, in my view, it is necessary that, as with the formal legislation of the Reich, so too the laws which are issued through decrees should be subjected to the control of a neutral agency which, in particular, observes whether all the Reich agencies which, in accordance with binding regulations are supposed to have participated, have in fact done so. Since this control over formal laws is the responsibility of your office, I would be obliged if you could examine how far it would be possible to extend this control to those laws which are issued in the form of decrees.

I would be grateful for an early response to my enclosed draft as well as to the suggestion at the end of this letter.

Yours sincerely,
MARTIN BORMANN

—

While Bormann's idea that the Reich Chancellery should vet the various decrees issued by the individual ministries was recognized as desirable, it was rejected by Kritzinger, in a minute dated 29 November, as unworkable on the grounds that the Reich Chancellery lacked the requisite personnel and expertise and (since the Reich Chancellery did not have the authority to reject them unilaterally) the draft decrees would then have to be circulated to all the Government departments. This would defeat the original rationale for delegating the right to issue regulatons to the individual ministries. However, in the final version of the decree, which was issued on 16 January 1942, Bormann had got a long way towards achieving his objective with the inclusion of the right of the Party Chancellery to participate in the drafting of Reich government supplementary decrees for the implementation of legislation (see II) but not departmental regulations:

**934** *Decree to Implement the Edict Concerning the Position of the Head of the Party Chancellery*

I. (i) The participation of the Party in legislation is to take place exclusively through the head of the Party Chancellery in so far as the Führer does not determine otherwise. Proposals and suggestions for legislation from the Party, its formations and associated leagues must also only be submitted to the responsible supreme Reich authorities via the head of the Reich Chancellery.
(ii) Similarly, the participation of the Party in the handling of personnel matters is to take place exclusively through the head of the Party Chancellery.

II. The head of the Party Chancellery has the position of a participant Reich Minister in all legislation. He is thus to be involved by the supreme Reich authorities from the beginning in the drafting of Reich laws, edicts, decrees of the Führer, decrees of the Ministerial Council for the Defence of the Reich as well as decrees of the supreme Reich authorities, including regulations for the implementation and execution of legislation. The same is true regarding the approval of laws and decrees of the states and the decrees of the Reich Governors (*Reichsstatthalter*).

III. In fundamental and political questions, in particular those concerning the preparation, alteration and implementation of laws, edicts, and decrees, the communications between the supreme Reich authorities and the supreme authorities of the states which contain several Gaus, on the one hand, and the offices of the Party, its formations and associated leagues, on the other, are to be carried out solely through the head of the Party Chancellery. Direct communication between the supreme Reich authorities of the states and other offices of the Party is in all cases inadmissible. The same applies to the handling of the personnel matters of civil servants except in so far as other regulations exist.

## (vi)  The Fragmentation of Government[9]

The result of the various attempts to rationalize and coordinate the governmental structures and processes since the first Defence Law of 1935 had in fact been to increase the complexity of government. Between 1 September and 30 December 1939, the *Reich Law Gazette* registered 14 Führer decrees, 1 Reichstag law, 8 Government laws, 58 Ministerial Council decrees, 29 decrees of the 'Group of Three' and 395 decrees issued by individual Government departments on the basis of previous legislation.

Above all, the problem of political and administrative fragmentation, which had already been developing before the war, grew steadily worse during the course of the war. Government departments increasingly acted on their own initiative, proposing legislation which had not been previously considered by other departments which were affected by it. This tendency was given an added impetus by Hitler's growing tendency to appoint new Reich 'commissioners' or 'delegates' to take over particular responsibilities, often at the expense of traditional government departments, hollowing them out until only the shell was left. The classic instance of this during the war was the Labour Ministry, which even before 1939 had lost responsibilities to the Four-Year Plan and the German Labour Front. After 1939, it lost further powers to Robert Ley, who was appointed Reich Housing Commissioner on 15 November 1940.[10] On 30 August 1941, Ley issued a decree establishing housing offices in the various Gau headquarters. This decree which created a separate administrative apparatus linked to the Party had not received the prior approval of either the Party Chancellery or of the Ministry of Labour, which was directly affected by it. Moreover, it contravened the decree establishing the Reich Commissioner for Housing. As a result, it created enormous administrative confusion and friction. Then, on 21 March 1942, in a crippling blow to the Labour Ministry, Hitler appointed the Gauleiter of Thuringia, Fritz Sauckel, Reich Commissioner for Labour Mobilization.

This process multiplied the number of agencies with the right to issue decrees and regulations, a trend which was accentuated by the growing autonomy of the Reich ministries. For, as a result of the collapse of cabinet government, each department tended to go its own way, issuing decrees as it saw fit.

---

[9] For the following see also Vol. 2, doc. 142.
[10] See also below, pp. 294ff.

The practice of heads of government appointing individuals, often cronies, to new posts was by no means unique to wartime Germany. The appointment by Churchill of his friend, Max Aitken (Lord Beaverbrook), to the new post of Minister of Aircraft Production in 1940 is a parallel development which shows that the practice was to some extent determined by the requirements of crisis government. However, the exceptionally personal nature of Hitler's rule turned this form of government from the exception into the norm for wartime Germany.

Moreover, the fragmentation was further exacerbated by the fact that ministries and other agencies were taking advantage of Hitler's tendency to favour laws and decrees which were very broadly framed, leaving the ministries to fill in the law with supplementary regulations. As a result, it was becoming increasingly difficult to retain an overview of what laws and regulations were actually in force at any one time. In 1941, for example, there were only 12 Government laws, which had been subjected to the regulation 'circulation procedure' of vetting by the relevant ministries, compared to 24 published Führer edicts, 9 Führer decrees, 27 decrees of the Ministerial Council for the Defence of the Reich and no fewer than 373 decrees issued by various Government departments with minimal or no consultation with other departments. Two years later, in December 1943, Department I of the Reich Interior Ministry prepared a detailed statement for the new minister, Heinrich Himmler, of the agencies which were entitled to make law and the forms by which laws could be made. They listed sixteen different authorities with the right to make law ranging from the Führer, whose basis was 'the emanation of his sovereignty' and whose sphere of competence was 'unlimited', to the Reich Commissioner for the Merchant Marine, whose basis was the Führer edict establishing a Reich Commissioner for the Merchant Marine of 30 May 1942 and which 'covered the tasks within his sphere of operations'.

**935** *Re: the agencies with legislative power and the forms in which legislation occurs*

. . . 2. The main difference between the forms in which legislation occurs, as set out in column 5 of the summary, lies in material terms, i.e. apart from the purely formal manner in which they were prepared, in the following:
(a) In the relationship between a Führer edict [*Erlaß*] and a Führer decree [*Verordnung*]. There are no fixed guidelines as to when one or other should be used. Recently, the Reich Chancellery has preferred to use the form of a Führer edict.

(b) In the relationship between a Führer edict or decree and a law. Here too there are no fixed guidelines. Over the course of time the practice has developed that, apart from the formal matters of State sovereignty, the Führer is exclusively responsible above all for matters of organization (e.g. the structure and administration of the eastern territories, the creation of the Protectorate of Bohemia and Moravia, the concentration of the War Economy, the appointment of a General Plenipotentiary for Labour Mobilization).

(c) At the moment, there is virtually no material difference between a law and a decree. All those legal rules which involve the fundamental regulation of a matter should take the form of a law and not be issued as a Führer edict or decree or as a decree of the Ministerial Council.

3. Until the outbreak of war, the situation which can be seen from Enclosure 1 was initially envisaged in accordance with a well-thought-out plan; but then, as a result of particular requirements which arose, it was extended in such a way that, very regrettably, legislation became fragmented and impossible to oversee.

The plan which was followed before the outbreak of war envisaged that the decree of the Ministerial Council would provide a substitute for the Government law and, above all, one which could be rapidly processed and that, furthermore, with the decrees of the Group of Three [*Dreierkollegium*] the whole sphere of civil administration could be combined under three supra-ministerial sectors. However, neither of these expectations was fulfilled. Since the Ministerial Council no longer meets and, therefore, its legislation is dealt with through the circulation procedure in just the same way as the Government laws, a decree of the Ministerial Council does not come about any quicker than a law. There is, however, a certain advantage in that fewer departments are involved. Since the individual departments have to a large extent received special powers, the importance of the legislation in the Group of Three has been much reduced. Often it is in fact merely a matter of chance what method is chosen for a particular piece of legislation.

Moreover, the powers employed for legislation are to some extent dubious . . . Thus, a reorganization of the legislative process in the direction of a tighter consolidation in favour of a few legislative powers, which would be adapted to all the changing demands of the war, appears highly desirable. At the very least, any tendency towards an extension of these powers must be prevented and no new general legislative powers should be granted to particular agencies. It is intended to contact the Reich Chancellery about this.

―――

## (vii) The Committee of Three

In fact there was growing pressure for a rationalization and simplific-ation of the administration deriving from the increasing need to transfer manpower and resources from the civilian sector to the armed forces and, during the course of the war, a series of measures were passed to try and achieve this. During 1942–3, these measures had the effect of temporarily strengthening the position of Lammers and the Reich

Chancellery. Thus, under Hitler's decree of 25 January 1942 for the further simplification of the administration, Lammers was given the job of coordinating and supervising the Government departments' attempts to save manpower and resources through rationalization, a task which had hitherto been the responsibility of the Interior and Finance ministries. A year later, in the context of the Stalingrad crisis, Hitler pressed for a major intensification of the mobilization of resources for the war effort and, on 13 January 1943, the Führer's 'Decree for the Comprehensive Deployment of Men and Women for Reich Defence Tasks' was issued.[11]

Lammers had proposed that, in order to ensure that the measures were implemented objectively, they should be coordinated and supervised by the 'Führer's leadership structures' rather than by Government departments with axes to grind. Hitler agreed and a so-called Committee of Three (*Dreierauschuß*) was established consisting of Lammers (Reich Chancellery), Bormann (Party Chancellery) and Keitel (OKW). Between January and the end of August 1943, the Committee of Three met eleven times in formal session. The departmental chiefs whose interests were affected by the topics on the agenda were invited to attend. The Reich Chancellery was responsible for the initiation and conduct of the Committee's business.

In fact there were severe limits on the Committee's ability to achieve an effective simplification/rationalization of the German administrative system. It had already been recognized during the Weimar Republic that the German political and administrative structures were in urgent need of rationalization. But before 1933 plans had never got further than the drawing board and, after 1934, Hitler had forbidden further discussion of *Reichsreform*, despite the fact that half-baked Nazi measures of centralization (1933–5) had only served to further complicate the situation. Above all, however, the nature of the Nazi system of government—the parallel rule of Party and State and the multiplication of offices as a result of Hitler's style of leadership—had greatly increased the manpower involved in various forms of government and administration and the complexity of government. Since Hitler was unwilling, indeed effectively unable, to make significant changes to his system of rule, there was little that could be done. Moreover, he proved extremely cautious when confronted with specific requests to abolish or merge Government offices, anxious above all not to stir up discontent among party officials or the population during wartime.

---

[11] See below, pp. 237ff.

The Committee of Three was not an adequate substitute for a cabinet but it did represent a more systematic form of coordination in the civilian sector and effectively assigned to Lammers the leading role within the civilian administration. Meanwhile, however, the Committee's existence had aroused envy and antagonism among those excluded from it and subject to its rulings. The Propaganda Minister, Joseph Goebbels, argued that the Committee was an inadequate institution for mobilizing the nation's resources for total war and that 'these three intend to establish a kind of kitchen cabinet and to put a wall between Hitler and his ministers'.

Goebbels was not alone with his discontent over the Committee of Three and its operations. His hostility was shared by others and, above all, by the Reich Minister for Armaments and War Production, Albert Speer. During the 1930s, as an ambitious young architect, Speer had established a close relationship with Hitler as a protégé whom Hitler seems to have regarded as a kind of surrogate for his own frustrated architectural ambitions. Speer, however, had not only proved his competence as an architect but had also demonstrated remarkable organizational skills and dynamism in completing complex and demanding projects. It was these qualities which had persuaded Hitler to appoint him to replace Fritz Todt as Munitions Minister when the latter was killed in a plane crash in February 1942. Building on his close association with Hitler and on Hitler's final recognition of the need for drastic action to increase war production, Speer had quickly been able to establish a dominant position within the German war economy.[12] However, like Goebbels, he felt frustrated at what he saw as the failure to mobilize Germany's resources for the war effort more effectively, a failure which he attributed in part to the ineffectiveness of the Committee of Three.

In March 1943 Goebbels took the initiative by launching an intrigue with Speer, Ley of the DAF, and Economics Minister Funk to try and get Hitler to revive the Ministerial Committee for the Defence of the Reich under Göring, expanded to include Goebbels, Speer, Ley and Himmler. Göring was won over and Goebbels persuaded Göring that he should be deputy chairman of the Council, no doubt hoping that Göring's indolence would ensure that he became the dominant figure on the home front. Lammers would be 'pushed back into the secretarial position intended for him from the beginning'. Goebbels recorded his thoughts and activities in his diary entry of 2 March 1943 reporting a conversation with Göring:

---

[12] See below, pp. 225ff.

**936**    ... There's the same trouble about our domestic policy. Everybody does and leaves undone what he pleases, because there's no strong authority anywhere. The Party goes its own way and won't have anybody interfere.

Here's where I introduce my proposals. I express the opinion that we'd be 'over the hump' if we succeeded in transferring the political leadership tasks of the Reich from the 'Committee of Three' to the Ministerial Council for the Defence of the Reich. This Ministerial Council would then have to be composed of the strong men who assisted the Führer in the Revolution. These will certainly also muster the strength to bring this war to a victorious conclusion.

I blamed Göring very seriously for having permitted the Ministerial Council for the Defence of the Reich to become inactive. He could excuse himself, however, with the fact that Lammers always torpedoed his efforts by constantly butting in and reporting to the Führer. This chicanery must be stopped. If Göring can muster the strength to surround himself with courageous, upright and loyal men, such a group would undoubtedly be able to relieve the Führer of most of the chores, thus setting him free again for his high mission of leadership. The Führer would certainly approve of such a solution as it would make his historic tasks much easier for him.

Göring was very much impressed with my statement that I had not come to get something from him but rather to bring something to him. I talked to him with all the persuasiveness at my command and finally succeeded in bringing him over to our side.

The Party must again be put on its toes and its ranks straightened out. The bothersome church question must rest for the duration of the war. The petty chicaneries still practised here and there in public life must be done away with. We must no longer waste time on side issues, but keep our eyes fixed on the main issue, war itself. Only thus can we succeed in concentrating the strength of the nation on a single aim.

While talking I gained the spontaneous impression that my presentation visibly pepped up Göring. He became very enthusiastic about my proposals and immediately asked how we were to proceed specifically. I suggested that he make a number of nominations and I would try to win over the rest. We won't tell any of these about our real intentions: namely, of gradually putting the Committee of Three on ice and transferring its powers to the Ministerial Council. That would only create unnecessary trouble ...

We have no other ambition than that of supporting each other and of forming a solid phalanx around the Führer. The Führer sometimes wavers in his decisions if the same matter is brought to him from different sides. Nor does he always react to people as he should. That's where he needs help.

Göring is fully conscious of his somewhat weak position today. He knows that it is decidedly to his advantage for strong men to come to his side and take upon themselves the task of relieving the Führer of his worst worries. We are all determined to make a new contribution to the war by our action.

Göring himself wants to win over Himmler. Funk and Ley have already been won over by me. Speer is entirely my man. Thus we already have a group that can be proud of itself. It certainly includes all those who today enjoy the greatest prestige and the highest authority in our political life.

Göring wants to come to Berlin immediately after his trip to Italy and there meet with us again. Speer is to speak to the Führer before then—and if possible I also. Questions of personnel and of division of work can, I believe, be disposed of relatively quickly. We want to show the greatest loyalty in forming this group, We shall pursue no other object save that of victory. We shall stand for no intrigue whatever. The fidelity of these men to the Führer is to be unparalleled.

I believe we shall render the Führer the greatest possible service by our action. One just can't stand by any longer and see how he is so weighed down with worries big and small that he can hardly breathe. The cause is greater than any of us, that goes without saying. The men who helped the Führer with the Revolution will now have to help him win the war. They were not bureaucrats then; they must not be bureaucrats today.

We still have many an ace up our sleeves. It surely isn't true that we are playing an empty game. If we make use of every possibility, we shall be able, I believe, to effect a fundamental change in the war within a relatively short time . . . Our problem today is not the people but the leadership. That has been true incidentally of nearly every war.

The Committee of Three was given a task with a time limit, as the Führer's decree expressly stated. The Ministerial Council for the Defence of the Reich, on the other hand, was given a task for the entire duration.

This first talk with Göring lasted almost four hours. I then had Speer brought in so that Göring could himself reveal to him what we had agreed upon.

We improved the occasion to touch upon a number of specific questions and thus to round out the picture. At the end of our talk each of us had the feeling that all problems that in any way come within our wide radius of action had found a solution in principle. As Göring put it, we shall manage the 'Three Wise Men in the East' in a jiffy, whereupon we shall go to work with a driving power and an enthusiasm that will put in the shade anything that ever existed.

I am very happy that a clear basis of mutual trust was established with Göring. I believe the Führer too will be very happy about this. I hope that we shall render him the greatest service possible.

---

Unfortunately for Goebbels and his colleagues, Göring's reputation with Hitler was by now so low, as a result of the poor performance of the Luftwaffe, that Göring and Speer felt unable to put forward their proposals. In fact, however, by the autumn of 1943, the Committee of Three had become dormant and such coordination within the government as existed was provided by informal contacts between the Reich and Party Chancelleries. But, in the meantime, the balance of power within this relationship had shifted even further in favour of Bormann and the Party Chancellery.

## (viii) The Reich Chancellery and the Party Chancellery 1943–1945

As far as the state was concerned, Bormann's ambition involved a challenge to the position of the Reich Chancellery which, although it possessed few formal powers, had acquired under its ambitious head, Hans-Heinrich Lammers, considerable influence as the official link between the Reich Government and Hitler. Although Lammers' position was undermined by the fact that some ministers or heads of state agencies (e.g. Goebbels and Göring) had independent access to Hitler, nevertheless the role of the Reich Chancellery, as the sole coordinating agency of the Reich Government and as the body which Hitler looked to to ensure that new legislation was properly prepared, guaranteed it a continuing influence. This influence had increased through the Reich Chancellery's role in the rationalization of the administration, which had culminated in the establishment of the Committee of Three. But, by 1943, the Reich Chancellery was becoming increasingly marginalized by Bormann. After the war Dr Gerhard Klopfer, the head of Department III of the Party Chancellery dealing with state affairs, outlined to his interrogators Bormann's mode of operation as follows:

**937** It was Bormann's job to keep the Führer informed about Party matters and to pass on his instructions to the Party offices. Bormann operated according to this principle in the sphere of legislation as well and that did not always benefit the Party or the cause in general. For, since initially he lacked confidence, he used to ask the Führer's opinion at a very early stage before any discussion could take place whether on the part of the Party or, later, on the part of the state offices. He evidently tried to strengthen his position within the Party by only expressing the opinion which he thought was that of the Führer . . .

I had the impression that Hess stuck very firmly to the principle which I referred to already, namely to listen to the Party agencies and then to give an opinion based on the views of the Party agencies which would then be put to the Führer together with the views of the Government departments for his decision. Bormann did not have the authority to represent the Führer in matters of the Party leadership. As a result—though things changed in the course of time—I had the impression that, initially, he was less concerned to form his own opinion on the basis of the process I have already outlined. Initially, he operated, broadly speaking, by passing on the views of the Party offices which he received. That was quite easy to do, often without putting it in writing, because there were officials seconded from the various ministries in the Office for State Affairs [of the Staff of the Führer's Deputy/Party Chancellery]. Thus, by making the views of the Party offices concerning the drafts [of legislation] available to these officials in the Department for State Affairs, he could inform the ministries of the views of those Party offices which were directly concerned without the need to adopt a high profile himself. And, in the great majority of cases, it was probably possible for Bormann and these Government departments to reach agreement on these viewpoints. Initially it was more of an informal process.

Q. But involving direct influence?

K. Yes, but only let's say, initially an influence without pressure. It was not the case that he said, for example: I—Bormann—support this point of view. Initially, he adopted an informal procedure by saying: the Gau headquarters thinks this. If the Ministry said: No, that's wrong, then he often restricted himself to referring this response back to the Party office. It's my impression that that is how he operated at the beginning. In the course of time, Bormann's position vis-à-vis the Führer grew stronger and I have the impression that he used the statements coming from the Party offices to strengthen his position with Hitler by reporting various Party statements to Hitler and then being able to secure the Führer's views on these statements. Once he was in the possession of these views of the Führer, Bormann then felt himself strong enough to express particular views, especially to the Party offices, with more vigour. For example, I had the impression that he used this method to curb the Labour Front, which under Ley was putting forward very far-reaching and wild demands, by asking for the Führer's view. He developed into a sort of secretary to the Führer, then adopted the title, and then in this capacity, repeatedly and at short notice, passed on the views and wishes of the Führer to the ministries as well as the Party offices without any prior consultation with any offices or departments having taken place.

Q. Departments within the Party Chancellery?

K. They were presented to us as the Führer's instructions in any case. No, I mean directly to the ministries in his capacity as the Führer's secretary. I have the impression that Bormann's main concern in his work was to express the opinion which he thought would in the end prove to be the Führer's opinion. He wanted to be in the right. As far as he was concerned, there was no other yardstick for the question of whether anyone was right than the fact that the Führer had approved or disapproved of an opinion. Thus, there were many occasions when he expressed various opinions to his colleagues or others in a very brutal way, only to change his mind if he only had the slightest fear that someone with a different viewpoint might be in a position to put this view to the Führer himself because he then might not have felt on strong enough ground to oppose it. In my view, if the Party Chancellery as an institution was to have a role, it should have been to express the viewpoint of the nation in the broadest way on the positions adopted by the Government departments. Since other institutions did not exist, this could very well have been secured via the Party Chancellery.

---

In the final sentence there are echoes of the Bormann–Lammers letter of 19 November 1941 (doc. 933), which Klopfer may well have drafted.

Lammers responded to this growing challenge from Bormann by endeavouring to establish a close relationship with him on the basis of mutual interests. Both were after all trying to introduce order into the regime and to resist its fragmentation into a polycracy of organizations with their own independent power bases. By working with Bormann,

Lammers could ensure his support against the interference in State matters by Party heavyweights such as Ley or the Gauleiters and, above all, he could hope to dissuade Bormann from encroaching any further on state terrain. The State Secretary in the Reich Justice Ministry, Franz Schlegelberger, made some interesting comments on the Bormann–Lammers relationship during his post-war interrogation:

**938** FS. The new ministries, e.g. the Propaganda Ministry etc., had much closer links with the Party Chancellery than the old ministries did.

Q. What were these links?

FS. They were personal links. We older ones never sought contact with the Party Chancellery. We didn't want to deal with these people. For a time we rested our hopes on Lammers in the Reich Chancellery.

Q. In what way?

FS. From 1941 onwards he tried to pull the threads together and to divert things away from the Party onto a more rational plane . . .

However, these hopes were soon disappointed. Lammers came under Bormann's influence . . . At any rate, Lammers didn't want to rebel against Bormann.

Q. What was the personal relationship like between Bormann and Lammers? Did they use the familiar 'you' form to each other?

FS. I don't know. But Lammers once said to me: 'I must have a good relationship with Bormann'.

Q. How did that work out in practice? Did he make concessions to Bormann?

FS. He largely conformed to Bormann's wishes. Here's one example: The last Minister of Justice was Thierack. I could see it coming and I had a talk with Lammers beforehand about this man and asked him what he thought of it. He replied: 'He's only good enough to be a provincial judge [*Landgerichtsdirektor*] at best.' When it happened, I asked him how he could have allowed it and he said: 'Bormann proposed him'.

[Schlegelberger was then asked what effect the Party Chancellery had on personnel matters:]

FS. It worked so that the Party Chancellery blocked us and we blocked the Party Chancellery. I once kept an important post vacant for 1 1/2 years. It was the appointment to the Higher Provincial Court [*Oberlandesgericht*] at Bamberg. I had a candidate who was unusually well qualified for this post because he had great professional experience. He was an upright man. I don't think he was a Party member. The Party Chancellery demanded another person simply because he was an old Party member . . . That was still in Hess' time. I refused and so the post remained vacant for 1 1/2 years. Then I made a report to Hitler and he decided that the appointment should be made in accordance with the wishes of the Justice Ministry. I then got my way. But hardly had I left when Thierack removed the man and so the person whom the Party Chancellery wanted got the job.

In April 1943 Bormann had moved an important step nearer his goal of exercising the decisive influence in matters of state when Hitler conferred on him the official title 'the Führer's Secretary'. On 8 May 1943 Lammers informed 'the supreme Reich authorities' of this development:

**939**    For some years the Führer has been accustomed to giving Reichsleiter Bormann special tasks of the most diverse kinds which do not form part of his responsibilities in his capacity as head of the Party Chancellery. They refer rather to matters outside the ambit of the Party, matters concerning which directives and opinions of the Führer are conveyed to leading and senior state figures on the Führer's orders. When dealing with such assignments Reichsleiter Bormann has hitherto intentionally avoided acting in his capacity as head of the Party Chancellery and has simply used the title 'Reichsleiter Bormann'—for example, at the top of his letters. However, particular incidents have shown that the significance and purpose of this practice have not always been correctly understood and that, therefore, a definite clarification is required. The Führer has, therefore, ordered that Reichsleiter Bormann, as the person designated by the Führer to deal with such special assignments, should carry the title 'the Führer's Secretary'.

This directive neither creates a new office nor does it grant new responsibilities; but rather it simply makes clear that, in addition to his role as head of the Party Chancellery, Reichsleiter Bormann carries out the special assignments of the Führer referred to. Reichsleiter Bormann will as a rule convey such Führer instructions to the responsible Reich Ministers or others involved via me, as he has done hitherto without this title.

Despite Lammers' assertion that Bormann's new title did not 'grant new responsibilities', in fact Bormann interpreted his ability to act as the 'Führer's Secretary' in matters outside his capacity as head of the Party Chancellery as a licence to intervene virtually at will in affairs of state. The Party Chancellery focused on issues central to Nazi ideology: eg. population policy, the churches (a topic of particular interest to Bormann) and the Jews. It tended to press for a radicalization of policy in these areas.

But the key to Bormann's influence was still, as indeed it always had been, his permanent proximity to the Führer. Bormann did not have complete control over access to the Führer. Appointments could be made with Hitler or communications passed on to him through his personal adjutants. This was how powerful ministers, like Speer, could get to see him without having to go through Bormann. Indeed, Hitler himself was aware of the danger of allowing Bormann too much control over access to him. For example, he told Winifrid Wagner to go through his adjutants and not through Bormann if she wanted to contact him.

However, the adjutants were well aware of whom Hitler wished to see and whom he did not and Bormann's constant presence ensured that he could choose the right moment to approach Hitler about a particular issue. From the very beginning of the war, Lammers had endeavoured to keep as close as possible to Hitler, establishing a branch or 'field quarters' of the Reich Chancellery attached to the Führer Headquarters, sometimes based in Himmler's special train. However, unlike Bormann, he was not one of Hitler's personal entourage and in the end this, combined with the growing political weight of the Party towards the end of the war, proved decisive in their struggle for influence. Lammers had his last proper interview with Hitler on 24 September 1944. After that he was only able to see him on a few occasions briefly to get his signature on documents.

On 1 January 1945, Lammers poured out his frustration in a remarkable letter to Bormann. It signifies the total collapse of the once proud Prusso-German state administration. Its senior figure is no longer consulted even about matters of great importance and has to humiliate himself before the head of the Party which it had tried simultaneously both to serve and to resist:

**940**  My dear Bormann,

... At the beginning of this new year, which is of such importance for the German nation and for every individual, I do not want to fail to wish you most sincerely, dear Bormann, all the best for your responsible work for Führer and people, but also for your personal prosperity and that of your family. I would also like to express the hope that our hitherto happy official collaboration and our personal friendly relations may remain the same as they have now been for years.

Our official and personal ties appear, however, to have somewhat loosened recently, to my very great regret, not through my fault, but for what are obviously not very important reasons, of which I am not fully aware and can only guess at. I would like to speak frankly in this connection, and I wish, in the first place, to talk about the problems of a general nature which are causing me great concern:

1. From the moment when, for perfectly justifiable reasons, I was ordered on 21 October last year to give up my field quarters attached to the Führer's Headquarters, I have been, so to speak, completely 'adrift' from the Führer and his Headquarters. My last official interview with the Führer took place more than three months ago, on 24 September of last year. Although I know that, owing to his preoccupation with the day-to-day direction of the war, the Führer has often been unable, for several months on end, to grant me, and us jointly, an interview, it was nevertheless my duty to press for this interview. For it actually concerns matters of which the Führer himself expects from me a final resolution, and for the early resolution of which I am answerable to him. I have, therefore, pressed, and still do so, by no means for my own sake, but only for the sake of the Führer and of the cause.

It does, after all, mainly concern matters which are important for the conduct of the war. And there are many other matters of which this cannot exactly be said, but which also must be dealt with one day during the war, if the number of little things not attended to is not gradually to cause disorder and damage, and finally to create the impression that the functioning of the state machinery has come to a standstill.

I am continually being pressed from all quarters to obtain the numerous decisions by the Führer which are urgently awaited. What I myself can deal with I deal with. What I can divert elsewhere I divert elsewhere. But the very things which are most important and most urgent, if they are settled at all, are not settled by me, because this is made impossible for me. But all the same I have to bear the whole or at least part of the responsibility for them.

A further consequence is that the Reich Ministers, the other supreme Reich authorities and other offices which come directly under the Führer and which, according to the Führer's instructions, are under my supervision, when they see that through me they get nowhere, choose other, not always desirable and right, ways to the Führer or address him directly. For the Führer this is an extra burden or, at least looked at from the point of view of time, a multiple burden!

I have to bear, both from the Führer and from the Ministers, etc., the odium of not having got things done! Further, it puts me in the unpleasant and often embarrassing position of having decisions by the Führer passed on to me in which I did not collaborate at all but for which I have to be responsible. Some of these I have to sign jointly and share responsibility for, without ever having been in a position to draw the Führer's attention to some essential aspects which might have brought him to a different decision . . .

I believe I can take it for granted that the Führer has not withdrawn from me the confidence which he has so far placed in me and assured me of. Indeed, I am of the opinion that the Führer is simply not told what a great many important matters I have been waiting to put before him and what harm and difficulties will arise if I continue to be excluded as I am at present. I therefore request you, my dear Bormann, to arrange a short interview with the Führer for me simply to clarify these questions. I would not bring any reports with me. I simply consider it my duty to place these questions before the Führer in detail and I hope that he will understand that I am bound to do this. If the Führer is, solely for reasons known to me, not in a position in the near future to take decisions himself as Reich Chancellor on matters the presentation of which he himself demands of me or which I am duty bound to place before him, it still remains my duty to explain the position in greater detail and leave him to examine the question of whether he will at least depute certain decisions to other authorities, in so far as they do not have to be taken by him, so that the machinery of state does not come to a standstill in those matters which must be decided in wartime too. I particularly emphasize that I am not aspiring to be the authority to whom this duty should be delegated. I would also like to place before the Führer a number of other suggestions which would serve to guarantee the faultless working of the state machinery during the further course of the war, without the direct participation of the Führer. I therefore request you once more to arrange a date for me to report to the Führer as soon as possible, just so as to sort out these questions . . .

I only wish you had recently taken account of my interest, i.e. my cooperation and participation, in the affairs which come within my competence or in affairs in which I must participate in the same manner as I normally used to. I am sorry to say that this has frequently not happened. I only wish to remind you of the Decree for the Creation of the Volkssturm [Home Guard][13], of your difference of opinion with Minister Frank about the construction of emplacements in the Protectorate and of the last Führer decree concerning the Youth Leaders of the German Reich without going into details here. Trustful cooperation is only possible if it is mutual. I have always observed this in my relations with you. I have never separately and one-sidedly reported to the Führer on any Party matter or any matter in which the Party was concerned, or in which it was merely interested. I even went so far as invariably to discuss with you in confidence numerous matters which did not require your participation and to deal with them in cooperation with you, because I considered this, not indeed necessary, but appropriate and expedient. I have never yet claimed to intervene officially in purely Party affairs. I think you must admit this. I am totally unaware of and unable to explain any other grounds you could have for being ill-disposed towards me or for your letting anything come between us, as is already giving occasion for comment by others. I would be most grateful to you if you would be kind enough to inform me frankly of any such grounds. After all, frank talk and honest discussion are always best. All insinuations from outsiders, who may have misinformed you or wrongly influenced you, would thus fall to the ground. Otherwise, they will rejoice at bringing about our estrangement. For our mutual cooperation to date has long been a thorn in the flesh of various people who would have preferred to have played us off against each other.

In conclusion, I should only like to repeat what I wrote at the beginning of this letter, namely to express my wish that our official and personal relations should remain in the new year the same as they have been in the past. I am not aware of having disturbed them. It is now your turn to say something—either by letter or by word of mouth. I am always at your disposal to talk things over.

———

The final eclipse of Lammers by Bormann during 1943–5 was paralleled by other developments which marked the takeover of the state by hardline Nazi leaders. The first was the replacement, on 20 August 1943, of the bureaucratic old Nazi, Wilhelm Frick, as Reich Interior Minister by the Reichsführer SS, Heinrich Himmler. This decision reflected Hitler's growing concern about the decline in popular morale which was reflected in the SD reports on popular opinion. Hitler was determined to avoid another 8 November 1918. The recent overthrow of Mussolini had only served to underline the vulnerability of dictators who had recently appeared impregnable.

Himmler was of course already head of the German police. However, as Reich Interior Minister he became responsible for the whole German

---

[13] See below, pp. 643ff.

internal administration. He had long had his eyes on the Interior Ministry and was already Frick's deputy as Reich Plenipotentiary for the Administration (GBV). It was, however, a position which placed him potentially in conflict with the Nazi Party apparatus which was challenging the state administration for predominance at regional and local level.

Himmler's position and the position of the Nazi movement vis-à-vis the traditional German establishment was strengthened still further with his appointment on 20 July 1944 as Commander of the Army Reserve with the authority to mobilize all available forces for front-line action. This appointment was closely linked to another important development, namely the appointment of the Propaganda Minister, Joseph Goebbels, as Reich Plenipotentiary for Total War Mobilization on 25 July 1944. The background to this appointment provides valuable insights into the workings of the German government during the war years.

## (ix) Goebbels as Reich Plenipotentiary for Total War

As we have seen, Goebbels had long been pressing for a more ruthless mobilization of Germany's resources in order to wage total war. In the spring of 1943, he and Speer had failed in their attempt to replace the Committee of Three with a beefed-up Ministerial Council for the Defence of the Reich with Göring as front man. During the early summer of 1944, with the collapse of Army Group Centre on the Eastern front and the successful D-Day invasion in the west, Germany's military situation became more and more critical and the shortage of manpower for deployment at the front and in the armaments industry increasingly acute.

In this situation Goebbels and Speer embarked once more on a coordinated campaign to press Hitler to take more drastic action to squeeze the home front. On 2 July Goebbels published an article in his flagship journal *Das Reich* with the title 'Are we fighting a total war?' Four days later, at a conference with Hitler, Speer advised him to order 'a significantly more ruthless stance on the total mobilization of the home front, one appropriate to the present situation'. In the minutes he noted: 'I therefore propose that the Führer should address a small group concerning the requirements for this increased mobilization. This group should consist of the Reichsführer SS Himmler, Reich Minister Dr Lammers, Field Marshal Keitel, Gauleiter Sauckel, Dr Goebbels, Reich Minister Speer. The Führer is in agreement with this proposal'.[14]

---

[14] See W. A. Boelcke, ed., *Deutschlands Rüstung im Zweiten Weltkrieg. Hitlers Konferenzen mit Albert Speer 1942–1945* (Frankfurt/M 1969), p. 390.

On 12 July Speer sent Hitler the first of two memoranda explaining how more manpower could be mobilized:

**941**  My Führer,

You are convinced that with the new technically superior weapons, aircraft, U-Boats, with the deployment of the A4,[15] and with the increase in production of tanks and anti-tank weapons, within three or four months we can overcome the worst of the crisis which confronts us and thus we must do everything to reduce its effects as far as possible.

In addition, you point out that 3–4 months of production would be almost sufficient to make up for the deficit if, during the same period, normal wastage occurs and there are no catastrophic losses.

*However, in order to achieve these armaments production goals and at the same time avoid catastrophes during the transitional phase, it is essential to mobilize our last reserves until our technical superiority is restored.*

To achieve this the main priority—despite the simultaneous additional pressures on armaments—is to provide the Wehrmacht with soldiers. This problem is difficult to solve, but I am convinced that what is required can still be achieved despite all the difficulties.

[After referring to the possible deployment of foreign workers Speer emphasized the importance of mobilizing domestic reserves:]

My Führer, of course many people doubt whether we still have reserves at home. However, the air raids have shown that a life lived amidst ruins—without pubs, without places of entertainment, without a congenial home life, in fact without the satisfaction of numerous daily human needs—is possible. It has shown that commerce and banking can survive with only part of their previous operations, that in all spheres the same experts who previously sharply rejected all changes and cuts suddenly find they can improvise, that, for example, passengers pay their fares even when no tickets can be issued since they have been burnt, and that the tax authorities still receive payments from people even when the taxation documents have been burnt in the tax offices.

Working people will accuse us of indecisiveness if we are not prepared to go to the limits in the present situation. The moment may come when the efforts of German workers may decline because they do not understand why we do not take vigorous steps temporarily to transform our life style in order thereby to mobilize new reserves. It is dangerous to proclaim total war, to discuss it, and then not to implement it in many areas. In the event of serious military setbacks which may confront us, the energy of German workers, which is necessary for them to carry out their work, may be sapped, not because they doubt the strength of the German nation, but because they doubt the determination of the German Reich government.

I am not alone in holding this view, my Führer; I have gained it from the numerous conversations I have had with workers during the past weeks. An underlying concern was repeatedly expressed as to whether the leadership was

---

[15] The VI rocket.

really determined to go to the limits and would carry out the necessary measures with the most extreme vigour. What would be the consequences, for example, if 30–40 per cent of our German domestic servants were withdrawn from their existing work for six months and, as a result, approximately 300,000–400,000 women were deployed in the war effort, or if 1/3 or 1/4 of the cleaning ladies, who are still working in German administrative offices, were withdrawn. Why in the present circumstances are there still female students studying philology, music, fashion, languages or other things which are now of absolutely no interest? Why should one not recruit these 30,000 intelligent young women for work? Why should the 100,000–150,000 strong air defence police not be deployed en bloc in German armaments' plants so that they can then be deployed locally in the event of air raids?

In the light of the experience which has been gained in those cities damaged by air raids, can one not cut back large parts of the administration and transfer the personnel to more important tasks in view of the fact that the German administration currently employs 3.851 million people? It is also certainly possible to redeploy 100,000–200,000 men from general war production. Also, in the view of the industrialists who were engaged to study this question, such as, for example, Röchling, Pleiger, Krauch, Vögler etc., it is possible through rationalization of the home-based administration of the armed forces, including the Waffen SS, the Todt Organization, and the Reich Labour Service to produce considerable savings and nevertheless improve the performance of these organizations so that not only soldiers but also workers could be released to become new soldiers.

Numerous examples could be put forward which demonstrate that simplific-ation of our complicated state apparatus, the Wehrmacht and our civilian life would be possible, above all if they were only temporary measures for six months to a year. However, the most vigorous measures must be implemented to achieve this; the success of the measures will only be possible if exceptional powers can be granted which apply to all ministries and the whole of the economy. It is only possible if the total commitment of the German home front and the conscious break with our notions of a civilized [bürgerlich] way of life is carried through in a revolutionary fashion.

All those who come from the administration or the business world and from the Wehrmacht itself are not at all suitable for carrying out comprehensive revolutionary measures, since they are handicapped by specialist knowledge and by their existing attitudes. They will be thwarted by their own misgivings. That has already been proved by the Committee of Three—Lammers/Bormann/ Keitel—which you appointed and which was not capable of implementing the total measures to strengthen our war potential. It is no longer appropriate to let such questions be decided by committees or commissions. Responsibility in the Reich must rather be allocated to those personalities who have the courage to take risky decisions and who at the same time can keep their nerve even in the most serious crises and not act rashly.

I can only see one possibility after the crisis of the next few months: we must be successful with the help of the new weapons but only *if we now undertake the total mobilization of the German people for our struggle.*

My Führer, the nation awaits that!

With the proclamation of your decision now to mobilize even the last reserves a deeply-felt enthusiasm will be unleashed such as the nation has not experienced since the Wars of Liberation [1813–15 against Napoleon].

Heil My Führer!
Yours,
SPEER

Then, on 18 July, Goebbels sent the following memorandum to Hitler using material on the manpower situation supplied by Speer. Not only does it illuminate Goebbels' view of the state of the war and of Germany's conduct of it, but it also provides a fascinating insight into how Goebbels handled Hitler:

**942** My Führer

At this critical phase of the war, when we are having to face the attacks of our enemies on all fronts, I feel obliged to inform you once again about my ideas on the total utilization of our national energies in order to ensure the victory of our arms. You know, my Führer, that I am not influenced by any scepticism or timidity. Throughout the war, even during its most critical phases, I have never doubted our final victory even for a moment. I am too much a man of faith to have ever harboured any doubts about you or your historic work. Moreover, the political and military circumstances of this war are such that at every new juncture it offers us new chances of success. Furthermore, do I still need to emphasize that I cannot and will not contemplate that I or the nation could survive in the event of our failure to win the day? I have stood by you for twenty years and believe that I have been a stronger support for you in difficult than in easier times. I want to make that clear right from the start.

As far as the situation itself is concerned, from my point of view it appears to be as follows: we are confronted by a world coalition of enemies, who in terms of numbers have an unattainable and in terms of matériel an almost unattainable superiority. Only one section of this coalition lacks an ideology; the other has been educated in a radical, uncompromising perspective. Moreover, it has embarked on the exploitation of its manpower and economic potential to an extent with which we have nothing comparable. Even if England and the USA are not going all out in this war, the Soviets certainly are. I am also convinced that the internal contradictions within the enemy coalition must in the end lead to a breach. But I sometimes ask myself the ominous question whether that will happen soon enough for us and whether at that moment we shall have enough trumps in our hand in order to exploit such a crisis in the coalition of our enemies to our advantage. Germany will have won this war if it does not lose it, if it isn't defeated. Our aim, therefore, must be to remain on the battlefield under all circumstances irrespective of when, where, how, and in what state we do so. To achieve this, one can never be too strong.

. . . Internally, we still possess huge reserves of manpower and economic strength which have not yet been mobilized let alone exploited. However, these reserves will not improve by being left unused; they will deteriorate. In my view our conduct of the war suffers from the fact that we expect too much of certain sections of the nation, e.g. those at the front, the cities subject to air attack, certain categories of armaments workers, the women who were already working in 1939 etc. and too little of the remaining sections of the nation. That will hardly be to our advantage in the long run either materially or psychologically.

. . . Our people have too sharp a political instinct not to draw their own conclusions from the situation as it is daily portrayed in our OKW reports. In the past few weeks I have spoken to countless people from all walks of life and all levels of education and have not encountered anybody who was not convinced that he could not achieve more than he is doing and who was not prepared in fact to do more if only he was shown how. We must be in a bad way if we National Socialists have not the organizational and improvizational talent to utilize such a surplus of national energy and goodwill for our war effort.

I have absolute faith in the Party. But my faith in the Wehrmacht and in particular in its generals is seriously shaken. The Wehrmacht is our great consumer of people; but it does not possess the requisite organizational elasticity to deploy the many millions of men which we have placed at its disposal correctly. Reecently, I had the opportunity to talk with a number of businessmen who had the task of inspecting the Wehrmacht's working methods. Their assessment was clear and unerring, but also lethal. It simply confirmed again my preconceived opinion, which I could back up with a hundred instances from my own sphere. I also do not expect much from a reform of the Wehrmacht by the Wehrmacht itself. Its apparatus is so rampant and bloated that one would need to take a knife to cut it back into a natural shape. But, in the nature of things, that cannot be the task for one of them; it must be done by an outsider, either from the Party or possibly from business. This is the absolute prerequisite for the rational deployment of personnel within the Reich. If it is not fulfilled we run the risk that even further additions of manpower to the Wehrmacht will not make a substantial difference. We shall be pouring water into a bucket without a bottom. As far as civilian life is concerned, in my view it ought to be possible to transfer it from the peacetime condition in which it is still to some extent operating to a true state of war. But, for this to happen, it will be necessary to grant powers over certain areas which should not be permitted to be restricted by existing powers, but, on the contrary, should have the effect of cancelling them. These powers should certainly be exercised by the Party since it alone has the requisite initiative and gifts of improvization for such a gigantic mobilization process. The organization responsible for directing the whole action should restrict itself to issuing the directives, getting the movement fired up, keeping it going and supervising the observance of the directives. I can imagine that one could unleash undreamt of additional amounts of energy from every Gauleiter if one took him on one side and made it absolutely clear to him where our most dangerous bottlenecks are. One would only need to give him the overall framework within which he may operate and leave everything else to his own entrepreneurial drive . . . I would rather not mention the slack which is apparent throughout the administration. There is hardly any sphere in our public life in which there are not three or four authorities governing alongside one another and whose main activity consists of making difficulties for each other, casting suspicion on each other's work or goodwill and thereby maintaining an army of personnel which could be deployed in productive work or even in the army . . . Friendly persuasion is no good anymore; the evil is dug in too far. Ruthless action must be taken. It is no good saying that that won't make any difference to the number of people we need. Every office, whether within the state or the Wehrmacht, has a trail of people who act or do not act in its name as the case may be, but who are exempt from military duties. When, during November and December, Berlin was so badly hit, the paper war suddenly stopped and a whole number of state and Wehrmacht offices disappeared from the scene for weeks on end. Nobody noticed their absence; at most people made jokes about it and it only manifested itself in the fact that the work suddenly went more smoothly.

What primitive conditions we used to work and fight under in the Party in the old days, but what success we had! Is this not a case of cause and effect? And why does the Party continue to have such successes during the war? Not simply because it works with idealism and faith, but because its apparatus is small and flexible and, therefore, can really lead. When I took over the office of City president of Berlin, this office had 600 personnel and yet it didn't work. I reduced its numbers to 50 and it worked like a dream. The same is true everywhere. An Unruh commission can establish that but it cannot eliminate it because it has no authority.[16] It is simply laughed out of court. The cuts made by General von Unruh are simply replaced while his back is turned. What is needed is a categorical order from the Führer and the delegation of responsibilities to men with backbone and character who implement the Führer's orders without any consideration for persons or offices and do not shrink from proposing to him the most severe penalties for those who go against his order. Such penalties need only be imposed and implemented a few times since they will have a deterrent effect.

My Führer, these measures must be delegated to men who enjoy your absolute trust and have blind faith in you and in victory and who have not been made tired and lethargic by the war having gone on for so long. These men can only achieve something if they are in possession of full powers. I myself, for example, have never felt so good about my work as in the Berlin blitz, however painful it may have been at the time because all those who had been fighting over responsibilities had left the scene under the impact of events and those who cooperated only did so in order to assist without questioning the chain of command. That would also be true in this case. I do not believe a committee would be any good. I was involved in the tragedy of the so-called 'Committee of Three' and would like to warn against reviving it. Every major decision was chewed over and prevaricated upon until, in the end, only a makeshift solution could come out of it. That is quite normal. On every occasion when great issues were at stake for the Party or the state you, my Führer, gathered men around you and not committees. Unfortunately, I can only put forward my own experiences as an example of what I mean because they are the most familiar to me. When

---

[16] A commission under General von Unruh had been appointed by Hitler on 22 November 1942 to comb through state and Wehrmacht agencies looking for men who could be deployed to the front.

you sent me to Berlin in October 1926, in order to sort out the mess in the Party in the capital, you didn't give me a committee but comprehensive powers[17]. I am sure that in the heat of the battle I may have had to do some people an injustice, but I built up a respectable Gau and thereby carried out your orders. Total war will also not be able to be mobilized without committing injustices. But what does injustice mean if the Fatherland is in danger! In 1941 we did not want to do women an injustice by compelling them to work because undoubtedly there were physical and moral dangers in doing so. Today the same women are sitting on the roofs in Berlin in storm, rain and heat and are nailing down their felt, if they've got any, without anyone asking whether that is just or unjust.

Thus I suggest, my Führer, that for every task that needs dealing with you assign far-reaching powers to someone who has your absolute confidence, something that can easily be sorted out in a joint meeting with you. Instruct him to work out a plan of procedure in short order. Give one of these men the task of coordinating these plans and then each one should get to work armed with your full authority. One will perform the supervisory role in the most collegial fashion as, for example, we have arranged in the case of the Reich Air War Inspectorate with conspicuous success. The quality of the men who have been assigned of whom there should only be a few, will guarantee loyal cooperation. You, my Führer, will be consulted regularly on the most decisive questions; but any attempt to bother you with ridiculous trivialities and with difficulties that can be resolved directly by those involved will be frowned upon. I have always considered it totally irresponsible, my Führer, to burden you with the detailed organization of resources in addition to your responsibility for war leadership. That is the same as if one required a regimental commander at the front to recruit his own regiment himself. When do you get the time, my Führer, to consider in peace and calm the decisive problems of the war, in view of the daily grind of work, although that is now, as it has always been, the most important thing of all? You are simply overwhelmed with work by men who lack initiative and imagination and then, in the end, one's physical strength is bound to give out. Each time that I visit you I look into your eyes and at your face to see how well you are . . .

One cannot allow you to be burdened with even the smallest responsibility simply to ensure that the person who should be carrying responsibility is covered. For that is usually the reason. So men must be appointed who combine imagination, political passion, a deep faith in you and your work with an eagerness to take responsibility, in fact a positive thirst for responsibility. They shall exploit and organize our national resources. They must carry out the reforms which the situation is crying out for. You, my Führer, will only experience satisfaction with such men. They should not be full of illusions but equally not be pessimists. In three or four months, my Führer, they will certainly provide you with fifty new divisions. The Armaments Minister will acquire additional manpower in order to intensify armaments production still further. During this period, we shall also have overcome our technical crisis. Then, my Führer, you will hold the fighting instrument in your hand with which you can win the final victory . . .

I have not discussed these ideas with anyone else; they have come from my own reflections and my own concern about the present situation. After all, my

---

[17] See Vol. 1, docs 36–37.

Führer, I have always been one of those who have stood by you faithfully and unshakeably during the critical hours when major and risky decisions have had to be taken. In March 1932, I was not a member of that group who urged you not to be a candidate in the second round of the Reich presidential election, but was one of the few who defended your decision to the contrary with burning fanaticism. I was the one who, on New Year's Eve 1932/3, enthusiastically greeted your decision to take part in the Lippe election by committing the whole strength of the Party and particularly of its leadership, and who worked out for you a programme and a campaign plan in the shortest possible time. I think that since then my temperament and my views have not altered one iota. If I now approach you, my Führer, in order to put forward these proposals, I know that you will be entirely willing to give them your consideration. You will also appreciate my concern . . .

After Stalingrad I proclaimed total war in the Sports Palace; but its effect was only superficial.[18] At the same time, the front and our blitzed cities got to know it. What is preventing us from extending it now to the whole nation, to the Party, Wehrmacht, the state, and the whole of public and private life? One could still discuss the modalities, but not I think the need to do it. Such measures could produce an unimaginable improvement in the morale of the whole nation. The nation would see that we're on the move again and would draw new hope from that. As far as the situation at home and abroad is concerned, the political consequences would only be positive. We would move carefully but ruthlessly. The measures to be taken would be comprehensive and effective. Some injustice might be caused; but in return the nation would once again acquire its right to exist. Our enemies are determined to destroy us. They use every conceivable means to achieve that end. We must confront them with a tougher determination. But this determination must not be limited to historical reminiscences; it must show itself in deeds and decisive action.

I am writing all this to you, my Führer, in order to get things off my chest. I know that you will receive it in the spirit in which I intend it. You know that my life belongs to you. More: each time when I am in Lanke with my six children I appreciate once again that not only I myself but my family as a whole could and must never live in a period which did not belong to us. That too makes me do everything which lies in my power in order to bring our cause to a successful conclusion. Our people await great decisions. The daily reception of the current news from the front can have a debilitating effect in the long run if nothing decisive is done about the crisis. So the moment to act has arrived. In war one can never be too concerned about one's strength and never possess too much strength. Let us throw everything that we call our own onto the scales of decision, then we shall be certain of victory.

If you, my Führer, give the command then your people will not only follow your orders but also obey them. But do give them orders. You will see what friends and comrades in arms, but also what a nation you have.

Heil my Führer!<br>
Yours faithfully<br>
JOSEPH GOEBBELS

---

[18] See below, pp. 490ff. and 545–46.

The Führer meeting proposed by Speer in his conversation with Hitler on 6 July took place on 22 July, though typically without Hitler. In the meantime, and particularly in the light of Goebbels' decisive role in crushing the attempted coup by the 20 July plotters, Hitler had decided to grant Goebbels the exceptional position which he had been seeking:

**943** *Minutes of the Meeting concerning the appointment of a Reich Plenipotentiary for Total War*

The following were present: Reichsleiter Bormann, Field Marshal Keitel, Reich Minister Dr Goebbels, Reich Minister Speer, Reich Minister Funk, Gauleiter Sauckel, State Secretary Stuckart [Interior Ministry], State Secretary Dr Klopfer [Party Chancellery], State Secretary Neumann [Four-Year Plan], Ministerial Director Dr Faust [Interior Ministry], Major General Weidemann (OKW), Director Dr Hillebrecht [Party Chancellery]. Present from the Reich Chancellery: Reich Minister Dr Lammers, Reich Cabinet Councillor Dr Killy, Reich Cabinet Councillor von Stutterheim, Ministerial Councillor Dr Boley.

Reich Minister Dr Lammers referred to Reich Minister Speer's memo to the Führer [doc. 941] which had prompted this meeting. The Führer wished for a short discussion of the issues touched on by Reich Minister Speer so that there should not be a detailed debate. Reich Minister Speer had himself expressed the view that the current war situation required the granting of comprehensive powers.

The Committee of Three had done as much as was possible with the means at its disposal, as the figures for the securing of manpower from the particular major actions demonstrate:

| | |
|---|---|
| Registration for Conscription | 1,126,000 |
| Checking of Reserved Status Workers | 830,000 |
| Plant Closure action | 150,000 |
| Combing through action | 400,000 |

In some cases measures which had been planned had not found the Führer's approval or had come up against decisive opposition from government departments. Now the situation was so critical that a commission was no longer adequate to fulfil the set tasks and it appeared necessary to grant comprehensive powers to a single individual. In the civilian sphere Dr Goebbels was regarded as the most suitable person for this. For the military sector it appeared advisable to grant special powers which it would be appropriate to transfer to Reich Minister Himmler.

Reich Minister Goebbels declared at the start of his lengthy statement that Reich Minister Dr Lammers had already said much of what he wanted to say. Now it was no longer a matter of individual measures but rather of turning total war from a propaganda slogan into reality. It would be completely wrong to blame the Committee of Three since it had done what it could with the means available. Even if a single individual had now been appointed he would still be very much dependent on the cooperation of all the Government departments. His task could not be to take particular measures but rather continually to press the responsible agencies to do what was necessary to provide the requisite momentum for their actions. The German people were unanimously of the opinion that, in contrast to the Soviet Union, we were not conducting total war and they explained the current situation in terms of this fact. It was incredible that major conferences, festivals and such like were still being held. Total war was not only a matter of matériel but above all a problem of psychology. The measures to be taken would only have an effect in 4–5 months but this was no reason not to endeavour to achieve maximum concentration of effort now. To achieve this, all opposition from whatever direction which a single individual might come up against must be broken. If no agreement can be reached with the relevant department head then he and the Reich Plenipotentiary must seek a joint interview with the Führer, who must decide. Other avenues of access to the Führer in such cases should no longer be open.

Reich Minister Goebbels then explained that the task should be seen in terms of three spheres:

1. Review of the Wehrmacht.
2. Review of the state apparatus.
3. Reforms in public life.

The Party no longer represents a reservoir of manpower since it can only just cope with its current personnel.

Re: 1. The Wehrmacht naturally tends to a somewhat luxurious use of manpower. This must be changed by granting comprehensive powers to the Reichsführer SS Himmler, who has a healthy attitude and sufficient experience. The Reichsführer SS must utilize the assistance of the Head of the Supreme Command of the Wehrmacht for this purpose. The apparatus at home and in the rear areas must be ruthlessly pruned for the benefit of the front line.

Re: 2. The task of reviewing the state apparatus is definitely unpopular but extremely important. Many rationalization plans in this sphere had failed because of opposition from Government departments. An individual like General von Unruh was completely unsuitable for carrying out such a task because he was no match for the department heads. Above all, it was vital to make cuts at the top of the administration, not so much in terms of people, who in total did not represent a significant manpower reserve, as in tasks. By reducing tasks one would achieve a remarkable reduction in the burden on the lower-level offices who would then themselves be able to release personnel.

Re: 3. The reform of public life would to some extent only be able to have a cosmetic character; however, the significance of such measures should not be underrated. Thus, to cite one example, orders had already been given not to rebuild theatres and cinemas which had been destroyed.

Reich Minister Dr Goebbels responded to Reich Minister Lammers' proposal of himself for the post by saying that he was prepared to undertake the tasks involved in 2 and 3, although he was by no means pushing himself forward. He believed that he would be in a position to master these tasks, particularly since he was continually in Berlin and possessed the requisite administrative apparatus. In the case of most of the special powers which had [hitherto] been allocated, countervailing powers had not been withdrawn. This was absolutely vital.

The task of the Party would be to secure the implementation of the project at the intermediate and lower levels. The Party already possessed all the necessary powers to do this. Everything that needed to be done must be done legally. The codification of the requisite legal regulations would have to be the task of the Reich Minister and Head of the Reich Chancellery. This must be combined with a major transformation of the situation with the aim of allocating manpower to armaments production, which must be carried out by the Armaments Minister [Speer] and, finally, a major general labour conscription programme must be carried out by the General Plenipotentiary for Labour [Sauckel].

On the basis of the results of this conference all participants should present themselves to the Führer as a body and declare that the crisis of the Fatherland demands major measures. The Führer must be freed from all minor details so that he can concentrate entirely on his great historic tasks.

Field Marshal Keitel thanked Reich Minister Dr Goebbels on behalf of the Wehrmacht for his remarks. He was in complete agreement with him and welcomed in particular the fact that special powers had been requested for Reich Minister Himmler. In view of its links with tradition, the Wehrmacht was often not in a position to overcome opposition to reforms within its own sphere. For example, it had come about that the Führer was continually requested to make decisions about the most insignificant military questions, which was quite intolerable. He, the head of the OKW, had suffered particularly under these circumstances and, in particular, had been unable to assert himself sufficiently vis-à-vis the chiefs of the individual branches of the Wehrmacht. He would, therefore, find it a relief if his responsibility could be transferred to a second pair of shoulders. Field Marshal Keitel then referred to the existing powers of General Ziegler who was delegated with the task of carrying out a rationalization of the Wehrmacht organizations. It would be desirable for Ziegler's powers to be strengthened and integrated into the general authority of the Reichsführer SS, since he had first-class talent at his disposal. Particular care must be taken that such powers were not rendered worthless by contradictory orders or directives from the superiors of those involved.

Reichsleiter Bormann recognized that tougher measures had to be taken. The difficulties lay in particular in the resistance of the Government departments and in the possibility of making objections to the Führer. A uniform national approach must be adopted and it must be ensured that the powers granted by the Führer were clear and unambiguous. As far as the interview with the Führer was concerned, the key question was whether the Führer would agree to the proposals in this general form or would prefer individual proposals. The former would only have a point if the whole project was carried out with incredible elan and tempo.

Reich Minister Speer agreed with the remarks of Reich Minister Dr Lammers, Reich Minister Dr Goebbels and Field Marshal Keitel. There were still huge reserves at home and they must be immediately exploited. The present manpower situation was still not as it should be with unproductive outlays still too high and organizational mistakes still too frequent. Armaments production was still too lightly manned in comparison with the administration, which operated with an apparatus of 3.851 million people. In the case of the Wehrmacht the fighting troops lacked soldiers, while there were too many in home bases and in the rear areas. It was different in the First World War when there had been many times the number of soldiers at the front.

State Secretary Dr Stuckart argued that Reich Minister Dr Goebbels' proposals represented the only way of getting out of the present situation. There must, however, be no general exemptions in any sphere and, furthermore, there must be clarification of how objections from Government department heads are to be dealt with. State Secretary Dr Stuckart also dealt once more with the question of the personnel situation in the administration in more detail. No further personnel could be obtained for the Wehrmacht and the armaments industry from the Reich railways and post office. In the administration too this was hardly feasible any more, since virtually only essential services were being carried on.

In reply to State Secretary Dr Stuckart's remarks, Dr Goebbels objected that the discussions should not become bogged down in details as Reich Minister Dr Lammers had indicated at the beginning.

Reich Minister Funk supported the maintenance and strengthening of the individual responsibility of the departmental heads.

Gauleiter Sauckel supported the remarks of Dr Goebbels but considered it necessary to discuss details in so far as it must be clarified whether and where there were people who could be deployed to carry out the required tasks.

Reich Minister Dr Goebbels emphasized once more that the meeting should stick to the following main points:

(a) Do we want major responsibilities transferred to individual personalities?
(b) Do we want to agree on the names of these personalities?
(c) Do we want to present the Führer with a uniform opinion?

There was no objection to these remarks. Since the figures given by the Reich Minister on the manpower in the administration had evidently given rise to detailed discussions, Dr Goebbels proposed that Reich Minister Speer should declare that these figures were withdrawn. Reich Minister Speer agreed to this.

Reich Minister Dr Lammers then declared that the only thing left to decide was who should be the spokesman with the Führer. He proposed Reich Minister Dr Goebbels. Reich Minister Dr Goebbels replied that he could hardly propose himself and requested that Reich Minister Dr Lammers should undertake to report. Reich Minister Dr Lammers agreed to do this and closed the meeting.

On 25 July 1944, Hitler issued the following Führer decree establishing the post of Reich Plenipotentiary for Total War Mobilization. Goebbels was appointed to the post under a separate decree, while Himmler had already been made commander of the Army Reserve on 20 July:

**944**    The war situation requires the comprehensive exploitation of all our resources for the Wehrmacht and for rearmament. I therefore decree:

I. (1) The chairman of the Ministerial Council for the Defence of the Reich, Reich Marshal Hermann Göring, will adjust the whole of public life to the requirements of total war in every respect. To carry out this task he will recommend to me a Reich Plenipotentiary for Total War Mobilization. This person will be responsible in particular for ensuring that all public events are appropriate to the objectives of total war and do not remove manpower from the Wehrmacht and from armaments production. He will inspect the whole of the state apparatus, including the Reich railways, the Reich post office, and all public bodies, institutions and utilities with the aim of freeing the maximum amount of manpower for the Wehrmacht and for armaments production through a completely rational deployment of men and equipment, by closing down or restricting activities which are of marginal importance for the war effort and through a rationalization of organization and procedures. For these purposes he may request information from the relevant Supreme Reich authorities and issue them with instructions.
(2) The legal regulations and basic administrative directives to be issued by the Supreme Reich authorities will be enacted in agreement with the Reich Minister and head of the Reich Chancellery, the head of the Party Chancellery, and the Plenipotentiary General for the Reich Administration [Himmler].

II. The head of the Party Chancellery will energetically support the measures ordered by me by deploying the Party on the basis of the powers granted to him.

III. Objections to the instructions the Reich Plenipotentiary for Total War should be referred to him. If an agreement cannot be reached then my decision should be sought through the Reich Minister and head of the Reich Chancellery.

IV. In so far as powers and commissions, which have been previously assigned by me, are not in accordance with this decree they are cancelled.

V. This decree is valid for the territory of the Greater German Reich and correspondingly for the annexed and occupied territories.

————

Hitler's characteristic way of operating was to try and solve crises by creating new agencies and new posts with 'special powers'. These agencies then invariably found themselves bogged down in trench warfare with existing departments and agencies, some of which were also new creations with special powers. The key question was whether Goebbels' new office would fare any better. It was clear from the meeting of 22 July that the representatives of the Government departments (Stuckart and Lammers) hotly disputed claims that the administration still had reserves of manpower available for deployment in the armaments industry or the Wehrmacht. And, in fact, only 78,000 of the one million employed there (excluding railways and post office) were under 43 years of age. Secondly, it was apparent that departmental ministers (Funk) and heads of agencies (Sauckel) would continue to defend their responsibilities against encroachments from the new authority. Under the terms of the decree establishing the new post the Reich Plenipotentiary was entitled to issue instructions but the legal provisions and basic administrative regulations would still be issued by the Government departments. Moreover, Hitler retained the right to make the final decisions on objections to the Plenipotentiary's measures. Also, according to a subsequent decision by Hitler, communicated to Goebbels by Lammers, neither the Reich Chancellery nor the Party Chancellery were answerable to Goebbels. Finally, the Nazi Party retained full autonomy.

In practice Goebbels' efforts were now concentrated on squeezing government bodies and industry to release personnel for the Wehrmacht. Inevitably, this brought Goebbels into confrontation with his previous ally, Speer, who was endeavouring to retain personnel in industry in order to maintain armaments production. In fact, the results of the measures introduced through the new initiative were, if anything, counterproductive, since the stripping of personnel from industry damaged industrial production without enhancing Germany's military capability, for most of those redeployed proved unsuitable for military service. After the war, Under Secretary (*Ministerialdirektor*) Boley of the Reich Chancellery reported that 'the whole action was an almost complete failure'. For the new agency to have succeeded in imposing its authority on the home front would have required the continuing active support of the Führer and this did not occur. The result was that, although Goebbels engaged in frenetic activity in his new role, the gains were minimal. This was partly because of Goebbels' lack of administrative experience and skill and partly because of the intractability of the problems which confronted him. The fact was that, by the summer of 1944, the German home front was already stretched to breaking point and there was very little that could still be done in the way of a more efficient allocation of resources. However, the fact that the responsibility for the 'mobilization for total war' had been granted to the Propaganda Minister was appropriate for a regime which set so much store on image rather than reality. Indeed, Goebbels himself had seen much of the importance of the project in precisely those terms, namely to give the appearance of action in order to raise morale. According to Boley, the effect of Goebbels' decrees had indeed been merely 'cosmetic' (*optisch*).

On 24 July 1944, Goebbels issued the following directives in his new role as Plenipotentiary for Total War:

**945**  1 . . . All theatres, variety shows, cabarets and drama schools are to close by 1 September. Repertory groups as well as private instruction of drama, singing and dancing will cease . . . Those who are released as a result will be called up into the fighting forces in so far as they are capable of combat. All orchestras, music schools and conservatories will cease their artistic activities apart from a few leading orchestras, which are also urgently needed by the radio for its programmes. In the sphere of fine art, exhibitions, competitions, academies, art schools, as well as private art and painting schools will be closed. All publication of belletristic and popular literature will cease. The only books still to be published will be academic, technical, armaments-related, school texts, and certain standard political works.
2. The Strength through Joy programme for entertaining the troops will be closed down . . .
3. In order fully to exploit our labour power, work time in the public administration and commercial offices will be fixed uniformly at 60 hours per week . . . The section of the retinue which is saved through such an increase in work time is to be immediately released for the Wehrmacht and the armaments industry . . .
A general ban on leave is to be implemented with immediate effect . . .

There was, however, one aspect of Goebbels' project which casts a significant light on political developments within the regime during the last period of the war. Right from the start, Goebbels decided that it would only be possible to carry out his task with the support of the Party and he set out to cultivate Bormann, thereby increasing his alienation from Speer. In a Regulation for the Implementation of Total War Mobilization of 16 August 1944 the Gauleiters in their capacity as Reich Defence Commissioners were given comprehensive powers of direction and information over all government offices, firms and businesses at regional and local level. The responsibility for combing through government offices and factories for surplus personnel was delegated to Gau and district (*Kreis*) commissions composed of government, Wehrmacht and Party representatives, in which, however, the local Party leaders had the real say.

This initiative was part of a major shift in power within the regime towards the Nazi Party cadre, which took place during the final phase of the war. It reflected an attempt to deploy the Party in the spheres of both propaganda and organization to mobilize the population for the war effort. The effort was made to recreate within the Party the atmosphere of the 'time of struggle' before 1933 and then use the Party to fire the German population as a whole with the same ardour. This in turn was the culmination of a growth in the influence of the Nazi Party throughout the war.

## List of Sources

919  *Reichsgesetzblatt* (RGBl.) 1939 Teil I, pp. 1539–1540.
920  Bundesarchiv Berlin (BAB) R 43 II/613 Bl.92.
921  International Military Tribunal Nuremberg (IMT) Vol. 11, pp. 64–66.
922  BAB R 43 II/604a.
923  Otto Dietrich, *Zwölf Jahre mit Hitler* (Cologne n.d.), pp. 150–154.
924  (a) Hauptstaatsarchiv Stuttgart (HStAS) E 151cI B 2.
     (b) BAB R43 II/613.
     (c) BAB R43 II/662.
     (d) BAB R3/001573.
925  G. Franz-Willing, *Die Reichskanzlei 1933–1945. Rolle und Bedeutung unter der Regierung Hitler* (Tabingen 1984), p. 77.
926  M. Domarus, *Hitler. Reden 1932–1945.* (Wiesbaden 1973), pp. 1874ff.
927  BAB R43 II/583.
928  BAB R43 II/604a.
929  *Völkischer Beobachter* 13 May 1941.
930  *Völkischer Beobachter* 14 May 1941.
931  RGBl. 1941 Teil I, p. 295.
932  BAB NS 6/785. Bl.1.
933  BAB R 43 II/1213. Bl.92–96.
934  RGBl. 1942 Teil I, p. 35.
935  BAB R 18/358.
936  *The Goebbels Diaries* ed. Louis P. Lochner (New York 1971), pp. 300–302.
937  BAB ZS/603.
938  BAB ZS/615.
939  HStAS Rep.142 O.5.50.
940  Nuremberg Document (ND) D–753-A.
941  W. Bleyer, 'Pläne der faschistischen Führung zum totalen Krieg im Sommer 1944' in *Zeitschrift für die Geschichtswissenschaft* 17.1969, pp. 1317–1319.
942  Peter Longerich, 'Joseph Goebbels und der totale Krieg. Eine unbekannte Denkschrift des Propagandaministers vom 18 Juli 1944' in *Vierteljahrshefte für Zeitgeschichte* 35. (1987), pp. 288ff.
943  Bleyer, op.cit., pp. 1326ff.
944  RGBl. I 1944, p. 161.
945  H. Michaelis, et al. *Ursachen und Folgen Vom deutschen Zusammenbruch 1918, und 1945 bis zur staatlichen Neurodnung Deutschlands in der Gegenwart*, Vol. XX (Berlin n.d.), p. 551.

# CHAPTER 41

# The Nazi Party

## (i) Introduction

The Nazi Party was intended to play a major role in the war effort; its prime function would continue to be the maintenance of popular morale. In his speech to the Reichstag on the outbreak of war Hitler declared: 'Let no one report that morale might be low in his Gau, district or local branch area. I am responsible for the morale of the German people. You are responsible for morale in your Gau or district!'[1] This involved different forms of propaganda, but also tasks of supervision and control designed to prevent activities which might undermine morale, such as blackmarket dealings, hoarding, listening to foreign broadcasts and the spreading of defeatist rumours, or activities which were contrary to Nazi ideological principles such as sexual relations with 'ethnic aliens'. Moreover, the Party's various ancillary organizations—and notably the Nazi welfare organization (NSV), the women's organization (NSF), and the youth organizations (HJ/BdM)—were to play an important part in maintaining the home front throughout the war. Finally, as the allied air attacks increased from 1942 onwards so the local Party cadres (Gauleiters, district and local branch leaders) acquired an increasingly important role in coordinating the measures to deal with the aftermath of the bombing: firefighting, dealing with the dead and injured, clearing away the rubble and re-establishing the basic utilities—gas, water and electricity, housing, food supplies etc. Often they alone had the political clout to cut through the jungle of responsibilities and take the requisite action in an emergency. However, the NSDAP cadres varied very much in their ability and willingness to take on this role. While some, like Gauleiter Karl Kaufmann of Hamburg, performed well, others like Gauleiter Karl Weinrich of Kassel proved incompetent and had to be replaced.

---

[1] Cf. M. Domarus, ed., *Hitlers Reden 1932 bis 1945*. Vol. II (Wiesbaden 1973), p. 1317.

## (ii) The Mobilization Orders

The Nazi Party headquarters in Munich had prepared the following orders for the mobilization of its members and cadres in the event of the outbreak of war. They set up standards of behaviour and performance of which, judging by numerous reports, most cadres fell far short.

**946**  The Führer's Deputy
Department M
SECRET

If war is declared—the German people have only one thought: Victory!
The Wehrmacht is responsible for the military effectiveness of the nation. The Party is responsible for the internal effectiveness of the German people.

Our weapons are unsurpassed in numbers and quality!

Our internal organization is exemplary!

The decisive factor in war is the belief in victory: the belief in the victory of the men who are fighting and the belief in victory of those at home who are a moral and material source of strength for the front.

*The NSDAP is the iron support of this morale*

It keeps the home front politically strong, materially effective and its morale unshakeable!

The plan of how best the Party can deploy the internal forces has been carefully considered. It is hereby communicated to the men of the NSDAP who carry responsibilities. The fulfilment of the duties assigned to them in this plan is a matter of course!

The World War proved the necessity of clearly and tightly defined responsibilities for leadership and command. The experience of the last world war has been utilized; a clear outline of the tasks has been secured!

The Party guarantees that the tasks assigned to it will be carried through to the letter!

The Party will be an unshakeable support for the fighting men at the front.

*If the Wehrmacht is the guarantor of victory at the front, then the Party is the guarantor of victory at home. Our faith is in victory—for its name is: Adolf Hitler!*

**947**  The Führer's Deputy
Department M
SECRET

### Your Duties

1. The Führer always does the right thing for the German people. Through him the Almighty shapes Germany's fate. Every order he gives is necessary for Germany's future.

2. Follow every order you are given unconditionally and to the letter.

3. Only give clear and unmistakable orders.

4. Do not use 'patriotic phrases' such as were current in the past.

5. Do not spread any illusions and avoid pessimism. In a crisis the word of a political cadre (*Hoheitsträger*) of the movement, and particularly one of the Führer's old comrades can carry ten times more weight than that of others.

6. Always remain on the offensive in your political actions. Never let yourself be forced onto the defensive.

7. Show yourself in every situation to be the most committed followers of the Führer prepared for any sacrifice. Be a model in your willingness to make sacrifices and to go without. Always be a good companion to your compatriots. Do not give them any grounds for thinking that your fate in the war will be different from theirs.

8. Always show courage, coolness and confidence. Your compatriots will be inspired by your calm and your unshakeable faith.

9. Commit yourself tirelessly to the completion of the tasks which have been assigned to you.

10. Be prepared to act quickly and on your own initiative and to take on major responsibilities if the situation requires it.

11. Do not fuss about your sphere of 'responsibilities'. Do not encourage jealousies between organizations outside and within the Party and do not tolerate such jealousies among your subordinates. Sort out friction at once and do not wait until your superior has to intervene. Do not practise or tolerate any bureaucracy.

12. Integrate your work into that of the whole. Do your duty and do not talk about it.

13. Never think that anyone will believe in you if you yourself or your family act differently. People will pay particular attention to your life style.

14. Always maintain a good grasp of the situation.

15. Be tough and energetic in supporting those measures of which the population and perhaps you yourself do not necessarily see the point.

16. Never believe that the least of your tasks is unimportant. Always act as if everything depended on you alone.

*The higher the grade of post—the better the example to be set—the tighter the discipline.*

———

 The Führer's Deputy
Department M
SECRET

*The Tasks and Duties of the Cadre and Political Leader in the War*

The cadre and political leader has particular duties in the fulfilment of his role as a leader.

1. He must *maintain absolute discretion and the greatest possible secrecy concerning all directives, measures and orders* whose further communication and publication has not been expressly ordered. He must exercise the greatest care in

the passing on of news, and important reports should only be sent via couriers whose reliability he can guarantee himself.

2. His *courage and confidence* must be an *example* to the population.

3. *He must confront his compatriots with the necessities of war.* Through his personal example and his own behaviour, particularly in situations which demand from him the greatest self-control and high idealism, he must demonstrate convincingly that the commitment of the German people is not only necessary but decisive and that he leads the way in making voluntary sacrifices and in accepting privations.

4. He must continually remind the population in clear and simple terms of the *purpose* and the *aim* of the war.

5. He must cooperate energetically in the *removal of all adverse conditions* and phenomena which could weaken the morale and commitment of the German people. In this connection, he must concentrate, in particular, on those phenomena which, during the World War, initiated the collapse in the people's morale: *black marketeering, hoarding, corruption, war-profiteering etc.* Where such phenomena are discovered they must be nipped in the bud straight away.

6. *He must recognize dangerous and recalcitrant activities in their* early stages so that they can be rooted out and eliminated in good time.

The Party must work in close cooperation with the offices of the Secret State Police [Gestapo]. They must be informed at once of such activities.

7. *He must pay particular attention to the starting of rumours.*

8. *He must vigorously deny unfounded, let alone false, assertions.* It is better to act ruthlessly to begin with than to let assertions become a matter of general discussion.

9. *He must deal ruthlessly with opponents of the war, grumblers, and defeatists in cooperation with the State Police.*

Every war can bring to light hidden opponents of the State, who feel secure since the homeland has been stripped of male forces, and who use the deprivations of war as the focus of their attack. The best method of neutralizing them is to act rigorously and with lightning speed.

10. *He must carefully observe the impact of the military reports,* correct misunderstandings and report any significant observations at once to his superior cadre through a secure channel.

11. *He must inform his superior cadre at once in brief reports of all important matters.*

All reports and information can be important to the enemy. The threat of espionage is always present. The only things that protect against it are carefulness, discretion and secrecy.

12. He must make the population unreceptive to the effects of enemy propaganda through *continual political education.*

In addition, to these tasks of directing and observing the popular mood, the Party will acquire the important task of taking personal care of those compatriots who have been affected by the war. Its fulfilment is of decisive importance for the attitude of the people.

The precondition for the fulfilment of this task is that the cadre and political leader becomes closely informed about the situation of the individual families.

The population's faith in the Party will be secured by his personal concern for the fate of the families which have been affected. *The soldier at the front must know that the leadership and care of his family lies in the secure hands of the NSDAP.*

The cadre and political leader must offer advice and help to families which have got into difficulties. He must offer sympathy, comfort and encouragement to the relatives of those killed in action: by giving them positive tasks to carry out he must take their minds off their sorrow. The bereaved must acquire new strength from the love which the Party shows them. Where domestic discipline suffers from the lack of the father or mother, the cadre and political leader must concern himself with the care of the children with special help from the NS Women's Organization.

He must also concern himself with the fate of small one-man businesses whose owners have been called up and whose control is often in the hands of helpless wives.

—————

**949**  The Fuhrer's Deputy
Department M
SECRET

*The Instructions and Directives for the Deployment of the
Local Branch Leaders in the War*

1. *The position and rights of the cadre*
The cadre (Gauleiter, district leader, local branch leader) is responsible for the *political leadership* and the *supervision/care [Betreuung] of the population of his area.* To carry out this task he is entitled to issue instructions, directives and assignments to those subordinate political leaders and members of the formations, as well as auxiliaries, in his area who are in the wartime service of the NSDAP. They are duty bound to implement the instructions and directives and to carry out the assignments. Failure to do so will be punished in accordance with the laws of war in so far as the use of special protective measures is not required.

2. *The deployment of personnel and equipment*
The tasks which devolve on the Party in the war require the *uniform deployment* and the *tight consolidation of all the personnel and equipment* which are available to the Party. Responsibility for the leadership of this overall deployment can only be located in one office. The office responsible is led at Gau level by the Mobilization Officer of the Gau headquarters acting for the Gauleiter, at district level by the district leader, and in the local branch by the local branch leader of the NSDAP.

The local leader of the Women's Group should be given extensive responsibility for dealing with requests for and the distribution and allocation of the *female* personnel.

3. *The tasks of the local branch leader*
The task of the local branch leader in war as in peace is the *political leadership* and *supervision/care of the population of his area*. He is responsible for carrying out the 'tasks and duties of the cadre and political leader in the event of war' referred to in the leaflet with that title and is responsible for ensuring that these tasks and duties become the intellectual property of every single political leader. The local branch leader should always warn of the need for care and discretion even about apparently unimportant matters.

*He should tirelessly encourage his colleagues to fulfil their tasks. In order to ensure the complete fulfilment of his leadership role the local branch leader should free himself from all tasks which another person could take over from him.*

The local branch leader should be concerned, in particular, to *deal with shortcomings and adverse conditions* with the help of his own offices and in cooperation with the State and military offices. If this proves impossible, then he should immediately inform his district leader.

The local branch leader must concern himself with the *smooth cooperation of all personnel* within his local branch. In carrying out measures he must observe the general directives.

4. *Advice and assistance*
In the event of war, the office of the cadre should become the centre in which all national comrades find advice and assistance. Thus, as far as possible, the advice centres of the cadre, the NSV, and the NS Women's Organization should be amalgamated in such a way that the person seeking help can be assisted quickly and without too much trouble.

5. *Training of the leadership of the local branch*
The local branch leader should, as often as necessary or as is required by his superior office, call together the leading men and important personalities in the area covered by his local branch to give them on a regular basis *a uniform political line* and a *uniform political goal*. The following personalities in the local branch will normally be involved: the mayor, the local branch Party officials, the local peasant leader, the head teachers, employers. The number of persons should not normally exceed twenty . . .

8. *Behaviour during the mobilization*
The smooth running of the mobilization procedure is of vital importance for the successful commencement of the war. The precondition for this is the sympathetic cooperation of all those involved.

*The local branch leader should cooperate in the smooth running of the mobilization within the local branch by lending it his political support.*

Cases of hardship are unavoidable in a mobilization. It is thus the task of the local branch leader to arouse the understanding of the population for those measures whose purpose and necessity is not immediately clear to the public. Nevertheless, the attempt must be made to avoid all measures which could produce a threat to morale.

Where the local branch leader feels compelled to intervene to mediate and conciliate he should do so tactfully and skilfully. If the local branch leader considers that the alleviation of unreasonable and unjust hardships is necessary, and if he is not in a position to deal with these faults himself, he should immediately inform the district leader.

### 9. *Behaviour in the event of an air raid warning*

In places where the boundaries of the local branch more or less coincide with those of the Air Defence district the local branch leader should, in the event of an air raid warning, leave his office at once and go to the command post of the local Air Defence commander or send a representative there. In places where there is no command post of the local Air Defence commander the local branch leader should go immediately to his office. He should secure communications with the district leader through a courier.

The *local leader of the Women's Organization*, the *local head of the NSV*, the *local steward of the DAF*, as well as the *local propaganda chief* must, in the event of an air raid, immediately go to the office of the local branch leader where they will be at his disposal.

The political leaders and their colleagues are to be given the green armbands with the words 'Air Defence—NSDAP'.

*The task of the local branch leader during the air raid and after the air raid is the political leadership and supervision/care of his branch. The local branch leader should urge the national comrades to follow the instructions of the local Air Defence leadership.*

The local branch leader carries out, within the framework of the directives given by the local Air Defence chief, all the measures which are required to deal with the emergency which has ensued or which is anticipated. In particular, he will order the deployment of the personnel and equipment available to the Party in his area. The district leader should be informed of vital measures.

### 10. *Behaviour during evacuation measures*

As part of the mobilization, evacuation measures will be carried out in certain parts of Germany. They are designed to secure certain important materials, objects and equipment; also those men liable to military service living in these districts will be removed to the interior of the country. This evacuation is a precautionary measure which is made necessary due to the proximity of the enemy's frontier.

*The task of the local branch leader is to convince the population of the necessity of these evacuation measures, to urge them to remain calm and to prevent any movement of refugees.*

The local branch leader should support all measures which have to be taken in the evacuation area for military reasons or for the protection of the population with all the personnel and equipment at his disposal.

The local branch leader should also follow the instructions of the district leader in the event of the need to carry out evacuation measures within the Party offices.

## 11. *Behaviour in the event of enemy invasion*

In the event of a sudden enemy invasion the political leaders and party comrades involved in the political leadership will act in the same way as the members of the Military District Commands; those Party officials involved in welfare duties (NSV, NS Women's Organization) will act in the same way as members of State offices. In the event of uncertainty the district leader should be contacted immediately.

All important documents are to be immediately destroyed. Important documents are handwritten and printed materials which are stamped 'Secret Reich matter', 'Secret', 'Strictly confidential', 'Confidential' and 'only for official use', in addition, all personal identity cards, personnel lists and card indexes.

## 12. *Party and Wehrmacht*

Whenever the opportunity presents itself the cadre should always demonstrate the close links which exist between the inner and the outer front, between the Wehrmacht and the Party:

*When the troops go off to the front.*
*When transports of wounded arrive.*
*When joint functions take place etc.*

*In addition, the local branch leader should concern himself with the psychological care of the wounded and sick in the hospitals.* He should convey to them the close links with the homeland and show them that the homeland is grateful for their commitment. The local branch leader should try to fulfil the wishes of the wounded and the sick and try to give them new strength and new courage by using whatever means appear appropriate.

## 13. *The tasks and deployment of the formations and associated organizations*

SA, NSKK, HJ

The formations (apart from the SS) will place their members at the disposal of the Party for the performance of its tasks in so far as they are not already committed for other war duties. The Young People and Young Girls are to be involved in so far as they are capable.

The *formations* remain responsible for the training, organization and discipline of their members.

*Requests for personnel* should be addressed to the local leader of the formation, in the case of requests for the BdM members by the Women's Organization, to the local BdM leader.

The members of the formations are to be deployed primarily for carrying out propaganda actions, to replace personnel who leave, as well as for special tasks for which their members are specially suited and in which they have been trained.

NSV

The NSV will be assigned the following tasks *in the context of the Party's wartime deployment.*

*1. The care of the population along the lines of the previous NSV work.*
*2. The care of those who have become homeless.*
*3. The care of the refugees.*
*4. The care of those national comrades who have been affected by air attacks.*

It is *the task of the NSV* official to pay particular attention to those families whose breadwinner has been called up or whose leadership has been endangered by other wartime circumstances.

THE NS WOMEN'S ORGANIZATION

The task of the NS Women's Organization is to train German women to the highest level of psychological efficiency and commitment. In addition, the NS Women's Organization and the German Women's Organization [*Deutsches Frauenwerk*] should support the NSV in its tasks with all its resources through the deployment of their members and equipment.

*Care for families* should be undertaken in the closest collaboration with the officials of the NSV. The NS Women's Organization should focus above all on the psychological side of the caring. The cadre must be informed about the measures which have been carried out to support families and other persons.

NSKOV [National Socialist War Victims Association]

The members of the NSKOV are to be involved primarily in *caring for the wounded and the sick in the hospitals*. Individual members of the NSKOV will be particularly suitable for the psychological care of the relatives of those killed in action as well as for providing advice and support for the relatives of the wounded, the missing, and those killed in action. The local branch leader should find out the names of suitable personnel from the local official of the NSKOV who is responsible and then deploy them as required.

———

On 3 September 1939 Hitler issued the following 'Address to the NSDAP', which was published in the *Völkischer Beobachter*:

**950** *The Führer's Address to the NSDAP*

Men and women of the National Socialist Party!

Our Jewish-democratic world enemy has succeeded in hounding the English people into war with Germany. The reasons put forward are just as mendacious and threadbare as were the reasons for 1914. Nothing has changed in that respect. But what has changed is the strength and the will of the Reich this time to carry on the struggle which has been forced upon us with the decisiveness which is necessary in order to prevent the new crime against humanity which is intended. The year 1918 will not recur. In a few weeks the German Wehrmacht will break the ring of encirclement which the English have laid down in the East. In the West it will defend German soil with the greatest fortifications of all time. The German nation will make every sacrifice in the knowledge that, given its numbers, its quality and its past history, it has no reason to fear this conflict. In the past, we have only been beaten when we were disunited.

Let us all vow that the German Reich and nation shall go into this war and come out of it again in an indissoluble unity. That is the highest task of the national socialist movement. Anyone who opts out of the work of the community, let alone thinks that he can sabotage it, will this time be mercilessly destroyed. The brave soldier at the front ought to know that his life is worth more to us than that of traitors. But he ought also to know that in this struggle for the first time in history it will not be the case that while some get rich others bleed to death. So anyone who thinks that they can enrich themselves during these fateful months or years will not acquire a fortune but will only secure his own death.

I make all national socialist functionaries responsible for ensuring that they set an example in their private lives by accepting the sacrifices which the community has to bear. What we possess today is completely insignificant; only one thing is decisive: that Germany wins! What we lose today is without importance; what is important is that our nation withstands its attacker and thereby gains its future. In a few weeks the national socialist community must have transformed itself into a united front sworn to live or die together. Then the capitalist warmongers in England and its satellites will recognize in a short time what it means to have attacked the greatest nation-state in Europe without any justification. The way that we are following is not more difficult than the way from Versailles to 1939. We have nothing to lose; we have everything to gain.

━━━

## (iii) Gauleiters as Reich Defence Commissioners (RVKs) 1939–1942

The outbreak of war saw the appointment of a number of Gauleiters to the new post of Reich Defence Commissioner (RVK) with the responsibility of coordinating civil defence matters in the thirteen military districts into which Germany was divided. The following decree was issued by the Ministerial Council for the Defence of the Reich on 1 September 1939. Like the decree creating the Ministerial Council for the Defence of the Reich itself, the decree appears to have been prompted by an initiative from Hitler. It was not the product of careful planning but rather a typical ad hoc decision which had to be hurriedly drafted in the Reich Ministry of the Interior to be in time for approval by the first meeting of the Ministerial Council for the Defence of the Reich on 1 September 1939:

**951** The Ministerial Council for the Defence of the Reich decrees with the force of law:

I 1. A Reich Defence Commissioner will be appointed in each military district for the purpose of the uniform direction of the civilian defence of the Reich. The Reich Defence Commissioners will be based where the headquarters of the respective military district is situated.

2. The Reich Defence Commissioners will not have staff directly assigned to them. They are to carry out their duties with the assistance of the administrative apparatus of the following agencies exclusively:

in Military District I:
the *Oberpräsidium* [Provincial Government] of the [Prussian] province of East Prussia—in Königsberg (Pr.) . . .

in Military District II:
the *Oberpräsidium* of the [Prussian] Province of Pomerania—in Stettin,

in Military District III:
the *Oberpräsidium* of the Mark Brandenburg—in Berlin,

in Military District IV:
the *Reichstatthalter* [Reich Governor] of Saxony—Ministry of the Interior of the State Government—in Dresden,

in Military District V:
the Württemberg Interior Ministry—in Stuttgart,

in Military District VI:
the *Oberpräsidium* of the [Prussian] Province of Westphalia—in Münster,

in Military District VII:
the Bavarian Interior Ministry—in Munich,

in Military District VIII:
the *Oberpräsidium* of the [Prussian] Province of Silesia—in Breslau,

in Military District IX:
the *Oberpräsidium* of the [Prussian] Province of Hessen-Nassau—in Kassel,

in Military District X:
the *Reichstatthalter*'s Office—in Hamburg,

in Military District XI:
the *Oberpräsidium* of the [Prussian] Province of Hanover—in Hanover,

in Military District XII:
the *Regierung* [district authority]—in Wiesbaden,

in Military District XIII:
the *Regierung*—in Ansbach,

in Military District XVII:
the Office of the Reich Commissioner for the Reunification of Austria with the German Reich (Reich Gau Vienna)

in Military District XVIII:
The Office of the *Landeshauptmann*—in Salzburg.

II  1.  The Reich Defence Commissioners are responsible for the direction of all branches of the civil administration in the area of the military district with the exception of the Reich Post Office, the Reich Railways, as well as the Reich Finance administration . . .

2.  The Reich Defence Commissioners are the organs of the Ministerial Council for the Defence of the Reich in their district. They are obliged to follow the instructions of the GBV and the GBW as well as those of the supreme Reich authorities in their respective spheres of operation and they are subject to the disciplinary supervision of the Reich Interior Ministry. The supreme Reich authorities are obliged to utilize the Commissioners for the implementation of fundamental measures of Reich defence and to keep them regularly informed of other defence measures.

3.  The Reich Defence Commissioners must work in the closest cooperation with the responsible offices of the Wehrmacht in their military districts and coordinate the measures of civilian defence with the requirements of the Wehrmacht. Within the framework of the responsibilities of the supreme Reich authorities, and in line with the instructions they have received from them, they can issue directives in all matters concerning the defence of the Reich to all those civilian authorities in their sphere of operation which are not supreme Reich authorities or supreme Prussian authorities.

4.   . . .

———

Göring appointed the following to the new post of Reich Defence Commissioner (RVK):

| | |
|---|---|
| Military District I | *Oberpräsident* and Gauleiter Koch (East Prussia[2]) |
| Military District II | *Oberpräsident* and Gauleiter Schwede- Coburg (Pomerania) |
| Military District III | *Oberpräsident* and Gauleiter Stürz (Brandenburg) |
| Military District IV | *Reichstatthalter* and Gauleiter Mutschmann (Saxony) |
| Military District V | *Reichstatthalter* and Gauleiter Murr (Württemberg) |
| Military District VI | *Oberpräsident* and Gauleiter Terboven (Essen) |
| Military District VII and XIII | State Minister and Gauleiter Adolf Wagner (Munich–Upper Bavaria) |
| Military District VIII | *Oberpräsident* and Gauleiter Josef Wagner (Silesia) |
| Military District IX | *Reichstatthalter* and Gauleiter Sauckel (Thuringia) |
| Military District X | *Reichstatthalter* and Gauleiter Kaufmann (Hamburg) |
| Military District XI | *Reichstatthalter* and Gauleiter Jordan (Magdeburg-Anhalt) |
| Military District XII | *Reichstatthalter* and Gauleiter Sprenger (Hesse-Darmstadt) |
| Military District XVII | Reich Commissioner and Gauleiter Bürckel (Vienna) |
| Military District XVIII | Landeshauptmann and Gauleiter Dr. Rainer (Salzburg) |

———

[2] These suffixes refer to their Gaus.

In fact, in *administrative* terms the creation of the office of Reich Defence Commissioner was unnecessary, indeed counter-productive. For the senior civilian officials in the military districts—the *Oberpräsidenten* in the Prussian provinces and the *Reichsstatthalter* in the states (*Länder*)—already had sufficient coordinating powers in an emergency. The new RVK layer was added to an already excessively complicated administrative structure. Moreover, the fact that the new post was linked to the military districts complicated matters still further, since the boundaries of several of the military districts did not coincide with either the existing State or Party (Gau) district boundaries. For example, Terboven was already Gauleiter of Essen and *Oberpräsident* of the Rhineland with his headquarters in Koblenz. Now, as RVK for Military District VI, which covered the provinces of both Rhineland and Westphalia, he was supposed to utilize the government agencies of the *Oberpräsidium* in Westphalia, based in Münster. But Dr Alfred Meyer, the Gauleiter of Westphalia-North, was also *Oberpräsident* of Westphalia! There was thus a built in clash between Terboven and Meyer.

The speed with which the decree had been produced resulted in anomalies which had to be corrected. In particular, the appointments immediately led to protests from those Gauleiters whose Gaus were within the boundaries of the various military districts, but who had not been made RVKs. On 22 September, therefore, a further decree was issued which aimed to pacify them. In the first place, a 'Defence Committee' was established in each military district to advise the RVK and to which the top Party and State officials belonged *ex officio*. Secondly, some Gauleiters who had been passed over for appointment as RVKs were appointed as 'delegates' who 'are to exercise the powers of the RVK in accordance with his instructions' in their Gaus. For example, in Military District X, which included Gau Hamburg, Gau Schleswig-Holstein, and Gau Weser-Ems, Gauleiter Karl Kaufmann of Hamburg had been appointed RVK. Now Gauleiter Hinrich Lohse of Schleswig-Holstein and Gauleiter Carl Röver of Weser-Ems were made his delegates for their Gaus. This of course simply had the effect of complicating the network of responsibilities still further, particularly since Gauleiter-'delegates' were unwilling to subordinate themselves to Gauleiter-RVKs.

The significance of the decree must be sought not in administrative but rather in *political* terms. In the first place, this decree reversed the practice in the First World War by which overall authority in the civilian sphere was exercised by the deputy military commanders in the various military districts. Now, the new RVKs would act as a civilian counterweight to the military commanders. Moreover, in future the military commanders were obliged to pass on proposals and requests to the civilian authorities via the office of the RVK rather than dealing with them directly, although this regulation was soon restricted to important defence matters.

Secondly, the appointment of Gauleiters exclusively to the new posts marked a significant strengthening of the position of the Party vis-à-vis the State authorities. For, although in theory the powers of the RVKs were circumscribed both by the provisions of the decree itself and by subsequent instructions issued by the Reich Interior Ministry during October 1939, in practice their new status and powers within the State apparatus provided tough and ruthless Gauleiters with further opportunities to strengthen their power bases within their Gaus. It is clear that this was Hitler's intention.

The result of this situation was the further erosion of the authority of the State authorities at regional level (*Oberpräsidenten* and *Regierungspräsidenten*) and the further exacerbation of the conflicts between Party and State at regional level which had already been prevalent before the war.[3] A typical example of such a clash occurred in Hessen between the RVK-Gauleiter Jakob Sprenger and the *Regierungspräsident* of Wiesbaden, Franz von Pfeffer. This was a particularly interesting example because, as head of the SA between 1926 and 1930, von Pfeffer had been a leading Nazi during the *Kampfzeit*. Now, however, as a representative of the State apparatus, this did not assist von Pfeffer in his confrontation with the RVK-Gauleiter, as is clear from the following correspondence. On 5 March 1942 von Pfeffer minuted that 'The Gauleiter had often given me and my officials instructions which were unlawful and which contradicted the minister's guidelines and the *Oberpräsident*'s directives.' On the same day he sent the following letter to Sprenger:

**952** My department is responsible for implementing the measures contained in your circular (re: the provision of coal, dated 4.3.42) in the government district and the regional economic district of Wiesbaden. My department is not subordinate to the Gauleiter. I am, therefore, not permitted to receive a 'directive' or 'instruction' from you. Directives to state or local government authorities from unauthorized departments can only create insecurity and confusion among those sections of the population which are affected, particularly if the [NSDAP] district leaders believe they must compel the

---

[3] See Vol. 2, Chapter 10.

implementation of your directives, while the county officials [*Landräte*] and mayors have received different instructions from me. The resulting legal uncertainty must in my view be absolutely avoided, particularly in wartime. When I received your letter, I had already discussed and agreed with my desk officer a relaxation of the measures initiated by me as a result of the coal shortage and had the support of the *Oberpräsident* in Kassel. These generally correspond with your wishes but will only be implemented at a later stage.

### Regierungspräsident *von Pfeffer to Hitler, 5 August 1942:*

My Führer!
On the initiative of the Party Chancellery I am to be immediately relieved as *Regierungspräsident* and not to be appointed to another post because my letter to Gauleiter Sprenger, although justified, was too bluntly worded (this letter is enclosed). Reich Minister Frick has only asked me to request my suspension on the assumption that this is your wish.

As a fifty year old, I am, however, loath to give up my work now in wartime when every person's labour is needed, particularly since the reports of all my superiors—and of Minister Frick—on my work here, as well as in the Todt Organization and the Wehrmacht, give me grounds for pride. Moreover, as an old soldier who is war-disabled, I would consider it a disgrace if I was sent away in the middle of the German nation's struggle for existence. As an old SA leader and long-time party comrade, I ask you, my Führer, to decide yourself whether or not I must now go.

If you require more information may I request, on the basis of the protection accorded to me in my terms of appointment, that you receive me or my local superior, the *Oberpräsident*, Prince von Hessen.

Yours,
FRITZ VON PFEFFER

### *Bormann to Lammers, 16 August 1942:*

*Regierungspräsident* Fritz von Pfeffer sent the enclosed letter of 5 August 1942, addressed to the Führer, together with the copy of his letter of 5 March 1942, addressed to Gauleiter Sprenger, which is also enclosed: both letters were placed before the Führer yesterday.

The Führer has long been aware of the differences between *Regierungspräsident* von Pfeffer and Gauleiter Sprenger; the Führer is in no doubt that Pfeffer can no longer remain *Regierungspräsident* in Wiesbaden. However, the Führer wishes that an attempt be made to see whether Pfeffer could not be employed in some function in the occupied eastern territories. Pfeffer is to be initially suspended from his duties in Wiesbaden pending his alternative employment.

*Frick to Lammers, 28 December 1942:*

In reply to your letter of 28 August 1942 I beg to inform you that my attempts to find alternative employment for the *Regierungspräsident* of Wiesbaden, von Pfeffer, have all come to nothing. The Party Chancellery has declared that it considers the appointment of Pfeffer to another post as *Regierungspräsident* inadvisable. The appointment of von Pfeffer to a non-political post in my sphere of operations is currently impossible because of the lack of a vacancy. The Reich Ministers Speer and Rosenberg have replied in the negative to my queries as to whether they are in a position to provide a new field of activity in their departments for von Pfeffer. I see no other possibilities of providing von Pfeffer with suitable employment at the present time. There is, therefore, regrettably no other alternative but to initiate his retirement.

————

Von Pfeffer was retired on 1 April 1943 and, on 1 July 1943, he was replaced by [NSDAP] district leader Schwebel of Frankfurt am Main, one of Sprenger's Gau clique.

On 16 November 1942 some of the problems produced by the overlapping jurisdictions were reduced with the publication of a decree which aligned the Reich Defence districts with the Party Gaus and appointed all the Gauleiters Reich Defence Commissioners. Thus, instead of thirteen there were now forty-two RVKs. This measure, which reflected the increased influence of the Party, introduced a measure of administrative rationalization, but it by no means solved all the problems. For example, in Gau Hanover-South-Brunswick the Gauleiter was Hartmann Lauterbacher. However, the state of Brunswick was subject to the Reich Governor, Rudolf Jordan, who was simultaneously Gauleiter of Magdeburg-Anhalt. So who was to play the leading role in Brunswick: Reich Governor-Gauleiter Jordan or Reich Defence Commissioner-Gauleiter Lauterbacher? This was just one example of the continuing problems caused by overlapping jurisdictions.

### (iv) The Assertion of the Party Chancellery's Control over the Party Apparatus

As can be seen from the von Pfeffer correspondence, Bormann invariably backed the Gauleiters in their confrontations with the State authorities with the aim of increasing the power of the Party. However, at the same time, he was anxious to try and assert his authority over the Gauleiters. Thus, following his appointment as head of the Party Chancellery in May 1941,[4] Bormann acted swiftly to try and assert his

---

[4] See above, p. 18.

control over the Party. On 15 May 1941 he sent a copy of the following letter, addressed to a certain Party comrade Zimmermann, to all Reichsleiters, Gauleiters, and leaders of the so-called Party 'Leagues' such as the DAF and the NSV:

**953** The work of the Party Chancellery will be carried on as hitherto, but now under the care and supervision of the Führer himself. I will of course keep the Führer regularly informed of all important events and I shall at the same time keep the Reichleiters, Gauleiters and League leaders regularly informed about the Führer's decisions and opinions. A large number of the directives issued by me during the past two years were in any case prompted by my work with the Führer.

Since I am a member of the Führer's personal staff, I will be continuing to accompany him on a permanent basis. This has the disadvantage that, during the war, I can sometimes only be reached by telephone or by post. On the other hand, this situation has the big advantage that during the war all important matters concerning the Party, the Reichsleiters, Gauleiters and League leaders can be regularly brought to the Führer's attention.

Moreover, my desk officers, Party comrade Friedrichs and Party comrade Klopfer, will be permanently available in Berlin to refer to.

If people say, as happened a few days ago, that they do not want to be bothered with desk officers, then I can only respond with a few personal remarks and the request for fairer treatment for myself and my men.

From 1933 onwards, I have been confronted with the task of securing the participation of the NSDAP in the preparation of laws and decrees. I have been faced with the further task of issuing the political directives to the Party offices and I have also been involved in the difficult task of achieving a uniform opinion among the various offices of the NSDAP which were dealing with countless matters. During all this time I have worked like a horse, in fact harder than a horse because a horse has Sundays off and rest at night, whereas during these past years I have hardly had a Sunday off and precious little peace at night. Despite this, I have not been able to do all the work on my own; I needed assistants. I have, therefore, asked the Gauleiters again and again to place their ablest and best people at my disposal; the better the men whom the Gauleiters send me, the better the work that can be performed at the centre. My men have for the most part also had to work hard during these past years because I could not spare them any more than I could spare myself. Apart from anything else, I believe that we have done some decent and useful work. Anybody who thinks differently should inform the Führer as soon as possible who he thinks would be better suited to take my job. I felt I had to make this personal statement.

In future I shall always inform the Reichsleiters, Gauleiters and League leaders when the Führer is staying in Berlin. The Führer is very pleased to invite Reichsleiters, Gauleiters and League leaders who happen to be in Berlin on these occasions to come to lunch or dinner in his Reich Chancellery apartment, provided they inform his adjutants' office beforehand (Tel: 120050).

As far as the challenge to Bormann's authority from elements within the Party was concerned, the immediate threat came from Robert Ley in his combined role as head of the Reich Party Organization (ROL) and head of the German Labour Front (DAF). The following minute by Martin Bormann, dated 6 June 1941, indicates the view taken of Ley by the Party Chancellery:

**954** *Minute for Party Comrade Friedrichs and Party Comrade Klopfer (Party Comrade Bärmann)*

Reich Minister Dr Todt was at Obersalzberg on 3 June. I took the opportunity briefly to outline to him the tendencies which Dr Ley is arousing and encouraging in the Reichsleiters at the moment. Dr Todt replied that Dr Ley's plans are not viable in practice because they would lead to a complete fragmentation of the Party and, conceivably, to a paralysis in the work of the state. The Labour Front already controls a huge sphere with all those who are employed in that sphere: a vast number of offices and officials are dependent on him. If Dr Ley's plans were implemented then there would no longer be any area of activity over which he did not have influence. Already the Labour Front has had to seek investment opportunities for hundreds of millions of Marks per annum and so it is buying up factories and industries, dockyards and real estate. Dr Todt has already observed how disadvantageous this is for the real task of the Labour Front in the case of the West Wall.[5] There the Labour Front started running the canteens itself. The result was that the workers often complained about the food to the Todt Organization. [Comment added in ink by a Party Chancellery official: 'to their employer about the people supposed to be looking after them!']

Bormann took advantage of the decree of 16 January 1942 to try and assert his control over the access of Party officials and agencies to the Führer. On 2 April 1942 he issued the following circular to the Party offices:

**955** In the decree of 16 January 1942 to implement the Führer's edict concerning the position of the head of the Party Chancellery of 29 May 1941,[6] the powers of the head of the Party Chancellery vis-à-vis the supreme Reich authorities were clarified. This has prompted me to summarize once more the decrees which have been issued so far which affect the sphere of the Party.

---

[5] The 'West Wall' was the fortifications built in 1938–9 against France.
[6] See above, p. 18.

The Party Chancellery is an office of the Führer. He uses it for leading the NSDAP, whose direction he has once more taken over himself completely and exclusively from 1 May 1941.

The head of the Party Chancellery has been delegated by the Führer to deal with all internal Party planning and with all vital questions affecting the survival of the German people which affect the Party and to do so in accordance with his basic directives. In addition, he is responsible for adjusting the proposals of the Reichsleiters, Gauleiters and leaders of the Leagues in accordance with overall political imperatives. Instructions and directives for the general political leadership tasks of the Party will be issued to the Party, its formations and associated Leagues in the first instance by the Führer himself or by the Party Chancellery on his behalf.

The Führer has reserved for himself the determination of the political line to be followed by the Party, its formations and associated Leagues. As the official responsible to him, it is my duty to keep him regularly informed concerning the current state of the Party's work and to bring to his notice all important matters relevant to the reaching of decisions in Party affairs. It is, therefore, necessary that I, as the head of the Party Chancellery, am kept regularly informed by the Reichleiters, Gauleiters and leaders of the Leagues about the plans and projects involving the work of the Party, as well as about plans and projects with political ramifications and that I participate in matters of fundamental importance to the Party from the beginning. On the other hand, I intend to keep the Reichsleiters, Gauleiters and leaders of the Leagues regularly informed about the Führer's decisions, directives and wishes. I believe that, as a result of this, the effectiveness of the NSDAP will be increased and its uniform opinion in all basic questions can be assured.

Furthermore, through the Führer's edict of 29 May 1941, as head of the Party Chancellery, I have been delegated for the sphere of the state with the representation of the Party vis-à-vis the supreme Reich authorities on the basis of the Law for Securing the Unity of Party and State.[7] The following powers derive from this and have once more been confirmed by the Decree for the implementation of the Führer's Edict concerning the Position of the Head of the Party Chancellery of 16 January 1942:

1. Participation in the legislation of the Reich and of the states, including the preparation of Führer edicts. The head of the Party Chancellery thereby ensures that the opinion of the Party as the guardian of the national socialist world view is taken into account. (Führer edicts of 27.7.34[8] and of 6.4.1935.)

The supreme Reich authorities must involve the head of the Party Chancellery from the beginning in the drafting of Reich Laws, edicts and decrees of the Ministerial Council for the Defence of the Reich, as well as of decrees of the supreme Reich authorities, including directives and instructions for their implementation. The same applies to the approval of laws and decrees of the states and decrees of the Reich Governors.

---

[7] See Vol. 2, doc. 156.
[8] See Vol. 2, doc. 161.

2. Participation in the personnel matters of the State officials and Labour Service leaders, whose appointment the Führer has reserved to himself. (Führer edicts of 24.9.1935[9] and of 10.7.1937.) The participation of the Party in personnel matters of the remaining State officials has been transferred to the Gauleiters through the Führer Edict concerning the Appointment of Officials and the Termination of Civil Service Status of 26.3.1942.

3. The securing of the influence of the Party on the self-administration of local government . . .

Since all the powers which belonged to the former Führer's Deputy in the state sphere according to the existing laws, decrees, edicts, orders and other regulations have been transferred to me, all the previous regulations governing communication between Party offices and supreme Reich authorities, and the supreme authorities of those states which contain several Gaus, retain their validity. As a result, the participation of the Party in legislation and in personnel matters dealt with by the supreme Reich authorities will take place exclusively via the Party Chancellery. Proposals and suggestions for legislation from the Party, its formations and associated Leagues may only be passed on to the responsible supreme Reich authorities by the head of the Party Chancellery.

Direct communication between the supreme Reich authorities and the supreme authorities of the states which contain several Gaus, on the one hand, and offices of the Party, its formations and associated Leagues, on the other, concerning basic political questions, in particular those which involve the preparation, alteration or implementation of laws, edicts, and decrees as well as the personnel matters of officials is, as hitherto, not permitted.

The Führer has made these regulations specifically in order to secure a uniform representation of the Party. They are, therefore, to be adhered to without fail. I myself have given instructions for the offices of the Reich [NSDAP] leadership to be informed at regular intervals in special meetings about pending legislation, for proposals and suggestions from these offices to be received at these meetings and for the Party offices which are responsible for the area covered by the particular bill concerned to be fully involved in all individual questions.

———

Bormann now set about enforcing these regulations against those Party leaders who failed to toe the line and, in particular, Dr Ley. On 2 August 1942, for example, he sent Ley the following letter:

**956** Dear Party Comrade Ley,

In a letter of 27.7.42 addressed to the Führer's chief adjutant you enclosed a copy of your letter to the former head of the [NSDAP] Reich Office for Agrarian Policy. You asked him to show this letter to the Führer and to send you the Führer's reply.

---

[9] See Vol. 2, doc. 162.

I must urgently request that in future you send such applications for presentation to the Führer to *me*, for, in accordance with a directive of the Führer, all letters which are concerned with the work of the Party must be presented by me. That is in fact obvious because that is the reason why I have been ordered to accompany him on a permanent basis.

As far as the presentation of such letters is concerned, the Führer has repeatedly decided—and repeated his decision only recently—that—in view of his enormous burden of work in dealing with the most important military matters and matters of state—only those matters should be put before him which he needs to know. In the case of disagreements, the Führer has repeatedly decided that, to start with, those involved must attempt to resolve the matters in dispute between themselves. If this is not possible, then, if the case in dispute is a state matter they should turn to Reich Minister Dr Lammers, and if it is a Party matter the head of the Party Chancellery should be involved. In the event that, despite the involvement of those persons, a clarification and agreement is not achieved, then the Führer should be informed at an appropriate time—by the head of the Reich Chancellery if it is a state matter and by the head of the Party Chancellery if it is a Party matter. The Führer will make his decision after studying the two points of view or, if in his view the matter has not yet been sufficiently clarified, he will order further discussions or a deferment.

The Führer by no means wishes simply to receive one-sided information, but wishes rather that, if something is brought to him for decision, then he will as a matter of course be thoroughly briefed, since only then is he in a position to make the right decision.

In the case in question I must initially decline to present your letter of 27.7.42 to the Führer since I am not yet aware of Party Comrade Backe's[10] point of view and, furthermore, because all the relevant files have not yet been sent to the Party Chancellery.

I urgently request that in future you respect the Führer's directives referred to above.

-----

## (v) The Gauleiters as Reich Defence Commissioners (RVKs) 1942–1945

The Party Chancellery's attempt to turn the Party into an effective political machine was faced, at least in the short to medium term, with an insuperable obstacle in the shape of the Gauleiters. The individual Gauleiters varied in terms of their importance from heavyweights, such as Adolf Wagner of Munich-Upper Bavaria, Fritz Sauckel of Thuringia, or Erich Koch of East Prussia, to relatively insignificant ones such as Carl Röver of Weser-Ems, Otto Telschow of Hanover-East or Karl Wahl of Swabia. Most of them, however, had managed to build up a strong power base in the 'period of struggle' before 1933 when, as they

-----

[10] Herbert Backe was head of the Reich Agriculture Ministry.

saw it, they had 'conquered' their area for the Movement. They were tough, ruthless individuals who had surrounded themselves with a loyal clique of Gau officials and district leaders. Above all, they saw themselves as the personal representatives of Hitler in the Gaus and directly responsible to him and, what is more, they were seen as such by Hitler, who was extremely loyal to his old Gauleiters, as is clear from the following minute of a conference with Albert Speer dated 5 November 1944:

**957** The Führer rejects my request to appoint a general commissioner for the West. He emphasizes that it is impossible for him to appoint another Gauleiter to be the superior of the old Gauleiters Florian [Düsseldorf], Meyer [Westphalia-North], and—despite his absence—Terboven [Essen] too. The Führer rejects my suggestion, despite his reservations, to appoint Gauleiter [Walter] Hoffman [Westphalia-South] on account of his efficiency and the understanding he shows for armaments and war production. He emphasizes that, although he sees the necessity for such a position, he cannot make this appointment on the grounds of personnel policy.

It was this direct link between the Gauleiters and Hitler which cut across the tidy hierarchical structure envisaged by Bormann, in which, while still being 'leaders' in their area, they would in effect become line managers of the Party Chancellery.

Bormann tried hard to control the separatist tendencies of the Gauleiters. However, during the second half of the war there were increasingly powerful centrifugal forces operating within the regime which combined to frustrate his attempts. In particular, this period saw an expansion of the role of the RVKs until they became effectively the dominant figures in their districts. In part this reflected the increasing extent to which the war impinged on the home front with 'defence' coming to subsume virtually all other matters and dominating the agenda under the slogan of 'total war'. This process manifested itself in two spheres in particular: first, in the civil defence measures necessary to cope initially with the impact of the massive Allied bombing raids and then with the threat of invasion; and secondly, in the mobilization of man/womanpower for the armed forces and for war production.

Although not directly in charge of the civil defence units—the responsibility of the local police chief, the RVKs played the major role in civil defence. They had overall responsibility among other things for coordinating the preparation and implementation of air defence, clearing up and restoring essential services after bombing raids and the evacuation of the population in areas threatened by constant bombing or imminent invasion. RVK-Gauleiter Karl Kaufmann of Hamburg, for example, dealt with the aftermath of the appalling raids on Hamburg in July 1943, while on 11 September 1944 RVK-Gauleiter Josef Grohé of Cologne-Aachen was responsible for evacuating the district of Aachen, which involved moving 246,000 people, 36,500 cattle and 33,000 tons of armaments material.

Secondly, the RVKs played the key role in implementing the unpublished decree of 13 January 1943 'for the comprehensive deployment of men and women for tasks of Reich defence'.[11] This involved the 'combing through' of offices and plants to secure manpower for the armed forces, the closing down of factories and businesses which were not given priority for war production, and the granting of UK (*unabkömmlich* = 'reserved') status to those workers who were indispensable. In this role, however, the Gauleiters were subject to conflicting pressures. For, apart from their ambition to expand their own power by extending their sphere of responsibilities, they also considered that the main task assigned to them by Hitler was to sustain the morale of the population of their Gaus and in this they were undoubtedly correct. Moreover, as the war situation became increasingly critical so the Gauleiters became increasingly anxious to sustain their own popularity and prestige. Thus, they were determined to defend their local economies from cutbacks and closures and to maintain the supplies of food and heating materials to their areas at all cost. This, however, threatened to undermine the overall coordination and rationalization of the war economy. Interference by the Gauleiters was to be the subject of frequent complaints from the Armaments Minister, Albert Speer. On 20 December 1944, for example, Speer wrote to the Reich Defence Commissioners as follows:

**958**   The sharp reduction in coal supplies resulting from the transport situation is producing considerable tension in various parts of the Reich when the existing coal supplies have been used up. The head of the Reich Coal Association, State Councillor Pleiger, receives regular directives from me which are intended to ensure that unacceptable disruption of armaments and war production and of the supplies to the population is avoided as far as possible. This sometimes necessitates the concentration of supplies, a fact which is not always entirely comprehensible from the point of view of individual districts which cannot be aware of the overall supply position.

---

[11] See below, pp. 239–40 and 331–34.

The total dependance of coal supplies on the current transport situation has necessitated the granting of far-reaching powers to the agencies which are responsible for the distribution of coal in their particular districts. However, in so far as binding directives from the Reich Coal Association exist, these must in all circumstances be followed.

During the last two weeks, in some parts of the Reich, Reich Defence Commissioners have interfered to such an extent that coal trains scheduled for other districts have been halted or diverted. In view of the tenseness of the overall situation such interference must have grave consequences whose extent cannot be assessed at district level.

I must, therefore, appeal to you urgently to avoid at all costs any interference with coal supplies not intended for your district or which have been allocated for a particular purpose. In the event of particular difficulties I request that you contact State Councillor Pleiger, who has been granted full authority by me and whose dispositions must be observed in all circumstances.

———

However, in addition to their primary concern with morale, arguably a stabilizing force, the Gauleiters were often influenced by a populist form of anticapitalism dating back to the *Kampfzeit* and tended to see themselves as defenders of small business, resenting what they saw as the dominance of Speer's industrial organization by the major firms, many of which were in any case based outside their own Gaus.

Faced with the insuperable obstacle posed by the Gauleiters to his plans, Bormann set about overcoming it in two ways. In the first place, he tried to convince the Gauleiters of the value of a strong Party Chancellery to them, in terms of the need to strengthen the Party vis-à-vis the State. The Party Chancellery would support their efforts to assert their predominance in their Gaus. Secondly, he operated through the next generation of Party officials. As the original group of Gauleiters died or became incapacitated through age, illness, drink, or (in a very few cases) fell out with Hitler, so he aimed to replace them with younger men who had been trained in the Party Chancellery. Thus, Carl Röver of Weser-Ems, who died of a heart attack in 1942, was replaced by Paul Wegener from the Party Chancellery.

Secondly, Bormann aimed to inculcate the Party Chancellery line in the Gaus by securing the secondment of Gau officials to the Party Chancellery: in the first place, the Gau Chiefs of Staff and Gau Inspectors and, secondly, the district leaders. This would ensure that the next generation of Gauleiters were house-trained. The following documents illustrate this process. The first is a minute by Walkenhorst, one of Bormann's subordinates, dated 18 May 1943:

**959**  The Gau Chief of Staff has a special position among the Gau departmental heads in the sense that he is not the head of a department dealing with a particular sphere of operation, but rather the right-hand man of the Gauleiter and deputy Gauleiter. Apart from his coordinating role, which covers virtually all spheres of operation of the Gau headquarters, he deals with many matters on his own responsibility, such as those to do with the mobilization for war, the organization of reports and information, Church questions, complaints, visits etc., tasks which at the Reich level are undertaken by the Party Chancellery. While all the other Gau departmental heads are answerable to a specialist office in the Reich headquarters: the Gau Propaganda Chief to the Reich Propaganda Department, the Gau Indoctrination chief to the Main Indoctrination Office, the Gau Finance Officer to the Reich Finance Office etc., there is no specific provision for such an office in the case of the Gau Chief of Staff. And it is not possible to limit him in such a way, since his role as the right-hand man of the Gauleiter and deputy Gauleiter is a coordinating one and so is concerned with every sphere. Nevertheless, in terms of his sphere of competence, he is in the first instance a representative of the Party Chancellery. One can see that from the fact that he, alone of all the Gau departmental heads, must have spent at least four weeks in the Party Chancellery. In order to ensure that the secondments to the Party Chancellery perform the function envisaged and in order to give the position of Gau Chief of Staff the appropriate designation, I consider it necessary for all those Gau department heads who have been given the title Chief of Staff to be officially approved by the head of the Party Chancellery. I enclose draft statements of approval for those Gau chiefs of staff who have already served a secondment to the Party Chancellery.

The next document is a report by Walkenhorst of a visit he paid to Gau Düsseldorf on 4 April 1944:

**960**  On the occasion of a visit to Gauleiter Florian I gave a detailed account of our aims in the sphere of personnel and recruitment policy. In this connection, I said that it was in the interest of the Gauleiters if they put their toughest and best men at the disposal of the Party Chancellery. On the one hand, this would solve the recruitment problem and, on the other hand, this was the only way in which the Party Chancellery could function really effectively. The precondition for strong Gauleiters, whom we wanted, was a strong Party Chancellery.

Gauleiter Florian was tremendously enthusiastic about my argument. He promised he would support us in every way. In this connection, he referred to his deputy, Party comrade O., who was too old (58) and, furthermore, was not a good speaker or leader. He was an excellent staff officer but could never become a Gauleiter. He was aiming in time to acquire a deputy who had it in him to become a Gauleiter himself one day. He had an excellent district leader, Party comrade K., who was young (born in 1910) and exceptionally active. K. had performed his military service with distinction and was in every way a model leader. I told Gauleiter Florian that it would be a good idea to second K. to the Party Chancellery soon. The Gauleiter replied that that was his intention. He wanted to second K. to the Party Chancellery at the end of this year or at the beginning of next year—he would let us know the date—with the aim that, in the event that he fulfilled expectations, he would appoint him as deputy Gauleiter. I told the Gauleiter that in any case it would be a number of years before he could be appointed. I myself know K. as a former Gau organization chief. He was considered by the other Gau organization chiefs as one of the best. I enclose his personal file.

I asked Gauleiter Florian to second an able district Party official as a desk officer for Department II [of the Party Chancellery]. He said he would be glad to do so. He would just have to think about who would be the best person. He cannot second too many people at the moment because he is in the process of subdividing large [Party] districts into smaller ones for which he needs new district leaders. He has already selected suitable men for this. They are heads of district subdivisions who had already been local branch leaders. I asked the Gauleiters to second these men to the Party Chancellery over a period of time before appointing them. Apparently Gau Inspector and Gau Chief of Staff L., who has already been seconded to the Party Chancellery and knows our policy and is an enthusiastic supporter of it, had influenced Gauleiter Florian. We can anticipate that Gau Düsseldorf will second all political leaders who are going to become district leaders to the Party Chancellery. Gauleiter Florian has for the time being declined to second the district leaders who are already in post in view of the intended reorganization of the Party districts and the air raid situation. Later, however, those district leaders who are in post and the Gau departmental heads will be placed at the disposal of the Party Chancellery to be briefed.

———

However, by no means all Gauleiters were as cooperative with the Party Chancellery as Florian.

## (vi) Party and State

Bormann pursued a dual policy of, on the one hand, trying to subordinate the party organization to the Party Chancellery, while, on the other, supporting the party officials in their attempts to assert their authority vis-à-vis the civil service. In fact, the years 1942–5 saw an increase in the power of the Party over the State, not only at national level, but also at regional and local level, where the Party seized the opportunity presented by the increasing problems caused by air raids and by the need to mobilize every available resource to claim the right to take decisions at regional and local level which had hitherto been the responsibility of the State officials. Significantly, although under the decree of 1 September 1939 the RVKs were supposed to use the existing State apparatus to implement their policies, increasingly they employed ad hoc 'commissions', 'staffs', and 'agents' to handle the various tasks. These were often led by and largely composed of Party officials from the Gau headquarters staff or, at district level, by the district Party headquarters staff. For example, at district level the district Party leaders and the district Party economic advisers played the key role in the commissions which decided which businesses were to be closed down. In other words, during the years 1942–5, Party officials and Party agencies were increasingly usurping the functions of the State.

The regime's reliance on the Party expanded after the bomb plot of 20 July 1944.[12] For example, Bormann assigned the task of organizing the building of defensive barriers to the Gauleiters rather than the Wehrmacht or the State. Indeed, on 23 August 1944 Bormann wrote to the Party cadres emphasizing that 'the task of the construction of fortifications was given to the Gauleiters and not to the Reich Defence Commissioners, i.e. to the man of the Party and not the man of the State', although of course the two were in fact identical.

An exceptionally interesting undated and unsigned memorandum concerning the Party, including its relations with the State, its organization and recruitment, written from the perspective of a senior party official, was prepared in the office of the Gau headquarters of Weser-Ems sometime during 1942. Its authorship is uncertain. It may have been written by Carl Röver, Gauleiter from 1929 to 1942, or—more likely—by his successor as Gauleiter, Paul Wegener, a young apparatchik, who had earned his spurs in the Party Chancellery. The author began by expressing his concern that the Party's official position had been defined as a 'public corporation' under the Law to ensure the Unity of Party and State of 1 December 1933 (see Vol. 2, doc. 156):

**961** I GENERAL MATTERS

1. *The legal position of the Party*
... The present laws prescribe that public corporations must be supervised by the State. If in practice this does not happen in the case of the Party at present, in my opinion one must not forget that in future generations when the leadership of the Reich may be weaker, which is possible even under our system, someone might have the idea of supervising the Party on the basis of its legal position as a public corporation. The authority of the Party today is based on—to put it bluntly—bullying tactics [*Schnauze*], on old Party men who know how to get what they want, and also on officials who think it will be to their disadvantage if they make difficulties.

---

[12] See below, pp. 620ff.

The NSDAP is a unique phenomenon; it has no precursors or models. Its legal position as a public corporation is unsatisfactory and undignified because it is derived from the legislation of the State and therefore incompatible with the sovereign position of the Party. The Party has fought for its position and conquered the State. For this reason it cannot be a public corporation but must, in accordance with its leading and special position, have its own position within the law.

For the same reason, I consider it wrong that the influence of the Party on legislation is made dependent on any appointment to the position of Reich Minister, as it was earlier on, or on the conferring on the head of the Party Chancellery the status of Reich Minister as it is now. This right must be given to the Party by virtue of its position and its entitlement to leadership and must be granted by the Führer for the future.

In my opinion the 'Law on the Winter Aid Programme of the German Nation' is a classic example of how not to do things. The Winter Aid programme has always been a purely Party matter and it is by no means clear why the State has to pass a law on this. If the cooperation of the State was necessary in this or some other case, the Party, by virtue of its position as granted by the Führer, should be able to require the State to carry out the necessary measures.

In any case, I regard the type of participation in legislation as carried out by the head of the Party Chancellery and in the Law on the Winter Aid Programme, which I chose as an example, as a concession to the State. This right must exist on the strength of the position of the Party. Otherwise the impression will undoubtedly arise that the offices conferred by the State are more important than the Party offices. Quite apart from that, and this is my main worry, the position of the Party could in the future be undermined to say the least.

For the same reason, the endeavour of so many high-ranking Party members to have their Party apparatus legally consolidated by the State must be rejected. The result so far has always been to the advantage of the State and the disadvantage of the Party. This is quite natural if one takes account of the greater powers of endurance which the State will always possess. It is indeed very easy and tempting to be able simply to use the State executive to carry out one's own measures. The leading Party members who seek their salvation in the State will in most cases forget the infinitely more important Party work involved with the people and, in their State posts, will either become more bureaucratic, that is to say, move away from the people, or pursue the quiet life of an official.

I must, therefore, reject the attempt to achieve the aim of controlling the State executive by establishing a personal union between Party and State offices. The supporters of this view always argue that, if this was carried out, all quarrels, controversies and other negative manifestations would be avoided. But against this it is arguable that, although the Party is in a leading position, it does not have to fulfil any executive tasks and that the objective airing of differences of opinion can only be advantageous for a cause. The Party has become great through struggle, and only continual struggle with problems and close contact with the people, such as the Party has, but which the State, of its inherent nature, can never have, will guarantee that our senses remain sharp and alert and that the dynamic and elasticity of the movement are maintained.

Thus I regard any unfounded personal union of Party and State offices as the surrender of a party position and a retreat into the State. The holders of offices at Gau level are an exception, because their functions are conceived from totally different considerations. On the strength of their Party office, they are leaders of large areas and because of their important tasks of leadership must always be able to affect State measures directly. To extend these exceptions to the district level or even further would, I think, be wrong for the reasons given above and I would advise strongly against it.

I am convinced that the bad developments described above would have been avoided if the legal position of the Party had given it a different basis from the start.

A demand should, therefore, be made for a Führer decree to give the Party a legal status, perhaps in connection with the Senate announced by the Führer at the Party Congress, corresponding to its struggle, its importance, and its mission of leadership, so that it may be in a position to demand from the executive authorities of the State the carrying out of certain measures for the fulfilment of its tasks, and to give them binding instructions in specific areas. This Führer decree, as the bequest of the creator of the movement, should secure the claim to leadership and the basic rights of the movement for all time.


2. *Fighting things out or defining spheres of responsibility*

The principle of letting things develop until the strongest has won is certainly the secret of the really remarkable development and achievements of the movement. But this principle too must be looked at from both sides. If both partners have the same character traits, the principle is right. If, however, one of the partners possesses character but the other one because of the weakness of his character operates the more craftily and slyly, the latter will usually be the winner.

As I said, the tremendous achievements and the rapid development of the Party are largely due to the system described above, and one must admit that this was certainly useful during the period when the Party was being built up. But now that the Party's position and tasks have acquired firmer outlines, now that it must be regarded as having attained full growth, the position here also must be consolidated; that is to say, a clear conception must be gained of its organizational structure, and spheres of competence must be precisely defined. Otherwise, conflicts over the boundaries of power and authority will be carried into the local branches, some of them possibly lasting for years; and we should not be blind to the damage that will be done. The flexibility and adaptability needed to counteract the establishment of a bureaucracy can be achieved in a different way. We must ensure a rapid consolidation of the position in this respect; for it cannot be denied that in many spheres of Party activity several offices are dealing with the same task: two or more seize upon the same task without as yet the intervention of any authority. Some outstanding personality may perhaps be able to assert himself through his superior abilities and thereby in time unite the various spheres under his control unless he is brought down by intrigue. But if all these men are more or less on the same level, they will continue to simmer in a permanent quarrel about spheres of authority, or else anyone who can will elbow his way forward and grab everything, and damage will be done to the cause. The number of different competencies means that many people are employed unproductively and unprofitably in continual disputes about authority, with a considerable wastage of resources. The success of the work is jeopardized and, in the end, the subordinate offices no longer know whom to follow. They become indifferent and in some cases they cannot even carry out the contradictory instructions they receive. The result is that important matters are treated in exactly the same way as unimportant matters; that is to say, important matters remain just as neglected and unfinished as unimportant ones. Moreover, it is not surprising that all this undermines respect for superiors. It is no secret that the higher the office, the more muddled is the demarcation of tasks within it. The block, the cell and the local branch are spheres of authority in which problems of competency are unknown. It is true that plenty of orders reach the local branch, but in the local branch things are arranged in such a way that the local branch leader has all the reins in his hand. In the district organizations confusion is more noticeable, but the district leaders through their personality know how to maintain uniformity. In the Gaus, on the other hand, confusion stares one in the face.

Thus a clear demarcation of tasks is urgently necessary in order to stop the considerable waste of energies caused by continuous disputes over competencies. Ways and means must be found, on the other hand, of letting the personality develop fully and thereby achieve its potential and, on the other, of securing a clear demarcation of tasks without transferring to the Party the bureaucratic system which exists in the State administration with all its adverse consequences in terms of restrictions. For it corresponds with the character and aims of the Party for the Party leader to be able to develop as freely as possible and independently of regulations and other obstacles. It must not be forgotten that in the administrative apparatus of the State a certain bureaucratic element is necessary and will be indispensable also in the future. But the task of leadership which has been given to the Party necessitates other methods in the work itself and in the demarcation of tasks, namely those outlined above.

### 3. *The leader principle*

The leader principle depends absolutely on the personality of the leader. The advantages of the leader principle itself have been sufficiently proved by the historical events of the past and the present, especially since the coming into existence of the National Socialist German Workers' Party, so that further discussion of it is unnecessary. But one cannot help recognizing the disadvantages of the leader principle, so that one can take suitable steps to eliminate the danger resulting from this as far as possible.

As already mentioned, the leader principle depends absolutely on the personality of the person entrusted with the office of leadership. This is true at a low level just as much as at a high one. The only difference is that the higher the authority, the more far-reaching are the effects whether positive or negative.

In the first place, the good leader excels through his achievements and, secondly, he tends to choose suitable people and experts as his assistants. These assistants grow in stature through the tasks given to them, adapt themselves to their leader and can take his place at any time. Through this process the succession to the leadership is automatically guaranteed and it is even possible to provide good people for other purposes. When the holder of a leading post is not a good leader and, in addition, has weaknesses of character, the position is usually completely reversed: to start with, there are no actual achievements; secondly, he usually chooses fools and blockheads as his assistants, who also have defects of character and act accordingly so that no results are achieved and, what is even worse, all the power lies in the hands of incompetents and people with defects of character. A change in the situation appears impossible since, on the basis of the leader principle, people of the same kind jealously see to it that they stay in power unless a superior authority intervenes. It is in the nature of stupid people who have been entrusted with an office on the basis of the leader principle to try to disguise their stupidity, put obstacles in the way of all progressive measures, and endeavour to consolidate their position by selecting assistants with a similar outlook; by the masterly staging of intrigue they usually succeed.

It is all very well to reward people's merits but the welfare of the nation must come first. It will not always be necessary to dismiss weak leaders who have performed meritorious service in the cause of the movement but who do not possess the requisite qualities for a leader. In most cases, if the faults which have been detected permit this, one will be able to give them other tasks where it will be impossible for them to do any damage. Certainly, loyalty is one of the noblest of virtues, but it cannot be used one-sidedly; that is to say, if a leader repays the loyalty shown him with neglect of duty, unprincipled actions or similar behaviour, the necessary conclusions must be drawn.

We must, therefore, demand that leaders who do not possess the prerequisites of ability, character and ideological reliability be replaced by better ones; for the damaging effect upon the nation and the State resulting in many fields from the silent toleration of such leaders must not be ignored.

The correct selection and choice of leaders and the building in of safety valves are of decisive importance for the removal of the faults which have been described . . .

II.  GENERAL QUESTIONS OF ORGANIZATION

1. *The Party comrade*
We have approximately 6 million Party members in the Reich. There is no question of their forming a unified combat group. One day, the Party will certainly be an elite order of the Führer; it is not one yet because the principles governing admission to it have obviously been influenced by the financial needs of the Party. Many have been admitted who merely needed Party membership to consolidate their social position or who wanted to gain professional or economic advantages through it. It must not be forgotten that, if the movement was to be able to master its various tasks, especially in those areas which from the Party's

point of view could only be called backward, many ideologically immature citizens had to be admitted, if only to enable the Party organization to be built up since the required number of ideologically mature citizens were simply not there, particularly in the so-called black [i.e. Roman Catholic] areas. The Party accepted these citizens in order, as I said, to be able to carry out the necessary work. Through the opportunities which the Party has gained for influencing such citizens, some have meanwhile become reliable National Socialists, but by no means the majority.

This development is regrettable. It will be necessary to overhaul the whole Party apparatus and to investigate every individual Party member, especially his ideological attitude and his sense of commitment. During the coming ideological conflicts, we must be able to rely on the Party members in all circumstances. But we should have no illusions about the fact that this is by no means possible at present . . .

The Party must be a minority of combative, determined and active people. Inactive people, who simply pay their subscriptions and ambitious people, who are out for what they can get, who exploit their membership for their own advantage, have no place in the leadership order of the German nation and must be excluded. Membership of the Party must involve active participation as a matter of course. Only the old and the sick can be exempted.

I am describing conditions in this connection in such detail so that the actual situation will be fully appreciated. One might come to the conclusion that the lower echelons are to blame for this development. But that is not the case. Certainly, some local branches have not always done their duty in this respect. But the whole trend and the overall situation such as, for example, the schematic allocation of a quota for Party membership of 10 per cent of all compatriots were responsible for this development . . .

*The political leader*
. . . The time of struggle [pre-1933] was simultaneously a natural process of selection. It produced a situation where every political leader had to prove himself as a political fighter. After the takeover of power that has radically changed because, on the one hand, there has been a complete shift in the tasks of the Party and, on the other, many new people became members. Some old Party comrades, who did their stuff in the time of struggle, couldn't cope during the period of reconstruction because, despite their willingness, they lacked the stamina, the knowledge and the ability. In the case of the new people who joined, it was impossible to tell whether they had done so out of conviction or calculation.

The task of leadership, which the Party has been set, requires that the political leaders should be closely linked to the people and remain so. It has proved beneficial that both the voluntary and the full-time political leaders are recruited from all sections of the nation.

In my view it is vital for the Party to ensure that the recruits for the positions as full-time leaders should not be trained in the *Ordensburgen* and similar institutions, but that the full-time political leaders should be acquainted with real life . . . In my view the methods of education employed in the *Ordensburgen* are wrong because I have frequently had the experience that Party comrades who basically had good qualities, after being at an *Ordensburg*, turned into conceited, in some cases arrogant, types. All those district leaders who have employed alumni of the *Ordensburgen* are unanimous that those boys have acquired a superiority complex which has nothing to do with a healthy and necessary self-confidence. They all had to be properly brought to heel.

Practical work in ordinary occupations as well as the voluntary and full-time work in the Party itself must provide and remain the basis for the selection of leaders. If one follows a different path one will undoubtedly produce a political priesthood [*Pfaffentum*] remote from life . . .

The leadership principle contains the danger that the individual leader will develop into a political despot, who does not tolerate any opinion other than his own, represses every justified criticism and every objection however well-founded. If a leadership personality has the necessary qualities for his office this danger is not so great, and as long as the Führer is still alive, it can in practice never come to pass. But, in view of later generations, one cannot ignore this danger . . .

The political leader must have appropriate freedom of action in order to fulfil his tasks. He cannot be constrained by fixed rules, as is possible in the Wehrmacht. However, this freedom of action, which is necessary for his work, creates the danger referred to above that he will develop into a political despot. This danger is less in the lower-level cadre positions than in the intermediate one, in the Gaus. The larger the Reich becomes the more remote does the top Reich leadership become from the Gaus, so that the necessary supervision cannot be carried out by the Reich alone. If the individual turns into a tyrant, nobody will dare to oppose him and in the long run he will be surrounded by toadies and sycophants.

So one cannot leave it to the individual to act abitrarily according to his own whims. We need certain clearly defined norms and clearly defined rights and duties not only for the particular cadre [*Hoheitsträger*] but also for his colleagues . . . I am thinking here of a Gau Senate, which is assigned certain powers and which must be composed of members of the Gau staff and a number of district leaders . . .

Since 1933, there has been no continuous unified concentration of the higher leadership corps. Apart from the gatherings which have taken place with the Führer himself, Rudolf Hess, whose job it was, did practically nothing in this sphere. The result is that everybody has more or less set himself up on his own and that there can be no talk of a combined and uniformly led higher leadership of the Party. The further result of this is that in the Gaus everybody rules in his own way and that opinions on basic questions are not formed in a unified manner. While it is true that the national socialist world view is the guiding principle for all action, there is a lack of guidance which is essential for the organization of day-to-day political activity in accordance with uniform principles. Moreover, the fact that *Reichsleiters* [Reich party leaders], as is frequently the case, carry differences of opinion down to the lower levels shows that there is a lack of tight coordination and strengthens my view that, in order to get rid of these defects, a close coordination of the higher leadership is necessary. The authority of the Reich Party leadership has suffered under the present conditions. One must expect from the *Reichsleiters* that they do not carry differences of opinion down to the lower levels on the basis of whose elbows are the strongest. They must dispute among themselves until they have come to an agreement. If no agreement is possible then the Führer must make a decision. In order that the Führer should not be bothered with everything, the head of the Party Chancellery, who is in certain respects the Führer's chief of staff, should take on the task of bringing the whole of the Reich Party leadership into line . . .

The author's concern about the fact that the Party had no legal status apart from the State according to the Law for Securing the Unity of Party and State of 1 December 1933 was dealt with by the following edict issued by Hitler on 12 December 1942:

**962**   I   The rights and duties of the National Socialist German Workers' party derive from the tasks which I have set for it and from the organizational status which is determined by them.

II   The internal order and organization of the Party are governed exclusively by the laws of the Party.

III   The Party participates in the general legal process in accordance with the legal regulations which are valid for the State, except in so far as a special regulation exists or is introduced.

IV   I hereby repeal the regulations in I (2) of the Law for Securing the Unity of Party and State of 1 December 1933 [see Vol. 2, doc. 156].

The author's views on the inadvisability of a 'personal union' of Party and State offices were shared by Bormann, who expressed them in the following illuminating circular to the Party:

**963**   *The Head of the Party Chancellery*               *7 August 1942*

*Circular No. 121/42*

Re: *The separation of the leadership of Party and State posts*

The frequent discussions about the advantages and disadvantages of a personal union of Party posts with those of the State, the sphere of economic self-administration, or other posts which carry executive authority prompt me once more to make a detailed statement on this very important problem.

In considering the pros and cons of a personal union one must always begin by considering the tasks of the NSDAP as the organization which has the responsibility of leading and supervising [*betreuen*] the German people politically, ideologically and culturally.

The NSDAP exercises decisive influence over the political direction and formation of the whole of public life.

If the Party were burdened with executive functions it would not only significantly complicate the fulfilment of these tasks which have been assigned to the movement by the Führer, but in many cases make it impossible. It is a well-established fact based on human inadequacy that, in order to reach a goal, the vast majority of people will follow a path which, in overcoming the least resistance, promises the quickest possible success, but one which often proves to be illusory. Thus some Party comrades who, in their role as political leaders, are simultaneously endowed with equivalent offices of state or offices of an official character, in many cases will try to achieve their political goal through the use of executive force which, as the head of an official agency, they have at their disposal. They can then dispense with the need for leadership in the sense envisaged by the movement. They need neither be a model for the national comrades placed in their care nor supervise them, let alone win them over. In other words, they no longer lead, but administer.

The negative consequences for the Party, which will in the long term result from this, are of such a serious nature that one cannot warn too often or too urgently against these dangers.

The task of the political leader, and in the first instance of the cadre [*Hoheitsträger*] himself, which is to lead, and that means, above all, to persuade, clearly indicates what preconditions it is necessary for him to fulfil in order to do justice to this particular task.

The value of national socialist indoctrination lies in the fact that a national comrade will fulfil his duties to the community of his own free will and from inner conviction.

It is a precondition for anyone who wants to act in a leadership role to recognize these fundamental differences between the tasks of a Party office and an official post . . .

[Bormann then discusses this distinction in terms of the inadvisability of a personal union between the Gau Economic Adviser (a party office) and the President of the Gau Economic Chamber (a quasi-official post). He then continues:]

Similarly, personal union between a district leader [*Kreisleiter*—Party] and a district counsellor [*Landrat*—State] can only be permitted in exceptional cases and for a limited period. The office of a Lord Mayor [*Oberbürgermeister*] or a district counsellor [*Landrat*] requires a man who possesses the requisite administrative skills; the office of a district leader, on the other hand, requires a Party comrade who can lead. The precondition for the successful activity of the first is the fulfilment of the necessary administrative work, which is mostly tied to an office desk; the precondition for the success of the second is the ability always to remain in lively contact with the compatriots of his district. The one necessarily precludes the other.

The Führer himself has, therefore, repeatedly refused to permit political leaders simultaneously to hold a corresponding State post. All the experience hitherto has underlined the correctness of this directive. Only the Gauleiter should and must be simultaneously a Reich Governor [*Reichsstatthalter*] or become one.

Thus, the combination of Party and State offices must be absolutely rejected, however attractive the personal union of a Party office and an official post may, at first glance, appear to be.

▬▬▬

In March 1943, this battle entered a new and interesting stage with the replacement as Reich Interior Minister, who was (together with the Reich Finance Minister) responsible for the civil service, of the ineffective Wilhelm Frick with the Reichsführer SS, Heinrich Himmler. Frick had fought a losing battle to try and overcome the fragmentation of the State and create a more effective Government apparatus by integrating the various Government agencies under the authority of the representatives of the Interior Ministry at regional and local level. However, his policy, which went under the slogan 'unity of the administration', was opposed by the other Government agencies which did not wish to lose any power over their officials to those of the Interior Ministry. Above all, however, his lack of influence with Hitler, who regarded him as too much of a bureaucrat, proved a crippling handicap in his attempts to reform the administration of the Reich.

Himmler's SS had been one of the main critics of the civil service and Himmler himself had little sympathy with the concern for legal and rational procedures characteristic of the bureaucracy. Indeed, it is clear that his plans for the civil service envisaged the introduction of a new culture closer to that of the SS than that of the traditional civil servant. However, Himmler believed in a strong state and, once he found himself in charge of the interior administration, he took on the responsibility for resisting the attempts by the Party to increase its power at the expense of the State administration. He found himself increasingly locked into a confrontation with the Party at various levels, although he had hitherto been on close terms with Bormann, with whom he used the familiar you (*Du*) form. For example, Himmler strongly resisted the attempts by one or two Gauleiters to establish their own armed units and so challenge the SS's monopoly of internal security.

It was significant for the close meshing of SS and Interior Ministry that it was the Chief of the Security Police and SD, Ernst Kaltenbrunner, who wrote the following report on Party/State relations for Himmler, which provides an illuminating description of the disintegration of the German administration in the latter stages of the war. It was dated 26 August 1944:

**964** With the intensification of total war there is an increased necessity for the measures introduced by the State to have an educative and stimulating influence on the population. This increased emphasis on the guidance of the population has increasingly led to local Party authorities claiming the right to take over the leadership from the State administration. This applies particularly to the relationship of the district leader to the district counsellor (*Landrat*) or Lord Mayor and to the heads of the special administrative bodies. The maxim 'only one person can give the orders' is used as a slogan to be applied at parish and district level, and is justified by reference to the present emergency caused by air warfare and to the efforts required in total war. I would like to refer in this context to the letter of 1.8.44 from Reichsleiter Dr Ley to the Führer. Numerous individual reports portray the following developments over the last few years:

1. The influence of individuals on administrative decisions, amounting in places to political pressure.

2. The takeover of administrative tasks by the Party.

3. Indirect influence on the administration through the formation of 'expanded district staffs' [of the NSDAP] in which the heads of the administration are included.

4. Direct influence through the formation of local or district 'triangles' or district action staffs for the air war (the holding of air raid practice, the compiling of plans for emergency action).

5. Putting the emphasis on the district leader [of the NSDAP] as the highest authority in the district ('the agent of the Reich Defence Commissioner'), the district leader as the 'representative of the executive power' (in the Moselle area). This claim finds expression in direct orders to the executive including on occasions the police.

6. The formation of a separate executive (e.g. political echelons). This development was furthered:

(a) by numerous Gauleiters who, as Reich Defence Commissioners, preferred to use the Party organization and thereby produced in the State administration a sense of being by-passed;

(b) by the Reich Party headquarters (Dept. II of the Party Chancellery) which gave official backing to this claim for leadership and influenced the district political leaders in this direction.

Undoubtedly tasks like the building of the East Wall, the evacuation of the border areas, and total war, demand a strong commitment of the Party organization. The best results have been achieved where the Reich Defence Commissioners used both apparatuses, each performing the function for which it was most appropriate. Faults occurred where one acted independently of the other (cf. my report on the effects of the military situation in the East on the eastern area of the Reich and on the *Generalgouvernement* [of Poland]).

The public does not appreciate it when, in the present situation, comradely cooperation does not always have priority and instead people take the opportunity of contriving shifts in the domestic balance of power. The constant necessity for the local Government organs to defend their position causes a loss of energy, inhibits initiative, and on occasion produces a sense of helplessness.

The following measures are worth considering in order to reduce the symptoms of tension:

1. The occasional exercise of influence on the Reich Defence Commissioners from an authoritative source.

2. The Reichsführer SS to express his views on suitable individual cases in order to clarify the situation and to provide backing for administrative heads against encroachments on their position.

3. The honouring of particularly deserving District Counsellors, Lord Mayors, mayors or other heads of State authorities (heads of Labour Offices).

——

## (vii) Party Activities

As the war continued, the Party became ever more heavily engaged on the home front, as is clear from the following 'Notes for a lecture' on 'The Party's Involvement in the War'. The piece is undated but was written in late 1943 or 1944 by the district leader of Berchtesgaden-Lauf in southern Bavaria and was published in a Party indoctrination pamphlet. The list of tasks is interesting as an indication of how the Party leadership saw its role, and the document illuminates the mentality of a Nazi district leader:

**965**   1. *Does the home front have the wrong attitude?*
What do people complain about? Do they complain about the demands made on them?
Hours of work—food shortages—withdrawal of the clothing ration book—shortages of consumer goods—the fact that their relatives are at the front—the dangers they face and sacrifices they make in the bombing raids?
No! People complain about those who could work and don't, who live better than others, who through their personal connections acquire goods which others haven't seen for years, who have never fought at the front, or who manage to escape the bombing raids by neglecting their duties. The attitude of people on the home front is excellent. The good ones are showing up the bad ones . . .

5. *The task of the home front in the war*
The home front has the task of providing the front line forces with weapons—munitions and supplies—and moral support. The home front must also look after all its own needs.

6. *The prerequisite for all these activities is the mobilization of a voluntary spirit*
Only when the German does something voluntarily, even better fanatically, does he achieve the highest level of performance.

*7. What have been the particular educational tasks of the Party since the beginning of the war?*
(a) To arouse a simple faith in the nation and in the Führer.
(b) To prove the correctness of the National Socialist world view.
(c) The practical application of the National Socialist ideology in life.
(d) The individual cannot escape the fate of the nation.
(e) The importance of the individual in the context of the nation, his responsibility for his actions, his responsibility for the fate of everybody.

The following questions require particular attention:

(f) Who is guilty of starting the war?
(g) When will the war come to an end?
(h) Longing for peace, the demand for peace at any price.

*8. The Party uses two methods for its task of education and leadership*
1. The training and education of the Party itself and its direct deployment via the political leaders, officials and wardens, as well as via the membership.
2. The leadership of compatriots through the methods of propaganda and indoctrination, through cultural supervision, through 'surgeries'. (Press, radio, books, family celebrations, village evenings, parent evenings, events put on by Strength through Joy.)
The importance of the experience.

*9. Particular wartime tasks for the Party*
(a) Improving performance.
(b) Filling gaps in personnel.
(c) Educating individuals to cut down their personal needs.
(d) Caring for soldiers at the front, in the barracks, in military hospitals, caring for soldiers' families.
(e) Informing people of the heroic death of their relatives, the carrying out of memorial ceremonies, the construction of memorial groves.
(f) Caring for the relatives of those killed in action.
(g) Caring for the war-disabled, returning them to civilian occupations.
(h) Air raids: early evacuation of mothers and children from the areas at risk. (For details see the sections on NSV, KLV, and mayors.)
(i) Direct participation by the Party in the air defence measures: education of the population, initiating the construction of air raid shelters, the deployment of the air defence forces; dealing with the effects of the air raid while it is in progress. Training the firefighters, setting up district task forces, setting up political teams for special tasks.

After the attack: providing food supplies for the population, evacuating those who have been bombed out, the wounded, digging out the dead.

Ensuring the continuation of activities important for the war effort, the fight against criminals, maintaining security against ethnic aliens and prisoners of war during and after an air raid.

10. *The particular wartime tasks of the most important formations and leagues of the NSDAP*

### THE GERMAN LABOUR FRONT (DAF)

People spend their lives at work and at home and so political leadership is just as important at the work place as it is at home.

The aim of the work of the DAF is to promote the highest level of performance by the individual and by the plant community. The preconditions are: to develop a political will (on a voluntary basis), the creation of a leadership core in the plant, the organizational penetration of the plant with the officials of the DAF, the influencing of individual members of the retinue through plant assemblies, the awakening of the creative abilities of the German man and woman—in the case of the individual through the Professional Competition, in the case of the plant community through the war efficiency competition (this creates the community spirit within the plant), the occupational training programme, the encouragement of a system of suggestions for improvements within the plant.

### FURTHER SPECIAL TASKS OF THE DAF:

The maintenance of the physical strength of the workforce through the supervision of catering, accommodation, the journey to and from work, conditions at the workplace, checking health conditions, the maintenance and increase in work morale through socially just treatment, through proper leadership in the plant, through provision for workers' recreation via the Strength through Joy and the adult education programme.

The DAF is the trustee for the maintenance of the strength of the worker, for the maximization of people's performance at their workplace.

### THE NATIONAL SOCIALIST WELFARE ORGANIZATION (NSV)

Not an operation for collecting money or a welfare organization of the traditional kind.

It looks after:

(a) Mothers before and after childbirth (grants, nursing care, home help, a period of residence in a home, childbirth in a home, care of mother and child).

(b) children as infants and toddlers (maternity home, crèche, kindergarten). The provision of work for mothers (made possible through the establishment of numerous new crèches).

(c) The Winter Aid Programme (WHW).

(d) The NSV is responsible, in particular, for the evacuees as well as those who have been bombed out. Arranging accommodation, help with getting hold of stoves and cookers, overcoming catering problems, the establishment of community kitchens (the cooker as the woman's theatre of war).

By means of cultural supervision one can overcome regional differences, and encourage understanding for the particular character of the host Gau and prevent an exploitation of hospitality by the evacuees. The importance of evacuation for the education of the German people for its role as a greater German national community.

11. *The Children's Evacuation Programme (KLV)*[13]

This institution was only set up during the war. Complete classes are evacuated from the areas threatened with bombing with their teachers together with a HJ or BdM leader.

Significant population movements occurred.

In addition to ensuring the security of the children, the KLV provides valuable opportunities for the national socialist education of these young people.

Previous experience with the KLV:

Superb state of health, increase in knowledge, creation of a strong sense of community, strengthening of the self-confidence of the children (nowadays the mothers no longer comfort the children, but it's the other way round: the children are comforting the yammering mothers).

The dangers—'epidemics, accidents, silly pranks'—naturally do exist, but so far have been very effectively overcome.

12. *The NS Women's Organization*

Women in wartime. Taking over the men's work, economic concerns and responsibility; solely responsible for education. Lack of time to recuperate physically or mentally. Dangers for marriages and families in the long absence of the men.

Individual tasks of the NS Women's Organization: Make new from old! From remnants make shoes, bags, utensils. Every woman a good cook in wartime. Caring for the soldiers and wounded as particular tasks for the Women's Organization, inspection of households in relation to the allocation of housemaids, compulsory service year girls, female Eastern workers, caring for small children (under 10) in crèches. Winning over the mothers via their children.

13. *The Hitler Youth*

Difficult leadership situation: the dangers have been overcome through the return of wounded leaders. Main task: political education of youth in a way appropriate for young people, support for school education and occupational training of young people, pre-military training particularly for male youth, deployment in anti-aircraft units, HJ fire brigades, signals organization in the air defence service; great Christmas toys programme; participation in the book collection for the Wehrmacht; collection of herbs, pine cones, brushwood; assistance for soldiers' wives, for evacuated and bombed-out families.

14. *The formations of the NSDAP: SA, SS, NSKK, NSFK*[14]

The formations have shrunk to a small size because of the call-up. The men who are still available are engaged at all key points as political leaders, as DAF wardens, as leaders of the plant defence units in factories, in the air defence organization, in the fire brigades, in the home guard (*Landwacht*), on special duties, in special task forces to deal with major air raids. Great attention is paid to maintaining their military strength and naturally also their political-ideological commitment.

---

[13] See below, pp. 421ff.

[14] The NS Fliegerkorps = NS Flying Corps.

15. *The NSDAP and cooperation with State and local government*

The mayors of small towns and villages today have some of the most important responsibilities. The mayor and the local branch leader of the NSDAP receive all the State and Party (Reich, Gau, and district offices) directives. The production battles in agriculture. The collection of the wood quota. The allocation of housing. The distribution of ration cards and coupons. Tax collection. The preparation of air defence and fire fighting services. The deployment of labour. All these are important tasks in which the mayors participate. The motto for the mayors is: you are responsible, you must do what you can yourselves.

The following tasks have acquired particular importance during the war: the military recruitment offices (the registration and deployment of those eligible for call-up); the labour exchanges (deployment of labour); the food offices and those responsible for rationed articles; the price inspectors; the office for family provision; and the building/planning departments . . .

The decisions made by these agencies have a major impact on the life of the individual (it does not matter so much whether or not the applicant receives anything, but rather how he is informed of the outcome; hundreds of mini-meetings every day). These agencies have a decisive influence on the leadership of people [*Menschenführung*]. The motto for all these offices is: justice; no favours, the proper treatment of people, keep your nerve!

16. *Further tasks for the NSDAP*

The NS Veterans' Association (In particular caring for the war wounded and bereaved). The comradeship groups (bringing together the soldiers of the 1914–18 World War). The political education and leadership of the civil servants, lawyers, doctors, teachers etc.—influence reaches into the associations.

17. *Examples of special war projects of the NSDAP*

Collection of furs, wool, winter equipment for the Wehrmacht; collection of old clothes and shoes, collection of paper, books, gramophone records; project to recycle copper and precious metals; education in being frugal with heating, reducing travelling, behaviour towards ethnic aliens and prisoners of war. Major involvement in the pursuit of escaped prisoners of war, criminals, crews who have baled out of enemy aircraft. The shadow action.

18. The tasks outlined above represent the major part of the practical activities of the Party during the war. One should emphasize once again the importance of political education as the basis of all success in every sphere. Voluntary activity alone achieves increased performance; voluntary action alone achieves the maximum success through the involvement of innovators and organizers in every sphere; voluntary action alone facilitates the carrying out of war measures; voluntary action and the fanaticism of the political leaders and of all activists in the NSDAP alone enables us to complete the overall tasks.

19. *Apart from the education of the 'good' member of the German nation, it is also important to remove the troublemaker and to destroy the enemies. A hundred meetings cannot kill off a bad state of affairs with speeches*

Particular weaknesses are: lethargy and complacency, selfishness, greed, negative opposition and corrosive criticism, the influence of hostile ideologies. For example, how do the following appear at the level of individuals: the Liberals, the Marxists (destructive criticism everywhere instead of positive achievements), the representatives of Americanism, individualists with the motto: I want to enjoy my life! What's the war got to do with me?!

We must prevent the activists in all these spheres from coming together in groups.

Importance of mateyness (*Kumpanei*) and buddiness (*Kumpaneitreue*). But comradeship and loyalty do not apply to those who sin against the community of the nation; the misuse of these values must be prevented. People who are enslaved to their own weaknesses must be compelled to fulfil their duties by an even stronger force of terror. Cowardice in the face of the enemy is only overcome through the fear of a court martial. If the educative measures of the Party are no longer sufficient then the compatriot will have to be delivered up to the courts and the educative measures which are most appropriate to his character. (No methods should be used which encourage the miscreants to get together and form a community.) If that does not work or if the dangers are too great, we demand the ruthless elimination of such elements. The loss at the front of those who are most racially valuable which is being experienced by the German nation must be countered by an equivalent elimination of criminals.

20. *The particular importance of setting a good example in the fifth year of the war*

Experience shows that the German people are ready to put up with everything which their leadership is prepared to do first. The great mass of the population, in particular, needs an inspiring example just as much as a warning example. The spirit and the performance of a village, a local branch, a platoon or a company is largely determined—in both the good and the bad senses—by only a few activists.

21. Despite the fact that, in the case of the Party as well, the best people are at the front, we have succeeded through unremitting political and ideological education in enabling the substitutes (sometimes even the third, fourth and fifth substitutes) to fulfil their tasks.

Political fanaticism compensates to some extent for a lack of professional competence. Nowadays, the best professional knowhow is worthless without the necessary commitment. If we on the home front have managed to achieve this success, then the same work will also prove itself in the German Wehrmacht.

22. It is of no importance whether we are soldiers at the front, trainers in a home base, political leaders in the Party, or doing our best as peasants or workers; anyone can be a fighter in the German people's army. But anyone who seeks a reward in external forms will always remain poor. Whereas the person who is conscious of fulfilling his duty to the limit and bears within him a fanatical combative spirit for the Führer and the nation and finds his reward in the continued existence of the German nation and Reich will be truly happy.

On 1 June 1944 the office of Robert Ley, Reich Organization Chief of the NSDAP, issued the following guidelines for the role of Block leader in the first of a new series of instruction pamphlets, entitled 'Service Directives Instructions', thereby answering one of the demands of the previous document:

**966** The Party's task of political leadership must be carried out as effectively as possible. The 'Service Directive' provides those actively responsible for the work of leadership, in particular in the local branches:
1. The Block leader
2. The Cell leader
3. The local branch leader
with *directives and binding instructions for their work.*

They will cover the implementation of
1. *Duties* such as house visits, the holding of cell evenings, meetings, the arrangement of ceremonies, the combating of enemy agitation etc.
2. *Important war measures* such as assistance during and following air attacks, deployment of labour, the collection of scrap etc.
3. *Caring/supervising measures* such as the care of bombed-out people and evacuees, the care of soldiers, the evacuation of children etc . . ..

*General Service Regulations for the Block Leader*

The Block leader has been assigned the right of political leadership for his area (Block).
He is responsible for:
(a) The overall political situation in his block.
(b) The maintenance of order in his block.
He is obliged:
(a) To maintain continued personal contact with the national comrades in his block.
(b) To promote and encourage the measures which are important for the war effort which have been ordained by Party and State.
(c) To implement supervisory measures.

*Instructions for the Block Leader*

1. *The house visit*
The Block consists of of 40–60 households. The most important method of leadership for the Block leader is the *regular house visit.* Basic principle: *Every* household is to be visited *once* a month. In order to carry out this task the Block leader should recruit suitable Party comrades or Party aspirants as Block assistants to work with him. He should deploy an assistant for every ten households: 4–6 Block assistants. The Block representative of the DAF. The Block

representative of the NSV and the Block leader of the Women's Organization are colleagues subordinated to the Block Leader.

Note: Every Party comrade is obliged to cooperate and can be called upon to do so at any time. *There are no such things as political pensioners.* Those who try to get out of it should be reported to the local branch leader. If his influence has no effect, then he should immediately request the district leaders to start exclusion proceedings. The regular home visits are intended to provide the Block leader and his colleagues with detailed knowledge of the situations of the various families, e.g.

(a) The social situation.
(b) The political and ideological attitude.
(c) The level of political commitment and occupational performance.
(d) Characteristics which affect the community either positively or negatively.
(e) Worries, wishes, needs.

In this way the Block leader will get to know and become familiar with every single family. Only direct and very close contact with the compatriots who have been entrusted to him will facilitate active leadership and supervision/care. Home visits should normally be carried out in the early evening. Sundays and public holidays can also be used for this purpose. Home visits should be combined with collections, with invitations to visit Party meetings, with the collection of dues, with requests to take part in community work or with the bringing of various bits of news. On these occasions the Block leader has to visit compatriots in their flats in any case. This gives him the best opportunity for striking up conversations with the compatriots entrusted to him, to strengthen them politically and to awaken the understanding which is required for all the important war measures.

*Important: The Block leader should not stay standing outside the door.* Don't just carry out the particular assignment but use the opportunity to discuss the needs of the day with compatriots! In this way home visits give the Block leader and his colleagues the opportunity of successfully influencing compatriots so that the effect lasts; *it is the most appropriate form of propaganda by word of mouth.* The Block leader should instruct the Block assistants very carefully in this task. The first visits of the Block assistants should be carried out in the company of the Block leader. The Block leader soon discovers after a brief period: *home visits are his most important means of leadership.*

### How do I go about a House Visit?

Today I want to visit the Paulus family at 29/I Gartenstrasse. I know that the head of the family works as a mechanic at Buderos & Co. and that he only gets home at 7.00. The two daughters aged 18 and 21, one of whom works as a nurse in the hospital and the other as a typist at the City Power Station, are usually at home at this time. The two eldest sons have been called up and are on the Eastern front.

So I go shortly after 8.00 in the evening to the Paulus family's flat. I ring the door bell and Frau Paulus opens the door. I give my name, greet her with Heil Hitler and tell her I am visiting her on behalf of the Party. I leave my coat in the hall and Frau Paulus leads me into the parlour where the family are sitting together after supper. I greet Herr Paulus and the daughters who are both present with a handshake and join the family at the table after I have been offered a chair. I first ask after their health and enquire when and what the sons have been writing from the Eastern front. I gather that their son, Robert, was wounded three weeks before by a bullet in the upper arm and that he is in hospital. I make a note of the address of the hospital. The youngest son Willi had just written the day before to say that he was in good shape.

The oldest daughter, Berta, who has just been listening to the conversation up until then, wants to go and visit a girlfriend. I ask her to stay and to postpone her visit to another evening since it's also important for her to take part in our conversation. At my request she stays and says that in the last few days a new batch of wounded have arrived at the military hospital attached to the general hospital. There is so much work that the hospital staff can barely cope. In the kitchen, in particular, there are not enough people to peel the potatoes, wash up, and prepare the meals. She thinks that the hospital management would welcome female volunteers just at the moment. I make a note to inform the branch leader so that the hospital can be given effective help. I will give him the names of five women in my Block who can then be asked by the Block women's leader to do voluntary work in the kitchen, even if only on an hourly basis. This proposal is warmly welcomed and even the youngest daughter, Mina, is willing to help in the kitchen on her free Saturday afternoon and on Sunday morning. The girls want to persuade their friends to join in so that the hospital can be helped out. Frau Paulus gives her full support to the plan because she says that she's sure that their brother is also being looked after by volunteers in the hospital where he is. And, as a mother, she knows best how grateful men are for a caring hand. I take up this idea and declare that, despite the heavy demands imposed by our jobs, every day we should all think of what extra things we can do to help and thereby make a small contribution to the final victory.

Herr Paulus says that that's all very well but in reality things are very different. He and his family want to help as much as they can and to accept all the restrictions which are caused by the war without grumbling, but the same must be expected of all other compatriots. He says that his neighbour, Schmidt, who lives in a four-room flat, has refused to take in a bombed-out family with three school-age children. I remember that this case was reported to the local branch leader, that he told Schmidt to come and see him and reminded him of his duty. Since Herr Schmidt refused to see that he'd made a mistake, following representations by the local branch leader he was instructed to vacate two rooms with the use of a kitchen for bombed-out people. Frau Paulus says that that was the right thing to do and that way we will make progress. And yet, although everyone is doing their duty, she still sometimes cannot avoid thinking that all these sacrifices are a waste of time because the enemy is so well armed. Although our soldiers at the front are making superhuman efforts, the terror bombing is causing massive casualties. I point out that we must be able to cope with this pressure as well, that the population particularly in our big cities is steadfastly resisting the terror attacks, that very quickly, and often only a few hours after the attack, life is back to normal and that, as a result of our preparations such as the evacuation of women and children from the big cities, and the creation of alternative depots for foodstuffs and production sites, we are in a position to prevent even the strongest terror attacks from having a decisive effect on the outcome of the war. The enemy knows that. But, because he is not strong enough to fight decisive battles on land, his military leadership has recourse to the desperate measure of attacking the civilian population by air. It's true that there will be plenty of sacrifices and perhaps some setbacks to come, but in four years of war we have shown that we have the strength to last the course and it is up to us to make sure that this strength is not weakened but rather increased.

The women say as one: 'Hearing you talking like that makes one feel a lot better'; and Herr Paulus says: 'Things'll turn out all right'.

He says that he thinks one of his workmates is listening to the English radio station, but he is only guessing and has no proof. He will keep a close eye on him for a time and report his observations to me. Frau Paulus also pointed out that the 16-year-old son of Frau Rausch, who has been running her husband's greengrocers shop at 26 Lindenstrasse since he was called up, had a road accident last week and had to go to hospital. The woman now has no help in the shop and there have been some unpleasant hold-ups in serving customers. I make a brief note of the case and will see to it in the next few days.

We have had a very lively conversation and the time has gone like a flash. Since we must be fresh for work next day, I say goodbye to the Paulus family and promise to call again in a few weeks' time.

That's how I carry out my home visits.

Limbach, 10 October 1943, Fritz Schroeder, Block leader

▬

While extremely interesting as a model example of *Betreuung Menschenführung* in action, this was clearly an idealized version of the role of a Block leader. A more common view of the Block leader emerges from the following complaint, of 17 July 1943, from the local branch leader of Ulm-Schlageter to the Party's district leadership about an article which had appeared in the local newspaper, the *Ulmer Tageblatt*, the previous day. The offending article had the title: 'The Local Branch Leader and his Colleagues':

**967**  As I briefly mentioned to the district leader, Party comrade Maier, today, I consider that the activity of the Block leader is portrayed in a totally one-sided way. It states:

'Our knowledge [of the local Party organization] is usually confined to the work of our Block leader: collecting contributions, selling tickets for meetings or other events, and now and again collecting books, old clothes or other objects for whatever collection happens to be taking place.'

In that description the Block leader appears like an official of a ten-pin bowling club or some such association. There is no mention of his important task as a political leader, i.e. leader and supervisor in political matters. It is disgraceful that an article like that can appear in a newspaper that claims to be National Socialist.

———

An important aspect of the Nazi Party's attempt to control and guide public opinion was its monopoly of the public sphere. This was jealously guarded, as a teacher in the Trier district in the Moselle valley discovered to his cost. On 31 January 1940, the local branch leader in W. reported to his district leader in Trier as follows:

**968**     On 31.12.39 teacher A organized a New Year's Eve party for villagers, soldiers and workers employed on the West Wall. I was neither informed about it nor invited to it. The local mayor and the mayor of the district were also not invited to this village evening. A was informed some days before this event by the local branch leader, Party comrade B, that he was obliged to inform his local branch leader about it. But A did not consider this necessary.

As I was later told by Party comrades, officers and soldiers, it seemed very odd on this evening that the Party had not even sent a representative to this 'village evening' and that teacher A of all people had made himself the spokesman of the parish. The local branch and the Party have undoubtedly been damaged by this. As you can see from the enclosed copy, I posed five written questions for teacher A to answer. I did not receive a reply. Such a breach of discipline is unforgivable. I request that you take the matter in hand yourself.

The district propaganda chief then wrote to teacher A on 5 February 1940:

Unfortunately, I have only heard today of the incident which is unique in the history of the Trier district. You seem to have forgotten that we have not been living in the time of the system [i.e. the Weimar Republic] for seven years but instead in the Greater Germany of Adolf Hitler. If you had felt the need to get involved in something—of which it must be said that up till now there has been no sign—you could have put yourself at the service of the movement or one of its associated organizations. But apparently you don't 'fancy' the movement of Adolf Hitler and imagine that you can express your need for recognition by holding special events and thereby working against the interests of the movement and, therefore, of the State. One would have assumed that those people who are apparently unsympathetic to National Socialism and yet receive a salary from the State might obey the instructions of the movement which sustains the State. Instead of which you have neither obeyed the various requests of the local branch nor considered it necessary to invite either the cadre or the district mayor to this 'village evening' and thereby convey to the guests from the

Wehrmacht an image of the unity of the nation. I shall inform the regional Government authorities of this incident and, in the event of future complaints about you, will take steps to ensure that the Party can continue to work fruitfully.

The teacher replied to the district propaganda chief on 12 February 1940:

I know as well as you do that we have been living for seven years in the Reich of Adolf Hitler but you are apparently not aware that there are people who sound off about National Socialism but who at heart have learnt little from it, while others do their duty to the nation as a whole calmly and quietly and do not see their main job as being to blacken other people's names.

I reject your letter which, from beginning to end, represents a crude insult to me on the following grounds: When the Führer came to power I was in the Eifel in a little place in the sticks in which one could only get the *Landeszeitung* [local newspaper] and had heard almost nothing of the movement. I did not do as so many of my colleagues did, namely become National Socialists overnight and not from conviction but for their own advantage. Instead, I got to know the movement and the Führer's deeds have won me over. I consider myself a National Socialist and not a 'system person' for . . .

[he then listed the following points: 7 children, member of the NSV since 1.6.34, member of the 'Self-Sacrifice Circle' (an organization making financial donations to the NSV) and, in any case, it was an event put on by the Wehrmacht in which he had simply participated. He made the same point to the school inspector who had been alerted by the district HQ of the Party and the regional Government authorities.]

An important function of the Party was to act as a recipient of denunciations by 'national comrades' not only of those who were breaking the law by, for example, listening to foreign broadcasts, but also those who were in breach of the norms of the 'national community' by, for example, fraternizing with foreign workers or POWs, grumbling about the war and its privations or not pulling their weight in the war effort. The following document provides a typical example:

**969**   *NSDAP Local Branch A, Ulm District, to the NSDAP District HQ, Ulm—6 September 1942:*

Re: *Conscription of M.F.*

The person referred to above has been staying at home for some time with her parents who do not have a farm but only a smallholding. Her father and mother are still able-bodied so that they can run the household. M.F. is still unmarried; she has no other employment apart from delivering some newspapers, which only takes an hour and could be done by a child.

M.F. can be conscripted at once. I request the district headquarters to take the necessary steps.

Re: *Conscription of A.J.*

A.J. possesses a small farm and a joinery. All the others in his age group have been called up into the Wehrmacht. The fact that A.J. is still at home continually prompts other national comrades to complain, pointing out that the others have gone and he too should go, and to some extent they are right. His mother, who is still able-bodied, his wife and a maid are still on the farm. He is not needed as a joiner since there are two other joiners in the village.

I would add that J. is a grumbler and malcontent of the first order and he deserves not only to be conscripted but also to be called up into the Wehrmacht like the others. It's precisely people like him who cause the most discontent in the village. I request the District headquarters to take the necessary steps.

——

## (viii) The Party's Response to the Crisis of 1943: An Attempt to Revive the Atmosphere of the *Kampfzeit*

The winter of 1942–3 with the German defeats at Stalingrad and in North Africa initiated a period of crisis which posed a major test for the Party's responsibility for sustaining morale. Bormann's response to this situation involved an attempt to revive the atmosphere of the *Kampfzeit*, the 'period of struggle' before 1933 when the Party had been so successful at generating a sense of elan and commitment which in turn had helped to mobilize large sections of the population in its support. On 18 December 1942 Bormann issued the following circular to all Gauleiters:

**970**   All doubts about a German victory and about the justice of our cause must at once be silenced with sound arguments and—if that does not work— with more violent measures on the model of the time of struggle. As in the days before the takeover of power, we are engaged in the toughest of struggles, our old opponents have got together again and the old methods are being employed against us once more.

The Führer expects that the Party too will once again deploy the spirit and methods of our time of struggle and will not confine itself to administering and governing but will lead.

——

In the autumn of 1943 Bormann tried once more to galvanise the Party with the old methods:

**971**  *Directive No. 55/43*

*The Head of the Party Chancellery*                    *Führer Headquarters, 29.9.43*

With the increasing intensity of the war, the defensive strength of the home front is being subjected to an ever-growing burden. The NSDAP must, therefore, continually steel the offensive morale of the German people; it must constantly influence the formation of public opinion in a positive direction and vigorously oppose all negative phenomena.

In order that all Party comrades can be deployed for this important task and appropriately prepared for it, I hereby decree the following:

From the 15 October onwards, all local branches will hold general meetings for the whole membership: where possible they should be held within four weeks. The cadres are responsible for holding these meetings in an effective manner and should call upon the cooperation of all available propaganda and indoctrination personnel. The Reich head of organization [Dr Ley] and the Reich head of Propaganda [Dr Goebbels] will provide the necessary speakers for this internal Party action.

The Gauleiters should if possible speak in one meeting in each district of their Gau; the district leaders are expected to conduct the meetings of the local branches in person. In those Gaus in which the number of districts and branches creates difficulties for the carrying out of this directive within the allotted time, the meetings should be combined in an appropriate manner.

Attendance of all Party comrades at these meetings is compulsory. The meetings themselves should be carried out in a dignified and above all focused manner. The individual Party comrades must be urgently and emphatically reminded of their obligation to act as a positive influence on the country's morale. Particular emphasis should be placed on the need for the exertion of greater influence on the mood and attitude of the population through personal contact. The bigger the impact of the enemy and of the current difficulties on our national comrades the more vigorously must the NSDAP, acting through all its members, strengthen belief in the correctness of our actions and in the certainty of a German victory. The ideas expressed in the enclosure should form the main theme of the meetings.

I request the Gauleiters to pay particular attention to these meetings. Further instructions will be given out centrally by the Reich head of organization and the Reich head of propaganda, who will oversee the implementation of the directive.

*Ideas for the General Membership Meetings*

The national socialist movement has so far mastered every situation! It has never allowed itself to be put off its stroke by occasional setbacks and problems. On the contrary, it has always risen to the tasks and emerged the stronger from all the challenges. Now, once more, the Party is faced with a historic challenge.

If the leadership remains firm and tough during this very difficult period, the bulk of the nation will remain unshaken. But the absolute prerequisite is for the leader to give the best example of strength of faith and resolution. The personal behaviour and quality of character of all Party comrades must always be irreproachable especially at this time. The Führer requires, as he particularly emphasized in his last address, that the Party set an example in everything. Never before have so many critical eyes been focused on it as today.

The Party is the political elite of the nation. In it those Germans with the greatest faith and political fanatics have come together. In becoming a member of the Party every Party comrade has taken on a particular responsibility towards the leadership and the nation. We conquered this state with incomparable toughness and energy. We must defend it with no less determination and doggedness. Every Party comrade must, especially now, feel himself to be a confidant of the Führer and a go-between between leadership and people. The Party must now in these testing times take the leadership of the people particularly firmly in hand. Our compatriots want to know that their opinions are being safely and reliably formed. Thus, the movement must not allow itself to be diverted for one moment, by the accumulation of other tasks, from the important task of the leadership and influencing of the people. The persuasion and political direction of our compatriots is one of the most fundamental tasks of the Party. In the time of struggle it was an honourable duty of the National Socialists to wrestle with every single person for the dissemination of our ideas. The same must still be true now! We must keep reminding our compatriots of the destructive aims of our enemies, which already emerged before the First World War in the encirclement policy of King Edward VII, in the fight against the German colonies etc. If the German people want to live then they must fight for their right to live until a victorious end to the war. Let us remember the post-war period, which, despite the fulfilment policy from Bell to Stresemann, imposed tougher and tougher conditions, concessions and debts on the German people. Every Party comrade must once more be persuaded to become an active participant in the movement. Only then will he feel that he is fully involved in what is happening today. More than ever before the Party must be a sworn band of fighters. Party comrades who have weakened or grown tired must once more be galvanized by the most active and fanatical ones. The elan and fighting spirit of the whole movement must at this time above all not waver for a moment.

It is essential that Party comrades remain unaffected by any fluctuation of mood. The flood of rumours and defamatory statements, which are systematically spread by the enemy in order to unsettle our people, must break against the calm and unshakeable spirit of all Party comrades! We have on occasion put up with much too much in the way of insults and abuse of our national socialist leadership. Any Party comrade who does not straight away and publicly stand up to fainthearts, wets and defeatists thereby brands himself as the greatest political weakling and, through his pathetic example, encourages the enemy's attempts to undermine morale. Now more than ever everything depends on the influence of every man and every woman on their fellow men and women. We must expect that every Party comrade has the guts and civil courage to shut up all malicious gossips. Every rumour-monger and unreliable compatriot must at once be confronted by a committed and combative Party comrade. Unfortunately, a number of Party comrades have become too comfortable and too posh to oppose the insidious wets with the requisite vigour.

We want to continue to help compatriots who are genuinely in search of advice and assistance. Fainthearts and despondent compatriots will be most effectively convinced by the example of the strength of our faith and our calm confidence in victory. But, in the case of shameless rumour-mongers and thoughtless gossips, politeness and restraint are out of place. They must be firmly put in their place or handed over to the police.

The leadership cannot always respond directly to every conceivable rumour and question that comes up. It gives out a line on the most important issues as far as possible. But, if no directives come from the top, then the resourceful Party comrade will have to look out for himself.

The movement can no longer be bothered with passengers and observers. The Party leadership makes no bones about the fact that it is ruthlessly determined to part company with insecure and fickle elements. Anyone who today no longer has the courage to declare their commitment to National Socialism is no longer one of us. But, if anyone is excluded from the movement, it is not as if they were being expelled from some association; they are being thrown out of the political order of the German people in its critical hour in disgrace.

If every Party comrade clearly and decisively exerts the necessary influence on the formation of the mood and opinion of his acquaintances and the section of the population led by him, then our nation's attitude and will to resist in this fateful struggle can never decline.

---

## (ix) Party Ceremonies

The Nazis believed that they were engaged in a revolutionary transformation of the values of the German people, replacing the Christian-humanist tradition with a new 'world view' based on 'scientific principles' reflecting 'nature' and, more specifically, on the particular ethnic (*völkisch*) qualities of the German nation. As part of this process, they had developed rituals, ceremonies and an official calendar of celebrations, which were clearly designed as a substitute for the traditional Church calendar. During the war the Party decided to institute a regular series of 'ceremonial occasions' (*Feierstunden*), or in modern parlance 'consciousness-raising sessions' to stiffen morale. On 17 November 1943, for example, the Gau newspaper for Upper Franconia, the *Bayerische Ostmark*, issued the following announcement:

**972**     *The Party to Arrange Ceremonial Occasions*
*a Requirement of the Times/Events in the Whole Gau*

In wartime a nation is driven by a strong need for inner strengthening and concentration of its will, for spiritual guidance and ideological consolidation.

Naturally, in the first instance it is the job of the Party, which created the preconditions for the insuperable defensive strength of the new Reich, to sustain all the energies of a nation which is struggling for its right to live and to convey to it the inner determination against which all the efforts of the enemy will come to nothing. In addition, the NSDAP has the task of conveying its condolences to the relatives of those killed in action and of providing them with assistance.

In order to carry out this great task which derives from the current situation, Gauleiter Wächtler has ordered the holding of regular ceremonial occasions for the NSDAP. They will provide edification, spiritual sustenance and honour the memory of those killed in action. No entry fee will be charged for the ceremonial occasions, which will be made lively and kept brief. In the case of the general ceremonial occasions the participation of the Party's youth will be particularly important. But the other sections of the Party, such as the SA, SS and the NSKK, will also be involved so that a community occasion will be achieved through the efforts of a variety of bodies. In addition, ceremonial occasions will be organized by the Party in association with the Wehrmacht.

The content of the ceremonial occasions will be determined by the basic ideas of the national socialist world view—for example, the idea of political soldiers and military songs, for which the use of well-trained choirs would be particularly appropriate. Moreover, the realization of the concepts of 'worker and soldier', 'youth and Wehrmacht', 'women in our time' etc. should form the focus of these occasions. The comradeship groups of the NS Veterans' Association will be heavily involved in the arrangement of these ceremonies, which will include an appropriate commemoration of those killed in action.

With ceremonial occasions having already been celebrated in the Gau headquarters city of Bayreuth, these ceremonies, which have already become an indispensable spiritual part of our wartime experience, will be introduced in all the districts of the Gau. In the countryside the assistance of teachers and the involvement of schoolchildren will be particularly important. The head of the [NSDAP] district cultural section will be responsible for arranging the NSDAP ceremonies and will coordinate all the organizations involved in cultural activities in order to implement this comprehensive community activity.

---

However, members of the Nazi leadership differed somewhat in their attitudes towards this development. Hitler himself, for example, was sceptical about the attempt to turn Nazism into a substitute religion as was made clear in a letter from Bormann to Alfred Rosenberg, the Nazis' 'official' ideologist, dated 29 May 1941:

**973**  . . . On no account, as the Führer has repeatedly emphasized, should National Socialism represent or help to create a substitute for ecclesiastical or religious activities. National Socialism is a scientifically based view of life from which everything mystical and cultic should be excluded. The Führer spelled out this basic principle and explained the reasons for it at length in his speech to the session on culture at the Reich Party rally in 1938. Only the application of the latest scientific knowledge can prevent the dogmatic fossilization of the national socialist world view.

———

Hitler's speech to the 1938 Party rally on 6 September had echoes of an Enlightenment manifesto:

**974** National Socialism is a cool doctrine of reality based on the most incisive scientific knowledge and its theoretical elucidation. In having opened and in opening the heart of the nation to this doctrine we do not wish to fill it with a mysticism which is external to the purpose and goal of our doctrine.

Above all, although National Socialism is in its organization a movement of the people, it is under no circumstances a cult. In so far as the enlightenment and the winning over of our people involved the use of certain methods which have now already become traditional, they are the results of a perception gained from an experience grounded in pragmatism. It makes sense, therefore, to retain them as customs. But they have nothing in common with methods or forms of expression which were borrowed or acquired for other reasons and which have adopted the designation 'cult'. For National Socialism is precisely not a cult but an ethnic-political doctrine deriving exclusively from racial theory. Its purpose is not a mystical cult but the care and leadership of a nation determined by blood. For this reason we do not have cult rooms but only halls of the people and we do not have cult shrines but assembly halls and parade grounds. We do not have cult groves but sports arenas and playing fields. And our meeting halls are characterized not by the mystical darkness of a cult shrine but by the brightness and the light of a hall which is both beautiful and functional. Thus no cult practices take place in them but instead exclusively demonstrations by the people in the form which we have learnt in the course of long struggles, which we have become used to and which we want to preserve as it is.

The intrusion of mystically-inclined occultists into the movement cannot therefore be tolerated. They are not National Socialists but something else, in any case something which has nothing to do with us. At the top of our programme are not mysterious ancestors but clear knowledge and therefore open commitment. By putting at the centre of this knowledge and this commitment the maintenance and therefore the continuation of a creature created by God, we thereby serve the maintenance of a divine work and thereby the fulfilment of the divine will and not in the secret twilight of a new cult shrine but before the open countenance of the Lord.

There were eras when twilight was the precondition for the effectiveness of certain doctrines and today we live in an era in which light is the basic condition for our successful action.

Woe betide us if, as a result of the intrusion of unclear mystical elements, the movement or the State sets unclear tasks. And it is enough for this lack of clarity to be in the words. It is already dangerous to order the creation of a so-called 'cult shrine' because then it will be necessary to devise so-called cult games and cult rituals. Our 'cult' is solely the encouragement of the natural and therefore what is divinely ordained. Our humility is the unconditional bowing down before and respect for the laws of existence, which we humans are coming to understand, and our prayer is: that we may courageously fulfil the duties which arise from them. Cult rituals are not our responsibility but that of the Churches.

Alfred Rosenberg had a rather different perspective on this issue and, on 6 March 1943, wrote to Bormann as follows:

**975** As I have already mentioned before, it must be accepted as a matter of principle that indoctrination and education must have the possibility of acting not simply through the spoken word in speeches and lectures, but should also appeal to the feelings of Party comrades through ceremonies. It seems to me necessary, particularly in the light of the struggle against the Church, for the Party to develop a ceremonial form which attracts Germans to the Party and allows them to dispense with what the Church has hitherto given them. In this connection it seems to me to be necessary above all initially to create within the NSDAP this new form and only when this new form has developed *within* the NSDAP for a few years to consider taking it further. Thus, I believe that there is nothing more necessary than to create a unified view on matters of ideology in the ranks of the Party and to deploy the efforts to achieve that rather than fragmenting them by extending them outside the Party, particularly in wartime. In my view it ought to be sufficient if the Reich Propaganda headquarters carries out the ceremonies which are contained in the draft proposal for the delimitation of the staging of ceremonies, namely: the Takeover of Power Day, the Heroes' Memorial Day, The Führer's Birthday, the Day of the German Nation, Mothers' Day, the Summer Solstice, Autumn Thanksgiving Festival, Memorial Day for the Movement's Martyrs, the Winter Solstice, Christmas celebrations of the NSDAP, the People's Christmas. If, in addition, there is at the most one ideological ceremony for the Party comrades per month, that would be all that could now be achieved in wartime.

It was at local level, and particularly in rural areas where the influence of the Churches tended to be greatest, that the battle between Church and Party was fought most vigorously. It took the shape of a struggle for influence between the local NSDAP branch and indoctrination leaders and the parish priest or pastor. One form taken by this struggle was the competition between the rival Party and Church ceremonies. For the Party tried to compete with the Churches by introducing rites of passage [*Lebensfeiern*]. On 9 August 1943 the SD reported on the state of play in this struggle:

**976**   *Views on the Activation of Rites of Passage: Their Staging and*
*Reception by the Population*

Church ceremonies and the rites of passage staged by the Party have developed very differently in the course of the war, as is indicated by reports from all parts of the Reich. While the Church ceremonies are gaining greatly in popularity, the national socialist marriage, christening, and funeral ceremonies, which even in peacetime were few in number, have declined still further.

*The state of the rites of passage is very varied in the various* Gaus, since the preconditions for a planned implementation of such ceremonies, in particular the attitude of the population and the activity of the people responsible for carrying them out in the different parts of the Reich, are by no means uniform. A great deal of work and a lot of practice are required and much experience needs to be gathered before the ceremonies will have acquired a form which will appeal to compatriots, will be convincing and will be able to stand up to the competition from the Church ceremonies. There are various reasons for the population still being unreceptive to the idea of national socialist rites of passage and often even hostile to them:

1. Rites of passage are still seen by the population as an internal Party matter.
2. The idea of the national socialist rites of passage has hitherto been almost completely neglected by the German media of guidance (press, radio, film).
3. There is a lack of ceremonial rooms (Community Houses) which turn the ceremonies into a real community experience such as is the case with the Churches.
4. The ceremonies naturally lack well-established forms and convincing customs, while the Church possesses a centuries-old tradition.
5. National socialist marriage or funeral ceremonies have often been rejected in many places on the basis of a completely one-sided reference to ceremonies which went off badly, whereas there is no such uncertainty about Church ceremonies.
6. A certain natural resistance to new forms, which is powerfully supported by the strong ties to the traditional Church ceremonies, particularly in rural areas.

1. *The number of ceremonies carried out up to now and the proportion of the particular types of ceremony within the total number of rites of passage*
The number of ceremonies carried out in the Reich as a whole is very small as is clear from the reports. Even in Gau Kurhessen, which with 100 ceremonies per month is at the top of the scale, the national socialist ceremonies are only a fraction of the large number of Church ceremonies. The majority of the ceremonies are restricted to the personal circle of colleagues and acquaintances of the indoctrination leader or other senior political leaders. Only in exceptional cases do compatriots ask for a national socialist ceremony for their circle and approach the Party with a specific request for support. *The proportions of the particular kinds of ceremony in the total number* are also completely different in the individual Gaus. While in the Eastern March [Austria] *funerals* form the largest group, Litzmannstadt [Lódź] and Reichenberg report a very small number

of funerals because 'the religious burials are more solemn and more comforting'. In the case of non-Church *weddings* most people do without a ceremony altogether, not least because the present form of registry office wedding guarantees a certain cermonial form.

2. *The reception of the new directives for the carrying out of rites of passage*
The uniform Reich directives which have been issued have been welcomed by those responsible for carrying them out without exception because they provide firm guidance and suggestions which have long been wanted . . .

3. *Rejection of the carrying-out of ceremonies because the Party agencies are overburdened with other tasks*
Most responsible Party comrades do not doubt the necessity for further work in the field of rites of passage as an essential means of ideological guidance—as is clear from the reports. But the majority of local branches regard the problem of carrying out rites of passage as a completely new task for which insufficient personnel, appropriate experience or positive response from the population can be anticipated. In addition, there is the current burden of other tasks of various kinds so that there is often a negative attitude towards the carrying out of rites of passage, sometimes also as a result of a certain lack of confidence and interest in cultural matters . . .

4. *The effect of the personal and ideological attitude of the person carrying out the ceremony on its success*
. . .'It is frequently the case that only a few national or Party comrades are in a position through their personal demeanour, their behaviour and their words to give expression to the dominant feelings at a rite of passage.' 'In most cases even in the district headquarters at the most one or two suitable people can be found. And you can forget about the local branches altogether, where—particularly in rural areas—many Party leaders still have strong church ties.'

5. *The creation of special ceremonial rooms as the precondition for the successful staging of a ceremony*
. . .'A major practical problem is the lack of suitable ceremonial rooms. Compatriots do not find the ceremonial atmosphere which the churches provide even in the rooms which have been specially decorated.'
. . .'If after twenty years I come back to a place I can say: I got married in that church and I will enter it with a certain sense of awe since this was the place where I experienced one of the most important events of my life. But, if I was married in any old room where tomorrow a play was going to be performed and the day after that a magician was going to do his act, then it would not be a place which one could seek out years later and be inspired with a sense of dignity'. . . .

6. *The lack of strong emotional and spiritual impressions as an obstacle to securing a powerful impact through national socialist ceremonial*
. . .'The failure of the national socialist rites of passage to make a deep impression is less the result of superficial flaws and inadequacies and more the

consequence of the lack of a religious element. By contrast, the priest knows how to answer all questions relating to God, fate, immortality etc. with self-assurance and thus in rural areas occupies a dominant position at all ceremonies, whereas the national socialist speaker normally takes care to avoid adopting any position on religious matters.' . . .

One problem with these ceremonies referred to in the next report of the Party Chancellery for 18-25 April 1943 was one which tended to apply to the Nazi propaganda effort in general:

**977**  If—as is the case this year—five ceremonies occur within one month (Heroes' Memorial Day, Hitler Youth Admission, Admittance into the NSDAP, Induction of the 10-year-olds, and the Führer's birthday) then these ceremonies tend to compete with each other and result in a fragmentation in the participation of the population.

It was in the most deeply Catholic areas, such as Eichstätt in Bavaria, that youth dedication ceremonies had least impact. Here, the Church was able to retain its hold over young people to a considerable extent, as the report of the Party's indoctrination office, dated 20 June 1944, makes clear:

**978**  Confirmation was celebrated for the town and countryside with great ceremony in the cathedral. Large numbers of people participated. The Corpus Christi procession followed the usual traditional church ceremony. The procession, which was held on Sunday in Eichstätt, was notable for the large number of young people who took part. Although the actual Corpus Christi Day (Thursday) had been officially declared a normal work day, the peasants in the countryside all stopped work . . .

In the countryside the youth dedication ceremony had little significant impact. Of course in the countryside these political ceremonies are held with an unexampled indifference and meagre display. The local branch leaders should at least have made clear to the Party members in the course of several evening sessions and on the basis of pamphlets the significance and importance of these ceremonies. Our numerous 'sleeping comrades' must finally be made aware of the ideological interests of the Party and be dragged from the depths of their Christian-Catholic rut. If our Party does not gather together a community of passionate advocates of a national socialist stance and life style then we shall make no ideological progress. The majority of schools showed no interest in the dedication ceremony.

If the Party failed to win over the population to its youth dedication ceremonies, this was even more true of its attempt to replace religious memorial ceremonies for those killed in action with special Party ceremonies, as is clear from the following report from the district indoctrination office of the Protestant district of Weissenburg in Bavaria dated 29 June 1944:

**979** It is impossible to carry out the instruction by Reichsleiter Party Comrade Bormann to hold a memorial service for every person killed in action. In our area a religious memorial service is held for almost every person killed in action; to try and suddenly introduce a Party ceremony would be more damaging than beneficial. Naturally, a special hero's ceremony is put on by the Party for any person killed in action whose relatives do not desire a Church ceremony. The Reich offices do not seem to be properly aware of the issue of the confessional commitment of the rural population when it says on page 7, paragraph 2, of the second issue of the Cultural Politics brochure: the relatives' desire to have a memorial service in many cases does not stem from a strong tie to the Church but rather from the need to see their dead honoured within the community . . . This is a misconception of the real position. The memorial service is an expression of the tie to the Church; it would almost never be dispensed with.

The work in the sphere of ceremonies to mark rites of passage must be pushed forward very carefully and circumspectly, particularly since the personnel to carry it out is lacking in the countryside. Nothing will be achieved by force or swamping.

## (x) The Attitude of the Population to the Nazi Party[15]

The population's attitude to the Nazi Party was sceptical from the start and to a large extent remained so. A report by the local government authority in Ebermannstadt in Bavaria dated 30 September 1939 noted:

**980** The relatives of those among the older age cohorts who have been called up, particularly those who fought in the 1914–18 war, are annoyed that young and single men, who are liable for call up, are still at home . . . It is in this atmosphere that indignation arises concerning the fact that the majority of the political leaders of the NSDAP have been given reserved occupation status, although, in the opinion of these grumblers, the 'old fighters'[16] would now really have a chance to do some fighting.

In its report on the mood of the population in November 1939, the Party district of Wiesbaden commented on the response to the

---

[15] For further information on this see Chapters 49 and 51 below.
[16] *Alte Kämpfer*, i.e. pre-1933 Nazis.

assassination attempt on Hitler, which took place in Munich on 8 November:

**981**   It made a deep impression to see how the ordinary man in the street in particular was affected by the news of the Munich assassination attempt. In this case it has once again been shown that the Führer is the inexhaustible spring of the National Socialist movement and that it is overwhelmingly through his person that the contact between Party and people is established. From this it is evident that we have a long way to go before the Party itself is firmly anchored in the nation.

The gap between the Party and the people increased during the war in part as a result of the blatant discrepancy between the ideals of national community proclaimed by the Party and the reality of corruption and privilege associated with much of its district and local cadres. The Party leadership tried hard to inculcate a sense of responsibility in its members with repeated appeals, of which the following circular issued by Bormann and dated 1 March 1943 is a good example:

**982**   The Führer has instructed me to make the following comment:
   The measures for the conduct of total war, which have been ordered by the Führer and which are decisive for the further development of the war, will only be able to be successfully implemented with the aid of the strength of the movement. As a result, a heavy responsibility rests on the movement. *Every leading Party comrade must be conscious of his responsibility.* The *personal example* of each individual Party leader is of decisive importance for the strengthening of such a commitment to the struggle. The whole nation will be given fresh heart by it and by its members. From now onwards, we have no more time for teas, for receptions and banquets except in so far as these have to be arranged for diplomatic purposes. Moreover, the nation has no sympathy for peacetime pleasures or for lengthy alcoholic sessions indulged in by individual leaders. People, who day by day have to give the best of themselves and who, for a long period, have given up various hobbies, must be certain that their leaders are setting a good example. This confidence will certainly be destroyed for hundreds and thousands of people if *a single* leading Party comrade behaves badly. We must assume that people will talk more about one night of carousing than about a hundred spent working. Since setting a personal example is psychologically of the highest importance, and since the task set for the Party requires the highest degree of commitment from every leader and sub-leader from early till late, every leading Party comrade must give up private pleasures, comforts, and special rights that do not serve the performance of duties both for himself and for his relatives in an exemplary fashion. The incorruptibility and correct behaviour of all relatives of the leadership are the first preconditions for the trust which must bind the leadership with the nation in difficult times.

Anyone who undermines this trust hinders the carrying out of the tasks which face us. Every National Socialist must be a representative of the will to resist to the last and, at his place of work, among acquaintances and relatives, in the Party work as in his private life, support with total dedication the fulfilment of the demands imposed upon us by the war.

Whatever is useful for the war and contributes to its speedy and victorious conclusion has our support; whatever disturbs and hinders the commitment of the nation will prolong the war and must be ruthlessly eliminated. We must train the National Socialists in the Party, its formations and leagues even more than hitherto to be activist individual fighters. Everywhere the Party comrade must be the motor for the adjustment of the home front to total warfare. The precondition for this is that a blameless, exemplary leadership gives it the inner strength necessary to achieve it. The Führer relies on the strength and steadfastness of the movement. He demands that the virtues which marked the National Socialists in the time of struggle are not only preached but are also practised.

The German nation must be able to look up to its leadership in critical hours filled with faith and trust; then it will possess the inward strength on which every power on earth must shatter.

However, two months later, probably referring not to the above document but to another appeal issued by Hitler to the Party on 10 May, the section of the Party Chancellery responsible for summarizing the reports of the various Gau headquarters included a devastating commentary on "the population's relationship to the Party" in its report for the period 9–15 May 1943:

**983**    In a recent proclamation the Führer said, roughly speaking, that the Party is the unshakeable embodiment of the power which now provides not only the internal guarantee for securing victory but, as a result, for ensuring the future of our nation. Unfortunately, it has become apparent that the measures which have been taken for this purpose, in particular by the Party Chancellery, have not as yet led to the desired end. Unfortunately, it must be said that the Party has become more and more ossified since the take-over of power. The elan and the ability to inspire enthusiasm are no longer there to the same extent as they were before.

The point has already been made that the enemy propaganda does not pass over the German people without leaving an impression and it must be said that the poison of these whisperings is beginning to eat into the deepest recesses of Germans' souls. Even if this process is as yet hardly visible on the surface, as is clear from the reports of the Gau headquarters, nevertheless there must be concern that it will appear at a critical moment.

We have not yet succeeded in completely neutralising this poisoning by enemy propaganda. For this reason, every effort must be made so that the political leadership are at all times in a position to refute the arguments of enemy propaganda in the simplest language. This requires that in future our propaganda no longer bases itself purely on the great public media, but that in addition it utilises Party comrades, and above all the political leaders and the members of the formations, to put over our slogans, as happened in the "time of struggle". The Party publications such as "The Cadre" (*Hoheitsträger*) "Indoctrination Pamphlet" (*Schulungsbrief*), "Confidential Information" (*Vertrauliche Informationen*), circulars etc. all reach only a particular and relatively small group. Under present conditions the district leader or the local branch leader does not in practice have the opportunity of giving the block and cell leaders written material. Oral instructions can only very rarely be given and can never achieve the desired goal. Thus, it is urgently necessary to give the block and cell leaders material which can tell them in skilful, simple and rousing terms how they must conduct the fight. This material should be phrased in the style which is used by the Supreme Command of the Armed Forces for its information for the troops, which finds the right tone and which can be understood by the ordinary person.

The Führer demands of the Party that it continually arouses the German nation to an awareness of the enormity of the dangers, that it strengthens the sacred faith that they can be overcome, that it instills strength into weak natures, that it ruthlessly destroys saboteurs, that it explains what is happening, that it breaks terror with terror which is tenfold as great, and that it exterminates traitors. Restrictions on the supply of paper, lack of personnel, lack of available rooms must not be allowed to prevent the achievement of this goal.

Many leading Party comrades have lost the courage to make a fair assessment of themselves. But this is necessary in order to understand the causes which have led us to our present condition. Many have become fat and complacent bourgeois and no longer recognise the rules under which they joined up.

These considerations are also the appropriate context in which to make it clear that the loyal and active Party comrades and also the mass of the decent compatriots do not understand why national socialist leaders who have broken our laws are not ruthlessly brought to book. The covering up and concealing of offences committed by national socialist leaders or the ignoring of and "not wanting to see" errors of behaviour do not pass without criticism. The motto "the little men are hanged while the big fish get off scot free" has once more become alarmingly popular.

It is clear from the many petitions we receive that the mood of the population would not be adversely affected if Party leaders, whose guilt has become public knowledge, were pilloried, dismissed or punished. On the contrary, a wave of renewed confidence would arise if some people were made an example of.

The Gau headquarters are continually making the point that there are great dangers in depriving vital Party offices of adequate personnel. It is being said that "either at this very time of fateful struggle we as a party have a great and decisive task, and then in that case we must act as if we do and make our weight felt, or we do not have this task, in which case it would have been better to have dissolved the Party three and half years ago, let all its men become soldiers and used the Womens' Organisation to make shells". A false modesty in this connection must produce false notions in the nation and contribute towards the dissolution which our enemies at home and abroad are so eagerly desiring.

The need to make the Party once more capable of carrying out its tasks and to secure the rebirth of the old community of struggle is one of the most vital goals of the present time.

The following two reports by the Security Service (SD) of the SS confirm the critical state of the Party's reputation during the spring and summer of 1943. The first is dated 8 July 1943:

**984** . . .3. A further phenomenon, which according to the reports can no longer simply be put down under the rubric "mood", is *the strong tendency to criticize the Party and state leadership*, which can be observed everywhere. Many national comrades viciously attack the performance of individual agencies of the state or the party ("The Party has failed"—"The administration is in total chaos") and meet with hardly any direct contradiction. The majority say nothing at all or even express agreement. *Apparently a section of our compatriots no longer experiences an attack on the institutions of the state and the Party or their personal representatives as something which concerns them but have inwardly distanced themselves.* This attitude explains the *bias* which many compatriots have against government measures and decrees. Certain *prejudices*, e.g. the opinion that the propaganda does not tell the truth or only part of it, or that the upper classes and above all the leading circles are spared certain cutbacks (the confiscation of housing space for bombed out persons, the allocation of housemaids, reductions in the provision of electricity, gas, and water) have become fixed in the minds of substantial sections of the nation. The rumours of the "Ritzy treatment" of the leading personalities cannot be quashed despite all the denials. A large section of the population still believes them. The following report is typical:

A bombed-out woman from the West commented in a discussion about the war situation that all the setbacks could have been avoided if the "brown bosses" were at the front instead of being at home and if they did their duty like the red commissars in Russia who were at the front. The Public Prosecutor's office takes the view that it would be unjust to prosecute this one woman. Similar comparisons come up in about a quarter of all the malicious attack [*Heimtücke*] offences being processed; again and again the bloated bosses are being compared with the commissars in Russia who are doing their duty. Moreover, it is the case that such remarks are common in substantial sections of the population and *so it is unacceptable to charge only this one woman, while it is impossible to press charges in the great mass of cases.* . .

7. Shopkeepers and officials dealing with the public report that the use of the "Heil Hitler greeting" has markedly declined in recent months. It has also been noted that many Party comrades no longer wear their Party badge.

On 16 August 1943, the SD reported further:

**985**    The decline in the use of the "Heil Hitler" salute and disappearance of the Party badge is reported as a fact from various parts of the Reich. People wearing the Party badge are frequently asked: "What? Are you still wearing that thing?". . .

The following "joke" was reported by several sources: Anyone who recruits 5 new members for the Party can resign himself. Anyone who recruits ten new members even gets a certificate to show that he was never in the Party. A joke which appeared some months ago has a new variation: "Exchange a gold Party badge for seven league boots".

But the most alarming report from the SD, as far as the Party's future prospects were concerned, had been made a few days earlier, on 12 August 1943, concerning 'young people's attitude towards the Party':

**986**    I.  The attitude of young people towards the Party is particularly evident each year at the admission ceremonies. The available reports on the admission of the 1924 and 1925 cohorts to the Party show in general a positive attitude on the part of young people towards the Party . . .

But there are reports from almost all parts of the Reich according to which a not insignificant number of young people have an attitude towards admission to the party which leaves much to be desired. The following detailed observations were made:

1. Indifference and a lack of inward commitment. Large numbers of young people see joining the Party not as a particularly desirable goal but rather as "good form", in fact as "a necessary evil".

'The opinion was frequently expressed that membership of the Party was the socially correct thing to do and, in addition, was *a good springboard for one's career.*'. . .

'The young people whose careers do not involve a position of dependence place hardly any value on joining the NSDAP'. 'Young people have a rather indifferent attitude to the Party. Only a very small minority see joining the Party as a mark of distinction. The vast majority regard membership of the Party as a necessity which one simply has to put up with. Thus a young Party comrade remarked: "If one wants to succeed in life one has to be a Party comrade, otherwise one isn't 100%." '

'Many young people believe that they absolutely have to be part of the adult world. The comments of an 18 year old that as a Party comrade one had to be admitted to everything and to be able to make a judgment about everything express the attitude of many young people. Occasionally, young people welcome admission to the Party because then "they were at last free of HJ service"; they hoped the Party would not make so many demands on them.'. . .'A characteristic remark by young people is: " I don't care in the least whether I'm admitted to the Party or not; it's all rubbish"'.

Many reports note that the lack of interest in the Party contrasts with a much greater interest in the *Wehrmacht*.

'Most boys and girls have not the slightest interest in becoming a member of the NSDAP. All attempts by the relevant authorities to get them involved have been in vain. For the boys it's the *Wehrmacht* which is now the thing not the Party.'

'The example is given that now many young people want to become officers because officers are an attractive role model, a desirable goal. The tasks which the block leader and the local branch leader have to carry out in their fields have little attraction for young people; clearly there is nothing which attracts them "to be in on the action" here in the way that a young man wants to be "in on the action" as a member of an elite military unit or a successful football team . . .'

Summing up, *the majority* of the members of the 1924 and 1925 cohorts are *positively* disposed towards admission to the Party. But the number of young people who are indifferent or opposed to admission is so great that it should not be overlooked [!] . . .

II. The reports refer frequently to the fact that a large part of the reason for this attitude of a section of young people is not the fault of the young people themselves.

1. The young people who are now in the HJ experience the Party as a historical fact. They are no longer bound to it by the experience of struggle which would make clear to them that the Party has fought for this state and so has acquired the right to place demands on this state and its people and to demand the right to set the ideological agenda. For many of these young people the Führer is not the representative of the Party but in the first instance the leader of the state and above all Supreme Commander of the *Wehrmacht*. Thus they have no inhibitions about approaching the Party in a critical frame of mind just like any other state institution. *They lack an organically developed relationship of loyalty to the Party* which formed the basis of the old Party comrades' actions. These [party comrades] also saw faults in the Party but nevertheless remained loyal followers. But these young people use the alleged mistakes and flaws of the Party to turn their back on it . . .

3. The reserve shown towards the Party is also encouraged by the unresolved Party-Church question. Since a large section of youth, and above all their parents, are still loyal to the Church, remarks aimed at the "sacred beliefs which they have held hitherto" by Party comrades, cadres and HJ leaders have a negative impact. This is particularly the case at the present time because, as a result of the current war situation, young people too notice that the Church pays great attention, for example, to caring for the relatives of those who have been killed, and that the priests give clear answers on questions concerning life and the present time. In addition, rumours about alleged positive remarks about the churches by leading personalities, soldiers who have been decorated etc. have a big impact.

---

## List of Sources

946   Bundesarchiv Berlin (BAB) NS 6/146.
947   Ibid.
948   Ibid.

949 Ibid.
950 *Der grossdeutsche Freiheitskampf* (Munich 1940), p. 35.
951 *Reichsgesetzblatt* (RGBl.) I 1939, pp. 1937f.
952 K.H. Müller, ed. *Preußischer Adler und Hessischer Löwe. Hundert Jahre Wiesbadener Regierung* (Wiesbaden 1966), pp. 313ff.
953 Jochen von Lang, *Der Sekretär. Martin Bormann: Der Mann, der Hitler beherrschte* (Frankfurt/M 1990), p. 464.
954 Ibid., p. 465.
955 Ibid., pp. 466–468.
956 BAB NS 22/714.
957 W.A. Boelcke, *Deutschlands Rüstung im Zweiten Weltkrieg. Hitlers Konferenzen mit Albert Speer 1942–1945* (Frankfurt/M 1969), p. 428.
958 BAB R 3/1573.
959 BAB NS 6/166.
960 Ibid.
961 BAB NS Misch Nr.1310.
952 RGBl. I 1942, p. 1256.
963 BAB R 18/5318.
964 BAB R 18/1263.
965 BAB Slg. Schumacher 382.
966 Staatsarchiv Ludwigsburg (StAL) PL 501 II Bü 116.
967 StAL PL 502/32/167.
968 F. Heyen, *Nationalsozialismus im Alltag: Quellen zur Geschichte des Nationalsozialismus vornehmlich im Raum Mainz-Koblenz-Trier* (Boppard am Rhein 1967), pp. 75–76.
969 StAL PL 502/32 Bü 78.
970 BAB NS 6/167.
971 Ibid.
972 *Bayerische Ostmark* 17.11.1939.
973 BAB NS 6/166.
974 M. Domarus ed., *Hitler. Reden und Proklamationen 1932–1945* (Wiesbaden 1973), pp. 893–894.
975 BAB NS 6/166.
976 H. Boberach, ed., *Meldungen aus dem Reich. Die geheimen Lageberichte des Sicherheitsdienstes der SS 1938–1945* Vol. 14 (Herrsching 1984), pp. 5583ff.
977 BAB NS 6/786.
978 M. Broszat, E. Fröhlich, F. Wiesemann, eds., *Bayern in der NS-Zeit. Soziale Lage und politisches Verhalten der Bevölkerung im Spiegel vertraulicher Berichte* (Munich 1977), pp. 587–588.
979 Ibid., p. 589.
980 Ibid., p. 134.
981 Hauptstaatsarchiv Wiesbaden (HStAW) 483/5543.
982 BAB NS 6/167.
983 BAB NS 6/786.
984 H. Boberach, op.cit., pp. 5446ff.
985 Ibid., p. 5621.
986 Ibid., pp. 5603ff.

# CHAPTER 42

# Law and Terror

## (i) Introduction

The function of the legal system during the war was seen by the Nazi regime in the light of two main considerations: the first was the concern to maintain the morale and strength of the home front by eliminating any political dissidence or criminal activity which might undermine the solidarity and efficiency of the 'national community'; the second was to ensure that the effects of the war on the 'national body' (*Volkskörper*) in terms of the losses of the best 'human material' at the front were not exacerbated by the survival or even proliferation of the worst elements at home, thereby producing a negative selection in terms of population quality. These aims were conveniently summed up in a letter from a desk officer in the Reich Justice Ministry to his opposite number on the staff of the Führer's Deputy for Party Affairs dated 26 January 1940:

**987** During the war, the task of the judicial system is the elimination of the politically malicious and criminal elements who, at a critical moment, might try to stab the fighting front in the back (e.g. the Workers' and Soldiers' councils of 1918). This is all the more important in that experience shows that the sacrifice of the lives of the best at the front has the effect of strengthening the inferior elements behind the front.

These objectives were implemented through various mechanisms. In the first place, new laws were passed introducing new offences. Moreover, these laws used the notion of 'offender types', e.g. so-called 'national pests', whose definitional vagueness gave wide scope to ideological and other forms of prejudice in reaching verdicts and deciding sentences. This elastic interpretation of offences was also encouraged through the use of vague language in the new laws, which gave considerable discretion to the judges to interpret the various legal clauses extensively.

The second legal mechanism designed to ensure the security of the home front was the use of various forms of pressure on the judiciary to pass the 'right' sentences, pressure which increased after the death of Franz Gürtner, the conservative Justice Minister, in 1941. Judges were encouraged to adopt an interpretation of the law which replaced the traditional emphasis on formal law by one on 'material law'. In other words, the legal system no longer operated largely on the basis of whether or not a particular law had been broken, a particular offence committed. Instead, what was considered important by the courts in considering their sentences was the question of what actual *effect* the offence had had, what damage it had inflicted on the national community and what the offender's *intention* had been. Indeed, intention was regarded more or less as important as the actual offence itself and so, even if an offence had not actually been committed, the intent should be punished equally severely.

Following on from this, the third legal mechanism was the encouragement of harsher sentencing. The use of the death penalty increased markedly. In an article with the title 'Thoughts on Correct Sentencing' published in a legal journal in 1939, Roland Freisler, the State Secretary in the Reich Justice Ministry responsible for penal affairs, made the following comment:

**988** If the community needs to be securely protected against the criminal personality for years on end, why not snuff it out and thereby ensure perfect protection at one blow? Why secure this protection for decades on end through the efforts of numerous valuable national comrades and expensive institutions and then for this additional price receive inadequate protection?

The following figures for death sentences do not include those executed in concentration camps:

**989**

| Year | Death sentences |
|------|------|
| 1938 | 85 |
| 1939 | 139 |
| 1940 | 250 |
| 1941 | 1,292 |
| 1942 | 4,457 |
| 1943 | 5,336 |
| 1944 | 4,264 |
| 1945 | 297 |

The highest monthly total reached during the war was 710 in September 1943. In addition, imprisonment was often replaced by penal servitude and there was a trend towards longer sentences.

This tougher sentencing policy was paralleled by moves towards shortening the legal process by cutting out various stages which had been designed to protect the interests of defendants. The most striking example of this was the increasing use of the Special Courts, which operated accelerated procedures and from which there was no right of appeal. They had first been introduced in 1934 with their main function being to prosecute 'malicious' comments about the regime and its leaders. Their scope was now extended through the assignment of new offences to their jurisdiction such as the ban on listening to foreign broadcasts issued at the beginning of the war. In September 1939, Freisler variously described them as 'the tank corps of the legal system and equipped with as much fighting strength' and as 'drum head court martials on the home front' designed to avert 'a stab in the nation's back'.[1] In one case an arsonist was sentenced to death by a Special Court on the same day he committed the offence. There was also an increase in the number of offences tried in the 'People's Court' (*Volksgerichtshof*), introduced in 1934 for cases of treason.[2] In August 1939 there were 1,347 people incarcerated on the basis of sentences passed by the People's Court, in August 1941 2,601, in April 1943, the last monthly total recorded, 4,128, and at the end of 1944 5,316.

All these developments—new offences, the direction of the judges, harsher sentences, accelerated procedures—were in part the result of an increasingly desperate attempt by the legal system to retain its sphere of jurisdiction in the penal field in the face of systematic attempts by the SS/Police to take over more and more of its responsibilities and in the face of constant criticism of the judicial system by the Führer himself, which sometimes resulted in direct interventions to 'correct' sentences he considered inadequate. In a regime in which all offences were regarded as essentially political, in the sense that they were challenges to the norms of the 'national community' and so threatened to undermine it, it was logical that the organisation which was successfully asserting its claim to be responsible for the defence of the 'national community'

---

[1] See L. Gruchmann, *Justiz im Dritten Reich 1933–1940. Anpassung und Unterwerfung in der Ära Gürtner* (Munich 1988), p. 1103, 956. This chapter owes much to this work. On the pre-1939 role of the Special Courts see Vol. 2, docs 350–52.

[2] On the founding of the People's Court see Vol. 2, doc. 353.

against all internal threats, namely the SS, should seek to acquire control over the prosecution and punishment of all those who, by offending, had placed themselves outside the national community. But the problem was that, in its attempt to prove itself as effective in dealing with such persons as the SS/Police, the judicial system became increasingly indistinguishable from its rival in terms of both attitudes and, by the end of the war even in its penal practice.

## (ii) New Penal Legislation

The first piece of legislation designed to crush dissent in wartime had already been drawn up on 17 August 1938 in the shape of the Decree on the Special Wartime Penal Code, which came into effect on 26 August 1939 just prior to mobilization. It contained the notorious §5, which introduced the new legal concept of 'undermining the war effort' (*Wehrkraftzersetzung*), which carried the death penalty:

**990**   *§5 Undermining the war effort*

The death penalty will be imposed for undermining the war effort on anyone

(1) who publicly invites or encourages people to refuse to perform their duty in the German or allied armed forces or otherwise seeks publicly to paralyse or undermine the will of the German or an allied nation to defend itself;
(2) who endeavours to provoke a soldier or a conscript on leave to disobedience, insubordination or violence against a superior or to desertion, absence without leave, or otherwise to undermine discipline in the German or allied armed forces;
(3) (a) who seeks to avoid military service completely, partially, or for a certain period or to assist another to do so by self-mutilation, by deceptive means, or in any other way:
(b) In less serious cases a sentence of penal servitude or imprisonment may be imposed.
(c) In addition to the death penalty and the sentence of penal servitude property may be confiscated.

The Reich Military Court (*Reichkriegsgericht*), which, until June 1940, was responsible for dealing with civilian offenders against this law as well as military personnel, introduced a broad interpretation of 'publicly', so that the clause applied to anyone who made defeatist remarks in a private context, such as a family situation or among friends, if he/she could assume that the remarks could be passed on to an indefinite number of people (a so-called *ersatz* public).[3]

Reports of cases brought under this clause appeared in the press as a

---

[3] See Gruchmann, op. cit., p. 901.

warning to others as in the following example, which was reported in the *Deutsche Allgemeine Zeitung* of 2 September 1943:

**991**   On 25 August 1943, the 52 year old *Regierungsrat*[4] Theodor Korselt from Rostock was executed. The People's Court had sentenced him to death for aiding the enemy and undermining the war effort. By making defeatist comments and by spreading rumours Korselt tried to damage the morale of the German people and thereby betrayed the fighting front. The death penalty is the only suitable sentence for traitors who are guilty of such a crime.

The first penal measure to follow the outbreak of war was a remarkable example of the frequently ad hoc and irregular nature of the legislative process in the Third Reich.[5] On 1 September 1939, Reich Propaganda Minister Goebbels sent Reich Justice Minister Gürtner and the Führer's Deputy for Party Affairs Hess a draft decree designed to prevent the German people from listening to foreign broadcasts. This was to be achieved not simply by imposing penalties but also by removing all radios.

Gürtner opposed the decree on the grounds that it would reflect badly on relations between the regime and the people by suggesting a lack of mutual trust. He also objected to the severity of the proposed sentences of penal servitude and the death penalty in serious cases. Hess objected to the idea of withdrawing all radios on the grounds that this would 'remove from the Führer himself the most important means of appealing directly to the nation', but otherwise approved the decree with the addition of a conciliatory preamble composed by himself and designed to deflect public criticism. Hess then showed the letter to Hitler who vetoed the removal of radios but otherwise approved it and ordered its immediate publication. This occurred on 2 September without either Gürtner or the Ministerial Council for the Defence of the Reich having approved it.

At this point, Reich Interior Minister Frick, who as General Plenipotentiary for the Administration (GBV) was a member of the Ministerial Council, persuaded Hitler to restrict the ban to *political* broadcasts and to certain specific radio stations and to limit the penalties for passing on information gleaned from such broadcasts to cases where this was done with intent and where such information could undermine national morale. This new version of the decree was then

---

[4] *Regierungsrat* is the title of a junior higher-grade civil servant appoximating to the British rank of Principal.

[5] For the following see Gruchmann, op. cit., pp. 902ff.

approved by the Ministerial Council on 4 September. However, on the following day, before Göring signed the decree, Goebbels persuaded him to drop the changes agreed between Hitler and Frick and which had just been approved by the Ministerial Council. Thus, the final version of the Decree concerning Exceptional Measures relating to Radio, which was still dated 1 September 1939 but was in fact issued on 7 September, was essentially the one originally agreed between Hitler and Hess on 1 September!

**992** In modern warfare the opponent does not only use military means but also methods which influence national morale and are intended to undermine it. One of these methods is radio. Every word which the opponent broadcasts is of course a lie and intended to damage the German people. The Reich Government knows that the German people are aware of this danger and, therefore, expects that every German will have the sense of responsibility to consider it a matter of decency to refrain from listening to foreign broadcasts. For those national comrades who lack this sense of responsibility the Ministerial Council for the Defence of the Reich has issued the following decree.

1. It is forbidden to listen to foreign broadcasts with intent. Contraventions will be punished with penal servitude. A prison sentence may be substituted in less serious cases. The equipment used will be confiscated.

2. Anyone who intentionally disseminates information gleaned from foreign radio stations which is liable to threaten the defensive capability of the German nation will be punished with penal servitude, in particularly serious cases with death.

3. The regulations of this decree do not apply to actions which are carried out in the performance of a duty.

4. The Special Courts are responsible for dealing with and passing judgement upon contraventions of this decree.

5. Prosecutions under §§1 & 2 are only to be initiated by the agencies of the State Police [Gestapo].

6. The Reich Minister for Popular Enlightenment and Propaganda will issue the requisite legal and administrative regulations for the implementation of this decree and, insofar as penal regulations are concerned, will do so in consultation with the Reich Minister of Justice.

> [Signed]: GÖRING,
> Chairman of the Ministerial Council
> for the Defence of the Reich,
> R. HESS, the Deputy of the Führer,
> FRICK, General Plenipotentiary for the Reich Administration,
> DR LAMMERS, Reich Minister and Head
> of the Reich Chancellery.[6]

---

[6] These were the standard signatories for domestic legislation.

The clause which placed the decision to prosecute in the hands of the Gestapo (§5), which had been proposed by State Secretary Neumann of Göring's Four-Year Plan Office to relieve the judicial authorities of being overloaded with trivial cases, in fact increased the Gestapo's power at the expense of the judiciary by giving it the discretionary authority which was exercised on the basis of the 'type' of offender. In 1941 there were 721 people condemned on the grounds of §§1 and 2, of whom one was sentenced to death. In the first half of 1942 two Germans and two Poles were given death sentences and in 1943 there were eleven death sentences, although others were simultaneously convicted of other offences which carried the death penalty, such as high treason, and so did not appear in the statistics. The following report in the official Nazi newspaper, the *Völkischer Beobachter*, dated 16 December, documents examples of court judgments:

**993**    Johann D from Leverkusen-Rheindorf was sentenced to one year's penal servitude under the ban on listening to foreign broadcasts because he repeatedly tuned in and listened to the news services of foreign radio stations. Also the Hanseatic Special Court in Bremen dealt with an accused person who listened to the Strasburg radio station on 7 September which was broadcasting the lie that the West Wall had been breached and that French troops were already at the Rhine and at the Moselle. The accused repeated these fairy tales the following day in his plant. In fact the law which bans listening to foreign broadcasts had been promulgated on 7 September, i.e. on the day the accused listened to the Strasburg radio station. Thus he was not sentenced for listening in but for spreading dangerous lies and he was given a term of penal servitude of one year and six months.
The sentences of penal servitude delivered by the Special Courts represent a serious warning to those incorrigibles who, out of curiosity or a lack of understanding, feel obliged to listen to the enemy's propagandistic insinuations.

Between 1 September and 31 December 1939, more than 1,100 people had been arrested, of whom 600 had been taken to court and the others reprimanded by the Gestapo. On 19 July 1940, Department IV of the Reich Security Main Office[7] produced the following Statistical Report on offences against the Decree concerning Exceptional Measures relating to Radio:

**994**    According to the available information, during the period 1 January to 30 June 1940 a total of 2,197 persons were arrested of whom the monthly totals were as follows:

---
[7] On the Reich Security Main Office see below, pp. 139ff.

January 453
February 471
March 327
April 309
May 368
June 269
Total 2,197

In 1,171 cases the accused persons were subjected to legal proceedings. 567 of the cases were dealt with by the political police and in 460 cases there are no reports yet of the measures that have been taken. Among those arrested were 59 Party comrades, 124 Communists, 80 SPD supporters and 19 clergy and others.

In the majority of cases the persons concerned have not been known to be politically active and have simply acted from a lack of a sense of national responsibility in the sense of doubting the German news reports.

Of the 1,166 cases brought to court sentence has been passed in 708 as follows:

| | | |
|---|---|---|
| Imprisonment up to 2 years | in | 208 cases |
| Imprisonment of over 2 years | in | 32 cases |
| Penal servitude of up to 2 years | in | 290 cases |
| Penal servitude of over 2 years | in | 92 cases |
| Found not guilty or case dismissed | in | 118 cases |

[The reports frequently make no mention of the accused's political stance so that the numbers listed cannot be considered complete.]

The introduction of strict controls on the supply of foodstuffs and other commodities on the outbreak of war obliged the regime to introduce strict penalties for those who tried to evade these regulations. These were contained in Section 1 of the War Economy Decree of 4 December 1939:

**995** *Section 1. Behaviour detrimental to the war effort*

§1 (I) Anyone who destroys, conceals, or hoards raw materials or products which are essential to the existence of the population and thereby maliciously endangers the supply of these goods will be punished with penal servitude or hard labour. In particularly serious cases the death penalty may be imposed.

(II) Those who hoard bank notes without good reason will be punished with hard labour, in particularly serious cases with penal servitude.

Offenders were tried in the Special Courts. The following judgment of the Special Court in Frankfurt am Main of 6 August 1941 is an illuminating example of the sentencing criteria used in such cases, introducing the model of the 'proper' or 'wartime housewife' against which the offender was judged:

**996**    Before the war, the accused acquired large amounts of foodstuffs, textiles and household goods and stored them in her house because she feared that, in the event of a war, she would suffer from shortages of these articles. She also wanted to invest her money in goods which would keep their value because she mistrusted the stability of the mark. At first she stored the foodstuffs in the attic of her house. But when, after the death of her husband, a conflict over the inheritance broke out between her and his children, she hid the food in tin buckets and boxes under coke and later in a compost trench in her garden, which she covered up with a board so that the goods were concealed from view but were not removed from the effects of the weather. As a result of this inappropriate storage of the approximately 23 hundredweight of foodstuffs 16 were so spoilt that they could not be used for human consumption.

The accused was found guilty of a crime under §1 of the War Economy Decree. Such a crime can also be committed in relation to goods which have been removed from the German distribution network and are already in the hands of a consumer.

While storing essential goods, the accused should have acted with the care of a proper housewife. All the more care could have been expected of her as a wartime housewife because, already during peacetime, a propaganda campaign had been running for several years under the slogan 'Don't let things spoil'. This had brought home to all compatriots, and therefore to the accused, in various ways and in memorable form the importance and the duty of preserving essential goods.

---

Perhaps the most striking example of the use of offender 'types' occurred in the Decree against National Pests of 5 September 1939, which originated in a draft put to the Ministerial Council by the Reich Chancellery and Reich Interior Ministry at Göring's request. This created three offender types—the plunderer, the black-out exploiter, and the anti-social saboteur. The vagueness of their definitions and of those of their offences gave enormous discretion to the judiciary. For, in reaching a verdict and deciding on a sentence, the judges were required to consider not simply whether or not the offender had committed an offence but whether he was a 'national pest' within the vague definition of the decree:

**997**    The Ministerial Council for the Defence of the Reich decrees the following with the force of law.

1. *Plunder in evacuated territory*
(i) Anyone who plunders evacuated territory or buildings or rooms which have been voluntarily cleared will be punished with death.
(ii) The sentence will be carried out by hanging.

2. *Crimes committed during air raids*
Anyone who commits a crime or an offence against life, limb or property by exploiting the measures which have been taken to protect against air raids will be punished with penal servitude for up to 15 years or with penal servitude for life or in particularly serious cases with death.

3. *Dangerous crimes*
Anyone who carries out an arson attack or another dangerous crime and thereby endangers the German nation's ability to resist will be punished with death.

4. *Exploitation of the war situation as grounds for increasing the sentence*
Anyone who commits any other offence with the aim of exploiting exceptional wartime circumstances will be punished in excess of the normal sentence with penal servitude for life or with death if this is required by the response of healthy popular feelings to a particularly heinous offence.

5. *Acceleration of the procedure of the Special Courts*
In all cases before the Special Courts in which the offender has been caught red-handed or his guilt is otherwise readily apparent, the sentencing procedure must occur immediately.

On 21 April 1941, the Hanseatic Special Court issued the following judgment:

**998** It corresponds to the general experience of life that a law breaker who systematically commits an offence in an area subject to black out, which has been thoroughly premeditated, will also include in his calculations the advantages which accrue to his plan from the existence of the black out measures. If the offender in such cases, who claims that he did not benefit from the black out measures, is to succeed in his claim, there must be special circumstances pertaining to the case.

On 25 November 1939 the Ministerial Council issued the following Decree to supplement the Penal Provisions for the Protection of the Military Strength of the German Nation:

**999** *§1 Damage to military equipment*
(1) Anyone who wilfully destroys, renders useless, damages, abandons, or gets rid of a piece of military equipment and thereby wilfully or negligently jeopardizes the effectiveness of the German Wehrmacht will be punished with imprisonment of not less than six months. In serious cases the death penalty, life imprisonment or a period of penal servitude may be imposed.

(2) Anyone who wilfully produces or delivers a faulty piece of military equipment and thereby wilfully or negligently jeopardises the effectiveness of the German Wehrmacht will receive the same punishment.

(3) The attempt to carry out these acts is punishable.

(4) Anyone who acts thoughtlessly and thereby negligently jeopardizes the effectiveness of the Wehrmacht will be punished with imprisonment.

(5) This clause replaces §143a of the Reich Penal Code.

### §2 Damage to important plants

(1) Anyone who damages or jeopardizes the normal operation of a plant which is important for the defence of the Reich or for the provisioning of the population by rendering useless or putting out of action either totally or partially anything which serves the operation of the plant, will be punished with penal servitude or in serious cases with death.

(2) In less serious cases the punishment is imprisonment.

### §3 Participation in an anti-military group

(1) Anyone who participates in or lends their support to an anti-military group will be punished with penal servitude, in less serious cases with imprisonment.

(2) Anyone who prevents the continued operation of the group or informs an agency of the state of its existence will not be punished under this regulation. This also applies in those cases where the group ceases to function not through the voluntary and serious efforts of the individual involved but for some other reason.

### §4 Forbidden contacts with prisoners of war

(1) Anyone who wilfully breaches a regulation concerning contact with prisoners of war or otherwise maintains contacts with prisoners of war in such a way as seriously to affront healthy popular feelings will be punished with imprisonment, in serious cases with penal servitude.

(2) In cases of negligent breaches of regulations concerning contacts with prisoners of war the punishment will be arrest and a fine of 150 RM.

___

The following decision of the Reich Supreme Court of 28 June 1940 indicates how this law was interpreted:

**1000**   §4 of the Decree to supplement the Penal Provisions for the Protection of Military Strength of the German Nation of 25.11.1939. (a) What are the regulations which have been issued to govern contact with prisoners of war? (b) Concept of contact with prisoners of war.

The court rightly saw in the fact that the accused let the prisoner of war S. drink from her beer bottle a contact with prisoners of war which seriously offended healthy popular feelings and thereby represented a breach of §4, sections 1,2, of the Decree . . . The fact that, before her temporary arrest, she wrote a letter to the wife of the prisoner of war asking her to send him some articles of daily use and then received a parcel and two cash remittances addressed to her and passed them on to the prisoner of war was regarded by the court as a negligent breach of a regulation issued to govern contacts with prisoners of war; the fact that the accused, after her release from arrest, once more accepted a letter and kept it in order to pass it on to S. was seen as a wilful breach of such a regulation (viz. §4, section 1) . . .

However, the court did not appreciate that the *whole behaviour* of the accused *including* the passing on of letters, the parcel and the cash remittances, thereby evading the camp controls, represented a contact with the prisoner of war, which seriously offended healthy popular feelings and thereby represented a breach of §4 of the Decree . . . Avoidance of such contact was a requirement both of national dignity and of consideration for the needs of the national community in its struggle for existence, which could be jeopardized by an exchange of post and the sending of money and other articles. Whether or not the accused was aware of this is not decisive since for the issue of whether or not healthy national feelings have been offended what is important is not the attitude and the perspective of the offender but the feelings of a decent conscientious compatriot. The court should, therefore, in accordance with the prosecution charge, have found the accused guilty of repeated breaches of §4 of the Decree of 25.11.1939 through banned association with a prisoner of war which seriously offended healthy popular feelings.

---

The next piece of penal legislation, the Decree against Violent Criminals of 5 December 1939, also created an offender type, namely the 'violent criminal' or gangster. The decree was a response by Gürtner to a case in which, on 30 September 1939, two bank robbers in Teltow had shot a bank employee who was pursuing them. The 'National Pest' law could not be used, since none of its conditions applied in this case and the offenders had been sentenced to ten years each. Hitler had then 'corrected' the sentence by ordering the two men to be shot. Gürtner responded to this 'gap' in the penal legislative armoury with the following decree issued by the Ministerial Council:

**1001** *§1 Violent acts committed with firearms*

(1) Anyone who uses firearms, knives or swords or equally dangerous means in the course of committing rape, a street robbery, bank robbery or another serious crime of violence or threatens another's person or life with such a weapon will be punished with death.

(2) Any criminal who attacks or fends off pursuers with a firearm will be punished in the same way.

*§2 Protection for those who assist in the pursuit of criminals*

Anyone who involves himself personally in the pursuit of a criminal will receive the same legal protection as police or judicial officials.

*§3 Responsibility of the Special Courts*

In the case of offences under §§1(2) or 2 of this decree the prosecution will be before a Special Court.

*§4 Tougher sentences in the case of attempted offences and assistance with offences*

In general an attempt to commit a punishable offence or assistance in committing it is eligible to receive the same punishment as is envisaged for the offence itself.

*§5 Retrospective law*

The decree also applies to offences committed before it came into effect.

*§6 Final regulations.*

The Reich Minister of Justice will issue the legal and administrative regulations necessary to implement and supplement this decree and will issue the more detailed guidelines for the application of the decree to the Protectorate of Bohemia and Moravia.

---

The following verdict of the Special Court in Breslau, dated 23 April 1941, is a good example of the way in which the vague definitions used in this legislation could be exploited by the judiciary greatly to expand the application of the laws:

**1002** With regard to 'other equally dangerous means', there is no doubt that in legal judgments and in the literature the term 'use of firearms' also includes the weapons and *means* referred to in Section 1. In the case of the break-in at Dr G.'s and the witness L.'s villa, the accused was discovered by the owners. In order to escape, he attacked the witnesses who were stopping his flight and seriously injured them with punches with his fists. The court decided the question as to whether punches such as were inflicted on the witnesses Dr G. and L. were to be regarded as dangerous means within the meaning of the Violent Criminals decree in the affirmative. In its decision of 12.9.40 the Reich Court pronounced that when an assailant simply uses the physical strength of his own body this can also constitute another equally dangerous means. The Reich Court gave as an example throttling round the neck. This view that dangerous means are not simply confined to the use by the assailant of means external to his own body should be supported. One has only to bear in mind that a weak assailant will use some means external to his body in order to fend off his pursuer but in other cases a robust strong assailant will intentionally reject such means because he can rely on his own physical strength and on his fists. If one confined the term 'means' to instruments used by the assailant then the tough criminal who relied only on his fists could never come under the Violent Criminals decree, whereas actually he is not less dangerous but in fact more dangerous than others from whom 'the means' can be removed from their hands in the course of pursuit or who may lose it in the struggle. Whether, therefore, the use of a person's physical strength should be regarded as 'a dangerous means' in the sense of §1 of the decree referred to depends on the particular case and, in particular, on the personality of the assailant and the method and aim of his attack.

If one takes into account the fact that the accused is a physically strong and robust man, that he inflicted well-aimed blows to the witnesses' heads and especially to the temples, then one must regard this form of bodily harm as a means which is equivalent in terms of danger to the use of firearms in the sense of the Violent Criminals decree.

---

The trend towards the progressive criminalization of all forms of behaviour which fell outside the norms of the 'national community', as defined by the Nazi leadership, and the increasing tendency to operate the penal system on the basis that there were criminal 'types', whose 'inclinations' were assumed to be largely biologically determined, culminated in the introduction of the concept of the 'community alien' (*Gemeinschaftsfremder*) and the attempt to introduce a Law on the Treatment of Community Aliens in 1944.

The law had been in preparation since 1940 but was delayed by disagreements between the various agencies involved and also by the fact that a new Reich Penal Code was being drafted as well as new provisions on criminal proceedings. By 9 August 1944, however, a final draft was ready to be signed and was only prevented from coming into effect by the deteriorating war situation. It provides, however, a clear indication of the extent of social control that would have existed under the Nazi regime in the future:

**1003**   *Article I. Community Aliens*

§1. A community alien is:
(1) anyone who, on the basis of their personality and way of life, in particular on account of abnormal defects of intellect or character, shows that they are incapable of fulfilling the minimum requirements of the national community through their own efforts (Inadequates);
(2) anyone who
(a) is workshy or dissolute and leads a useless, unproductive or disordered life and thereby threatens or imposes burdens on others or on the community.
Or shows an inclination towards begging or becoming a tramp, being idle at work, thieving or swindling, or other misdemeanours, or towards causing disturbances when drunk, or who fails to fulfil their family obligations as a result of such behaviour (Good-for-nothings); or
(b) through cantankerousness or quarrelsomeness persistently disturbs other people's peace (Troublemakers); or
(3) anyone who, on the basis of their personality or way of life demonstrates that they are disposed to commit serious offences (Anti-social criminals and the criminally-inclined).

*Article II. Police Measures against Community Aliens*

§2 (1) Community aliens will be kept under police observation.

(2) If such observation proves inadequate, the police will transfer community aliens to the Gau (State) welfare agencies.

(3) If a community alien requires more careful supervision than is possible in the institutions of the Gau (State) welfare agencies, the police will accommodate them in a police camp.

___

## (iii) Crime Statistics

German crime statistics during the Second World War are deeply problematic and even more unreliable than usual. There were the problems of continually moving geographical boundaries; the different spheres of jurisdiction—civil, military, and SS/police; and varying degrees of enforcement of particular offences, often dictated by political criteria, but often also by shortage of personnel. Furthermore, the range of acts which were defined as 'criminal' changed all the time, which makes the figures hard to interpret. Finally, much crime undoubtedly remained unrecorded. However, in spite of these and other problems, the following statistics give some indication of trends such as the increase in female and juvenile crime:

**1004**  (a)

| Year | Total | Adult males | Females | Juveniles | Previous offenders |
|------|-------|-------------|---------|-----------|--------------------|
| 1913 | 561,805 | 19,171 | 8,462 | 54,172 | 252,127 |
| 1914 | 460,858 | 35,860 | 8,008 | 46,990 | 209,113 |
| 1915 | 425,598 | 39,702 | 117,045 | 68,841 | 132,619 |
| 1916 | 341,283 | 45,137 | 115,228 | 80,918 | 105,104 |
| 1917 | 357,808 | 26,346 | 135,112 | 96,350 | 94,498 |
| 1918 | 406,113 | 45,721 | 159,052 | 100,340 | 95,126 |
| 1919 | 402,434 | 35,640 | 101,679 | 65,115 | 86,901 |
| 1937 | 444,036 | 50,912 | 68,531 | 24,593 | 171,430 |
| 1939[a] | 298,851 | 34,943 | 46,450 | 17,458 | 114,254 |
| 1940[b] | 266,223 | 85,291 | 59,614 | 21,318 | 86,668 |
| 1941[c] | 320,766 | 93,851 | 89,028 | 37,887 | 85,833 |
| 1942[d] | 343,601 | 74,186 | 116,946 | 52,469 | 77,847 |
| 1943[e] | 177,019 | 0,521 | 67,097 | 29,401 | 35,953 |

[a] The 'Old Reich'.
[b] The Old Reich and the Sudetengau.
[c] The Old Reich and the Sudetengau + Silesia, Danzig, Posen and German judicial authorities in Bohemia and Moravia.
[d] The Greater German Reich without Austria.
[e] The Greater German Reich without Austria for the first half of 1943.

A continual increase in the number of sentences occurred in the case of the following offences from 1939 to the first half of 1943:

(b)
Simple theft from 48,252 to 82,828 = 71.0%
Receiving stolen goods from 4,432 to 13,822 = 126.9%
Gambling and lottery offences from 2,540 to 5,170 = 103.5%
Treason from 663 to 1500 = 126.2%
Illegal association with prisoners of war from 3 to 10,600 = 353333.3%
Breaches of labour discipline from 74 to 29,634 = 3945.9%
Breaches of consumer regulations from 2,194 to 26,550 = 198.5%
Breaches of the War Economy Decree from 9 to 13,338 = 148,100%
Sentences on the basis of the National Pests Law from 170 to 7,596 = 4,215.9%

A continual decrease in the number of sentences occurred for the following offences from 1939 to the first half of 1943:

Obstructing an officer in the performance of his duty from 4,343 to 1,836=57.7%
Escaping arrest from 801 to 184 = 77%
Sexual offences with children under 14 from 6,285 to 2,480 = 60.5%
Unnatural intercourse from 7,614 to 2,126 = 72%
Rape from 642 to 224 = 65.1%
Pimping from 656 to 150 = 53.4%
Malicious arson from 233 to 78 = 66.5%
Racial disgrace[8] from 365 to 62 = 83%

(c) *Specific wartime offences*

|  | 1939 | 1940 | 1941 | 1942 | 1943 |
|---|---|---|---|---|---|
| Offences *v.* the consumer regulations |  | 2,194 | 7,806 | 18,645 | 13,275 |
| Offences *v.* the War Economy Decree | 9 | 743 | 3,063 | 8,121 | 6,669 |
| Offences *v.* the National Pests Decree | 170 | 2,943 | 3,168 | 5,060 | 3,798 |
| Offences *v.* the Foreign Radio Decree | 36 | 830 | 721 | 1,017 | 510 |
| Illegal association with POWs | 3 | 1,909 | 4,343 | 9,113 | 5,300 |
| Offences *v.* the Violent Criminals Decree | 2 | 81 | 172 | 197 | 97 |
| Total | 220 | 8,700 | 19,273 | 42,153 | 29,649 |
| Total crimes | 298,851 | 266,223 | 320,766 | 345,150 | 177,332 |

----

[8] i.e. sexual relations between a Jew and an 'Aryan' see Vol. 2, doc. 403.

## (iv) Intervention by Hitler and the SS/Police in the Legal Process

The series of new penal measures passed between September and December 1939 represented, at least in part, an attempt by the judicial authorities to demonstrate to Hitler their effectiveness and to pre-empt attempts by the SS/Police to encroach any further on their responsibilities. Before Hitler went off to the Polish front, on 3 September 1939, he told Himmler to maintain order at home 'with all means'. Reinhard Heydrich, the Chief of the Security Police and SD, responded to this injunction by issuing the very same day the following 'Basic Principles for Maintaining Internal Security during the War':

**1005** In order to secure the commitment of all the resources of the nation against any disturbance and sedition, which is essential for the realisation of the Führer's aims, the following principles are laid down for the security organs of the Reich to ensure the internal security of the state.

1. Any attempt to undermine the unity of the German people and its determination to fight must be ruthlessly suppressed. In particular, any person who doubts the victory of the German nation or questions the justification of the war is to be arrested.

2. Those compatriots, however, who are guilty of mistakes of some kind through personal distress or in moments of weakness must be treated with psychological understanding and efforts must be made to strengthen their will by educative means.

3. Particular attention must be paid to all attempts to influence other people in public in a hostile direction towards nation and Reich—in bars, on public transport etc. In the same way, drastic measures must be taken against any attempt to form groups and rings with the aim of spreading such views and information. If instances occur of public activity or the formation of rings, the suspected persons must in every case be arrested.

4. After the arrest of the suspected person all inquiries necessary to clear up the case must be made without delay. In the course of this it must be established as thoroughly as possible through files available at the State Police offices and at subsections of the SD and by interviewing witnesses, and through enquiring at local Party offices, what general attitude and what particular motives were behind the actions of the persons concerned. The Chief of the Security Police must then be informed without delay and a decision requested on the further treatment of the arrested persons, since the ruthless liquidation of such elements may be ordered at a high level.

5. Compatriots who are guilty of lapses not wilfully but for excusable reasons must, after thorough interrogation on the point, be taken to the head of the State Police office in person, who shall lecture them and admonish them thoroughly. This lecture and warning must be carried out in such a way as to produce loyalty and to strengthen their will. While they must be left in no doubt that they are to expect tougher measures in the event of a repetition, the result

of this warning should not be mere intimidation; it should rather have the effect of convincing and encouraging the person concerned. The attention of the relevant Party offices must then be drawn to the compatriot concerned and they must be requested to provide political supervision and supervision in material matters.

6. Appropriate steps should be taken at once against informers who for personal reasons make unjustified and exaggerated reports about compatriots, in the form of a serious warning and, in cases of malice, of transfer to a concentration camp.

7. The chiefs of the State Police offices are personally responsible for the effective suppression of any sign of defeatism in their area.

▬

Already, on 7 September 1939, Himmler ordered an offender on remand transferred to the SS and shot, an event of which the Justice Minister, Gürtner, only learned the following day from a press report. Several other such cases quickly followed, including, on 15 September, a Jehovah's Witness who refused to do military service. In vain Gürtner pointed out that the Special Courts could deal with such cases with exceptional speed.

On 20 September 1939 Heydrich issued the following instruction to supplement the 'Basic Principles':

**1006**   To clear up all misunderstandings I would like to state the following:

1. As is stated in the Basic Principles of 3.9.1939 every attempt to undermine the unity of the German people and their determination to fight must be ruthlessly and harshly suppressed.

2. On the other hand, those cases which are due to personal distress or a moment of weakness should be treated with psychological understanding and efforts must be made to strengthen their will by educative means.

3. I leave the assessment of the borderline between sections 1 and 2 to the Stapo regional and district offices.

4. In the cases covered by section 1 a distinction must be drawn between those which can be dealt with in the ordinary way and those which must be assigned for special treatment.[9] The latter case covers those for whom, in view of their reprehensibleness, the threat that they pose, or through their propaganda effect, it is appropriate that they should be eliminated through ruthless action (namely through execution), irrespective of the persons involved. Such cases are, for example, sabotage attempts, the encouragement of members of the army to mutiny or of large numbers of people to rebel or to undermine their morale, hoarding on a large scale, Communist or Marxist activities etc.

---

[9] *Sonderbehandlung*, a Nazi euphemism for execution.

These cases should only be used as examples and have no claim to being comprehensive. Here too it must be left to the Stapo regional and district offices to make a preliminary decision, using psychological and political sensitivity, as to whether this or that case is appropriate for special treatment. If the Stapo regional or district office believes that in a particular case special treatment is appropriate, they should at once impose protective custody and report back as quickly as possible (express telex). In this event, the guidelines mentioned above should be adhered to so that enquiries are reduced to a minimum. They should then await further instructions. Any doubtful cases should be reported to this office.

5. Those cases which, on the basis of the facts, are not appropriate for special treatment are to be dealt with as before within their sphere of responsibility, i.e. it should be a matter of protective custody, prosecution, a warning etc. Reports to this office should be made as usual.

6. Reports on those cases which are appropriate for special treatment should be made conscientiously and very thoroughly so that any wrong decisions are excluded.

7. Care should be taken so that the district and local police authorities immediately report particularly serious cases to the relevant Stapo regional and district headquarters so that an instruction can be given not to transfer the arrested persons to the investigating judge until the arrival of the decision

The district and local police authorities should not be informed of this edict.

▬▬▬

On 27 September 1939, Himmler issued the following order for the reorganization of the SS, SD, and state security agencies to form a new Reich Security Head Office (*Reichssicherheitshauptamt*). Essentially it represented the consolidation of the SD, the Gestapo and the Reich Criminal Police Department into one agency:

**1007**   Re: *The composition of the central departments of the Security Police and SD*

1. The following departments: the Security Police Head Office, the Security Main Office of the RFSS, the Secret State Police Office, the Reich Criminal Police Office will be combined to form the Reich Security Head Office in accordance with the following guidelines. The position of these offices in the Party and in the state administration will not be affected by this merger.

2. For the purpose of internal communications the following organizational structure and office titles will be valid from 1.10.1939:

(a) The administration and legal department of the Security Police Head Office, Department I of the Security Head Office, Department I of the Secret State Police Office, as well as Department IV of the Secret State Police Office (in so far as the responsibility of another office is not prescribed by the office

plan) will form Department I of the Reich Security Head Office, headed by
*SS Brigadeführer* Dr Best. [10]

(b) The Central Department II/I of the existing Department II and I/3 of the
Security Head Office of the *Reichsführer SS* will form Department II of the
Reich Security Head Office in the altered structure and with the responsibilities
laid down in the office plan. It will be headed by *SS Standartenführer* Professor
Dr Six.[11]

(c) The Central Department II/2 of the existing Department II of the Security
Head Office of the *Reichsführer SS* will form Department III of the Reich
Security Head Office in the altered structure and with the responsibilities laid
down in the office plan. It will be headed by *SS Standartenführer* Ohlendorf.[12]

(d) The Political Police Department of the Security Police Head Office and the
Sections II and III of the Secret State Police Office will form Department IV of
the Reich Security Head Office headed by *SS Oberführer* Reich Criminal Police
Director Müller.[13]

(e) The Criminal Police Department of the Security Police Head Office and the
Reich Criminal Police Department will form Department V of the Reich
Security Head Office headed by *SS Oberführer* Reich Criminal Police Director
Nebe.[14]

---

[10] Dr Werner Best (1903–89), a lawyer, was Heydrich's deputy as Chief of the
Security Police and SD and as personnel chief did much to build up the Gestapo
and SD. He left the RSHA in June 1940 after differences with Heydrich and in
November 1942 became Reich Plenipotentiary in Denmark. See the important
book by Ulrich Herbert, *Best. Biographische Studien über Radikalismus,
Weltanschauung und Vernunft 1903–1989* (Bonn 1996).

[11] Franz Alfred Six 1909–?). A typical young SS intellectual who rose through
the Nazi student organization (head of the Heidelberg University *Studenten-
schaft)*, joined the SS at the beginning of 1935 and was soon appointed head of
Central Department II of the SD ('Combating ideological enemies'). 1938
appointed a Professor of Königsberg University. He played an important part in
the SS's intellectual/academic activities.

[12] Otto Ohlendorf (1908–51). A lawyer by training, after active participation in
the Nazi student organization he became assistant to Professor Jessen at the
Institute of World Economy at Kiel University in 1933. He joined the SD in
1936 and in 1938 became head of Department III responsible for domestic
intelligence, gathering material on popular opinion. From June 1941 to June
1942 he was head of Task Force (*Einsatzgruppe*) D responsible for murdering
thousands of Jews in southern Russia. Executed in 1951 by the Allies.

[13] Heinrich Müller (1901–45?). A professional Bavarian policeman who had
been in charge of the surveillance of Communists under the Weimar Republic.
With the merger of the Bavarian Political Police with the Prussian Gestapo in
1934 Müller was assigned to head the Gestapo, despite the fact that he was not a
member of the NSDAP. On Müller see Vol. 2, doc. 372.

[14] Arthur Nebe (1894–1945?) A professional policemen in the Prussian Criminal
Police Department before 1933, Nebe joined the NSDAP in 1931 and acted as

(f) Department III of the Security Head Office of the *Reichsführer SS* will form Department VI of the Reich Security Head Office in the altered structure and with the responsibilities laid down in the office plan. It will be headed by *SS Brigadeführer* Jost.

3. The responsibilities of the departments of the Reich Security Head Office and its organization into groups and sections will be defined in the office plan.

4. The staffing and salaries, the budget and the day-to-day financial running of the departments listed under 1 will not be affected by this edict.

5. The Chief of the Security Police and SD will issue the necessary guidelines (office plan etc.)

▅▅

Meanwhile, even more ominously from Gürtner's point of view than Himmler's actions in shooting prisoners on remand, in October 1939, Hitler had begun intervening to 'correct' sentences passed by the courts considered inadequate, ordering the offenders to be transferred to the SS and shot in the nearest concentration camp. Between 1 September 1939 and 20 January 1940, at least eighteen such executions had taken place, half before sentence had been passed by the courts and half after. By 20 October 1942 there had been at least thirty cases of Germans having their sentences 'corrected' in this way and even more Poles.[15]

Typically, Hitler would have his attention drawn to some press report of a case by his adjutant, Julius Schaub, usually in response to prompting from an outside source, and then would 'blow his top' and, often without seeing the case papers, would order the execution of the offender(s) involved. The following case in which a Jew was convicted of hoarding a large quantity of eggs illustrates the process:

**1008** (a) Reich Minister and Head of the Reich Chancellery [Lammers] to State Secretary Schlegelberger, Acting Minister of Justice 25.10.1941:

The Führer has been shown the enclosed press cutting concerning the sentencing of the Jew, Markus Luftgas, to $2\frac{1}{2}$ year's imprisonment by the Special Court at Bielitz.

The Führer desires that Luftgas should be sentenced to death. I would be obliged if you would make the necessary arrangements as soon as possible and report to the Führer through me on the measures you have taken.

---

their liaison with the criminal police. After 1933 he was appointed to head the Prussian criminal police and then given the task of creating a national criminal police force (*Kripo*) out of the various state (*Land*) forces. Between June and November 1941 he was in command of Task Force (*Einsatzgruppe*) B responsible for killing Jews in central Russia. He appears to have been later involved in the Resistance.

[15] For these figures see Gruchmann, op. cit., pp. 682, 688.

(b) Lammers to *SS Gruppenführer* Julius Schaub, Hitler's adjutant:

On receiving your letter of 22 October 1941 I contacted the Reich Minister of Justice and requested him to make the necessary arrangements.

(c) Schlegelberger to Lammers 29.10.41:

On receiving the Führer command passed on to me by the Minister of State and Head of the Chancellery, I handed over the Jew, Markus Luftgas, who was sentenced by the Special Court at Kattowitz to $2\frac{1}{2}$ years' imprisonment, to the Secret State Police for execution.

━━━

Before the war, unnatural deaths occurring in concentration camps had to be reported to the authorities. Although, in practice, the investigations were largely token or were invariably blocked by higher authority, including on occasion Hitler himself, the legal authorities were responsible for prosecuting offences committed by concentration camp guards and this was clearly irksome to the SS. In June 1939, therefore, Himmler persuaded Hitler to allow the SS and the police to establish their own independent court system.[16] This was finally introduced by a decree of 17 October 1939, which thereby effectively removed the concentration camps from the jurisdiction of the civil courts.

The judicial system was not only faced with direct intervention by the SS/Police in its cases, it was also subjected to a constant barrage of criticism from the SS newspaper, *Das Schwarze Korps*, for its allegedly lax attitude towards offenders and to pressure from the SS Security Service (SD), which used its regular reports on popular opinion to imply that the judiciary was out of touch with 'healthy popular feelings'. The following report of the Reich Security Main Office on the checking of sentencing by the SD, dated 3 November 1941, illustrates this process:

**1009**   Numerous further reports from the [SD] sections have been sent as individual reports to the Reich Ministry [of Justice] or to other Reich agencies. Here too the situation reports are proving quite effective. For example, in several cases the Reich Ministry has been sent copies of incomprehensible sentences for review. The Reich Justice Ministry has then frequently prompted the Supreme Reich Prosecutor at the Reich Court to initiate their annulment[17] or instructed the presidents of the Higher State Courts and General State Prosecutors to press for tougher sentencing in particular penal areas.

━━━

---

[16] Initially only when on special assignment, from 1942 in all cases.

[17] The Supreme Reich Prosecutor could suspend sentences of the lower courts within one year through an 'annulment objection' (*Nichtigkeitsbeschwerde*), if he felt a sentence was unjust 'because of a failure to apply the law to the established facts'. The case then had to be retried. See below, pp. 143–44.

The judicial authorities in the field increasingly resented the interference by the SS/Police in the legal process, which placed them in an invidious position vis-à-vis the local population, since it assumed that they were responsible for what was happening. This is clear from the following documents. The first is a query from the President of the Higher State Court (*Oberlandesgericht*) in Hamm to the State Secretary in the Reich Justice Ministry, Dr Freisler, concerning the legal status of police actions, dated 31 March 1941:

**1010**   The hangings of Poles which, as far as I can see, are disturbing the population of my area are regarded as arbitrary acts by the police. From the main points in your address[18] it appears that the *Reichsführer SS* bases his actions on instructions from the Reich Marshal [Göring] and has issued a directive to the administrative agencies with leaflets for the Polish workers and their employers. I consider it necessary that this justification for the executions carried out by the police as well as the contents of the instructions given to the administrative agencies and of the leaflets should be communicated in confidence to the judges at least orally. Otherwise, if this matter is referred to in a public hearing, a judge might reject such an assertion as completely unbelievable. If the administrative agencies and the employers are informed then presumably those judges who are necessarily interested in the matter can also be informed . . .

The shootings 'while resisting arrest' are, as far as I can see, generally regarded as arbitrary acts by the police and weigh heavily on the population's sense of justice. What can the judges be told in confidence about the legal basis for the shooting?

The second document is an excerpt from the monthly report from the General State Prosecutor in Berlin to the acting Reich Minister of Justice 31 March 1942:

**1011**   In the Berlin State Prosecutor's office there have been 12 death sentences during the period covered by this report. As far as we are aware, 11 of those sentenced were handed over to the Stapo and shot. In this connection I would like to emphasize in particular the case against Gomolinski and others, on which I reported under . . . [ref. no.] The eleven condemned men, who were all without previous convictions, were executed on 10 February 1942. Seven of them had received sentences of penal servitude of ten years down to one year nine months, the others, on the other hand, prison sentences of one year nine months and one year six months.

---

[18] This refers to an address by Freisler to the presidents of the Higher State Courts on 20 March 1941 in the Reich Justice Ministry.

One of those condemned, named Johannes R., who had been given a prison sentence of one year and six months, is the father of six children. The relatives of those who were shot have repeatedly been to see the desk officer of the State Prosecutor's Office in Berlin, State Court Councillor D, and demanded an explanation as to why the State Prosecutor's office had them shot. The councillor kept replying that the shootings were not initiated by the State Prosecutor's office and that he could give no further information. But the petitioners did not believe this and stated more or less bluntly that the official was not telling them the truth. Furthermore, the relatives of those condemned have filed a number of written petitions with the State Prosecutor's office in Berlin.

———

One method by which the legal system tried simultaneously to pacify Hitler and the SS/Police and to retain responsibility for sentencing was to introduce two mechanisms for revising sentences which had already been through the normal judicial procedures. The first was the so-called 'Exceptional Objection' (*ausserordentliche Einspruch*), which was introduced by a law of 16 September 1939. This was in response to Hitler's desire to revise a particular sentence in a treason case, which had been passed by the People's Court, despite the fact that there was no right of appeal against sentences from that court. This new law permitted the Supreme Reich Prosecutor (*Oberreichsanwalt*) to appeal against any sentence, which had the immediate effect of quashing the sentence. The case was then reviewed by either the special bench of the Reich Court or the special bench of the People's Court, depending on where it had been first tried. In future most of the cases were initiated by other agencies than Hitler. In 1939/40 four such appeal cases came before the Reich Court and in 1941/2 14 cases with 31 accused. Although it was possible for appeals to result in milder sentences, in practice this rarely happened and there was only one case of the mechanism being used to seek such a result—in the case of a policeman accused of forcing a confession out of a prisoner! No more exceptional objection cases were brought before the Reich Court after 1942; however, the mechanism continued to be used by the People's Court and more and more to increase sentences. Thus, in 1944, there were 84 such cases of which 75 resulted in death sentences.

The fact that relatively little use was made of the 'exceptional objection' by the Reich Court, and none after 1942, was because the second mechanism came to be employed much more frequently.[19] This was the so-called 'plea for annulment' (*Nichtigkeitsbeschwerde*). Whereas

---

[19] For the following see Gruchmann, op. cit., pp. 1081–88.

the 'exceptional objection' was designed for major political cases, the main function of the 'plea for annulment' was to permit a revision of sentences passed by the Special Courts, which were not subject to appeal through the normal procedures, but where the sheer speed of the proceedings could easily produce errors. Like the 'exceptional objection', the 'plea for annulment' had been included in the new penal law code, which was being drafted in 1938 in order to avoid the looming threat of direct political interference where sentences did not accord with 'healthy popular feelings'. But the code was never in fact implemented.

On 21 February 1940 a decree was issued which came into effect on 15 March, of which Article 5 laid down that the Supreme Reich Prosecutor could issue an annulment to the Reich Court against a sentence passed by a lower court or a Special Court 'if the sentence is unjust on account of an error in the application of the law to the established facts of the case'. The case would then be considered by the Reich Court but, unlike with the 'exceptional objection', in the meantime the sentence would still stand. The Reich Court could then either confirm or quash the sentence, or refer the case back to the original court or another court.

During the Gürtner period (1940–41), the Annulment procedure was frequently used to reduce sentences, many of which involved cases of minor misdemeanours or offences by Nazis. Indeed, between March 1940 and March 1941, of 509 applications to the Supreme Reich Prosecutor for an annulment, 205 led to a annulment appeal on which the Reich Court reached 170 decisions of which only 28 were to the disadvantage of the accused. However, from 1941 onwards, not only did the number of such applications increase but they were used more and more to increase the sentences on the grounds that they did not accord with 'healthy popular feelings' as defined by the authorities. The following letter from a public prosecutor to the Reich Justice Minister, dated 28 April 1942, suggests how the procedure was then operating:

**1012**  The defendant Paul Krüger was condemned to fifteen years imprisonment by the Special Court here in its session of 4 March 1942; furthermore, this was to be in the form of protective custody. I demanded the death penalty. I enclose the file containing the sentence.

I have heard from the head of the local criminal police office that the local police in a report sent to several State authorities have expressed their regret that Krüger was not sentenced to death. He recommends me to try and influence the Reich Ministry of Justice to change the sentence to the death penalty by plea of annulment, *otherwise another authority might possibly intervene.*

As things are I recommend that an appeal for annulment should be arranged with the Supreme Reich Prosecutor, particularly since sentences of over ten years are regarded as undesirable according to the latest guidelines.

———

However, rather than having to revise sentences, which had already been passed, under pressure from the SS/Police, let alone have them 'corrected' on Hitler's orders, it was clearly better for the legal system if the 'right' sentences could be passed in the first place, thereby avoiding outside intervention. An attempt to achieve this was made through a further mechanism which was increasingly employed during the war years, namely direction or in the Nazi euphemism 'guidance' or 'steering' (*Lenkung*) of the judiciary.

## (v) The 'Guidance' of the Judiciary

This took various forms, for example: articles in professional journals, personal contacts between officials of the Justice Ministry and the judiciary at meetings and conferences, unpublished circulars and published regulations. Thus, on 12 September 1939, Freisler sent the following circular to the presidents of the Higher State Courts (*Oberlandesgerichtspräsidenten*):

**1013** Re: *The handling of cases which come under the Decree against National Pests of 5 September 1939*

Germany is engaged in a struggle for honour and justice.

The model for every German in terms of fulfilling his duty is the German soldier.

Anyone who, instead of following that example, sins against his nation no longer has a place in our community.

The Ministerial Council for the Defence of the Reich has created the requisite legal bases for the ruthless combating of these national pests.

I expect all judges and prosecutors to implement the decree with the same ruthless, speedy and rigorous determination with which it was issued.

Not to employ the most extreme strictness against such pests would be a betrayal of the fighting German soldier.

All participants must also cooperate in ensuring that the deed, the indictment, the court proceedings, the sentence and its execution follow each other in quick succession.

All judges and prosecutors who are involved should be informed of this instruction at once.

———

Again, on 24 October 1939, *Ministerialdirektor* Crohne of the Justice Ministry told a conference of Public Prosecutors at the Ministry, with specific reference to the same decree, that 'against hardened criminals in war time the death penalty is not only permitted, it is at the same time on principle the most appropriate one'.[20]

Under Gürtner as Reich Justice Minister, the pressure on the judges tended to be more indirect through the public prosecutors, who would be instructed before the court hearing what sentence to request and then inform the judge before the main hearing, but *confidentially*. Under his successors the pressure became more systematic and direct.

Following his death, on 1 February 1941, Gürtner was replaced by an opportunist career civil servant, Franz Schlegelberger, as acting Reich Justice Minister. On 10 March 1941, he wrote to Hitler that he saw it as his duty 'to draw it to the attention of the judges if a sentence does not accord with the wishes of the leadership of the state'.[21] On 15 July 1941 a law was passed which enabled the legal authorities to influence the sentencing of *civil* law judges who, in their opinion, required 'guidance and leadership', and permitted the Supreme Reich Prosecutor to apply for a review of civil cases if he considered it 'necessary in view of their particular significance for the national community'.

However, Hitler, the NSDAP and the SS remained dissatisfied with what they considered soft sentencing by the courts and unimpressed with the legal system's attempts to meet their wishes by, for example, speeding up trial procedures. On 1 September 1941, the legal department of the RSHA commented on this as follows:

**1014**  It goes without saying that the aim of a national socialist penal policy must be to sentence the offender as quickly as possible. However, speed must not be at the expense of a just consideration of the sentence. The legal process suffers both when the individual is sentenced without a proper examination of the question of his guilt and if, as a result of the additional acceleration of the proceedings, facts are ignored which are important in assessing the offender as a particularly dangerous person. You will be aware that the RJM [Reich Justice Ministry] has recently issued instructions which have virtually turned summary trials into the norm. This represents a reaction to certain interventions by the police in the judicial system . . . The judiciary aims to pre-empt the police by extending the use of summary trials as far as possible. That is, of course, an approach which can seriously jeopardise due process . . .

---

[20] Ibid., p. 1103.

[21] M. Broszat, 'Zur Perversion der Strafjustiz im Dritten Reich. Dokumentation', *Vierteljarshefte für Zeitgeschichte*, 6 (1958), p. 417.

You will no doubt have gathered from my preceding remarks that the judicial system has not succeeded in adjusting its sentencing to the political requirements for our national security. I have outlined the reasons for this. They can be found, in the first instance, in the personnel situation. The fact that my assertion is no exaggeration is repeatedly demonstrated by the sentences passed by the judiciary, for example, on Polish civilian workers who have periodically appeared before the judges for engaging in sexual intercourse with German women, although according to the *Reichsführer's* instructions, they should only have been dealt with by the State Police. They are given ridiculously mild sentences.

The criminal court in Bielefeld sentenced a Polish farm labourer to $1\frac{1}{2}$ years for a rape offence but since he was not *compos mentis* it confined him to a lunatic asylum for life and removed his civil rights for three years. (The Pole concerned has meanwhile been eliminated on the Führer's orders.)

——

The Nazi leadership encouraged the notion that there was 'a crisis in the judicial system' (*Justizkrise*). This found its most striking expression in Hitler's Reichstag speech of 26 April 1942, which further demoralized the judiciary.[22] In response, Schlegelberger introduced a system of so-called *Führerinformationen*—regular reports to Hitler on particular cases and sentences in order to demonstrate how effective the judiciary really was. On 21 May, for example, he reported: 'I have made the senior officials [i.e. the Presidents of the Higher State Courts] personally responsible for steering even the individual cases in their districts and at the same time ensured that I will be kept continually informed about all important cases'[23]

During Schlegelberger's tenure of the Reich Justice Ministry, a further mechanism of control was introduced following the initiative of the President of the Higher State Court in Hamburg, Dr Curt Rothenberger.[24] From 7 May 1942 Rothenberger required the judges in his district to inform him of all cases 'in which there is a possibility of a degree of contradiction between the formal law and popular feelings or national socialist views' so that he could discuss the case with the judges concerned. In addition, every 8–14 days, he held a meeting with the presidents of the State Courts subordinate to him in order to discuss the sentences which had been passed in the meantime, and they carried out the same procedure with the judges subordinate to them. This system of

---

[22] See above pp. 14–16.

[23] See H. Weinkauff, *Die deustche Justiz und der Nationalsozialismus. Ein Überblick.* (Stuttgart 1968), p. 148.

[24] For the following see W. Johe, *Die gleichgeschaltete Justiz.Organisation des Rechtswesens und Politisierung der Justiz am Beispiel des Oberlandesgerichtsbezirks Hamburg* (Frankfurt/M 1967), pp. 180ff.

so-called 'preliminary case reviews' and 'post-mortems' (*Vor-und Nachschau*) initiated in Hamburg was then adopted by the Reich Justice Ministry for the whole of Germany.

However, Schlegelberger's attempts to ingratiate himself with the Nazi leadership were unavailing and, on 20 August 1942, he was replaced by the hardline Nazi and President of the People's Court, Otto Georg Thierack. Prompted either by the SD or the Party Chancellery, Thierack immediately took the practice of guiding or 'steering' (*Lenkung*) the judiciary a stage further by instituting, on 7 September 1942, the practice of circulating to the judiciary so-called 'Judges' Letters' (*Richterbriefe*). These letters commented on what he, as Minister, regarded as good and bad examples of sentencing. In a circular to the Presidents of the Reich Court, and the People's Court, the Higher State Courts and the State Courts, dated 7 September, Thierack described their purpose as follows:

**1015** I do not wish to, cannot, and must not, tell a judge who has been given a case how he is to decide in an individual instance. The judge must remain free to carry the responsibility for his decisions. I cannot order him, therefore, to follow a particular interpretation of the law but can only convince him of the way in which a judge must help the community in order to regulate behaviour which has become disordered or requires ordering with the help of the law.

To this extent the profession of the judge is related to that of the doctor who also has to bring help to his fellow citizen who asks for it or to protect the community from injury. In the same way, a judge must, like a doctor, eradicate centres of infection or be able to carry out the operations of a surgeon. This conception of the legal sphere has now been widely accepted among German lawyers. But its practical effects on the administration of justice have not yet been realized.

In order to help the judge to fulfil his high office in the life of our nation, I have decided to publish 'Judges' Letters' which are to be sent to all German judges and public prosecutors. These 'Judges' Letters' are not meant to create a new casuistry, which would lead to increased rigidity in the administration of justice and would put the judges under tutelage. They are intended merely to illustrate how the judicial leadership envisages a national socialist application of the law and in this way to give the judge the inner security and freedom to make the right decision. The contents of the letters are confidential; the official in charge must look after them personally and hand them out to judges and prosecutors in return for a receipt.

The cooperation of all judges and prosecutors is needed for the publication of the Judges' Letters. I expect to be given suitable sentences from all spheres of law for publication. In making use of these neither the judge nor the relevant court will be mentioned by name.

I am convinced that the Judges' Letters will contribute greatly to a uniform alignment of justice in the spirit of national socialism.

The following is an example of a Judges' Letter:

**1016**    Judges' Letter No. 13

Refusal of the German greeting by a child of school age. Guardianship Court judgement of 21 September 1941.

An eleven-year-old girl has been noticed in school continually refusing to give the German greeting.[25] She gives her religious convictions as the reason and quotes several passages from the Bible. At school she shows a complete lack of interest in matters concerning the Führer.

The parents, who have another daughter of six, approve of this attitude and stubbornly refuse to influence the child in the contrary direction. They also refuse to give the German greeting, referring to the biblical passage: 'Do nothing with a raised hand for this displeases the Lord.' They stick to this despite instructions from the court and from the headmaster of the school. The mother utterly refuses to speak to the child about it. The father is willing to do so but says the child must decide for herself. The parents show themselves to be opponents of the national socialist state in other ways. They do not possess a swastika flag. They have not put down their child for the Hitler Youth. They are excluded from the NSV because they have not joined in contributing although the father could afford it. Nevertheless, they deny being opponents of the movement.

Because of their attitude the Youth Department has proposed the removal of both children from the care of their parents. The Guardianship Court has turned this down and has only ordered supervision, arguing in its judgment that it has not been proved that the parents are opponents of the national socialist movement or even have fought against it; they 'simply do not regard the movement sympathetically and are not inclined to further it'. The judgment goes on to say: 'The parents are responsible for their personal attitude towards the national socialist movement only in so far as they break laws that relate to the movement.' The parents have to agree that the children must be brought up in the national socialist spirit and that the school is bound to give this education. If the children do not want to bring their children up in this spirit themselves or, from religious convictions, think it impossible for them to do so, they must be asked at least not to counteract the national socialist education given by the school. Since the child is otherwise well brought up and the parents give the impression of having 'reliable characters' it may be assumed that they will make no further difficulties for the school in future.

The Court of Appeal has revised the verdict of the Guardianship Court and removed the guardianship of both children from the parents because they are unsuitable to bring them up.

---

[25] i.e. the Hitler salute.

*Comment by the Reich Minister of Justice*
The verdict of the judge of the Guardianship Court shows a misunderstanding
of the principles of national socialist youth education.

Those responsible for the education of German youth today are the parents,
the school and the Hitler Youth (Law on the Hitler Youth of 1 December
1936[26]). Working together, each in its own sphere, these fulfil the educational
mission given to them by the community. The aim of the communal work of
education is to educate youth physically, mentally and morally in the spirit of
National Socialism for the service of the nation and of the community. The aim
can only be achieved through cooperation between parents, school, and Hitler
Youth. Every conflict and deviation in education endangers the common aim.
Parents have been given a decisive role in education and a special responsibility.
They are connected with the child by ties of blood. The child lives near them
and continuously watches his parents' habits and example. Education means
guiding. Guiding means setting an example by their way of life. The child shapes
his life according to his parents' example. What he hears and sees there,
especially in early youth, he gradually adopts as a habit and a standard for his
life. Thus, the educational aim of the national socialist state can be achieved
only if parents are conscientious and responsible in thought and action and give
the child a model example of how to behave in the communal life of our people.
Part of the education of the German man and woman is the early conveying of
respect and reverence for the symbols of the state and the movement. Here too
the community expects active cooperation on the parents' part. Reserved
neutrality here is just as damaging as combating the national socialist idea.
Indifference towards education in patriotic citizenship, therefore, means a
neglect by the parents of their duties and endangers the education of the child,
even if this is not immediately apparent. Accordingly, it is not sufficient for the
parents in this case not to oppose the child's future education by the school; they
must take an active part in the communal education. The parents' educational
responsibility, then, does not begin only at the point at which their violation of
it becomes punishable. The danger for the child becomes apparent when the
parents openly oppose education through the community. This was so here.
Those who stubbornly oppose the German greeting because of wrong doctrine,
who exclude themselves for no reason from the socially constructive work of the
NSV, purposely keep their children away from the Hitler Youth and are
inaccessible to all advice, can no longer be said only to be 'not sympathetically
disposed' towards the movement or not to be furthering it. Through their
resistance they are fighting it and are its enemies. This is shown by their attitude
and inclination.

The guardianship judge should, therefore, have deprived them of their
guardianship with the simple explanation that parents who openly profess the
ideas of the Jehovah's Witnesses are not suited for the education of their
children in the national socialist spirit.

▬▬▬

---

[26] See Vol. 2, doc. 299.

Thierack summed up his views on the role of judges in the Third Reich and on the question of 'guiding' them through such mechanisms as the Judges' Letters in a speech to a conference of German legal academics held at Cochem Castle, where he had established an indoctrination centre for legal personnel, on 16–18 September 1944:

**1017**  The key question with which I was confronted was whether the judges' freedom from direction is compatible with the bases of our state structure. You know that my reply to this, of which I am totally convinced, is in the affirmative—but on one condition: that our judges' decisions reflect the fundamental ideas of our movement's world view. Our judges' freedom from direction, which is an indispensable feature of the image of a judge as far as our people are concerned, can only be maintained in our Führer state if the judges are committed and knowledgeable National Socialists.

The time of the emphatically unpolitical 'neutral' judge is past. Nowadays, in contrast to the past, judges must be politically aware and active people. Only then can they adequately fulfil their task in the community and their role as immediate vassals of the Führer and aides of the political leadership.

The basic view of the position of a judge is closely connected with the change in the judge's position vis-à-vis the law in the national socialist state. For us the law is a Führer command, is an expression of the will of the leadership. The liberal type of legal positivism, which believed that one could achieve a just verdict by using the method of conceptual logic and with laws which went into great detail has been replaced by a more elastic form of legislation which appears to give the judge greater discretion in reaching a verdict which is appropriate to the requirements of national life, but which in reality is limited and bound by the interests of the community and the basic principles of our world view.

In order for the law to retain its effectiveness as an instrument of leadership it has to be continually developed in accordance with the national political development. This development of the law is not only possible through new laws, but, even in the case of antiquated regulations, the application of our world view as a yardstick can permit verdicts which reflect the overall national sense of justice. This only recognizes judges' verdicts as just if they further national life.

In this way, the law can be kept elastic and adjusted to the changing conditions of national life. In this manner, without altering the wording of the law, one can achieve the effect of legislative innovation on a small scale.

Such a phenomenon, which is an important political process, cannot be left to the judiciary itself; it must be steered. This raises the much-discussed topic of the steering of sentencing.

The aim of the guidance must be above all to remove the isolation in which the judges easily find themselves as a result of their position by providing wide-ranging information about the aims and the needs of the political leadership, in other words, by providing a closer link to the political leadership. The abstract way in which laws are formulated makes it necessary for those responsible for the implementation of the laws to be informed about the political leadership's concrete intentions and goals. That is, of course, only possible to a limited extent. The political function of the legal system, the position of judges as the direct aides of the political leadership, requires in addition that they know the guidelines followed by the political leadership in the various spheres of life, in order for them to be able to assess a case within the context of the totality of national life. For the judicial system is not a discrete sphere of life. Its function of ordering and purging, which makes it an instrument of national leadership and racial care, covers all spheres of life. Thus, perhaps more than any other institution the legal system must work together with the other agencies of the Party, the State, and the Wehrmacht and learn from and utilize their experience.

All that is in addition to the exchange of information within the judicial sphere itself, which must occur both horizontally and vertically. I refer, for example, to the meetings which I hold at least every six months with the heads of the provincial authorities and the highest courts. Apart from these meetings, and apart from the general guidelines and directives for the legal system contained in general instructions and circulars of the Reich Minister of Justice, there is a permanent information service, which is also designed to inform the heads about political events. In addition, the presidents of the Higher State Courts and General Prosecutors hold meetings with their district heads and court chairmen in which current issues and important verdicts are discussed. Other methods of guidance include articles by ministerial desk officers designed to give a lead, reviews of verdicts, the duty to make reports, and particular edicts. The reserve with which the Judges' Letters were initially received has long since given way to warm approval of the assistance which they provide for judges. The Judges' Letters are in my view a particularly striking example of the fact that it is possible to guide sentencing without interfering in the judges' freedom from direction.

Moreover, the conferences in Cochem Castle, introduced this year, and which I shall talk about later, represent a new method of guidance but also of general political leadership [*Menschenführung*]. Thus, firm and regular methods have been devised for steering sentencing. We no longer see guidance as a problem. Only malicious people can maintain—and now I return to what I was saying at the beginning—that this is a way of giving orders; guidance as we practise it does not represent any interference in the judges' freedom from direction but simply assistance which is intended to enable the judge to come to the right verdict in the interests of the nation as a whole.

▬

While some judges welcomed the introduction of the Judges' Letters as relieving them from some of the responsibility for passing sentences in what was an increasingly politicized judicial climate, a few deplored what they saw as the undermining of the whole position of the judiciary. In his monthly report to the Reich Justice Ministry, dated 3 December 1942, the President of the Higher State Court in Cologne delivered what, particularly given the constraints under which he was required to

express his opinions, represents a remarkable and damning indictment
of the state of the judicial system in wartime Germany:

**1018**    What I have to say about this in detail derives partly from my own
experience and partly from a number of conversations with professional
colleagues, in particular old Party comrades, whose opinions I am summarizing
in what follows. My comments are not only concerned with the oral and written
criticisms of sentences, but with the Party's whole attitude to judges and
prosecutors and, therefore, also include the issue of Party and State. It is
disputed that there really is a crisis in the judicial system. While it cannot be
ignored that large sections of the Party, including the Führer himself, have
expressed their dissatisfaction with the judicial system, and especially with
particular sentences, with increasing frequency, and that, in particular, the
Führer's well-known speech of last April[27] has revealed an unmistakable threat
to the future work of judges, nevertheless, apart from and alongside this
criticism is the fact that large sections of the nation have by no means lost their
old faith in the honest work of the German judiciary. On the contrary, apart
naturally from the endless complaints of discontented grumblers, the fight
against the judiciary and the judicial system is, in reality, being directed
exclusively by the Party and, in particular, by the district leaders and, in
addition, by certain sections of the press, and so a kind of artificial crisis has
been created. In so far as the Führer has also to a limited extent criticized
sentences for being too mild, the unanimous view is that this statement was the
result of the Führer being given one-sided information by subordinate Party
organizations. The fact that there have always been poor and inadequate
sentences and always will be is in the nature of things and is the result of the
varied dispositions and different levels of competence of the judges. The fact
that a number of these sentences can be attributed to the failure of some,
particularly older, judges to move with the spirit of the new times is also
undoubtedly true. But this does not provide the true reason for or remotely
justify the continual criticism of so many Party organizations, which goes way
beyond the mark.
      Apart from the point, which is often made, that many of the old Party
comrades had unpleasant experiences with the courts during the time of struggle
[i.e. pre-1933], the most profound reason for this phenomenon lies above all in
the fact that the district leaders [of the NSDAP] (and I refer primarily to them
because they and the members of their staffs form the main front with which the
judges come into contact during their day to day work) in terms of their
background and education completely lack any understanding of the essence of
the law, of its important place in the life of the nation and the State, and of the
professional work of judges. They stick to the slogan about sentencing
according to the letter of the law [*Paragraphenurteil*] and thereby negate law and
justice. The cadres have been politically indoctrinated but this indoctrination
does not include the basic principles of state law and public administration.

---

[27] See above, pp. 14–16.

They lack knowledge and they often lack superior ability as well, which they ought to possess for such a multifaceted and responsible position as a cadre. And—this point must not be ignored—they often lack tact, which has nothing to do with education. The importance of their position and the way in which they parade it and represent it to the outside world encourages many compatriots and many of the least desirable ones to utilize the power of the cadre for not always honourable private interests. Moreover, and this is what is really wrong, one invariably finds that the person who succeeds in getting the cadre's ear first has his side of the story accepted without his opponent getting a hearing. This then results in those numerous and often insulting interventions in the legal process, either when the proceedings are still continuing, or indeed after they have been concluded, which justifiably so annoy the judges, since no attempt has been made beforehand to form an objective judgment about the truth of the matter. The attempt by the beleaguered judiciary subsequently to get to the truth of the matter often fails because of the damage that is caused to the self-esteem of the particular Party official, who cannot bring himself to admit that he was in the wrong, and normally the clarification comes too late and cannot make up for the damage, the offence, and the annoyance that has been caused. I have never heard that a cadre has ever apologized to an official or a judge for the obvious injustice done to them. To what extent this is due to an often misconceived socialist viewpoint, which believes that the 'simple compatriot', whose rights have allegedly been infringed, has to be protected against a jurist is open to question. The dislike of graduates, which sometimes manifests itself in such cases, is similar to the thoughtless criticism of the civil service as such, which has been going on for so long and which has led to the current evident and ubiquitous unwillingness of our young people to become civil servants. It is only since people have become aware of this damage and perhaps since they have realized that the Party work depends on the almost 100 per cent involvement of civil servants for its survival that they have begun to put the brakes on in this respect and started systematically recruiting civil servants. The fact that it is the inadequate education of many cadres which is the main reason for the Party's distorted view of the judicial system is apparent among other things from the fact that, where a district leader is himself a graduate or even a lawyer, one finds a much more positive and, above all, more just assessment and it is much easier to reach an understanding concerning the unavoidable differences of opinion. The most important task for the future will, therefore, be to provide the Party officials, and in particular the cadres—but also the group of Party secretaries—with a better education and, in particular, more understanding of the importance of the law and the position of judges, of their work and their way of working . . .

I and the General Prosecutor continue to regard the 'steering of sentencing', which is closely connected with the 'crisis in the judicial system' and is presumably a consequence of it, as an increasingly serious burden from the point of view of both the work load involved and our professional consciences. To intervene in the process by which a judge decides on a sentence, at a stage and with methods which do not permit a full assessment of the deed or of the accused, strictly speaking represents a sin against what we, more than any other professional body, should regard as sacred, namely the law. The requirement for an oral hearing with all its provisos and the reaching of the decision on the sentence only on the basis of this hearing is after all, and not without reason, an integral part of every judicial system. Every attempt to direct a judge in advance of a trial contains a whole number of possibilities of error, which cannot be removed by the objection that the judge concerned is not strictly bound by the directive he has received, but can, and indeed sometimes must, deviate from it. For what authority can tell the judge whether the conviction about the guilt or degree of guilt of the accused which he has gained from the main court proceedings will subsequently be approved by and will coincide with that of his superiors, the President of the Higher State Court or even the Justice Ministry, who will determine his professional future? The less robust judges will give in and pronounce the sentence which has been indicated; but how often will they do so against their better conscience? The tougher ones will risk a reprimand. But if they are reprimanded and the reprimand is repeated this will certainly not encourage them to take firm decisions, nor will it improve their professional morale. People are simply too different from one another for it to be possible to reach the same or even roughly the same judgment on a case among the various authorities involved (President of the Higher State Court, Justice Ministry). I have known cases where the verdicts which could have been given and the sentences which could have resulted from them covered a grotesque range of possibilities; where does justice lie in such cases? Are we not removing from the judges all the nobility of their high calling if we force them to act against their consciences? Moreover, there is another point: the practice of directing judges represents for the President of the Higher State Court and the General Prosecutor a burden of work which bears no real relation to the rewards for this labour of Sisyphus . . .

Up to now the tough sentences which, apart from anything else, are the goal of the guidance process, have not produced a noticeable reduction in criminality. The mail robberies are still taking place, despite the fact that in these cases in particular long sentences of penal servitude and on several occasions even death sentences have been passed. The same is true with contacts with prisoners of war . . . Black market slaughtering and similar war economy crimes are also hardly declining, despite the fact that draconian punishments have also been imposed in these cases. Their number would doubtless be even greater if the prosecutors and the police had more personnel and could pursue these cases more effectively. As it is, only a relatively small number of the offences are actually prosecuted. Barter trade, particularly among retailers, is virtually a no-go area for the prosecuting authorities. It is an open secret that in Germany too an awful lot can be obtained through barter. Anyone who can supply game or poultry can receive cloth in exchange, and anyone who can get hold of some tobacco products will not lack for other rationed goods in short supply. Although the rationing regulations are making the retailers more and more dependent on having to come up with the coupons which he has received [from customers] in order to acquire new goods, nevertheless the majority of retailers still have a certain store of goods which is kept from the normal customers and used for private bartering. Since civil servants in particular cannot produce such things, this situation creates a lot of bitterness. The fact that civil servants and those on fixed incomes are getting much thinner than the more fortunate business classes is only too apparent.

On the question of the war economy and on that of the judicial crisis I would like to make an observation which needs to be mentioned. The fact that the Economic Offices have their own penal powers is very disadvantageous for the judicial system. The Economic Offices have their own rules and apparently also often special guidelines according to which they operate. Cases are dealt with under their own penal procedures which would have been better handed over to the public prosecutor. Quite often, farmers, butchers, and innkeepers are brought before the courts, while their customers, particularly those from the higher bourgeois social circles, get away with a fine. In this way they do not register in the court records but continue to figure in the memory and gossip of the public, who are extremely interested in all this. There are then lively discussions about why *Regierungsrat* X or the wife of Colonel Y or district leader Z did not appear before the courts and only the master butcher had to go to jail. And, along with all this criticism, it is often the judicial system which gets the blame for these double standards, although in fact it is not responsible for these unfortunate results.

▄▄▄▄

However, even more serious than these points were the observations made by the President of the Higher State Court in Karlsruhe in his report to the Reich Justice Ministry of 13 September 1943:

**1019**    The further expansion of the powers of the police is causing concern because people anticipate a further reduction and limitation of justice, indeed consider that in practice this has already occurred. Apart from the loss of the power to prosecute Jews, Poles and Russians to the police (the domestic political reasons for this are not generally known),[28] people are aware of the arrest by the police of those who have been sentenced by the courts, or who have been released having served their sentence, or the transfer of accused persons to police custody when the charges against them have been dropped. In Alsace, in particular, this is considered to represent a marked deterioration in legal protection and negative comparisons are drawn with the previous French system. A [court] president has pointed out—I was not hitherto aware of this—that, according to a recent edict of the *Reichsführer SS* and Chief of the German Police, the criminal police departments can now keep an arrested person in custody for up to 21 days without having to inform the State Prosecutor or bring him before a court. The justification given for this is that 'other authorities should not be unnecessarily bothered'. This instruction from the *Reichsführer SS*, together with other indications of an expansion of police power, such as, for example, the article by Professor Dr Maunz, published in the *Frankfurter Zeitung* on 6.7.1943, No. 338, with the title 'The Police in the State',

---

[28] See below, pp. 159–61.

prompt fears that the prosecution, indeed perhaps the whole criminal legal process, is being taken away from the judiciary. I too must say that the police practice up to now of imposing police custody for lengthy periods in political cases has been difficult to reconcile with the notion of justice, and that the extension of this system to all penal proceedings (if it is true about the edict referred to above) would make a farce of §128 StPO.[29]

In 1944, the Reich Justice Minister, Thierack, summed up his views on the role of the judicial system as follows:

**1020**   In the fifth year of the war, in which the enemy has been attacking the Reich on all fronts, and in which the best members of our nation are risking their lives at the front and the homeland is standing behind them with all its strength, the penal system must keep a sharp eye on the attitude of the home front and make sure that the community remains steadfast in its will to resist. Anyone who offends against this internal order on principle deserves a harsher punishment than in peacetime even if his deed does not appear to differ from one committed in normal times. For what is essentially new is the fact that our nation's wartime situation requires different assessment of the offence . . .

The life of the nation in all its aspects and its need for protection is, therefore, the guiding principle for the assessment of every offence and the sole valid criterion for just punishment The offender will receive the appropriate response from the community via the judge to the same extent and the same degree with which he offends against the community. In the event of a real breach of loyalty, it will be harsh; but if it is a case of an odd misdemeanour, which does not seriously affect the community, it may be mild.

Penal justice is also determined by a further consideration in the fifth year of the war. Every war inevitably produces a negative selection. Where the most valuable blood is sacrificing itself on the battlefield, the degenerate, socially and mostly biologically inferior criminal cannot expect the community to tolerate his living among them any longer even if the offence for which he is being judged does not appear to justify the most severe sentence. His exclusion is in fact a requirement for the maintenance of the nation's value. The penal system fulfils the hygienic national task of a progressive purging of the national body so that in the end the bad elements do not outgrow and smother the good ones.

In accordance with the task assigned to the judicial system by the Führer of dealing with traitors, saboteurs, national pests, violent criminals, and asocial habitual criminals in the harshest possible way, the number of death sentences

---

[29] §128 of the Penal Code stated: 'The arrested person, in so far as he is not released again, must be brought before a magistrate of the district in which the arrest occurred without delay . . . 2. If the magistrate considers the arrest is not justified or considers the grounds for it no longer apply, then he is to order the prisoner to be released, otherwise he is to issue a custodial order'.

has steadily increased since the outbreak of war. The following figures cover this period:

| 1939 (from 1.9 to 31.12. 1939 | 99 |
|---|---|
| 1940 | 926 |
| 1941 | 1,292 |
| 1942 | 3,660 |
| 1943 | 5,336 |

From at least the late 1930s onwards, the Reich Justice Ministry was fighting a losing battle with the SS for control over the prosecution of criminals. Given the nature of the regime and the increasing expansion of the definition of criminality, it was inevitable that political concerns and political criteria should increasingly determine priorities in the judicial field and that, in turn, the political police (Gestapo) should increasingly expand its authority at the expense of the judiciary and the penal system.

In practice, however, this did not make a great deal of difference. For the penal authorities had already been willingly cooperating with the Gestopo in facilitating the transfer of certain categories of prisoners to concentration camps at the end of their sentences, since many of the officials involved, such as prison governors, shared the same 'mind set' in terms of their views about 'community aliens' as the SS. In fact, already in 1936/37, the SS/Police had taken the initiative in arresting large numbers of so-called 'professional criminals' and 'asocials' and consigning them to concentration camps. However, the penal system still had a considerable number of such people under 'security confinement' (*Sicherungsverwahrung* as opposed to *polizeiliche Vorbeugungshaft*= police preventive custody).

On his appointment as Reich Justice Minister on 20 August 1942, Thierack received a lecture from Hitler about the iniquity of criminals being allowed to survive in prison while the valuable elements risked their lives at the front and the consequent need 'to exterminate the vermin in society' in order to prevent the dysgenic effects of the war resulting in another November 1918.[30] Responding to this on 14 September, Thierack then consulted Goebbels who suggested that all Jews, Gypsies, Poles serving more than three or four years penal

---

[30] See *Hitler's Table Talk* (Oxford 1988), pp. 638–45. The following section of the commentary is largely drawn from the important recent London University PhD by Nikolaus Wachsmann 'Reform and Repression: Prisons and Penal Policy in Germany, 1918–1945'.

servitude, and Czechs and Germans sentenced to life imprisonment or permanent security confinement, should be transferred to concentration camps and that 'the idea of destruction through labour was best'. Four days later, Thierack met Himmler and reached an agreement with him on transferring certain categories of prisoners to the SS. Thierack no doubt hoped that in yielding up responsibility for dealing with racial inferiors and 'community aliens' to the SS he would facilitate the Justice Ministry's attempt to retain control over the reminder of the penal system dealing with 'reformable compatriots'. However, it was also because he shared Hitler and Goebbels' views about the need to eliminate certain elements and, as he also told Bormann in a letter of 13 October, because 'in spite of the harsh penalties imposed there is little that the law can do towards eliminating them . . . My idea is that we shall get better results if we hand them over to the police, who can then carry out their measures untrammelled by the criminal law.'[31] The 'them' here referred to the Jews, Poles, Gypsies, Russians and Ukrainians. The following document contains Thierack's record of the meeting with Himmler at which this agreement was reached.

**1021** Discussion with *Reichsführer SS* Himmler on 18.9.1942 in his Field Headquarters in the presence of State Secretary Dr Rothenberger, *SS Gruppenführer* Streckenbach and *SS Obersturmbannführer* Bender.

1. Correction by special treatment at the hands of the police in cases where judicial sentences are not severe enough. At the suggestion of *Reichsleiter* Bormann, the following agreement was reached between the *Reichsführer SS* and myself:

(a) As a rule the Führer's time is no longer to be burdened with these matters.

(b) The Reich Minister of Justice will decide whether and when special treatment at the hands of the police is to be applied.

(c) The *Reichsführer SS* will send the reports, which hitherto he has sent to *Reichsleiter* Bormann, to the Reich Minister of Justice.

(d) If the views of the *Reichsführer SS* and those of the Reich Minister of Justice coincide, the final decision on the case will rest with them.

(e) If their views are not in agreement, the opinion of *Reichsleiter* Bormann will be sought on the case, and he may inform the Führer.

(f) In cases where the Führer's decision on a mild sentence is sought through other channels (such as by a letter from a Gauleiter) *Reichsleiter* Bormann will forward the report to the Reich Minister of Justice.

The case will then be decided as already described by the *Reichsführer SS* and the Reich Minister of Justice.

---

[31] See M. Broszat, 'The Concentration Camps', in H. Krausnick, M. Broszat, *Anatomy of the SS State* (London 1970), p. 98.

2. The following anti-social elements are to be transferred from the prison where they are serving their sentence to the *Reichsführer SS* to be worked to death: persons under preventive detention, Jews, Gypsies, Russians and Ukrainians, Poles with sentences of more than three years, Czechs and Germans with sentences of more than eight years, according to the decision of the Reich Minister of Justice. First of all, the worst anti-social elements amongst those just mentioned are to be handed over. I shall inform the Führer of this through *Reichsleiter* Bormann . . .

3. Participation of the people in sentencing.

This should be introduced step by step as soon as possible, initially in villages and small towns of up to about 20,000 people. It is difficult to implement in big cities. I shall . . . encourage the Party in particular to become involved. We are clear about the fact that the legal system must not be in the hands of the Party . . .

4. It is agreed that, in view of the plans of the Government for settling the eastern problems, in future Jews, Poles, Gypsies, Russian, and Ukrainians are no longer to be judged by the ordinary courts, so far as punishable offences are concerned, but are to be dealt with by the *Reichsführer SS*. This does not apply to civil lawsuits, nor to Poles whose names are announced or entered in the German racial lists.[32]

———

(3) It has been estimated that, by the summer of 1943, around 17,300 state prisoners had been handed over to the police for 'destruction through labour' including 1,700 women.[33] The largest group were prisoners in preventive detention, mainly petty criminals convicted for repeated property offences; the largest group of 'ethnic aliens' were Poles. Later, another 3,000 odd were transferred, mainly political offenders and violent criminals. In general, the prison directors either passively obeyed orders or cooperated willingly in the transfers, provided they did not interfere too much with the economic production of the prison for which they were responsible. It was up to the prison governors in the first instance to decide whether or not particular prisoners should count as asocial and so be transferred. Around 95 per cent of these prisoners were so classified. Apart from their ideological professional sympathies with the programme, it helped to ease prison overcrowding and enabled them to get rid of prisoners who were unproductive because of age or sickness, the latter often brought on by inadequate food rations and overwork, or recalcitrant.

A bleak future awaited those sent to the concentration camps under this agreement.

———

[32] i.e. Poles who were racially acceptable.
[33] For the following, see Wachsmann.

### (vi)  Concentration Camps[34]

The concentration camps (KZs) had originated in 1933 as institutions for neutralizing, and in some cases eliminating, political and ideological enemies—mainly Communists, Socialists, and politically and culturally prominent Jews—during the critical period of the 'seizure of power'. By 1936, however, with the regime well established, this function was becoming increasingly superfluous. However, the Nazis increasingly tended to see society in terms of loyal 'compatriots' (*Volksgenossen*) and those who were outside the 'national community' through racial origin or congenital disability or 'placed themselves outside it' through outright resistance or through a failure to conform to its norms. Thus the SS now broadened the role of the KZs to concentrate increasingly on the 'hygienic' task of purging the 'national body' of those elements considered to be undermining its health and efficiency. On their arrival at the camps prisoners were divided into separate categories denoted by the wearing of a piece of coloured cloth in the shape of a triangle on their striped uniforms: red for political prisoners, green for 'habitual criminals', black for 'asocials', pink for homosexuals, violet for Jehovah's Witnesses, and a yellow-red Star of David for Jews.

The concentration camps constituted an extraordinary distinct world with its own social structure, hierarchy and value system. After the war, Benedikt Kautsky, the son of the leading SPD theorist, Karl Kautsky, who between 1938 and 1945 experienced Dachau, Buchenwald, and Auschwitz concentration camps, provided one of the most remarkable descriptions of this world:

**1022**   *The Top People* [Die Prominenten]

This term was used by the camp to describe the aristocracy. It contained various ranks. There were the camp leaders (*Lagerältesten*), the office capo, the capos of the work details, of the storerooms (personal effects, clothing, tools), the mail room, and the cashier's office. The kitchen and the canteen (both the ones for the prisoners and the ones for the SS), the men responsible for the sick bay, those from the Commandant's office (Political Department, Photography Department), then a few 'great' block leaders and capos, above all those in charge of particular workshops and work details, but also a few people who were well-regarded such as officers' lackeys, sometimes also hairdressers and tailors. All these people, who owed their rank to the most varied causes, constituted a very diverse society. In some cases it really was due to their efficiency, in others it was their ability to curry favour with the SS or with prisoners who had already gone up in the world which proved decisive. There

---

[34] For the extermination camps see Vol. 3, docs 852–916.

were extremely hard-working and efficient people alongside lazy and incompetent ones. Some shamelessly exploited their office at the expense of their fellow prisoners; others showed complete integrity.

In every camp there was a bitter struggle going on among these people. Since the majority of prisoners continued to have absolutely no influence, these struggles took the form of palace revolutions. The most despicable intrigues were sometimes launched, in which people did not shrink from involving the SS. There were also numerous occasions on which the SS cliques fought out their own battles with the aid and at the expense of the prisoners.

The struggles were particularly tough and ruthless where the Reds and the Greens were fighting for supremacy. The Greens were naturally absolutely unscrupulous in using the most vicious methods. They were particularly fond of doing down their opponents [*platzen lassen*], i.e. they reported alleged or real offences to the SS and got them to intervene. The Reds naturally had to respond in kind, although they mainly relied on their superior efficiency and honesty. But their opponents liked playing the trump card of accusing them of political unreliability and that worked on more than one occasion.

The prize for the winner was a big one. In the first place, it took a material form: better food, better accommodation, better clothing, more freedom at work, the realization of cultural aspirations even against the background of the most acute need. Many found that attractive. But even more attractive was the social aspect. Power and status had an enormous impact, particularly in these surroundings which were designed to oppress people. Naturally, one could not feel free, but one felt the lack of freedom much less keenly if one could give orders to others. The power that one exercised was incredibly great and the social distinction between this upper class of the top people and the dregs of the prisoners was crasser than that between bourgeoisie and proletariat in a democratic state.

Thus, it was understandable that people for whom these values were important strove to acquire such positions. But it was also understandable that political prisoners, who felt that they were up to holding these positions, claimed this power not for themselves but for the prisoners as a whole. If they had not done so, then the life in many camps would have been even less bearable than it was already. Thus, it was definitely in the interests of the prisoners for the politicals to get these positions. However, getting involved in this web of intrigue represented a major threat to one's personal integrity and it required remarkable strength of character not to let oneself be corrupted by either the power or the material advantages. It must be said that a number of Communist functionaries in Buchenwald and a number of Jewish functionaries in Auschwitz-Buna deserve this accolade. However, alongside these shining examples of the triumph which the human spirit could achieve in overcoming the most difficult conditions, there were also manifestations which showed how far people of absolute personal integrity could go astray when they believed it served their cause . . .

The same phenomena which occurred in the highest ranks of the top people were also present among the rest of the camp aristocracy and, if less intensively, then more generally. These included the remainder of the Block Leaders as well as most of the Capos, a few important foremen and authoritative functionaries in the offices and workshops, the sick bay etc. Here too there were continual intrigues going on. But, since they had less access to the SS the place of the SS was taken by the top ranks of the prisoners. That made the intrigues somewhat less tense and dangerous, but, since the group involved was much larger, the number of possible combinations was much higher.

It was by no means unusual for people to fall from the heights of being top people to the deepest depths of the punishment company and punishment details. But it was usually not irrevocable. I saw many fall and rise again, and do so more than once, without the fall being considered dishonourable any more than in the case of the camp punishments. Most of them experienced these ups and downs; there were of course others who remained in the same positions for years so that they were considered part of the furniture, like the watch towers or the bunker. But they were well advised to watch out and not to rely on their ability to hang on—on the contrary. When, on one occasion, such a prisoner responded to his removal from office by referring to his years of service in this function, he was told: 'then it's high time that you picked up a shovel and went out on a work detail'.

Right up until the end of the war, the top rank of the top people was almost exclusively German; in Auschwitz the Poles played a major role for a time. The Germans also dominated the remainder of the camp aristocracy, although here a considerable number of nationals from other countries played a part, as towards the end of the war did even Jews in increasing numbers.

### The Middle Class

Beneath the top people there was a fairly broad layer which we can call the middle class. They were the room leaders, the foremen, the workers in the workshops and the lower-level clerks and functionaries in the offices, the nurses, clerks and other functionaries in the sick bay, but one could also add the 'junior' capos and block leaders. This group was very numerous. In Buchenwald, even before the great influx of foreigners, it consisted of 2,000–3,000 prisoners out of a total prisoner population of 10,000. Even in Auschwitz-Buna, where there were no significant workshops, there were around 1,000 out of a total of 10,000.

This group had far less power and prestige than the top people but also less responsibility. The material advantages were quite varied—cooks naturally had enough to eat, the prisoners in the clothing store were well clothed, whereas, many foremen only had few advantages compared to the men in their work details. Nevertheless, this group was quite distinct from the mass. This resulted from the type of work they did. Either these prisoners worked in the workshops, i.e. under cover, and were employed in their own trades, or, as foremen, they did not have to do physical work, or they worked in offices or in the sick bay and, therefore, under cover, were seldom supervised and could have long breaks.

In the early years German 'Aryans' were given priority. But, after the influx of the foreigners, they too secured numerous positions and, in the final period, as the distinctions began to disappear, even the Jews, although only the specialists and the long-term prisoners. A knowledge of German was not absolutely necessary, whereas in the case of the top people, it was more or less required for all posts.

In view of the general camp conditions, the life of the middle class can be described as comfortable. Even if the post did not of itself—as in the kitchen, the sick bay or office work—provide more food, then working for the SS, contacts with sources of food or with civilians, barter and doing deals on the side, all provided opportunities for acquiring 'rations through the back door'. The work was sometimes hard—for example, the nurses often had a hard time and in some workshops there was a lot to do—but that was more than compensated for by the fact that the SS almost never controlled this work and could not control it, so that this group did not have too much mental stress.

The very fact that the SS had fewer possibilities of controlling them prompted many 'middle-class people' seriously to neglect their duties. That in turn had an impact on the camp as a whole. Apart from the cases of actual theft from comrades, such as the purloining of food from the kitchen or linen from the clothing store, it was not a matter of indifference for the great mass of ordinary prisoners whether the barrack-room cleaners kept the block clean and used all the available opportunities to acquire fresh linen or shoes or whether the nurses in the sick bay looked after the sick properly; it was also important how many pairs of shoes the colleagues in the shoe workshop repaired each day and whether the laundry met the camp's needs.

All this depended on the top people performing their duty of supervision. In this connection one can give the Buchenwald prisoners in the camp leadership the highest praise. The laundry, for example, can be described as a model operation, which performed its responsible task right to the end, despite apparently insuperable difficulties. Also the development of the sick bay in Buchenwald was remarkable, as indeed was the Auschwitz sick bay, which, in the most difficult times, was turned from nothing into something very respectable. In both cases this was entirely the work of the prisoners.

### The Great Mass

The large number of remaining prisoners lived under the 'normal conditions' of the camp. This meant in general: normal rations, work in the open air, and continual supervision by higher-ranking prisoners and SS. In the course of time, however, marked differences emerged in that workers were selected for armaments plants.

There were major differences in the types of work. These existed even before the war. The question of whether one worked in the quarry or in a building detail could in certain circumstances be a matter of life and death. It was not only the question of how heavy the work was but also its social status. There were heavy types of work, such as, for example, working in the Buchenwald haulage column, which were highly regarded socially, and there were much heavier ones, such as carrying rocks or pulling carts in the quarry, which were considered low-status.

In general the law of the camp was: to him that hath shall be given and from him that hath not shall be taken. The heaviest and dirtiest jobs were given to the weakest, who, as compensation, got the least rest and the smallest number of perks. The lightest and socially most highly regarded jobs were done by the strongest prisoners who, in addition, had bonuses and the opportunity of getting extra rations by the back door. We should also bear in mind that youth was considered a definite advantage and age was mostly regarded as a crime . . . then we can see the 'master morality' [*Herrenmoral*] in its pure form.

However strange it may sound, there was a justification for this morality. Nietzsche's motto: 'whatever falls one should kick' contains a truth for normal circumstances. In the camp it was almost entirely valid. When applied to conditions there it meant that in the camp only a few have a chance of coming out alive and those are the strongest ones. Everybody who is old, weak and sick is condemned to death. The possibilities of helping anyone are minimal; whatever I give to anyone I am taking away from someone else. If I give to the weak then I will be keeping them alive for a bit longer, but in the end I can't save him; at the same time, I am taking that away from a strong person and thereby weakening him so that he too will become weak and ill. The upshot is that I will plunge both into misfortune.

One can hardly object to this kind of logic. However, who was to judge the ability and above all the worthiness of the people being considered? In reality youth was not a definite advantage, not even in a physical let alone a moral sense. In my experience, people in early middle age with a healthy constitution and firm nerves, with a broad experience of life and strong ties to wife and children had much better chances of coming through than physically strong young men whose nerves were no stronger than their moral views and who had nothing to tie them to normal life outside in freedom.

The point of view expressed in the camp along the lines of: 'old boy you've had your day; we young ones want to have something from life after this is all over' sounded much more logical than it was; and if one considers that the selection of the prisoners was based on personal feelings—often on the lowest level—and on materialist motives, one can easily work out how distorted the 'selection of the fittest' turned out to be. This explains how such a variety of people survived the camp—valuable politicals as well as scum and nonentities. Chance and arbitrary factors played the main role in this connection as in every other.

Before the war, the majority of the lower class consisted of Jews and the Germans of inferior status, mainly the Blacks, with the bulk of the heavy and despised jobs being placed on the shoulders of the Jews. They remained the pariahs of the camp during the war as well, while foreigners replaced the lower status Germans, particularly from those nations which had larger numbers of prisoners and who, because of their lack of German, played a less significant role in running the camp. 'Vitamin B', as personal contacts [*Beziehungen*] were called in Hitler's Germany, was vital in the camp as well and the lack of it was extremely disadvantageous for Russians, Poles and the French. Otherwise, a number of factors determined which nations belonged to the lowest classes in the individual camps.

If one combines the fact that Jews and large groups of foreigners had to do the heaviest work with the fact that they were most exposed to organised theft and that they had to live in the worst accommodation, then one can envisage the gap which existed between them and the top people. In the same period in which the Jews and foreigners were dying within four to six months in the temporary accommodation, the death rate among the upper class was nil and in the middle class not much above the norm for these age groups.

Within a few weeks, hunger, overwork and having to live in impossible conditions produced a discrete group among the lower class, the:

### Moslems [Muselmann]

I am unable to explain why this name was chosen in Auschwitz or why in Buchenwald, where they were much less common, they were given the name 'tired sheikhs' until the Auschwitz expression was adopted there too.[35]

The Moslem was on the lowest level to which a prisoner could sink. The sight of the daily marches in and out of Auschwitz, when thousands of these miserable wretches dragged themselves off to work in the morning only in many cases to be dragged back home in the evening, was appalling. Tired, hungry, morose, filthy and in rags—that is how one saw them march past the fat camp leader who took the parade all dressed up with his hair smarmed down, smelling of good soap—from 'Kanada',[36] well-fed and complacent, ready at any moment to make a few patronising remarks and play the camp father or, just as easily, to dole out the most brutal kicks and blows if some poor human wretch aroused his disgust. He was, which in the case of Auschwitz it is unnecessary to mention, invariably a Green. Even the richest tycoon or the most powerful statesman in a democratic state is not so far superior to an unemployed person, who has to sleep on a bench in the open air covered with a newspaper and perhaps has not eaten for days, as this man was to a Moslem. For the rich and powerful can let the poor starve or die; they can rob them of their freedom; they can enjoy everything while he goes miserably to the dogs. But the camp leader in Auschwitz-Buna could do all that and more: he could eat and drink to his heart's content; he had his own cook and what the camp kitchen did not have was supplied by 'Kanada' or the 'black stock exchange' in Buna. Clothes, linen, shoes—as many and as nice ones as he liked. For why else were the Jews dying in the gas chambers of Birkenau? Women—the camp brothel or the thousands of girls in Buna supplied every type desired. Art—the camp orchestra with first-class musicians: the leader of the orchestra of the Berlin State Opera, graduates of the Vienna Conservatory were at his disposal. Painters and draughtsmen fulfilled his every wish. In his own sphere he could realize his architectural fantasies just as much as Hitler. The camp supplied personal poets of every quality desired, both for the physical and for the spiritual realms. The fact that he had a group of actors at his disposal was just as much a matter of course as the fact that he could order any books he wanted. He had specialists from every country at his disposal to treat his real and imaginary ailments—a Polish surgeon, a French internist, a Hungarian eye and a German ear specialist. It is true that he could only move in a restricted sphere, though not confined to the

---

[35] One suggestion is that the name is derived from pictures of starving Africans from the famine-affected areas of North Africa, which had appeared in the German press during the 1930s.

[36] The store in Auschwitz where the prisoners' possessions were stored.

camp, and of course under supervision. But his escort would have hardly cramped his style any more than personal detectives restrict millionaires or politicians. But what they could not do, he could and did: when he had the urge—and that was not infrequently—he could express his sadistic impulses and beat or kill without any compunction and with impunity until he had fully satisfied his urges.

And if one wants to object that the camp leader was after all dependent on the SS and could be brought down by them—well, even the most powerful dictator is dependent on somebody and the Auschwitz camp leaders, whom I saw overthrown, landed very softly in comparison to the other dictators. They disappeared into a satellite camp and, even if they did not play the same role there, nevertheless, as members of the German master race, they were still top people.

A concentration camp was in reality a world, a world full of contradictions and pitfalls, with a hierarchy which was admittedly shaky, but which could always be defined and in which everybody had his place. He could rise or fall depending on luck and ability, but at any one time he had to take up the position allotted to him and to respect that of others.

_____

As part of the SS/Police's project of using terror as a weapon of social discipline, on 26 October 1939, the Gestapo (now Dept IV of the RSHA) issued the following edict on increasing the deterrent effect of protective custody:

**1023**    Re: *The implementation of protective custody.*

On the orders of the *Reichsführer SS* and Chief of the German Police all prisoners taken into protective custody during the war and consigned to a concentration camp will be transferred to a particular punishment section. The only exceptions are those prisoners in protective custody who have been assigned to a camp by the police for preventive detention (especially the A file category), or who are expressly exempted in the transfer document. However, these exemptions require the approval of the Secret State Police Office [Gestapo] and, if necessary, should be requested from department II.

In order to ensure a further deterrent effect the following procedure should be followed in every individual case:

1. If the prisoner in protective custody in a concentration camp was employed in a plant and his behaviour was hostile to the state or alien to the community and calculated to influence discipline or the work morale of the retinue, then care should be taken to ensure that his transfer to a concentration camp is publicised by putting up a notice.

2. In more serious cases this announcement can include the statement that, in view of his behaviour, he has been transferred to a punishment section of the camp.

3. On no account should the period of detention be mentioned, even if the *Reichsführer SS* and Chief of German Police or the Chief of the Security Police

and SD has determined the length of the sentence. As far as the public is concerned, the period of detention in a concentration camp should always be referred to as 'for the time being'.

On the other hand, there is no objection in serious cases to spreading rumours designed to increase the deterrent effect by, for example, suggesting that one has heard that, in view of the seriousness of the case, the person will not be released for two or three years.

4. In individual cases the *Reichsführer SS* and Chief of the German Police will order corporal punishment in addition to assignment to a concentration camp. Here too there is no objection to spreading news of this as in section 3, paragraph 2 in so far as this is calculated to increase the deterrent effect. In future the relevant State Police offices will be informed of such instructions.

5. Naturally, especially suitable and reliable persons should be selected for spreading such information.

6. The Stapo regional headquarters must send me a short progress report by the 1.11.1940.

---

In 1941 Himmler decided to categorize not only the prisoners but also the concentration camps. On 2 January 1941 Heydrich issued the following directive to the top officials in the Security Police and SD and concentration camp administrations:

**1024**   Re: *Categorisation of concentration camps.*

The *Reichsführer SS* and Chief of the German Police has agreed to the division of the concentration camps into different categories, which take account of the personality of the prisoners and degree of threat they pose to the state. In accordance with this, the concentration camps will be divided into the following categories.

Category I: For all those prisoners in protective custody who are not serious offenders and are capable of improvement and, in addition, for special cases and for solitary confinement:

Dachau, Sachsenhausen and Auschwitz I (the latter also partly comes into this category) camps.

Category Ia: For all prisoners in protective custody who are old or only partially capable of work who can be employed in the medicinal herb garden: Dachau camp.

Category II: For more serious offenders who are nevertheless educable and capable of improvement:

Buchenwald, Flossenbürg, Neuengamme and Auschwitz II camps.

Category III: For serious offenders, in particular those who simultaneously have previous convictions and are asocial, i.e. prisoners in protective custody who are barely educable: Mauthausen camp.

A rearrangement of the prisoners in accordance with the new categories cannot be carried out for the time being because of the current measures being taken to employ prisoners. In future, however, new prisoners will be assigned according to these categories. I request, therefore, that in the case of all future requests for the imposition of protective custody and transfers to concentration camp, suggestions should be made about what category of camp they should be sent to in the light of the prisoner's personality and the threat posed to the state by him. I insist that it should be a requirement that the whole political and criminal record, previous punishments, behaviour since the takeover of power etc. should be taken into account and, in particular, that every request for assignment to Category III should be individually justified in detail.

This edict is not intended for the district and local police authorities.

In practice, however, this scheme could not be systematically implemented and is interesting primarily in providing an insight into the systematizing mentality of Himmler and the SS and as an indication of what the future would have held had the outcome of the war turned out differently. For example, the existing prisoners were not rearranged in accordance with these categories and the treatment of different categories of prisoners within the individual camps differed more than that between the camps. Only in the case of Mauthausen was the scheme more or less effectively implemented in the sense that conditions there tended to be—with the partial exception of Auschwitz—worse than the other camps and the death rate correspondingly higher. It was there that most of the prisoners in 'preventive detention', who were transferred from the penal authorities to the SS under the Himmler–Thierack agreement of September 1942, were sent to be 'worked to death' in its quarry. Of 12,658 such prisoners 5,935 had died by 1 April 1943.[37]

However, the main reason why Himmler's new categorization of the KZs could not be properly implemented was the fact that it was soon overtaken by events which radically transformed the concentration camps from being penal institutions for outlaws from the national community or 'community aliens' into being, primarily, suppliers of slave labour for German industrial production.

There were in fact three main developments in the history of the concentration camps during the war, all of which were mainly concentrated in the years 1942–5. The first was the enormous expansion in numbers which took place. The first phase of this expansion occurred between September 1939 (c.25,000 prisoners) to 88,000 in December 1942. However, the main increase occurred during 1943 and 1944. By 15 January 1945 there were around 714,211 KZ inmates (511,537 men and 202,674 women). The following figures for admissions to Buchenwald

---

[37] See Broszat, op. cit., p. 244.

concentration camp, which were typical of other camps as well, indicate this development:

**1025**

|                  | Admissions | Deaths  |
|------------------|-----------|---------|
| 1939             | 9,553     | 1,235   |
| 1940             | 2,525     | 1,772   |
| 1941             | 5,890     | 1,522   |
| 1942             | 14,111    | 2,898   |
| 1943             | 42,177    | 3,516   |
| 1944             | 97,867    | 8,644   |
| 1945 (3 months)  | 43,823    | 13,056. |

The second main development was the growing numbers of foreigners who were consigned to the camps and who soon greatly outnumbered the German prisoners of war. By 1945, for example, Buchenwald had contained prisoners from at least thirty different nationalities and, on the liberation of the camp, there were 4,380 Russian, 3,800 Polish, 2,900 French, 2,105 Czech compared to 1,800 German prisoners.[38] Hitler's notorious (OKW) 'Night and Fog' decree of 7 December 1941 resulted in the transfer of captured resistance fighters to concentration camps. The agreement between Thierack and Himmler, on 18 September 1942, to consign certain categories of foreign offenders (Russians, Ukrainians, Poles and Czechs) wholesale to the SS[39] had been both preceded and was followed by an increasing tendency to send Russian and Polish civilian workers to KZs.

The third main development, to which the other two can be attributed, was the increasing use of concentration camp prisoners for industrial work.[40] The SS had already begun to exploit concentration camp labour for its own business operations in the late 1930s. Stone and bricks were much in demand for the pre-war construction boom, notably for the regime's prestige building projects such as the Nuremberg Party Rally complex. On 29 April 1938, the SS established the German Quarrying Company (*Deutsche Erd- und Steinwerke GmbH* = DEST). The selection

---

[38] *The Buchenwald Report* (Boulder/San Francisco/Oxford 1995), pp. 7–8.
[39] See above pp. 160–61.
[40] For the following see Enno Georg, *Die wirtschaftlichen Unternehmungen der SS* (Stuttgart 1963).

of the sites of several new concentration camps (Flossenbürg near Weiden/Upper Palatinate and Mauthausen-Gusen near Linz in 1938, Gross-Rosen in Silesia in 1939, and Natzweiler/Alsace in 1940) were largely determined by their proximity to substantial quarries, while brickworks were established at Buchenwald and Sachsenhausen in May 1938. During 1941 DEST achieved a turnover of RM 5,169,000 compared with 1,589,000 in 1939. A year later, on 3 May 1939, a new firm, the German Equipment Company (*Deutsche Ausrüstungswerke GmbH*) was established which integrated the numerous metalworking and carpentry workshops, bakeries etc., which had sprung up in the various KZs, while, on 21 June 1940, the Textile and Leather Processing Company (*Gesellschaft für Textil und Lederverarbeitung GmbH* = Lebed) was established, which concentrated on making uniforms for the Waffen SS and the KZ prisoners. On 26 July 1940, these various businesses were integrated into a holding company German Business Plants Ltd. (*Deutsche Wirtschaftsbetriebe* = DWB), which was subordinated to the SS Administration and Business Main Office under the former naval paymaster, *SS Gruppenführer* Oswald Pohl. These business operations were designed to reinforce the SS's autonomy by making it partially self-sufficient, and to provide an additional function for, and therefore justification for the expansion of, its concentration camps.

This latter point acquired a new urgency as the labour shortage in Germany became increasingly acute after the failure of her *Blitzkrieg* strategy in Russia in the winter of 1941. One can sense the growing pressure from the following circular from the head of the Concentration Camps Inspectorate, *SS Brigadeführer* Richard Glücks, to the concentration camp commandants, dated 12 February 1942:

**1026**  All the camps are asking me for prisoners since the commandants no longer know how they are going to meet the increasing demands for labour being placed upon them with the prisoners they already have. While the total number of prisoners has more or less remained the same, the tasks being imposed by the *Reichsführer SS* have multiplied several times.

Thus, it is necessary for the number of prisoners employed within the camp to be significantly reduced in order to release prisoners for these tasks and for the increasing labour deployment.

I request the camp commandants, in association with the protective custody camp leader and the protective custody camp leader 'E'. to carry out personally a sifting through of the camp and to release all prisoners for labour deployment who are not absolutely essential for maintaining the camp. In making the selection I request that a figure of 10 per cent of all prisoners fit for work should be laid down in the future as the maximum for the operation of the camp. Since in every camp there are a number of prisoners who are only partially fit, these can be used for clearing up and cleaning operations in addition to the 10 per cent of healthy prisoners which has been agreed.

---

In this situation there was the danger that other agencies—the Labour Ministry or the new Armaments Minister, Albert Speer—might try and gain control over the employment of KZ inmates and this became particularly acute when, in March 1942, the decision was taken to appoint a new Plenipotentiary for Labour Mobilization.[41]

Himmler responded to this threat by reorganizing the concentration system in order to prioritize its economic function.[42] First, more in order to clarify a confusing situation rather than to initiate a major new departure, on 1 February 1942, the SS Head Offices 'Budget and Buildings' (*Haushalt und Bauten*), responsible for administering the Waffen SS and the Death's Head Units, and the Administration and Business Head Office (*Verwaltungs-und Wirtschaftshauptamt*), responsible for administering the General SS and the SS business enterprises, were formally integrated into a new office under Oswald Pohl, the Business and Administration Head Office (*Wirtschafts- und Verwaltungshauptamt* = WVHA). In fact, in practice they had already been functioning as one agency since 1939.

Secondly, and more important, on 3 March 1942, the hitherto autonomous Concentration Camp Inspectorate, responsible for running the concentration camps, under its head, *SS Brigadeführer* Richard Glücks, was integrated into the new WVHA as D Branch (*Amtsgruppe D*). Thus Glücks, his deputy, *SS Standartenführer* Maurer, and his assistant *SS Hauptsturmführer* Karl Sommer were all now subordinate to Pohl.

This subordination of the concentration camps was designed to ensure a more effective coordination of their security/penal and economic functions, and the effective assertion of the new economic priorities. This significant shift in emphasis in their role was reflected in a string of orders which went out from Himmler and Pohl in March and April 1942. In order to maintain control over the labour deployment of concentration camp inmates, Himmler was anxious to try and concentrate production in and around the camps and if possible carry it out within the SS's own plants. The following document contains the minutes of a meeting in the office of Speer's deputy as Armaments Minister Karl-Otto Saur on 17 March 1942, attended by representatives of the WVHA:

---

[41] See below, pp. 241ff.
[42] See Georg, op. cit., pp. 25ff.

**1027**    Re: *Transfer of the finishing stage of armaments production to concentration camps.*

Following a meeting in the Führer's headquarters, the concentration camps are to become more involved in the armaments industry. At yesterday's meeting *Brigadeführer* Glücks announced that the following camps were envisaged for such a deployment:

| | |
|---|---|
| Buchenwald | with roughly 5,000 capable of work |
| Sachsenhausen | with roughly 6,000 capable of work |
| Neuengamme | with roughly 2,000 capable of work |
| Auschwitz | with roughly 6,000 capable of work |
| Ravensbrück | with roughly 6,000 capable of work (women) |
| Lublin | is being filled up |

A large influx of prisoners is expected at the end of this month. All the craftsmen and those in related occupations will be removed and assigned to those camps which are taking on armaments production.

According to a decree issued by the *Reichsführer SS* the work must be carried out in the camps. The firms involved must, therefore, transfer their production to the area of the camp and ensure the temporary provision of engineers and foremen for training the prisoners . . .

The whole task of mobilizing the concentration camps for armaments production has been taken on by State Councillor . . . He will initiate two pilot projects as soon as possible in Buchenwald-Weimar and Neuengamme camps.

───

On 30 April 1942, Pohl reported to Himmler on what he had done since he had taken over the concentration camps on 3 March:

**1028**    I am reporting to you today on the current situation of the concentration camps and on measures which I have taken to implement your order of 3 March.

I. 1. At the outbreak of war the following concentration camps were in operation:

| | | | | | |
|---|---|---|---|---|---|
| (a) Dachau | 1939 | 4,000 | now | 8,000 inmates |
| (b) Sachsenhausen | 1939 | 6,500 | now | 10,000 inmates |
| (c) Buchenwald | 1939 | 5,300 | now | 9,000 inmates |
| (d) Mauthausen | 1939 | 1,500 | now | 5,500 inmates |
| (e) Flossenbürg | 1939 | 1,600 | now | 4,700 inmates |
| (f) Ravensbrück | 1939 | 2,500 | now | 7,500 inmates |

2. In the years 1940 to 1942 nine more camps were established, namely

| | | |
|---|---|---|
| (a) Auschwitz | (d) Natzweiler | (g) Niederhagen |
| (b) Neuengamme | (e) Gross-Rosen | (h) Stutthof |
| (c) Güsen | (f) Lublin | (i) Arbeitsdorf |

3. Apart from these 15 camps which, in terms of their functions and operation, in the composition of their command staffs and their protective custody camp

duties, correspond exactly to the organization of the old concentration camps, additional tasks were assigned to the following:

(a) SS Special Camp Hinzert: the command staffs and guards are subordinate to me. The protective custody camp is subordinate to the Reich Security Main Office. No plants, no opportunity for work.

(b) Moringen Youth Detention Camp, no plants.

(c) Uckermarck Youth Detention Camp, under construction.

(d) Litzmannstadt [Lodz] Youth Detention Camp, planned.

4. In recent weeks the Reich Security Head Office and the commandant of the Waffen SS has requested SS leaders for the camps planned by these departments in Riga, Kiev, and Bobrusk.

I think such plans should be referred to the SS Economic Administration Office so that they can be uniformly planned and implemented for the SS by one agency. Otherwise there may be a duplication of effort and, as a result, confusion may occur.

II 1. The war has produced a marked change in the structure of the concentration camps and a fundamental alteration in the tasks on which prisoners should be employed.

The incarceration of inmates simply on grounds of security or for educative or preventive reasons alone is no longer paramount. The main emphasis has shifted to the economic side. The mobilization of the labour resources of all inmates, initially for wartime tasks (to raise armaments production) and later for peacetime tasks is becoming increasingly important.

2. This obliges us to take the requisite measures to secure a gradual transition of the concentration camps from their previously one-sided political form into an organization appropriate to their economic tasks.

3. Thus, I assembled all the leaders of the former Concentration Camp Inspectorate, all camp commandants and all directors of works on the 23 and 24.4.1942 and explained the new developments to them personally. I have summarized the essential things, which need to be urgently implemented, in order that the armaments work can be got under way without delay in the enclosed directive.

4. The transfer of the Concentration Camp Inspectorate to the Economic Administration Head Office has been implemented with the full agreement of all the main offices involved. All the agencies are cooperating smoothly; the elimination of the parallel operations in the concentration camps is generally welcomed as the removal of fetters which were hampering progress.

■■■

In order to effect this shift in priorities from security to economic production, it was necessary to involve the concentration camp commandants, who had hitherto shown little sympathy for the needs of the local SS plants. Thus, on the same day, Pohl issued the following order to the concentration camp commandants:

**1029**    1. The camp commandant is responsible for the leadership of the concentration camp and all business operations which come within its scope. He alone, therefore, is responsible for the maximum productivity of its business operations.

2. The camp commandant will utilize the works director for running the business activities. The works director must inform the camp commandant if he fears that a particular order from him will cause economic problems or disadvantages.

3. This duty ensures that the works director will share the responsibility for any economic damage or failure.

4. The camp commandant is solely responsible for the deployment of the workers. In order to maximize performance this deployment must be, in the true sense of the word, exhausting.

Work will only be assigned centrally through the Head of Department D. The camp commandants are not permitted to take on work from third parties or conduct negotiations on their own initiative.

5. There are no limits to the hours of work. The length of work time depends on the structure of the plants in the camp and on the type of work to be carried out and is solely a matter for the camp commandant.

6. All factors which may shorten work time (meals, roll calls etc.) are, therefore, to be reduced to an absolute minimum. Lengthy marches to work and lunch breaks simply for the purpose of eating are banned.

7. The old methods of guarding prisoners are to be replaced and made more flexible in the light of the future peacetime tasks. Mounted guards, the deployment of guard dogs and mobile watch towers and barriers are to be developed.

8. The implementation of this order will impose considerably greater demands on every camp commandant than hitherto. Since few camps share the same characteristics, no generally applicable directives will be issued. Instead, the camp commandant will be made wholly responsible. He must combine clear professional expertise in military and economic matters with a shrewd and wise leadership of those groups of people whom he is to bring to a high level of performance.

———

Initially there were to be two test projects for the location of plants in concentration camps, one at Buchenwald camp near Weimar and the other at Neuengamme near Hamburg. At Buchenwald, for example, the Gustloff works, controlled by the local Gauleiter, Fritz Sauckel, established a large plant making rifle barrels. There were a number of other instances of firms establishing plants in and around concentration camps, most notoriously the artificial rubber or 'Buna' plant built near Auschwitz by the giant chemical combine, IG Farben, which came to be known as Auschwitz III.[43] However, Himmler was anxious to try and

———

[43] On Auschwitz III see Vol. 3, docs. 887–904.

secure armament production facilities located in and around the camps under the control of the SS, thereby increasing its self-sufficiency.

However, the Armaments Ministry was determined to resist the SS's attempts to acquire substantial production facilities and, in any case, by 1943, it was becoming clear that, such was the demand for labour, that the idea of requiring firms to relocate their production facilities to the camps on a large scale was simply not feasible. Instead of the plants moving to the prisoners, the prisoners would have to move to the plants. The result was the creation of large numbers of satellite camps (*Aussenlager*) or 'external work details' (*Aussenkommandos*), often a long distance away from their base camps (*Stammlager*). Camps like Buchenwald and Auschwitz functioned like monstrous fungi spawning camps all over Germany, camps in which the conditions were often even more barbaric than in the main camps. By October 1944, for example, Buchenwald had 66 external work details in which 65,000 prisoners were employed by armaments firms. The procedure whereby industry recruited concentration camp workers was described in a statement made on oath to the Nuremberg Tribunal in 1947 by *SS Hauptsturmführer* Karl Sommer, the deputy head of the WVHA section responsible for the deployment of concentration camp prisoners as workers in industry.

**1030**     The deployment of KZ [concentration camp] prisoners in German industry began in the months of August–September 1942. It happened as a result of pressure from the Armaments Ministry which wanted thereby to enable the industrial plants to fulfil the orders they had been given. I recall that concentration camp prisoners were deployed in almost all German industrial firms which were capable of employing large numbers of KZ prisoners. The number of KZ prisoners employed by the individual firms varied. They were not deployed unless at least about 500 KZ inmates could be employed in a plant. The largest number of KZ prisoners employed in a plant was between 40,000 and 50,000. In total there were about 500,000 KZ inmates employed in the whole of German industry at the height of the deployment.

The KZ prisoners, who were placed at the disposal of an industrial firm, were housed in specially constructed camps on the site of the plant. Such camps were called work camps . . .

The selection of KZ prisoners as industrial workers was done purely on the basis of their manual and technical capabilities. For this purpose a commission from the plant was often brought into the concentration camp before a work deployment which examined the individual inmates in terms of the particular skills and abilities required. If it became clear in the course of the deployment that individuals were not up to the technical demands made on them then the KZ exchanged them for other workers . . .

At this time (roughly since spring 1943), a firm paid the Reich Treasury a fixed sum of 4 RM per day for an unskilled labourer and 6 RM for a skilled worker. But the prisoners got no benefit from these higher scales since this so-called wage was passed on to the Reich via the WVHA. Plants in private industry approached us if they needed workers and we directed the appropriate concentration camp to supply them with so and so many prisoners, provided the Speer Ministry had confirmed the priority status . . .

As far as I can remember concentration camp inmates were deployed at the following work places:

From Buchenwald concentration camp: . . . [There follows a list of firms, including BMW, Junkers, Rheinmetall Borsig, and Bochumer Verein AG].

Various plants from the private sector were located directly in concentration camps or directly outside them, e.g. Krupp in Auschwitz, where fuses were produced under the supervision of Krupp engineers and foreman. The Siemens concern had a plant in Ravensbrück camp and another one in Auschwitz camp. The Walther Weapons Works Zella Mehlis ran a plant in Buchenwald making rifles. The Gustloff Works AG had a plant next to Buchenwald. Zeppelin Airship Construction produced barrage balloons in a works next to Sachsenhausen. The Metal Works Neuengamme (Walther, Zella-Mehlis) ran a works in Neuengamme concentration camp . . .

IG Farben was given priority in the provision of KZ inmates over all other armaments plants for its Buna production. Maurer informed me of the instruction only to assign inmates to other plants when the Buna needs had been met.

Firms regularly applied to WVHA Section D/Maurer for the assignment of inmates as workers, in individual cases to Glücks, and only if they had a personal contact to Pohl direct. Now and again firms applied to the commandants of the individual KZ camps to get prisoners, contrary to the procedure described above. When the section had approved the use of KZ inmates, the accommodation and security arrangements in the plants were inspected either by Maurer or by a commandant of a KZ camp. If the preconditions for the employment, particularly in relation to security had been met, then the relevant KZ camp was instructed to supply an appropriate number of inmates. The firms concerned were requested to select from the available material in the relevant KZ camp or, if necessary, from several KZ camps the most suitable workers.

Their representatives then entered the camps for this purpose, accompanied by the camp commandant or his representative, and in the process could see the conditions which existed in the KZ camp concerned.

Thus, the Armaments Ministry and the SS became locked into a kind of alliance from which each drew benefits but which was marked by tension. This tension forms the subject of the following letter from *Brigadeführer* Dr Walther Schieber to Albert Speer, dated 7 May 1944. In theory Schieber was Himmler's contact man in the Armaments

Ministry but as a department head in Speer's ministry his loyalty was more with Speer:

**1031**   In the last few weeks the increasingly difficult labour situation has become intolerable as a result of the removal of highly trained workers from the branches of the finishing industry whose production benefits the armaments sector as a whole.

As a result of an agreement between the Reich Minister of Justice and the General Plenipotentiary for Labour Mobilization, it had been settled that those prisoners with lengthy sentences working in the armaments industry should continue to be employed in their existing plants after their release by being conscripted. But this agreement is being increasingly broken on the basis of an earlier arrangement between the *Reichsführer SS* and Minister Thierack, in that those prisoners who have completed their sentences are being transferred to employment in SS plants. In particular, the so-called asocials, but also other species of prisoners who, after years of employment in the armaments industry, have been trained to become skilled or semi-skilled workers, are thereby being lost to the plants of the armaments industry. In view of the continually increasing labour shortage, their removal represents a serious disruption and damages the completion of important military equipment.

In this connection, I feel obliged to inform you of a still greater disruption of work in our plants and a very serious threat to production, which I already mentioned to you in Merino. We are losing a significant number of the high percentage of foreign, and in particular Russian, workers in our armaments plants through their gradual transfer to the SS plants. You know that we have been satisfied with the work of the Russian workers—particularly of the women —when they have been sensibly treated. Many of them, who understandably tend to favour moving jobs, are now being assigned to SS plants on the grounds that they have committed some offence and so do not return to their old workplace. This withdrawal of labour is being caused by the increasing enlargement of the SS business concern, which is being consistently pursued by *Obergruppenführer* Pohl in particular. To the numerous plants already producing civilian goods are being added increasing numbers of well-known and also secret weapons-producing and general armaments plants.

Following on from the technical and economic successes in the big wood-working plant in Dachau, the *Reichsführer SS* has decided to get involved in a big way in business activities and to establish an increasingly large number of plants as a financial basis for the various tasks carried out by the SS. This has a lot to do with the SS's marked hostility to the concept of business self-administration.[44] This expansion is much facilitated by the virtually unlimited control over workers—some of them highly trained—attached to the KZ camps. This development was accelerated by your previous refusal to provide the SS directly with a specific proportion of our weapons production. I would like to mention here as examples: the transformation of the large SS brick

---

[44] On business self-administration, see pp. 207 and 221ff.

works at Oranienburg, the reconditioning plant in the Oranienburg camp, the
SS decision to start manufacturing electrical products near Getewend,
the pistol production in Karlsruhe, the arms production in Buchenwald,
Mauthausen and Neuengamme, the attempt to produce chemical products
(nitrogen etc.), which has so far been resisted, the production of motor vehicles
in the Protectorate etc.

The development referred to above was fortunately limited and virtually
stopped by last autumn's agreement with the *Reichsführer SS* that, in return for
the provision of workers from the SS camps, depending on the numbers of
hours worked, a certain proportion of armaments and weapons production
would be assigned to the *Waffen SS* and the police. In return, however, we had
to put up with the establishment of the KZ departments in our armaments
plants with all the friction they cause. However, the practical and human success
which has been achieved far outweighs the disadvantages which are mainly
caused by the jealousy of the lower ranks of the SS leadership. However, the
current policy of the SS is not only destroying the initial success which has been
achieved, but a large number of foreign workers are being removed from us
because the number of KZ inmates is being increased at all costs; it is being
done by transferring foreigners from the foreigners' camps to KZ camps on the
grounds of their having committed some offence however insignificant. In
addition, there is the SS's demand that we hand over the many Jewish and, in
particular, female workers who are working in the supply industry and here in
the electrical industry and who, as I am happy to admit, work gladly and very
hard. In view of the food supplies, which our plant leaders keep managing to get
hold of for the camp workers they employ, despite all the difficulties, and in view
of the decent and humane treatment of the foreign and KZ workers, the
Jewesses and the KZ inmates will presumably work hard and do everything in
order not to be sent back to the camps. These facts suggest that really we should
transfer even more KZ inmates to the armaments industry.

The need to maximize production obliged D Branch of the WVHA to
introduce a more relaxed and somewhat less brutal regime in the
concentration camps. The camp commandants were ordered to cease the
continual harassment of prisoners through such practices as the lengthy
and exhausting roll calls, which forced the prisoners to stand at attention
for hours in all weathers, and the camp doctors were ordered to pay
more attention to trying to heal sick prisoners instead of having them
killed. As part of this new policy, on 15 May 1943, Pohl issued the
following Service Instructions for the KZ commandants:

**1032**    The extent and urgency of all the work which is being carried out by
prisoners requires the highest level of performance from every prisoner. The
current results must, therefore, be improved. This will be achieved through the
leadership and education of the prisoners and by granting them privileges.

For this purpose I am issuing the following

*Service Instructions*

Prisoners who demonstrate hard work, prudence, and good behaviour will in future receive privileges. These consist in the granting of:

1. Relaxation of confinement conditions. 2. Additional food. 3. Financial rewards. 4. Tobacco. 5. Brothel visits.

2. Relaxation of confinement conditions . . . Reich German prisoners may, with the consent of the Commandant, be permitted to let their hair grow . . .

5. Only the best workers should be permitted to visit the brothel on request and as a special reward. The prisoners concerned should make a brief request to the camp commandant via the Protective Custody Camp Leader, who should consider the request and reach an immediate decision. The Camp Commandant is empowered to grant permission in individual cases for a maximum of a weekly visit to the brothel. I emphasize, however, that only prisoners with exceptional performance records should be permitted to do so. Prisoners must pay a fee of RM 2 to visit the brothel. The payment will take the form of a ticket for this amount which the prisoner will receive at his place of work in return for the additional work he has performed. The brothel inmate will receive RM 0.45, the female prisoner in charge RM 0.05 and the remaining RM 1.50 will be retained for the time being and the accumulated sum reported every six months to the Head of D Branch, for the first time on 10.1.1944 to cover the period up to 31.12.1943.

---

This change of policy was to some extent reflected in generally declining mortality rates in the KZs during 1943, although the situation varied from camp to camp. However, as the military situation further deteriorated, so the regime increasingly turned to miracle cures in the shape of crash programmes to produce the V weapons and the new jet fighters, which were designed to turn the tide in Germany's favour. These crash programmes involved new secret industrial facilities often built underground, whose rapid construction was carried out by concentration camp inmates since their labour could be ruthlessly exploited with a total disregard for their welfare. The most striking example was 'Dora' camp, which began as a labour camp attached to Buchenwald and then, on 29 October 1944, achieved independent status with 32,532 inmates. After the war, two former German prisoners described their experiences in Dora to a Nuremberg trial court:

**1033** We, the undersigned former prisoners of Buchenwald concentration camp state the following freely and without being compelled to do so:

In August 1943 transports of several thousand inmates from KZ Buchenwald were organized to construct the new camp, Dora. Dora camp was located not far from Nordhausen in the Harz [mountains] near the railway station at Niedersachswerfen. Over the years, as a result of the extraction of ammonia, a tunnel with chambers leading off it had been created, which was originally intended for the storage of fuel. It was now the task of the prisoners who had been transported there to turn these tunnels and chambers into a factory for the production of the V weapons (V1,V2). At that time, there was not yet a camp there for accommodating the prisoners. Thus, these chambers functioned as the prisoners' sleeping quarters and their workplace; they had to sleep on the bare rock with no straw and without blankets. Because of the continual blasting being carried out . . . the gases which were created could not escape. There were absolutely no arrangements for ventilation at all. There was a twelve-hour working day. Meals consisted of a piece of bread, about 20 grams of margarine and a litre of warm soup which was only provided every three or four days. As a result of this inadequate supply of food and the fact that there was absolutely no water to drink or to wash with, because of the inhuman accommodation and the fact that the prisoners were not allowed into the open air for weeks or months at a time and, as a result of the poisonous gases which accumulated in the immediate proximity of the prisoners because of the blasting, around 200 prisoners a day died a miserable death. The tunnel and chambers were covered with the corpses of prisoners which were then loaded on to wagons or trucks and taken back to Buchenwald to be cremated.

The treatment of the exhausted prisoners by the SS during their twelve-hour shifts was almost indescribably inhuman. The prisoners were beaten to death on the spot with rubber cables, bull whips, shovel handles, iron bars and such like for the slightest offence. Prisoners who had collapsed from exhaustion were beaten and then thrown on to the heap of those who had already died. Then, after a few hours, they died a wretched death. The guards were equipped with police dogs which had been trained to attack the striped uniforms of the prisoners and they arbitrarily unleashed their dogs on the prisoners who could hardly protect themselves from the bites of these animals. During the months of November 1943 to January 1944, the number of deaths increased so much that the transport facilities proved inadequate for removing the dead. So they coped in a way which was typical of the SS mentality. They made wooden pyres and poured oil on them and then burned the bodies. It was only in March 1944 that they built a crematorium.

Since sanitary facilities were totally lacking in the tunnels and because people could not change their clothes for months at a time, since there were not enough supplies, the tunnels were covered with myriads of lice and fleas . . . Almost every day prisoners were hanged for alleged acts of sabotage or because of attempts to escape. In the case of these acts of murder too the SS proved how 'inventive' they were. In the roof of the tunnel there was a crab on which two beams were fixed and thirty nooses were slung over each of them, which were then put round the necks of those who had been condemned to death. The hangman then climbed onto the platform of the crab, started up the crane and so raised all sixty prisoners off the floor in one go. If there were a large number of prisoners who were to be hanged and if this 'pleasure' lasted too long for the SS, then the people who had just been lifted up were let down again half dead and beaten with stools and iron bars or shot in the back of the neck with a pistol.

Although, with the possible exception of Auschwitz III, 'Dora' was the most notorious of the Nazi KZ labour camps, its horrors were only marginally greater than those in many other such camps. In general, between 1942 and 1945, atrocious living and working conditions in the camps had produced high death rates, which had further fuelled the demand for labour. With the SS desperate to increase the number of KZ inmates 'at all costs' the concentration camps had turned into a moloch consuming more and more prisoners from all parts of Europe.

## List of Sources

987  L. Gruchmann, *Justiz im Dritten Reich 1933–1940. Anpassung und Unterwerfung in der Ära Gürtner* (Munich 1988), p. 921.

988  Ibid., p. 924, f.n. 38.

989  R.J. Evans, *Rituals of Retribution: Capital Punishment in Germany 1600–1987* (Oxford 1996), pp. 916–17.

990  *Reichsgesetzblatt* (RGBl.) I 1939, p. 1456.

991  *Deutsche Allgemeine Zeitung* No. 419, 2 September 1943.

992  *Reichsgesetzblatt* I 1939, p. 1683.

993  *Völkischer Beobachter*, 16 December 1939.

994  Bundesarchiv (BA) Potsdam Film No. 1, 124.

995  RGBl. I 1939, pp. 1609ff.

996  *Höchstrichterliche Rechtssprechung* 1942, No. 36.

997  RGBl. I 1939, p. 1679.

998  *Höchstrichterliche Rechtssprechung* 1941, No. 834.

999  RGBl. I 1939, p. 2319.

1000  *Höchstrichterliche Rechtssprechung* 1940, No. 1140.

1001  RGBl. I 1939, p. 2378.

1002  *Höchstrichterliche Rechtssprechung* 1942, No. 330.

1003  Bundesarchiv Berlin (BA) R 22/943. There is an English translation of part of the justification for the law in N. Frei, *National Socialist Rule in Germany: The Führer State 1933–1945* (London 1993), pp. 182–6.

1004  (a) B. Blau, 'Die Kriminalität in Deutschland während des zweiten Weltkrieges', in *Zeitschrift für die gesamte Strafrechtswissenschaft*, 64 (1952), p. 34; (b) ibid., pp. 56–7; (c) ibid., p. 58.

1005  T.W. Mason, *Arbeiterklasse und Volksgemeinschaft* (Cologne 1974), No. 180.

1006  *Vierteljahrshefte für Zeitgeschichte* 6, 4 (October 1958), pp. 405–7.

1007  *Der Prozess gegen die Hauptkriegsverbrecher vor dem Internationalen Militärgerichtshof*, Vol. XXXVIII (Nuremberg 1949), pp. 102–3.

1008  M. Broszat, 'Zur Perversion der Strafjustiz im Dritten Reich. Dokumentation', *Vierteljarshefte für Zeitgeschichte*, 6 (1958), pp. 422–3.

1009  BAB R 58/990.

1010  BAB R 22/3367.

1011  BAB R 22/3370.

1012  I. Staff, *Justiz im Dritten Reich* (Frankfurt/M 1964), pp. 102–3.
1013  H.A. Jacobsen and W. Jochmann, eds., *Ausgewählte Dokumente zur Geschichte des Nationalsozialismus 1933 bis 1945* (Bielefeld 1966), Document 12. IX.
1014  BAB R 58/990.
1015  H. Boberach, ed., *Richterbriefe. Dokumente zur Beeinflussung der deutschen Rechtsprechung 1942–1944* (Boppard 1975), pp. 1–3.
1016  Ibid., pp. 48–51.
1017  Ibid., pp. 469–72.
1018  BAB R 22/3370.
1019  Ibid.
1020  BAB R 22/4692.
1021  Nuremberg Document (ND) PS-654.
1022  Benedikt Kautsky, *Teufel und Verdammte. Erfahrungen und Erkenntnisse aus sieben Jahren in deutschen Konzentrationslagern* (Vienna 1961), pp. 159ff.
1023  BAB R 58/1027.
1024  *Der Prozess gegen die Hauptkriegsverbrecher vor dem Internationalen Militärgerichtshof,* Vol. XXXVIII (Nuremberg, 1949), pp. 695ff.
1025  *The Buchenwald Report* (Boulder/San Francisco/Oxford 1995), p. 109.
1026  *Buchenwald. Mahnung und Verpflichtung. Dokumente und Berichte* (East Berlin 1983), pp. 248–9.
1027  Ibid., pp. 249–50.
1028  Ibid., pp. 250–2.
1029  Ibid., pp. 256–7.
1030  Ibid., pp. 253–6.
1031  Ibid., p. 260.
1032  ND NO-400.
1033  *Buchenwald. Mahnung und Verpflichtung,* op. cit., pp. 274–5.

# CHAPTER 43

# The Economy

## (i) Introduction

The most striking feature of the history of the German war economy is the contrast between its early phase, 1939–41, marked by a poor productive performance in which output per worker in the arms industry actually fell by 24 per cent and Germany was outperformed by Britain in the production of most types of weapon, and the period 1942–44, when German production grew by leaps and bounds despite the growing problems created by the air war. The change is illustrated by the following figures:

**1034** (a) *The Index of German armaments production 1940–1944* (January–February 1942 = 100)

| Year | Total production | Weapons | Tanks | Motor vehicles | Aeroplanes | Ships | Munitions |
|------|------|------|------|------|------|------|------|
| 1940 | 97  | 79  | 36  | –   | –   | 11  | 163 |
| 1941 | 98  | 106 | 81  | –   | 97  | 110 | 102 |
| 1942 | 142 | 137 | 130 | 120 | 133 | 142 | 166 |
| 1943 | 222 | 234 | 330 | 138 | 216 | 182 | 247 |
| 1944 | 277 | 348 | 536 | 110 | 277 | 157 | 306 |

(b) *Comparison of the rate of armament production of the combatant powers* (1944 = 100)

|         | 1938 | 1939 | 1940 | 1941 | 1942 | 1943 | 1944 |
|---------|------|------|------|------|------|------|------|
| USA     | 2  | 2  | 6  | 11 | 47 | 91  | 100 |
| Canada  | 0  | 2  | 6  | 27 | 73 | 102 | 100 |
| Britain | 4  | 10 | 34 | 59 | 83 | 100 | 100 |
| USSR    | 12 | 20 | 30 | 53 | 71 | 100 | 100 |
| Germany | 6  | 20 | 35 | 35 | 51 | 80  | 100 |
| Japan   | 8  | 10 | 16 | 32 | 49 | 72  | 100 |

In the past it was thought by many historians that this discrepancy in production between the two periods was produced by two different strategies pursued by the German leadership. During the first phase, Germany allegedly followed a Blitzkrieg strategy of short 'lightning wars', designed to plunder industrial plant and raw materials, which did not require the full mobilization of German economic resources through a switch from civilian to military production. Then, as a result of the difficulties encountered in Russia in the winter of 1941–2, Germany was forced to confront the fact that its Blitzkrieg strategy had failed and so it was obliged to follow a new economic policy of total mobilization for war. Thus, in the view of these historians, the massive increase in German war production during 1942–4 was primarily the result of the switch in German resources from civilian to war production.[1]

However, research over the past decade or so has shown that this analysis is flawed.[2] For it is now clear that, while Hitler was anxious wherever possible to fight short 'lightning wars', his economic policy was geared to the belief that one must prepare for long wars. As he told his top military chiefs on 23 May 1939: 'Everybody's Armed Forces and/or Government must strive for a short war. But the Government must, however, also prepare for a war of from ten to fifteen years duration.'[3] In short, Hitler believed in pursuing a Blitzkrieg strategy in the *military* sphere, wherever possible, but a total war strategy in the *economic* sphere. With the Four-Year Plan of 1936 he had aimed to provide the raw materials for a massive rearmament drive which envisaged Germany becoming involved in a major war at some time in 1943–5. Thus in 1938–9 he launched the Air Force Plan 8 designed to achieve a fivefold increase in the Luftwaffe, the 'Z Plan' intended to produce a battle fleet, and a large-scale motorization plan for the army.

The outbreak of war in September 1939 came at a time when these various plans with their huge and competing claims on German resources were in the process of being implemented. A partial mobilization had already been achieved in the sense that the economy was governed by numerous regulations geared to war. However, full mobilization did not proceed nearly as smoothly or effectively as suggested by Nazi propaganda. As we have seen, even before the outbreak of war, German economic mobilization for war had been

---

[1] See in particular Alan Milward, *The German War Economy* (Oxford 1965).

[2] See in particular the work of Richard Overy referred to in the bibliography and of Rolf-Dieter Müller (see n. 6) to both of whom the present chapter is much indebted.

[3] See Vol. 3, doc. 539.

bedevilled by a lack of coherent planning and organization.[4] The main problem was the lack of a central agency which could coordinate the various military and civilian departments involved in armaments production and issue clear guidelines and authoritative instructions. The Reich Defence Council established in 1938 met very rarely and, in any case, Göring had announced that he and his Four-Year Plan organization were responsible for gearing the economy for war. In practice, however, they failed to do so. Nor had the problem been solved by the creation, on the outbreak of war, of the Ministerial Council for the Defence of the Reich under Göring, since, as we have seen, the new organization failed to develop into an effective war cabinet.[5] Hitler envisaged Göring as the man to drive through economic mobilization. However, Göring was preoccupied by his role as head of the air force and as such was in any case *parti pris* in the struggle for resources and so part of the problem rather than the solution.

Instead of being subject to a single coordinating and directing agency, therefore, economic mobilization was subject to the continued existence of two agencies competing for control, each of which had its own field organisation—the GBW/Economics Ministry under Walter Funk with its District Economic Offices (*Bezirkswirtschaftsämter*), and the Wehrmacht Economics and Armaments Office (*Wehrwirtschafts- und Rüstungsamt*=WiRüA) under General Georg Thomas with its regional Armaments Inspectorates and its district Armaments Commandos, which exercised supervisory powers over armaments plants. Moreover, the WiRüA itself faced the problem of trying to coordinate and balance the demands of the three branches of the Wehrmacht, each of which was competing fiercely for allocations of raw materials, factory space and labour to produce the weapons which it claimed were essential and whose specifications it had determined. Similarly, within the civilian sector there were divisions between the officials of the Economics Ministry and Funk's staff in his role as GBW. The problem was that, in addition to the usual rivalries deriving from departmental self-interest, the military and civilian sectors were governed by somewhat different priorities. While the Wehrmacht was interested in absolute priority for arms production, the Economics Ministry was under pressure from the Party and the Propaganda Ministry to avoid placing undue burdens on the civilian population and to avoid imposing too many bureaucratic regulations, a position for which the Führer himself on occasion

---

[4] See above, pp. 2ff.
[5] See above, pp. 4ff.

expressed sympathy. Meanwhile, industry was caught between these two organizations. A leading industrialist had already made the point in March 1939 'that business did not mind whether it was governed by a helmet or a top hat but they ought to decide in favour of one or the other kind of headgear'.[6] In fact, industry had its own agenda which was concerned with avoiding being dragooned into a straitjacket of state controls in a militarized economy and being forced to commit itself to a major reorganization of its plant and a massive capital investment for the production of military equipment if—as for much of 1939–40 seemed to be the case—peace was just round the corner.

The history of the German war economy between 1939 and 1942 is essentially the history of the gradual emergence of institutional arrangements which ensured effective coordination of the competing demands on resources and enabled a more or less coherent prioritization to be carried out. It is also the story of how the top hat replaced the helmet in the sense that the dominant influence of the Wehrmacht, which had characterized the war economy at the beginning of the war, was progressively eroded through the growing influence of businessmen and engineers (technocrats) who were integrated into the new administrative machinery. It was these developments which in turn facilitated the rationalization processes at plant level, which contributed so crucially to the astonishing increases in the production of war matériel between 1942 and 1944. Finally, the history of the German war economy provides an excellent case study of government in the Third Reich.

## (ii) The Attempt at a Full-Scale Mobilization of the Economy for War 1939–1940

(a) *The War Economy Decree of 4 September 1939*

As a result of Hitler's hope that war with the West could be avoided, full economic mobilization was delayed until 3 September when Hitler issued his Directive No. 2 for the Conduct of the War, which decreed 'the conversion of the whole German economy onto a war footing'. On the following day, a War Economy Decree was issued. This represented an

---

[6] Cf. Rolf-Dieter Müller, 'Die Mobilisierung der deutschen Wirtschaft für Hitlers Kriegführung', in B. Kroener, R. D. Müller and H. Umbreit, *Das Deutsche Reich und der Zweite Weltkrieg,* Vol. 51: *Organisation und Mobiliserung des deutschen Machtbereichs. Kriegsverwaltung, Wirtschaft und personelle Resourcen 1939–1941* (Stuttgart 1988), p. 375. The present chapter owes much to this piece.

attempt by the authorities to use the crisis to reverse the trend towards rising wages and increasing bonuses, which had resulted from the growing labour shortage during the pre-war period, while at the same time raising taxes on the better off:

**1035** The safeguarding of the frontiers of our fatherland necessitates big sacrifices from every German citizen. The soldier is protecting our homeland with his weapons at the risk of his life. In view of the extent of this commitment, it is the obvious duty of all citizens at home to put all their strength and resources at the disposal of the nation and Reich and thereby to guarantee the continuation of an orderly economic life. This means above all that all citizens must impose upon themselves the necessary restrictions on their standard of living. Therefore, the Ministerial Council for the Defence of the Reich decrees with the force of law:

SECTION I: BEHAVIOUR DETRIMENTAL TO THE WAR EFFORT

(i) Anyone who destroys, conceals, or hoards raw materials or products which are essential to the existence of the population and thereby maliciously endangers the supply of these goods will be punished with penal servitude or hard labour. In particularly serious cases the death penalty may be imposed.
(ii) Those who hoard bank notes without good reason will be punished with hard labour, in particularly serious cases with penal servitude.

SECTION II: WAR TAXES

*War surtax on income tax . . .*
2. *Those liable to tax*
(i) The Reich will levy a war surtax on income tax.
(ii) Those liable to income tax at the standard rate whose income does not exceed RM 2,400 are exempt from the war surtax.
3. *Amount of war surtax on income tax*
(i) The war surtax on income tax is 50 per cent of the income tax for the tax collection period . . .
(ii) The war surtax on income tax may not amount to more than 15 per cent of income, income tax and war surtax on income tax may not amount to more that 65 per cent of income . . .
[Special war taxes were also imposed on beer and tobacco.]

SECTION III: WAR WAGES

. . . 18. The Reich Trustees and Special Trustees of Labour, on instructions from the Reich Minister of Labour, will adjust wages immediately to wartime conditions and will fix a compulsory maximum limit for wages, salaries and conditions of work.
(i) If new plants or administrative offices are established or reorganized, or if workmen or employees carry out a different form of employment than hitherto after this decree has come into effect, the same wage or salary levels apply as for

similar plants or administrative offices as those which are standard for the new occupation. If any doubts arise as to which wage and salary scales should be used, the Reich Trustee or Special Trustee of Labour will make the decisions.

(ii) Bonuses for overtime work, and for Sunday, national holiday, and night shifts are no longer to be paid.

(iii) Paragraphs 1–3 apply equally to remuneration and other work conditions in home labour.

19. Regulations and agreements on holidays are temporarily suspended. More detailed instructions on their reinstitution will be given by the Reich Minister of Labour.

20. The Reich Minister of Labour can make decisions on the announcement and content of wage scales and regular hours of work which deviate from existing regulations. For public administrative offices and plants the Reich Minister of Labour makes these decisions in agreement with the Reich Ministers concerned.

21. (i) Anyone who promises or grants wages or salaries or accepts a promise or grant contrary to paragraphs 18–20 of this decree will be punished with a disciplinary penalty in the form of an unlimited fine for each violation. The same punishment will apply to those who demand or grant more favourable working conditions than are permitted according to the regulations of this decree. Appeals to the Reich Minister of Labour against disciplinary penalties are permitted.

(ii) In serious cases the sentence will be hard labour or penal servitude. Prosecutions will be instituted at the request of the Reich Trustee or Special Trustee of Labour. The charge can be withdrawn . . .

SECTION IV: WAR PRICES

Prices and charges for goods and services of all kinds must be fixed in accordance with the principles of the war economy.

23. (i) Prices and charges for goods and services of all kinds are to be reduced in so far as savings in wage costs for goods and services occur as a result of Section III of this decree.

(ii) Prices and charges for goods and services of all kinds must in future be based on the wages and salaries permitted according to Section III of this decree, these being treated as the maximum.

(iii) Social benefits for the retinue, which are not prescribed as compulsory in laws, decrees, or wage scales, must be used to determine prices and changes only in so far as they are customary for that particular business and are not contrary to the principles of economical business methods.

(iv) It is forbidden to demand or permit higher prices or charges than those laid down as permissible in paragraphs 1–3 . . .

However, the wage provisions of this decree caused widespread discontent among the labour force. Martin Mutschmann, the Gauleiter and RVK of Saxony, one of the largest industrial areas, wrote to the Ministerial Committee for the Defence of the Reich on 2 October 1939:

**1036**  In his express letter III 16591/39 of 4 September 1939 the Reich Minister of Labour has instructed the Reich Trustees of Labour to adjust wages in accordance with the requirements of the war economy.

The Reich Trustees of Labour in the Defence Economy District IV have consequently introduced a new system of wages and working conditions for all existing wage scales. In the heavily industrialized Gau Saxony a particularly large number of wage scales are due for readjustment.

This measure has produced unrest in the economy which is politically undesirable and has not only economic but above all social side effects in that the workers fear they are now going to be subjected to strong pressure on wages. This rigid fixing of upper limits for piecework is felt especially acutely since the consumer goods industries, which predominate in Defence Economy District IV, are still understaffed and, on account of the war, have to work increasingly long hours. The planned rigid restriction of piecework wages is, moreover, uneconomical since it has a negative influence on people's enthusiasm and productivity. This danger exists particularly in the metal industry, which is so important for the war economy, because, in the context of the new wage scales, a drastic reduction in average piecework rates is planned even for this industry.

The fact that the readjustment of wage scales is increasing the previous number of wage group subdivisions causes scales to become unduly complicated whereas they should be fixed as simply and clearly as possible, especially in the present situation, in order to avoid all possibilities for differences and difficulties.

The plan to pay women less in future, instead of the previously approved equal pay for male and female labour, provides an undesirable inducement for the excessive employment of women, particularly in the metal industry.

It seems to me particularly unacceptable that, according to guidelines given by the Reich Ministry of Labour, e.g. the fixing of maximum wages for skilled workers in the metal industry, Gau Saxony, the most important industrial area in Greater Germany with a relatively high cost of living, is to be worse off than other industrial areas with more favourable living conditions.

For these reasons I request that you decree that an extensive alteration of the wage system should not be carried out at present and that only a wage freeze should be ordered, to reduce the exaggerated top wages and enticement wages. Such measures will meet with understanding from the workers.

▬▬▬

Such was the sensitivity of the regime to discontent among the working class that the suggestions of Gauleiter Mutschmann to replace the reduction of wage rates by a wage freeze was adopted by the Government. At the same time, the regime was considering retreat on another provision of the War Economy Decree—the abolition of night and holiday bonuses in Section III, para. 18 (3). This whole question was aired at an interdepartmental conference which throws interesting light on the labour situation at the beginning of the war and on the way in which the political process operated in the Third Reich. The workers had clearly responded to the cancellation of the bonuses by absenteeism and the Government was forced to adjust itself to that fact by restoring the bonuses, although 'the authority of the State would undoubtedly suffer a severe blow' (Thomas[7]). The attempt to compensate for this by reducing the level for income tax exemption could not disguise the fact that the Government had been forced to retreat by pressure from below, which had been supported by various Gauleiters. The bonuses for Sunday, holiday and night work were restored by a decree of 16 November with effect from 27 November 1939. Also, §5 of the Decree on Labour Protection of 12 December 1939 laid down that, with effect from 18 December 1939, 'members of the retinue can claim an appropriate overtime payment for time worked in excess of ten hours per day' and, on 3 September 1940, the ban on overtime payments was lifted altogether with effect from 8 September:

**1037**    *Minutes of the interdepartmental conference with the GBW on 10 November 1939*

Subject of discussion: Bonuses for overtime, night work, and Sunday work.

Participants: State Secretary Posse (Economics Ministry), State Secretary Neumann (Four-Year Plan), State Secretary Syrup (Labour Ministry), *Ministerialdirektor* Mansfeld (Labour Ministry), General Thomas (WiRüA), *Ministerialdirektor* Hedding (Finance Ministry), Flottmann (Reich Price Commissioner), *Ministerialrat* Josten (Economics Ministry), Dr Rigler (Economics Ministry).

State Secretary Posse opened the meeting with the declaration that the Reich Minister of Economics felt obliged to consider the reintroduction of bonuses for overtime, night and Sunday work: (1) because the workers' incomes were no longer sufficient to buy the foodstuffs allocated to them by the rationing regulations; (2) because it had been observed that the ban on bonuses had led to a refusal to do overtime, night and Sunday work and to phenomena which constituted actual sabotage. State Secretary Posse pointed out at the same time that a cancellation of the ban on bonuses would constitute the first official deviation from the War Economy Decree. Simultaneously, this raised the question of the advisability of lowering the level at which incomes become liable to the war surtax on income tax.

In the ensuing debate the following points were made. In the armaments factories the majority of workers had in fact stayed away on Sundays. Similarly, a decrease in night shifts had been noted (Thomas). In addition to this, the usual absenteeism among building workers on Saturdays after they had received their wages on Fridays was now up to 80 per cent (Mansfeld). Only Sunday and night work was regarded as having any importance (Syrup). Moreover, the bonuses were unjust because they were not uniform. They did not correspond to the

---

[7] See below, p. 193.

actual additional expenditure; very often they did not take into account the double amount of food required by workers, e.g. during night shift, which made a tremendous hole in the workers' budget. In the graphics trade, for example, the cancellation of bonuses amounted to 45–50 per cent. This had already required special regulations (against Amann[8]).

The statement that the workers could not even buy everything due to them on their ration cards could not be true for the average worker. (But it could apply to wages actually below average.) It was a fact that sometimes a worker's large family was entitled to more than they had ever bought before. The growth of black market food ration card agencies was proof of that. The very heavy workers were entitled to receive more food than they could use. This was proved by the Pohl memorandum (Labour Research Institute of the DAF), though it was disputed. So far the attempts to achieve the necessary increase in productivity had been made through wage increases. At the moment business was once again demanding such wage increases on a large scale. But today this form of incentive was bound to fail. The average worker did not lack the will to work, but just could take no more. For years he had had to stand up to too hot a pace. This was proved by the sickness reports which had shown a rise in some places of up to 50 per cent of the retinue (Mansfeld).

On the other hand, there had been no wage cuts, so that if the ban on bonus rates, the only sacrifice the workers had had to make so far, was cancelled, the workers would be exceptionally favoured; they would even profit from the war. War could not be waged if one section of the population, the workers, was wrapped in cotton wool. Moreover, the amount of purchasing power was not being matched by the level of production. It must, therefore, be skimmed off, otherwise the result would be inflation (Josten).

In this context, the reintroduction of all bonus rates was discussed, together with the simultaneous imposition of the war surtax on all incomes down to subsistence level, thereby cancelling the previous level of RM 2,400 (RM 234 per month) at which incomes became exempt from the tax. Dr Ley would then probably emphasize the unavoidable cases of hardship in which, for example, a previous surtax of RM 3 could be replaced by one of RM 6. Such a regulation would hit both the small tradesmen and the artisan hard.

Accordingly, a reduction of the exemption level from RM 234 to only RM 150 could be approved, although the reduction of the exemption limit would have undesirable repercussions on people's willingness to work, since no worker would want to work so that his earnings came to slightly over this limit. *Ministerialdirektor* Hedding declared that the reduction in tax revenues with the reintroduction of Sunday and night work bonuses amounted to RM 100–150 million, or, including overtime bonuses, to RM 250–300 million. As a tax specialist, he would welcome the reintroduction of bonuses with a simultaneous reduction in the exemption limit from RM 2,400 to RM 1,800.

The authority of the state would undoubtedly suffer a severe blow if the bonuses were introduced (Thomas). To counteract this impression, the most suitable way would have to be found of compensating for such a concession. In

---

[8] Max Amann, the head of the Eher Verlag, the main Nazi publishing company.

the drafting of the War Economy Decree, which incidentally was done without the participation of the relevant Government departments, the question of bonuses for overtime had been treated from a psychological, not from a material point of view. Undoubtedly it would have been better if the bonuses had never been abolished and if instead the war surtax had been imposed on the workers.

As a result of the discussion, State Secretary Posse will suggest to the Reich Minister of Economics that the Ministerial Council should introduce a decree: (i) to reintroduce the bonuses for Sunday and night work; (ii) to lower the level of income giving exemption from the war surtax from RM 2,400 to RM 1,800.

The Government was of course obliged to bluff in order to disguise its retreat, as is clear from the following extract from the *Völkischer Beobachter* of 20 November, which is also interesting for the pseudo-socialist slant which it gives to Germany's war aims. Moreover, the impression of life returning back to normal was not one which corresponded to the requirements of the full-scale economic mobilization for war, which the military leadership was trying to implement:

**1038**    . . . That is the balance sheet in the social sector of our people after ten weeks of war. At the beginning of the war, the severest sacrifices, the tightening of belts; after ten weeks life back to normal, only a fraction of the powers have had to be used. That was not because the leadership yielded to your demands, workers, but because everything had been so well prepared that these sacrifices were unnecessary. We should almost be ashamed of our small part in the nation's war sacrifices, particularly when we think of the sacrifice in blood made by the soldiers. All the more reason, then, workers, plant leaders and retinue, why we must vow to do everything which the Führer demands of us . . .
Workers! Plant leaders and retinue!
I have tried to give you a balance sheet of our fighting nation after ten weeks of war in telegram-style descriptions of the situation.
*However, the greatest credit factor in this balance sheet is the fact that the Führer lives!*[9]
*Germany's position has never been better and that of England has never been so bad. This time we're going to do it! England will be beaten and you and Germany will be free!*

*Work versus Money-bags!*
*Freedom is ours!*

*Editorial comment*

*Socialist war*
. . . The path which the National Socialist Reich has followed since 1933 has been a path of work and hardship, the path of a poor nation. But, at the same

---

[9] Presumably a reference to the failed assassination attempt on 8 November. See below, pp. 592–94.

time, in this poverty lay our wealth: conscious of the difficulties opening up before us, the whole nation became one big community. We have struggled out of the poverty of the fifteen years of Versailles because all Germans were gripped by the spirit of socialism, because we did not use our minds and our hands for the advantage of individuals or particular classes, but because the rise of the Reich was to the profit of every working German.

It is because of this that Great Britain has declared war on us. The regime of money grubbers, the bastion of capitalism seeks to strangle the Germany that has given the world the example of a socialist order. They fear the effects on their position in England itself, even more they fear for their huge colonial empire. Their subjects inside and outside are no longer to have the National Socialist state before their eyes which, by its mere existence, might turn them into rebels against their exploiters.

This means that Germany is waging the war not only for its own existence, but at the same time for *all* oppressed nations of the world.

▬

(b) *The munitions crisis and the appointment of Fritz Todt as Reich Munitions Minister on 23 March 1940*

In fact, economic mobilization for war proved relatively ineffective and the first six months saw the emergence of what came to be known as the 'munitions crisis'. The end of the war with Poland saw Germany's supplies of munitions seriously depleted and considered inadequate for Hitler's projected campaign in the west (although this point was to some extent played up by generals unwilling to risk war with France at that stage). On the basis of the available figures, new munitions production for the army was only enough to equip one infantry army and one Panzer division per quarter-year. This 'crisis' was not the result of a lack of resources but of a failure to mobilize them effectively, and this in turn was the result not of a lack of will on the part of the authorities but rather of the weaknesses in the system which had already revealed themselves before the war: a lack of clear and coherent leadership from the top; inflated and uncoordinated demands from the three branches of the Wehrmacht; the failure to integrate business effectively into the war economy; and, last but not least, the failure on the part of business to gear its plants fully to war production and to use the most rational methods for the mass production of armaments.

The man responsible for coordinating the military side of economic mobilization, General Thomas, the head of the Economics and Armaments Office of OKW (WiRüA), expressed his frustration over the situation at a meeting with representatives of the Economics Ministry and the Army Weapons Procurement Office (HWaA) to discuss iron and steel quotas held on 21 October 1939:

**1039** *General Thomas*: The [Army] Procurement Office has expressed the opinion that the iron quotas for the armed forces could be increased if the quotas already allocated to the civilian sector of the economy were cut further. Although the distribution of iron supplies was justified in detail at the meeting on 4.10, it still appears necessary to clarify the matter so that General Thomas and General von Hanneken cannot be accused of not doing enough to help the Wehrmacht.

*General von Hanneken*[10]: I have been accused of being to blame if the war is lost. I feel hurt by this accusation and must defend myself against it . . .

*General Stud*[11]: Please may I be provided with the same amount of iron for the first quarter of 1940 I had for the fourth quarter of 1939. Then I could start using this now and that would ease the situation somewhat.

*General von Hanneken*: Please don't keep simply making demands but for once tell me how I can meet these demands . . .

*General Thomas*: At the moment, there is a war of all against all in Germany. That is all the more regrettable since I have made an effort to explain the situation to the Commanders-in-Chief and have pressed urgently for the individual branches of the Wehrmacht to establish priority projects and to utilize the available raw material supplies for these . . .

The general staffs and Weapons Procurement Offices have also had it all explained to them. Everyone responded by demanding that no reserves should be held back and instead that all available supplies of raw materials should be distributed.

So what's the result? New requests have come in from all three branches of the Wehrmacht and that doesn't surprise me when the responsible officials simply regard themselves as commission agents. For example, if no one objects to a direct order from the Führer to transfer 1.9m anti-tank ammunition to the air force then that just shows that neither the top leadership [i.e. Hitler] nor the Army Chiefs have a clear view of the current situation. One cannot expect that. But we must be expected to put our cards on the table and to work together to persuade the Commanders-in-Chief to support a clear solution. I cannot understand how such large amounts of iron are still being put into fortifications. Our iron situation is such that we can either prepare an attack or build fortifications we can't do both.

The same is true of the U-boat programme. First twenty were ordered, now it is thirty. As long as the Commanders-in-Chief go along with all this without objecting we shall never find a solution . . .

I consider it impossible for the army to free up further supplies of iron. The air force has also asked for more but after discussion Colonel-General Milch has accepted that it's impossible to fulfil these demands.

---

[10] General Hermann von Hanneken, head of Department II in the Economics Ministry and Plenipotentiary for Iron and Steel Allocation.

[11] General Erich Stud, a department head in the Army Weapons Procurement Office.

The Commanders-in-Chief must not allow themselves to be side-lined by Todt[12] and Speer[13] but must use their influence with the Führer just as they do . . .
*Colonel Waeger*[14]: The Wehrmacht High Command must achieve a compromise. It is up to Colonel-General Keitel to inform the top leadership.
*General Thomas*: Colonel-General Keitel does not have an overview of how the branches of the Wehrmacht allocate their raw material supplies in detail. It is the responsibility of the Commanders-in-Chief of the individual branches of the Wehrmacht and it is up to them to object if they are given new tasks which cannot be fulfilled.

▬▬▬

General Thomas was anxious to justify his role in the light of the growing criticism of the relatively slowness of German economic mobilization for war and so, on 19 November 1939, he produced the following minute for the record. It reflects his own perspective but does not address some of the key underlying problems, notably the failure to involve business more effectively:

**1040**     *Enclosure 38 dated 19.11.39 RE*

*Reasons for the Slow Start to Economic Mobilization:*
I have gained the impression from my recent interviews with Colonel-General Keitel and Field Marshal Göring, as well as from remarks by the Führer which Keitel passed on to me, that the responsible departments are being blamed for the slow mobilization of the economy for war and in particular the slow increase in munitions production.
    I am, therefore, stating now—19 November 1939—the reasons for the slow start:
1. The failure of the GBW to prepare industry. The fight over plants for the past two years. FM Göring's decision on the Armaments and K.u.1. plants.
2. Inadequate preparation of the munitions factories. The Führer's directive (that munitions production was not that important—what date?).
3. The raw materials situation—steel and non-ferrous metals.
4. The fact that industry was overstretched with orders and the blocking of deliveries as a result of the naval programme.
5. The division of responsibility for mobilization between the Wehrmacht and the rest of the economy.
6. The political view of govt. and people that it would not come to a war with the West. The false hopes of a speedy peace.

---

[12] Dr Fritz Todt was head of the Nazi Party's Main Office for Technology, Inspector General of the Highway System (creator of the autobahns) and responsible for army and naval building projects.
[13] Albert Speer was Hitler's favourite architect and responsible for air force building projects. See below, pp. 225ff.
[14] Colonel Waeger was a representative of the Army Procurement Office.

7. The gunpowder and explosives situation.
8. The labour problem.
9. The other reasons—prices and wages situation . . .

------

Ten days later, Göring read the riot act to the representatives of the Wehrmacht at a meeting on 28 November 1939. The following minutes were prepared for the Commander-in-Chief of the Army:

**1041**    Present: Göring, Reich Economics Minister Funk, the chiefs of the Weapons Procurement Offices of the three branches of the Armed Forces, Major-General Thomas, Major-General Dr Todt, Professor Speer, the Commander of the Reserve Army [General Fromm], the responsible state secretaries.

Field Marshal Göring opened the meeting by saying that the Führer had complained to him that the transition to a war economy was going much too slowly. The armaments projects were not properly organized. There were flaws in the munitions finishing plants. Furthermore, the present organization revealed certain inadequacies in comparison with the armaments planning during the First World War.

Field Marshal Göring urged all the agencies involved to engage in more extensive cooperation, otherwise he would be compelled to appoint an independent munitions minister . . .

In addition, Field Marshal Göring said that industry had still not understood the situation. They were still dreaming of an immediate peace. As a result, they were not changing their approach. This undoubtedly represented a failure on the part of the Reich Economics Ministry. The Reich Economics Ministry, in agreement with the economic warfare staff [i.e. the Wehrmacht agencies] must now at last take a tough line. The only thing that would work was rigorously to close down those plants which were not vital for the war effort or for civilian life. The larger armaments plants must then be instructed as far as possible to subcontract work to the smaller factories which have been closed down. This process should also involve a decentralization in the allocation of Wehrmacht contracts but this would have to be handled unbureaucratically. This would also avoid the problem of workers having to wander round the country like gypsies.

------

The day after the meeting with Göring, on 29 November 1939, General Thomas addressed the main official organization of German industry, the Reich Industry Group, to persuade them to focus more on the war effort:

**1042**    SECRET

Gentlemen! To put you in the picture right away, to start with a few words about our political, military and economic situation. Both Field Marshal Göring and

Colonel-General Keitel have instructed me to tell you in all seriousness that we are at a fateful turning-point in the war. Germany is engaged in a life and death struggle. England has been badly hit by our operation involving the planting of mines and hopes to shake us off through a long-drawn-out war. The Führer, on the contrary, is determined to increase the pressure by all the means at our disposal and to secure victory for Germany through the toughest of military measures. For this purpose the political and military leadership is demanding an expenditure of effort on the part of the German economy, which, in extent and rapidity of implementation, must go far beyond the Hindenburg programme.[15]

Gentlemen, what we have been doing up to now has not represented a war economy but rather a transitional economy [*Übergangswirtschaft*]. It is not up to us to investigate the reasons why this has happened. They are in the first instance political and may have derived from the false hope of the German people that the war will be over by Christmas. Thus the economic mobilization planned for the outbreak of war took a very different course from that we envisaged. In particular, we abandoned its basic principles for fear of unemployment. Thus Directive No. 22 of the Reich Agency for Iron and Steel was relaxed. The production bans were not issued; the majority of plants continued with their peacetime production; raw materials continued to some extent to find their way into production which was not important for the war effort; every plant leader tried to retain his group of skilled workers, all in the hope of an imminent peace. I have been observing this course that our war economy has taken for several weeks, for it could not produce a satisfactory result for us. In the first place, the armament firms did not receive the increase in skilled workers necessary to implement second and third shifts, so that the production of military equipment, and particularly munitions, is insufficient. Furthermore, the changeover of plants to war production, above all in the case of the subcontractors of the armaments firms, has not proceeded and has not been as energetically pushed forward as was required. Industry has not, therefore, managed to start completing the individual programmes of the Wehrmacht branches in a satisfactory manner. I therefore considered it my duty to point this out at the highest level and the Führer has now given instructions for the reorganization of the German economy to proceed with the greatest possible energy and for it to be called upon to make the most vigorous efforts.

Before I turn to details, I would like to begin by referring to the main points which, in the unanimous opinion of the Economics and Armaments Office [*Wehrwirtschafts-und Rüstungsamt = WWiRüA*], the GBW, the Reich Economics Ministry, and the Reich Labour Ministry, require major readjustment.

Restrictions and bans must be imposed in a number of spheres of production not vital to the war effort. The bans must be clear and unequivocal. If they are to achieve their purpose they must not be subsequently relaxed. Regional interests must also be subordinated to the wider and general interests.

By restricting non-essential production, it should be possible to free up workers for the armed forces and to improve deliveries. Sufficient freed-up

---

[15] The crash industrial programme launched in 1916 to solve the munitions crisis.

capacity will also enable the Wehrmacht to distribute its orders and thereby to contribute towards a healthy and sensible spread of the orders. The result of that will in turn be that the workers will remain employed in their home districts and that labour conscription with all its socially and psychologically damaging effects will only need to occur to a limited extent . . .

I would like to use this opportunity to refer to the injunction of Field Marshal Göring that it is treason against the Fatherland to hoard workers where they are not necessary for the completion of projects which are vital to the war effort. Anyone in business who fails to act in accordance with this law must be brought to account. Entrepreneurs must now put aside their understandable efforts to maintain their civilian production as far as possible in the expectation of an imminent resumption of it and must place their plants fully at the service of war production in so far as they are suitable for it. In so far as they are not suitable for it, entrepreneurs must make the major sacrifice of accepting a partial or complete closure so that capacity is freed up for war production. For we shall never be able to defeat England with radios, vacuum cleaners and kitchen utensils.[16]

We must not repeat the mistakes of the First World War when the need for maximum concentration on the production of war materiel was only recognized in the fourth year of the war and then, because of flaws in the organization, was not even implemented. Maximum concentration on the production of materiel of direct and indirect benefit to the war is absolutely vital, particularly in the light of the lessons of the First World War in this sphere. Every breach of this priority for the benefit of economic and social requirements or regional interests should be rejected in so far as it would result in an increase in the use of raw materials, coal and other fuels, transport and labour. Running a war economy means reorienting the economy towards the single goal of winning the war without allowing this to be affected by any consideration for the damage which this may cause . . .

I now come to the question of the changeover of industry to war production and so to the method of allocating orders. During the past three months two concepts have been at the centre of discussion: the concentration or the spreading of orders. In my view, neither of the two concepts meets the current requirements, for, in the first place, the situation in each plant is different, and secondly, the distribution of orders is entirely dependent on the product which is being acquired.

The following principles are fundamental:

(a) The sector of industry which already produced weapons, war material and munitions in peacetime is in no position to cope with the requirements of the Wehrmacht in wartime.

(b) The overall situation requires that an expansion of these plants through new construction can occur only where this is absolutely necessary. All unnecessary construction is a mistaken commitment of raw materials and people.

---

[16] This last comment echoed a statement by Hitler to the Army Weapons Procurement Office in November: 'We shan't defeat England with refrigerators, washing machines and agricultural implements'. See R. D. Müller, op. cit., p. 409.

(c) All avenues must therefore be explored in order to shift those parts of industry which have not hitherto been involved in armaments production towards the fulfilment of their new tasks. This should be done by giving these plants orders either for complete products of for parts or subcontracts. I see the only way of achieving this reorientation as being through close cooperation between the procurement agencies and the professional business organization and by involving the personal initiative of the individual entrepreneur.

Gentlemen, please tell the members of your Economic Group who are eligible for the shift to war production that, in a very short time, they will have their supply of raw materials ruthlessly cut off if they do not succeed in reorienting their production towards armaments. In the last war price was the attraction; this time we must do without that lure. Tell your members in addition that every plant must use its own initiative to find the ways and means of acquiring the machine tools, the gauges and other materials necessary for achieving the changeover. Link the small plants which are shifting production with the large firms which have the experience. In any case we must ensure that the German economy is operating fully on a war footing in the shortest possible time. Wherever the orders can be spread around, as for example in the textile industry, then this should of course be carried out for socio-political reasons. However, here too there are limits to what can be done because it is not acceptable to use raw materials, energy and people in small and very small plants in wartime without a really positive result coming out of it . . .

3. Now a few words about labour deployment. Unemployment, which was feared by many agencies on the outbreak of war, has not materialized. At the moment, there is a labour shortage, which, according to State Secretary Dr Syrup,[17] exceeds the figure of 150,000 by a considerable margin. It is worst in the Labour Office districts of Nordmark [Schleswig-Holstein and Hamburg], Brandenburg, Central Germany, and Lower Saxony. The shortage of skilled workers is partly due to the fact that, at the time of the preparation for mobilization, workers were secured for W[defence]-Plants, which then in fact, after the outbreak of war, were not allocated orders as a result of a change in the procurement situation, and yet those plants hung on to their workers.

The Economics and Armaments Office has tried to resolve this problem by securing a directive from the Chairman of the Ministerial Council for the Defence of the Reich [Göring]. According to this directive, all skilled workers who are not required for urgent production are to be released by their plants. Furthermore, the demand for skilled workers is to be kept to a minimum. This is intended to ensure that the rigidities in the labour deployment process deriving from the assignment of the status of W-Plants are relaxed and that it is made possible to withdraw workers from those W-Plants which are not being fully utilized. As yet, these measures have not produced significant results. As a result, systematic investigations will need to be carried out shortly into the state of plants' order books and the numbers of skilled workers required to fulfil them. The results which have emerged from the initial investigation in Berlin have shown that individual plants

---

[17] State Secretary Dr Friedrich Syrup, President of the Reich Labour Deployment Office and a State Secretary in the Reich Labour Ministry.

have given priority to private economic interests over the requirements of national defence in a completely irresponsible manner.

<hr>

Industry, however, was unimpressed by such exhortations owing to the confusion produced by the conflicting demands from the various Wehrmacht agencies and the Reich Economics Ministry. It also took a dim view of his statement that 'in the last war price was the attraction. This time we must do without that lure.' A number of leading industrialists poured out their complaints to General Thomas at a meeting with him on 18 December: 1939:

**1043**    *Privy Counsellor Bücher*[18]: What is necessary above all is unified leadership of the economy and as simple an organization as possible. Then one will get the optimum performance from industry, which is a very cooperative body. A single agency must be aware of all the demands of the Wehrmacht, have an overview over all the available raw materials and make the final decisions about their allocation; a single agency must clearly and unequivocally determine the extent and priority of requirements in accordance with uniform principles.

Furthermore, there must be consistency in the allocation of orders. Maximum output from industry depends on the regular utilization of its capacity and on the possibility of making one's plans over a long period on the basis of a normal level of performance. There are enough official agencies which can work out the details; what is lacking is leadership. The fact that it takes sixty-six days to acquire a metal permit is the sign of a flawed organisation . . .

*General Director Kissel*[19]: Industry could achieve much more if it was given clear tasks. The most effective deployment of skilled workers is also dependent on this . . .

*General Director Pleiger*[20] and *Dr Bingel*[21] repeat their demands for a unified leadership and a clear allocation of tasks because otherwise the planned increase in performance will not be achievable . . .

*General Thomas*: Summing up, one can say that, in the course of the discussion, the main issue to emerge was the request for a unified and clear leadership because otherwise the demands of the state cannot be fulfilled or at least not on schedule. I myself have always put forward this demand and will continue to do so in the future. The influence of the Economic Armaments Office is, however, limited because it has no authority to give instructions to the Weapons Procurements Offices [of the Wehrmacht branches] . . .

<hr>

[18] Hermann Bücher, a director of the electrical firm AEG.

[19] Wilhelm Kissel, Chairman of Daimler-Benz, the big car and lorry manufacturer, now also making marine and aero-engines.

[20] Paul Pleiger was the managing director of the Reichswerke 'Hermann Göring', the new coal, iron and steel combine established by Göring in 1937 to exploit Germany's low-grade iron ores.

[21] Rudolf Bingel, head of Siemens, the major engineering and electrical firm.

Meanwhile, Hitler had been becoming increasingly preoccupied with the contrast between the current levels of armaments and particularly munitions production and that of the last two years of the First World War. He now demanded that Germany should reach the same level of production as had been achieved in 1917–18, which involved tripling output. He had decided to concentrate all Germany's resources on a crash programme to provide the requisite weapons in order to secure victory in 1940. General Thomas, who had hitherto been an advocate of armament in depth, i.e. the provision of adequate manufacturing and raw materials capacity for fighting a long war, was informed of Hitler's views by Göring at a meeting at Carinhall, Göring's country estate, on 30 January 1940:

**1044**   Field Marshal Göring began by informing me of the Führer's intentions and of the economic measures resulting therefrom. He stated:

The Führer is firmly convinced that he will succeed in reaching a decision in the war in 1940 by a big attack in the west. He reckons that we shall gain Belgium, Holland and northern France and he, the Führer, had estimated that the industrial areas of Douai and Lens and those of Luxembourg, Longwy and Briey could replace the supplies of raw materials from Sweden. The Führer had, therefore, now decided to utilise our reserves of raw materials from Sweden without regard to the future, at the expense of possible subsequent war years. The Führer is convinced of the correctness of this decision since in his view the best way of building up stocks is the building up of stocks not of raw materials but of finished war materiel. Furthermore, one must bear in mind that, if the air war were to begin, our factories could also be destroyed. Furthermore, the Führer is of the opinion that the main thing is to reach maximum effort in the year 1940 and that one should therefore postpone programmes which only produce results later on, in order to accelerate those producing results in 1940.

So far as our work is concerned, therefore, the conclusion is to exploit everything to the utmost in 1940 and thus to exploit reserves of raw materials at the expense of later years. It will be necessary to act in future according to this principle.

I replied to Field Marshal Göring that I was grateful for this clear programme, but that I advised him to build up reserves of finished war materiel also, as experience shows that war materiel which is ready to hand is always put into action at once and used for setting up new formations. We would, therefore, have to put on the brakes in this respect so that one day we are not faced with big surprises. Field Marshal Göring agreed.

But Hitler was uncertain how to proceed. On the one hand, he was unwilling to assign full powers of coordinating the war economy to the military, as was being urged by OKW, since he believed that military bureaucrats were unsuited to business activities, while he was particularly distrustful of the Army High Command (OKH), of whose commitment to the war at that stage he was rightly suspicious. On the other hand, he was wary of giving further powers to Göring and the Four-year Plan organization since the *dirigiste* policies pursued by its technocrats were in danger of alienating industry, which, by contrast, trusted Funk and the Economics Ministry. Moreover, he was unwilling to subordinate the civilian sector of the economy entirely to military priorities for fear of adverse repercussions on morale on the home front. On 7 December 1939 he abolished the post of GBW and gave Göring and his Four-Year Plan a new and vaguely defined commission to direct the war economy, but only within his existing responsibilities, a move which solved nothing, since Göring's creation of an expanded General Council of the Four-Year Plan was no more effective as a coordinating agency than the Reich Defence Council had been.

In January 1940 Dr Fritz Todt, the head of the Nazi Party's Main Office for Technology and the Inspector General of the Highway System, a confidant of Hitler's, had been complaining to him about resistance by the Army Weapons Procurement Office (HWaA) to the rationalization of industry. These criticisms confirmed Hitler's own views of military incompetence in business matters and they were further confirmed by more criticism of the HWaA from industry, notably from Krupp's artillery specialist, Erich 'Cannon' Müller.

In a decision which was typical of him, namely to solve a crisis by appointing a personal confidant to head a new agency, on 26 February 1940 Hitler decided to appoint Todt to the new post of Minister of Armaments and Munitions. Over the next three weeks there was hard bargaining over the responsibilities of the new agency with the WiRüA trying in vain to establish itself as its new executive arm, since Hitler did not want it to have an elaborate organization. Hitler intended Todt to act as a 'slave driver' for industry with the aim of involving industry more in the organization of munitions production. Todt had the advantage of being a strong Party man, a technical expert and someone with good relations with business, which he had already actively involved in his organization of the construction of the West Wall. Hitler signed Todt's appointment on 17 March 1940 and it was published on 20 March together with its implementation decree:

On 29 March 1940, in a speech to his Armaments Inspectors, Thomas reviewed the background to the appointment, which represented a severe setback for the WiRüA. The following are the notes for his speech:

**1045** Fought for armament in depth. Rejected by Führer. Doesn't want a war, only bluffing. 'For that I need breadth.'

My statements in the General Staff pamphlet (?) concerning breadth and depth provoked hostility. Only FM [Göring] sympathized with them and got the message, otherwise I had no joy with them and all the measures to do with factory construction were rejected. All the emphasis continued to be put on breadth (weapons), munitions remained a poor cousin.

Then the day of the Munich [conference] arrived. I received instructions by telephone: all preparations now to be focused on war with England, target date 1942! The munitions production plan put forward in response was rejected, since machine tools, raw materials among other things would be necessary for it, which would require considerable amounts of foreign exchange as well as workers etc. Comment: munitions are the last things to be considered since shells can be produced rapidly. My reference to the munitions issue in relation to the 'Western operation' meets with the response: out of the question. So here too we couldn't secure what we wanted and considered necessary.

Early 1939, directive: War against Poland in the autumn. Renewed attempt to push ahead with the munitions situation. Reply: Poland will be finished off in 4 weeks. There are enough reserves for that. When there were increasing signs of an imminent start to the war with Poland I requested simultaneous military and economic mobilization in view of a possible war with the West. Reply: No war with the West—only the war with Poland.

Before the start of the war against Poland: memorandum to the Führer. Contents: we are still weak in munitions. The same is true of fuel. My warnings are noted.

Saturday, 26.8, before the start of the Polish campaign, once again to Col.-Gen. Keitel. Explained the situation on the basis of sketches and tables. Was more or less sent packing but K. was going to speak to the Führer.

27.8 Sunday, before the start of the war with Poland, when the telegram arrived from England: renewed representations! Mentioned that a munitions crisis was on the cards, in particular with regard to P[owder] and Expl[osives]. Was sent packing. Response: I was thrown out. Führer: Don't bother me any more with talk of a damned war with the West.

After the outbreak of the war with Poland I pointed out to the branches of the Wehrmacht that it was impossible to complete all the programmes simultaneously and demanded that priorities should be set. Memorandum. Reply: No priorities necessary now since no one knows how the war will turn out.

On 29.11.39 I made a speech to the business community.[22] I was taken to task by Göring, claiming it was an attack on him. Explanation! Success. G. takes up the matter. Since the branches of the Wehrmacht were making great demands, G. got the idea of proposing that the Führer should make him Munitions Minister. I made a counter-proposal (??). As a result of the Göring proposal the Führer takes up the munitions issue and compares the current production

---

[22] See above, pp. 198ff.

figures with those of the First World War (Schwarte) [*sic*]. Result: Huge programme. Did not take account of the fact that: in those days industry was lacking orders, not pumped full of them and overburdened as it is now (civilian orders were cancelled, unemployment, motorization, tanks, aircraft, U-boat programme were smaller etc.) Complains to Becker.[23]

One day before Christmas Führer mentions the idea of appointing a munitions minister. Keitel opposed it. Führer produced his own munitions programme—figures that simply could not be achieved. K[eitel] suggested appointing a leading industrialist to the Army Weapons Procurement Agency [WaA] to stop the practice whereby industry only had contact with desk officers from the WaA. General Director Borbet[24] only wanted to cooperate with the OKW, but offered to place one of his directors, Plampe [?], at our disposal. Führer appeared reassured, which, however, was not the case. After Christmas he returned to the issue of the, in his view, inadequate munitions production. K. proposed that he should be given the responsibility for carrying out munitions production. The proposal was rejected. Production did not get going as expected because of the weather conditions (cold, transport) and interventions by the Führer.

When the Führer saw the January and February production figures and made comparisons with the First World War amounts he summoned industrialists and Todt. Industry complained about the WaA. Shortages of raw materials, workers, machines. Continual complaints from the branches of the Wehrmacht. The Führer sticks to his system. K. rejects all proposals that he should explain the situation to the Führer. In addition, there is the tense relationship of Führer–OKH, to which the WaA belongs. So it is blamed for a lot which it can do nothing about. Complaint that in the air force everything works all right, which proves that the army is going about things in the wrong way.

In appointing Todt the Führer was working on the assumption that industry needed a slave driver. A business and Party man could choose many possible ways of operating unfamiliar to an officer. The Führer couldn't expect the latter to be up to all the tricks in the way the former would be.

The slave-driver system, one pitted against another is fine as long as sufficient raw materials, machines, labour etc. are available. But if that is not the case then such a system leads to friction etc. and output will not be 100 per cent but only 80 or 70.

Those are the reasons for the appointment of a munitions minister or for the Führer's secret assignment to Todt. K. informed but ban on speaking about it.

Saturday before Palm Sunday in the Reich Chancellery where K. was already there and a decree was prepared which was much tougher than the one later published (among other things the Wehrmacht subordinated). This was because, in the Führer's view, it wasn't appropriate to subordinate part of the OKW (the Economics Staff) to a ministry . . .

---

[23] General/Professor Karl Becker, head of the Army Weapons Procurement Office 1938–40.

[24] Walter Borbet of the Bochumer Verein, an important arms manufacturer.

Todt is reaping what was sown by the WaA. Possibility of putting thousands of workers from his autobahns in the munitions plants.

Did we make mistakes? Let's think back a year. The potential performance of industry for the production of munitions was underestimated. Perhaps our preparations were on too small a scale. We should at least have made them on paper. Direct preparations would only have been possible if orders could have been placed.

―

Lacking his own executive arm and surrounded by rival agencies resentful of an interloper, Todt had to move cautiously towards his goal of reducing the role of the military in arms and munitions production and increasing the role of business. His two most important moves were, first, to introduce an element of the profit motive by using a payment system he had already successfully operated in the construction of the West Wall. This involved a mixture of the traditional arrangement whereby firms had been paid according to the costs incurred plus a standard rate of profit with a new fixed-price system which encouraged business to cut costs through rationalization in order to increase profit margins. However, opposition from the military and business establishment prevented this from being carried very far.

The second measure introduced by Todt, on 6 April 1940, was to adopt a proposal from the Reich Industry Group that it should establish 'working groups' at district level in which representatives of those firms involved in munitions production would meet to allocate the orders to the various plants in the district and exchange experience to encourage best practice. The chairmen of the various working groups in a military district then formed a 'munitions [later armaments] committee' and the chairmen of the munitions committees in turn formed a 'munitions [later armaments] council', based in Berlin, which was responsible for balancing the munitions and later armaments contracts between the various districts.

### (iii) The Period of Incoherent Planning: June 1940–November 1941

This proposal for the greater involvement of business in munitions— soon extended to armaments—production through working groups and committees, which introduced for the first time an element of 'self-administration' or autonomy (*Selbstverwaltung*) for business into the armaments production process, was adopted against strong opposition from the military agencies. However, Todt was unable to solve the central problem of the German war economy, namely the lack of a strong central planning, directing, and coordinating agency, because the various institutions involved—the OKW's WiRüA, the OKH's HWaA, the Four-Year Plan, the Economics Ministry, and the three branches of the Wehrmacht—all continued fiercely to defend their autonomy, and Hitler failed to give the necessary support to Todt in his attempts to turn the new Munitions Ministry into such a central agency. With Hitler's connivance, Göring continued to insist on his overall responsibility for the economy without actually being able to fulfil the role.

Todt's efforts were not helped by the new situation created by the unexpectedly rapid and easy success in the western campaign. This encouraged a mood of complacency within the German economic agencies which was not conducive to the full-scale mobilization of the economy for war. This over-optimism was then compounded by an initial underestimation of Soviet capabilities. Hitler was himself partly responsible for this with his initial response to the victory in the west, namely ordering a partial demobilization of the army and signalling the need to improve civilian conditions. This message was underlined by his order to restart the prestige building projects in Berlin and Nuremberg. Although he rapidly reconsidered the situation once it became clear that Britain was not going to make peace and plans went ahead for an attack on the Soviet Union in 1941, the damage had been done. When the German army began the invasion of Russia in June 1941, it was ill-prepared for what was to come and, as a result of a combination of complacency, lack of planning, and the need to keep the attack secret, munitions shortages developed in the winter of 1941–2. Instead of mobilizing for war, German business began to plan for the peacetime exploitation of the opportunities which had opened up in Germany's new European empire. The parlous situation which existed within the German economic leadership in the autumn of 1940 is well caught in the following devastating passages in the memoirs of Hans Kehrl, at that stage head of the textiles department in the Four-Year Plan and soon to become a major figure in Albert Speer's Armaments Ministry:

**1046**  The attempt to get any kind of sense of direction or guidelines for my future work from within the Ministry [of Economics] proved fruitless. State Secretary Dr Landfried had only a modest conceptual ability as far as economic matters were concerned and certainly lacked the imagination to develop new ideas. Essentially, he restricted his activities to making sure that whatever occurred was done according to the book and to carrying out instructions from the Four-Year Plan whenever there were any. A conversation with Walter Funk revealed that he had no contact whatsoever with Hitler since, following the outbreak of war, the latter had been entirely preoccupied with military-political considerations. No directives had been issued by the Four-Year Plan and none were expected. As Commander-in-Chief of the Air Force, Göring had been concentrating his attention on the military actions in Poland, Norway and the western campaign. All his energy and thoughts were focused on military events. As a result the Four-Year Plan, which had been conceived as a control centre for the whole economy, was almost completely inactive. A conversation which I had with State Secretary Körner[25] revealed that I could not expect even the most limited guidance or any suggestions from them. Only ongoing matters were being dealt with. Funk was concentrating mainly on his role as President of the Reich Bank because he was primarily an expert in financial and currency matters.

The comparatively frequent meetings of the departmental heads, which were held by General von Hanneken were my only opportunity of getting any information from the Ministry. When I presented a report, following my return from my trip to the occupied western territories, I tried to initiate a general discussion about guidelines for our future work. The military actions and their outcome, which had certainly not been anticipated by the majority of the officials, had produced a kind of wave of euphoria, particularly among those who had previously been extremely sceptical about the future prospects of the war. At one of the first meetings of department heads after the start of the western campaign *Ministerialdirigent*[26] Holtz had remarked smugly that he knew exactly how long the war would last. In reply to my question as to how he did so he replied: 'our copper supplies will only last six months and so we can't go on fighting any longer than that'. But that was completely untrue. For, at the time, the assumption was that even in war time the needs of the non-armaments sector would continue to be met in full. The significant opportunities which existed for making savings in industry and in the consumer goods sector, which had played such a major role in the First World War, had not been attempted at all.

Possibly in response to my remarks, General von Hanneken, who had close links with the Army Procurement Office and with Thomas's Economics and Armaments Staff, reported that during the war in the west weapons consumption in particular, but also fuel consumption, had been far less than envisaged. A few weeks later, he reported to us on the preparations for the 'Sea Lion' operation, an invasion of England with strong forces planned for August or September. That was the only military operation which could be expected in the foreseeable future, if at all. The requirements for materiel which were envisaged were comparatively small since one could not deploy millions of men for an invasion of England but only hundreds of thousands. Hanneken reported further that, on account of these experiences, the production of munitions, bombs and normal weapons had been sharply reduced since '*there would be no need for them in the foreseeable future*'. Tank production, on the other hand, would be stepped up, which in Hanneken's opinion' was complete nonsense. He considered we had 'enough' tanks. Finally, he informed us that he had 'heard' from State Secretary Körner that it was Hitler's wish that restrictions on the

---

[25] Paul (Pilli) Körner, Göring's deputy in the Four-Year Plan.

[26] A rank roughly equivalent to Deputy Secretary in the British Civil Service.

civilian population and on the civilian economy should be implemented as gently as possible and harsh cuts should be avoided. He told me personally that the tough measures in the clothing sector, some of which had been implemented and some of which were in preparation, had 'made an unfavourable impression'.

It seemed to me completely pointless to try and influence General von Hanneken. Despite his martial appearance, he was timid, avoided responsibility and was anxiously concerned not to cause offence by raising objections. One could not expect any initiatives to come from him. I considered the trends hinted at by Körner or considered correct by Hitler were wrong and posed a serious threat to our nation. Increasingly I gained the impression that we were in the process of fighting a world war without a Reich government which contemplated mobilizing the economic and human resources of the whole nation. Certainly, the Reich Economics Ministry was the most important civilian Government department in this sphere and so if there was a complete lack of leadership here then things would hardly be any better in other departments. But I wanted to try and find out . . .

I then spoke to State Secretary Stuckart from the Reich Ministry of the Interior . . . I explained to him my great concern that, to put it bluntly, while fighting a life and death struggle, we did not have a functioning Reich government, but only the performance of fragmented functions by the individual Reich ministers, who were simply operating as department heads without any awareness of the overall picture. Hitler was almost never in Berlin, did not hold any cabinet meetings, nor did he exercise what we would now call 'control over the main lines of policy' [*Richtlinienkompetenz*]. The Führer did not even seem to be kept adequately informed from below. According to my impression, only ad hoc and often chance pieces of information reached him and only ad hoc directives were issued. And thus, in my view, the 'Führer and Reich Chancellor' could only be being inadequately and certainly not systematically informed.

I hoped to provoke Stuckart into contradicting or correcting me. But, unfortunately, while expressing himself cautiously, he basically agreed with me. He himself was trying to improve this unsatisfactory situation and was in contact with Lammers about it. If the political and military events became less turbulent, which could be anticipated for the next period, then improvements could no doubt be made. He tried to reassure me. So there was nothing doing there either!

▬

The friction which existed between the various agencies responsible for the war economy is well illustrated by the following letter from Todt to Keitel, dated 24 January 1941:

**1047**  Dear Field Marshal,

For a long time I have wanted to ask you to accept my proposal that both of us try wherever possible to eliminate the unfortunate cases of rivalry which keep cropping up between the agencies of the OKW and those of the Reich Minister for Armaments and Munitions, and to ensure that, while the Wehrmacht is responsible for putting forward military requests, the Reich Minister for Armaments and Munitions is responsible for their implementation, and that this should occur in an atmosphere of mutual respect as indeed is envisaged in the Führer's first directive. For a time, I believed that mutual consideration would gradually develop naturally between our two agencies through a sense of tact on both sides. However, now that in the New Year things have once again got off on the wrong foot I must ask you to concern yourself personally with the maintenance of the sense of tact which is the precondition for comradely co-operation. Above all, I wish to avoid the Führer being confronted with behaviour such as is alleged to occur in Italy, whereby everybody uses every opportunity to report to the Führer a few days before someone else was going to report on the matter to him. I propose that, on every occasion when I am going to report to the Führer on a matter which touches on military affairs I will inform the Wehrmacht adjutant beforehand so that either he can participate himself or, if he considers it appropriate, he can inform someone else. However, in return I must request that matters which are concerned with factory production and not armaments should be referred to me as the person responsible and that reports to the Führer on these matters should not be made before they have been cleared by me.

What finally prompted me to make this request was the note for the head of the OKW, dated 21.1, a copy of which is enclosed. In this the Economics and Armaments Office [of OKW] requests the Führer's agreement to eleven measures, of which all but points 10 and 11 are economic measures, the majority of which do not affect the armaments sector but are concerned with the civilian sector of the economy. After our joint report to the Führer I initiated detailed discussions on measures 1–9 with the representatives of the Economics Ministry, the Four-Year Plan, and of course also the OKW. If the Economics and Armaments Office now proposes that such questions should be put to the Führer for a decision by the head of the OKW, then that is another of the typical cases in which, in order to have the prestige of making the first report to the Führer, other agencies are treated without the requisite tact.

I would be grateful if you would refrain from making this report and would inform the Economics and Armaments Office that these matters are dealt with by the Reich Ministry for Armaments and Munitions in consultation with the responsible ministries. The Führer should not be asked for his decision unless it proves impossible to reach a satisfactory agreement or if the Delegate for the Four-Year Plan, Reich Marshal Göring, does not make a decision.

——

In the spring of 1941 Hitler's mind was increasingly focused on Operation Barbarossa, the attack on the Soviet Union, and in this context he was becoming somewhat concerned about what he saw as flaws in German armaments production. On 18 May 1941 he addressed a meeting of top armaments officials at his house near Berchtesgaden, making a number of points which from now onwards became a constant refrain in his comments on the armaments issue. The following is an excerpt from a WiRüA report of the meeting, dated 21 May 1941:

**1048** 1. *The armaments situation on the basis of the 'Overview of the Armaments Position' of the Wehrmacht branches*

The Führer complained about the, in some cases, sharp decline in the munitions and weapons production which was evident from the army's Red Books, as well as about the fact that the mechanical production capacities which were cited were not remotely reflected in the actual output. Above all, he did not understand why the large reduction in munitions production for the army was not reflected in corresponding increases in other areas (air force and naval munitions) . . .

5. . . . Even allowing for the need for a permanent superiority over the equipment and weapons of the enemy, the construction of equipment and weapons must be considered too complicated and over-sophisticated. Excessive requirements in this respect place too many burdens on industry and in consequence damage the whole armaments sector in view of the labour situation (skilled workers). Furthermore, the maintenance and renewal of this complicated equipment is made significantly more difficult. A return to more primitive robust designs is, therefore, in many cases highly desirable for all three branches of the Wehrmacht.

Despite these concerns, however, Hitler was convinced that the Soviet forces would be defeated within a couple of months. Indeed, so confident was the German leadership of victory that, even before the launching of Barbarossa, they were planning a reorientation of armaments production for the next phase of the war in the autumn. This would involve a shift away from the army towards a massive build-up of aircraft production to deal with the threat from the remaining enemy, Britain, and possibly also the United States. It would also involve focusing the naval programme on U-boat production and the army programme on tank production. On 20 June 1941, two days before the start of the Russian campaign, Hitler issued an order from which the following extract is taken:

**1049** If the armaments allocated to the army are curtailed, manufacturing plant and labour reserves will become available. Those resources which have become available are to be put at the disposal of the expanded air force programme under the direction of the Minister for Armaments and Munitions. Arrangements must be made as soon as possible for the air force to contact firms regarding the transfer of production. The Reich Minister for Armaments and Munitions will regulate the allocation of these available resources between the special air force programme and the most urgent requirements of the army and navy.

However, although Todt was apparently given greater coordinating authority under this order, in practice it did not amount to much. His one concrete success at this point was to persuade Hitler to agree to the removal of tank production from the Army Procurement Office (*Heereswaffenamt* = HWaA) and place it in the hands of a new Panzer Commission under the control of his Ministry. The new Commission, which was responsible for the whole production process from model development to delivery of the finished product, was headed by the brilliant industrial designer Ferdinand Porsche. It marked one more step in Todt's laborious attempt to acquire control of armaments production for his Ministry and to replace the military bureaucrats of the HWaA and the WiRüA with the 'self-administration' of business.

However, a major obstacle to Todt's ambitions was posed by the air force, which, with Göring's political weight behind it, was able to assert its independence both from the OKW and from Todt's Ministry. Now, with the focus on armaments production shifting in its favour under the new Göring Programme, which involved quadrupling its size, the air force seized the initiative. Göring appointed his able State Secretary, Field Marshal Erhard Milch, to head the new programme and gave him 'the right to requisition every factory in Germany for the air force armaments programme'.[27] Milch immediately set about following Todt's example in involving business. For each aircraft model he formed the industrialists involved in its construction into 'rings' and encouraged them to rationalize production by introducing standardized parts and serial production methods on American lines.

This independent initiative by the air force under Milch threatened Todt's strategy and forced him to seek allies. At the end of June 1941, therefore, he approached the head of the WiRüA, General Thomas, as Thomas informed his superior, Field Marshal Keitel, in the following letter, dated 29 June 1941:

**1050**    On Friday afternoon, after lengthy attempts to set it up, I at last succeeded in having a substantial conversation with Minister Todt. I began by telling Dr Todt that unfortunately a large number of directives had gone out which should definitely have been cleared with us beforehand, and that, above all, the Führer's order about which he had written to the Field Marshal [Keitel], should have been issued with the agreement of the head of the OKW. Dr Todt admitted that, because of the pressure of business, he had neglected to involve the OKW and that he now wished to try and work more closely with the

---

[27] See: Chief of Staff of the Economics and Armaments Office, Re; The Air Force Armaments Programme, 26.6.1941 in G. Thomas, *Geschichte der Wehr- und Rüstungswirtschaft (1918–1943/45)* (Boppard 1966), pp. 448–49.

Economics and Armaments Office. The further discussion took a very interesting turn.

An hour earlier, Dr Todt had had a row with Field Marshal Milch about the powers which Field Marshal Milch had received from the Reich Marshal for putting into effect the great air force programme. Apparently Todt threatened to offer his resignation to the Führer if Milch were to retain these powers. For his part Field Marshal Milch expressed the view that he would have to give up his assignment if he were not given greater powers. Field Marshal Milch takes the view that the army and naval programmes should be considerably reduced if he is to carry out his air force programme. I agreed with this view. Dr Todt takes the line that the panzer and U-boat should be carried out in full and that the Führer will not accept anything less. However, Dr Todt does not consider it possible to increase the panzer programme from 600 to 900 vehicles as the Führer wishes. The upshot of the conversation was that Todt said to me:

'I have told the Führer that this situation in which the branches of the Wehrmacht work at cross purposes is no longer viable since the economy is so over-stretched that the optimum armaments production can no longer be achieved. An office must be created which can ruthlessly override the three Commanders-in-Chief.'

I had the impression that Dr Todt had proposed himself for this task to the Führer and was astonished when Dr Todt told me frankly:

'The Führer replied that that was a task for the Supreme Command of the Wehrmacht [OKW] and that no one else could give directives to the Commanders-in-Chief.'

Dr Todt then told me that, since everyone had been given powers, there was nothing else for it but for me, General Thomas, to acquire a general authority and to decide the issues in the name of the Field Marshal [Keitel]. The main thing was for the OKW to assert itself with all means and no longer to tolerate these continual interventions [*Attacken*] by the Commanders-in-Chief with the Führer.

Colonel Neef, who accompanied me, and I had the clear impression that Todt was calling on us to assist him against the air force. We parted having agreed that the OKW should rapidly work on transforming the programmes and that we should then seek a joint interview with the Field Marshal [Keitel].

Yesterday, Field Marshal Milch asked me to see him and I had exactly the same experience. Field Marshal Milch told me that things could not go on like this. The competing programmes running side by side could not continue; the Reich Marshal had two hearts in his breast: one for the air force and one for the Reich Defence Council. So there was now only one thing to be done, namely, the OKW should assert itself ruthlessly and take the decisions. Field Marshal Milch asked for my help and declared that he would work very closely with me if we managed to assert ourselves and supported him as far as we could.

I naturally promised him this assistance.

It seems to me, therefore, that now is a particularly favourable moment for the OKW to take firm control of armaments matters. We are in the process of clarifying the effects of the air force programme as rapidly as possible and of preparing a new plan for you, Field Marshal, which I will personally report on.

A few days later, on 10 July 1941, Thomas tried to take advantage of the new situation by proposing to Keitel that the OKW should take the initiative in establishing a central coordinating agency for the German war economy based around its Economics and Armaments Office. However, as his minute at the end of the document makes clear, Keitel was sceptical about such an initiative and, given Hitler's previous unwillingness to give consistent backing either to OKW or to Todt in their attempts to rein in the branches of the Wehrmacht or to permit the military to control the civilian economy, he was no doubt right to be:

**1051** *General Thomas: Report on the performance in the sphere of Wehrmacht armaments in the period from 1.9.40 to 1.4.41 for Keitel, dated 10.7.41*

. . . The more difficult the situation becomes in the sphere of labour and raw materials the more their deployment needs to be planned. Because of this it is necessary to subject all Wehrmacht plans as early as possible to an investigation as to whether and in what time scale they can realistically be implemented and whether or not they represent pipe dreams. Only when we succeed through such central Wehrmacht planning in deploying the main factors of production, namely labour, raw materials and machinery, in the most efficient way possible will we secure the implementation of the most important programmes. Such central Wehrmacht planning will also be in a position to establish a realistic set of priorities in the armaments sector as has unfortunately not fully been the case hitherto.

I thus propose that the head of the OKW should give the Economics and Armaments Office the task of immediately establishing a Wehrmacht Planning Office. Each of the three branches of the Wehrmacht as well as the Wehrmacht Procurement Office would delegate a representative to the Central Wehrmacht Planning Office.

How far the Central Planning Office can be expanded though the inclusion of those offices which, although outside the Wehrmacht, nevertheless influence the armaments sector of the economy, e.g. the Four-Year Plan, the Reich Economics Minister, the Reich Labour Minister, can be left to future developments. [Keitel minute: . . . Because of the continual interventions by the Führer I fear that it will be purely a paper exercise and we shall be running to catch up with the Führer orders.]

—

It rapidly became clear that Hitler's attempt to quadruple the air force, while simultaneously expanding the U-boat and panzer programmes, was beyond the capacity of German armaments production as currently organized. General Thomas was the architect of this system, which had been introduced in June 1940, and which was based on priority categories. Whereas previously the Wehrmacht branches had worked out what weapons/munitions they wanted and then they had set out to acquire the raw materials, labour and plant capacity to produce them, under the new system the Wehrmacht branches were allocated a certain amount of raw materials etc. by the OKW and then had to gear their requirements to what could be produced, instead of the allocations being based on their requests. Moreover, they were expected to place their orders in one of four priority categories. In theory this allowed for more realistic planning; in practice, however, the raw materials allocations increasingly became a straitjacket and the priority system was subject to inflation, since, given the competition for resources, orders which did not carry high priority ratings would not get produced. The following report for Keitel, dated 6 July 1941, indicates Thomas's assessment of the problems and shows his lack of awareness of how more rationalization of production through the greater involvement of business could transform the situation:

**1052**    The implementation of the expanded air force programme, ordered by the Führer, makes especially heavy demands on the German war economy. In view of the high level of employment and the raw material situation of the German economy, the solution of this task will only be possible through extensive and far-reaching measures. In order to carry out a successful reorientation of German armaments to meet the requirements of future military action the Supreme Leadership must be aware of the bottlenecks which will influence the required reorientation.

[Thomas then described the various raw material shortages and continued:]

The overburdening of Germany's economic potential naturally had a very adverse effect on the completion of war contracts and was a main reason for the increasing pressure for all important military products to be given a higher priority rating. The result was such an inflation of priority-rated production that the purpose of giving priority to the production of the most important equipment was vitiated.

All the measures which were taken to relieve these blockages, such as rationalization of plants, closure of productive capacity not important for the war effort or the transfer of contracts, were unable to improve the situation; for the tasks which have been given to the economy by the military leadership have in the course of time not become any smaller but in recent years have gone far beyond what such ameliorative measures were capable of achieving.

The armaments industry will no longer receive any notable gain from trying to move into the remaining civilian production capacity. For example, if one takes the iron and metalworking industry: around 68 per cent of all employees are employed either directly or indirectly in producing for the Wehrmacht. The majority of the remainder are also engaged in areas which serve the war effort (mining, railways, energy etc.)

Within the armaments industry proper the following are the percentages of those who work for the various branches of the Wehrmacht:

| | | | |
|---|---|---|---|
| For Army | production | " | 38% |
| For Navy | " | " | 19% |
| For Air Force | " | " | 38% |
| Other Wehrmacht | " | " | 5% |

Thus the expanded air force armaments programme which will be decisive for the outcome of the war can only have a prospect of being completed on time, while maintaining the tank, U-boat and Krauch programmes[28] if the armaments planners can themselves find a way of ensuring the essential reduction in the burdens on industry, i.e. that all Wehrmacht contracts which can no longer be regarded as decisive for the outcome of the war should be ruthlessly cancelled.

[He then proposed a number of cuts, including a drastic cut in weapons and munitions production for the Army.]

▬▬▬

However, although Hitler was aware that there were problems with armaments production, at this stage he was still confident that conquest of the Soviet Union would soon resolve all the difficulties caused by raw materials and labour shortages and, on 14 July 1941, he confirmed the reorientation of armaments policy in the following major directive, 32a:

**1053**    On the basis of the intentions announced in Directive No.32 for the future conduct of the war I hereby issue the following guidelines for armaments in the spheres of personnel and equipment.

1. *General*

Our military domination of the European continent after the defeat of France will shortly permit a significant reduction in the size of the army. Within the limits of the reduced army, panzer forces will be greatly increased.

Naval armaments are to be strictly limited to those measures which directly serve the prosecution of the war against England and America.

The main focus of our armaments production will be transferred to the air force, which is to be greatly strengthened.

▬▬▬

However, it rapidly became apparent that the new armaments pro-grammes ordered by Hitler were unrealizable with Germany's current resources. At a major meeting in the OKW from 14 to 16 August 1941 it was, therefore, resolved to cancel the preparations for Operation Sea Lion (invasion of Britain), to withdraw a new panzer programme (III), to reduce the anti-aircraft gun programme and, above all, to postpone

---

[28] The synthetic oil and rubber (Buna) plants being constructed by the Four-Year Plan under the supervision of the chemicals supremo, IG Farben director Carl Krauch.

the air force's Göring Programme (4x) until summer 1942 and to implement the Elch Programme, which merely envisaged restoring the air force to its pre-Barbarossa state.[29]

Under pressure to meet Hitler's armament programmes, the OKW sought a way out by squeezing the civilian sector of the economy. A week before the OKW meeting, on 10 August, Keitel had written to the Economics Minister requesting further civilian cutbacks. However, confident in the knowledge of Hitler's unwillingness to impose further burdens on the German population at a time when he was claiming imminent victory on the eastern front, Funk could afford to delay his reply for a couple of months and then brush Keitel off with a letter dated 21 October 1941, which the head of the OKW peppered with caustic minutes:

**1054** With your letter of 10 August you have requested additional directives from the Reich Marshal and from the ministers responsible for business in order to facilitate the increased armaments programmes. I can assure you that no effort will be spared on my side to commit all the resources available within Germany's sphere of influence to achieve this goal. On the other hand, I believe that I may claim that hitherto I have already done everything to utilise the available raw materials, production capacity and labour for the benefit of armaments . . .

According to the agreement reached between the Reich Marshal and the departments involved, the cuts imposed by me were intended to last six months and, with the ending of military operations envisaged for the autumn, they were intended to be lifted again where necessary. If, in view of the war situation and the resources required for the new air force armaments programme, I now refrain from doing so I nevertheless feel obliged to point out with all seriousness that the indirect requirements for the war effort, for which I am responsible, cannot in the long term remain so severely restricted. The iron allocations for the maintenance and renovation of industry do not meet the requirements caused by the wear and tear on industrial equipment caused by the high work rate and the use of unsuitable labour. Many repair contracts and orders for spare parts, tools etc. can already no longer be fulfilled or only with long delivery dates because the plants are full up with Wehrmacht contacts with high priority ratings.

The Reichsführer SS attributes the rising curve of fatal traffic accidents to the shortage of lighting equipment. According to the reports of the Reich Minister for Food and Agriculture, large amounts of butter have spoiled because of the shortage of containers. Even the Wehrmacht itself often requests that production plants which have been deprived of workers should be protected again because the troops need to be supplied e.g. with tobacco or typewriters. [Keitel minute: not decisive for the war effort!]

---

[29] See the minutes of the meeting with Field Marshal Keitel, 14–16.8.41 in Imperial War Museum (IWM) E78 AL 14982.

The growing shortage of furniture and household equipment has restricted the settlement of those being resettled in the east who thus became unavailable for agricultural labour. Those hit by air raids can often no longer be equipped with the most necessary household effects. The Gauleiters report that, as a result of the shortages, employees' willingness and enthusiasm to work, particularly in the armaments industry, is beginning to decline. I have countered such arguments by pointing out that, at the moment, it is completely out of the question to support the efforts of the political agencies by providing labour for the production of goods to satisfy the needs of the population. However, in the long run, we shall not be able to ignore the objections of the Gauleiters that the war cannot be won simply with shells and bombs. [Keitel minute: no slogans, please!]

In pursuit of the directives issued by me Inspection Commissions of the Reich Minister of Armaments and Munitions and the offices of the labour administration have provided the armaments sector once again with more than half a million workers. It is the unanimous judgment of the Inspection Commissions, in which the Armaments Inspectorate have the dominant voice, that the workers still employed in civilian production cannot be transferred to the armaments industry. On the contrary, the Inspection Commissions have unanimously declared that the workers required for the new armaments programmes can only be provided through cutting the less urgent Wehrmacht production.

I welcome the fact that you yourselves have now taken steps in this direction from which an easing of the situation can be anticipated for the civilian sector as well. [Keitel minute: not my intention!]

The fact, for example, that a single [Wehrmacht] provisions store submitted an order for 150,000 liqueur glasses which was described as urgent, or that in dozens of cases household equipment, for example pokers 'of a particular design' were ordered as a special priority contract and, as a result, workers are committed, while at the same time 'civilian' plants of the importance of the Lauta aluminium oxide plant or the Rheinfelden aluminium smelter have to be closed from time to time because of a shortage of labour—all this was very difficult to understand for those involved. [Keitel minute: why are we not informed of this in time?]

As far as I can see from the production for indirect war requirements overseen by me, in the final analysis the unlimited piling up of armaments programmes without any consideration for the actual capacity of the German economy simply has the effect of damaging armaments production itself. The delivery dates get longer. The consumers fight in the plants to secure the completion of every single contract. As a result, the plant leader finds it virtually impossible to ensure an orderly system in accordance with rational production procedures. The system of priority ratings, which becomes daily more complicated, simply focuses on trying to cure the symptoms but cannot provide any real assistance so long as the programmes of the Wehrmacht branches are not geared to the capacity of the economy and the priority ratings, which are by now accorded to some 70 or 80 per cent of the Wehrmacht contracts waiting to be completed in the plants have been reduced to a peak which can be controlled. [Keitel minute: unfortunately true!]

Meanwhile, Hitler had been becoming increasingly frustrated by the failure of the military bureaucrats and, in particular, the Army Procurement Office (HWaA), to deliver the goods in terms of increased armaments production. He had become convinced that the reason lay in a combination of excessive red tape imposed on business and the tendency of the army weapons experts to demand too high quality and specialized weapons, which in turn prevented the rationalization of industry and the introduction of modern mass production methods. On the afternoon of 21 November 1941 he addressed these issues at a top-level meeting held in the Reich Chancellery attended by, among others, Keitel and Jodl from OKW; the C.-in-C. Army, Brauchitsch, and the head of the HWaA, General von Leeb, from OKH; the Armaments Minister, Todt, and the heads of the panzer programme; the designer Ferdinand Porsche, and Walter Rohland, director of the Vereinigte Stahlwerke (United Steel), both from industry. The minutes were prepared by Hitler's adjutant Colonel Schmundt:

**1055**　Turning to the question of production, the Führer stated: it is a serious error to believe that we are a leading state in terms of manufacturing performance. Our designs get in the way of the practical requirements of production, e.g. for exploiting the possibilities of stamping and casting etc. Thus our designs must pay much more attention to production requirements. Above all, one should turn to private industry for advice in this respect. For it is compelled to calculate profit and loss and to work economically, whereas state plants generally go ahead regardless of cost because their civil servants and white-collar employees are maintained by the state.

Mass production must be encouraged by simplifying designs. It is by no means the case that this will result in neglect of the function or the effectiveness of the weapon concerned. By standardizing, one facilitates the cannibalizing of vehicles which are no longer roadworthy. In the process we will create a natural source of spare parts which we are at present seriously lacking as a result of the variety of types in use. The parts of one vehicle . . . must be freely interchangeable with another.

It is not acceptable that we should now be building vehicles which can last 120 years while we know that after two or three years they will be out of date. Towing vehicles must become very basic in type. Aesthetic considerations should not come into it; function is much more important and what will permit mass production. In the East we shall find that grasshopper-like vehicles work well.

The fact that moving to simplified designs can bring benefits is shown by the design of a new machine gun which, despite a simplified design and a reduction in costs, works better and is more suitable for action in the field. We should think twice about new designs. If we can keep our designs up to scratch for one or two more years then I shall be content. Then, when we go over to the defensive, our hollow shells will prove superior to all offensive weapons.

The Führer then talked of the need to shorten the distances in the transport of materials which have got out of hand. We should also seek to ensure less wastage of materials in the production process.

The lack of necessary raw materials must not result in a failure to use poorer substitutes and a decision to give up producing the equipment. The soldier at the front would prefer to have a weapon with a lower level of performance than not to have a weapon at all. *The fateful struggle of the German people must not be put at risk because weapons are being dreamed up which cannot be mass produced.*

After the discussion, in which Minister Dr Todt, Colonel Fichtner [Weapons Inspectorate] and other gentlemen took part, the Führer emphasized that the German soldier deserved the best weapons and that we were not going to capitulate to lack of technical possibilities.

Minister Dr Todt assured the meeting that 30 per cent of workers could be spared through simplifying production.

———

## (iv) The Todt–Speer Rationalization Programme 1941–1942

Although a number of measures had already been taken during the previous months, it was not until December 1941 that a more systematic programme of rationalization began to emerge. This was primarily in response to a memorandum dated 3 December 1941, in which Hitler elucidated his views at length and which functioned as a general instruction. It does not appear to have been purely Hitler's own work since there is an earlier draft in the files of the WiRüA headed 'old draft not accepted by Dr Todt', who thus seems to have had some input:[30]

**1056**  *The Simplification and Improvement of the Performance of our Armaments Industry*
The current and future war and economic situations require the planned concentration of all our design and production capacity in order to fulfil the armaments tasks ordered by me. An increase in armaments production simply by the use of labour measures can only be achieved in Germany through the employment of more prisoners of war unless the remaining productive capacity in Europe is effectively integrated into our economy either directly to produce armaments or to relieve our own industry by producing essential articles of everyday use. Moreover, an increased supply of raw materials is only possible to a very limited extent at any rate for the time being.

The required increases in the performance of our production of arms and equipment must, therefore, be achieved:
1. through an alteration in the design of our weapons and equipment in the sense of facilitating as far as possible mass production on modern lines, which is the only way of achieving a rationalization of our production methods;

———

[30] In Bundesarchiv/Militärchiv (BA/MA) RW 19/122.

2. through the allocation and concentration of contracts on those plants which are best equipped for the required purpose and, therefore, will operate in the most economic fashion;

3. if necessary, through the establishment of new factories which are confined to the production of a single piece of military equipment which is most suitable for mass production.

Hitherto, the requirements made of the individual weapons and pieces of equipment by the Wehrmacht agencies originated in a smaller Wehrmacht with a lower level of wear and tear; in addition, the demand was for a technically and aesthetically perfectly crafted product. The design features and the factory methods used in their construction, therefore, reflected these features. By contrast, the required shift to mass-production necessitates a fundamental change so that the designs are geared to mass production methods.

The task is, therefore, to examine the design features of our weapons and equipment and to alter them in such a way that they are suitable to be produced with much simpler methods. This will facilitate the work methods both in general and in particulars, and thereby save on raw materials, skilled labour and time. This will require a careful examination of individual weapons and pieces of equipment in the light of the materials available to us, the performance that can reasonably be expected of them and the simplest design appropriate to their function.

Further significant savings must be achieved through a reduction in all other excessive technical requirements which may exist. Thus contractual conditions must be relaxed where the tolerances which have been required hitherto go beyond the absolute minimum required for the use of the equipment either in general or in particular. As a matter of principle, the effectiveness, the ease of production as well as the saving in materials must be given priority over aesthetic or any other criteria which are not required for use in war.

Finally, every piece of equipment which actually exists, even if it has only a modest performance, is better than an ideal solution which, because of the high demands it makes, cannot be produced as a result of the limits imposed by our raw materials and labour situation. A large amount of military equipment and, above all, the whole of the general Wehrmacht equipment has not yet been subjected to such an examination.

The working groups which have been established by the Reich Minister for Armaments and Munitions, as well as the Air Force Industrial Rings, have already been given the task of improving the production of certain weapons and equipment through the simplification of designs and the resultant possibilities for the increased rationalization of production. The work which has already been initiated is to be further expanded to include all other military equipment which has not hitherto undergone such examination.

I therefore order:

I The Wehrmacht branches must examine the existing performance requirements for weapons and equipment with the aim of:

1. limiting their technical requirements to those which are sufficient to ensure adequate performance on the battlefield;

2. reducing their requirements in terms of aesthetics, durability and levels of equipment to those which are necessitated by the war;

3. stripping the equipment down to the minimum necessary for combat and refraining from making any further demands on it.

II   To ensure that these demands for simplified production are met the relevant experts must be involved already at the development stage of new weapons and equipment.

III   All firms producing military equipment as well as other businesses suitable for the purpose and individual experienced engineers are to be requested in an appropriate way to make suggestions for such improvements in production which should above all cover the following:

1. removal of obvious technical flaws and weaknesses in designs which already exist, are in the process of being introduced or are being developed;

2. simplification as far as possible of the individual design features in favour of simple forms suitable for mass production;

3. extension as far as possible of the standardization of individual parts in so far as this does not detract from the effectiveness and usefulness of the particular weapons and pieces of equipment;

4. avoidance of excessive requirements which will delay steady and rapid production;

5. elimination of excessive production requirements and contractual conditions, particularly in relation to tolerances in parts of weapons and equipment which could easily be made more generous.

Above all, however: proposals for the saving of labour through stopping the exaggerated reworking of inessential parts of weapons and equipment, which is primarily designed to please the eye rather than serve a useful purpose.

These proposals should be met with a generously receptive response. However, it is essential to prevent the effectiveness and usability of the weapons and military equipment from being damaged resulting in important disadvantages which may even be decisive for the outcome of the war.

Directives for the implementation of this order will be issued, after consultation with each other, by the Supreme Command of the Wehrmacht for the military sphere and by the Reich Ministry for Armaments and Munitions for the production sphere in agreement with the Wehrmacht branch involved. The head of the Supreme Command of the Wehrmacht and the Reich Minister for Armaments and Munitions will report to me regularly on the success of these measures.

———

However, although this order indicated the direction of Hitler's thinking and stimulated the formation of various rationalization 'commissions', without a more clear-cut allocation of responsibilities, in particular without establishing a central agency with real authority, which could direct the other agencies, the 'war of all against all' (Thomas) was bound to go on. In the event, it required the crisis produced by the serious reverse experienced by the German armies before Moscow, which began during the next few days, to force Hitler at last to take decisive action. Even then, he began hesitantly, with limited backing for Todt's initiatives and, arguably, it was only with the death of Todt on 8 February 1942 that Hitler was prepared to throw his political weight fully behind the creation of a new structure for the German war economy.

On 13 January 1942 Todt explained his programme to a session of the Grand Council of the Reich Industry Group:

**1057** 1. *Todt*: We came to a halt before the gates of Moscow presumably because the Russians had a huge base behind them in the shape of the 4 million-strong city of Moscow. If we draw conclusions from that, it means that not only the Wehrmacht but the whole German people must be made to feel the harsh effects of war more than hitherto in order to prompt them to give of their utmost.

Contrary to the practice hitherto, in future the watchword must be: concentration of production.

Contrary to the practice hitherto in which production costs were met in full, in future the motto must be: we shall only pay for performance. And so there must be fixed prices. The factory which works in the most rational way will make the most profit.

To achieve this, we must involve the self-administration of business. Business must itself make proposals as to how the concentration of production, i.e. the most efficient outcome, can be achieved . . .

It has proved necessary to tighten the reins in the sector of general Wehrmacht equipment as well and to make a central agency responsible for ensuring that this sector operates efficiently as well. This task has been given to Herr Zangen, who has taken it on on behalf of the Reich Industry Group and, as the head of the Group, he has delegated it to the heads of the Economic Groups . . .

It is not our task to transform the economic structure, the issue is rather: how can we best serve German armaments production in order to secure victory? We don't want to hurt people for the sake of hurting, but only to close plants when there is no other alternative. In order to take account of the regional implications, the Armaments Inspectorates should if necessary be informed beforehand and their agreement secured.

Todt has already written to Generals Thomas and Leeb with the request to support Herr Zangen in the task which he has been set . . .

3. *Zangen*: Herr Zangen repeatedly quoted a remark made by Ministerialdirektor[31] Mansfeld of the RAM[32] in his earlier speech . It was a remark of Frederick the Great: Battles are won with bayonets, wars are only won through the economy.

---

[31] A rank approximating to that of Under-Secretary in the British Civil Service.
[32] *Reichsarbeitsministerium* = Reich Labour Ministry.

Zangen referred to the successful rationalization in the armaments sector carried out by Herr Kessler's committee. This process must now be repeated in the civilian sector under the responsible leadership of the Economic Groups. The only people suitable for appointment as heads of the working groups were factory owners acting in an honorary capacity and ideally the heads of plants or designers. Priority must invariably be given to the most efficient factory.

---

The rationalization issue was then taken up within industry itself, as is clear from the following excerpt from the secret minute taken by Karl Albrecht, Secretary of the Economic Group Fine Mechanics and Optics, at the session of the Council of the Reich Industry Group on 5 February 1942:

**1058** Herr Zangen emphasized once more that the whole of industry must be regarded as involved in armaments and therefore is confronted with the task of realizing the Führer's order [of 3 December 1941]. The Economic Groups should nominate suitable men for this purpose. They need not necessarily do the job themselves. The main thing is to appoint first-class specialists from the best plants who are in a position to carry out the tasks energetically, if necessary in the face of tremendous opposition. We must rationalize radically on the model of the best plants. He is eagerly awaiting the arrival of individual proposals. Every wastage of working time must be rigorously rooted out. Zangen is pressing for maximum speed and rejects bureaucratic methods. Todt demands that our aims should be ruthlessly realized and will grant any authority required to achieve this.

The action was in no sense directed against medium-sized and small plants but rather exclusively against uneconomic plants. He [Zangen] wished to state that one could assume that there would be a greater deployment of Russians and the French . . .

In the discussion Lange[33] described the task roughly as follows: first phase, reduction in the number of types; second phase, completion of the production programme of the individual firms and coordinating it with the other firms; third phase, complete reorganization of production or closure.

---

On 8 February 1942, however, Todt was killed in an air crash. Hitler replaced him as Reich Minister of Armaments and Munitions by his protégé, Albert Speer. Speer had established a relationship of remarkable intimacy with Hitler largely based on Hitler's admiration for Speer's architectural gifts. He evidently saw in Speer the architect he might have become himself and the man through whom he could realize his archi-

---

[33] Karl Lange, Secretary of the Machine Building Economic Group and Plenipotentiary for Machine Production under Todt.

tectural ambitions, which were in turn an expression of his megalo-
mania. But Speer had also impressed Hitler with his organizational
skills, demonstrated, for example, in his supervision of the construction
of the new Reich Chancellery on schedule. Speer had been made
responsible for reconstructing Berlin for its future role as the capital city
of a world power (Germania) and, at the beginning of the war, he had
been put in charge of construction projects for the air force. Now, with
Hitler's full support behind him, Speer was able to put into effect and
develop further the policies initiated by Todt.

On 18 February 1942 the main outlines of the new organization were
agreed at a meeting at the Reich Ministry for Armaments and
Munitions attended by representatives of the army (Fromm,), navy
(Witzell), air force (Milch), OKW (Thomas), Reich Economics Ministry
(von Hanneken), Reich Industry Group (Zangen):

**1059**    2. The contracts given to business by the various consumers are to be
directed via the Main Committees which have been or are to be established for
the various spheres . . .

3. In the case of numerous production processes, (e.g. forged pieces) which need
to be carried out in the production spheres covered by several Main Committees,
difficulties in meeting the demand will arise in the course of the allocation of
contracts by the Main Committees in association with the department heads
and section heads of the Wehrmacht branches. It is, therefore, envisaged that,
alongside the vertical organization of the Main and Special Committees and the
working groups, a horizontal organization will be introduced in the shape of
Industry Rings. The leadership of each Industry Ring will be assigned to a
single firm which can provide the best specialist for the task . . .

The Industry Ring has the right to give instructions to all firms in its sphere of
operations. In addition, the Industry Ring has the task of distributing the
contracts in such a way that they are completed at minimum cost; it must
undertake technical rationalization and cut the number and variety of types in
collaboration with the consumer . . . The head of the Reich Industry Group is
responsible for coordinating the Industry Rings.

The whole self-administration organization of business consisting of the Main
Committees and Industry Rings is subordinated to the Reich Ministry for
Armaments and Munitions. The representatives of the consumers who are
participating in the meeting commit themselves to ensuring that, within their own
spheres of operation, the procurement agencies and their officials will respect this
self-administration organization of business and will refrain from initiating any
measures which are calculated to disrupt the process of armaments production in
accordance with this scheme. In particular, the consumers will refrain from
issuing directives to business either directly or indirectly which contradict the
directives of the Main Committees and Industry Rings without prior
consultation with the relevant Main Committees and industrial leaders.

A few days later, on 24 February 1942, Speer explained the new arrangements in a speech to a meeting of Gauleiters. He urged them to support him in mobilizing the economy for war, but at the same time made clear that his Ministry was now in charge:

**1060**    During the war, the armaments sector must establish and determine the priorities for the rest of the industrial economy. Improvement in the performance of plants is primarily a technical and economic matter. Thus, as the Führer has established through a directive, the Party is only to involve itself in this sphere when I consider it necessary . . . Naturally the leadership of the people, i.e. in this case the need to increase the German workers' willingness to work, is not my task but quintessentially that of the Party and, in particular, of the German Labour Front. It is also the task of the political leadership to help overcome the lethargy of industry which, by no means with negative intent, will undoubtedly stand in the way of these efforts . . .

In order to achieve an improvement in performance, in the past few days I have created the following organization, which, in agreement with the Reich Marshal, the three Wehrmacht branches, the Reich Economics Ministry, various General Plenipotentiaries of the Four-Year Plan and industry itself, will now be established under the leadership of my Ministry.

The various important mass products such as weapons, munitions, tanks, Wehrmacht equipment, aero-engines and fuselages for the air force, motor vehicles and locomotives, or communications equipment are being placed under the control of Main Committees, which in turn are subdivided into Special Committees. For example, the Main Committee for tanks has Special Committees for tank production, development, engines and gearbox production, for traction vehicles or special vehicle programmes.

As a matter of principle, the Main and Special Committees will only employ industrial designers or mechanical engineers. The plant leaders, in so far as they are not experts and the official administrators in the Wehrmacht offices, are, therefore, excluded on principle.

The Main Committees, together with the Special Committees, have the task of receiving the constructive requests of the Wehrmacht branches and then making the necessary practical suggestions. Hitherto, the designs put forward by the weapons procurement offices were often completely 'oblivious to the needs of factory production' [*Betriebsfremd*], i.e. without any consideration for the limits imposed by schedules and supplies of material. At the same time, the Main Committees have the task of allocating contracts in such a way that, through mutual exchanges, as far as possible plants only manufacture one product but do so in large numbers.

In the work of the numerous Main Committees and Special Committees various common tasks arise which need to be carried out simultaneously. They need to be dealt with jointly. Thus, for example, crank shafts are a particular bottleneck for almost every Main Committee and this has a considerable influence on the decisions of the designers.

In order to coordinate the various interests here as well, 'Industrial Rings' have been established. Here all the common issues which arise in the spheres of operation of the Main Committees are brought together and the individual specialists of the Main and Special Committees simultaneously fulfil the role of specialists in the Industrial Rings. Thus, hitherto Industrial Rings have had to be created for forged pieces, armour plating, steel plating, steel tubes, engines, cogs, screws, crankshafts, ball bearings, machine tools, optical equipment etc.

This whole organization would not be worth much more than a scrap of paper if one did not ensure that now, for the first time, technicians really acquired freedom of action in these matters. In a speech on 13 February the Führer declared that among individual designers and engineers there is a huge number of the most notable brains which are not being utilized. They only needed to be employed in the production of weapons and Wehrmacht equipment. The tremendous amount of inventive genius available had hitherto not been sufficiently utilized for military purposes. I am confident that our new organization for which, by the way, Dr Todt laid the foundations, will at last achieve the necessary changes here.

Unfortunately, nowadays the leading figures in our industry are too old. In order to avoid this excessive age from having any adverse effects on our rationalization measures, instructions have been given that, in the case of all important posts which are occupied by people over 55, the permanent deputies should all be at most 40 years old.

The improvement in performance through the improvement of plants or through the reallocation or centralization of contracts already produced remarkable results during Dr Todt's period of office. Here are a number of examples:

The Munitions Ministry began by focusing on trying to improve the production of the 8.8 shell. The time taken to improve this shell varied between the individual firms by up to six times and in the case of individual work processes even by as much as thirty times. By simplifying numerous work processes during the past year output was increased by 100 per cent, although the number of workers employed only increased by 25 per cent, i.e. 80 per cent more is achieved than a year ago with the same number of workers.

----

By mid-1944, there were twenty-one Main Committees and twelve Rings, in addition to the Special Commissions.

However, arguably the most important reform which Speer persuaded Hitler to introduce—Speer himself described it as 'the most important war economy measure of all'[34]—was the establishment of a new central organization For the main problem of the German war economy had been the lack of a coordinating body which could develop and enforce a programme of priorities for the allocation of resources. This new organization was called the Central Planning Board. Its influence was

----

[34] In a speech to Gau Economic Advisers on 17 April 1942. See BA/MA RW 19/967.

based on its control over the allocation of raw materials and planning decisions for new plant. Hitherto this task had been divided between the Reich Economics Ministry, which provided the raw materials, and the WiRüA, which in turn allocated them to the three branches of the Wehrmacht through a rigid quota system, which effectively placed the war economy in a straitjacket. Hitler agreed on 4 April 1942 to the formation of the Central Planning Board and ratified it by decree on 15 April. For the sake of appearances and to give it even more political clout, the Central Planning Board was placed within Göring's Four-Year Plan Office and Paul Körner, Göring's right-hand man, was made a member of the triumvirate running it. But power lay essentially with the other two members, Field Marshal Milch of the air force, and above all Speer, who not only had direct access to Hitler but for the next eighteen months or so was on exceptionally cordial terms with him.

**1061**    On the proposal of Reich Minister Speer in his capacity as Plenipotentiary for Armaments in the Four-Year Plan, the Reich Marshal has established a 'Central Planning Board' within the Four-Year Plan. The contents of the decree are as follows:

Berlin, 22 April 1942

In order to guarantee the priority for armaments which has been ordered by the Führer and in order to concentrate in one decision-making body all the demands which must be made on the economy as a whole during the war, as well as to coordinate the requirements of the armaments industry with those of the supply of foodstuffs and with the availability of raw materials and manufacturing facilities within the economy, I decree:

1. A Central Planning Board shall be established within the framework of the Four-year Plan. It is to be directly subordinate to me.

2. The direction of the Central Planning Board shall be undertaken by Reich Minister Speer, Field Marshal Milch, and State Secretary Körner working in collaboration.

3. The sphere of activity of the Central Planning Board embraces the whole economy and has among others the following responsibilities:

    (a) the power of decision over whether or not new plans are required or whether existing plans should be continued;

    (b) the power of decision over whether or not to create new raw material manufacturing plants or whether existing plants should be extended;

    (c) the allocation of existing raw materials, in particular of iron and metals, to those requiring them;

    (d) the distribution of coal and energy to manufacturing plants;

    (e) the co-ordination of the requirements for transport throughout the whole economy.

4. Except where I have reserved for myself the power of decision in individual cases, the Central Planning Board makes the final decisions on its own authority on the basis of the powers delegated by me.

5. The Central Planning Board will decree the requisite regulations for the implementation of this decree.

6. The powers which were delegated to the Plenipotentiary-General for Armaments in the Four-year Plan by my decree of 1.3.42 are not affected by this decree.

▬

The formation of a body with such far-reaching authority was bound to reduce the powers of the other economic agencies, notably the WiRüA and the Reich Economics Ministry. On 7 May 1942 the sections of the WiRüA responsible for implementing the armaments programme were transferred to the Armaments Ministry and, although Thomas was still nominally in charge of the new 'Armaments Office', in practice he had been sidelined and, in November 1942, was forced out altogether, thereby finally ending military influence over the economy. Then, on 2 September 1943, a Führer edict transferred civilian production from the Economics Ministry to the Armaments Ministry. Funk was appointed to the Central Planning Board and a Central Planning Office was established to handle the board's increasingly heavy workload, to prepare its decisions and supervise their implementation.

One of the problems which had bedevilled armaments production during the first two years of the war had been the conflict between the various agencies in the field—the Armaments Inspectorates and Commandos answering to the WiRüA, the State Economic Offices (*Landeswirtschaftsämter*) subordinate to the Economics Ministry, the State Labour Offices under the Reich Labour Ministry, the Todt working groups etc., not to mention the representatives of the three branches of the Wehrmacht. On 17 September 1942 an effort was made to co-ordinate armaments activities at district level (*Mittelinstanz*) by creating so-called Armaments Commissions under the control of the Armaments Ministry and containing representatives from the various bodies.

The following letter from the Gauleiter of the Lower Danube, Dr Hugo Jury, to Bormann, dated 2 April 1942, presents a stark picture of the weaknesses of German economic organization at the time the Todt–Speer reforms were in the process of being introduced. Among other things he criticized:

**1062** 1. The imposing of continually increasing burdens on people's commitment and ability to perform effectively in the form of unproductive tasks caused by:

(a) An overstaffed centralized administration. Every industrial plant is subject to professional supervision by its Economic Group. Its raw materials are administered by a Reich agency. As far as economic self-administration is concerned, the plant belongs to the Chamber of Industry and Commerce, but as an armaments plant it is subject to the Armaments Inspectorate and the Armaments Commando. The State Economic Office [*Landeswirtschaftsamt*] is responsible for its civilian production. The political leadership [*Menschenführung*] is in the hands of the DAF, its labour supply in those of the State Labour Office. Wages are dealt with by the Reich Trustee of Labour, price issues by the Price Inspectorate. If the plant is in the foodstuffs industry then there are, in addition, the organizations of the Reich Food Estate to contend with. Co-operation with these agencies is complicated by the fact that their spheres of operation overlap both in terms of the duties they perform and geographically. The result is an unproductive toing and froing which reaches grotesque proportions if the plant is in a frontier district or is involved with several geographically distinct administrations.

(b) The lack of a central and unified economic-political leadership, which is reflected in the minimal or total lack of coordination between the measures and plans of the individual centres of leadership and which encourages the perpetuation of irrational conflicts over competencies from the top down to the lowest office. For example, I keep feeling ashamed to see how not even the three Wehrmacht branches can coordinate their plans and demands . . .

(c) Lack of clarity and confusion of the price regulations and directives . . .

3. A lack of ideologically-based, focused economic-political guidance and, as a result, the major goals become obscured by an exaggeration of the importance of day-to-day issues. A lack of awareness of context, a narrow vision, conflicts over competencies as a result of unprofessional personal motives . . .

———

Despite the Todt–Speer reforms, many of these problems remained. Moreover, Speer's Ministry was unable to get control of air force production until 1944 and faced constant interference at district level from the Gauleiters, who, as we have seen, became increasingly influential during the last phase of the war.[35] Nevertheless, the transform-ation in armaments output between 1941–2 and 1944–5 was remarkable.

At the end of the war, the Allies were anxious to discover how the Germans had organized their war economy and, during 1945–6, subjected its leading figures to lengthy interrogation in the prison camp known as 'Dustbin'. The records of these interrogations provide one of our best sources for the history of the German war economy. The following excerpts are from the interrogations of Karl Otto Saur. Saur, a mechanical engineer and originally a senior figure in the major steel firm, United Steel (*Vereinigte Stahlwerke*), was Todt's right-hand man while he was Munitions Minister and then, after his death, became Speer's deputy and eventually his rival:

---

[35] See above, pp. 89–91.

**1063**    (a) . . . In the further course of our work under Reich Minister Todt up
to winter 41/2, following the takeover of munitions and tank production,
Special Commissions led by industrialists were also created for weapons, motor
vehicles and general Wehrmacht equipment. This form of organization was
characterized by the fact that leading figures in industry each took over responsibility for the entire planning and implementation of production in a particular
sphere of military equipment. It was an essential task for the Committees
through rationalization to find ways of securing significantly more production
from the existing amounts of material, labour and plant. The Führer's decree of
3.12.1941[36] was of fundamental importance in this respect . . .

On the basis of this decree (Implementation Decree of 22.12.1941) engineers
acquired a large sphere of operations. Within the framework of Commissions
every piece of armaments equipment was examined by the military procurement
agencies, the technical experts and the practical men in the plants. However, in
addition to savings on labour and material an essential task of our technical
experts was to find ways of solving the raw materials problem. Locomotives
provide an example of our mode of operation. At the beginning of 1942, a
locomotive needed 2.3 tons of copper. After this action had been implemented,
in 1943 it only needed 237kg, i.e. the amount of copper was reduced to 1/10. At
the same time, the construction of locomotives was expanded from 117 per
month on average in 1941/2 to 500 in June 1943. Thus, these 500 locomotives
used only half the amount of copper needed to produce the 117 before.

Another example is the U-boat. Because of a shortage of copper the
construction programme was going to be reduced from 24 to initially 20 and
later even down to 16. At that time, each boat required about 56 tons, later only
about 26 tons . . .

Previously, there were constant alterations. No programme ran for longer than
two to three months until, in spring 1942, the Führer banned any alteration of
programmes on account of some day-to-day event. But, at that time, the Führer
only concerned himself with army matters because he knew about them from his
own experience. As a result, even in 1944, the air force was still continually
altering its contracts. We had plants which, as a consequence, for years on end
never produced a single plane. When we formed the Fighter Staff on 1.3.1944 we
had about 45 different types. In the first three months we came down from 45 to
20, then to 9 and finally to 5 types . . .

In 1943, Speer had to take civilian production away from the Economics
Ministry and place it under the Armaments Ministry.[37] The preconditions for
production of the two sectors were so bound up with each other that one could

---

[36] See above, pp. 221–23.

[37] §2 of the Führer's decree concerning the concentration of the economy of 2
September 1943: 'The responsibilities of the Reich Economics Minister in the
spheres of raw materials and production in industry and handicrafts are
transferred to the Reich Minister for Armaments and Munitions. In view
of his extended range of duties, the Reich Minister for Armaments and
Munitions carries the title Reich Minister for Armaments and War Production.'

not conduct armaments production with modern methods on its own without taking account of the reserves in the rest of production. But, in order not to kill off civilian production in the process we had to take it over ourselves and increase its performance through rationalization.

For example, we had 117 carpet factories of which 5 produced 90 per cent of the demand and the remaining 112 firms 10 per cent. To close these 112 firms and transfer their workers to armaments production would only produce a loss of 10 per cent, particularly since the other five firms were far more economical in their use of materials than the smaller firms.

And so, despite extensive reallocation of plant capacity and raw materials to the armaments industry, we succeeded through countless similar measures in sufficiently sustaining the production of other goods vital to the life of the population.

(b) . . . During the first years of the war, most plant capacity was under the control of the individual branches of the Wehrmacht. Each Wehrmacht branch anxiously tried to make sure that nothing was produced in its plants which was not to its benefit. At the beginning of the war, the Wehrmacht branches also built entirely separately from each other. In the case of the army and navy construction was in the hands of Todt; Speer was in charge of air force construction. As a result, capacity being used for programmes which had finished or been stopped and for which the particular Wehrmacht branch no longer had any use was paralysed. In Labant, for example, in 1940 a large plant was built for making bombs which was finished in 1941/2. But since we already had a large supply of bombs the plant never went into production and since the air force had no other use for it remained idle. A few kilometres away the army was proceeding energetically to build plants for heavy munitions. It was not yet possible to achieve coordination and to balance up the various demands . . .

Previously industry was in many cases hostile to rationalization . . . The mass production of guns was not initiated by the large firms but by the medium-sized and smaller plants. Markstedt was the only example of an attempt to involve a large concern in mass production and this attempt failed. Big industry had no interest in mass production since previously Krupp, Rheinmetall, Skoda, Deutsche Waffen u. Munition did not make their money from mass production but through the continual development of new and complicated types. One knew, therefore, that mass production could only be introduced on a large scale if one could find a way of providing large profits through mass production. This way was found through a simple measure: fixed prices . . .

(c) . . . Once the fixed price was introduced rationalization made an unexpected step forward. It was established as a basic principle for the fixed price in Government contracts that the first price group did not pay taxes, the second group [with a higher price] had to pay taxes, and the third group with an even higher price had to supply proof of special circumstances and bases for costs— for example an unfavourable establishment, excessive distance for transport, encumbrance with mortgages and loans, extraordinary expenditure. Yet all the departments that had anything to do with the matter were at first vigorously opposed to the idea of a fixed price.

As early as the first part of 1940, with the establishment of the Ministry for Armament and Munitions, an attempt was made to introduce the fixed price. In that we were working from the practical experience of one of our colleagues, Schaede—at that time Major Schaede, in his own factory; he asserted that if such a limit were set, it would be possible to adjust oneself to it to carry on business. But the order was not signed by Göring until October1941 (the agreement of the Four-Year Plan Office was required). Government departments vigorously fought against the proposal; the industrialists themselves were not consulted.

The previous basis for pricing had been the 'LSO' [*Leitsätze für die Selbstkostenabrechnung bei öffentlichen Aufträgen*: Guiding Principles for Settling Prime Costs in Public Contracts]. According to that, the total expenditure was recompensed, plus a profit of 3–6 per cent based on the expenditure. Consequently, no one was interested in reckoning a lower expenditure; the higher the cost the higher the profit. The 'LSO' quite consciously brought higher costs . . .

It goes without saying that, in addition to the fixed price we took various other steps in the field of armaments. We were spurred on by Director Heynen of the Gustloff Werke,[38] who, in the summer of 1941 gave a lecture to our armaments people on the occasion of an armaments meeting in Berlin. At one point he compared the cost of the individual processes in the manufacture of a machine gun in the various production firms. Previously, it had been the custom to say, 'Such and such a factory is the best', and other factories were adjusted accordingly. Heyden analysed in detail the twenty or thirty different steps. In this way it could be shown that the best factory produced at least 10 per cent of the processes in the most expensive way, and the most expensive factory produced 10 per cent of the processes in the best way, so that it was not correct to compare factory with factory, but only the individual process of one factory with the corresponding process of another. Thus comparisons cannot be made in a lump, but only by breaking down the whole into its component parts and then comparing part with part. It then became apparent that the most expensive factory was only expensive because it was perhaps not on the railway line or had some sort of special expense for equipment in contrast to another factory which had cheap water transport; or another factory was in the same combine with a steelworks and consequently got its steel at production cost.

After this lecture it became quite clear that, in addition to the comparison of factories there must be a comparison of the industrial programmes within the factory and, on the basis of the detailed work times, one must establish the best possible work plan . . .

In a short time the factories had been standardized in this manner to such an extent that the original ratio of difference between plants was reduced from about 1 : 5 to about 1 : 1.5, and in some cases even the average of all factories put together was better than the previous performance of the best factory.

___

The following document contains excerpts from the interrogation of Dietrich Stahl, Managing Director and owner of the munitions firm

---

[38] A big armaments firm.

T.H. Bergmann AG, Berlin, and from July 1943 Head of the Main Committee for Munitions in the Speer Ministry:

**1064** Remarkable results were achieved in the rationalization of the munitions industry. Through the introduction of the self-administration of industry the compulsory cooperation of firms using the same equipment and with the same categories of products was ensured. The manager or the technical director of the most efficient firm was appointed head of the respective 'Committee' or 'Ring'. The enquiry started in the price-examining centres and in similar supervisory organizations which acquired a fairly accurate estimate of the technical production capacity of the factories through the calculations they made when determining the fixed prices. It was the duty of the head of the Committee to raise the production of other firms of the same category to the same level as his own. By this means the experience gained in the various factories was discussed in a way that was impossible in the military procurement offices on account of the lack of people with practical experience and specialized knowledge. In this way specialists, engineers and technicians of proven ability were appointed as honorary members to work with the committees, and all trade secrets, private improvements and methods which might have been withheld by firms were made public for the benefit of all. This idea of compelling firms of the same category to cooperate under the leadership of the most competent one was the first big step towards the realisation of successful rationalization . . .

I recall that, as a result of the rationalization of the munitions industry the total average saving in materials, machinery and labour amounted to 30–40 per cent.

The following is an excerpt from the interrogation of Wilhelm Schaaf, a director of BMW and the Head of the Armaments Supply Office in the Speer Ministry:

**1065** The most important thing which the Armaments Supply Office did was to switch the components industry, with its 51,000 plants or thereabouts and 4 million workers from the production of vast quantities to producing only as much as was required by the army. The German components industry had expanded quite considerably during the latter years before the war. In order to satisfy the various export markets (which was its strongest line) the industry showed little standardization and even less rationalization. Apart from the larger concerns of international repute in the electrical, optical and machine-tool industries, there existed tens of thousands of moderately important and smaller firms, in particular in the field of iron and metal machining, and the production of machine elements and production aids, which had firmly established their place in the export trade, largely due to the excellence of their skilled workers and craftsmen. Through a combination of this wide production base and the new construction caused by the demands of armaments production, the necessary increase in capacity produced no great problem. By effecting rationalization and standardization in the works which already existed, a considerable increase in output was achieved without a substantial concurrent increase in the number of workers, in factory space or in expenditure on machinery.

The switch to the production of normal parts had to be given priority. At the same time, plants of a similar nature were brought into close cooperation. A monthly report on their work had to be produced by the Rings and the Committees. Thus, a very standardized type of material was in fact obtained, which when it was introduced to related firms served as a further stimulus and guidance in the work of simplification and rationalization.

For this work, the heads of the Rings had specially selected rationalization engineers on their staffs, who kept in constant personal contact with the responsible engineers at the individual companies within the scope of the Ring and had to guarantee an exchange of experience on a very broad basis . . .

I can only quote a few examples from memory, e.g. in the optics and precision instruments industry:

In 1942 300 different types of prismatic glass were produced and in less than one year these had been reduced to 14 different types. Simultaneously, 23 different plants were combined to form only 7. It was possible to reduce 3,000 types of articles to 180 and the 35 factories producing them were reduced to 6.

The fire-fighting apparatus required by the air force was manufactured at 334 different factories in 1942/3. By the beginning of 1944 these had been reduced to only 64. This coordination resulted in an economy of 360,000 productive working hours per month.

Through large-scale introduction of serial and assembly-line production, and even more by using seamless fittings, we achieved a substantial production increase with the same number of workers. The following figures from the Main Committee for Electrical Engineering Apparatus serve to demonstrate the results:

*Monthly output of 200cm searchlights*

at the end of 1942 . . . . . . . . . . . . . . .    20 searchlights
at the end of 1943 . . . . . . . . . . . . . . .    80 searchlights
at the end of 1944   . . . . . . . . . . . . . .    150 searchlights

## (v) Labour Mobilization 1939–1944

There was, however, one section of the economy which lay outside the control of Speer's Ministry and Central Planning but which was crucial to the full mobilization of the economy, namely the supply of labour. Here too, the German reverse before Moscow in December 1941 brought matters to a head. While, on the one hand, it became vital to draft more men into the armed forces to replace the mounting losses, on the other hand, it was equally essential to maintain or even increase the supply of labour for industry and, in particular, for the armaments industry. The problem was that attempts to secure additional labour for the armaments industry would involve withdrawing it from other sectors of industry. This was something to which the Gauleiters, who took a considerable interest in the economies of their areas, often objected.

To deal with this crisis Speer advocated the establishment of a post with special powers over the mobilization of labour to which, in his view, a Gauleiter should be appointed, since he would have the necessary weight within the Party to enable him to resist the other Gauleiters. Speer nominated Karl Hanke, the Gauleiter of Lower Silesia, who had been his district Party leader in Berlin and had given him his first architectural assignment for the Party. Bormann, however, wishing to reduce Speer's influence, persuaded Hitler that Hanke was too young and suggested one of his own protégés, Fritz Sauckel, Gauleiter of Thuringia. Thus, on 21 March 1942 Sauckel was appointed Plenipotentiary General for Labour Mobilization.

There were basically two possible solutions to the problem of labour supply, though they were not mutually exclusive. The first was the maximum utilization of all available labour resources within Germany; the second was the extensive use of foreign labour.

(a) *German labour 1940–1943*

There had already been a considerable shift of labour from the consumer goods sector to the armaments sector and even within the civilian sector many were working indirectly for the Wehrmacht. Already, on 9 January 1941, a deputation from the consumer goods industries had impressed on General Thomas the problems this was causing:

**1066**   *Dr Guth:* The consumer goods industry has already lost a large number of its workers as a result of them being called up into the Wehrmacht and through the combing through actions. The reduction was biggest in the following economic groups:

*Reduction in the male workforce in consumer industries in the first year of the war*

| Economic group | Pre-war | 1 June 1940 | Decline | |
|---|---|---|---|---|
| | | | absolute | % |
| Foodstuffs industry | 169,478 | 151,015 | −18,463 | −10.9 |
| Sugar industry | 24,926 | 24,432 | −494 | −2.0 |
| Spirits industry | 17,571 | 21,391 | +4,320 | +24.6 |

Reductions were much smaller in the foodstuffs sector with the exception of the breweries. In the spirits industry the number of those employed actually increased to some extent because of the increased production of spirits for fuel. In the course of the war the retinues in the consumer industry have been increasingly deployed to work directly and indirectly for the Wehrmacht . . . For example [the proportion] so employed in the leather industry at the end of the first year of the war was 55 per cent, in the textile industry 43.6 per cent. The glass industry (34.6%), the ceramics industry (27.3%), the spirits industry (29.4%) and the food industry (17.9%) are also employed in provisioning the Wehrmacht to a considerable extent.

While the number of those in the consumer industry who are working for the Wehrmacht is continually increasing, the number of those available for other purposes has gone down drastically:

*Male work force in consumer industries working on civilian contracts, June 1940*

| Economic sector | Pre-war | June 1940 | Decline | |
|---|---|---|---|---|
| | | | (nos.) | (%) |
| Leather industry | 98,515 | 45,437 | 53,078 | 53.9 |
| Textile industry | 360,795 | 165,819 | 194.976 | 54.0 |
| Clothing | 44,302 | 18,598 | 25,704 | 58.0 |
| Woodworking | 178,833 | 71,351 | 105,482 | 59.7 |
| Ceramic industry | 47,013 | 32,202 | 14,811 | 31.5 |
| Brewing | 70,742 | 48,720 | 22,022 | 31.1 |
| Paper | 39,987 | 26,047 | 13,490 | 34.9 |
| Metal goods | 94,371 | 49,991 | 44,380 | 47.0 |
| Glass industry | 59,909 | 38,491 | 21,417 | 35.7 |
| Printing | 143,300 | 103,019 | 40,281 | 28.1 |
| Foodstuffs | 166,478 | 124,015 | 42,463 | 25.5 |
| Sugar industry | 24,427 | 20,432 | 3,995 | 16.4 |
| Spirit industry | 14,571 | 15,891 | +1,320 | +9.1 |
| TOTAL | 1,343,243 | 760,014 | 583,229 | 43.3 |

The reduction in the number of workers who are still available for the war economy, apart from Wehrmacht contracts, is in some cases so large that individual economic groups are already fearing considerable damage. Thus we are faced with the alternative of either generally refraining from a further removal of workers—exceptions may be made in the case of individual plants— or of transferring considerable numbers of contracts to the occupied territories.

However, the authorities were convinced that a more ruthless pursuit of the 'combing through' policy was required and a year later, with the defeat of Stalingrad in January 1943, the problem came to a head once more. At a top-level meeting in the Reich Chancellery on 7 January 1943 Field Marshal Keitel reported that the eastern front had a shortage of 700,000 men and that while 'the monthly reinforcements sent to the Eastern front comprise 60,000–65,000 men, by contrast the losses on the Eastern front in terms of deaths, those missing, the wounded, sick etc. comprise 150,000 per month'.[39] Speer offered 200,000 men from the armaments industry but these could not really be spared, since it required 800,000 new workers for the first quarter of 1943.

This situation formed the background to the issuing of the Führer Decree for the Comprehensive Deployment of Men and Women for Reich Defence Tasks of 13 January 1943, involving the setting up of the 'Committee of Three' (Lammers, Keitel and Bormann) to organize the more effective allocation of man/woman power between industry and the armed forces and within industry itself.[40]

The Führer decree of 13 January 1943 was immediately followed by two further important measures: first, on 27 January 1943, a decree introducing for all men between 16 and 65 and all women between 17 and 45 years of age, with certain exceptions, the duty to register with their local Labour Office for work.[41] Three days later, the Committee of Three issued a so-called Closure Decree which ordered the closure of trade and commercial businesses, which were not considered essential to the war effort. The decisions on closure were made by the Reich Defence Commissioner/Gauleiters acting on the advice of the local Party district leaders and the Party's district economic adviser and representatives of the official business organizations.

This measure produced a remarkable negative response since it involved thousands of members of the *Mittelstand,* the small business/ retailer section of the community which had been most supportive of the Nazi Party before 1933, suddenly finding themselves forced to close their shops and businesses and accept assignment to factory work or some other dependent and more or less menial employment. Moreover, they feared that this was not simply a temporary wartime measure but was part of a fundamental restructuring of the economy at their expense. The Gauleiter of Mark Brandenburg described it as 'certainly one of the greatest moral and political burdens which I have had to bear

---

[39] See Besprechung in der Reichskanzlei am 7 Januar 1943, 12 Januar 1943 in Bundesarchiv Berlin (BAB) R 43 II/655.

[40] For further details on the background to this decree see above, pp. 26ff.

[41] For further details on this decree, which was aimed mainly at women, see below, pp. 330ff.

in my long years of Party and public activity'.[42] In his Gau alone, by 9
May, some 9,000 businesses had been closed down. And he reported the
huge numbers of appeals and attempts to evade closure by, for example,
transferring the business to sons, grandsons, nephews etc. who were at
the front, in the hope that this would force the authorities to back off.
Such was the threat to morale by this action that, partly under pressure
from the Propaganda Ministry, it had to be concluded by September
1943.

Those involved on the ground with labour matters were sceptical from
the start about the value of these measures. Thus the Reich Trustee of
Labour for the Württemberg district told a meeting of experts in
Stuttgart that 'it is wrong to expect a significant increase in the amount
of labour from the new laws on the duty of labour. One cannot increase
armaments production with old people and women who are not used to
work. The biggest current difficulty is in the lack of skilled workers. We
are short of 350,000 skilled workers, who will have to be secured from
French industry'.[43] Indeed, the other, and more effective, solution to the
labour problem was to increase the use of foreign labour.

(b)  *Foreign Labour*[44]

By 1943, foreign labour was already being used to a considerable extent.
However, it was a controversial issue from the start since many within
the regime regarded the employment of large numbers of 'ethnic aliens'
(*Fremdvölkische*) as both a security and a racial threat. Its development
had not followed any coherent plan or any consistent principles but had
proceeded in an ad hoc fashion. It had emerged from the interaction of
economic, security and racial priorities whose relative significance
shifted depending on the state of the war. When the war was going well
racial and security priorities achieved greater weight; when the military
situation deteriorated more emphasis tended to be given to economic
priorities.

---

[42] See Emil Stürz to Lammers 5.5.1943, BAB R 43 II/662.

[43] See 'Vortrag des Reichtreuhänmders der Arbeit Dr Kimmich bei der
Arbeitstagung der SB am 5.2.43 in Stuttgart' in Staatsarchiv Ludwigsburg
(StAL) PL 502132 Bü 107.

[44] For further material on foreign labour see Vol. 3, doc. 638 and docs 695–99
and pp. 326ff. below. This section owes much to Ulrich Herbert's *Fremdarbeiter.
Politik und Praxis des "Ausländer-Einsatzes" in der Kriegswirtschaft des Dritten
Reiches* (Berlin/Bonn 1985).

After the conquest of Poland, the German authorities began to recruit Poles for work in the Reich, mainly on the land to replace the German land workers who had left for more lucrative employment in the armaments industry. There was already a long-standing tradition in Prussia's eastern provinces of hiring Polish labour, a tradition which had included legal and social discrimination against Polish workers. This was now reinforced by Nazi racial dogma leading to the issuing of harsh codes of behaviour for Polish workers during 1940.[45] When voluntary methods of recruitment proved inadequate, in May 1940 the German authorities began to introduce coercion and also to convert Polish prisoners of war into civilian workers. As a result, by the spring of 1942 there were approximately 1,080,000 Polish workers in the Reich.

Between the end of the campaign in the west and the spring of 1942, the recruitment of foreign labour was mainly among West European prisoners of war and unemployed workers recruited from the western countries and from Germany's allies, particularly Italy. This policy proved extremely successful and, by 1 October 1942, there were some 3,507,526 foreign workers and prisoners of war employed in Germany.

With the invasion of the Soviet Union vast numbers of prisoners of war were captured. But since the assumption was that the Soviet Union's defeat was imminent and Soviet prisoners were regarded as sub-humans, they were allowed to die of starvation and ill-treatment. By February 1942, of the original number of 3,900,000 Soviet prisoners of war only 1,100,000 were left. In October 1941 Hitler had finally agreed to the use of Russian prisoners of war for labour in Germany, but the food rations allocated to them were so minimal and the conditions in which they were housed were so poor that even those who had arrived in Germany in good health were soon in no fit state to work.

Sauckel had been appointed Plenipotentiary General for Labour Mobilization in March 1942 to recruit the large amount of labour which was necessary to replace the increasing numbers of workers being drafted into the armed forces. On his appointment, he was given orders by Hitler to recruit the necessary workers primarily from the occupied territories and in particular from the east. Sauckel embodied these instructions in a programme which he issued on 20 April 1942:

**1067**   The aim of this gigantic new labour mobilization is to use the rich and tremendous resources, conquered and secured for us by our armed forces under the leadership of Adolf Hitler, for the armament of the armed forces and also to provide food for the homeland. The raw materials as well as the fertility of the

---

[45] On the treatment of Polish workers see Vol. 3, docs 696–99.

conquered territories and their manpower are to be exploited completely and conscientiously for the benefit of Germany and its allies . . .

All prisoners of war, actually in Germany, from the territories of the west as well as of the east must be completely incorporated into the German armaments and munitions industries. Their productivity must be raised to the highest possible level. It must be emphasized, however, that a tremendous additional quantity of foreign labour must be found for the Reich. The occupied territories in the east will provide the greatest pool for this purpose. Consequently, it is absolutely essential to use the human reserves of the conquered Soviet territory to the fullest extent. If we do not succeed in obtaining the necessary amount of labour on a voluntary basis, we must immediately institute conscription of forced labour. Thus, apart from the prisoners of war still in the occupied territories, we must requisition skilled or unskilled male and female labour from the Soviet territories from the age of 15 upwards for the labour mobilization programme.

On the other hand, as things stand at present, one-quarter of our total needs of foreign labour can be procured from the occupied territories in the west. The procurement of labour from friendly and also from neutral countries can cover only a small part of our total requirements. In this connection, virtually only skilled workers and specialists can be considered.

In order to provide significant relief for the German housewife, especially for mothers with many children and farmers' wives who are extremely busy, and in order to avoid any further danger to their health, the Führer has charged me with procuring 400,000–500,000 picked, strong and healthy girls from the eastern territories . . .

The employment of all prisoners of war, as well as the use of a tremendous number of civilian workers, has become a prerequisite for carrying out the labour mobilization programme in this war. All the men must be fed, housed, and treated in such a way as to exploit them to the greatest possible extent at the absolute minimum of expenditure. It has always been natural for us Germans to refrain from cruelty or mean chicanery towards a conquered enemy, even if he had proved himself the most bestial and implacable adversary, and to treat him correctly and humanely, even when we expect useful work from him.

So long as the German armaments industry did not make it absolutely necessary, we refrained from using either Soviet prisoners of war or civilian workers, men or women from the Soviet territories under any circumstances. It has now become impossible to maintain this attitude, and the manpower of these people must be exploited to the greatest possible extent. Consequently, my first measures have been to arrange the feeding, housing and treatment of these foreign workers, in conjunction with the competent Reich authorities and with the consent of the Führer and Reich Marshal of the Greater German Reich, in such a way that maximum productivity will be demanded and obtained. It must be remembered, however, that the output even of a machine is conditioned by the amount of fuel, skill and care given to it. In the case of men, even of a low type and race, how many more factors must be considered than in the case of a machine!

I could not justify it to the German people, if, after such a tremendous number of men had been brought to Germany, these men, instead of doing highly necessary and useful work, were to become a burden on the German people or even a threat to their health because of blunders made regarding their nutrition, housing and general treatment. The principles of German cleanliness, order and hygiene must, therefore, be carefully applied to the Russian camps. Only in this way will it become possible, without any trace of false sentimentality, to exploit their labour so as to achieve the maximum advantage for the production of arms for the front and for our programme of wartime nutrition.

━━━

In fact, despite Sauckel's comments, although there was a slight improvement in the treatment of the so-called Eastern workers (i.e. Russians) in terms of diet, basically they continued to receive exceptionally poor treatment, dictated by official and unofficial racial prejudice.[46]

From 1942 onwards, broadly speaking there emerged two rival approaches to the employment of foreign labour and, specifically to the treatment of the 'Eastern workers'. On the one hand, there were those whose responsibility was to maximize production—the Speer Ministry and business organizations. This group, while not uninfluenced by racial considerations—they were Nazi managers, not unpolitical technocrats—nevertheless favoured somewhat better treatment of foreign workers in terms of food rations, accommodation and freedom of movement, in order to improve their health and raise their morale and so improve their productivity. However, any improvements increasingly took the form of incentives specifically tied to increased individual output. On the other hand, there were those for whom racial and security priorities came first and who were loath to make any but the most minimal concessions to the Eastern workers, notably the Reich Security Head Office (*Reichssicherheitshauptamt* = RSHA) and the Party Chancellery. They feared and resented the presence of 'ethnic aliens' in Germany and wished to assert the racial superiority of Germans and to maintain maximum distance between them and the foreign workers at all costs, even that of productivity. Sauckel was to some extent caught between the pressures from these two positions. While making rhetorical gestures towards the humane treatment of foreign workers, he shared the Nazi ideological prejudices and in practice did little to improve matters. Moreover, his recruitment policies countenanced extreme ruthlessness as he sought to meet the quotas which he had promised to fulfil.

At the beginning of 1943, the first group, the pragmatists, acquired a powerful new ally in the shape of the Propaganda Ministry. For, as a consequence of the German defeat at Stalingrad, Goebbels had

---

[46] See below, pp. 326ff.

concluded that the war could only be won or at least defeat avoided if absolute priority was given to the war effort and racial policies were for the time being played down. In consequence, he launched a two-pronged strategy: on the home front a campaign for total war;[47] and, secondly, a campaign of 'Europe against Bolshevism' designed to portray Germany as the only defender of Europe against the threat of a Bolshevik conquest. As part of the second campaign he aimed to differentiate the 'Russians' from 'Bolshevism' and to woo the former to support the German war effort.

Early in February 1943, Goebbels persuaded Hitler to endorse his new line and grant him the authority to ensure a uniform treatment of foreigners by all German agencies. On 15 February, he produced a set of propaganda guidelines which laid down that the Eastern peoples were no longer to be treated as 'beasts and barbarians'. However, the RSHA and the Party Chancellery were unhappy with the new course and on 10 March, a conference took place in the Propaganda Ministry at which they objected to Goebbels' new guidelines. The matter was then referred to the permanent working group which dealt with the treatment of foreign labour. On 6 May 1943, Ernst Kaltenbrunner, the new head of the Reich Security Head Office (RSHA), reported to Lammers on the outcome of these deliberations, a set of rules drawn up on 15 April 1943:

**1068**    Re: *Directives for the treatment of foreign workers employed in the Reich*

I opposed the guidelines for the treatment of the workers employed in the Reich proposed by the Reich Minister for Popular Enlightenment and Propaganda in the conference on 10.3.43 because these guidelines:

1. were intended to cancel all previous directives in the sphere of foreign labour,
2. as far as most of their points were concerned, had already been the subject of appropriate instructions from the relevant agencies, or, following intensive discussions, had been declared unacceptable,
and
3. completely ignored the security of the nation and the state.

Further discussions of the issue by the working group which meets in the Reich Security Head Office, in which all the agencies involved in the deployment of foreign labour are represented, have led to a re-examination of the draft proposed by the Reich Propaganda Ministry. After all the relevant points had been taken account of, a set of rules was issued by the working group which is based on the original draft of the Reich Propaganda Ministry. As a result, the matter has now been settled.

I enclose a copy of the set of rules for your information.

---

[47] See below, pp. 487ff.

[The Reich Chancellery desk officer minuted the Kaltenbrunner letter as follows:]

The enclosed new set of rules concerning the treatment of the ethnically alien workers largely corresponds, to some extent word for word, with the guidelines proposed by the Propaganda Ministry in the meeting on 10 March. The difference is that consideration of Reich security and the need to maintain a distance between Germans and ethnically alien workers are emphasized as the most important points.

*Rules concerning the general principles governing the treatment of foreign workers employed in the Reich*

The Reich's struggle against the destructive forces of Bolshevism is more and more becoming a European affair. For the first time in the history of this continent the outlines of a European solidarity are beginning to emerge, albeit in some countries only vaguely. A visible practical result of this development is the employment of millions of foreign workers from almost all states on the European mainland including a large number of those belonging to the conquered enemy powers. However, this fact imposes a number of obligations on the German people which arise above all from the following principles:
1. The first priority is the security of the Reich. The Reichsführer SS and his agencies determine the security measures for the protection of the Reich and the German people.
2. Naturally, humane treatment of the foreign workers designed to increase their productivity and concessions made to them can easily lead to the obscuring of the clear line of separation between the ethnically alien workers and German compatriots. German compatriots are to be instructed to regard the maintenance of the requisite distance between themselves and the ethnic aliens as a national duty. German compatriots must be aware that, if they ignore the basic principles of the national socialist conception of race [*Blutsauffassung*], they will face the severest penalties. Awareness that it is a matter of victory or Bolshevik chaos must prompt every German to draw the necessary conclusions in his relationship with ethnically alien workers.

Everything must be subordinated to the goal of a victorious conclusion of the war. The foreign workers employed in the Reich are, therefore, to be treated in such a way that their reliability is maintained and encouraged, that negative effects for the Reich in their home countries are kept to a minimum and that their full labour potential is maintained for the long term, indeed that their performance is increased. For this purpose the following points are to be regarded as decisive:
1. Every person, even the most primitive, has a delicate sense of justice. Thus any unjust treatment must have a devastating effect. Injustice, insults, chicanery, mistreatment etc. must, therefore, be avoided. The use of corporal punishment is banned. The ethnically alien workers are to be kept suitably informed of the harsh measures applied in the case of recalcitrant or rebellious elements.
2. It is impossible to gain someone's support for a new idea if one simultaneously offends his deepest sense of personal worth. One cannot expect a high

level of performance from people who are called beasts, barbarians and sub-humans; on the contrary, every opportunity should be taken to encourage and promote their positive characteristics, such as a willingness to fight Bolshevism, the desire to protect their own lives and their homelands, commitment and willingness to work.

3. In addition, everything must be done to encourage the necessary cooperation of the European nations in the struggle against Bolshevism. Words alone are not going to convince the foreign workers that a German victory will also be beneficial for him and his nation. The precondition is appropriate treatment.

Based on these principles, the Plenipotentiary for Labour Deployment, as well as the other agencies responsible for the deployment of foreign workers in the German Reich have issued the following directives. Among these directives the following are to be given particular emphasis: . . .

[There follows a list of eight points dealing with such matters as 'clean and hygienic accommodation' and a ban on 'prison-like conditions and barbed wire', adequate clothing for the climatic conditions, food rations related to those of comparable German workers, provision for medical treatment etc.]

Since they have been issued as directives by the relevant agencies, the principles enunciated above are binding on all organizations, agencies and individuals. All agencies which are involved in the deployment and supervision of foreign workers, in particular the plant and camp leaders, are responsible for ensuring that these principles are put into practice and kept to. They must be clear about the fact that breaches of the above principles will damage the German war economy, and thereby indirectly the front, and, therefore, are not going to be prosecuted simply as political [*sic!*] offences (e.g. bodily harm, embezzlement, corruption) but in certain circumstances are even to be considered as aiding the enemy. It is not only the offenders themselves who may be called to account but also the heads of the agencies responsible The provision of inadequate information can also lead to disciplinary proceedings.

All existing orders and instructions for the treatment of foreign workers are to be examined by the responsible agencies to see whether they are compatible with the above principles. Where this is not the case they are to be immediately amended to bring them into line.

*Berlin, 15 April 1943*

---

The issuing of this document represented a setback for the RSHA and marked something of a turning point in the treatment of foreign workers. In practice, however, foreign workers and, in particular, Poles and Russians were still subject to varying degrees of discrimination and poor treatment. From 1943 onwards, responsibility for the treatment of foreign workers increasingly shifted from national to local level. Here it was up to the local camp commanders, employers, shop-floor managers and foremen how well foreign workers were treated. Conditions varied from industry to industry (with coal mining, for example, being particularly poor), from plant to plant, and even within plants depending, for example, on the skills and efficiency of the individual worker and the attitude of the supervisors. There was, however, a marked hierarchy of treatment both within plants and outside, a hierarchy which reflected the racial dogmas of the regime. The most marked division was between west European workers whose pay and conditions were not much inferior to those of German workers and those from eastern Europe, particularly Poles and Russians. But even among the workers of western Europe fine distinctions were made. Thus Flemish-speaking Belgian workers were treated better than their French-speaking compatriots since they were considered more Germanic. The Jews of course were at the bottom of the hierarchy, though few remained in Germany by 1943.

While there were cases of Germans giving food and showing kindness towards foreign workers and cases of brutality and contempt, the majority seemed to have responded with indifference, accepting their presence as a natural part of wartime existence. But this acceptance represented a form of adjustment to the new racially-determined society envisaged by the regime. Those German workers who suddenly found themselves in supervisory positions varied in the way they exercised their new power over the foreign workers but all had effectively become an integral part of the racist system.

The figures in doc. 1069 show the distribution of the labour force by origin and occupation.

(c) *Discipline and incentives*

Despite the concessions forced by labour militancy in response to the War Economy Decree of 1 September 1939,[48] the regime continued to keep a tight control on labour. This was reinforced by its most notable measure, namely the Directive of the General Plenipotentiary for Labour Mobilization against Breaches of Labour Contracts and the Poaching of Labour as well as the Encouragement of High Labour Earnings in the Private Sector of 20 July 1942. This not only prevented employers paying higher wages (only limited rises of 3–4 per cent per annum for a restricted number of workers in each plant were permitted) but also prevented workers from refusing work or leaving their jobs without permission. At the same time, there was shift to piece work and a rearrangement of wage scales to induce higher performance levels. Finally, as part of Goebbels' total war measures, on 11 August 1944 a

---

[48] See above, pp. 190ff.

**1069** *Labour force distribution 1919–1944, as of 31 May each year ('000)*

| | 1939 N | 1939 F | 1940 N | 1940 F | 1941 N | 1941 F | 1942 N | 1942 F | 1943 N | 1943 F | 1944 N | 1944 F |
|---|---|---|---|---|---|---|---|---|---|---|---|---|
| GRAND TOTAL | 39,115 | 301 | 34,403 | 1,154 | 32,716 | 3,033 | 31,157 | 4,137 | 30,267 | 6,260 | 28,984 | 7,126 |
| I AGRICULTURE | 11,104 | 121 | 10,007 | 680 | 9,262 | 1,459 | 9,252 | 1,978 | 9,008 | 2,293 | 8,708 | 2,478 |
| II INDUSTRY AND TRANSPORT | 18,482 | 156 | 15,857 | 401 | 15,206 | 1,379 | 13,836 | 1,878 | 13,324 | 3,566 | 12,489 | 4,132 |
| (a) Industry | 10,836 | 110 | 9,551 | 256 | 9,200 | 965 | 8,370 | 1,401 | 8,170 | 2,828 | 7,640 | 3,162 |
| (b) Handwork | 5,307 | 29 | 4,122 | 108 | 3,730 | 310 | 3,207 | 296 | 2,957 | 430 | 2,745 | 537 |
| (c) Transport | 2,109 | 16 | 1,982 | 35 | 2,072 | 97 | 2,064 | 171 | 2,010 | 289 | 1,927 | 407 |
| (d) Power | 230 | 1 | 202 | 2 | 204 | 7 | 195 | 10 | 187 | 19 | 177 | 26 |
| III DISTRIBUTION | 4,595 | 8 | 3,719 | 20 | 3,358 | 58 | 3,124 | 95 | 2,933 | 147 | 2,679 | 188 |
| IV ADMIN. AND SERVICES | 2,670 | 7 | 2,605 | 21 | 2,626 | 50 | 2,373 | 48 | 2,340 | 62 | 2,228 | 94 |
| V ARMED SERVICES | | | | | | | | | | | | |
| ADMIN. | 689 | 2 | 710 | 11 | 804 | 39 | 1,184 | 60 | 1,292 | 120 | 1,294 | 163 |
| VI DOMESTICS | 1,575 | 7 | 1,505 | 21 | 1,460 | 46 | 1,388 | 78 | 1,370 | 72 | 1,307 | 72 |
| VII HOME WORK | – | – | – | – | – | – | – | – | – | – | 279 | 1 |

N = Native      F = Foreigners, including Jews and PWs

total ban on vacations was introduced and, on 31 August, the 60-hour week was made mandatory for all plants and administrative agencies and overtime payments were abolished.

Breaches of discipline by foreign workers, particularly by Polish or 'Eastern workers' were harshly punished—often with beatings or consignment to a concentration camp or a 'work re-education camp' where conditions were little better. From 1942 onwards, the SS were eager for an excuse to transfer foreign workers to their concentration camps where they could exploit them for the factory production which was increasingly becoming the main raison d'être of the camps.[49]

The discipline of German workers remained generally good with the partial exception of female and young workers. Fear of having their reserved (*unabkömmlich*=uk) status removed and being sent to the eastern front was a distinct disincentive to bucking the system. But also they depended on their employers for their eligibility for additional food rations and work provided a valuable point of stability in an increasingly chaotic world. Employers were loath to use imprisonment as a weapon against German 'slackers' (*Bummelanten*) since they were so short of German workers; they preferred to impose fines or withdraw privileges as in the following example of the Untertürckheim plant of Daimler Benz:

**1070** [50]    To all Department Heads and Foremen of the Plant

Re: *The Combating of absenteeism through the withdrawal of additional food allocations*

All available measures must be taken to combat absenteeism. I refer you in particular to the relevant decrees of the Reich Minister for Food and Agriculture of 7 April 1942 and 20 October 1943 according to which, in cases of unexcused absence from work (absenteeism) and irresponsible reduction in work performance, the plant leader is not only entitled but is even duty bound to withdraw the offenders' bonus food ration cards, since in such cases the preconditions which are necessary for the provision of bonus food ration cards are no longer fulfilled. The bonus cards which have been withdrawn should be returned to the Food Office stating the reasons for the action taken.

· These decrees of the Reich Minister for Food and Agriculture are valid for all German and foreign workers in employment . . .

Every week the Welfare Department must provide me with a list of the cards which have been withdrawn broken down into departments and foreign and German workers.

*Untertürckheim, 4 May 1944*                                   THE PLANT LEADER

---

[49] See above, pp. 171ff.
[50] I owe this document to Dr Neil Gregor.

The Gestapo was also loath to get involved in the vast majority of cases which only affected individuals and where there was no political motive involved. However, in cases regarded as incorrigible or sometimes as a deterrent they would make an example of such an offender as in the following case of a German typist in a Daimler-Benz plant:

**1071** *NOTICE*[51]

Re: *Punishment for absence from work without leave*

The typist Maria S. employed in Department 60 KS, had to be reported to the Reich Trustee of Labour for frequent absence from work without leave on the basis of the first directive of the General Plenipotentiary for Labour Deployment of 1.11.1943 §5. He ordered her imprisonment where she remained until the prison was destroyed by fire. Subsequently she was transferred to the Rudersberg Work Re-education Camp from where she was released after seven weeks.

I wish to bring this to your attention and to remind you of the First Directive of the General Plenipotentiary for Labour Deployment for Ensuring Order in Plants of 1.11.1943, which was already announced some time ago, and take this opportunity to refer you to the second directive of 23.9.1944, which was put up on the notice board in the last few days in the hope that in future punishments will not need to be imposed on members of the retinue of our firm.

*Untertürckheim, 27 November 1944*                    THE PLANT LEADER

In addition to the employment of foreign labour on a massive scale by 1944, the authorities also tried to improve German labour productivity by a combination of material incentives and disciplinary measures, including an elaborate restructuring of the wage system in the iron and metal industry initiated by the personnel experts of industry and the German Labour Front along the lines of the latest personnel management techniques. Dr Theodor Hupfauer, an efficiency expert employed by Todt and later the head of Speer's Central Office, explained these to Allied interrogators after the war as follows:

**1072**     The skilled workers were shifting more and more from hourly paid wages to semi-skilled piece rates because this method led to higher total wages. The agreed times per piece were wrong, as they did not expect of any piece worker even a normal effort let alone a high level of efficiency. Fear of the notorious cutting of piece rates led to a constant concealment of the actual effort that was feasible. One of the usual results was that piece workers whose output was higher than the average let their piece-ticket disappear 'into the drawer' in order to hand it in and cash it at a later date, just before a holiday or

---

[51] I owe this document to Dr Neil Gregor.

leave. This tit for tat of 'cutting piece rates' in retaliation for 'concealment of piecework' was in no way conducive to a good atmosphere amongst the employees. The amount of labour reserves that was concealed in these false statements about piecework in 1942 and the negative effect the cutting of piece rates produced is brought out by the following concrete example:

When a factory in Saxony was investigated it was found necessary not only to change the organization of that factory but also to alter the agreed times for piecework. The actual state of production at the factory was explained to the entire workforce in a lecture and at the same time those on piecework were asked to reduce voluntarily the agreed, albeit too high, piece timings. With the foremen and works council acting as intermediaries the staff agreed on its own initiative to reduce the timings by 20 per cent.

Another innovation introduced by us was as follows. The classification of workers into three categories: 'skilled, semi-skilled, and unskilled labour' as adopted up till then was abolished. From that time on, all work in the iron and metal industry was graded into eight groups, called 'wage groups'.

Wage group I included the most primitive manual labour, whilst wage group VIII covered the highly qualified. All the other activities were classified into the wage groups II to VII, according to their value in relation to I and VIII. With the help of this grading of labour, any activity could be judged in a much fairer way than by merely applying the rough kind of classification of skilled, semi-skilled and unskilled. Various firms carried out a still more detailed grading by creating sub-groups within each wage group. For the firms in question this introduction of the new wage groups created considerable work, as every single activity performed by the firm had to be studied very carefully. For the valuation itself every possible factor which could influence the quality of work performed had to be considered. The trade skills, which were essential for carrying out any sort of work, everything which could impede the work process had to be studied. It must be emphasized that it was not only the worker but also the work that was graded. A proper classification could only be achieved if a uniform procedure for classification of activities was guaranteed throughout the country. For this reason the so-called Catalogue of Wage Groups was drawn up by representatives of the State, the trade organizations and the German Labour Front, with the assistance of first-class experts on industrial organization, that is industrialists and workers, who were organized in the Work Committees. This catalogue was issued to factories as a handbook. It contained numerous examples for each wage group, according to which a firm was able to grade the types of work it carried out. It was obvious that not every kind of activity could appear in the same wage group, as working conditions were entirely different in each firm..The 'factory wage group catalogue', submitted by the factories on the basis of the main catalogue, was checked by the German Labour Front and handed over to the Reich Trustee of Labour for the purpose of authorization and for the fixing of wages. The Reich Trustee of Labour fixed, within the limits (local classification) laid down by the Reich Minister of Labour and/or the General Plenipotentiary for Labour, the so-called average wage for a factory. The average wage was the wage of group V, according to which the amount to be paid out for the other groups was fixed.

The following is of interest with regard to wage groups. Under the former classification the difference between basic wages of unskilled and skilled labour was about 25 per cent at most. If, however, the basic wage of group V is fixed as 100 under the new scheme, then group I would be approximately 75 and group VIII 125. Accordingly there is a margin of about 50 per cent between the basic wage of unskilled and skilled labour.

The purpose and value of these wage measures can be seen from the following points:

1. The system of wage groups was a precisely constructed scale of valuations, which showed a clear relationship between each activity. As those immediately affected by this, i.e. employers and employees, drew up this scale themselves, one can indeed call it an absolutely impartial valuation.

2. The wage groups were the basis of the amounts paid out and they made it possible to fix wages at a level appropriate for the work done and in proportion to other work performed. Consequently, the basic wage varied according to every more or less well-defined skill required, indeed even in the kinds of work performed, both of which were subsumed under the old scheme under the three main categories: unskilled, semi-skilled and skilled labour.

3. The difference in basic wages between the most simple work, or even the simple skilled work, and the most complicated specialist work was so great that it took account of the training of the worker and, at the same time, offered an incentive for specialist work from the financial point of view, which up till then was not possible because of the small variation between the different wages.

4. The proper payment of work performed made every worker, and above all the skilled worker, interested in getting into the wage group in which he could best use his knowledge and ability. This was the best way to counteract the flight of the specialist workers into the better paid semi-skilled piecework, which up till then had taken place on a large scale.

5. At the same time, the wage groups represented a visible means of advancement for everyone. It was an incentive to those who were ambitious enough to perfect their training and to achieve a higher efficiency because of probable promotion and a rise in their standard of living.

6. As a result of the wage group system, the factory had a first-class check on the rational use of labour. The employment authorities also had a means of precise control, in that it was quite easy to find out, for example, whether a firm had a surplus of specialists or not.

7. The wage groups covered all types of work irrespective of their being based on hourly-paid wages or piece rates. Thus the wage groups fixed not only basic wages for hourly-paid work but also basic rates for any kind of piecework.

I have already stressed that we linked the idea of a 'just wage' with the idea of 'just output'. So that for a normal salary everyone expended a normal amount of effort. Originally, it was intended to create an atmosphere of increased integrity and mutual confidence in relation to piecework, but this would only have been possible if problems like the cutting of piece rates and the concealment of work done had been overcome. However, this was very difficult. In spite of that we started, in connection with the new wage policy and rationalization of the factories, to 'clean up' piece rates. This was easier to plan than to carry out, especially if it was honestly intended not just to do it roughly but to carry out a thorough job and to fix piece times which would be permanent. We wanted to guarantee the permanence of the agreed times per piece laid down, and only to allow a future change (in the sense of decreasing its agreed times) in those cases where, by reason of organizational or technical improvement, work was made considerably easier, permitting the piece worker to work and earn more without using more energy. Such a correction to agreed times would be obvious to everyone and even if not liked it would be considered to be completely justified. Such a guarantee was absolutely essential if one wanted to give the piece worker confidence in this whole plan and to do away with that constant source of distrust, the 'piece rates cut'. However, the implementation of this plan was fraught with difficulties. Total success was far from achieved. The plan covered only those firms which had experts available, who were in a position to establish proper piece times. There were, however, comparatively few such men ('Refa' engineers) in Germany. Our training programme could only achieve a gradual success, owing to the difficulty of the project and in most cases it had to be limited to elementary training. The 'assault troops' employed by us could only cover a limited number of firms.

The following point was important in this connection. After the 'normal agreed times' were laid down (i.e. times which corresponded to the average efficiency of an ordinary working man and not the time which exploited the maximum effort of a piece worker), the development of individual efficiency should not be interfered with and no maximum limit should be put on wages. The Government met this demand by issuing decrees accordingly. In spite of that, this matter was not entirely cleared up and quite a number of Reich Trustees of Labour made rulings about these decrees in such a way that the piece worker was left with doubts about these regulations . . .

It is difficult to say how important these measures were as regards the increase in output per man. Those firms which had to submit reports to us, showed variations in most cases between 8 and 25 per cent. Besides, a correct assessment could never be made as the wages measures were carried out more or less in conjunction with the general rationalization measures . . .

With regard to 'actual hours worked' and 'theoretical hours of work' I would like to emphasize the following points:

The normal working period with us was the 48-hour week. Hours worked in excess of this were paid for by special bonuses. This rule held good even when, in the summer of 1944, the 60-hour week was officially introduced. The 60-hour week was, like the approved 69-hour week in various other industries, nothing else but a measure to increase efficiency and labour potential, in order to compensate for the lack of manpower. It was clear that the increased number of working hours resulted in a higher output, although in the long term the output per hour continually decreased. The consumption of energy was much higher because of overtime and consequently it is better to limit overtime, otherwise, judged overall, efficiency will decline. The fixing of 'hours of work' is in itself of no value unless at the same time one makes certain that these 'hours of work' are in fact worked and represent 'an efficiency period'. Most firms seldom had a clear picture of the proportion of the hours actually worked to the theoretical hours of work. Here too the investigation of firms provided very interesting information. The figure of actual hours worked by women in a large Berlin firm was 36 compared with a theoretical work period of 48 hours and for men a figure of 46 hours actually worked compared with a theoretical work period of 54 hours (the period in question was 1942–3). The actual hours worked were naturally influenced to a large extent by the constant air raids; this was particularly noticeable each time there were large-scale air raids on particular cities.

I remember a census that was taken in the summer of 1943 about three to four weeks after a heavy air raid on Cologne. At that time, about 75 per cent of the labour force was at work in the iron and metal industry, about 68 per cent in the construction industry and often less than 60 per cent in factories which had a majority of female workers such as textiles, clothing etc. Later on, however, attendance improved very much—a fact which can be traced back above all to the excellent behaviour and spirit of the workers, who were conscious of their duty to go to work in spite of being bombed out and in spite of interruptions to the communications system. Secondly, it was due to measures taken by the works management and the aid given to those who had been bombed out, which also helped to increase the actual hours worked.

1. Based on the experience gained from the Ruhr, we developed the system of 'factory labour control' [*betriebliche Mannschaftsführung*]. We used the groups (Blocks and Cells) created by the German Labour Front for the purpose of political leadership, and appointed in each case the foreman of such a control unit, or any other sub-leader suitable for such a position, as personnel controller. This man was responsible to the works manager for the attendance of his men. Every day, and especially after air raids, he had to report to his superiors the number of those who had come to work. Furthermore, if normal work could not be resumed because of the damage inflicted on the workplace, he had immediately to mobilize those of his men who were present into a 'clearing-up squad'. (There was a clearing-up squad in every firm.) He had to find out for himself, or with the help of intermediaries what had happened to those who had not come to work, and to see that those who had lost all their personal belongings got leave. He also had to fetch back to work those who were absent without good cause.

2. In the course of the war we established more and more 'works canteens' as a measure to increase the war effort. These canteens had to supply an additional meal, generally a 'one pot' meal. It was important that the canteen should start functioning again immediately after an air attack. For this purpose a large scale, so-called neighbourhood aid system was organised with the purpose of securing food from 'field kitchens'. In large industrial areas, notably the Ruhr, food was supplied to large firms by 'railway food trains'. The daily food capacity of such a train was about 25,000 litres [of soup]. The chief function of the trains was to bridge over the four days until the works canteen could be reopened. These food distribution measures were particularly effective and undoubtedly were an incentive to make people return to work. In addition, there were regulations in

existence in those areas which were constantly exposed to air raids allowing food distributed by the official depots of the NSV to be given only to those who could prove by means of a certificate that they had reported to their firm, and were either at work or had been granted leave.

3. Absenteeism can only be overcome if the causes are known. As the firms could give information in only a few cases, and then merely the number of absentees, we introduced the personal 'work time card' for plants. On this card the firms had to put down all absence from work, both 'unavoidable', such as annual leave (granted according to a roster), illness, or when reporting to the authorities etc. and 'avoidable' absence which could be reduced by measures taken by the firms themselves, or by higher authorities. These 'monthly statements' covering every individual and the entire staff of the factory gave the management and the authorities a clear picture of the proportion of the hours actually worked to those theoretically worked, so that it could be seen whether or not anything should be done to increase them.

It was the firms' task to reduce absenteeism. This was done by abolishing methods which wasted work time and by controlling those workers who showed a desire to take breaks, often lasting for days, by being absent without excuse and by reporting sick.

4. A very important role was played by the factory doctors. The employment of factory doctors became more and more frequent during the war as, with their help, quite a number of working hours could be saved. Many doctors were called up to the armed forces, so that the delay in getting appointments became longer and longer. To prevent a waste of time on this account an examination of all workers on the staff who felt sick was carried out by the factory doctor. In the last years of the war the factory doctors obtained permission to treat the sick as well. In some cases they even went as far as to make the factory doctor a 'panel doctor' (i.e. free choice of a doctor was removed from all invalids who were able to walk). The factory health service also included 'inspectors of the sick'. These were mostly women who had received basic hygiene and first-aid training; their function was to look after those unable to work. They were supported by the management and had to visit workers who had reported sick and, if necessary, see that a doctor was called in to treat them. They had to look after those whose health could not stand the strain of the work and had to see that they were given an easier job. On the other hand, another duty of the inspectors of the sick was to report anyone who was a 'malingerer'.

5. Air raids and other hardships caused by the war resulted in a waste of work time. People who were bombed out had to obtain a permit to get the necessary ration cards at the War Damage Offices to purchase essential goods such as clothing, shoes or household articles.[52] They had difficulty in buying the goods as in most cases the shops in the town were also bombed out. The housewife who did war work also had the worry of the daily shopping for food and household utensils, repair of shoes etc. In these cases too the firms had to help in order to avoid too much waste of work time.

---

[52] See below, pp. 559–60.

Many firms, therefore, instituted Welfare Offices [*Betreungsstellen*]. They were generally incorporated in the personnel department and provided the bombed-out members of staff with the necessary ration cards from the War Damage Office, in most cases in the form of a combined list. In addition, the local tradesmen were given the chance of selling their goods inside the factory. In the Ruhr, for instance, we organized the sale of shoes via the factories. More and more firms started to take over food stores in order to relieve the working housewife from her daily shopping worries. She could hand in her orders before beginning a shift, and after the shift she could collect the goods which were waiting for her. For the same reason we initiated the order for essential shops to remain open until 21.00 or to open on Sundays. Similarly repair shops for consumer goods were set up in factories.

6. An important step, not only towards avoiding any waste of time, but also towards increasing the willingness to work was the Emergency Homes Scheme [*Behelfsheim-Aktion*]. This scheme was to provide, where possible, all bombed out workers (and in addition their evacuated families) with a temporary home within easy reach of their factories. The vast number of bombed-out people shows the importance of this scheme. But the plan for 1943–4, and the one for the later period, could not be carried out. Altogether, about 200,000 provisional [pre-fab] homes were to be erected of which about 35,000 were to be in the Ruhr. However, this scheme collapsed in the end because of the increasing transport difficulties due to the constant air raids, which rapidly brought the production of building materials to a standstill, as coal had to be taken to the more essential armament industries.

7. In addition to these management and welfare measures, there were quite a number of Government decrees, which dealt with the strengthening of work discipline and the fight against notorious shirkers. I should like to point out here that the number of 'shirkers' was always very exaggerated. It was a mistake to categorise the large amount of absenteeism (this can be estimated at an average of 19 per cent for the last year of the war) as 'shirking' in every case, i.e. disloyal absence from work. At the beginning of 1944, with the assistance of the Reich Trustee of Labour, I instituted a general inquiry, since firms were constantly complaining about an increase in the number of 'shirkers'. All factories with a staff of more than fifty had to report the names of the shirkers who were continually absent without any reason (i.e. those who showed a really disloyal attitude and were termed 'inveterate shirkers') and for whom educational measures initiated by the Government were necessary. The five regions of the Ruhr reported altogether about 1,200 cases, of which after a careful examination, only 700 were proved to be really notorious shirkers. In spite of this result a careful watch had to be maintained, as even negative examples like these had an increasingly bad effect on others.

In order to stop further shirking the Government issued many decrees. I recall the following:

(a) Fines of up to a day's pay in the case of repeated early departure from work.
(b) Fines of up to a week's pay in the case of repeated disobedience to orders of the management.

(c) Days absent from work were deducted from leave entitlement (in this case the consent of the Reich Trustee of Labour had to be obtained).

(d) Stoppage of allowances and additional ration cards (decree of the Ministry of Food) for absence from work without permission; or for intentional slackness. Under these circumstances there was no obligation to issue additional rations.

(e) Extra work, if absent without cause within the regulations laid down for work time, and stoppage of holiday pay if absent without cause immediately before and immediately after holidays, because those shirkers worked during the actual holidays mainly to get the 100 per cent higher pay, and took their time off before or after the official holiday (Decree issued in 1940 by the Reich Labour Ministry) . . .[53]

For all genuine overtime, that is work performed over and above the normal time specified for any particular wage, there were corresponding extra money payments. The original rate of overtime payments (10–25%) was calculated according to the length of time spent on such additional work. Later, however, the system was simplified in order to cut down wage accounting and office work. In the autumn of 1944 the Plenipotentiary General for Labour issued an order on the following lines:

Overtime was considered as any work which, calculated within the framework of the normal regulations for hourly paid wages, produced a total output exceeding the average for an eight-hour working day. The decisive factor, therefore, was the amount by which the total number of hours actually worked exceeded the figure reached by multiplying the working days by eight. However, it was not permissible to count hours worked on a night shift as overtime as no extra payment was due for this.

For such overtime, a uniform supplementary payment of 25 per cent was made; for workers paid on an hourly basis the percentage was calculated on the earnings by the hour of the current or most recent wage period. For Sunday work, extra payment amounted to 50 per cent, and for public holidays 100 per cent.

Owing to the length of the war and the fact that all resources were pooled, this overtime payment gradually lost its power as an incentive to increased effort, but other privileges such as extra food for long hours, special rations for particularly long working periods, 'Speer bonuses' for work done, became more effective . . . The following is a short account of the 'Speer bonuses':

These were granted to workers, including foreigners, who had distinguished themselves by exceptional commitment and efficiency: for example, any foreman or master craftsman who had shown a good example to his subordinate workers, or any worker who while working overtime in an emergency programme etc. had been obliged to work under particularly hard conditions. It might happen that in

---

[53] Absentee workers were sometimes also arrested by the Gestapo and imprisoned or sent to Re-education Camps, which were little better than concentraion camps. However, the shortage of German labour meant that these camps were increasingly used to discipline foreign rather than German workers.

any given industrial concern as many as 20 per cent of the staff would receive such bonuses. The mining industry was an exception, as miners were in any case entitled to special welfare treatment. Among the different kinds of bonuses for work performed were the following: (a) Tobacco and spirits; for women and young persons preserved vegetables and condensed milk. (b) Articles of daily use of all kinds. (c) Health tonics rich in vitamins. (d) 'Speer parcels' for persons engaged in mental work. (e) Camping outfits etc.

In addition to these, the Reich Food Minister frequently provided special rations at Speer's request. If, on working days (i.e. not Sundays or rest days) men worked 60 hours and women at least 57 hours per week, they would receive as much as an extra 250g of cereals, 250g of vegetables, and 250g of tinned vegetable soup per person for each food allocation period. These provisions were sent to the canteen. Special rations for 69- or 66-hour weeks were allocated to the works canteen as additional supplies and, as far as I can remember, were distributed at the rate of 15g of vegetables and about 25g of cereals per person per day . . .

Factories employing women installed crèches with trained children's nurses. These crèches were either set up by the factory or by the NSV . . .

At the beginning of the war, serious consideration was given to the idea of introducing total warfare measures and making all men into soldiers subject to military law, the factory workers becoming labour soldiers. At that time it was not possible to foresee the length or the extent of the hardships involved in the war. The above idea was only considered from the point of view of output and it was rejected because it was found that the output of the army construction companies was always considerably less than that of independent firms. It was felt, therefore, that the worker in private companies was probably producing to the limit of human capacity. In addition, there appeared to be no necessity for such a drastic restriction on personal freedom of movement; this liberty was, however, to be strongly limited by the war. Towards the end of 1944, when the air raids became continually heavier and the workers' discipline weakened, the proposals for militarizing labour were revived but this time rejected on the grounds that they would be too difficult to put into effect.

---

## (vi) Economic Collapse

Despite the remarkable productivity gains achieved by the rationalization programme, by 1944 at the latest, Allied bombing was having an increasing impact on the German war economy and as the Allied forces began occupying sources of German raw materials (e.g. Romania) and manufacturing capacity so the problems increased. By the end of January 1945 the man responsible for German war production composed the following memorandum for his Führer. It met with a cool response and Hitler ordered Speer not to show it to anybody else; he was obliged to withdraw the circulated copies. But the facts could not be so easily ignored:

**1073** *Memorandum to Adolf Hitler* 30.1.1945

For information to Martin Bormann
Colonel-General Guderian[54]
von Poser[55] with 8 copies for the Gen. St. of the Ar.

Re: *The armaments situation February–March 1945*

While the loss of Upper Silesia has meant some reduction in armaments production capacity, its effects are being felt exclusively in terms of the loss of coal production; for Upper Silesia was still the only area on which the economy could rely for the production and transport of quality coal in large quantities.

All armaments production capacity in the Reich can now only be *partially* exploited, since it can neither be provided with the necessary coal and electricity, nor with the necessary gas . . .

*Because of the currently unfavourable transport situation in the Ruhr area which has not improved as a result of the recent air raids, the coal production capacity can only be exploited to the extent of 5.5–6 m tons per month = 26% of that of January 1944.*

In order to spare the population the serious effects of an economic collapse the following amounts of coal must be diverted from the coal supplies currently available . . .

. . .*It is impossible to maintain German economic life in the long run with the available coal supplies and with the amount of steel that can still be produced . . .*

This impending collapse of the German economy can be delayed for a few months

*That will mean that armaments production in January, February, and March will simply be using up the large supplies previously built up . . .*

The actual [future] output figures, which correspond to current steel production can only be a fraction of the January output.

*After the loss of Upper Silesia German armaments production will no longer be remotely in a position to fulfil the requirements of the front for munitions, weapons and tanks or to make up the losses at the front and equip new forces.*

*As a result, the courage of our soldiers can no longer compensate for the enemy's material superiority.*

▬▬▬

In his post-war interrogation in 'Dustbin' Saur responded to questions about the reasons for the collapse of the German war economy by pointing out that, in terms of armaments output, the collapse only occurred in 1945, although already in 1944 there was a sharp reduction in what might have been produced without air raids. In late 1944–1945 it was the impact of bombing on the transport facilities which proved crucial:

---

[54] Heinz Guderian, Chief of the General Staff since July 1944.
[55] Lieut.-Col. Manfred von Poser, Speer's liaison officer to the general staff.

**1074**    Before discussing the causes of the decline in production in autumn 1944, I would like to make my basic position clear. The question refers to a widespread industrial collapse throughout the whole of Germany in the autumn of 1944. This is true as regards the oil industry, the raw materials industry and parts of the armament components industry. End-production of armaments, however, taken as a whole was able to maintain output at a satisfactory level up to the end of 1944 owing to the more or less lengthy period taken to process the primary material (i.e. a long production gestation period). In certain fields of production there was a decline beginning to make itself felt, but this was balanced out by increases in other spheres. The following figures for the end-production of armaments will illustrate this point:

(a) The total output of *weapons* increased continuously throughout 1944 and only reached its absolute peak for practically all types in December that year . . .
(b) The highest production of *tanks and assault guns* for the whole war was reached in December 1944, when 1,804 vehicles were produced, i.e. 1,201 assault guns and 603 tanks. This figure was also very nearly maintained in January 1945, when the output was 1,705 vehicles of which 1,201 were assault guns.
(c) In the naval sector the peak production for *U-boats* was reached in December 1944, with 38 boats accepted, of which 28 were of the new model. Even in January 1945, when 27 U-boats were delivered, a higher output was obtained than in the previous months.
(d) As regards aircraft, the production of all *high-performance planes* increased compared with the yearly average during autumn and particularly in December and continued to increase until February and even March. The number of old types admittedly decreased already as from September, a fact which had been foreseen and incorporated in the programme, owing to the increasing difficulties in the prerequisites of production.
(e) The production of *ammunition* of 290,000 tons in December 1944 was only about 10 per cent below the peak production reached in September, although it declined very rapidly at the beginning of 1945.
(f) Production of *motor vehicles* was very low in December. This branch of armaments production as opposed to all the other branches was not able to recover again from the damage caused by the direct air attacks of 1943.

In this connection, the figures from the production record of 1944, issued by Speer on 27 January 1945, may be of interest. It contains a comparison between the output of the fourth quarter of 1944 (i.e. average of the three months October, November, December) and the monthly average for the whole of that year. According to this report, the figures for Autumn 1944 are as follows:

|  |  |
|---|---|
| For weapons from 7.5cm calibre | 22.0% higher |
| " Armoured fighting vehicles | 8.0% higher |
| " Day fighters | 36.0% higher |
| " Ammunition | 2.5% lower |
| " Lorries | 46.0% lower |

1. As regards the cause of the decrease in production in 1944, next to the further loss of territories the decisive factor were the ever-increasing effects of air attacks.

2. In the beginning only production centres were bombed and later, with far greater effect, the transport system and to some extent the communications system (telephone, telegraph etc.). The attack on the *means* of transportation was, however, less effective; as late as the beginning of 1945 there were still about 2,000 locomotives in reserve.

3. With the bombing of factory installations and towns the direct damage to the plants was of far greater effect than the loss of labour through absenteeism or stoppage of work through a temporary lack of power. The reason for this was that the workers and their families, German and foreign alike, tried with almost incredible perseverance to get to their places of work as usual in spite of all the difficulties. The stoppages caused through the breakdowns of the power supply were in the majority of cases reduced to a minimum by the excellent working of the compensatory system and the outstanding repair work.

4. The ratio between the effects of bombing through direct attacks on the factories and the indirect attacks on the transport reached by November 1944 a proportion of 50:50. From then onwards, the effects of the fast-increasing number of attacks on transport installations reached by the beginning of 1945 a proportion of at least 80 per cent in indirect and only 20 per cent in direct attacks. Naturally, by far the greater problems caused by the attacks on transport arose in connection with raw materials and semi-finished products. The reason for this lies in two facts:

(a) The demands on transport facilities as regards weight are about seven times as great before end-production as those for the finished commodity.

(b) The extraordinarily widespread decentralization of production enforced by the air offensive was much more vulnerable from the transport angle than the former output of large compact groups of factories . . .

5. As regards the relative importance of other factors causing this decline in production, the output of crude steel was decisively affected by the loss of occupied territories. The production capacity of 3.5 million tons per month, with a peak output reached in spring 1944 of 3.15 million tons, stood in approximately the same relation in January 1945, when the capacity was 1 million tons with an output of about 825,000 tons. The result was that already from summer 1944 onwards the use of steel was further limited for any non-direct armament production and was stopped altogether by the end of 1944. Ammunition production provides a significant example of the dislocation. Its share of a crude steel production of 3 million tons was about 450,000 tons input weight. It still received 350,000 tons when total production was only 1 million, and finally, in February 1945, it had an allocation of 250,000 tons for a total output of half a million.

The development of the effects of air raids on production shows clearly that the effects of direct bombing, although still increasing (in spite of the very heavy raids in the first months of 1944) progressively declined in significance and in its proportional share in causing the decline in production when compared with the extensive effects caused by transport difficulties. The extent of these effects can be seen from the number of railway wagons allocated for armaments end-production. In November 1944 this amounted to 225,000 (the demand was for 240,000); in December 1944, with the same demand, there were only just over 140,000, and in January 1945 the number sank far below 100,000. The effect in the munitions field was, for example, that in February 1945, although the quantity of crude steel had considerably decreased, only about 160,000 tons out of 235,000 could be delivered by road or rail to the munitions plants.

To sum up, I think I should stress the fact that the absolute under-production in 1944, as compared with the programme, was very pronounced. In the production report of 27 January 1945 an attempt was made to ascertain these figures working on the assumption that neither direct nor indirect air attacks had taken place. The arrears thus assessed, as compared with the production target figures for 1944, which were admittedly set very high, amounted to:

(a)  for armoured fighting vehicles about 35 per cent less;
(b)  for aircraft about 31 per cent less;
(c)  for lorries about 42 per cent less.

The output attained in 1944 was, however, sufficient, as stated in the annual report, to equip fully about 250 new divisions. [In practice of course the equipment was required to replace the equipment lost by the existing divisions.]

## List of Sources

1034  H. A. Jacobsen, ed., *1939–1945: Der Zweite Weltkrieg in Chronik und Dokumenten* (Darmstadt 1962), pp. 380–1.

1035  Hans Volz, *Dokumente der deutschen Politik. Das Werden des Reiches,* Vol. 7 (Berlin 1940), pp. 403ff.

1036  T. W. Mason, ed., *Arbeiterklasse und Volksgemeinschaft* (Cologne 1974), no. 201, pp. 1132–4.

1037  Ibid., no. 224, pp. 1183ff.

1038  Ibid., no. 229, pp. 1192ff.

1039  Bundesarchiv/Militärarchiv (BA/MA) RW 19/513.

1040  BA/MA RW 19/567.

1041  BA/MA RW 15/159.

1042  G. Thomas, *Geschichte der deutschen Wehr- und Rüstungswirtschaft (1918–1943/45)* (Boppard 1966), pp. 498–503.

1043  D. Eichholtz and W. Schumann, eds., *Anatomie des Krieges. Neue Dokumente* (East Berlin 1969), pp. 238–9.

1044  Nuremberg Document (ND) 606–EC.

1045  BA/MA Wi 19/512.

1046  H. Kehrl, *Krisenmanager im Dritten Reich. 6 Jahre Frieden–6 Jahre Krieg. Erinnerungen* (Düsseldorf 1973), pp. 202–5.

1047  BA/MA RW 19/967.

1048  BA/MA RW 19/122.

1049  Thomas, op. cit., pp. 533–4.

1050 BA/MA RW 19/122.
1051 Ibid.
1052 Ibid.
1053 Thomas, op. cit., p. 452.
1054 BA/MA RW 19/122.
1055 Ibid.
1056 Imperial War Museum (IWM) E 53 Mi 14/433 (2).
1057 Eichholtz and Schumann, op. cit., pp. 373–4.
1058 Ibid., pp. 377–8.
1059 Ibid., pp. 381–2.
1060 BA/MA RW 19/959.
1061 Nuremberg Document (ND) Speer-7.
1062 Bundesarchiv Berlin (BAB) R 43 II/706a.
1063 (a) Interrogation of 8 August 1945 IWM E 529 AL 1571.
     (b) Interrogation of 10 August 1945 IWM E 529 AL 1746.
     (c) IWM FD 5445/45 Box 368 Report 90 V.
1064 Ibid., Report 65.
1065 Ibid., Report 67.
1066 IWM E 629 AL 1745.
1067 BAB R 36/554.
1068 BAB R43 II/605c.
1069 IWM FD 3056/49.
1070 Archiv der Mercedes-Benz AG Stuttgart Best, Haspel 3, 32.
1071 Ibid.
1072 IWM FD 5445/45 Box 368 Reports 85 I & II.
1073 BAB R 3/1573.
1074 IWM FD 5445/45 Box 368 Report 67.

# CHAPTER 44

# Welfare and Social Planning

## (i) Introduction

The war enormously increased the burdens on the German welfare system. Not only was the normal provision of various kinds of facilities, such as 'Mother and Child' clinics and kindergartens, and of benefits for those in need placed under greater strain as the result of, for example, the increase in female employment, but the war created a range of new problems. There were, for example, the needs of bereaved families, the problems of large-scale evacuations from frontier districts and from areas threatened by air attack, and the social effects of the air raids themselves. Providing solutions to these problems was crucial for the maintenance of morale on the home front.

Responsibility for dealing with these matters was shared by local government, church bodies, notably the church welfare organizations *Caritas* (Roman Catholic) and the *Innere Mission* (Protestant), and an organization which came to play the major role and whose contribution to sustaining the German home front cannot be overestimated, namely the Nazi welfare organization, the *Nationalsozialistische Volkswohlfahrt* (NSV) under its little-known leader, Eric Hilgenfeldt.

## (ii) The NSV

By 1939, with several thousand health and social work professionals, over half a million unpaid block wardens, each of whom was responsible for thirty to sixty households, and over 1 million local voluntary workers, the NSV had the expertise and organizational stretch, reaching right down to grass roots level, to develop and implement coherent and effective responses to the increasingly urgent social problems thrown up by the war.

## (a) The ideological priorities of the NSV

The NSV conceived of welfare primarily in biological rather than ethical terms. A central concept was the notion of the *Volkskörper*, literally the 'national body', whose health it saw itself as responsible for sustaining. The principles of NSV welfare policy had already been defined in a book published by Hermann Althaus, a leading official of the NSV in 1936, from which the following extract is taken. Significantly, he had formerly been a member of the *Innere Mission*, the Protestant church's welfare organization. In fact, in certain respects, notably in the common use of eugenic criteria, the welfare policies of the two organizations were not that far apart:

**1075**  The National Socialists do not recognize welfare for welfare's sake. All activities—economic, intellectual, artistic, and also social and welfare ones—must serve the whole community to which they are geared. That is indicated by the term 'People's Welfare' [*Volkswohlfahrt*]. It is not a matter of the welfare of the individual but of the whole nation. The individual national comrade is aided in the interests of the nation and the individual's only claim to rights is based on the duties to the general public which he is prepared to recognize and to fulfil. Thus the principle of performance prevails in the sphere of the people's welfare as indeed all theories and ideas within National Socialism seek their realization, and should do so, in a permanent dynamic.

Biology not economics provides the guiding principles for national welfare policy . . . According to National Socialism the nation is a chain of clans bound together by the families in whose wombs the individual members of the nation are conceived and brought up and are integrated into the context of national life. The nation reaches out from the present into the past and the future, to the ancestors whose biological inheritance is carried by the present individuals and which they in turn are obligated to pass on to the coming generations so that these unborn, who through conception are called into existence, can bear the holy shrine of the hereditary values of their nation into the future on strong and healthy shoulders to ensure its preservation and honour.

Geared to this ideological perspective, a national socialist welfare programme is fundamentally governed by the principles of genetics and racial hygiene. It does not recognize the notion of equal citizenship. It knows that the genetic inheritance makes people unequal in terms of their value for the well-being of the community. Environmental conditions are not decisive for the development of individuals.

A welfare programme which is geared to the nation's well-being will, on the contrary, repress the inferiors through an eliminatory genetic policy. Based on this perspective the national socialist state has ensured the exclusion of the genetically sick from the genetic strain of the nation through the Law for the Prevention of Hereditarily Diseased Offspring.[1] The inferior individuals who are

---

[1] See Vol. 2, docs 334–335.

alive should only receive the minimum amount of welfare and, furthermore, should be removed as far as is necessary from the life of the nation through detention in a welfare institution or through preventive detention under the criminal law. This is particularly the case for those individuals whose status as bearers of genetic illnesses is not clear but which can be inferred from their antisocial behaviour . . .

All welfare provision by the national socialist welfare organization is geared to the genetically healthy. It does not provide welfare for the genetically sick which is pointless and wastes national resources, but rather constructive welfare for the genetically healthy. No environmental conditions (milieu) however favourable can remove the damage caused by genetically sick individuals if they lack a healthy genetic constitution.

The Propaganda Minister, Joseph Goebbels, then summed up these principles rather more concisely and brutally in a speech to the NSV rally at the Nazi Party Congress in Nuremberg in September 1938:

**1076**　Bourgeois social theory is primarily concerned with the individual. It is thus essentially determined by pity, or compassion, or the Christian love of one's neighbour or similar convictions. Our Socialist ideas and actions have nothing whatsoever to do with such notions. Our starting point is not the individual; we do not support the idea that one must feed the hungry, give water to the thirsty and clothe the naked—we have no use for such beliefs. Our aims are very different: they can be summed up most succinctly in the following sentence: we must have a healthy people in order to get our way in the world. And a healthy nation is represented not only by weapons, ideas or convictions; a healthy nation is also represented by the strength of its body and through the strength of its soul. And the strength of the body and the strength of the soul of a people need to be fostered and above all require foresight. In other words our socialism lies in the community.

### (b) The tasks of the NSV

By claiming responsibility for *Volkspflege* (lit. care of the people/nation) or social welfare, a new vague and all-embracing term corresponding in the welfare field to the term *Menschenführung* (lit. leadership of people) used by the NSDAP in the political field, the NSV aspired to take over all spheres of welfare, replacing the activities of local government, the Churches, and the Red Cross. By August 1944 it had succeeded in establishing its preponderance in the welfare field, a situation which was formalized in a decree issued by Hitler on 22 August 1944:

**1077**　The maintenance and strengthening of the life force of the German people is one of the basic tasks of the NSDAP. Social welfare is of decisive importance to this.

I therefore decree that:

1. The NSV is in charge of and responsible for social welfare. Its work is primarily concerned with the education of the individual to participate in the welfare of the community. All its measures must serve this biological and educative task.

2. The NSV takes care of the genetically healthy German families who are worthy of support in its 'Mother and Child' aid programme. It establishes and directs the institutions which are necessary for the recuperation and care of mothers, expectant mothers, infants and young people. The NSV provides economic assistance to those who are in need.

3. After air raids the NSV is responsible for the provision of food and accommodation for those who have been bombed out. It has the task of looking after the national comrades who have been evacuated from those districts threatened by air attack and establishing war maternity hospitals and hostels for mothers, babies and infants.

4. The NSV is responsible for providing the means (including gifts) for looking after the Wehrmacht. It has a particular responsibility to look after the wounded.

5. In order to carry out its tasks it will recruit and train suitable specialists in addition to its voluntary personnel. If there are insufficient specialists to carry out its wartime tasks, the head of the Main Office for National Welfare is empowered to regulate the deployment of specialists in order to achieve an appropriate balance between the various demands.

6. The Head of the Party Chancellery will issue the necessary regulations.

—

On the same day, Martin Bormann, the head of the Party Chancellery, defined the spheres of activity of the NSV and the principles governing its welfare measures in a lengthy memorandum. The following extracts contain the preamble and a list of specific wartime tasks. Also included is the final paragraph in which Bormann emphasizes that this list is not definitive and that the NSV is in a state of continual development:

**1078**   The NSV is responsible for national socialist social welfare (*Volkspflege*). Social welfare in this sense means planned and organized assistance by the community to ensure the maintenance and encouragement of the healthy elements of the German national community as well as the removal of social need.

The aim of this community assistance is to look after the genetically healthy, socially efficient German family on the basis of the principles of the population policy of the NSDAP.

The community assistance of the NSV is predicated on

(a)  the genetic health

(b)  the worthiness

of the family which is to be cared for. Genetic health is assessed in accordance with the racial-political principles of the NSDAP. Worthiness is determined by the general behaviour within the community of the family which is to be looked after. A formal request is not necessary for community assistance to be granted; the NSV can—in accordance with its function—act prophylactically and initiate the requisite welfare measures itself if this appears necessary in the particular case concerned . . .

IV   WAR-TIME TASKS OF THE NSV

During the war, the NS People's Welfare Organization carries out the following additional tasks:

1. The extended children's evacuation programme in which the NSV is responsible for the evacuation of mothers and children up to the age of 10.

2. Evacuation

The NSV has the task of assembling the people who are being evacuated, looking after them on their journeys and providing accommodation for the evacuees in the Gaus where they are being resettled. In the case of mothers and mothers with infants the following accommodation is provided:

(a)  War maternity homes.
(b)  War mother and child homes.
(c)  War children's homes.

3. The provision of gas masks for the civilian population.

4. Immediate assistance in the event of air raids. In this case the NSV, as the organization responsible for communal catering for the bombed-out population, will provide both permanent and mobile kitchens, catering trains and catering ships.

5. The transfer of those injured in air raids to hospital.

6. The issuing of additional bread coupons to those in need and the distribution of food ration cards to the population in those areas under the threat of air raids.

7. The distribution of cards to pregnant women, mothers with infants and the severely disabled to secure them preferential treatment in shops.

8. Looking after members of the Wehrmacht.

(a)  Looking after the wounded in hospitals, in transports and in recuperation units through the provision of additional necessities and semi-luxuries [e.g. cigarettes] for the sick and wounded.
(b)  Looking after soldiers.

The NSV secures the material preconditions for the NSDAP cadres to look after soldiers and takes on the responsibility for looking after those on leave in accordance with the cadre's instructions.

(c)  Providing parcels for soldiers who are single.
(d)  Sustaining the morale of soldiers through the supply of letters and newspapers.
(e)  Sustaining the morale of the soldiers' relatives through cultural events.
(f)  Granting economic assistance to the seriously wounded to enable them to establish a household.
(g)  The provision of hospitals and institutions of the NSV for the Wehrmacht for receiving the wounded.

(h) the establishment and maintenance of officers' hostels for the reception of wounded officers who are studying.

(i) The provision of Adolf Hitler free places,[2] as part of the care of soldiers on leave.

(j) The provision of recuperation holidays in Italy for soldiers recovering from wounds.

9. The training of war wounded to become welfare workers.

10. The special role of the NSV in evacuations and the return from evacuations.

V   SOCIAL WELFARE TASKS IN OCCUPIED AND ANNEXED TERRITORY

The activity of the NSV in occupied and annexed territory covers:

1. Responsibility for public welfare work for Reich and ethnic Germans .

2. Looking after the relatives of those who are ethnically related [to Germans].

3. Looking after the relatives of ethnic aliens in so far as the preconditions are met. These measures are to be implemented in accordance with prescribed regulations.

VI   NSV AND WINTER AID OF THE GERMAN PEOPLE INCLUDING THE WAR AID PROGRAMME OF THE GERMAN RED CROSS

1. The NSV is also responsible for the Winter Aid Programme of the German people [WHW]. The WHW provides economic assistance to families and single persons who are in need. During the period of the WHW economic assistance is granted in the form of

(a) Cash payments.

(b) The provision of tinned food from the fruit and vegetable collections.

(c) The provision of toys and Christmas biscuits.

(d) The provision of clothing (second hand clothes off-ration).

The measures of the WHW designed to raise morale include artistic events and entertainment. The official directives of the WHW are applied to the individual cases.

2. Other organizations are provided with the means of fulfilling tasks beneficial to social welfare from the proceeds of the Winter Aid Programme (War Winter Aid programme).

3. The War Aid Programme of the German Red Cross is a component part of the war Winter Aid Programme . . .

The fulfilment of the tasks of the NSV represents work beneficial to the living national body. The above listing of its spheres of operation cannot, therefore, be definitive and final. The sphere of its operations is in a state of continual development and will, therefore, receive frequent additions.

The Head of the Main office for National Welfare will issue the necessary instructions to implement this directive.

[signed] M. BORMANN

---

[2] This was a scheme begun in 1934, whereby German families offered to put up those in need of a holiday (originallly mainly SA men) in their homes for a short stay.

The main focus of the NSV's campaign to improve the 'national body' was on measures to reverse the decline in population, to prevent infant mortality and to improve the health and material and moral welfare of mothers, children and adolescents. As part of this programme it determined to try and take over the local government, church and Red Cross health centres and to establish new ones where none existed. By 1942, there were 6,349 local NSV health centres and also 30,000 NSV 'Mother and Child' advice centres, which had 10,300,000 visits.[3]

### (c) The NSV Nurses, Local Health Centres, 'Mother and Child' Advice Centres and Kindergartens

Given the importance of the role of nurses in the national health field, and given the fact that the vast majority of the nursing profession belonged to either the Protestant (*Innere Mission*), the Roman Catholic (*Caritas*) organizations, or the Red Cross, the NSV was determined to recruit and train a new corps of national socialist nurses who would implement its racial and eugenic agenda. These NSV Nurses (commonly known as 'Brown Nurses') were required to be 'of German or related blood', not to have a criminal record, and to be committed National Socialists. One author compared their role to that of the SA before 1933. However, the NSV Nurses suffered severe problems of recruitment as a result of the competition provided by other careers for women, particularly during the war. There were also financial problems, since, whereas the material expectations of the Church nurses were low, the NSV nurses had to be provided with proper remuneration and career prospects. The result was that by 1943 there were only 12,000 NSV nurses, and, although they took over the Reich Association of Free Nurses in 1942, the combined total of 40,000 still compared unfavourably with the 120,000 total of the two church nursing organizations. In fact, the NSV was obliged to continue to employ 1,300 Protestant and 596 Catholic nurses in the 2,330 health centres taken over from the Red Cross in 1937 until the end of the war.[4]

A typical example of the operation of the NSV is provided by its policy and actions with regard to kindergartens. Kindergartens were considered important partly because of the possibility they offered of

---

[3] Eckhard Hansen, *Wohlfahrtspolitik im NS-Staat. Motivationen, Konflikte und Machtstrukturen im 'Sozialismus der Tat' des Dritten Reiches* (Augsburg 1990), p. 159.

[4] Ibid., p. 160.

influencing children's upbringing from an early age, an opportunity which in the past had often been seized by the churches. Thus, in April 1942, a senior NSV official pointed out that the NSV's efforts to secure a monopoly of the provision of kindergartens was based mainly on the fact 'that kindergarten work was the best means of reaching families and especially mothers and in this way to be able to perform deep ideological indoctrination [*weltanschauliche Tiefenarbeit*]'.[5] Furthermore, in wartime kindergartens played a particularly important role in enabling women with infants to take up employment. At the end of 1938, there were some 10,800 kindergartens and crèches of which about half were permanent and half were temporary 'harvest crèches'. By the end of 1942 there were 31,000, of which around half were permanent and the remainder temporary, the majority of them 'harvest crèches'. In 1942 there were around 1.2 million places and 73,736 personnel, many of them voluntary.[6]

At the beginning of 1940, Karl Fiehler, the head of the NSDAP Main Office for Local Government reached the following agreement with Eric Hilgenfeldt, the head of the NSV, which was contained in a circular dated 4 January 1940:

**1079** 1. The existing local authority kindergartens will remain under the control of local government.
2. The existing NSV kindergartens will remain with the NSV.
3. The kindergartens which have hitherto belonged to religious and other organizations will gradually be taken over by the NSV.
4. The NSV will be responsible for newly established kindergartens.

In fact, and typically for the Third Reich, this agreement was not worth the paper it was written on. For the NSV had no intention of permitting the local authorities to keep control of their existing kindergarten. Six months later, in a NSV draft for a Interior Ministry decree on kindergartens, dated 26 June 1940, Hilgenfeldt was insisting that 'the running of kindergartens is a task of *Menschenführung* and, therefore, essentially a task for the party'.[7] On 21 March 1941, the Reich Interior Ministry was forced to accept this point by agreeing to a preamble to its kindergarten decree which stated that the 'care of children in the kindergartens is a matter for the NSV in the context of the Party's

---

[5] Ibid., p. 238, n. 112.
[6] Ibid., p. 170.
[7] Ibid., p. 235.

overall task of *Menschenführung*'.[8] Although the rest of the decree
appeared to confirm the existing division of responsibilities between the
NSV and the local authorities, it not only reaffirmed that the establishment of new kindergartens was a matter for the NSV, but went on to lay
down that the costs of setting them up and running them should be
borne by the local authorities. This produced strong protests from the
local authorities. For, as the *Oberbürgermeister* of Erfurt indignantly
pointed out, this meant that the local authority would have to

**1080**   pay for everything but is not responsible for building them and, as a
result, would not have the say and also, as far as the public is concerned, will not
appear to be involved. The public will assume that the NSV has produced
something marvellous, but in reality it will have been paid for by the city out of
taxes.

Nor did the NSV rest content with its responsibility for new kindergartens. A year after the appearance of the decree, a senior official in the
Party's Local Government Office was reporting that

**1081**   Despite the wartime conditions, indeed in some cases by exploiting
them, a battle is going on for almost every kindergarten in a way which does not
correspond to the dignity either of the Party or of the local authorities. In the
process it is often the case that reference is made to the general clause in
Paragraph I concerning the 'Party's task of *Menschenführung*' while the rest of
the decree is ignored.

Only the most influential *Oberbürgermeister* such as Karl Strölin of
Stuttgart or Fritz Krebs of Frankfurt am Main were able to resist the
ambitions of the NSV and hang on to their municipal kindergartens.
   In a similar fashion the NSV set out to take over the religious
kindergartens as the following example indicates:

**1082**   *Instruction by the Secret State Police Office, Aachen, 5 April 1941
to Father Göttscher, Aachen*

On the basis of the Reich President's Decree for the Protection of People and
State of 28.2.1933 and in conjunction with the Law on the Secret State Police of
10.2.1936 the following injunction is hereby issued:

The kindergarten in Reumondstrasse, Aachen belonging to the parish of St
Mary, together with all its equipment and other accessories, is being seques-
trated with immediate effect.

---

[8] Ibid., p. 236.

Those who have hitherto been in charge no longer have any authority over the building and its contents with immediate effect. Authority over the kindergarten with all the rights appertaining to it is hereby transferred exclusively to the NSV from the moment of the police sequestration.

Any actions contrary to or designed to evade this order will be punished by police or penal measures in accordance with §4 of the Decree of 28.2.1933.

There is no legal remedy against this injunction of the State Police.

▄▄▄

However, following vigorous church protests at the widespread confiscation of church and monastic properties by numerous Party agencies, Hitler became concerned about the possible damage to popular morale produced by these actions and so, on 30 July 1941, Bormann issued the following order:

**1083**    The Führer has instructed that the confiscation of church and monastic property must cease for the time being with immediate effect. Independent actions by Gauleiters must on no account occur even when special circumstances in individual cases urgently necessitate the use of church and monastic property on the basis of existing legal regulations. If a Gauleiter considers that such a situation exists in a particular case, then a report must initially be made to the Führer through me.

▄▄▄

In fact, personnel shortages placed limits on the extent to which the NSV could take over church and local government kindergartens. However, varying from district to district and depending partly on the attitude of the local Gauleiter, by 1943 the NSV had succeeded in seizing control of a large number of them. The *Caritas* lost 1,200 out of 4,300 and the *Innere Mission* a similar number. The losses were concentrated in particular in the Gaus of Saxony, Thuringia, the two Hesses, Upper and Lower Silesia and the Rhineland, whereas Westphaliaa, Pomerania, Baden, the Saar/Palatinate and East Prussia remained largely unaffected.[9]

Whereas in the case of the churches there was to some extent an 'ideological' basis to the defence of their kindergartens, with local government it was more a defence of their organization against a rival organization with little or no disagreement about how kindergartens should operate and what values they should instil.

The NSV was anxious to use the opportunity provided by its kindergartens for the early indoctrination of the children attending them and it laid down clear guidelines for the training of its kindergarten

---

[9] Ibid., p. 229.

teachers. In 1941 a syllabus was issued for training kindergarten teachers, of which the following is an extract:

**1084**    III.   Health Education

This group of subjects is responsible for communicating in both a theoretical and a practical way basic knowledge about the natural interrelationships in life, about racial identity, and about the conditions for a healthy national life, and thereby to encourage a clean personal life style and the practical application of these insights into the laws of life to children's education. It is closely linked with the 'National Political Education' group of subjects and provides so to speak a concrete explanation of the national socialist world view in that it demonstrates in detail what its implementation in the form of a new mentality and a new moral code demands of each individual compatriot.

1. Genetics and racial awareness

This subject has the function, in close association with the Group I subjects, namely National Political Education, of encouraging a genetic and racial-biological approach as the basis of the national socialist view of the world and of human beings. It aims to begin by arousing the basic feeling for the natural links which people have with blood and soil, the family, the clan, and with race and nation and is designed to lead on to the great racial-political questions concerning the maintenance of the life force of our nation. This perspective should inform as clearly as possible the maternal tasks which every woman must undertake as the guardian and educator of the coming generation by ensuring that she adopts a responsible, healthy way of life and brings up her children along the same lines.

A.  Natural laws of development and inheritance and human genetics

Comparison of human life with the lives of plants and animals.
Similarities and differences.
Demonstration of growth in the plant and animal worlds, its conditions, processes and genetic laws.
The application of the basic principles of human genetics.
Sharp differentiation between inheritance and breeding through selection in the plant and animal worlds and inheritance and selection through education as the decisive factor for human beings.
(To be done in close collaboration with 'Pedagogics and Anthropology').

B. Racial theory

Inheritance and the racial laws of life.
The European races.
The racial composition of the German people and the tasks of racial improvement.

C. The encouragement of racial awareness

Clarification of the concepts: Nation [*Volk*], race and alien blood.
Basic principles of the German racial laws in the national socialist state.

Racial-political laws and rules for behaviour towards alien nations.

Encouragement of racial awareness through state measures and through national-political education.

D.  Racial-political education and the biological task

The threat to national strength and Germany's population situation.

The responsibility of the individual towards ancestors and descendants as a link in the chain of generations.

Marriage and family as the germ cell of a strong and healthy nation and the particular responsibility of women as mothers and educators.

The basic requirements for a healthy way of life and for bringing up children so that one's responsibility to the nation is fulfilled.

The maintenance of people's natural ties to blood and soil.

The mind as the special mark of human beings and the task of achieving a harmonious development of body, soul and mind.

In particular, the treatment of the task of achieving racial-political education and the discussion of the biological threat should be linked as far as possible with the subjects covered in 'National Order—National Service', 'National Welfare and Youth Aid' on the one hand and 'Physical Education and Gymnastics with Children', and 'The Care of Children and Children's Nutrition' on the other.

The whole subject of Genetics and Race should form the basis of national-political education giving it depth and should lead on to the topics of personal attitude to life and bringing up children which are directly linked to 'Pedagogics and Anthropology'.

———

A similar emphasis on genetic and racial issues was present in the syllabus for training NSV nurses.

However, as the war continued,the NSV found itself obliged to focus more and more of its efforts on the immediately pressing tasks of coping with the social effects of the continual large-scale air raids and the mass evacuations which increasingly came to dominate life on the home front.

*(d)  War-time Tasks*

Among the remarkable range of tasks carried out by the NSV on the home front was its Railway Station Service. Railway stations were a hub of activity during the Second World War, as a contemporary subsequently recalled:

**1085**   Railway stations and trains had a strange magical power of attraction during the war. Despite the dangers of bombing and strafing, despite long journey times and the endless delays, millions of people travelled right across Germany during these years. In those days almost everybody had a particular task, was going on a particular mission: soldiers, functionaries, BdM auxiliaries or teachers who were going to their KLV classes somewhere; women travelling to meet their men who were on a short leave from the front; widows on their way to a recent grave. In between came long military trains, trains carrying the wounded, trains carrying children, closed wagons containing Jews being deported.

At every station women would be standing with great tureens of soup and tea urns, nurses were meeting children or cripples in order to put them on the next train. When the air raid warning went, people who were complete strangers hurried side by side through the darkness, helped each other into the air raid shelters, told each other about their lives which had been turned upside down and then, hours later, travelled on other trains with other people.

On 19 May 1942 the NSV issued the following directives for its Railway Station Service:

**1086**	. . . Tasks of the Railway Station Service:
The NSV railway station service has the task of advising and where necessary of looking after compatriots who are passing through, arriving or departing.

The work of the NSV railway station offices is essentially a morale-boosting [spiritual] rather than a material one. The main task is to look after mothers with babies and toddlers, children and young people travelling alone, old and infirm compatriots as well as to look after and provision the transports organized by the NSV. In addition, all other German compatriots who make enquiries should be given advice. As a result, Jews, Poles, Gypsies, asocials etc. should not be looked after.

The following measures are envisaged:

(a) Giving advice and information, e.g. concerning travel, accommodation and general matters.

(b) Assistance at the station itself, e.g. dealing with transports, provisioning the transport, handing over children or young people travelling alone to the guard or receiving them from the guard and then transferring them to their relatives or, if they are changing trains, handing them over to the guard on the next train. Particular care should be taken of children travelling by themselves . . .

Assistance when people are changing trains. Since there are often not enough porters on the stations because of personnel shortages, such assistance must include carrying small pieces of luggage. Fare money should only be provided where it can be proved that a crisis has arisen through no fault of the passenger.

(c) Assistance outside the station, e.g. informing the relatives of young people travelling by themselves, the provision of food and accommodation in special cases etc. Particular attention should be paid to ensuring that suitable and decent accommodation is available. Compatriots must under no circumstances be sent to dirty or dubious boarding houses or hotels.

The NSV's contribution to sustaining morale, indeed life itself, on the German home front cannot be overestimated. And, although in practice it often simply took over responsibilities from existing bodies—local government, religious, or Red Cross—substituting its own services for theirs, it did have some success in introducing common welfare standards where previously welfare provision had been spread rather unevenly across the country and, in particular, had tended to be concentrated in urban areas. For example, the NSV brought welfare services to hitherto neglected and often socially deprived rural districts. Unlike in the First World War, Germany now had a comprehensive welfare system which could cope reasonably well with many of the major social problems created by the war. The fact that it was driven by inhumane ideological imperatives which confined its services to the racially and eugenically acceptable elements of the population is clear from the documents printed above. However, for most Germans, facing an increasingly desperate situation, the NSV was the first port of call offering a helping hand in time of need, providing temporary shelter, a bowl of hot soup, bedding, clothing and other necessities for those who had lost everything. It was probably the most popular Nazi organization. Indeed, in the autumn of 1943, frustrated by the fact that the Party had to fulfil 'numerous difficult, thankless and unpopular tasks', Bormann insisted in a letter to Robert Ley in his capacity as 'Head of the Reich Party Organization' that 'all those measures and institutions which are favourably received by the population should also operate under the party's name'.[10] On 7 January 1944 Ley responded by issuing the following directive:

**1087** Re: *The designation of the NSV agencies as official Party organizations.*
In agreement with the Head of the Party Chancellery, the Reich [NSDAP] Treasurer and the Head of the Main Office for National Welfare, I hereby issue the following instruction:

From now onwards, the NSV and the Reich League of German Nurses will carry out all their work in the name of the NSDAP. In so far as exceptions may be necessary in individual cases these will be decided by me in agreement with the Head of the Main Office for National Welfare.

This instruction does not alter the legal status of the NSV as an officially registered association or that of the Reich League of Nurses. The 'NSV rune', which has become a popular emblem will continue to be used.

My Main Organisation Office will issue the detailed regulations in agreement with the Head Office for National Welfare.

DR R. LEY

---

[10] Ibid., p. 353.

## (e) The War Winter Aid Programme

Much of the finance for the activities for the NSV came from the Winter Aid Programme (WHW), which continued during the first four years of the war. In 1939/40 631.58 million Reichsmarks were collected and, by 1942/3, the sum had grown to 1.587 billion RM, of which 1.21 billion was used for the 'Mother and Child' programme and other wartime tasks, a huge sum.[11] Collections for this programme, now called the War Winter Aid Programme, in the form of the sale of badges, involved street collections, collections from house to house on the basis of lists (this method was discontinued during the war), collections from businesses, deductions from wages, and Sunday collections held once a month during the winter, in which families were expected to have a simple stew instead of a full Sunday lunch and contribute the money saved. During the war, these 'one-pot Sundays' were renamed 'self-sacrifice Sundays'. Apart from their function in helping to finance the NSV, these collections were intended primarily as demonstrative gestures of the 'national community' in action and of national morale, as is clear from the following excerpts from Hitler's speeches opening the Winter Aid campaigns of 1939–40 and 1940–1:

**1088**    (a) . . . And so the Wartime Winter Aid Programme, in particular, must help to make the German national community tougher than ever: a community for struggle, a community for victory and then, in the end, for peace.

The more determination and the more toughness we demonstrate in accepting the sacrifices which this war may bring the more surely will we achieve the peace which our nation needs. Because, at some point, and this is my view as well, the period of insecurity must come to an end. It must be possible for the German people too to arrange its life within its own living space in accordance with its own wishes and its own ideas without being continually bothered by others, and for the German people to receive the share of the goods of the world which it can and will claim on the basis of its numbers and its worth.

On this basis I hereby inaugurate the Wartime Winter Aid Programme 1939/40 and ask the helpers to work hard for it just as I ask the German people to show that those on the home front are worthy of the heroes of today and thereby to make up for the sins committed against the German people by the home front in the years 1914–18.

(b) When the English entered the war a year ago, they said: 'we have got an ally'. People were curious as to who it was. They said: 'it is a general. His name is General Revolution'. Ha! They haven't got a clue about the new national socialist German workers' state . . .

We educate people to have a uniform outlook on life, to have a common view

---

[11] Ibid., p. 28.

of duty . . . It is an arduous task rubbing off the rough edges and training . . . But we can see from the Winter Aid Programme that it's making progress. Gradually, even the most stubborn representative of the old order has come to see: first, that there's no point [in refusing to make a donation]—they'll keep coming back, and when one has left, the next one will arrive. So that, secondly, it's better if I accept it and stick it on; thirdly, well actually they do a lot of good things with it...

So that if I now, once again, thank all the people who have contributed to the first Wartime Winter Aid programme and who have helped with it in other ways, I want to appeal to you all: do your duty once again now in the second wartime Winter Aid programme, some of you as voluntary helpers and others as voluntary contributors. Let us ensure that once again it becomes a demonstration to the world of our indissoluble sense of community so that they finally come to recognize that, in place of their general stands another general, the General of Common Duty who commands us all.

———

These collections also provided something for the party membership to do, a target to keep the members up to scratch, and a reassurance of the Party's value and popularity and of the morale of the German people. In 1940, for example, Goebbels interpreted the results as proof 'that the German people was determined not to shirk making sacrifices when the national existence of the Reich was at stake. From the extent to which we are willing to make sacrifices depends to a large degree whether we can bring this war that has been forced upon us to a victorious conclusion within a reasonable timespan'.[12] League tables were prepared on the basis of data showing the sums collected by the local NSV branches in every village and every Gau compared with their population size, and NSV branches were continually being urged by the local Party officials to improve their results.

On 24 November 1939, for example, the Winter Aid Programme official for the Offenbach district in Hessen-Nassau issued the following circular:

**1089** In my WHW [Winter Aid Programme] directive No. 20/39 I gave you a summary of the results of the first self-sacrifice Sunday. In this circular I declared that the self-sacrifice Sunday had not produced the result I wanted. The district leader [of the NSDAP] was also very surprised by the poor result that I reported.

The results of the collection for the Wartime Winter Aid Programme must go far beyond those that have been achieved hitherto in order to provide evidence that, in this sphere too, the whole German nation is unequivocally and joyfully supporting the efforts of the State and the Party . . .

———

[12] Ibid., p. 41, n. 11.

The summary of the results of the last self-sacrifice Sunday clearly demonstrate that the results of the self-sacrifice Sunday *could be considerably improved if some of the local branches were to deploy their efforts more effectively in carrying out this collection.*

The local branches in Buchschlag and Obertshausen once more produced very good results *both of which far surpassed the result of the first self-sacrifice Sunday, which was itself a good one.* Apart from the Buchschlag local branch, whose economic structure provides the preconditions for good collections, the Obertshausen branch achieved a result which will not easily be matched by any comparable branch in Gau Hessen-Nassau. This was because of the superb efforts of the party and the NSV. *In Obertshausen each household pays an average of RM 1 . . .*

It must be the job of the cadres and local representatives of the Winter Aid programme to make all the necessary preparations to ensure that, on the next self-sacrifice Sunday, no local branch falls below the average of RM O.45 per household . . .

*In various branches it was clear that particular sections of the population are mainly to blame for the overall result of the local branches.* They are invariably families who are comfortably off and who give a self-sacrifice Sunday contribution which cannot really be called a proper contribution.

It is the task of the cadre, together with the local Winter Aid programme official, to keep a check and to point out to those Party members and compatriots who behave in such a manner the error of their ways. This has been done in various local branches and it produced the required result.

An examination of the results of the second Reich street collection also clearly showed that it is always the same local branches which deliver the goods.

▬▬

The circular enclosed the following sample letter to be sent to those whose contributions were regarded as inadequate.

**1090**    Re: *The WHW One Pot Collection:*

You are presumably not unaware of the tremendous achievements of the Winter Aid Programme.which is officially recognized by the Führer, and which will go down in history as the greatest aid programme of all time. Thus, in approaching you now I do so simply to draw to your attention the fact that examination of the One Pot lists in the last few days has produced an unsatisfactory amount compared with the level of donation that was required. The donation made by you in no way corresponds to your circumstances. If you consider that every day thousands of comrades risk their all and their lives at the front, you ought to be ashamed of your unwillingness to make sacrifices.

I expect you to re-examine your donation and your willingness to make a sacrifice to ensure that your donation corresponds to your circumstances and represents a real sacrifice.

▬▬

While many were happy to contribute to what was widely seen as a good cause, the continual, indeed growing, pressure imposed on the population by these repeated collections caused growing resentment. On 27 November 1942 Ley told the Reich Party Treasurer, Schwarz, that 'the ways in which the collections for the WHW have developed damage the reputation of the Party and are no longer acceptable'. He criticized the attitude in the NSDAP, which he had become aware of during 'numerous inspection visits', namely that 'the quality of the Party's work and the mood of the population' could be documented on the basis of the results of the WHW collections.[13] On 16 September 1943 the following directive was issued by the Wehrmacht to those of its members involved in the WHW collections, a directive prepared in the Party Chancellery:

**1091**     The collections can only fulfil their two special tasks of influencing and educating the population propagandistically and of informing the leadership if the *voluntary principle is absolutely adhered to*. Recognition of this fact is part of the political alphabet of every national comrade who has anything to do with the political leadership.

## (iii) Social Planning

*(a) The DAF social policy programme*

Before the war, the German Labour Front (DAF) under its ambitious leader, Dr Robert Ley, had tried to extend its influence into any sphere of economic or social activity which could be remotely justified by the vague and all-embracing definition of its role contained in Hitler's Decree on the Nature and Goals of the Labour Front, dated 24 October 1934, namely 'to create a true national and productive community of all Germans'. Among its more important initiatives had been the creation of the organizations 'Strength through Joy', covering leisure activities; 'Beauty of Labour', for improving working conditions; and the 'Reich Occupational Competition', to improve occupational skills.[14] However, the DAF's social engineers employed in its Labour Research Institute (AWI) had even more far-reaching ambitions, and the prospects of a victorious peace for a Great German Reich fired their imagination. They envisaged a comprehensive social programme embracing wage structures, occupational training, health, housing, and even provision for old age— a kind of technocratic utopia.

---

[13] Ibid., p. 38.
[14] See Vol. 2, doc. 222ff.

Superficially, this programme bore certain similarities with the plans put forward at the same time in Britain by Sir William Beveridge for a comprehensive post-war welfare scheme covering old age pensions, a national health service and unemployment benefits. Certainly, part of the motivation for the two programmes was similar, namely to sustain popular morale in wartime by presenting a vision of a post-war order in which many of the cares which had traditionally plagued ordinary people would be removed. However, a very different ethos informed the two schemes. For, whereas the Beveridge scheme reflected a combination of Christian, liberal and humanitarian values, the DAF project was inspired by a very different set of beliefs. Influenced by a combination of the latest personnel management techniques ('Taylorism'), first imported from the United States by leading German employers in the 1920s, and eugenic and racial concepts, they aimed to create a model society, a German 'national community' whose members would be 'new men and women' [*Menschen*], highly productive and efficient, healthy in body and mind, and socially contented. This would be achieved through a combination of incentives and rewards for those who fulfilled their obligations to the national community by doing their best to remain healthy, to perform whatever tasks they were asked to do both enthusiastically and efficiently, and penalties for those who failed to meet the norms of the national community through fecklessness or conscious opposition, or who were designated racially or eugenically unfit and, therefore, excluded from the nation. Thus, under the DAF scheme the old age pension was not the right of every citizen who had paid their national insurance contributions, but rather a reward for long service and good behaviour as a 'compatriot' within the 'national community'.

Before the war, the national energies and resources had been focused on rearmament and so the realization of this programme had to be postponed to an uncertain future. However, with Germany's victories in the West in 1940, the end of the war appeared to be in sight and the officials of the AWI set about drawing up their plans with renewed enthusiasm. The aim now was to provide the socio-economic foundations for a consolidation of the new territory or 'living space' which had been gained and to prepare for future national challenges, including war. In the Annual Report for 1940/1 they published a comprehensive plan setting out 'The Social Tasks for the Post-War Period', from which the following excerpts are taken:

**1092**    . . . After it is over every war requires a greater concentration of political energies on the internal construction and consolidation of the living space which has been acquired, so that at the end of every war—and in particular at the end of a successful one—there is a need for increased activity in the field of social policy. That has always been the case and it is characteristic of the most successful statesmen that they have managed the transition from the politics of war to the peacetime work of social construction.

Such a transformation of the general political line is inevitable. For, if the aim is to maintain and exploit the benefit of a military victory then, in the first instances, the inner forces of the state must be mobilized. And that is the essence of social policy.

The war has changed not only the external but also the internal position of the state. This new situation requires an adjustment of policy. Although it will not determine the ideological goals, it will substantially determine the pathways or diversions which lead to them. In any case, the list of political priorities will be different. So long as a military confrontation is in the offing all internal political measures have to be concentrated as far as possible on the confrontation which is about to take place. In some cases this must happen to the extent that more distant socio-political goals have to be consciously neglected in order to achieve a more immediate concentration of forces to the maximum possible extent.

After a war things are different. Then the main concern is to organize the existing and newly acquired forces so that, in the course of the following period, they provide the broadest possible basis for new national efforts. That does not by any mean imply that one must definitely prepare for a new war. However, all forces must be mobilized with maximum care and speed to secure for the nation as rapidly as possible a cultural, economic, and social superiority over the other nations. Only such a superiority will in the long run provide the basis for the political claims to power.

The aim of social policy after the war can, therefore, be summarized roughly as follows: the life of the community is to be organized in such a way that a maximum standard of living is achieved with the available national energy on the available living space. In this context the term standard of living is to be defined in the broadest possible sense. It includes all the aspects of life of a nation from the satisfaction of its daily needs to the expression of its national military strength . . .

II   THE COMMUNITY ORDER AND THE DISTRIBUTION OF GOODS.

*1. The social order*

. . . In the future the task of social law will be to bring the legal framework into line with the national community's spiritual and emotional sense of justice. The old ideal according to which the legal and the just corresponded to each other must shape the social constitution of the future. The social constitution will in this way—irrespective of whether it is in the form of written or unwritten law— form the basis of the social life of the community. If, for example, one of the basic ideas of the sphere of work is the duty to work, then this basic concept must be reflected in all the individual laws dealing with social matters. It is inconceivable, for example, that a right to claim benefits could be established which relegated the duty to work to the background let alone legalized the receipt of 'an unearned income'.

Hitherto, social law has been based essentially on the definition of the rights of the individual both vis-à-vis others as also vis-à-vis the community. Like the rest of the law, social policy also concentrated on delimiting as clearly as possible the position of the individual vis-à-vis the state to the absolutely essential cases. Thus, social law was also dominated by the fiction of the fundamentally free individual. National Socialist law, by contrast, will derive law and obligations not from the individual but from the community. *All things which are beneficial to the community will thereby become just . . .*

V   THE PRESERVATION OF FITNESS AND VITALITY

*2. The health service*

If the benefit system operates on the fundamental principle of the obligation to work and the right to work, the principle of the health service will be: every national comrade is obliged to maintain his health at the highest possible level for the sake of the community; the health service will provide him with all the necessary preconditions to achieve this . . .

*3. Leisure and recreation*

If old age pensions and the health service are designed to bridge the pitfalls along the social pathway the efforts to secure leisure and recreation for productive people are no less important in the efforts to improve performance. The programme has long been defined in the term 'strength through joy', even though final decisions have not yet been taken over the form, content and extent of the various particular spheres.

The efforts which are combined in the NS organization 'Strength through Joy' [KdF] serve a single goal: to unify the German people not only as a productive community but also as a community of experience. KdF is no cultural consumers' association; its ultimate aim is not to provide cut-price entertainment or holidays. That is only a means to an end: the overcoming of barriers which now stand between work and recreation . . .

An essential aspect of our current social problems is the unsatisfactory way in which work and leisure relate to one another. Not the least of the contributory factors to this situation has been the struggle between capitalism and Marxism which has been continuing for decades between two ideologies each of which claims for itself a certain totality.

If work is regarded as slavery for overmighty capital and, on the other hand, leisure is seen as the useless waste of energy, then inevitably an unbridgeable gulf will emerge. But, as soon as work is seen as service to the national community and leisure no less as an expression of the life of the national community, this will produce an entirely different assessment. Work and recreation are just different manifestations of the same life and it is clear that this life will be all the more balanced and all the more valuable the more harmoniously these two sides are geared to one another. It may be true that tensions are the driving force of life; but these tensions are only valuable if their total effect is beneficial and if they do not cancel each other out.

The aim will never be to blur the boundaries between recreation and work. Each of these spheres of life obeys its own laws. But the whole national energy would suffer if, for example, a senseless use of leisure depleted work energy and efficiency, while on the other hand, the meaning of recreation would be lost if inappropriate working methods and working conditions depleted the energies which were intended for leisure. The collective term 'leisure' implies not only the satisfaction of personal needs but also the fulfilment of essential national political tasks, in particular family life. It is absolutely inconceivable how a community life could come about if the fulfilment of the national comrades' obligations only applied to their worktime; the community, indeed the life of the nation altogether, would soon die out.

In short, the socio-political task is: *to develop the style of national community life and community experience from the subspheres of work and leisure from which the nation can draw the necessary strength for its future tasks.*

Applied to the practical tasks, this means four problems in particular: 1. The Leisure Service. 2. The Recuperation Service. 3. The Cultural Service. 4. Beauty of Labour.

### 4. *Housing*

The German people live in conditions which represent a serious political threat. The border areas are depleted of ethnic Germans; millions of dwellings are necessary simply to settle the East. On the other hand, the mass of the population concentrate in the interior of the Reich in the most confined and inadequate living space. This poses a threat not only to morality, culture, health and social peace, but above all to the birth rate. Some 300,000 children each year are not being born simply because miserable living conditions have removed their potential parents' incentive to have them. If the deterioration in the age structure which threatens to establish itself from the 1960s onwards is to be prevented then within the next decade there must be a change in housing conditions.

Six million dwellings must be built and they must be sufficiently large; at the moment there are 1.5 million more so-called small dwellings available than can be justified on the basis of the priorities of our population policy. If this building programme is to be achieved within a decade, which is necessary for reasons of population policy, it will require a doubling of housing activity by comparison with the highest level that has been attained hitherto. That raises the question of the competition for resources between house-building and the rest of the building sector; in view of the urgency of the housing needs for reasons of population policy, it will be essential to subject the construction industry to careful planning. Equally, it will need completely new ways of financing . . .

Healthy and adequate dwellings are, therefore, the first preconditions of a social policy which is aiming for continuity and stability. If families are considered to be the cells, the building blocks of the nation and if the morale of the family is the driving force behind personal performance, then it is essential to provide them with sufficient housing space. House-building has, therefore, been designated, again not by chance but logically, as one of the first projects to emerge from our social policy programme. As a defence against social deprivation, it will encourage economic performance and social peace just as effectively as the Western Wall promoted the military strength of the Reich by providing it with a strong defence.

## C. Summary

The Führer's determination to develop the German Reich as a model state in terms of its social provision requires social policy to adopt a new rhythm. The myriad of stopgap remedies implemented by the social policies of the past will be replaced by the creative ideas of national socialism. Planning will be substituted for the ad hoc practice of social policy. So long as social policy was limited to the sporadic alleviation or combating of poor conditions it was more or less irrelevant in what order or in what context the particular measures were implemented. The system of social practice that was applied, if one can call it that, was not driven by an internal coherence but was 'initiated' by external contingencies.

The desk officers in the government offices and organizations dealt with their 'cases' in the chance order dictated by the arrival of the post or—which was even worse—according to the power rankings of the interest groups supporting a particular request. Cobbling things together became a system.

As far as national socialist social policy is concerned, operating on the basis of a hierarchy of priorities dictated by chance is not only unacceptable because of a dislike of the party goings-on of the past. If one builds a new house, one cannot just pile beams on bricks at random. One has to build up from the foundations to the roof according to a plan . . . The same is true of social policy.

It is not a matter of indifference which of the great social problems is tackled first and how the laws are dovetailed together and delimited from each other.

Old age pensions, the health service, the wage structure and the housing situation, Strength through Joy, occupational training, performance-based selection, management, the settlement of the East, the Four-Year Plan, and pre-military training are not unconnected matters. They all have an impact on each other; they only have a purpose as a totality carefully balanced against each other.

That makes sense. But from which end should one begin to unravel this tangle of relationships without it getting into a knot? The aim of cutting through the Gordian knot is after all not to divide things that belong together but simply to remove senseless confusion.

Social policy has two sides: an economic side and a political one. The socio-economic problem is determined by the concern to provide the economy with an adequate and appropriate supply of raw materials, production plant, and consumer goods. Without them prosperity cannot be secured. The larger, the more effective, and the better the supply of goods, the better will be the social conditions. But that is only one side of the issue; the other, the socio-political aspect is no less important: the place of the compatriot in the community, his legal and social relationships to the totality (not only to the production process) as well as to his neighbours and workmates . . .

. . . Thus, it is quite clear that the great social schemes must begin at the same time as the economic construction of the Reich gets under way on a massive scale. Four-Year Plan and social policy are not in conflict with one another but products of the same constructive impulses. Social policy creates the work morale which is essential for tackling the economic problems; the economy reciprocates with an increasing provision of goods. And now to the socio-political tasks in particular. They have in common—as has been said—the aim of regulating the links between compatriots and the nation . . .

One thing really does influence another. Morale is not a particular problem for which the KdF warden has exclusive responsibility but the outcome of social policy in general. Only the people who are content in their whole being can develop the work morale which the nation must demand of them in view of the tasks which lie ahead. If, simultaneously with the drafting of an old age pensions scheme, the housing question is being addressed, a health service is being prepared, and a wage structure is being worked out, that is not the result of an ambition to make a mark in the social field or a sign of going completely over the top. The totality of our social planning is the logical effect of national socialist dynamic. In the first years after the takeover of power the political foundations were secured. Some people may have asked themselves why the social development seems to be going more slowly than the turbulent political construction. Well, the systematic and consequential nature of National Socialism forbade the start of the social revolution before the political one had borne fruit. With the political and military victory of the Reich the building site has been acquired; with the victory of the national socialist ideology the foundations have been dug on which the social edifice will now be built. The social revolution is reaping the fruits of the political one. Now that the way is clear, the social sphere can be organized in its totality. Particular topics will no longer be addressed out of context and dealt with in a makeshift way. The structure will grow brick by brick in accordance with the laws not only of logic but above all of national needs.

The economic requirements of this social structure are in a political sense productive plant. As such, they are bound by the needs and possibilities of the political and economic situation in just the same way as other forms of investment in the narrow sense of the term. They reinforce each other to produce increased economic performance This harmonious relationship between the economic and social factors is all the more necessary in the future because the economic reserves, which hitherto lay dormant as a result of unemployment, have finally disappeared thanks to the economic policy of recent years. The opportunities for technical rationalization depend very largely on whether we are successful in training a nation to be capable of embracing technical progress. The more complicated the technology of the production process becomes, the bigger the demands it places not only on intelligence and expertise but also on the willingness to take on responsibilities and on the commitment of the producers. These qualities are, however, not only the result of education but also to a large extent of the social situation. Thus, technical and social progress are linked together in an indissoluble if not fateful process of interaction. One is not, therefore, subordinate to the other, but rather, and particularly in a period under economic pressure, they are of equal importance.

———

In fact, the first part of the DAF social programme to be tackled was the plan for a new old age pensions scheme. The DAF plan differed from the existing old age pension scheme in that it followed the existing arrangement for civil servants, firstly, in being financed not by insurance contributions but by general taxation and, secondly, in that it would embrace all occupations replacing the existing distinct professional/ occupational schemes. In its commentary on the plan the AWI rejected the 'division of the productive compatriots into workers of the hand and workers of the brain', which, it claimed, had only had the purpose of 'elevating as many productive compatriots as possible from the mass, irrespective of how difficult their job was, in order to prevent the working class as a whole from successfully achieving its aspirations and demands within the class state'. By contrast, the new scheme was designed to realize 'the notion of the national community in the social sphere' and to secure the removal of 'every barrier within the community of producers which cannot be rationally justified'.[15]

Ley claimed the scheme was in the tradition of Bismarck's 'state socialism' of the 1880s, a tradition which had now reached its apotheosis with Hitler. One aspect was certainly in the tradition of Bismarck's social policy, namely the fact that, according to a member of the Economic Armaments Office, 'the primary purpose of the scheme' was 'to bind the great mass of the workers more closely to the n.s. state'.[16]

The removal of the insurance feature from old age pensions also removed the individual's right to a pension to which he or she had contributed. Under the new scheme the pension was awarded by the state only to those who had fulfilled their 'duty of work' and were otherwise loyal and dutiful 'compatriots'. Those whose behaviour had placed them outside the national community were liable to lose their pension.

On 15 February 1940 Hitler issued the following commission to Dr Robert Ley to implement a comprehensive old age pension scheme for the German people:

**1093**   To Dr Robert Ley, Berlin.

For the purpose of realizing the National Socialist Party programme I hereby commission you, party comrade Dr Ley, in cooperation with the responsible agencies of the Party and the State, to examine and to elucidate the bases and conditions for the implementation of a comprehensive and generous old age pension scheme for the German people, to produce proposals and to present them to me without delay.

---

[15] See Marie-Luise Recker, *Nationalsozialistische Sozialpolitik im Zweiten Weltkrieg* (Munich 1985), p. 101. This section owes much to this book.
[16] Ibid., p. 99.

This new legislation for the construction of the National Socialist national community is intended to remind our nation for all time of our common struggle at the front and at home for the freedom and independence of the Great German Reich.

Berlin, 15 February 1940                                    signed: ADOLF HITLER

▬▬▬

Ley managed to sell the scheme to Hitler primarily on the basis that the prospect of a secure old age would help to reconcile the German population to their current wartime privations. It would be projected as a future reward for their efforts. Four days later the Security Service reported on the response of the population to Hitler's announcement:

**1094**    The announcement of the Führer's instruction to establish an old age pension scheme for the German people has met with a marked response from a large section of the population, above all among the workers. The fact that the measures ordered by the Führer are to be carried out now while the war is on has caused particular astonishment. There has been some discussion about whether the planned measures would include those who lost their life savings in the inflation and who are getting older.

▬▬▬

Ley and the DAF envisaged the old age pensions scheme as merely one part of their social programme and, on 15 September 1940, he outlined the project to a press conference. The following is a report of his speech from a Swedish newspaper.

**1095**    *The German people are going to be rewarded for their wartime sacrifices with an old age free from cares.*
*In eighteen years Germany will not be recognizable. A proletarian nation will have become a master nation.*
*In ten years' time the German worker will look better than an English lord.*

The meeting started late because the Reich Chancellor, Hitler, was spending the evening with Dr Ley as his guest. Hitler regularly rings up his closest colleagues and invites himself for a few hours. This evening he told Dr Ley among other things that house construction methods were completely out of date. We are still building in exactly the same way as a thousand years ago by putting brick upon brick. Building technology has never modernized or rationalized. Germany will have the task of reforming the construction industry. Prefabricated materials will have to be used. If in the future everything has been standardized and prefabricated then later on it will only be necessary to put the materials together at the building site so that a house can be built in a few days. According to Dr Ley, this type of building will be 50 per cent cheaper than hitherto.

The starting point of the interview was the creation of a new old age pensions scheme which has been in preparation for a year. And which is apparently now ready. It is intended to be the reward for the war-time sacrifices made by the German people. I asked Dr Ley if it would be based on some kind of insurance scheme. His reply was:

It will be based on completely new principles, since the whole nation will guarantee that the old age pensions are paid for by the national community. A social contribution will be paid as part of income tax and it is now my task through rationalization to achieve a more effective use of the same amount of money. I rejected an insurance-based system; it creates too large an administrative apparatus and, in any case, is a compulsory savings system to which the poor do not have access. The financial apparatus of the state will take over responsibility for collecting the money for the old age pensions and also for payment. In this way there will be no administrative costs. The pensions will be three times higher than hitherto because the administrative costs will have been saved. Thus, invalidity pensions will be increased from RM 33 to RM 90 per month. The old age pension will increase from the current minimum of RM 60 to a maximum of RM 250. In addition to the normal pensions, there will be an honorarium for the victims of the war and for those injured at work, for example for miners who have become invalids through their work. Mothers who have at least four children will receive an equivalent subsidy. They will not only be decorated with the Mothers' Cross but get their honorarium in old age.

All in all, we will need 8 billion for the new old age pension scheme. Up to now this sum has been spent on insurance schemes. Thus, no new burdens will be placed on the nation. The administrative costs will now be completely eliminated since the tax system will take over the scheme. This will save 2 billion. Furthermore, I have devised a scheme to utilize the unemployment insurance for the old age pensions, which will bring in another 2 billion. As is well known, the former will no longer be needed, since there will not be any unemployment in Germany.

In future, the workers will not receive their long wage slips as they do now with the numerous deductions for insurance and unemployment benefit. All these figures made the workers suspicious; now this will all be done via taxation.

If we take over the insurance capital, Dr Ley continued, then we hope that we can reduce interest rates to 2 or 1.5 per cent and, when this is achieved, it will benefit the individual consumer. We will no longer need the insurance companies' money, since the housing construction industry, for which it was needed hitherto, is going to be financed by the state.

The health insurance offices will also disappear and be replaced by a health service. The party will build Community Houses in all towns. Doctors and dentists will work there. The health of every German will be examined once a year just like a car engine is serviced once a year. There will be three groups of doctors:

1. General practitioners, who know the genetic history of every single family and who have the families' trust.
2. Company doctors who are employed in the factories.
3. Specialists who will be treated as artists and, as a result, will have a special position in the national community.

The practice of medicine will be licensed. Its economic basis will be secured and, in addition, there will be the opportunity for private practice.

The post-war national socialist reforms will revolutionize social conditions, continued Dr Ley, in that in future there would be no difference in the payment of workers of the hand and workers of the brain. Hitler wants payment in future to be made in accordance with three principles: the danger involved in the work (for this reason miners will be paid the most), the difficulty of the occupation, and, finally, according to performance. In future, the piecework rates will be set not by the plant managers but by independent agencies. The wages principle will be radically reformed. The wage will be divided into a tied and a free sum. In future, people will not be able to buy just what they want. Just as at the moment the rationing system prevents people from buying more than a certain amount of many goods, the same will be true in the future. The goods which Germany has to import will be controlled by the state. The use of wages will be directed in accordance with the interests of the state. Since Germany has too little wool, it is not on for certain people to buy ten suits and hang them in their wardrobes. Similarly, it is not on for people to drink twenty-five cups of coffee when one is enough. The demand for imported goods will be restricted, whereas people will gladly purchase what we ourselves produce in quantity, such as, for example, the Volkswagen from German steel. It is Hitler's plan to pay wages in coupons so that people can have wage rises but only on condition that they use the higher wages to buy a Volkswagen or a house on an estate. So the state will say: OK you can have more money but you must invest this extra income in a house.

In future there will an eight-hour working day in Germany. The laws which currently prevent workers from freely choosing their place of work will be repealed. The weekend will go from Saturday midday until Monday morning. Everybody will have holidays and over the next ten years Dr Ley intends to build ten spa hotels, as well as the new large complex in Rügen with 20,000 beds, and finally KdF hotels with 2,400 beds each in every city.

The training period for young people will be shortened. The apprentice period will be reduced through rationalization from four years to two.

Finally, a major building programme will be carried out. Very shortly Hitler will sign a decree to this effect. Three rooms with a large kitchen and bathroom will become the norm. They will cost RM 30 per month since the rents are going to be halved and it will be 50 per cent cheaper to build prefabricated houses.

During the course of the press conference, Dr Ley repeatedly emphasized that power means money. After the war the role of London will have been played out and Germany will have the power. Then Germany will be rich enough to realize its programme so that in ten years time the German worker will be better off than an English lord.

▬▬▬

Ley could afford to be even more frank about the thinking behind the Nazi plans for an old age pension scheme, first in an interview with a group of German editors probably in the autumn of 1940 reported by Dertinger, and then in a speech to the Gau leaders of the German Labour Front in Munich in February 1941:

**1096**     (a) Yesterday, Reich Organization Chief Dr Ley gave a strictly confidential briefing to a small group of editors in the Reich Press Centre concerning the
new old age pensions scheme. The following information is solely for personal
information and must on no account be published.

The Führer has given Dr Ley the responsibility of implementing the NSDAP
programme point regarding old age pensions because he wants socialism to be
realised in Germany after victory has been achieved. National Socialism has a
positive attitude towards life. People have duties; they should work at their jobs
for the general good. But, corresponding to this duty is the right to enjoyment
and pleasure: 'sour weeks; happy festivals'. Many people stay in their jobs long
after they are up to them because they cannot afford to retire from work. In the
process they bar the way for younger and more efficient people, since there is
only room for one person in a job. If someone's physical strength declines then
so does their mind. All claims to the contrary which point to 'ripe experience'
are rubbish. Experience is simply a burden. Nobody should be in a senior
position who is no longer physically fit. In the Party and the state we shall
certainly come round to making leading figures retire at around 60. The Führer
has repeatedly emphasized that he himself will set an example by retiring at the
right time. He would not dream of remaining at the head of the nation and the
Reich if he started showing signs of physical decrepitude. In Dr Ley's view this
might be the greatest decision which the Führer would have to make as a human
being . . .

Dr Ley explained further that the question of an old age pension scheme had
been preoccupying him and the Party for many years. But the objection had
always been made that it would cost too much money and that it would be
impossible to introduce further contributions. Now the war offered a unique
opportunity. The costs of the war had to be met by the German people; income
tax would be increased to the limit of what was possible and then when the war
costs had been gradually covered income tax would be reduced again, which
would make people happy, and then one day one would stop reducing it and
then income tax would cover what was needed for the old age pensions. The
British will also alleviate our burden of war costs since they will have to make a
considerable one-off reparations payment.

On the reorganization of the old age pension scheme, for which a suitable
name was still being sought, Dr Ley stated that here for the first time a model
and very close relationship between Party and state would be established. There
will be a small supreme Reich authority and, apart from that, the Party agencies,
NSV etc. will be involved and receive full state powers to carry out these
functions. He is already in full agreement with the Reich Finance Ministry (State
Secretary Reinhardt). It was, however, clear to him that he still had some battles
to fight and he must, therefore, request that none of his remarks be made public
because he did not want unnecessarily to arouse more opposition. He did not
doubt for a moment that the whole thing would come about as he had broadly
sketched it out. The basic decision had been made . . .

The opposition presumably comes not only from the private insurance
companies for whom the social insurance provision in its existing form had been

their propaganda cloak, but also from the Reich Labour Ministry, which has hitherto been responsible for social insurance.

(b) The German national pension scheme will require a contribution from all Germans in work. Anyone who has an income must contribute to this social welfare plan. Thus, there can be no more old age insurance; the insurance idea is dead. However, this scheme implies that there must be an upper limit of provision. For if it is intended to benefit the propertyless there must be an upper limit of provision. At the moment, we have fixed this at RM 400 [per month]. At the same time, there must be a lower limit. We consider this to be around RM 80 per month. This lower limit is a biological boundary; below it a German cannot survive. For the German simply requires more than the Pole or the Negro or whoever. The higher the race, the higher the preconditions for human life. A further principle for the old age pension scheme and for our social welfare programme in general is: work takes precedence over benefits. We do not want to create a benefit law; rather we want to ensure that every bit of capacity for work, no matter how small, is preserved for the nation. Thus, in the case of an invalid—whose invalidity has, for example, been caused by ill health or an accident—we will not pay him a pension but compensation for the work capacity he has lost. We shall put him back to work, i.e.—as I said before—it is a question of labour deployment and not of benefits. Thus, the administration of it must lie with the Labour Office. Sickness pay will be based on the same principle. We shall only make an exception in the case of old age. If the person reaches a certain age which the state has designated as the upper limit, then they can receive their old age pension without any problem. Everybody else must accept that they will be returned to the labour market by the Labour Office and the state—the old age pension scheme, invalidity benefit and health service—will pay the difference. In addition, we shall differentiate between an old age pension and old people's pay. The old person can—and that will even be encouraged— continue to work. Nobody will stop him and he can thereby increase his income to provide more than his pension. We shall pay 60 per cent of income as a pension with RM 50 as the lower limit. If the income was lower, let us say: RM 800 or lower and he would only get RM 48 or less, then of course we would pay the lower limit of RM 50. The same is true for widows and orphans. For war victims and others we envisage an honorarium which will be paid separately from the pension and will also be paid to the mothers who have the Mothers' Cross. Thus, the pension will be between RM 50 as the lower limit and RM 250 as the upper limit and be RM 90 per month on average. The current average for the invalidity benefit is RM 32 per month.

———

In fact, the DAF old age pensions scheme was strongly opposed by the government ministries, notably the Finance and Labour Ministries, and there is no guarantee that it would have been implemented in this form after the war. Moreover, as the war continued so doubts grew about the wisdom of making promises which might raise people's expectations. Thus, on 17 June 1941 Goebbels noted in his diary: 'We mustn't make people's mouths water. We mustn't go on about it, particularly given the impossibility of doing anything now . . . In wartime one should talk above all about war not about peace.'[17] Aside from the propaganda and morale-boosting functions of the old age pensions scheme, what the Nazis really thought about old age pensions and their recipients is suggested by a comment from the Reich Doctors' Leader, Dr Conti, who remarked on 28 March 1943 that the old age pensions scheme has 'not very much to do with the biological fate of the German people'. It was a 'duty of honour' but involved those who 'from a biological perspective' 'have become less important for the fate of the nation'.[18]

## (b)  The housing programme

One of the most important parts of the 'great social project' envisaged for the post-war era was 'social' or welfare housing. This programme provides important insights into the nature of Nazism as it had developed by the early 1940s.

Housing had been neglected since the late 1920s, initially because of the depression and then because of the priority given to rearmament. During the 1920s, initiatives had emerged for the rationalization of the construction industry, which had led to the establishment in 1927 of the Reich Research Society for Economical Practices in the Construction and Housing Sector (*Reichsforschungsgesellschaft für Wirtschaftlichkeit im Bau- und Wohnungswesen*) based in Berlin. The aim of this body was to rationalize and standardize all aspects of construction—construction techniques, building materials, and ways of organizing housing projects—with the aim, first, of reducing the costs of mass housing and, secondly, of ensuring quality. However, the German construction industry was so fragmented and localized that it was difficult if not impossible to implement such measures. But, in the course of preparation for war and the associated pressures for rationalization, and even more so after the introduction of tighter controls associated with the war economy in 1939, conditions became much more favourable.

In the early summer of 1940, with a German victory apparently within sight, attention was increasingly focused on the need for a post-war housing programme. However, a number of different organizations had claims to responsibilities within the housing sector. There was the

---

[17] Ibid., p. 154.
[18] Hansen, op. cit., p. 53.

Reich Labour Ministry under Seldte, which was traditionally responsible for public housing policy at Reich level. There was the General Plenipotentiary for the Regulation of the Construction Industry under the Four-Year Plan (Fritz Todt), who controlled the allocation of labour, building materials and transport and the German Labour Front (DAF), led by the head of the Nazi Party organization, Robert Ley and its recently established housing organization, *Neue Heimat*. Albert Speer was responsible for the reconstruction of Berlin, while Heinrich Himmler was in charge of construction in the conquered eastern territories. Most of these organizations had programmes for rationalizing the house construction industry through the encouragement of standardization and mechanization in order to facilitate mass housing projects, and the first three in particular were in competition for the lead role in this process.

In the event, Ley was able to exploit his superior contacts with Hitler and his Reich-wide organization to acquire the dominant position. With his first Decree on Post-War German House Construction of 15 September 1940 Hitler set up a committee involving all the various bodies, under Ley's chairmanship, to put forward proposals for post-war housing. The upshot of these discussions was the following second Decree for the Preparation of the Post-War German Housing Programme dated 15 November 1940. This separated 'social housing' from the remaining forms of housing and assigned responsibility for its planning and organization to Robert Ley in the new role of Reich Commissioner for Social Housing, thereby removing the existing responsibilities of the Reich Labour Ministry in this area:

**1097**    The successful conclusion of the war will confront the German Reich with tasks which it will only be able to carry out with an increased population. It is necessary, therefore, for the wounds which the war has opened up in the national body to be closed by an increase in births. Thus, the new German housing programme must create the preconditions for a healthy life for large families. It is necessary to introduce preparatory measures now in order to ensure that a housing programme can be launched immediately after the end of the war. I therefore hereby issue the following instructions:

I. The fulfillment of the requirements laid down by me is a task for the Reich. In order to carry it out I hereby appoint a Reich Commissioner for Social Housing, who will be directly subordinate to me.

II  HOUSING PROGRAMME

House building will be carried out in accordance with a housing programme which will be arranged on an annual basis, I will decide the total number of dwellings to be built in any one year. For this purpose the Reich Commissioner, together with the General Plenipotentiary for the Regulation of the Construction Industry [Todt] will present me with an annual plan. The General Plenipotentiary for the Regulation of the Construction Industry will be responsible for ensuring that the total amount of house-building envisaged for any one year is in accordance with the general construction programme of the Reich which in turn must be geared to the capacity of the construction industry.

Housing for agricultural labourers should be given priority within the total housing programme. The same applies to the construction of family houses and smallholdings. Plans should be made for the construction of a total of 300,000 dwellings in the first post-war year.

### III IMPLEMENTATION OF THE BUILDING PROGRAMME

The private sector should be involved as far as possible in the provision of finance. The construction work and its administration will be carried out by non-profit making housing organizations or other appropriate bodies under licence in so far as it is not undertaken by local government. The tenants will be selected by the local authorities with the prior approval of the Party in accordance with principles concerning which sepcial guidelines will be issued.

### IV RENT

The costs and rents of the new German housing programme are to be fixed in such a way that they take into account the income of the compatriots concerned. In order to achieve this aim Reich funds are to be used as far as is necessary in order to ensure tolerable rents and costs . . .

### VII PLANNING

(a) *Types of housing.* The new German post-war housing will take the form of blocks of flats, individual family houses and smallholdings. The particular form chosen will depend on the location of the building site.

(b) *The interior of the dwellings.* During the first five years after the war, the dwellings will be designed along the following lines:

(aa) 80% of the new dwellings will have a kitchen-cum-living room, three bedrooms, a shower room with a separate WC. Flats in two- or more storey buildings should ideally have a balcony.

(bb) 10% of the new dwellings should have one room more and 10% one room less.

(cc) Furthermore, in every case there should be a larder and a boxroom.

When planning new towns or major construction projects which radically alter a locality, these proportions can be altered with the permission of the Reich Commissioner.

(c) Size of rooms. The rooms/flats should have the following minimum dimensions which should not be reduced:

(aa) Three-room flat including kitchen-cum-living room:

| | |
|---|---|
| 1 Kitchen-cum-living room | 22 sqm |
| 1 Parents' bedroom | 16 sqm |
| 1 Additional bedroom | 10 sqm |

|                                       |        |
|---------------------------------------|--------|
| 1 Shower room with separate WC        | 5 sqm  |
| 1 Hall                                | 6 sqm  |
| 1 Balcony                             | 3 sqm  |
|                                       | 74 sqm |

(cc) Four-room flat including kitchen-cum-living room.

|                                       |        |
|---------------------------------------|--------|
| 1 Kitchen-cum-living room             | 24 sqm |
| 1 Parents' bedroom                    | 16 sqm |
| 2 Bedrooms of 10 sqm each             | 20 sqm |
| 1 Shower room with separate WC        | 5 sqm  |
| 1 Hall                                | 6 sqm  |
| 1 Balcony                             | 3 sqm  |

(dd) Five-room flat including kitchen-cum living room

|                                       |        |
|---------------------------------------|--------|
| 1 Kitchen-cum-living room             | 26 sqm |
| 1 Parents' bedroom                    | 16 sqm |
| 3 Further bedrooms of 10 sqm each     | 30 sqm |
| 1 Shower room with separate WC        | 5 sqm  |
| 1 Hall                                | 6 sqm  |
| 1 Balcony                             | 3 sqm  |

Minor variations are permitted in so far as the nature of the site requires them.

(d) *Taking account of the experience gained from air raids.* The experience gained from air raids is to be used in the choice of building sites, in the housing density, in the construction of the houses and in the inclusion of air raid shelters. In so far as the building plan includes air raid shelters they are to be made bomb-proof and large enough to provide sleeping accommodation for all residents . . .

VIII  STANDARDISATION AND RATIONALISATION

A reduction in the construction costs of the dwellings must be achieved with all means without damaging their design quality. Ground plans for the dwellings should, therefore, be worked out and be provisionally declared compulsory for a period of five years. In addition, the number of storeys, the thickness of walls, and the types of construction of roofs, ceilings and staircases should be standardized.

The fixed service instalations as well as the windows and doors are to be standardized as far as possible. The work on the building sites should be mechanised with the aim of excluding manual labour as far as possible . . .

XI  GAU HOUSING COMMISSIONER

The area supervision of the housing programme and its direction within the context of the overall construction activities within the Gaus is the responsibility of the Gauleiters as Gau housing commissioners. To carry out this task they will operate through state agencies to be designated by the Reich Interior Minister and, within the framework of existing legislation and in accordance with the directives given to them by the supreme Reich authorities, they can give instructions to all those official agencies within the Gau which are either directly or indirectly involved in housing construction.

In the first issue of the official journal of the office of the Reich Commissioner for Social Housing, *Der Soziale Wohnungsbau*, dated 1 January 1941, Heinrich Simon, one of Ley's closest aides, spelled out the new agency's agenda in an article entitled 'German Post-War Social Housing Construction':

**1098**    There has hardly been a social issue which has figured so prominently in the day-to-day political work of the Gauleiters as the housing question. It has been the subject of their daily concern. In every Gau the failure of past governments to make provision for the future and the defence requirements of the recent past have combined to produce the housing shortage with which we are familiar. What has been done in terms of meeting housing needs could only deal with the most urgent requirements and had to be subordinated to the need to achieve economic and military freedom.

Now, in the middle of the war, as the first stage of the great social programme, the Führer has brought the solution of the housing problem a decisive step nearer with his decree of 15 November 1940. It is part of the great comprehensive social project with which the Führer will express the nation's gratitude to its sons returning victorious from the front, a social project of which no other nation on earth can boast and which will make Germany the first truly Socialist people's state in the world.

The development and future of our nation depends to a decisive extent on the solution of the housing question. After this war the German people must:

1.    produce sufficient offspring to achieve the population numbers required to penetrate the newly-won territories;

2.    to prepare housing for the settlement of compatriots in the newly-won territories;

3.    to bring the housing conditions in the old as well as in the new Reich territories into line with the nation's cultural standards and thereby create an increase in happiness and efficiency.

Given the cultural level achieved by the German people, a sufficient number of offspring is only possible with satisfactory housing conditions. Although the provision of housing will not by itself increase the desire to have children, it is clear that inadequate housing conditions will ensure the failure of all other measures to increase the birth rate . . .

With the Führer's decree a path-breaking transformation in the function of flats has occurred. The flat is no longer merely a matter of housing but rather it has now acquired an ethical purpose. It is subject to the law of population growth and must serve this law. For this reason, in his decree of 15 September 1940, the Führer already said how many rooms such a flat must have if it is to serve the designated purpose. Then, in the final Führer edict of 15 November 1940, the minimum size of the rooms was decreed. In the course of numerous meetings with Reichsleiter Ley and Professor Speer the Führer also expressed his opinions on other details of the arrangement of the rooms. It is in fact these aspects of the edict which in particular reflect the Führer's detailed considerations and thoughts. Thus, it was his express wish that the flats should not have a parlour and a small kitchen but a living room-cum-kitchen, i.e. a room in which the whole family could gather during the day and in the evening and which would simply contain a small kitchenette.

Also, the much-debated question of bath or shower was decided by the Führer in favour of the shower—not because he was concerned about saving space or money but because he considered showers more hygienic, since he wants to avoid the whole family using the same bath water in order to save money. Naturally, the showers will have to be constructed in such a way that they provide a 60-70cm high plinth on which babies can be bathed in the same way as in a baby bath.

The Führer has given further instructions that in every flat there should be a larder and a boxroom. In this connexion one should mention the fact that, as a further development from the use of larders, the Reich Commissioner is to address the question of providing people's refrigerators, since they are the best weapon in the *battle against spoilage*. The boxrooms will be complemented by enabling prams and bicycles in future to be stored on the same level as the front entrance instead of having to be taken into the flats via the staircase.

Finally, every flat should, if possible, have a balcony which can function as a kitchen balcony, as a place for rest in the evenings or on Sundays, or as a place to put the baby in the pram and which enhance people's cosiness in 'their own four walls'.

The Führer has viewed ground plans drawn up in accordance with his wishes and has already decided in favour of one of the proposals presented to him.

In the context of the interior decoration of the flats the Reich Commissioner will address the question of furnishings which has often been dealt with in a very unsatisfactory manner. What is nowadays offered to the German worker in terms of furniture, interior fittings and suchlike is not in the least attractive or functional. It is not at all the case that attractive and functional furniture must inevitably be expensive, must be the kind of pompous stuff that is currently being foisted on them. It is much more a question of organization and education and business must adjust itself to our current cultural attitudes and, on the other hand, the workers' taste must be educated to see that what is simple and unfussy is generally the most attractive.

----

In effect the DAF had adopted the rationalizing agenda of the architects and town planners of the 1920s but subjected it to the criteria and requirements of the new 'national community' and of the 'Greater German Reich' which was being created through the settlement of conquered territories in the East. Thus, housing would become an article of mass consumption—'people's flats' like the 'people's car'.

It was clearly impossible to build the vast number of dwellings required within the designated time span of ten years without resorting to intensive housing developments. Thus, despite the hostility of elements within the Nazi movement to modern urban mass housing developments, blocks of flats would be built as well as more traditional individual houses and smallholdings. However, in an approach which ran directly counter to the advocates of 'blood and soil', the agrarian romantics within the Nazi movement with their intense hostility to big cities—an attitude shared to some extent by Hitler himself—Ley insisted on the need for a more positive attitude towards cities:

**1099**    We are used to seeing cities as a threat to the nation, as sources of disease and biological dangers. Cities tear people away from the ties of the local community which still exist in villages and offer them the opportunity of leading their own lives in the way they want, in a certain sense anonymously, outside the community's control. The reason for this impression lies mainly in the fact that our cities have developed inorganically, that they have lost the communal context of the local unit [cell]. But if we are confronted with the fact that we have cities and must build new ones then we must develop a more positive attitude towards cities. I am convinced that a city, even a big city, if it is properly planned, need not represent a biological and political threat for a nation.

The DAF envisaged cities containing planned housing estates focused on community centres run by various party organizations. The latest techniques of industrial design, manufacture and construction were to be employed—for example, using prefabricated sections—in order to maximize economy. This technocratic emphasis on rationalization in the interests of efficiency leading inexorably to standardization through the increasing use of large-scale building operations and industrial prefabrication rather than craft work ran directly counter to the Party's previous ideological emphasis on the importance of the *Mittelstand*—the small builder and craftsman—enshrined in Point 16 of the 1920 Programme.[19] But the new mass housing would not sacrifice quality to economy. For a high uniform standard of quality was considered necessary: first, to retain and maximize labour and procreative efficiency by ensuring healthy conditions; secondly, to sustain morale by providing a sufficient degree of comfort and contentment; and, last but not least, to reflect and encourage an awareness of the high level of civilization which was considered quintessentially German and a crucial part of the German nation's claim to be a 'master race'. As one contributor to the DAF journal on social housing put it: 'We will all be obliged to adopt a new attitude towards building so that we build in a national socialist way in order that we can dwell in a national socialist way.' The new social housing policy was intended to play a crucial role in the creation of the 'new man' who would be fit to rule the new Reich. Ironically, after 1945, many of these new building techniques and town-planning schemes were used, now stripped of their Nazi connotations, to rebuild post-war Germany.

---

[19] See Vol. 1, doc. 3.

# List of Sources

1075 H. Althaus, *Nationalsozialistische Volkswohlfahrt. Wesen, Aufgaben und Aufbau* (1938), pp. 10ff., in H. Vorländer, *Die NSV. Darstellung und Dokumention einer nationalsozialistischen Organisation* (Boppard 1988), pp. 382–3.

1076 H. Vorländer, op. cit., p. 369.

1077 Ibid., pp. 515–16.

1078 Ibid., pp. 516, 520–1.

1079 E. Hansen, *Wohlfahrtspolitik im NS-Staat. Motivationen, Konflikte und Machtstrukturen im "Sozialismus der Tat" des Dritten Reiches* (Augsburg 1990), p. 149.

1080 Ibid., p. 237.

1081 Ibid., p. 238.

1082 H. Vorländer, op. cit., p. 479.

1083 E. Hansen, op. cit., p. 226.

1084 H. Vorländer, op. cit., pp. 438–40.

1085 C. Larass, *Der Zug der Kinder KLV—Die Evakuierung 5 Millionen deutscher kinder im 2. Weltkrieg* (Munich 1983), pp. 144–45.

1086 H. Vorländer, op. cit., pp. 412–14.

1087 Ibid., p. 514.

1088 (a) Ibid., pp. 393–4.
(b) Ibid.

1089 D. Rebentisch, ed., *Dreieich zwischen Parteipolitik und 'Volksgemeinschaft'. Fünf Gemeinden in Dokumenten aus der Weimarer Republik und der NS-Zeit* (Frankfurt am Main 1984), pp. 153–4.

1090 Ibid.

1091 E. Hansen, op. cit., p. 42.

1092 *Jahrbuch 1940/41; 1. Die sozialen Aufgaben nach dem Kriege* (Arbeitswissenschaftlichen Institut der DAF Berlin 1987), pp. 32ff.

1093 Bundesarchiv Berlin (BAB) NS 22/655.

1094 H. Boberach, ed., *Meldungen aus dem Reich. Die geheimen Lageberichte des Sicherheitsdienstes der SS 1938–1945*, Vol. 3, p. 775.

1095 Translation from the *Berlinske Titende* of 15 September 1940 BAB R 41/649.

1096 (a) BAB ZSg.101/41.
(b) *Dokumente der deutschen Politik,* ed. Meier-Benneckenstein (Berlin 1943), pp. 714–15.

1097 T. Harlander and G. Fehl, eds., *Hitler's Sozialer Wohnungsbau 1940–1945. Wohnungspolitik, Baugestaltung, und Siedlungsplanung* (Hamburg 1994), pp. 131–2.

1098 Ibid., pp. 150–3.

1099 Ibid., p. 158.

# CHAPTER 45

# Women

## (i) Introduction

Women bore the brunt of the war on the home front. Not only did they—literally in many cases—keep the home fires burning, but they also kept the wheels of industry and transport turning; they sustained the health and welfare services, even more vital in war than in peacetime; they helped maintain the morale of the fighting men at the front and, by providing home comforts both physical and emotional, they sustained the male workers who remained in Germany.

The war enormously increased the burdens on women, particularly on married women with children. Rationing and shortages of food, clothing, household goods and fuel necessitated time-consuming queuing and caused women constant worry about how to feed and clothe their families and keep them warm during a series of particularly harsh winters. Continual air raid warnings and increasingly frequent and serious air raids robbed them of sleep and kept them in a permanent state of anxiety. Many were forced to abandon bomb-damaged homes and seek refuge with other family members or to be evacuated to distant parts of the country, staying with often resentful strangers in overcrowded accommodation. There was the nagging concern about the well-being of husbands, sons and brothers at the front, whose absence imposed on them additional responsibilities such as for the family finances, children's discipline and other important decisions which previously would have been shared or taken by their husbands. Many had to cope with the stress of bereavement.

Finally, in addition to their household responsibilities, most women had some kind of job, whether full-time or part-time. As more and more males were drafted into the armed forces so the demand for female workers increased. By 1942, 52 per cent of the German labour force was female. These women workers had to get to work and back often over quite long distances using transport that was increasingly disrupted by the effects of air raids. Then, on their return from a hard day's work they were faced with their usual household duties. Many had never previously been employed or found themselves in jobs and working environments of which they had no previous experience. Particularly badly hit were the wives and daughters of the self-employed, whether peasants or small businessmen, who now found themselves burdened with running the farm or small business on their own and were forced to work excessive hours.

To cope with all these burdens women depended on family and neighbourhood networks of support, mostly female, to look after children and the aged, to help in times of sickness or when bombed out and in numerous other ways. They also had to summon up reserves of energy, resilience, initiative and independence, which many did not realize they possessed and the experience of which transformed lives in various ways, not least relationships with their husbands, often producing tension when they returned home. The war challenged gender roles and affected sexual mores in other ways that caused growing concern to the authorities. The awareness, for example, that they might be killed at any moment in an air raid or at the front encouraged some to make a quick marriage or seek a sexual encounter after only a brief acquaintanceship.

Developing appropriate policies for women posed serious problems and the hesitant and often contradictory policies pursued by the regime in this field reflected conflicting pressures and priorities and a changing military situation. For example, there was growing concern about the effects of increasing mortality rates in the armed forces on the numbers and quality of Germany's future population. The desire to increase the number of births prompted some Nazi officials to consider changes to sexual mores by encouraging illegitimate births, provided the parents were of 'good blood', and contemplating new forms of marriage such as polygamy. However, most Germans shared traditional moral values and these received powerful reinforcement from the Christian Churches, and so the regime was obliged to consider the effects of such ideas and proposals on popular morale.

However, it was in the field of work that the contradictions and shifts in policy were most apparent. For, while, on the one hand, the Nazis were conscious of the need to mobilize female labour to fill the gaps left by the men drafted into the armed forces, at the same time, they were anxious not to alienate women and their husbands at the front by compelling them to work. At the beginning of the war, by international standards, Germany already had a very high proportion of women in gainful employment. Thus, it was not so much a question of tapping a large pool of unemployed female labour, but rather one of deploying those women most effectively and increasing numbers of women employed at the margins.

On the one hand, there was pressure from the economic agencies— Todt, Speer and the Armaments Ministry, the Wehrmacht Economics Section, and the Labour Ministry—for a tougher policy geared towards mobilizing women for work, particularly in the armaments industry. There was also pressure from the Nazi Party, from the SD, and from Goebbels and the Propaganda apparatus, who were concerned about popular discontent with the unfair distribution of the burden of work among women from different social groups. But, on the other hand, the leadership was governed by certain notions of what work was appropriate to women, notions which, in some cases were reinforced by class prejudice. Few Nazi leaders came from the working class, and the new Nazi elite operated on the assumption of the existence of a social hierarchy, newly legitimated by the application of Nazi criteria, whose upper ranks deserved to be privileged. They were also influenced by ideological concerns about population policy, namely about protecting women's health to ensure that they could perform their primary role as mothers. There was the further consideration that married women might be more usefully employed at home looking after their husbands and children and sustaining the home front in this way rather than in factory work for which they were not trained and in some cases not suited. Moreover, employers generally preferred where possible to employ foreign workers, both male and female, who were not subject to the same restrictive regulations governing hours and conditions of work as German women and would not require expensive investment in new facilities which would probably not be needed in the future if the war was about to end. Finally, and above all, however, there were concerns about morale, both that of the women themselves and that of their husbands, if coercion were used.

Policy towards women emerged out of the conflicts and compromises produced by these contradictory pressures depending on the respective influence of the contenders and what were regarded as the priorities at any given time. The balance between these pressures and priorities was in turn influenced by the changing military situation, which affected the availability of foreign workers to fill the gaps left by the increasing numbers of German males being conscripted into the armed forces to replace those who had been killed, injured or captured. Policy towards female labour was thus the product of a complex set of pressures and changing circumstances from which even the Führer himself was not immune.

Hitler's views reflected his opinion about the 'nature' of women, the ideological priority of population policy, social prejudice and concerns about morale, and on occasion he intervened decisively. While he reluctantly accepted the need during the war for women to work in jobs hitherto considered male work, he was not prepared to conscript married women with children, older women or middle class women unused to factory work. But, ultimately, he too was subject to the constraints imposed by a deteriorating situation.

## (ii) The Nazi Female Organizations

The Nazis had two organizations which were directly concerned with women's role in the war: the National Socialist Women's Organization (NSF), with its adjunct, the German Women's Work (DFW), and the women's section of the German Labour Front (DAF). The number of women in the NSF/DFW grew from roughly 3.3 million at the beginning of 1939 to 6.2 million in 1942, in other words approximately one in five German women was enrolled in these two organizations.[1] Well before September 1939, the Nazi women's organizations had been preparing German women for war. Through its section 'Economy-Home Economics', for example, the NSF taught women to use the available foodstuffs in the most economical, efficient and digestible manner by showing them how to bottle fruit and vegetables and providing advice on cooking and recipes. It also organized sewing courses so that women could repair and alter their clothes and thus limit the effects of the clothing and textile shortages. By 1938, 1.8 million women had attended the section's various courses.

After the outbreak of war, the NSF/DFW had two main functions: first, to continue, but now with even greater urgency, its previous work preparing women for war. Between 1939 and 1941, for example, it gave out 70 million brochures and leaflets with recipes in a campaign which it styled as 'the Household Battlefront'.[2] However, it now had additional tasks. Through its sections 'Mothers' Service', and 'Aid Service' it carried out a range of useful activities, some of which overlapped with those of the NSV. For example, it provided help with the harvest; it sent parcels to men at the front and helped to entertain them when they were

---

[1] See Hans-Jürgen Arendt, 'Zur Frauenpolitik des faschistischen deutschen Imperialismus im zweiten Weltkrieg', in *Jahrbuch für Geschichte* 1982, Vol. 26, p. 322.
[2] Ibid., p. 319.

lying wounded in hospital; it helped with the evacuees; it helped with Winter Aid (WHW) collections and to distribute ration coupons. The list is almost endless. Its second function was to try and indoctrinate German women with the regime's main ideological themes and its particular day to day propaganda line. Both of these tasks were deigned to help sustain the morale of the female population.

The following report by the NSF branch of Söflingen-West in Württemberg for the month of January 1943 gives some indication of the range and extent of activities undertaken by the NSF at local level:

**1100** Women's work in the households of large families and working women, as well as looking after children: 340 hours.

Railway Station duties: 34 women. Total: 60 hours

Work for the Wehrmacht: 5 women (socks darned). Total: 36 hours.

Hospital care: 10 women plus 4 girls (BdM)

Accommodation secured for the relatives of wounded soldiers: 2 women.

Distribution of clothing coupons: 3 women. Total 16 hours.

Distribution of food rations cards: 12 women. Total 28 hours.

16 women worked in the two sewing rooms for 3 hours each. Total: 48 hours.

The cell and block leaders have been reminded of the need to visit the relatives of those killed in action and soldiers' wives.

With all its flaws, the significance of the NSF/DFW should not be underrated. For its leadership corps it was able to mobilize the energies and exploit the idealism and gifts of some of the most dynamic and able women in Germany. In a society in which career opportunities for women were severely restricted, not least by the ideological precepts of the regime, paradoxically the Nazis' own women's organizations, with their hundreds of thousands of posts, provided an outlet for the abilities and ambition of women. One captures a sense of this in the following letters from the head of the NSF district organization of Kronach-Stadtsteinach in a largely rural but quite heavily industrialized part of northern Bavaria: The first, dated 23 October 1939, was to the Gau headquarters of the Women's Organization, the second, dated 28 October 1939, to colleagues:

**1101** (a) During my visit to the State Peasants Organization (*Landesbauern-schaft*) in Bayreuth, it emerged that the position of female desk officer IC in the *Landesbauernschaft* office was to be refilled . . . I have been chosen as the replacement . . . After long deliberation I have decided to accept the post, since I cannot afford to reject such an opportunity for professional advancement and because the job of looking after the spiritual and cultural needs of peasant women is something which appeals to me. At the same time, the dual job of having to do my full-time job and be head of the Women's Organization is too much for me. I simply had to do something about it. It has been a very difficult decision for me to leave my leaders, who have faith in me and my work, and my close colleagues.

(b)  My dear colleagues,
Quite unexpectedly, I have to inform you of a change in my duties. The *Landesbauernschaft* has appointed me as a desk officer 1E in Bayreuth . . . With [NSDAP] District Leader, Dr M's approval I have accepted the post for an [initial] period of 1¹/₂ years and must now ask for leave . . .
    Thank you all for the loyalty which you have always shown to the Führer's work. I myself can no longer imagine my life without this content and say, to you, therefore not 'farewell' [*Lebt wohl*] but good bye [*auf Wiedersehen*].
▬▬▬

In fact, this change of jobs indicated one of the weaknesses of the NSF, namely the fact that few of its personnel were salaried; most had to make do with expenses.
    As far as most members of the NSF were concerned, their main regular involvement with the organization was, or was meant to be, through the so-called 'community evening', which occurred at varying intervals depending mainly on the keenness of the local branch and constraints imposed by the time of year (e.g. demands of harvest etc. in rural districts). The importance of community evenings during wartime was spelled out in a circular from the NSF headquarters in Gau Bavarian Eastern March to the local branches dated 11 October 1939:

**1102**    In these grave times it is more than ever necessary to carry on with our community evenings. After all, the aim of these get-togethers is to strengthen the feeling of belonging and the sense of mutual support among all our women. The community evening should be for every woman the source of strength with which to cope with her often serious personal cares as a German woman and, at the same time, to keep in sight the great goal to which all our efforts and all our sacrifices are dedicated, namely our nation's freedom.
    . . . Now, in time of war, the spiritual care of our women is a particularly important task of the local women's leader which she can best carry out through the community evenings. Here, with us, women should be able to recharge their energies and be edified. Our community evenings should contribute towards ensuring that we grow ever closer together in our common aims and actions. Everything for the Führer and nation.
▬▬▬

The reality of these community evenings varied very much depending above all on the quality of the local leader, but also on the nature of the local community. If the local leader was popular and respected within the community and if she was skilful enough to sweeten the indoctrination pill with cosy socializing, the evenings could be quite successful, as is suggested by the following excerpt from the monthly report for February 1941 for the NSF local branch of the village of Stockheim in the district of Kronach-Stadtsteinach:

**1103**    Our community evening took place at member L's house; it was well attended. The evening's topic was the Führer's speech which he gave on 31.1.1941 and from which we read aloud some excerpts. We sang songs of the movement [NSDAP] and folk songs to accordion accompaniment. Then we had a coffee evening at which we all cosily got together.

Elsewhere, however, the evenings were less successful, partly for reasons outside the control of the local leadership, as the following monthly report for the same month from the NSF branch in the village of Mitwitz in the same district:

**1104**    The general report on morale is as follows:
Everybody is quite confident about a definite victory, although every woman knows there will be a struggle. My concern is that so few women attend the evenings that are arranged. Whenever I ask why that is, the reply is almost always the same: they have no *time*. Everybody here is doing something: housework in the evening, writing letters. In the case of older women the black-out is a real problem. But there is more to it than that. On Saturdays and Sundays the cinema is open and $^3/_4$ of the NSF go there. One can really see that the women want to be entertained. For example, if I had a big spread every fortnight the attendance would be brilliant. People are earning quite a lot here and they want a treat.

How wrong things could go if the conditions were not right is suggested by the following NSF reports from the strongly Catholic village of Steinwiesen in the same district:

**1105**    *June 1941.* We in K really miss Fräulein Z. She definitely knew how to attract people. I don't think I have it in me to do the same. I will of course do my best but it's very difficult. I very much need the support of the NSF district leadership so that I can be effective. Since the war began people no longer want to attend evenings. There's no real impetus any more.

*August 1941.* Every day there are losses on the eastern front and the population is beginning to complain. Wherever one goes there are little huddles complaining, crying and grumbling. The black blood really comes out here. They run off to the church like mad to seek comfort.

*September 1941.* You have no idea how much complaining there is here. People are no longer ashamed about it. Mainly in the butchers' shops and even about the films put on by the Gau Propaganda Department, e.g. *Ohm Krüger*.[3] Of course these people are too stupid to understand its significance. The people here are much too unenlightened about everything. When the Party puts on something they never attend, so how can they know about anything. Everyone just thinks of 'me' and not of the 'wider whole'.

*May 1942*. Our people have no interest in anything any more. On the 23rd of this month, our District Leader [NSDAP] spoke here and there were only 12 women there. Everybody charges into the church like mad. If the priest holds a service 10x a day then they go running in 10x and the meetings and evenings are only attended by a few people and always the same ones. They're so furious with me because I don't go to church. Even members of the NSF get cross about it. What can one do?

The above documents indicate one of the weaknesses of the NSF, namely the fact that many of its officials were the wives and daughters of sometimes 'foreign' Nazi leaders, e.g. village teachers, and their ideological zeal was liable to alienate local women, particularly in rural areas where the influence of the church was still strong.

What really attracted the women to the 'Community Evenings' and what really enabled the NSF to reach them was the provision of tasks or information which women felt were beneficial to their menfolk fighting at the front or which helped to alleviate their own day-to-day problems. Women welcomed, for example, the provision of courses on sewing, cooking and baking and they welcomed the opportunity to knit and darn socks for the Wehrmacht. In her monthly report for February 1942 the NSF district leader in Kronach-Stadtsteinach observed that:

**1106**    Last month our women's meetings took a practical form. The short courses put on by the Department for Economics-Home Economics (V-H), above all the tasting of sample dishes, were popular and are being widely copied. Since we have a very big dearth of instructors, our local women's leaders, together with the V-H section heads, are going ahead on their own. They are organizing sessions in their branches on darning, slipper-making and baking. We are very glad if this can be done by the people out there themselves because the demand for courses, above all courses put on by the Mothers' Service section, is growing month by month and it is intolerable that the only instructor in our large district with 74 local branches is the head of the Mothers' Training Unit.

Particularly at the present time, courses are the best thing for winning our women. There are after all here and there signs of people getting tired of the war: one person says they're becoming resigned because they cannot understand why at such a grave time one can go on holding community evenings, another because, having sacrificed her son, she feels she's made enough sacrifices, others can't face hearing the youth group laughing and singing. But one thing always

---

[3] An anti-British film about the Boer War.

.

brings them together again, namely work, particularly work for our soldiers. Thus, at the moment, we are being bombarded about socks. Let's hope they come soon because otherwise work will begin elsewhere and many hard-working hands here will not be able to get going.

▬▬▬

The last comment about socks was true. For example, even the embattled NSF branch leader in Catholic Steinwiesen was able to report in the same month that 'the women show great enthusiasm for the proposed sock-darning sessions for our soldiers. So please send us some supplies'.

A classic case of the successful mobilisation of women for the war effort by the NSF was the collection of winter clothing for the troops on the eastern front in December–January 1941–2.[4] In her report for January 1942 the NSF district leader in Kronach-Stadtsteinach commented on its importance:

**1107**    The woollens' collection produced close cooperation with all the Party agencies. The DAF made available its training room as a third sewing room. Almost all the community evenings last month were cancelled  and replaced by work evenings in which our women were busy working on the wool and fur clothing which had been collected. From all the local branches came reports that women and girls had immediately and enthusiastically volunteered. On the last day of the month, we could close our K sewing rooms in which the many damaged garments from the whole district had had to be repaired. 2,170 women and girls were working there in the period from 30.12.41–31.1.42, a total of 10,675.5 hours. But they were proud when they heard about the results of their work. Out in the country too a number of branches worked until late in the night. 'A peasant's wife was sitting until 12 o'clock at night knitting socks, gloves, and mittens'. We also used the children's group assistants, the Young Girls, the BdM, and even the schools for the work. The girls plucked wool or sewed, while others unravelled old unusable garments and then knitted new warm things from them.

Finally, one should make the point about the woollens' collection that it was *the* sphere of activity for which our women had long been calling. At last their cry of 'we want to help our soldiers' had been listened to. I am convinced that with the 'Sock Action', which is envisaged, our goods will be 'snapped up'. The 30 January was a particular day of celebration for us because the Führer spoke to us again.

▬▬▬

### (iii) Female Labour

Apart from its intrinsic interest and importance, the issue of female labour during the Second World War provides an excellent case study of policy-making in the Third Reich. The First World War had

---

[4] See below, pp. 481–85.

demonstrated the essential contribution of women to the workforce and, from the very beginning of their planning for the next war, the Nazi leadership had envisaged the large-scale deployment of women. Thus, the first paragraph of the Reich Defence Law of 21 May 1935 stated: 'In wartime every German man and woman has a duty of service for the Fatherland.' The decree of 22 June 1938 enabling labour to be conscripted for projects of special political importance, which was revised and extended in February 1939, applied to women as well as men. However, the ambivalent attitude of the regime towards the employment of women is apparent in the following 'Directives for the Employment of Women in the Event of Mobilization' which the Reich Labour Ministry issued on 16 September 1938. They established restrictions for the employment of women 'where it would otherwise threaten the nation's life spring' by jeopardizing 'the fulfilment of their task of motherhood':

**1108**    In the event of war women must be extensively employed in industry and in the administration in order to release men for combat. In the process peacetime habits and considerations, which in other circumstances would have prevented the deployment of women, must be decisively put aside in the interests of the defence of the Reich. At the same time, during wartime too women's work must be subject to restrictions where it would otherwise threaten the nation's life spring. Thus, in wartime too women must not be exposed to threats to their health, which sooner or later would jeopardize the fulfilment of their task of motherhood. Moreover, in the deployment of female labour consideration must also be given to the fact that, as a result of their mental and physical nature, women are not capable of performing all the types of work carried out by men and that assignment to the wrong type of work would also have negative results in terms of work performance. Thus the deployment of women requires very careful preparation and must be carried out through close cooperation between the plant, the factory inspectorate, and the Labour Office. In particular, the factory inspectorate must ensure that the way in which women are employed is appropriate to their particular need for protection. For this purpose the plant must inform the office of the factory inspectorate of the type of employment of those women who are being deployed in place of men. Notice of this is not required where women have already carried out the same work in the plant before the war. Notice must be given at the latest three days after the work has begun with a detailed description of the women's activity.

On the basis of its legal responsibility, the office of the factory inspectorate can make the employment of women dependent on certain conditions and in those cases in which serious threats to health appear unavoidable can ban it altogether. The following points, whose practical implementation will be elucidated by a number of examples, are intended to serve as indicators for the feasibility of employing women . . .

I. GENERAL POINTS.

1. Women may not be employed in work which involves a serious threat to health (poisons, corrosives, and gases, health-threatening vapours and dust, great heat and vibration).

2. Women may not be given heavy work for which they are not physically suited.

3. Women should not be employed in work which requires a high degree of presence of mind, decisiveness, and a rapid response.

4. In general women should not be employed in work which requires a high level of technical understanding and technical knowledge. Employment in such work is, however, possible in the case of:

   a) women with high intelligence after special technical training.

   b) increased technical supervision.

Women may often be able to be employed by means of altering equipment or work processes in the plant (lifting gear for heavy materials, conveyor belts, automatic mechanisms for feeding in materials, simplification of clamping procedures, introduction of automated machinery, the breaking down of work into separate simple routines, the provision of gadgets and templates for mass production, technical instruction, increased supervision) . . .

———

In fact, despite the Nazis' ideological preference for women to stay at home, the numbers of women in employment had increased markedly since the Nazi takeover of power in 1933 from 11.4 million in 1933 to 14.8 million in 1939 and, in particular, since the introduction of the Four-Year Plan and accelerated rearmament in 1936. On the outbreak of war, women made up 37.4 per cent of the total labour force in Germany (12.4m.) and 27 per cent of the industrial labour force. These figures included 6.4 million married women (36 per cent of all married women), while 8.7 per cent of all single women aged 15–60 were already employed. However, the Nazis were wary about conscripting women for work and, up to June 1940, only a quarter of a million women had been conscripted, the majority of whom were simply transferred from one firm to another regarded as more important to the war effort. The following table shows the development of the female labour force during the war:

**1109**

*The Employment of German Women in Germany 1939–1944 according to Economic sectors (thousands)*

|  | May 1939 | May 1940 | May 1941 | May 1942 | May 1943 | May 1944 |
|---|---|---|---|---|---|---|
| Agriculture | 6,495 | 5,689 | 5,369 | 5,673 | 5,665 | 5,694 |
| Industry/ Handicrafts/ Energy | 3,836 | 3,650 | 3,677 | 3,537 | 3,740 | 3,592 |
| Commerce/ Banking/ Insurance/ Transport | 2,227 | 2,183 | 2,167 | 2,225 | 2,320 | 2,219 |
| Domestic Service | 1,560 | 1,511 | 1,473 | 1,410 | 1,362 | 1,301 |
| Administration/ Services | 0,954 | 1,157 | 1,284 | 1,471 | 1,719 | 1,746 |
| TOTAL | 14,626 | 14,386 | 14,167 | 14,437 | 14,806 | 14,808 |

The basic policy regarding the employment of women was laid down at the beginning of the war by the Reich Ministry of Labour:

**1110**

(a) 7 September 1939: State Secretary Dr Syrup has decided that married women who have hitherto not been in employment will continue not to be liable for labour conscription unless they wish to volunteer for the labour mobilization programme entirely of their own free will. The regional labour offices are to be informed accordingly.

(b) To the Presidents of the Regional Labour Offices (personal)
Re: Circular of 3.vii.39

In the circular referred to above I have laid down that in peacetime women who have domestic and family responsibilities are not to be called up unless they were previously in employment and unless their family circumstances and health have changed in the meantime.

Even under the present circumstances I do not consider it advisable to utilize married women who were not previously in employment unless the women volunteer for the labour mobilization programme entirely of their own free will. I request, therefore, that you ensure that the above-mentioned instructions contained in the circular continue to be applied.

The manpower requirements for plants engaged on projects of national importance must be met by exploiting all other possibilities (the employment of labour from plants engaged on non-priority projects, particularly of female workers and employees who become available through the closing down of such plants, by exchanging labour between the different areas, volunteers etc.). If this should prove impossible please inform me of the fact.

▬▬▬

Initially, the labour requirements for mobilization were largely achieved through the transfer of workers from the consumer goods sector to the production goods sector, a process which affected women workers in particular, as the following table makes clear:

**1111**

*Distribution of Female Labour in Germany May 1939–May 1943 (thousands)*

|                              | May 1939 | May 1940 | May 1941 | May 1942 | May 1943 |
|------------------------------|---------|---------|---------|---------|---------|
| *Production Goods*           |         |         |         |         |         |
| Chemicals                    | 184.5   | 197.4   | 204.7   | 215.8   | 255.9   |
| Iron and steel               | 14.7    | 18.4    | 29.6    | 36.6    | 64.9    |
| Metalworking, machinery      | 216.0   | 291.3   | 363.5   | 442.0   | 603.0   |
| Electrical                   | 173.5   | 185.4   | 208.1   | 226.3   | 264.7   |
| Optical Industry             | 32.2    | 37.2    | 47.6    | 55.6    | 67.2    |
| Metal goods                  | 139.1   | 171.3   | 172.0   | 191.2   | 259.5   |
| TOTAL                        | 760.2   | 901.3   | 1,025.7 | 1,168.4 | 1,515.4 |
| *Consumer Goods*             |         |         |         |         |         |
| Printing                     | 97.2    | 88.8    | 92.6    | 73.9    | 60.1    |
| Paper goods                  | 89.5    | 84.3    | 79.2    | 71.9    | 73.1    |
| Leather                      | 103.6   | 78.7    | 85.0    | 81.8    | 95.6    |
| Textiles                     | 710.1   | 595.4   | 581.3   | 520.9   | 546.3   |
| Clothing                     | 254.7   | 226.5   | 225.3   | 212.8   | 228.9   |
| Ceramic goods                | 45.3    | 41.4    | 39.3    | 37.1    | 42.8    |
| Food                         | 324.6   | 273.5   | 270.9   | 236.8   | 238.0   |
| TOTAL                        | 1,625.3 | 1,388.7 | 1,364.0 | 1,235.4 | 1,284.5 |

However, the table also indicates that the number of women working in industry dropped between May 1939 and May 1940 by some 236,000 and the bulk of this drop occurred after the outbreak of war. The main reasons for this were: first, the fact that, in an attempt to sustain morale in the light of the negative experience of the First World War, on 2 October 1939, the Government had introduced generous allowances for the families of those drafted into the armed forces. The allowance was assessed on the basis of the conscripted husband's income and comprised a combination of a cash sum, rent, insurance payments etc.

up to 85 per cent of the previous income. However, women who were employed lost up to 45 per cent of their family allowance depending on their income, a clear disincentive to remaining in employment. The second reason for women leaving their jobs or failing to enter the labour market was that conditions had deteriorated since the outbreak of war as hours were increased and protective measures on women's work were partially removed. Concern about the trend in female employment was increasingly expressed by officials in the field as in the following letter from Gauleiter Mutschmann, the Reich Governor of Saxony and Reich Defence Commissioner for Military District IV to Lammers, dated 27 May 1940:

**1112** Re: *The increased labour mobilization of women*

It can be seen from repeated reports from the regional labour offices that there are still considerable difficulties with the deployment of female labour. The number of women registered for health insurance [i.e. in gainful employment] in Saxony on 31.8.39, i.e. at the beginning of the war was 777,332; by 31.3.1940 this had been reduced by around 77,000. Domestic difficulties or the prospect of the receipt of family allowances for members of the Wehrmacht are not only used as an excuse for not taking up jobs but often encourage people to give up their jobs, ignoring work discipline in the process.

The extraordinary reduction in female employment can be attributed to the following three main reasons:

1. The reduction in the opportunities for employment in the textile and clothing industries as a result of which a large number of older women, who are not readily employable elsewhere, have become unemployed.

2. The increasing domestic demands on women as a result of wartime conditions.

3. The lack of incentive for going to work as a result of the family allowances for members of the Wehrmacht.

However, the possibility that working women are in fact disadvantaged in comparison with those who are not working, as suggested in the enclosed letter from Dr Lauterbach, cannot be dismissed out of hand. Thus, I consider it necessary that, when women are being deployed, these difficulties should be taken into consideration as far as possible. In particular, one must be generous in not removing their family allowances from working women whose husbands have been called up into the army or cutting them as a result of taking their wages into account.

Provided this is done, there can be no objection to requiring married women to register for work. In this way, many women who have left their jobs during the war will be prompted to start work again. One must expect increased work from this group of women in particular. The majority of single women are in employment or are already deployed elsewhere in the interests of the defence of the Reich. A noticeable increase in the number of those prepared to work can only come from married women.

I would like, therefore, these considerations to be taken into account by the Ministerial Council when it introduces a duty to register for work.

*Dr Lauterbach, head of a horticultural centre to Mutschmann 17.5.40:*

... The women who do not go to work can sleep longer, they need less to eat and do not wear out their clothes, although they get exactly the same rations as the working women. If there are any unrationed foodstuffs available in a particular store, such as fish, these women have time to get them. The working women cannot do that. And, when they really do have time, the shop has sold out. And so in this way too they are disadvantaged by comparison with the women who do not work. Furthermore, they cannot look after their health so well as those women who are not employed. Those women, therefore, who want to help to replace the men who have been called up into the army by working willingly not only do not have the advantages mentioned above, but even have part of the wages deducted through taxes. This makes people very bitter and threatens labour peace, for the working women feel themselves disadvantaged compared with the women who do not work. It would, therefore, be desirable for the soldiers' wives who go out to work not to have any more wage deductions.

▬▬▬

In April 1940 a draft Decree for the Increased Deployment of Women for Reich Defence Tasks was drawn up by the Reich Labour Ministry envisaging a duty of registration for work by all women between 15 and 40 for the purpose of checking their employability. However, the Nazi leadership regarded the issue as highly sensitive as is clear from the following statement from the Reich Interior Ministry, in a letter to the Ministerial Council for the Defence of the Reich in May 1940:

**1113**   ... The compulsory recruitment of women to work is calculated to influence popular morale to a remarkable degree. One should be particularly cautious in recruiting women. Mistakes in this area can have a damaging impact on morale both at home and at the front ...

▬▬▬

In fact, encouraged by the emerging military successes in France, on 4 June 1940, Marotzke, an official in Göring's office, wrote to his opposite number in the Reich Chancellery, Kritzinger, as follows:

**1114**   I am returning the enclosed Decree for the Increased Deployment of Women for Reich Defence Tasks. The Field Marshal [Göring] is not disposed to sign the decree since, at the moment, the requisite numbers can be achieved through the use of prisoners of war. According to the Field Marshal, the decree would at the moment still arouse too much concern among the population.

▬▬▬

Nevertheless, the authorities remained concerned about the difficulty of persuading women to return to work or take up jobs in industry. In place of compulsion they now tried propaganda. On 16 March 1941, the Führer's Deputy for Party Affairs, Rudolf Hess, issued the following instruction to his Gauleiters:

**1115** On the fundamental question of whether the present need for female labour and the need that will arise through the further drafting of men should be met by compulsory state measures or through a voluntary action the Führer has decided in favour of voluntary action. Following this decision, the NSDAP will carry out a comprehensive action in the Greater German Reich under the motto 'German Women aid Victory'. It has the aim of bringing about the voluntary registration for work of all women and girls who are eligible for war work. I shall make an appeal to these women and girls and request them voluntarily to sign their names in lists. The success of all these measures will essentially depend on the cooperation of the Gauleiters. I therefore call upon you to engage in this decisive action in the same way that we used to engage in the NSDAP's political struggle of old. I am particularly concerned that the NSDAP sub-leaders should not exercise any pressure on the women and girls in question, but instead should make a strong appeal to their sense of honour.

However, neither this campaign, nor a direct appeal by Hitler in a Reichstag speech in May for more women to become industrial workers, had a significant effect, as the following undated report on industrial labour statistics from the summer of 1941 makes clear:

**1116** *The Reduction in Female Labour in the Military Districts*

The deployment of female labour has in general not produced the anticipated relief for industry. The total number of female workers employed in industry declined markedly in the first months of the war since the consumer goods industry released numerous women, some of whom found work in the transport sector and in the administration, while others gave up gainful employment altogether. In the course of the war the deployment of women in the iron and metal industry and in the raw materials industry has increased. Nevertheless, in May 1941, there were 80,000 fewer women employed than shortly before the outbreak of war. By contrast, the number of female white-collar employees has considerably increased. Thus, the tendency for women to work in administration has manifested itself in industry as well. The decline in female labour is apparent in almost all the military districts. The largest reductions are in the military districts of Nuremberg, Hanover, Dresden and Stuttgart. It was only in the coastal districts [Stettin and Hamburg] and in Breslau that the number of female industrial workers could be increased. Here they were successful in taking over the female workers released from the consumer goods industry and immediately redeploying them in the armaments industry. In the military districts of Stettin and Hamburg there were additional female workers from outside.

According to the detailed figures, in July 1939 there were 2,284,000 female workers employed in industry, whereas in May 1941 there were only 2,199,000, a drop of 82,412 of which the Dresden military district alone provided 28,587.

Two steps were taken to remedy the situation: first, from 1 July wages were no longer counted against family allowances. Secondly, on 20 June 1941, Göring issued a secret decree according to which all those female workers in receipt of family allowances, who had given up employment since the outbreak of war and had not subsequently become mothers or were obliged to look after sick or infirm relatives, should be forced to register for work or lose a substantial portion of their allowance.

However, the effects of this decree were very limited with only about 20 per cent of the women, who were being investigated by the Labour Offices on the grounds that they were receiving family allowances, being assigned to jobs. Moreover, the decree was clearly socially discriminatory, since it only applied to those women employed pre-war and not to the better-off women who did not need to work. This caused understandable resentment of which the following letter, dated 21 September 1941, from an irate husband at the Russian front to his local Labour Office in Görlitz, Saxony, is a good example:

**1117**   My wife has written that she has received from you a demand that she report for work. Just to make matters quite clear, I have forbidden my wife to go out to work, i.e. as long as our baby is not yet two years old, and, as far as I know, women who have small children shouldn't go to work, at least that's how our Führer wants it to be. But I wanted to ask politely whether your wife goes out to work yet. I'm sure she doesn't because otherwise you wouldn't have the orderly household which enables you to recover from your hard work. Of course what we're doing out here is nothing compared with your work and deprivation. My dear sir, I haven't slept in a proper bed for 2 years or rather I've had 28 days' leave during this time. But we do our duty gladly in the mud here and happily put our lives at risk because it's for Germany. But then, I reckon, we can demand that our wives are not bothered with such rubbish. How about you giving up something and sending your wife out to work. I bet there are men in your office whose wives are childless and who don't go out to work. In your place I would be ashamed to ask a soldier's wife who has a six-month-old child to go out to work. But there's no point in writing to you like this because you always have it warm and cosy. But just to put you in the picture: my wife receives no state benefit, she only gets my salary and I imagine my life is worth those few marks. At any rate, my wife is not going out to work even if I have to go and see my divisional commander who is at least a human being and is sympathetic. You're just a bureaucrat and not a human being. I'd like to get you over here for four weeks' square bashing; that would really make you sweat. But I can give you some good advice. Come out here and relieve me. I could put up with being at home for a bit. But what's the point of arguing with you. My wife is not going out to work. I hope you realize that I'm going to make a complaint and I think you understand that I'll get my way! I think you're having it a bit too easy. You could do with a bit of fresh air.

———

This discontent was taken up by Dr Ley, the head of the German Labour Front, who wrote to Göring on 10 September 1941 as follows:

**1118** I feel I must contact you once more concerning the integration of women into the labour process. Not only are there an increasing number of reports from my offices, but I am continually receiving letters from Party members and national comrades who should be taken seriously, including leaders of model plants, which refer to this matter.

As is well known, the Reich Minister of the Interior issued a circular on 30 June 1941 which regulates the issue, particularly the administrative technicalities raised by your edict of 20.6.1941.

Since roughly the middle of June, one has been able to assess the effects of these decrees and, in connection with this, I feel bound to draw your attention to phenomena which are calculated to produce unrest and discontent, and thereby to disturb the social peace. The two edicts referred to envisage the reintegration into the labour process of those women who left employment after the beginning of the war. These are mostly women who are relatives of soldiers and thus receive a family allowance.

There can be no doubt that most of these women could have stayed on in work and to this extent this measure is right and necessary, provided that one is not too mean-spirited in recognizing important reasons why individuals cannot start work again.

It is also true that the Führer's appeal to German women to show themselves willing to work, made in his statement to the Reichstag on 4 May 1941, met with a lively response and induced many women to apply for work. Nevertheless, a large number of women have not responded to the appeal and in many cases they are those who would not only be capable of taking a job but of whom one could expect that they really ought to do so.

However, this group of women are not covered by your decree because before the war they neither gave up employment nor were ever employed. Also, those women are not covered who, while not receiving family allowances, nevertheless receive equivalent payments from the public purse, such as, for example, the wives of civil servants and public employees who have been called up, professional soldiers etc. There are, however, continual complaints about the attitude of these women and people do not understand why nothing is done to hold them to the fulfilment of their clear duties and if necessary to compel them to do so.

Numerous childless women are staying in districts not subject to air raids and in spa towns—often for several months—whose circumstances enable them not only to maintain their regular domicile but also pay the costs of staying in a spa and, in addition, to follow an extravagant life style. There is also evidence of an unusual growth in the number of so-called 'lady's companions'—above all in the households of landed estates. While they pay substantial sums for their board, they are staying there less for the purposes of learning and more in order to avoid the possible requirement of having to take a job. There are also incredible numbers going to boarding and finishing schools. This demonstrates a lack of the right attitude which has often led to—unfortunately not unjustified—feelings of discontent.

While, on the one hand, it is precisely those women who, for the whole of their lives have been compelled to contribute to the maintenance of their families through their work, who are now being hit the hardest and who, in addition to their work also have to face the danger of the frequent air attacks in the districts threatened by air raids, on the other hand, it is possible for those women who have never been in gainful employment and who have always been better-off, to leave the districts threatened by air raids in order to recuperate in spas, rest homes etc.

It is no exaggeration to say that in the districts subject to air raids whole localities are stripped of women. Either they have sought safety somewhere at their own expense—as described above—or they have been sent away, e.g. by the NSV 'Mother and Child' organization. The only women left are mainly those who are in employment.

These phenomena, which are becoming increasingly evident, are calculated to produce a mood whose effects should not be underestimated and, if these conditions are not fundamentally changed soon, I can no longer be held responsible for the maintenance of social peace in these districts.

In view of the almost invariably model attitude of German women and the great personal sacrifices which are being made by the working women in particular, I consider it urgently necessary, in order to maintain the social peace, for the causes of this remarkable degree of discontent to be removed as soon as possible.

I wish, therefore, Herr *Reichsmarschall* to request you once again to take up the question of the labour deployment of women. I propose that you initiate the following:

1. The extension of your edict of 20.6.1941 to all women who receive a family allowance or equivalent payments from public funds.
2. The mobilization of all healthy, childless, married and single women between 18 and 40 years of age, even if they do not receive family allowances or the equivalent in so far as they are not fully employed in the care of sick and frail family members or in running a substantial household in accordance with the Defence Law of 21.5.1935 Section I §1 Paragraph 3.
3. To comb through all spas for childless women who have established their wartime domicile there.
4. The registration and mobilization of all childless women who, while maintaining their flats, have given up their normal place of residence and are staying with relatives without pursuing an adequate occupation.
5. To comb through private educational institutions, substantial households etc.

for girls who are older than 17 and are not employed or in a recognized apprenticeship, or have a training place and require them to take a job.

The labour deployment agencies should be instructed that cases of refusal to work on the grounds of ill health should be examined by an official doctor.

I am aware that these measures will be considered tough and unpleasant by a small number of compatriots. The new labour resources mobilized by these measures could be deployed primarily in order to:

1. reduce the existing labour shortage by providing further full- and part-time employees.
2. release men for work places for which women are completely unsuitable.
3. alleviate the intolerable shortage of maids in households with numerous children.
4. to initiate a more generous provision of leave for women in the armaments industry in need of recuperation, which was hitherto prevented by a shortage of replacements.
5. gradually give all those women in work with at least three children under 14 years of age the possibility of giving up work.

I do not believe Herr *Reichsmarschall* that I need to go into further detail on the political and socio-political reasons for my proposal and, in recognition of their necessity, request you to initiate the appropriate measures as soon as possible.

Hitler, however, remained unimpressed by Ley's arguments, as Bormann made clear to Lammers in a letter dated 25 September 1941:

**1119**   I enclose a photocopy of a letter from *Reichsleiter* Dr Ley to the Führer dated 19.9.1941, together with a copy of a letter of the same date to *Reichsmarschall* Göring. I enclose a copy of my letter to Dr Ley dated 22.9.41.

Reich Minister Dr Goebbels also raised this question again with the Führer during his visit. For your personal information only I wish to inform you that the Führer only wishes to consider the introduction of labour conscription for women in the event of a possible entry into the war by America.

However, it was not only Ley and Goebbels who pressed for female labour conscription for reasons of morale. In its reports on popular opinion the Security Service (SD) repeatedly drew attention to the resentment among working women caused by the regime's policies towards female labour as, for example, in the following report dated of 26 February 1942:

**1120**   1. *Material difficulties for women in employment*
According to the reports, working women increasingly complain about shortages, long hours of work and long journeys to and from work, about inadequate provision for their children, wage problems etc . . . .

The difficulties referred to above have a negative impact on the morale of working women. The women affected are nevertheless aware that it is not possible to remove these difficulties just like that. Working women are, therefore, prepared to make the sacrifices necessary in wartime. The fact that, despite the urgent need for additional female workers—both to increase production and to relieve working mothers—up to now there has been no regulation issued to pull in women who are not yet working and yet are available for work is increasingly a source of discontent, indeed of bitterness. The difference in the treatment of women when it comes to pulling them in for war work is also strongly criticized by front-line soldiers whose wives do not receive any consideration, despite their maternal and housewifely duties. According to the reports received here, the edict of 20 June 1941 only permits the Labour Offices to pull in women who have already worked before, i.e. possess a work book. However, this largely affects the less well-off people who are dependent on gainful employment. Also, the reduction in family allowance in the event of their not taking on a job only affects the economically disadvantaged sections of the population. In our experience up to now it is clear that this edict has not produced a significant increase in the number of female workers; on the other hand, in terms of morale it has produced more of a deterioration than an improvement.

In the context of the urgings in the Führer's Christmas message that German women should get more involved in the work process than they have done up till now, it has been reported from all over the Reich that workers—above all those in the armaments industry—express the opinion that a law for female labour conscription is necessary and would be socially just. Workers repeatedly point out that it is still possible for large numbers of women to live a life totally devoted to their own interests. Cafes and bars in the big cities are full of women from the early afternoon onwards who spend hours there. And yet not a thing happens to such women to punish them for their laziness and behaviour. Whereas working women who, for example, want to leave their jobs because of domestic responsibilities or physical ailments run into great difficulties. Those who have already left are compulsorily brought back and deployed elsewhere or conscripted. The difference in the kind of 'employment' which exists on the other side of the tracks and which the working population find incomprehensible is evident in a report from Berlin which is just one example among many. It states:

Working women condemn the fact that people are still continuing to practice equestrian sport, particularly in the Grünewald and Dahlem districts. The fact that the ladies then walk through the streets in their riding gear is considered provocative. This fact is also strongly criticised by those on leave from the front. For example, a soldier on leave was travelling on a tram down the Kurfürstendamm a while ago and witnessed a conversation between two young ladies who were discussing the purchase of the necessary gear and then discussed at length where they were going to spend this year's winter holiday. They also had to visit a few fashion shows. The soldier then vigorously upbraided the two women which resulted in a big argument.

These and similar incidents are happening every day and have a wearing psychological effect on working women, who are already physically very much under the weather, because they cannot understand why the sacrifices which are necessary cannot be distributed equally among all women . . .

. . . The introduction of a duty of registration for work as a precondition for the mobilization of all those women who, on the basis of a fair assessment, are considered available for work is regarded as essential, above all because the war and the economic situation are imposing ever greater sacrifices and cuts on the working population. It is true that views differ about the extent of the reserves of female labour which can be mobilized. However, in general, the impression is that the number is not inconsiderable. But, apart from the question of numbers, it now appears essential at least to demonstrate the 'will' to redistribute the burden of work to those women who have not yet been employed . . .

For years the Party and the DAF have been sharpening the German worker's sense of social justice through propaganda. It is precisely for this reason that German male and female workers cannot understand why, when they are having to improve their performance, they should be asked to make more sacrifices and suffer more cuts when numerous women belonging to those classes which are not used to having to work for their living have, in this sphere at least, not yet made any sacrifices.

The Nazi Women's organization (NSF), were also unhappy about the situation, as is clear from the following letter to Himmler, dated 2 April 1942, from *Gruppenführer* Berger, head of the SS Main Office. In it Berger reported on a meeting with senior members of the NSV at which they complained about their leader, Frau Scholtz-Klink, and about Göring's attitude to the conscription of women for labour:

**1121** The Women's Organization felt itself completely abandoned and did not know where to turn. The NSF speakers who were recently scheduled to speak in Berlin plants had been whistled down and had not been able to speak. The women who had been deployed, some of them with 3 or 4 children, who had been conscripted for six months or up to a year, had had their additional food rations withdrawn.

The fact that the Reich Marshal's wife had invited 70 or 80 generals' wives to a coffee party at which the table had been groaning with delicacies had caused tremendous resentment. It was the talk of all the Berlin plants and making morale even worse.

They had always thought the *Reichsführer SS* would support Frau Scholtz-Klink and for this reason had put up with her poor work habits and her duplicitous methods of leadership. After a meeting with the *Reichsführer SS* at the end of February, Frau Scholtz-Klink had announced to them that the RF-SS would in future only work with her on formal terms and that there would be no more personal links between them. That was the worst blow for her. Moreover, they would have expected that her marriage to SS Ogruf Heissmeyer would have improved and altered matters. But the opposite was the case and they were shocked when Frau Scholtz-Klink—admittedly in a temper about some failed negotiation with the Reich Education Ministry—referred to her husband in their presence as an idiot.

Gauleiter Sauckel had been to see Reich Marshal Göring and told him that there was a shortage of 2 million workers, 1.2 million in the armaments industry and 800,000 in agriculture. They had then discussed the possibility of labour conscription for women and its problems. Reich Marshal Göring was against it. At the meeting he stated: 'work horse and thoroughbred. If a thoroughbred is harnessed to a plough it gets exhausted quicker than a work horse and so one can never have general labour conscription for women. The main task of women of good breeding is to have children'. This principle was absolutely recognized by the Reich Women's Leadership. It was only depressing that the high-quality women were not going to have children.

The mothers with 3 or 4 children who were now deployed and whose husbands were often at the front complained that the coffee houses in Berlin's West End and the tennis courts were still full of women who had nothing to do while they worked themselves to death.

. . . Reich Marshal Göring commented further 'that these women are the culture bearers and should not be exposed to the stupid remarks and the cheek of ordinary women'.

I pass on these comments with reservations. The women made a good impression on me and seem at the moment to be feeling incredibly depressed because of the Reich Women's Leader and the Reich Marshal's remarks. They don't know what to do.

———

With the crisis caused by the military reverse in front of  Moscow in December 1941 German economic policy underwent an agonizing reappraisal which led, among other things, to the appointment of the Gauleiter of Thuringia, Fritz Sauckel, to the new post of General Plenipotentiary for Labour Mobilization with the task of providing the German economy with the necessary labour force.[5] Sauckel was a supporter of female labour conscription, but as a Gauleiter was sensitive to the morale issue. In any case, Hitler was still determined to resist female labour conscription.

Sauckel gave the following assessment of the issues in a statement on 20 April 1942:

**1122**    . . . The mobilization of German women for labour is extremely important. After  having acquainted myself thoroughly with the views of both the Führer and of the Reich Marshal of the Greater German Reich [Göring], and having examined this most difficult problem through my own extremely careful investigations, I must reject absolutely the idea of conscripting all German women and girls to work in the German war and food industries.

———

[5] For more on this see above, pp. 241ff.

Although initially I myself and probably the majority of the leading figures in the Party and in the women's organization had particular reasons for believing in the need for the conscription of women, all men and women in responsible positions in the Party, in the state, and in business should now accept the view of our Führer, Adolf Hitler, with the greatest veneration and the deepest gratitude. For his greatest concern is the health of German women and girls, in other words of the present and future mothers of our nation.

I cannot enumerate all the reasons which have made me come to this decision. I ask only for confidence in myself as an old and fanatical Gauleiter of the National Socialist Party and that you should believe that this was the only decision possible.

We all agree that this decision may appear unjust towards millions of women who are working in the defence and food industries under the most strenuous conditions, but we also realize that an evil cannot be remedied by expanding it to the ultimate extent.

The only possible way of eliminating the existing injustices and hardships lies in winning the war so that we shall be in a position to remove all women and girls from jobs regarded as unsuitable for women—jobs which are a danger to their health, to our nation's birth rate, and to family and national life.

We must also bear in mind that it makes an enormous difference whether or not a woman or girl has been used to working in the fields or in a factory from an early age and whether or not she has proved herself capable of standing this kind of work. Apart from physical harm, it is the Führer's wish that German women and girls must be protected under all circumstances from moral and mental harm . . .

It is doubtful whether these conditions could be fulfilled in the event of mass conscription and employment. In this connection, it is impossible to compare German women with the German soldier because of the basic difference between men and women, a difference which is determined by nature and race. Considering the countless men fighting bravely at the front, especially those who have been killed, we cannot accept responsibility for the dangers which would threaten the life of the nation as a result of the labour conscription of women.

▬▬

Instead of imposing compulsory registration for work on upper- and middle-class German women, Sauckel adopted the alternative of recruiting large numbers of foreign workers, many of whom were women. By the end of 1944, there were some 7.6 million foreign workers in Germany. Some were volunteers, but the vast majority had been forcibly conscripted. At the end of November 1942, 30 per cent of the civilian foreign workers from western Europe and around 50 per cent of those from Russia and Poland were women. By the end of May 1944, there were 1.7 million female foreign workers in Germany, most of them from the east, and 58 per cent of all the eastern workers were women. The treatment of these workers varied depending primarily on their ethnic origins. The following report by an eighteen year old French woman, who volunteered for work in Germany at the beginning of 1944, gives a good insight into the conditions of these foreign workers, which reflected the racial hierarchy imposed by the regime, with the West European workers at the top and the Poles and Russians at the bottom:

**1123**   I was sent to a so-called 'Free Work Camp' in Frankfurt Hoechst and was employed by IG Farben as a labourer. The day began at 4 o'clock in the morning. For breakfast we got ersatz coffee with saccharin in an iron mug. Then we went to the wash rooms. Although men and women were accommodated in separate barracks, they had to wash together. After roll call, at 5 o'clock, we marched several kilometres to the factory. There we worked until 5 o'clock in the evening with an hour's lunch break—at any rate those were my hours of work; others had a night shift. After we had washed ourselves with a sandy type of soap we marched back to the camp.

If we had a free day we slept in because we were so exhausted. Then we washed our clothes, although with this sandy type of soap everything always stayed dirty; it was a labour of Sisyphus. Every foreign worker only possessed one set of clothes with which they had to make do: a crude jacket, a primitive pair of trousers and wooden clogs. Although everyone had arrived at the camp wearing their own clothes, when these were worn out there was nothing else to wear but these primitive work clothes often worn next to the skin without any underwear so that one got sore.

Although we foreign workers were officially allowed to go out, in fact that turned out to be an illusion. Wherever we went there was a notice saying 'Germans only' or 'Foreigners and dogs forbidden'. One was not allowed to sit in trams. If a German offered you a seat he risked being arrested. We went around as if in a ghetto. Things were even worse for the eastern workers. They were not allowed to go out at all. The aim was to make distinctions between the workers; it was like a staircase: right at the bottom the Russians, then the Poles, and on top were the workers from the western territories. Comparatively speaking we were treated the best. On the surface, we were paid the same wages as the Germans. But the deductions were so large that, for example, I only got 8 RM for two weeks. And the eastern workers got almost nothing at all. Everything was organized so that we foreigners should be separated off from one another and not show solidarity with each other. Thus, for example, the western workers in the Free Work Camp were given sheets to make it clear that we were treated as human beings. The eastern workers, on the other hand, only got straw and a blanket; they were considered to be subhuman. The food was also different. A French woman, for example, was not allowed to go into a canteen for eastern workers. When I on one occasion passed such a canteen I smelt a horrible smell. I went in and tried something on a plate; the food was bad, rotten. When I complained about this to the Germans, they forbade me to visit the eastern workers' canteen again. I did go again. Then they said: if you're so concerned about the people from the east why don't you go and work with them.

And so I had more and more personal experiences. For now I was with the eastern workers who had the hardest work to do. For example, we used to carry pieces of sulphur from one plant to another, often quite a distance. We only had gloves and had to press it to our chests which burned our skin.

Also foreigners and Germans were strictly segregated. The doors between the departments in the factory were barred so that there was no contact between us. The German department was as far away from us as a distant planet. We only dealt with the foreman. If I asked him: 'Can I go to the toilet?' he would reply: 'OK. Three minutes.' If one stayed longer it would be knocked off one's pay. Everything was so organized that we could not help but equate all Germans with the Nazis and learn to hate them. Hate was the Nazis' weapon with which to control everything; that was the Nazis' method of rule.

—

Inevitably some of these foreign women workers became pregnant. The response of the German authorities again reflected their ideological prejudices. On 27 July 1943, Himmler issued the following directive to his Higher SS and Police Leaders:

**1124**   Re: *The treatment of pregnant foreign female workers and the children of foreign female workers born in the Reich.*

1. Foreign female workers who become pregnant are not to be sent back to their homelands until further notice. This regulation is based on the urgent priority for labour provision. All directives to the contrary (including, in particular, those issued for Polish women and eastern female workers) are hereby suspended. After giving birth, the female foreign workers are to be sent back to work as soon as possible, in accordance with the orders of the Plenipotentiary for Labour Mobilization.
2. According to the directives of the Plenipotentiary for Labour Mobilisation and the Reich Health Leader [Dr Conti], the births should, where possible, take place in special sections in the sick bays of the residential camps or the transit camps. They can only be admitted to a hospital barrack for foreigners in a German hospital or, quite exceptionally, in a German hospital, if there has been a breach of the regulations or if it is necessary to provide material for training medical and midwifery students. In such cases the separation from pregnant Germans must be guaranteed. The Plenipotentiary for Labour Mobilization has issued the labour authorities with regulations concerning costs and the provision of a special allocation of linen, clothing etc. as well as food supplements.
3. The children born to the foreign workers must on no account be looked after in German institutions, be admitted to German children's homes, or otherwise grow up with and be educated with German children. Thus, special infant care units of the simplest kind will be established within the accommodation, to be called 'Foreign Children's Care Units', in which these foreign children will be looked after by female members of the particular ethnic group concerned . . .

4. The need to prevent the loss of German blood to foreign nations [lit. national bodies] is increased by the loss of blood during the war. Thus, the children of foreign female workers, who have some German or ethnically similar blood and can be regarded as valuable, should not be sent to 'Foreign Children's Care Units' in accordance with Section 3 above, but if possible be preserved for the German race and, therefore, be brought up as German children. For this purpose plants should report all pregnancies to the Youth Office via the Labour Office.

(a) The Youth Office will attempt provisionally to establish the father's identity in those cases in which it has been suggested or appears probable that the procreator is a German or a member of a related, similar (Germanic) ethnic group. If the father's identity cannot be established, the Youth Office will provide a short account of the case and state whether, in view of the particular situation, it is probable that the father is a German or a member of a related similar (Germanic) ethnic group. If the pregnant woman declines to make a statement about the procreator, the Youth Office may request an interrogation by the State Police Office.

(b) The Youth Office will report the cases which come under 3a to the Higher SS and Police Leader on a form for racial assessment. For this the following procedure should be observed:

The medical, genetic, and racial examination will be carried out by Health Office doctors. At the same time, the SS Leader in the Racial and Settlement Office, as the representative of the responsible Higher SS and Police Leader in his capacity as the delegate of the Reich Commissioner for the Strengthening of the German Race will be given the opportunity to reach his own conclusions on the basis of the directives of the *Reichsführer SS* . . .

The SS Leader in the R & S Office will make a preliminary selection before the examinations are carried out. The Health Office will produce a report on the result of the examinations (with photos) which will be sent to the SS Leader in the R & S Office.

The SS Leader in the R & S Office will decide how the pregnant woman and the children should be treated in the light of the results, in accordance with the directive issued by the *Reichsführer SS,* Race and Settlement Main Office.

5. In those cases in which, on the basis of the racial assessment as well as the genetic and medical examination of the procreator and the pregnant woman, offspring of good race can be anticipated, the children will be looked after by the NSV in order to ensure they are brought up as German children, in accordance with the statement in Section 4, paragraph 1. They will be placed in special children's homes or placed with foster parents. If the assessment is negative the treatment will be in accordance with section 3 . . .

B. The Higher SS and Police Leader will remain in touch with Office L in the RFSS's Personal Staff. Office L may instruct the *Lebensborn* [lit. life spring] organization to assign racially particularly valuable expectant mothers, who meet its criteria, to SS maternity homes and to act as guardians for the children.[6] In so far as cases are referred directly to the *Lebensborn* organization, this will proceed in the usual manner but the Higher SS and Police Leader will be informed.

6. The transfer of a child of good race to the care of the NSV or the *Lebensborn* organization will normally require that it be separated from the mother, who will remain at her place of work. For this very reason, it is only possible for the children of good race to be transferred to their care with the consent of the mother. She will need to be persuaded to agree by the caring institution through a description of the advantages it will bring, but should not be told the aim of this care. It is, however, being considered whether, in the case of female eastern workers, workers from the General Government, and pro-tected persons the need for agreement can be dispensed with if the persuasion is unsuccessful; in such cases, therefore, a report should be made before further action is taken.

In order to reassure the mother about the care, it will be the task of the caring agency to concern itself with the mother in the last stages of pregnancy and, above all, to provide her with the best possible location for the delivery within the framework of the possibilities outlined in Section 2.

The question of whether a child of good race should be taken on by the NSV or the *Lebensborn* organization straight after birth or later (possibly after weaning) will depend on the individual case. Thus, even in cases in which the mother is in principle prepared to transfer her child, the child of good race will stay for some time in a Foreign Children's Care Unit, for example in order not to bring about a premature separation of mother and child.

If mothers of children of good race wish to return with these children to their homelands, they should where possible be kept in the Reich by means of conscription by the labour administration. However, if the possibilities of doing this have been exhausted, the children cannot be kept here by force; another way of proceeding is being considered in the case of female eastern workers, workers from the General Government and those under our protection . . .

---

[6] The *Lebensborn* organization was established on 12 December 1935 on Himmler's orders. Its task defined in its statutes was '1. To support racially and genetically valuable large families. 2. To accommodate and look after racially and genetically valuable expectant mothers to whom, after careful investigation of their families and the families of the procreator by the SS Race and Settlement Main Office, it can be assumed that equally valuable children will be born. 3. To care for these children. 4. To look after the children's mothers.' It maintained fifteen maternity homes where the wives of impecunious SS men could go before and after birth. Single women who expected a child from an SS man or Wehrmacht soldier were also welcome. During the war, *Lebensborn* also established maternity homes in German occupied territories with the aim of 'capturing' the 'good German blood' of the offspring of liaisons between German soldiers and the local women. See G. Lilienthal, *Der 'Lebensborn e.V.'. Ein Instrument nationalsozialistischer Rassenpolitik* (Stuttgart 1985), pp. 38–9 and *passim*.

9. Children, both of whose parents are members of Germanic peoples, can also be admitted to institutions for German children if the racial examination does not indicate otherwise . . .

10. Since the presence of ethnic aliens who are incapable of work imposes heavy burdens on all agencies and increases the threat to the nation posed by the employment of foreigners, foreign mothers with racially undesirable children should be deported as a matter of priority when the labour situation makes this viable . . .

12. The Higher SS and Police Leaders will receive further instructions from the SS Race and Settlement Main Offic on the implementation of racial examination procedures and on the registration of the children of good race . . .

▬▬

The regime had no interest in the survival of 'children of bad race', i.e. Russian and Polish babies. Thus, on 23 July 1942, Bormann informed Rosenberg, by then Reich Minister for the Eastern Territories (Soviet Union), of Hitler's view that 'if girls and women from the occupied eastern territories abort their children that is fine by us, since we have no interest in an increase in the non-German population'.[7] In 1943 the legal penalties for abortion were removed first for Russian and then for Polish women. In the summer of 1943, *SS Gruppenführer* Hilgenfeldt, head of the NSV, reported to Himmler on a visit to one of the 'Foreign Children's Care Units' as follows:

**1125**   On my visit I noted that all the babies in the home are undernourished. On the basis of a decision by the state Food Office, the home is allocated a daily ration of only 0.5 litre of full cream milk and 1.5 pieces of sugar for each baby. With these rations after a few months the babies will die of malnutrition. I was informed that there are differences of opinion about the babies' treatment. Some people are of the opinion that the children of the eastern female workers should die; others believe they should be raised. Since a clear statement of policy has not yet emerged, and—as I was informed—it was desirable to maintain our reputation in the eyes of the female workers, the babies are given insufficient nourishment, as a result of which, as already said, after a few months they inevitably die.

▬▬

At the beginning of 1943, with the German offensive in Russia suffering another major setback in the shape of the Stalingrad defeat, demands for a 'total' mobilization of German labour became irresistible. Under pressure from Goebbels, Speer and others involved in the war economy, Hitler reluctantly agreed to Sauckel issuing a decree on 27 January 1943

---

[7] See N. Westenrieder, '*Deutsche Frauen und Mädchen*'. *Vom Alltagsleben 1933–1945* (Düsseldorf 1984), p. 107. This section owes much to this book.

'concerning the Registration of Men and Women for Reich Defence Tasks'.[8] According to the decree, with certain exceptions, all women between the ages of 17 and 45 were obliged to register for work. However, Hitler was anxious to restrict what he envisaged as its negative consequences as far as possible, as is clear from the following note from Lammers to Sauckel, dated 25 January 1943:

**1126**  Re: *Comprehensive mobilization of men and women for Reich defence tasks.*
Dear Herr Sauckel,
The Führer has ordered that women who have reached the age of 45 should for the time being be excluded from the duty of registration and requests you to include an appropriate regulation in the decree which you have prepared. If the inclusion of women between the ages of 45 and 50 proves necessary later on then I would ask you to inform me of the fact so that I can approach the Führer for another decision.

Moreover, there were a large number of exemptions to the decree. Thus, the following were excluded from its effects: employees in the public service, the Wehrmacht, Agriculture, the Health services, women who had worked at least 48 hours a week since 1 January 1943, the self-employed who were employing at least five persons on 1 January, pregnant women, women with a child not yet of school age or with two children under 14, as well as school pupils and members of the Labour Service.

The regime launched a propaganda offensive to try and defuse opposition and persuade women to register. The following excerpts from a radio talk by Hans Schwarz van Berk, given on 10 February 1943 with the title 'What do we do not expect of German Women', provide an example of the kind of rhetoric used:

**1127**  . . . In Berlin, as in every German town, thousands of shops will be closed down in the coming weeks. Shop girls will become conductresses, conductors will become soldiers or armament workers. Milliners will get into uniform and shorthand typists will go into the electrical industries. Many flower shops will close, but the hairdressers will go on working for there is scarcely a woman with a permanent wave who would not lose her enjoyment of work and pleasure if she had to go around with her hair untidy and uncared for. We want our girls and women to remain pretty; we have every reason to see that they do not become ugly and grey, and sad and listless. But we do not want them to be out of touch with the times, and with us men and soldiers. It must be clearly realized: either we win this war all together, or we shall all go together to where Stalin would like us to go. We are not making life difficult because we think it

---

[8] For more information on this decree see above, pp. 239–40.

heroic, but because we can no longer win this hard war by easy living. Although uniform suits many a young woman quite well, none of us men would like to become the commander of a woman's battalion—and certainly none of us wants anything to do with women who do their work unwillingly or with a bad grace. What we now want to do is to convince the girls and women that we cannot manage without their help.

But this help must be given where it is really needed. It is not a question of seeking any occupation, a job which serves as protection against further demands. It is a question of seeking an occupation which has real meaning. A few days ago a young photographer telephoned me. She asked me whether she should go into market gardening. I said yes, but naturally into vegetables, because vegetables are more important than a little picture and better than the most beautiful bunch of flowers. She said: 'but physically I'm not very strong'. I replied: 'You will probably soon feel fresher and healthier than ever in your life.' Women and girls in towns as a rule are inclined to think they are not particularly strong. Many men in offices feel the same, but once they get out of their badly aired, unhealthy indoor way of living, after a few weeks they feel they could uproot trees.

I must correct another error. Most women and girls have a horror of factories. They think to themselves: 'Anything but a factory.' They think war service means turning and dragging shells, means performing the same action from morning to night at the same machine, or standing between the machines a mere number in the dirt and the noise. Most of those who think like that have never seen the inside of a factory, or at least not in the past five years . . . Nowhere in the world are there such model factories, so clean and rationally equipped as ours. Nowhere are women so much in their place at work as with us . . .

I mention this because it seems to me that many reasoning women are seeking work but think it must be something better. What is a better sort of job? What is necessary must be done . . . No soldier can in wartime select the spot where he would like to receive the enemy—so no woman can pick and choose where she will help him in this war. What is necessary must be done.

During the next few weeks life in Germany will change considerably. It will become more serious, just as the situation at the front has become more serious. No soldier who comes home from the east in the future would understand us if we at home took the war as lightly and carelessly as we did and could do in the years of swift successes. No woman must look at what another woman is doing, or not doing. Neither can she wait until one or the other has been called up for work and make her own will to work dependent on that. In dangerous situations personal decisions must be taken. It is certain that those women and girls who fail to pay attention to the gravity of the High Command reports will very shortly expose themselves to general contempt. All those among our people who for years past have been working hard—and that is most of them—and all those who now go into war work from inner conviction will discover the small minority which may still be trying to shirk it. Anyone who does not take the present hour seriously will be dealt with very seriously. There is still time to join in voluntarily. But consideration will only be given to voluntary action which is not evasion into camouflaged comfort. At this time we say to the women: we should not call upon you unless we had to. We are in the midst of the most severe trial of this war. We do not talk of war and politics to our womenfolk if it can be avoided. Now it is no longer possible to avoid it. We are all in danger. If we were silent about it, the women could justifiably say later: why didn't you tell us what it was all about? But now we know that all men should be at the front, all the men who can be dispensed with at home, and there is no other solution but for our women to take their places at home. In the name of our dead comrades, of the many comrades who have been wounded several times, we demand that you should not shirk this work, that you will not seek a comfortable hiding place, but that you will remain worthy of every decent man who will one day come home from a hard battle.

Unfortunately, however, women who had hitherto been able to escape employment on the whole proved reluctant to take a job and there was resentment on the part of working women about what was seen as the weakness of the decree as is clear from an SD report of 4 February 1943:

**1128**    The reports note that, in particular, *those national comrades who have long been employed in important war work had expected tough regulations.* However, after the publication of the details of the decree they were astonished that *so many exemptions had been given.* The disapproval of this manifested itself in some cases in quite drastic remarks such as 'rubber decree' etc. The question was frequently raised as to whether all those groups who up to now had succeeded in 'avoiding all work' would be caught . . .

*Already women and girls from every social class have been contacting numerous Labour Offices to try and prove that they are not available for labour mobilization* . . . It was already evident that some of these women were trying to claim they were suffering some illness or other with a doctor's certificate in order to evade recruitment. The extent of this attempt at evasion by these women is apparent from the large numbers consulting gynaecologists as mentioned above . . . In addition, people are thinking up the numerous possibilities of 'phoney employment' with relatives and acquaintances which simply 'feigns' fulfilment of the legal requirement of registering for work . . . Almost all the reports emphasize as a particular problem the fact that large numbers of *requests for their release from employment have been made to Labour Offices by those women who, although they have been in employment for many years, belong to that category of women who, according to the new decree, are not liable for registration.* (Women who are over 45 or have a child under school age or two children under 14) . . . Other cases have been noted in which women who are affected by the duty to register try and get hold of a foster child in order to become unavailable for work.

But the campaign to mobilize more women for work was undermined not simply by the reluctance of many women to take on the added burden of employment and the reluctance of the regime to act in too draconian a fashion in enforcing the decree. It was also due to the reluctance of employers to take on untrained women who were subject to much more stringent employment regulations than foreign workers and who often necessitated extensive alterations to plant facilities and production processes. Moreover, as time went by and Germany's defeat became increasingly likely so the increased investment required to accommodate female workers appeared  less and less justified in terms of the future requirements of the post-war era. A year later, at a conference in the Armaments Ministry on 10 August 1944, a participant reflected on this aspect of the campaign as follows:

**1129**  . . . Plants must quickly consider what types of production and what production processes they can transfer to women and where they can get more out of them. If you walk through plants you can see an enormous number of work places, including peripheral work places, which are predominantly staffed by men or by foreign women where German women could be employed without difficulty. Gentlemen! We can't have another situation like that which occurred last year with the so-called Sauckel Action, with the duty of women to register for work, namely that the armaments industry was offered a large number of women and then either didn't accept them or spat them out again. At that time, Sauckel mobilized 1.6 million women, 800,000 of them on a half-day basis. After a few weeks, of these 1.6 million, 500,000 were once again no longer employed. And, what is more, it was primarily the larger firms and, in the first instance, the armaments firms which let them go. The women were kept on in the less valued firms working in the civilian sector and in other firms which are less valued. This is a sign that the armaments firms have not taken enough trouble to ensure that the women get fulfilment from their work. The women lost enthusiasm, switched from one department to the next and finally got themselves a doctor's certificate and left.

In fact, the results of the attempt to mobilize more women under the Labour Registration Decree were less  than impressive as is clear from the following table prepared by Sauckel's office in early July 1943:

**1130**

| | | |
|---|---|---|
| 1. Registered persons | 3,048,000 | |
| 2. Processed persons | 2,703,000 | = 88.7% |
| 3. (a) Of those in 2 who were employable* | 1,462,000 | = 54.1% |
|     (b) Not employable | 1,241,000 | = 45.9% |
| 4. Persons actually employed | 1,260,000 | = 86.2% of 3a |
|     (a) for less than 48 hrs p.w. | 684,000 | = 54.3% of 4 |
|     (b) as workers in | | |
| 1. Agriculture and forestry | 262,000 | = 20.8% of 4 |
| 2. Armaments industry | 537,000 | = 42.6% of 4 |
| 3. Rest of the economy | 461,000 | = 36.6% of 4 |

*Of whom more than 50 per cent on a half-day basis.

Hitler, however, remained unenthusiastic about the conscription of women for work and was not prepared to extend it to older women, as he informed Sauckel, according to a minute of Sauckel's office, dated 21 November 1943, which recorded a meeting between the two men three days previously:

**1131** On Point 2. The Führer immediately rejected an increase in the age at which women become liable to labour conscription to 50 years. This decision by the Führer corresponds to the Gauleiters' view because he believes that an increase in the age limit to 50 would in practice not increase the labour capacity. A preliminary investigation has shown the following: by increasing the age limit, approximately 1 million women would be included. According to the experience of the labour mobilization programme begun in the spring, of these only 250,000 would be capable of being deployed even in the most favourable circumstances, in fact probably only 140,000–160,000. Since most of these women are the wives of men in employment aged between 50 and 60, their removal from their households would seriously affect the care of their husbands, some of whom are engaged in heavy work, so that whatever would be gained from the women in terms of a new labour reserve would be lost again through the loss of the men's labour.

By the summer of 1944, however, the military situation was such that Hitler was forced to overcome his qualms about the mobilization of women for work and yield further to the pressure from Goebbels, Speer and others for 'total war'. On 29 July 1944 Lammers wrote to Goebbels as follows:

**1132** Dear Party Comrade Dr Goebbels
I have just received the following piece of information from *Reichsleiter* Bormann:
'I wish to inform you that the Führer has agreed to the extension of the duty of registration for work for married women from 45 to 50 years of age.'
Gauleiter Sauckel, who wishes to prepare the requisite legal measures, has already been informed.

## (iv) Welfare at Work

The regime showed considerable concern for the welfare of women workers. This was partly for population policy reasons, partly in order to persuade women to enter or return to employment and partly for propaganda reasons to confirm National Socialism's 'socialist' credentials. The lead here was taken by the DAF-Women's Office. During 1939–40, the DAF doubled the number of female Plant Social

Workers, of whom there were a total of 2,370 in 1941, including trainees, and over 3,000 by 1943. The number of its Works Women's Groups increased from 5,420 in 1941 with 82,000 members to 7,300 with 120,000 members a year later.[9] These organizations were designed to improve working conditions for women, advise on household and family matters, for example through recipes—also for the factory canteen—and generally indoctrinate the women. It was largely in response to pressure from the DAF and the Propaganda Ministry that the regime issued a new Law for the Protection of Mothers in Gainful Employment on 17.5.1942, which introduced new measures to protect women and, in particular, mothers at work:

**1133** German women can only realize their greatest achievement for the national community, giving birth to healthy children, if they are protected against all pre-natal and post-natal harm and disadvantages. This concern for adequate protection applies to all German women. The most urgent need, however, is for special protection for the mothers who are in gainful employment and who, despite having to cope with more difficult circumstances, present the Fatherland with children. In order that they can fulfil their maternal duties without coming to any harm, the Government has decided on the following law which is promulgated herewith: . . .

§2 *Employment bans for expectant mothers*
1. An expectant mother may not be employed if, according to a medical certificate, this poses a threat to the life and health of the mother or child.
2. Expectant mothers may not be employed in heavy and physical labour, e.g. the lifting and carrying of heavy weights, or in work where they are subjected to the damaging effects of materials or rays which endanger health, dust, gases or vapours, heat or cold, dampness or vibrations. Their employment is not permitted on piecework, on commission, or on an assembly line if the average work rate is beyond the strength of the expectant mother. The Factory Inspectorate can determine whether a job comes under these provisions; it can also ban employmemt in certain other types of work. When these provisions are applied or, in the case of a change of work imposed by a medical certificate, the expectant mothers should be granted their average earnings of the previous thirteen weeks in cases where they are unable to receive a birth allowance (§7 Para.1, Sentence 1); those involved may agree an alternative arrangement.
3. Expectant mothers are to be exempted from all work for the last six weeks before the birth at their request.

§3 *Post-natal Employment Bans*
1. Mothers who have just given birth may not be employed until six weeks after the birth. For mothers who are breastfeeding this period extends to eight weeks, for breastfeeding mothers after premature births to twelve weeks.

---

[9] Figures quoted in Arendt, op. cit., p. 320.

2. The Factory Inspectorate can order measures for the protection of breast-feeding mothers and women who, according to a medical certificate, are not fully capable of work in the first months after giving birth.

§4. *Ban on overtime, night work, and work during official holidays* . . .

§5. *Time for breastfeeding*
Mothers who are breastfeeding should at their request be given time to do so.

§6. *Ban on dismissal*
Women may not be dismissed against their will as a consequence of their pregnancy. Dismissals for other reasons during pregnancy and up to four months after birth are also ineffective if the employer was aware of the pregnancy at the time of the dismissal, or if he was immediately informed of it. This does not apply if the woman declares her agreement with the dismissal. The Reich Trustee of Labour can make exceptions if a dismissal is requested for an important reason.

§7. *Birth and breastfeeding allowance*
1. Women who are insured in the official insurance scheme will receive a birth allowance during the last six weeks before and the first six weeks after the birth, which amounts to their average earnings of the previous thirteen weeks, or at least two Reich marks per day. The claim to a birth allowance ceases for the period during which a woman works for financial reward. Women who are not in the official insurance scheme will receive their regular pay during the protected period.
2. Women who are breast feeding who are insured in the official insurance scheme will receive, as long as they are breastfeeding, a daily breastfeeding allowance of 0.50 Reich Marks until the twenty-sixth week after the birth.
3. Other benefits of the official insurance scheme will continue to be granted.

§8. *Protective period, duty of informing*
1. A certificate from a doctor or midwife is decisive for the calculation of the six week period before the birth (§2 Para.3 and §8. Para.1). If the doctor or midwife makes a mistake about the date of the birth then this period will be shortened or lengthened accordingly.
2. As soon as they become aware of their condition, expectant mothers should inform their plant leaders about their pregnancy and the assumed date of the birth. They should present a certificate from their doctor or midwife at his request. The costs of the certificate will be borne by the plant leader.

§9. *Crèches*
The Reich Labour Minister can determine that plants and offices must contribute to the costs of crèches of the National Socialist Welfare Organization or of local government ones in order to ensure sufficient supervision for the children of mothers in gainful employment. Where such crèches are not available or are not being established the Reich Labour Minister can also insist

that crèches (cribs, kindergartens, or crèches) are established and maintained by the plants or offices.

———

In addition to these improvements on the 1927 law, the protective measures were for the first time extended to female agriculture, forestry, and fisheries workers. However, civil servants, domestic servants, home workers and family workers on farms were not included, as indeed was inevitably the case with female Jewish and foreign workers.

## (v) Gender Issues

The fact that large numbers of women were required to become involved in the public sphere, to replace the men who had been deployed at the fighting front, meant that the war on the home front raised a number of issues affecting various aspects of gender. The first and most sensitive of these was how far women should engage in military activities.

### (a) Women in the armed forces[10]

Although foreign labour could be used very widely as a substitute for German women, there was a whole range of jobs associated with the armed forces which, for security reasons, could not be given to foreign workers. However, the idea of women being involved with the Wehrmacht was an extremely delicate matter. Hitler had very strong views on gender issues in general and on women's relationship to the military in particular and he had already outlined them in a speech to the Nazi Women's Organization (NSF) at the Nuremberg Party Congress on 13 September 1935:

**1134** If National Socialism has now given women a different position to that which was the case with liberal and, in particular, Marxist, parties the reason is it has a different valuation of women. We see in women the eternal mothers of our nation and the companions of men through life, in work, and in struggle. These two aspects form the basis for the particular attitude which National Socialism adopts towards women.

The so-called 'equal rights' of women, which Marxism demands, are in reality not equality of rights but a deprivation of women's rights because they will draw women into areas where they are bound to be inferior because they will put women in situations which cannot strengthen their position vis-à-vis both men and society but only weaken it. Among the Germanic nations women have

———

[10] This section owes much to Westenrieder, op. cit., pp. 86ff.

always been accorded equal rights. Both sexes had their rights, had their tasks and these tasks were of completely equal value and, therefore equal . . .

If they are now setting up *women's battalions* in Marxist countries, one can only say: *we will never do that. There are some things which are for men to do and for which they alone are responsible.*

I would be ashamed to be a German man if ever, in the event of war, a single woman had to go to the front. Women have their battlefield. With every child which they bring into the world for the nation they fight their fight for the nation. Men support their *nation* in the same way that women support their families. Female equality consists in the fact that they enjoy in those spheres of life which nature has defined as theirs the respect which is due to them.

Women have always had respect for *courageous, decisive and bold men* and men have always shown admiration and sympathy for *feminine* women. Those are the two opposites which attract each other in life; and if, by good fortune, two such people find each other, then it is no longer a question of equal rights because it has already been answered by nature: it is no longer equal rights, it is a unity.

Men and women represent two quite different essential characteristics. In the case of men the intellect is dominant. In the case of women emotion is preeminent.

———

At the outbreak of war, the Wehrmacht employed about 160,000 women as secretaries, telephonists, cooks, cleaners etc. and in the armouries and clothing stores. After the outbreak of war, to meet the new demand created by the occupation forces, the Wehrmacht began to recruit more women and to employ them in new roles such as air warning personnel. But the recruitment was not publicized and, with the exception of the air warning personnel and those working in occupied territories, the women were not put in uniform.

After the invasion of the Soviet Union and the high casualty rates which it produced, there was an increasing demand for women to replace soldiers who had been drafted to the front but initially in the same functions as before. This growing demand for female personnel in the armed forces was increasingly met by young women who had been conscripted into the women's section of the Reich Labour Service (RAD). Although in theory young women had also been subject to labour service under the 1935 law, by the outbreak of war only 36,219 'Work Girls' (*Arbeitsmaiden*) had been recruited. The introduction of mandatory labour service had been vigorously opposed by the Wehrmacht, the Labour Ministry, and the Four-Year Plan, who did not want the valuable pool of potential young female workers to be taken out of the labour market for six months' indoctrination and inefficient deployment in agriculture. However, the leader of the RAD, Konstantin

Hierl, had succeeded in persuading Hitler of its educational value and so, on 4 September 1939, Hierl received instructions from the Führer 'to enlist for labour service single women between 17 and 25 years of age, who are not in employment or in training or education or are not urgently needed to help on the family farm'.

In July 1941, the six months' labour service was extended by a further six months' 'War Service', as announced by the *Völkischer Beobachter* on 6 August 1941:

### 1135 *Girls' War Service*

As is well known, the Führer decree of 29.7.41 lays down that the war service of the Reich Labour Service for female youth is to undergo a considerable *expansion*. In the first place, the total number conscripted into the Reich Labour Service for female youth will be increased initially from 100,000 to 130,000 and, at the same time, orders have been given for an increase of 150,000 (including permanent staff) to be prepared. Secondly, the girls subject to labour service will be *conscripted* for a further six months' *War Service* after they have completed their half year of labour service. Through this war service they will release male workers for deployment elsewhere and will be deployed in particularly important spheres.

The introduction of War Service in the form ordered by the Führer represents for the parents of those conscripted the comforting knowledge that their daughters will continue to be under the care and supervision of the RAD. For the work girls the War Service represents the continuation of the happy camp comradeship with all its many joys both large and small.

The following points can already be made about the practical implementation of the War Service:

Deployment will only occur in the territory of the Greater German Reich. The deployment areas should be as close as possible to the existing camps. The War Service conscripts will as a rule be divided into accommodation groups and will be accommodated and fed as a group. Every accommodation group will be subordinate to a supervisory office of the RAD which will look after the War Service conscripts, in particular during their free time. Apart from free board and lodging, the War Service conscripts will receive pocket money, a clothing allowance, and social insurance. They will wear the special War Service badge on their civilian clothes both on and off duty.

The initial intention is that the War Service should enable male workers in the offices of the Wehrmacht and government offices to be relieved as far as possible by suitable female workers so that they can be deployed elsewhere. Apart from the Wehrmacht and government offices, War Service will be carried out in hospitals and other medical or social institutions. The relief which this will provide for doctors and nurses will make a significant contribution to the health of the nation.

Furthermore, there is the possibility in individual cases for those girls who are finishing their Reich Labour Service to perform their War Service in families which are in need of assistance, in particular those with many children. This type of War Service is also of great national importance. Although housemaids are not currently being called up into the Reich Labour Service, the Führer's edict provides the opportunity for additional help for large families which are in particular need.

The current work girls, who without exception will continue their service from 1 October, will justify the Führer's faith in them in just the same way as our soldiers have done in this war. For the welfare of the nation is more important than the personal wishes of individuals.

▬▬▬

Initially, Hierl, protected by Hitler, succeeded in resisting pressure from the economic agencies to deploy the 'work girls' in the armaments industry, although the Wehrmacht estimated that, as a result of the changes, the economy and especially the armaments sector would lose 260,000 girls compared with the 80,000 hitherto.[11] But, in the crisis of December–January 1942, he was finally forced to give way and agree to the deployment of 'work girls' in the armaments sector and, increasingly, in the armed forces as 'Female Wehrmacht Auxiliaries' (*Wehrmachthelferinnen*).

The Wehrmacht was anxious to insist on the avoidance of any 'militarization' of the women employed in the armed forces. Thus, on 22 June 1942, OKW issued directives 'for the deployment of women in the Wehrmacht's sphere, in particular in the territories outside the Reich's borders', of which the following excerpt forms the introduction:

**1136**   Increasingly, nowadays, women have to replace soldiers who are needed at the front in the service of the Wehrmacht. It is the Führer's wish that all German women, particularly when they are acting as Wehrmacht auxiliaries, far from their parents and homeland, should be provided with care and supervision to protect them and to facilitate the fulfilment of their duties. However, the measures which are necessary to implement the care and supervision must be appropriate to their feminine natures and must on no account lead to a militarization of women which might tend to happen within the Wehrmacht. The 'female soldier' does not accord with our national socialist view of womanhood.

▬▬▬

But, despite the fact that they did not wear a military uniform (except abroad), in practice the lives of these Wehrmacht auxiliaries became increasingly regimented, since they lived in hostels under the supervision of NSF personnel. Moreover, they were increasingly assigned to military

---

[11] See General Thomas, Minute for the Head of the OKW, 16.8.1941 in Imperial War Museum (IWM) E79AL1571.

duties. From the middle of 1943 onwards, they were deployed as 'anti-aircraft auxiliaries' to replace males in servicing (though not firing) the anti-aircraft batteries. And, in 1944, they replaced males manning the searchlights. By the end of the war, 50,000 'work girls' were involved in anti-aircraft defence operations and 30,000 in searchlight batteries. In the summer of 1944, it was decided to establish a formal organization to integrate all the various 'auxiliaries' of the various armed forces into a 'Wehrmacht Auxiliary Corps'. But it remained largely a paper exercise. At the beginning of 1945, there were approximately 80,000–100,000 female members of the Labour Service involved in Wehrmacht duties. In addition there were approximately 470,000 female Wehrmacht auxiliaries. Of these, roughly 300,000 were with the Reserve Army (150,000 of them conscripted), 20,000 as signals and staff personnel with the Field Army, 130,000 with the Luftwaffe, and 20,000 with the Navy. Finally, there was an unknown number with the Waffen SS.[12]

Unlike those conscripted into factory work, for many of the young women drafted into the various services the unpleasant compulsory aspects of their new lives were compensated or more than compensated for by the liberating and in some cases personally empowering experiences acquired through escaping from what were often narrow and restricted lives, broadening their horizons and acquiring new skills and responsibilities free from the constraints imposed by family and local community norms and expectations.

In the critical last months of the war the regime went even further in dumping its ideological objections to the militarization of women. On 28 February 1945, Bormann minuted the following order from Hitler:

**1137**    Women must be trained as quickly as possible. A women's battalion is to be raised in liaison with the Reich Women's Leadership. If this women's battalion proves itself then more should be raised. The Führer is hoping that the establishment of this battalion will have a salutary effect on the attitude of the men.

___

### (b) 'Women's work'

Another gender issue, which has already been touched on in a different context, was the question of the suitability of certain types of work for women. This issue emerged in various forms. One, which preoccupied the planners in the German Labour Front, was the question of women's role in industry, not simply in the context of the war, but also because

___

[12] See Arendt, op. cit., p. 316.

they were aware that German industry would continue to be dependent on female labour in the future peace as well. They were concerned with how what were regarded as 'natural' female physical and mental qualities and attributes could be most appropriately and productively utilized. The following excerpts from the 1940/41 Year Book of the Labour Research Institute of the DAF illuminate their thinking on these matters. Their views are dominated by the conventional wisdom on the 'nature' of women in relation to work, a set of ideas widely held in the Western world at the time. Their aim was to use these 'scientific' insights to rationalize women's work to produce maximum efficiency:

**1138**   The recognition that differences exist between male and female work performance must be the guiding principle of employment. Only success in relating the work required to women's biologically determined capabilities will refute the view that women's performance is inferior to that of men. On the contrary, they will become equal work comrades if they are given work appropriate to their particular nature.

At this point it must be observed that those professions and activities which are natural to women (social, welfare, educational professions etc.) are completely excluded from consideration since they do not raise any basic problems which need to be solved.

. . . If we now have to focus on the employment of women in particular it is because we have the feeling that biologically determined differences exist between the kinds of work that can be done by men and by women, differences which we must take account of.

Traditionally, in general, all those jobs which were felt to be female were assigned to women, namely those which were to do with the fulfilment of housewifely duties, or which were closely associated with them, whereas men were given those jobs which were felt to be male, namely agriculture, business, trade and industrial production or commercial gain. We can, at least on the basis of our feelings, distinguish between male and female jobs.

We must now concern ourselves with the problem of female labour because, as a result of recent developments in our forms of production, women are, on the one hand, increasingly capable of being employed in spheres of work which were originally male and, on the other, because the current war situation requires women to be employed to replace male workers. A positive social policy will thus have to focus on these issues and ensure that women are not employed arbitrarily . . . The guiding principle for all discussions and measures must be the maintenance of female strength and womanhood for the real task of women, namely as the bearers of coming generations, so that any damage to the growth of our whole national body can be avoided, despite the current need to employ women . . .

. . . The female intellect is different from that of the male. Although both sexes have a practical sense, women's interests are more determined by emotion and directed at personal things and also more dependent on sympathies for people and things than men's are. Imagination takes priority over calculating intellect. That is the reason why most women prove incompetent in technical matters and are inferior to men in abstract thought and observation such as, for example, in the intellectual planning of a piece of work. Thus women are less suitable for all jobs which require technical understanding or the ability to plan. Men are thus preferable as superiors when it comes to organisationally or technically complicated jobs, whereas, by contrast, women in these situations are capable of very effective performance as assistants to men. Women are more easily blind to danger. They usually respond to danger on the spur of the moment, lose their heads, are more readily subject to the dangerous influence of moods than men are. This fact substantially limits the employability of women on technical assignments on complicated machines and in dangerous plants, or at least requires increased protection at the work place or in the plant as well as special selection and training . . .

. . . Where there is a division of labour it should always be borne in mind that women have greater manual dexterity and a better sense of touch. For this reason they are particularly suited to work within the whole field of measurement and testing. In fine handicrafts, which can require great speed, with practice and given talent there is no difference in their performance compared with that of men. Women are, however, more suitable and their performance is superior if the work can be carried on automatically with no great demands being placed on an understanding of its context. Women are less sensitive to monotony. They can also cope well with work which remains the same and does not engage their minds if it leaves them free to think about their lives outside employment.

They lack, and presumably always will lack, real interest in normal industrial work. Women are, therefore happy to be semi- or unskilled workers. Where it is possible to change jobs easily one can often observe that women are prompted to do so by external factors such as the fact that other women make their own jobs sound particularly attractive or that relatives are employed in that particular workplace or some similar reason. In general, women work particularly well when it is a case of reproducing something, where it is a monotonous activity not requiring any changes but mainly needing manual dexterity . . .

Women want work which in every respect is as simple as possible, can be quickly grasped, carries little responsibility, provides a regular income and, apart from that, enables them to have maximum freedom to organize their own work environment and to pursue their own thoughts . . .

———

Hitler had very strong views on what kinds of work were or were not appropriate for women. In 1936 he had banned women from becoming lawyers and from most senior posts in the civil service.[13] With the outbreak of war, the shortage of lawyers and civil servants, as a result of military conscription, encouraged requests for a reconsideration of this policy. In January 1940, the Reich Interior Ministry reported to the Supreme Reich Authorities on the response to these requests as follows:

---

[13] See Vol. 2, doc. 340.

**1139**    The NS Lawyers' League has approached me with regard to the appointment of probationary female judicial assessors and civil service assessors [*Assessorinnen*] to posts in the higher ranks of the service. My response to this query, made in consultation with the Führer's Deputy, is as follows:

As the Reich Justice Minister informed the Supreme Reich Authorities in his letter of 16.1.1937, following a decision of the Führer, the appointment of women to judgeships or as lawyers is not permitted. In accordance with a further decision by the Führer, communicated to the Supreme Reich Authorities in a letter from the Reich Interior Minister of 24.8.1937, as a matter of principle only men are to be appointed to the administrative grade of the civil service. However, even after these decisions by the Führer, it is still permissible to appoint women to administrative grade posts for which they are peculiarly suited . . .

In accordance with this, there are no objections to the appointment of female probationer judges and administrative grade civil servants if they are better suited to the particular posts than men. Such posts will be available in particular in the welfare field. However, in other cases which are predominantly involved in the care of women and children it may also be more appropriate to appoint women than men. There will be, for example, such posts in the female branch of the Reich Labour Service or in the Reich Trusteeship administration. To what extent the appointment of probationary female lawyers (and civil servants) may be appropriate in other individual cases must in the first instance be left to the discretion of the relevant body.

The assessment whether a particular post, which is especially appropriate for a woman, would be better filled by a woman than a man may in certain circumstances be influenced by the prevailing shortage of civil servants. However, the appointment of women to permanent posts must always be approached with the requisite caution.

For this reason, the creation of new permanent posts designed to be filled by women on a regular basis does not appear desirable. An exception to this can only be made in the event that a change in current conditions produces an urgent need for the creation of such posts.

━━━

On 20 February 1942, the acting Reich Minister of Justice, Franz Schlegelberger, wrote to Lammers asking whether, in view of the shortage of legal personnel due to their being drafted into the armed forces, women might be permitted to act in a judicial capacity in guardianship cases and to deal with wills, 'since in these cases they do not have to appear in public'. He also asked whether female probationer lawyers, whose husbands had been killed in action, might not exceptionally be permitted to become lawyers, in order to be able to provide for their families, particularly given the small numbers potentially involved—sixty married female probationers of whom three had petitioned for admission following their husbands' deaths.

Lammers replied to Schlegelberger on 13 March 1942 as follows:

**1140** I raised the question of whether, and to what extent, women should be employed in the judicial and legal professions with the Führer. The Führer has accepted your first proposal as a *wartime measure*. However, the Führer does not wish that probationer female lawyers, whose husbands have been killed in action, should be admitted as fully-qualified lawyers, since this measure would have an effect in the post-war period. The Führer has no objection to women acting as judges in civil cases during the war as outlined in your first proposal, provided they fulfil the legal preconditions.

---

*(c) Female students*

The question of what kind of work was appropriate for women also raised the question of women's place in higher education. Just before the Nazis came to power 18 per cent of German students were female. Since the Nazis disapproved of academically trained women on principle, except in certain specifically 'female spheres', on 25 April 1933 they introduced a *numerus clausus* of 10 per cent for female students. By 1939, the number of female students had declined to 11.2 per cent of the total. However, because of a growing shortage of students, partly for demographic reasons and partly because students' life under the Nazis proved less appealing and the prospects for graduates less attractive, the regime had to lift the *numerus clausus* in 1935 and, in 1938, they began a recruitment drive among school leavers. After the outbreak of war, a series of measures facilitated the entry of women into universities, with the result that the number of female students rocketed. Already in the winter semester of 1942/3, there were more female students than in 1933 (20,000) and, since male students were being increasingly drafted into the armed forces, by 1944 nearly half the students in German universities were women (28,400). On 2 January 1943, the Reich Chancellery minuted that women would have to fill the graduate gap during the war and in the immediate post-war period until 'there was a sufficient number of male graduates again'.[14]

The sensitivity of this issue for the regime is reflected in the following excerpt from a report of the Reich Women's Leadership on 'The Deployment of Female German Students in Wartime', published in their 1941 Year Book, which endeavours to alleviate concerns about a perceived invasion of a male sphere:

**1141** Since the first trimester of the war, the vacation factory work, which was hitherto voluntary, has become compulsory for every student in their first three semesters.

---

[14] Westenrieder, op. cit., p. 104.

*Issues concerned with female students in wartime*
The report is preceded by a brief overview of the numbers of girls studying in German universities before and during the war.

At the beginning of the war there were around 13,000 female students at Germany's universities; this number increased to around 17,000 by summer 1940 and increased further to around 18,500 by December 1940. This figure does not include the vocational students of whom there are approximately 1,500.

We are seeing a repetition of a development which is familiar from the First World War: the number of those women who decide during the war to start a university or vocational college education increases considerably. We know that after the World War women were blamed for this fact and that it seriously damaged female studies. At that time, men returned from four years of war. Disappointed, despairing, without hope that their sacrifice had meant anything, they returned to the universities from which so many of them had set out years before with such enthusiasm. In the lecture halls they came across women, many of whom were now ahead of them in terms of numbers of semesters attended and exams passed. They believed that this was an undeserved advantage, which the war had given to women, because in their bitterness they overlooked the fact that these women had had the same hopes, indeed even greater hopes, removed from them. This development was understandable in human terms but the conclusion drawn from it was erroneous.

The female students of today know that, because of this human response, there is still the danger that, after the end of the war and perhaps even now, in the minds of many [male] students, who have fallen behind them in their studies by some semesters or even years, the same psychological process is repeating itself.

But, because we are aware of that, we want to discuss it with them, with those who as our comrades are closer to us than ever before. We want to ensure that there is clarity and honesty between them and us. Those who are at the front should know that we do not wish to play down their personal sacrifice. But they too should recognize from our behaviour and our work that the motto for women studying during the war is not personal gain but personal commitment.

All those who have seriously looked at our work and who understand the spirit which underpins it must recognize this. They will be able to recognize it all the more because we are already convinced that this war will end with the prospect of a happier future than was the case with the World War: a future which can give every German man and woman space and work.

The figures mentioned earlier seem to us, therefore, to justify not a negative but rather a positive interpretation. They are a sign that gifted young German women have become conscious of their intellectual abilities and, stimulated by the war, have decided to train them so that they may be able to utilize them if need be.

One can earn money quicker from a shorter and cheaper course of study and the question of professional success does not arise for a woman because she will end her career when she gets married. For a woman the decisive factor is always in the first instance the need for intellectual training and knowledge and the intention to acquire a qualification  appropriate to her intellectual ability in order to use it if her life circumstances require her to do so.

Thus, viewed in particular from the standpoint of the students' work, female studies remain in wartime a period of strict spiritual training, not in an intellectual sense, but in terms of the quality of the personality. This is guaranteed by the training in the ANSt.[15] The aim of the ANSt training is that our female students should develop into women who are characterised by a marked historical awareness and who understand how to master life's difficulties with cleverness and tact and with real feminine dignity. Women who have a strong and understanding heart but also a clear view of the needs of daily life.

*War work in addition to study*

If we presuppose that this aim will be achieved, it is illuminating to see how important is the fact that over 90% of German female students belong to the ANSt.

At the beginning of the war, the ANSt comprised 370 groups with around 7,000 active members. It now comprises, i.e. in the 1st Trimester of 1941, 513 groups with 13,070 active members and 5,034 old comrades, in other words a total of around 18,105 students. These students are both reliable and indispensable for German female labour. Let us for the moment ignore the fact that, after their exams, they can perform necessary work in important areas with the knowledge they have acquired, areas for which men are either unsuited or in which, for whatever reasons—perhaps as a result of the war—men are unavailable. Everyone is aware of this fact. Much too little known, however, is the huge amount of work that is done by our female students in addition to their studies: the real war work done by students which contradicts and refutes every accusation and every dubious query about how far students are in touch with and aware of real life.

In the war trimesters 1940/1:

3,000 students carried out factory service. That means 750,000 hours of additional leave for German female workers.

55,000 students helped with the harvest.

600 students acted as helpers, kindergarten teachers, school assistants, and medical assistants in the resettled ethnic German villages in the Warthegau. That represents 20,000 work days assistance for the returnees.

300 students were involved in settlement actions in Lorraine. That represents 14,000 hours of preparatory work for later settlement in the Western area.

In the war trimesters 1940/1 German female students looked after 17,000 soldiers and workers on the West Wall fortifications. They sent around 50,000 parcels and letters to the front.

One cannot dispute these figures. They show clearly that the female students are not concerned with their own lives, their own gain, their own health and their own pleasure, but rather with the whole community, with that same Germany to which our male students are committed whether fighting at the front or in strict military training. The figures refute the objection that the political education of

---

[15] The *Arbeitsgemeinschaft nationalsozialistischer Studentinnen*, the Working Group of National Socialist Female Students.

female students does not fulfil its purpose and is basically a waste of time and at the expense of their studies.

This is contradicted not only by the actual work which has been carried out and is reflected in the figures and which is real war work and, therefore, real political work, but above all by the fact that among the thousands of students involved there are not even 20 cases where the students have failed in terms of either their attitude or their work. This is true of the factory service as much as of the harvest service or the caring work. All the reports we have received hitherto are unanimous in commenting on the enthusiasm and joy, on the reliability and efficiency, on the hard work and the comradely spirit of our female students.

One must bear in mind the fact that the figures mentioned here are only an incomplete record of the work performed by the students in addition to their studies. These figures do not cover the work which the students perform in their university towns when conscripted as tram conductresses, assistants with the German Red Cross, as air warning assistants, in hospitals etc. Without the political education of German girls which has been going on for years and for semesters such a result would have been inconceivable. It is apparent from these quite concrete facts that this education has shaped the German female students into women who think historically and act politically.

━━━

### (d) Equal Pay

Equal pay was a particular bone of contention. The DAF had long campaigned for the principle of equal pay for equal work. With the outbreak of war and the replacement of large numbers of males by female workers doing the same job, the issue became acute. The DAF continued to press for equal pay with morale and its own reputation among its clientele as key considerations. However, the economic agencies were concerned about its potential harmful effects on the wage structure leading to demands by men for a restoration of differentials, thereby stoking inflation at a time when consumer goods were in short supply. Employers were concerned about the effect on their profit margins and about possible discontent among male workers.

The Reich Labour Ministry laid down guidelines soon after the outbreak of war and clarified them in the following letter to the Trustee of Labour for the Economic District of Middle Elbe, dated 2 November 1939, a copy of which was sent to all the other Trustees of Labour, the state officials responsible for wages and working conditions:[16]

**1142** Re: *Women's wages in the German Railways.*
In my edict of 27.10.39, of which a copy has meanwhile reached you, I have

---

[16] On the Trustees of Labour see Vol. 2, doc. 222ff.

established that male wages in the public sector should only be paid to female employees in those cases in which the woman

1. does exactly the same job as the man;
2. achieves the same level of performance in every respect; and
3. performs *particularly* responsible or *particularly* physically demanding work.

These principles, which are valid for the public sector, should also be applied—although with certain crucial qualifications—in the private sector. The basic principle should be that female workers should receive lower wages than male workers. When in doubt the guideline is that women should receive 75% of the pay which the equivalent male worker would receive. If, however, the preconditions for equal pay for women, which have been laid down for the public sector, exist in a branch of the private sector, then, before equal pay can be permitted, the question must be examined whether or not price rises would result therefrom. In the process of this examination, consideration must be given further to whether such favourable wage rates for women would produce discontent in other trades with low male wages and yet which impose heavy physical demands. Care must also be taken to prevent excessive wage differentials vis-à-vis trades in which female labour has long been customary but in which female wages are relatively low. It is only in those cases where such repercussions are not to be feared and in which the preconditions outlined here have been met that, in a deviation from the principle of differential pay, equal pay for male and female workers can be recognized in the private sector

———

However, requests for equal pay continued to flood in and so, on 21 December 1939, the Labour Ministry wrote to Göring setting out its views on the matter:

**1143**  Re: *Female wages—in reply to letter of 13.12.39.*

I have recently received numerous requests for as close as possible an equalization of pay between male and female members of the retinue. These demands are generally based on the fact that women are replacing men in the workplace and in many cases the women perform as well as the men. It may be the case that in some professions and trades women's performance is equal to or almost equal to that of men. However, it is undeniable that in the majority of cases where women replace men at work, their performance is in the long run inferior to that of men.

But, even where one can accept that the level of performance is the same, there are in my view very pertinent reasons why the repeated calls for the equalization of male and female members of the retinue should be rejected. If performance was to be the sole criterion determining wages, then, quite apart from the fact that a demand for equal pay for juvenile and adult members of the retinue could be justified in the same terms, this would produce wage conditions which would lead to social discontent. I need only remind you of the high earnings of young people of both sexes during the First World War, which had an extremely negative impact on morale at the front as well as at home. If one is to avoid a situation where in a family the wife gets the same or even a higher wage than her husband or the daughter than her father, then, in order to avoid an intolerable situation within individual families, one will have to keep female wages below those of males even if their performance is the same. Exemptions from this principle can only be made in individual cases for which there are very special reasons.

There are also economic reasons for differential pay. Female labour is customary above all in the textile industry, in the clothing trade, in the porcelain industry, in the shoe industry, in the confectionery and baking trades and to some extent in the metal refining industry. Thus women are predominantly employed in the weakly-performing consumer goods industries. If equal pay for men and women was introduced here, it would result in considerable cost increases which could only be borne by corresponding price increases. Such a price movement was, however, even in recent years, unwelcome and is even less justified at the present time. If one has to avoid equal pay for male and female members of the retinue in these trades, then one will not be able to permit it in the other industrial sectors where such an equalization might be economically bearable. If, for example, one was to pay women in the metal industry the same wages as men on a regular basis, not only would they receive a considerably higher wage than their work mates in the consumer goods industries, but they would also in some cases receive a higher wage than the male workers employed in the consumer goods industries with their customary low wage levels. In the light of the experience of recent years, it can be assumed with certainty that such wage conditions would lead to social tensions.

For these reasons I continue to insist that, as a rule, female wages should be fixed at a lower rate than those of males. In general, I believe that a differential of around 25% is justified. This also takes into account the fact that, as a rule, women's earnings represent in part or in total an additional income for the family, which supplements the husband's wages, a pension, or assists the maintenance of a family.

---

It was then agreed to raise female wages in the public sector from 75 to 80 per cent of male wages from 1 June 1940. However, there were particular instances where the authorities were prepared to grant equal pay in the public sector, as in the following case of which the details were reported in the internal newsletter of the local government umbrella organization, the DGT, of 5 February 1941:

**1144**   *67. Wages of women drivers*

The Reich Trustee of Labour for the Public Sector has issued the following regulation dated 30.11.40:

According to the Reich Minister of Labour's regulation concerning the employment of women on vehicles, dated 30.10.40, women may not be employed as drivers of trams, buses and lorries of more than 1.5 tons in weight. Exemptions can be granted by the offices of the factory inspectorate in agreement with the Plenipotentiary for Local Transport. In this case work time must not exceed 8 hours a day.

In view of the fact that the working hours of the female drivers are restricted and thus their income may be below that of the conductresses with longer working hours, and the fact that a driver's job may be considered, all in all, to be a particularly responsible one in the sense of the Reich Labour Minister's edict of 27.10.39 . . . I hereby approve in accordance with . . . in general that the wages of female drivers of trams and buses should be set to ensure they receive up to the full wage of comparable male members of the retinue.

——

In the meantime, the Reich Labour Ministry had also made limited concessions in the private sector. On 15 June 1940, the Ministry issued the following instructions to the Reich Trustees of Labour:

**1145**   The transformation of the German peacetime economy to meet the demands of the war has resulted in an increased deployment of women in jobs which were previously exclusively, or at least with few exceptions, confined to men. This unusual deployment of women necessitates a survey of their wage conditions.

I. The survey must be restricted to those economic branches which are particularly vital to the war effort, namely the iron and metalworking and chemical industries. In the event that it proves necessary the survey can be extended to the mining and iron and metal production industries. The other economic branches, such as in particular the textile and clothing industries, the food industry, the wood and paper industries are not to be included in the survey.

II. In the survey of female wages a distinction must be made in reviewing the plants of the iron and metal working industries and those of the chemical industry as to whether it is typical women's work or whether the work is only being carried out by women to replace the absent men.

1. Typical women's work is defined here as work which has traditionally been carried out by women and in the assessment of which the normal worker is assumed to be a woman and not a man. For these types of female jobs the existing wage rates are to be retained without exception . . .

2. Where, on the other hand, women have taken on jobs which have hitherto been customarily restricted to men, investigation must be made as to whether they must complete the work under the same technical conditions as the men. Any easing of the work load through the provision of extra helpers, through the use of special equipment etc. must be taken into account when setting wage rates. If the women's work is equivalent to the men's in terms of the technology used, the following procedures should be adhered to:

(a) *Piece work*

If men and women work together on the same pieces of work then  women should be granted the same piece work conditions as men. Women must also be granted the same conditions if they are brought together to work in special departments in the plant provided they perform the same work as the men.

(b) *Work on commission*
The principles laid down for piece work apply correspondingly to premium work.

(c) *Hourly paid work*
In general it must be assumed that, in the long run, women will not perform these types of work to the same level as men and that, therefore, until the opposite has been proved, a lower wage—80% of the corresponding male wage—is justified.

III. The wage regulations envisaged here are thus essentially to be restricted to the iron- and metalworking plants and to those of the chemical industry. Within these plants they do not affect the wages for typical female work, but only those jobs which hitherto have been carried out by men and are now being done by women under the same technical conditions. Finally, in the first instance, they are intended only to ensure an appropriate payment for piece work.

These essential restrictions are necessary so that these special regulations do not provide an excuse for a general increase in wages for female labour, which inevitably would destabilise all wages and salaries.

------

Despite repeated appeals by Robert Ley, the leader of the DAF, the regime resisted further concessions on equal pay. The issue was finally resolved at a high-level meeting in the Führer's headquarters on 25 April 1944 at which Hitler laid down the law. The proceedings were recorded by Lammers in the following minutes:

**1146**   On the 25th of this month there was a meeting with the Führer in my presence and in that of *Reichsleiter* Bormann, and which was attended by the head of the Reich [NSDAP] Organization, Dr Ley, the Plenipotentiary for Labour Mobilization, Sauckel, *Oberbürgermeister* Liebel, representing the Reich Minister for Armaments and War Production [Speer], and, in addition, Price Commissioner Dr Fischböck and Ambassador Abetz.

Dr Ley reported to the Führer as follows:

In order to increase the work performance of women and thereby to enhance overall efficiency, i.e. to mobilize all labour reserves, it was necessary to equalize the wages of women with those of men on the principle of equal pay for equal work and equal results. The problem of the 'social wage', i.e. measuring the wage only according to the *pure work performance*, but at the same time taking account of the worker's position in the national community as a national comrade and state citizen (husband, father)—a problem which inevitably leads to the granting of different wages to men and women—must be ignored during the war in the interests of a massive increase in efficiency.

The Führer responded to the issue raised by Dr Ley with the following fundamental statements:

'Wages in the national socialist state have two tasks to fulfil:
(a) To reward the basic work performance.
(b) Wages have social tasks to fulfil, namely their level must take into account

the position of the employee within the national community. For this reason the man whom the state requires to marry and start a family must be paid a higher wage than the man who is not married and than women. It is not acceptable to assess wages simply on the basis of work performance. For, if one did that, then one would have to pay a younger man, whose work performance is undoubtedly better than that of an older man, a higher wage than an older one. There can be no doubt, for example, that a young 25-year-old worker will achieve a considerably better work performance than a 50 to 60-year-old man. But, at the same time, as a father and in the light of his other contributions to the state, the latter must be given a higher wage than the former. Thus, if one operates on the basis of granting wages simply on the basis of work performance one must reach the false conclusion that with increasing age wages must decrease.

To take the line on the question of the relationship between male and female wages that there should be 'equal pay for equal work' is wrong. For, during the war, there is no basis of comparison for stating that the work performance of women is the same as that of men. The work performance of a woman cannot now be tested in relationship to a healthy man of average age working in peacetime, but only in relationship to the men currently working with women, namely the older men who are no longer fully capable and to the younger men whose performance is also less since they are not yet fit for combat. If one was to equate the wages of women with men then this would be in total contradiction to the national socialist principle of the maintenance of the national community. Men and, in particular, older men who are married and fathers must be paid more than women in the interests of the national community for social reasons because they must make more sacrifices for the national community; in the main women simply have to look after themselves, whereas men have to care for their families and the national community. It is the national socialist ideal, which must be realized in peacetime, that only men should be the earners and that even the most humble worker should have a three-room flat for himself and his family. Women must then work at home in order to look after their families and their flats. If the work performance of family men is rated higher than that of women for social reasons this does not represent a negative comment on women's work. Now, during the war, it is true that we have to get women to work, but in peacetime hopefully women in general can be removed from plants so that they can devote themselves to their families. Thus, even during the war, this national socialist ideal should only be breached as far as is absolutely necessary. One cannot anticipate a significant improvement in performance by equalizing the pay of men and women. Money is not worth as much as it used to be because there is a dearth of consumer goods which can be bought. An increase in women's wages would in practice simply mean strengthening the black market. If one wanted to achieve a general improvement in performance that could only be done by improving food supplies and the supply of the most important commodities. Unfortunately, that is impossible at the moment. There may indeed be cases in which justice requires that a woman should receive the same income as a man if she is engaged in typical men's work, e.g. that of a heavy or very heavy worker and if, in addition, she has to care for children in place of a husband. But then one should achieve the equality not by increasing the basic wage, but through child allowances or, even better, through an appropriate reduction in taxes. For such a woman is contributing to the maintenance of the national community in the same way as a family man.'

Finally, the Führer commented more or less as follows: 'The principles I have outlined must be adhered to even during the war. Otherwise, we would pre-empt the implementation of our peacetime plans along national socialist lines; indeed, we would run into difficulties even during the war. For a complete equalization of female with male wages would inevitably result in the tendency for an increase in male wages to occur. Thus, we must stick to the existing regulation which does not exclude the possibility *in particular exceptional cases* for a female wage to be equalized with a male wage. A complete equalization of female wages with male wages would ignore male contributions to the national community which I wish to avoid at all costs.'

In addition, the following may be noted:

In the course of the meeting mention was made of the fact that in a number of plants, e.g. in high precision engineering, men and women carry out the same relatively light and clean work side by side. Dr Ley remarked that in such cases unequal pay seemed unjust. The Führer commented that in such plants where typical women's work was carried out only women should be employed, since then not only would there be no inequality in wages but the men who had been working there hitherto could be transferred to work which was more appropriate for them. The Führer added that one must start thinking whether, when peace comes, certain occupations should be banned for men, e.g. the occupation of waiter, which could just as easily be carried out by women, or this was even more the case with women's hairdressing, for it was a thoroughly undignified occupation for a man to be a women's hairdresser. Above all, one could employ female teachers to teach children up to a certain age.

———

### (e) A problem of trousers

The extent to which women had invaded male spheres on the home front clearly disturbed many Nazis. A typical example was the frequency with which women wore trousers. This prompted the authorities to ban the practice in various parts of Germany, notably in the south-western state of Württemberg, where the Gauleiter-Reich Governor-Reich Defence Commissioner, Wilhelm Murr, a former minor business employee in his fifties clearly had very traditional views on such matters. On 23 September 1941, he wrote to the Württemberg Interior Minister as follows:

**1147**   The increasing unpleasant tendency for women to walk the streets wearing men's trousers is considered by the public to be incompatible with the seriousness of the situation. I request, therefore, that the offensive clothing should be banned in built-up areas with the justification that it is incompatible with the seriousness of the situation for women to dress in such a provocative manner. This also applies to women wearing riding gear in public outside riding establishments and events.

The wearing of work clothes does not of course come under the ban.

I request a report on what has been done in this matter.

―――――

The Interior Ministry responded by issuing a ban along the lines suggested and announced that the police had been instructed to prosecute breaches of the ban with fines or imprisonment or in certain circumstances with labour service.

However, the fact was that, as a result of clothing shortages and the extent to which women were now in various kinds of employment (postal workers, tram conductresses etc.) for which wearing trousers was the norm, trousers had become no longer a fashion garment but a very convenient form of dress for many women. As a result, the police who had to enforce the unpopular ban were put in an invidious position, as is clear from the following letter from the police chief in the university town of Tübingen to the county commissioner (*Landrat*) of Tübingen dated April 1942:

**1148**    Following the edict, the wearing of men's trousers by women on the streets is banned on the grounds that it is offensive and incompatible with the seriousness of the situation. Only the wearing of work clothes and sports trousers during sport is permitted. After this edict became known I was approached by the head of the local riding stable who asked for permission for women to wear riding gear on their way to and from the riding stables, since there were no changing facilities. I gave permission on condition that these women wore a coat over their riding gear. This was adhered to.

On the question of wearing 'training and ski trousers' the position was rather different. In view of the period of extreme cold and the deep snow, many women—mostly students but also women from older age groups—were observed wearing such clothing on the streets. When questioned they all declared that they could only keep out the cold by wearing such clothing. In most of the cases complained about the women involved were in my view those who did not possess long boots and long galoshes. Since this was obviously an emergency I did not prosecute these cases. Furthermore, it was often impossible to establish whether or not they were wearing work clothes which do not come under the ban, particularly since the claims by employees that such clothing was work clothes which they were required to wear could not be verified on the basis of visible signs such as the uniforms worn by women employed by the Post Office or the railways. In addition, there was the problem that, when challenged, other women claimed that they were on the way to do sport.

All these circumstances finally persuaded me to instruct my officers only to take action if it was a case of someone wearing trousers with the usual male cut which had become the fashion shortly before the Interior Minister's edict and which were occasionally seen here. Since the local riding stables are now shut, the question of the wearing of riding gear has now been sorted out as I indicated above, and the coming of spring will make the further wearing of 'training and ski trousers' unnecessary for the time being, one might think there was nothing more to say.

However, since we can reckon with the same things happening next winter, I would be very grateful if you could request the Interior Minister to permit the wearing of 'training and ski trousers' in future, particularly since this clothing is normally worn legitimately and in any case it dominates the street scene and so the sight of 'training and ski trousers' should not give offence. I have seen a number of young women walking the streets of Stuttgart in such clothing and assume that it was not objected to.

Those who wear such clothing and other people as well have repeatedly expressed their discontent about the action being taken. I have decided to put forward my proposal because I take the view that at the present time one should try to avoid the impression of any chicanery (and this is how the ban was regarded in an emergency such as last winter) and because the cautious line, which we have taken through experience and for other reasons which prevented us from acting, has the effect of reducing the prestige of the authorities and thereby cuts across attempts to prevent a weakening of the fabric of the state.

▬

However, by no means all Nazis shared the conservative views of men like Murr. The SS tended to have a more 'modern' attitude in such matters and a writer in the 27 January 1944 issue of the SS newspaper *Das Schwarze Korps* poured scorn on such bans:

**1149** Re: *Worries about trousers*

If one has a lot of time and nothing at all to do, one can, dear people in D and in the rest of the German fatherland, happily quarrel over whether the increasingly frequent practice of wearing long trousers suits our women or not . . . But even if trousers do not suit every woman . . . this is entirely a matter of taste which is solely the concern of the person wearing that particular article of clothing or at most of the man whose opinion she may value. At any rate, it has nothing to do with morality, decency, good conduct and such like. Hitherto, morality has always been cornered by those who have maintained that women wear too little. If they are going to remain logical they should not find it immoral that a woman is wearing too much. But no garment can possibly be longer than a pair of long trousers.

But in fact our Frau F. did not put on her long trousers to be immoral, indeed she did not even do it to prove her good or poor taste. She did it for *practical* reasons. Such a pair of trousers not only covers up non-existent stockings, it also replaces half a dozen other garments. That is one reason why so many women nowadays wear long trousers even if it may not suit any part of their anatomy. It is one of the not very frequent concessions made by female vanity to good sense.

Thus one should not scold women but praise them. They are doing us a good turn when they utilize textiles which have been used for men's trousers for a more appropriate purpose, one indeed which is useful to the war effort.

More important . . . the doctors say that the wearing of trousers has spared them having to treat a large number of bladder complaints. For decades they have railed in vain against the wearing of excessively thin stockings, short skirts, the invisible inadequacy of the less official garments. Long trousers have removed their concerns as a stroke.

These and other reasons—one need only consider how useful long trousers are for our tram and train conductresses and postal workers and other women who are doing their stuff for the war effort—suggest that one should leave the question of long trousers for women alone, at any rate in wartime. Later in peacetime, when we can afford the time for other cares, one can once again discuss the issue of women's trousers as a matter of taste, provided, that is, our fair women's need for variety has not by then placed quite other matters in the foreground of public interest.

▬

As the problems on the home front mounted, so Murr was forced to modify his decree to take account of the new situation, but it was not lifted. On 24 March 1944, the Württemberg Interior Minister wrote to the Higher SS and Police Leader South-West as follows:

**1150**　Re: *The Württemberg Interior Minister's decree concerning the wearing of long trousers by women of 27.9.1941.*

I have learned that a number of women who wore men's or training trousers have recently been punished on the basis of the above decree. These were women who had put them on for practical reasons, namely to clear away debris caused by air raids. The decree does not of course apply to these cases. The wearing of work clothes and the wearing of sports trousers during sport was expressly excluded from this ban at the time it was issued. The exemption must also apply to those cases in which women wear trousers for the practical purpose of clearing up after air raids. However, the ban remains in force for the type of women who wear men's clothing in public with the clear aim of attracting attention. I request that you instruct the police force accordingly.

▬

At the end of 1944, however, Himmler stepped in:

**1151**　The *Reichsführer SS* and
　　Chief of the German Police

To the State Governments, the Reich Governors etc.　　　　　13.12.1944
Immediate!

The police authorities in various places have issued　regulations banning the wearing of long trousers by women and imposing punishments for doing so. The

*Reichsführer SS* and Chief of the German Police has personally ordered that at the present time no action should be taken in the event of a breach of such regulations. I request that the subordinate offices should be informed. This instruction is not to be published.

[Signed p.p.] DR DIEDERICHS

## (vi) Evacuation

As the Allies stepped up their bombing campaign so the effects of air raids began to have an ever greater impact on the lives of women, not least through the experience of evacuation, which had an enormous impact, both on those being evacuated and on the communities to which they were sent. Clashes of class, religion, and the different ways of life of town and country between hosts and guests added to the burdens and stresses of being uprooted from one's home environment and forced to live cheek by jowl with relatives or strangers, or having relatives, let alone strangers, imposed on one in what was usually a very restricted living space and often over lengthy periods of time. In her monthly report for April 1944 the NSF local branch leader in the village of Unterrodach in northern Bavaria made the following comment on some of the problems created by the arrival of Hamburg evacuees:

**1152** It is always the people who've been bombed out who are responsible for the general mood. There are always some of them who have something to grumble about and are continually discontented. Big city people and country people simply don't suit each other. One woman says: 'we're left to starve here in the sticks'. Another complains that there's no entertainment here; another says to a shopkeeper: 'I'll buy anything off you but not your Bavarian stupidity.' One often has to step in and sort things out.

Above all, evacuation posed a threat to the family unit, which had gained greatly in importance for its members during the Third Reich as a kind of shelter from the growing pressures and threats which developed in the public sphere. This role of the family as a psychological shelter, particularly for men, became especially important from 1942 onwards as the effects of, on the one hand, military and labour conscription and, on the other, bombing with its destruction of neighbourhoods, enforced relocation of plants and the accompanying mass flight and evacuation, undermined or destroyed job, neighbourhood and wider family ties and networks, leaving the individual much more dependent on his or her immediate family. In this situation it is not surprising that families increasingly resisted the evacuation of close family members.

In its report of 18 November 1943, the SD set the evacuation issue in the context of a broader assessment of 'the effects of current events on women's mood and bearing':

**1153** According to the available reports, women are feeling calm but quite depressed because of the heavy fighting and the continual withdrawals in the east. They are worried about what is going to happen in Russia.

The retreat of our troops is interpreted by many women as a sign of the general weakening of our resistance. On the other hand, women in particular wonder why there are so many troops to be seen in the towns of the Reich and why they are not being sent to the front, particularly in view of the call-up of older male age groups and the recruitment of female anti-aircraft auxiliaries.

Women show little interest in the day-to-day events of the war. Young women, in particular, appear quite indifferent. Women often show they are tired of the war. They are anxious to avoid anything which may remind them of the war. Thus, they avoid the relevant radio programmes and newsreels and ignore the political section of the newspapers. In general, it is only those who have close relatives at the front or women from intellectual circles who show a significant interest in political events. They follow the war reports closely and, for example, paid attention to the development of the political situation in Sweden and in Turkey, as well as the reports about the Indian declaration of war, which most women, however, do not take very seriously. Women are generally sceptical about the reconstruction in Italy for 'trust in anything' coming from Italy has completely disappeared.

Many women are also concerned that the stability of their marriages and the mutual understanding with their partners is beginning to suffer from the lengthy war. The separation which, with short breaks, has now been going on for years, the transformation in their circumstances through total war and, in addition, the heavy demands which are nowadays made on every individual  are changing people and filling their lives. When on leave, the front-line soldier often no longer shows any understanding for his family's domestic circumstances, which are governed by the war, and remains indifferent to the many daily cares of the home front. This often produces an increasing *distance between the married couple*. Thus, wives often point out that, having looked forward to being together again during their husband's leave, the occasion is spoilt by frequent rows caused by mutual tensions. That even happens in marriages which were previously models of harmony.

It is particularly striking that many measures carried out by the Party and leading personalities are criticized more vigorously by women than by men and yet most women always support the Führer. Generally, women always take the line that the Führer would definitely sort it out if he knew about it all.

But most women focus their minds on the immediate practical tasks. Among the current pressing needs the potato and vegetable shortages cause women the most concern. Many women with growing children have sleepless nights because 'they often do not know what they are going to put on the table'. Women also find the different shopping hours for foodstuffs and household goods a serious complication . . .

Women continue to complain about the often *unfriendly service* in the shops. Shopping is frequently like running the gauntlet. The shopkeepers no longer find it necessary to treat their customers with a minimum of politeness.

At the moment, women are complaining in particular about the withdrawal of clothing coupons, pointing out the urgency of the need to end the shortage of stockings and bed linen in view of the cold weather and that woollens must be provided without fail. (In the meantime, the request for stockings has been satisfied by the release of one pair each.) . . .

However, political and economic events, indeed the whole war, are currently being overshadowed by the evacuation measures and their effects. A substantial number of the evacuated women and children have found a satisfactory place to stay in the reception areas. These women have accepted their lot and behave generally calmly. Another group of women, perhaps smaller in number than the other group, is rightly or wrongly discontented with their accommodation and with their whole new situation. These women make all sorts of comments about the way in which the evacuation was carried out; they exert an unfavourable influence on the other evacuated women and convey a partly false impression of the situation of the evacuated national comrades to the rest of the Reich.

The [SD] reports stress the following points in particular:

The *splitting up of families* without the possibility of making visits with all the accompanying problems is in the long run felt to be an intolerable situation both by men but in particular by women In the first place, men suffer from the separation since nobody is there to look after them and to take care of their flats. The experience of coming home after a hard day's work to a cold and lonely flat, the lack of loving care and a better diet provided by their wives and, above all, the absence of their children's laughter removes their will and also their strength to work In particular, one often hears workers saying that if one wants to retain their work morale and their strength then one should let their wives stay put. But if they were evacuated then one could forget it because the men would soon be so depressed that they would no longer be in a position to cope with the heavy demands of their work. These comments are supported by authoritative spokesmen of industry to the extent that *already* they have observed a *reduction in performance* to some degree as a result of the evacuations that have taken place.

The suggestion of organizing *neighbourly assistance* through which the husbands themselves, but also their flats, gardens, and in some cases their animals could be looked after is often considered unviable, since the women who have been left behind have largely been recruited by the Labour Office and thus are fully occupied with their own concerns and their own households. Furthermore, this assistance would produce jealousy among the wives and create a lot of bad blood in the families. Such fears are seldom expressed in public, but the following comment by a worker's wife is typical: 'if that old biddy heard that I was going to light his stove for him then the stove would soon be cold again because she'd arrive on the next train even if she had to travel through the night and pay for the journey herself.'

In addition to the economic worries, there is the great mental strain which is caused by a long separation. Above all, the married men say that their family is the only compensation they have for their heavy work load. One shouldn't take away from them the only thing that makes life worth living. But the wives are no less subjected to a heavy mental burden because they want to live in their own homes, to look after them and to care for their husbands and children. To know that their husband is alone and uncared for and that they themselves are the guests of strangers and have to ask for every utensil is in the long run intolerable. Reference is frequently also made to the *sexual problem* and the danger of *marriage break-up.* (There are already reports to the effect that the morals of evacuated wives are anything but satisfactory.) However, in general it is *the separation from children* which is felt to be a particularly intolerable burden in the long run. The longing of the parents and of the children for each other is getting everybody down. There are hardly any opportunities for visits so that in some cases they have begun to drift apart. The fear was that if they were separated for long then this could become the norm.

Moreover, religious women express concern that their children will lack the necessary *religious* instruction. Sometimes one hears the opinion expressed that the evacuation has only been organized in order to have a better opportunity of influencing them in an anti-religious direction. On the other hand, women who are *gottgläubig* [believers in a God but not the Christian one, i.e. supporters of Nazi ideology] express the fear that, by being evacuated to Catholic areas, their children will be subjected to religious influence and so will be brought up in a way they did not approve of. Above all, mothers are worried that the Catholic Church will try hard to influence vulnerable children's minds. It is no longer a rare event for even Hitler Youth boys to join Church processions attracted by their impressive style.

In particular, *national socialist women* find the obvious attempt by the Catholic Church to influence their members politically intolerable since each is trying to convert the other to their way of thinking and this results in unpleasant tensions. Remarks by the locals after air raids on Munich and Nuremberg such as: 'We've got you Hamburgers to thank for this. It's because you don't go to Church' or 'You should've prayed more' are considered to be the result of *political education* by the Catholic Church.

In addition to the mothers' fears that the children in the reception Gaus will lack the necessary care and supervision, there is concern about their health care. According to the available reports, the conditions in the reception Gaus are often inevitably not conducive to reducing let alone removing the dislike of evacuation. The majority of the evacuated women and children are accommodated in small villages and rural parishes under the most primitive conditions. They have to cook in the same kitchen with their hosts, which often gives cause for conflict, since people look into each other's pots and get jealous if the other family has something better to eat. In a number of cases there can be no question of family life, since sometimes not all the children can be accommodated with the mother in the same house, and furthermore often the only living room that is available has to be shared with the host family.

The difficulties involved in acquiring the most basic utensils further compli-cate life away from home. The mood of the available negative reports is expressed in the following report of a female evacuee:

'We are harried from pillar to post if we want to get something to which we are entitled. Every office turns us away and sends us to another one. First, we go to the NSV; they send us to the mayor, again to the [NSDAP] local branch leader, to the contact man for us evacuees; then we go to the *Landrat,* from there to the district head of the NSV or to the [NSDAP] district leader himself, who then promises us help, which then doesn't come. No office is prepared to accept responsibility and if someone happens to consider themselves competent then their decision is overturned by someone else and everybody claims to have more authority than everybody else. Or is this all simply an argy bargy over competencies between the State and the Party?'

In order to buy food people often have to go for kilometres even in wind, rain, ice and snow. The children then usually stay at home unsupervised and so are a source of worry and concern for their mothers. In addition, there are regional character differences between the indigenous population and the evacuees in terms of the way they think, feel and act. News of those cases in which the latter have had a bad deal spreads like wildfire and creates a mood of hostility to evacuation, This has sometimes found visible expression in remarks being entered in the NSV house collection lists for the WHW instead of contributions.

All the available reports mention that one of the *vital factors* which has a *very negative* impact on people's mood and in terms of their trust in the NSDAP is the fact that, despite the *Reichsleistungsgesetz,*[17] well-off people who have a number of rooms *remain unaffected,* whereas ordinary people, who have limited accommodation, are forced to take in evacuees.

Further points which are made against evacuation are the fact that: (a) nowadays there is hardly a Gau or a country district which is safe from air raids; (b) that, in the event of evacuation, people's flats may be lost for good; and (c) there has been a lull in the air war. Taken together, these factors are the reason why large numbers of evacuees have gone back home and would, along with those who have hitherto stayed behind, refuse to let themselves be sent away again. This has resulted in them having their food ration books withdrawn, e.g. in Gau Westphalia-South, presumably in order to persuade those women who have returned to go back to their reception Gaus. But the women concerned have tried to force the return of their ration books. Thus, according to a report from Dortmund, on 11.10.1943 roughly 300 women in Witten *demonstrated* in order to protest publicly against the measure.

There were shameful demonstrations so that the Witten local authority was compelled *to call on the police to restore order.* However, they *refused to intervene,* since they claimed the women's demand was rightful and the decision not to hand out ration books to returning compatriots was by no means legal. In Hamm, Lünen and Bochum there were also noisy demonstrations in front of the municipal Food Offices. Angry crowds waited for the ration books to be handed out. Since some of the women brought babies and infants with them and some miners came in place of their wives, while they were waiting they swapped evacuation experiences and made the most hair-raising statements. Miners declared that *they would not go down the pit* until they had secured the necessary food ration cards for their families. Women declared that they would

---

[17] This law issued on 1 September 1939 permitted the Government to requisition property for war purposes.

rather suffer air raids there than travel back to the place where they had been evacuated. The announcement in the newspapers, which was also posted up in the ration book office on 12.10.1943, to the effect that not only would no ration books be issued to those who had returned but that also the food ration books for all children of school age would be withdrawn, produced a virtual riot by the women who were ready to do anything without the slightest constraint or concern for the consequences. Attempts to talk them round had the opposite effect.

Abuse of officials and leading figures was widespread. Comments like: 'They'd better keep out of my way. My children aren't going to be sent away and if I have nothing to eat then I can bloody well die with them.'

'We'll see about whether I don't get anything for my children to eat. I can leave my children where I want. After all they're *my* children.'

'The people from the Food Office will first have to show me the law which says that my children have to be sent away. If there's no law for it and there isn't one, then no one can take my food ration book away from me.'

'That doesn't come from the top; it's just the mayor here and the Food Office or the Gauleiter who are responsible. They think they know it all but we'll show them.'

'They might just as well send us straight to Russia, point machine guns at us and have done with it.'

'If I have to go then my child must come with me and not have to be alone in the world. We'll stay together. That would be something if they could do with us what they want. After all, it's still voluntary.'

People said that in other Gaus, which were even more badly affected by enemy planes, such as the cities of Essen and Cologne, there had not been a compulsory evacuation and that the children there were going to school again. In addition, it was pointed out that once again it was only the working population which was affected by the evacuation, whereas the wives and children of the financially better off had found accommodation in spas at their own expense . . .

Since the authorities responded uncompromisingly to all these attacks, women adopted the subterfuge of going to the Labour Office and seeking work. They provided the proof that their children were being looked after by someone else during their working hours, although whether this was really true could not be ascertained. As a result, they were assigned to a place of work and received ration books. In this way the women secured their entitlement. An inevitable result of this toing and froing was that, in some cases, the children went without milk for fourteen days.

The miners' families were able to help themselves in that initially they thought they could do without ration books and live off the generous supplements for heavy workers and very heavy workers. However, it was explained to them that if they were not able to carry out their work because of an inadequate diet they would simply have to be off sick.

The measures which were taken in the sphere of school education were also not always calculated to persuade the women to agree to evacuation. These measures consisted essentially in not giving the children in the cities any opportunity of going to school so that, if they wanted to attend a proper school they would have to let themselves be evacuated. To ensure the success of this measure the authorities further laid down that private tuition could not be regarded as fulfilling the duty of school attendance and that the children would have to catch up with any schooling they had missed and that, if they had been absent from school for longer than ten months, they would be demoted to the class below. But the parents were now responding to this measure by saying that it did not matter at all to them whether the children would still have to continue at school after they had reached 14 years of age. They were determined to keep the children at home and would never let themselves be persuaded otherwise. Moreover, they presumed that when the children were 14 years old a sufficient number of people would be needed in Germany so that one could easily avoid the measures now being threatened. They could calmly wait to see what happened.

The reports point out that the *hostile attitude* adopted by large sections of the population towards the *evacuations* cannot be demonstrated more clearly than by these stubborn attempts to sabotage all the measures which the authorities have taken to implement the evacuation . . .

Authoritative sources in industry declare that it would be in the interests of the workers' work performance if it could be arranged as soon as possible for the workers to have their wives and children back home with them. The following statement is relevant here:

The evacuations were intended to remove the workers' concern about their relatives in order to raise their work morale. Unfortunately, however, in the light of experience so far, often the very opposite has been achieved. For example, at the end of his shift, a miner remarked:

'Once more I'm dreading the evening. As long as I'm at work I don't think about it, but the moment I get home I start worrying. I miss my wife and my children's laughter.'

As he said it, the man cried without any shame.

## List of Sources

1100   Bericht der NS Frauenschaft Ortsgruppe Söflingen-West für Monat Januar 5.2.1943 Staatsarchiv Ludwigsburg (StAL) PL 502/32/171.
1101   (a) Staatsarchiv Bamberg (StAB) M 33/144.
         (b) StAB M 33/138.
1102   StAB M 33/76 IV.
1103   StAB M 33/36 I.
1104   StAB M 33/71.
1105   StAB M 33/36I, 36 II.
1106   StAB M 33/144.
1107   Ibid.
1108   Ursula von Kardorff, *Frauen im Kriegsdienst 1914–1945* (Stuttgart 1969), pp. 286–7.
1109   D. Winkler, *Frauenarbeit im 'Dritten Reich',* (Hamburg 1977), p. 201.
1110   Nuremberg Document (ND) 1456-PS.
1111   R. Wagenführ, *Die deutsche Industrie im Kriege* (Berlin 1955) pp. 145–7.
1112   R 43 II/652.
1113   N. Westenrieder, *'Deutsche Frauen und Mädchen'. Vom Alltagsleben 1933–1945* (Düsseldorf 1984), p. 89.

1114 Bundesarchiv Berlin (BAB) R 43 II/652.
1115 Ibid.
1116 Ibid.
1117 Ibid.
1118 Ibid.
1119 Ibid.
1120 H. Boberach, ed. *Meldungen aus dem Reich. Die geheimen Lageberichte des Sicherheitsdienstes der SS 1938–1945,* Vol. 9 (Herrsching 1984), pp. 3382, 3386–7, 3391.
1121 H. Heiber, ed., *Reichsführer! Briefe an und von Himmler* (Munich 1970), pp. 140–2.
1122 ND 016-PS.
1123 Westenrieder, op. cit., p. 108.
1124 *Aus deutschen Urkunden 1935–1945* (n.d., *c.*1945), pp. 136–40.
1125 Ibid., pp. 108–10.
1126 BAB R 43 II/654.
1127 Imperial War Museum (IWM). BBC Monitoring Transcripts 1A Home (xi).
1128 Boberach, op. cit., p. 4756–8.
1129 BAB R 3/1740.
1130 W. Schumann, ed., *Deutschland im Zweiten Weltkrieg*, Vol. 3 (East Berlin 1982), p. 217.
1131 BAB R 43 II/654.
1132 Ibid.
1133 *Reichsgesetzblatt* (RGBl.) *I 1942,* p. 321.
1134 *Die Reden Hitlers am Parteitag der Freiheit 1935* (Munich 1935), pp. 53–4.
1135 *Völkischer Beobachter* 6.8.1941.
1136 von Kardorff, op. cit., p. 361.
1137 Westenrieder, op. cit. p. 122.
1138 *Jahrbuch 1940/1.* Vol 1. Arbeitswissenschaftlichen Institut der DAF, Berlin. Rep. (Munich 1987).
1139 BAB R 43 II/427.
1140 Ibid.
1141 von Kardorff, op. cit., pp. 352–4.
1142 BAB R 36/515.
1143 BAB R 41/69.
1144 Ibid.
1145 BAB R 41/69.
1146 BAB R 43 II/542.
1147 Hauptstaatsarchiv Stuttgart (HstAS) E 151 CII Bü 754.
1148 Ibid.
1149 Ibid.
1150 Ibid.
1151 Ibid.
1152 StAB M 33/80.
1153 Boberach, op. cit., Vol. 15, pp. 6025–33.

# Sex and Population Policy

## (i) Introduction

The interest shown by the regime in the position of women in work was part of a more general preoccupation with gender issues and population policy. The war had a major impact on relations between the sexes. The absence of the majority of the male population for long stretches of time combined with brief periods of leave often produced tensions between husbands and wives as heightened expectations of their relationship often failed to be realised because of the difficulty of readjustment to being together again under conditions of great stress for both partners. The strain on marriages was increased by sexual frustration and increased opportunities for new relationships. The mobilization of large numbers of women into various forms of employment, the increased mobility produced by conscription and evacuation tore them out of their existing social networks and facilitated the creation of new liaisons which could be conducted without the customary close supervision of family and neighbours. The continual awareness of the fragility of such relationships, which could easily be ended by relocation or death, encouraged an intensity which removed inhibitions. Marriage breakdowns, precipitate marriages and illegitimate births were the frequent result. The fact that the absence of husbands and fathers to some extent liberated women from various forms of male control was perceived as a threat to the social order and to the morale of the men at the front. Fears of rampant female promiscuity and, in particular, sexual relations between German women and foreign workers leading to 'racial pollution' were a constant concern of the authorities. At the same time, however, the persistence of traditional moral values was increasingly seen as an obstacle in the way of responding to the demographic and eugenic imperatives created by the war. For it was the demographic and eugenic effects of the war which created the greatest anxiety for the regime.

## (ii) Population Policy

Between 1933 and 1939, the Nazis had been endeavouring to adopt a systematic population policy involving both a quantitative approach, i.e. a desire to increase the number of births, and a qualitative approach by applying the principles of eugenics or in German terms 'racial hygiene'. The quantitative aspect had been covered, positively, by such measures as a marriage loan scheme, increased child allowances, improved maternity advice and welfare facilities and a propaganda cult of motherhood, and, negatively, by the official discouragement of birth control, the vigorous prosecution of abortion, except where eugenically indicated. The qualitative aspect of population policy had consisted of the application of rigid criteria of entitlement to benefits, thereby excluding the allegedly genetically unfit and 'asocial' and in many cases enforcing their compulsory sterilization.[1]

After the outbreak of war the obvious concern was that the deaths of men in their prime and the long periods of separation between husbands and wives would have a serious impact both on the birth rate and on the quality of those being born. This issue was tackled on a number of fronts. First, the regime stepped up its propaganda campaign on motherhood, which had been under way long before the war. Thus, for example, on 15 December 1939 an exhibition was held in the Kaiser Friedrich Museum in Berlin on 'Woman and Mother—Lifespring of the Nation'. The issue was also addressed shortly after the outbreak of the war in the following order issued by Himmler to his SS:

**1154**  The *Reichsführer SS* and
Chief of the German Police  Führer Headquarters, 28 October 1939

To all men of the *SS* and Police

The old proverb that only he can die in peace who has sons and children must again hold good in this war, particularly for the SS. He can die in peace who knows that his clan and everything that his ancestors and he himself have wanted and striven for will be continued in his children. The greatest gift for the widow of a man killed in battle is always the child of the man she has loved.

---

[1] On this policy see Vol. 2, docs 327–335.

Beyond the limits of bourgeois laws and conventions, which are perhaps necessary in other circumstances, it can be a noble task for German women and girls of good blood to become even outside marriage, not light-heartedly but out of a deep moral seriousness, mothers of the children of soldiers going to war of whom fate alone knows whether they will return or die for Germany . . .

During the last war, many a soldier decided from a sense of responsibility to have no more children during the war so that his wife would not be left in need and distress after his death. You SS men need not have these anxieties; they are removed by the following regulations:

1. Special delegates, chosen by me personally, will take over in the name of the *Reichsführer SS*, the guardianship of all legitimate and illegitimate children of good blood whose fathers were killed in the war. We will support these mothers and take over the education and material care of these children until they come of age, so that no mother and widow need suffer want.

2. During the war, the SS will take care of all legitimate and illegitimate children born during the war and of expectant mothers in cases of need. After the war, when the fathers return, the SS will in addition grant generous material help to well-founded applications by individuals.

*SS-Men and you mothers of these children which Germany has hoped for show that you are ready, through your faith in the Führer and for the sake of the life of our blood and people, to regenerate life for Germany just as bravely as you know how to fight and die for Germany.*

▬▬

The issue was also addressed by the Führer's Deputy for Party Affairs, Rudolf Hess. On 22 December 1939 the following instruction was transmitted by a journalist to his editor:

**1155**    At a press conference with Rudolf Hess we were informed that this evening the letter of an unmarried mother and Rudolf Hess's reply will be released to the newspapers via the DNB.[2] This material is about five pages long and should be published in the Christmas editions of the newspapers—either in the Christmas supplement or, if this has already been prepared, in the inside pages in the form of an article or somewhere else where families are likely to read it.

The material is of fundamental importance, since the problem of unmarried mothers and illegitimate children is addressed from a national socialist perspective. Legal regulations dealing with the care of and provision for unmarried mothers and children can be expected shortly. Rudolf Hess's letter is preparing the way for these regulations.

The most important section of the letter concerns the fact that, when dealing with the problem of unmarried mothers, traditional views, customs and social

---

[2] DNB = Das Deutsche Nachrichten Büro (German News Agency).

views should be suspended during wartime and the post-war period in so far as this is required to maintain the nation's strength.

The material should appear under neutral headings such as 'Rudolf Hess writes to an unmarried mother'. There should be no commentary. Qualified pens, above all well-known male and female authors such as Ina Seidel, Agnes Miegel etc. will comment later on this topic.

All families should read these basic views of the national socialist state leadership over Christmas.

▬

The letter read as follows:

**1156**     Dear Frau H——

Your personal lot is the reason for our issuing an appropriate regulation which, as a matter of principle, will apply to all young mothers in your position. The national socialist movement sees in the family the germ cell of the nation. It will no more depart from this principle than from any other. The NSDAP has done many decisive things for the family, for its maintenance and its care, and above all for the joy of having a child in the family, and it will continue to do so. That is part of its unalterable programme!

Conscious of the fact that the national socialist world view has given to the family the role in the state which is its due, in times of national crisis measures may be taken which depart from basic norms. Especially in time of war, which causes the death of many of the best men, every new life is of particular importance for the nation. Thus, if racially impeccable young men who go into battle leave behind children who transmit their blood to future generations, children of equally genetically healthy girls of equivalent age, with whom marriage is for some reason not immediately feasible, this will secure the maintenance of this valuable national possession. Scruples, which in normal times might be justified, must be put aside.

If a marriage has not yet taken place when these children's births are registered at the Registry Office, 'war father' will be entered instead of the father's name or as the father. The mother will be registered as 'Frau' with her maiden name and be addressed as 'Frau'. Mother and child will be able to respond to questions about the father frankly by saying that he was a 'war father'.

If the mothers so wish, the NSDAP will arrange guardians for the children of 'war fathers' who will consider it their national socialist duty to look after them. However, I believe that in many cases the grandparents of the 'war child' will see this as their most pleasant task. Where there are material difficulties the state will provide assistance.

I am convinced that before long my attitude will be shared by the whole German people and that the whole German people will support all those mothers who, by going beyond the bounds of bourgeois norms and customs, which may normally be necessary, are helping to make up for the losses of the war—just as the rural population has long adopted a more liberal attitude to the problems of illegitimacy.

You can believe me that it has not been easy for me either to free myself from traditions which for the whole of my life I have accepted unquestioningly. But, as a National Socialist, I know that the highest law in peace as in war is to maintain the nation. All other laws, customs and views must subordinate themselves and adjust themselves to this highest law. In time of war the attitude to killing undergoes a complete transformation as a result of the nation's instinct for self-preservation. A similar transformation must occur in wartime and in the post-war period in the public's attitude to unmarried mothers and to children born out of wedlock, equally out of the nation's instinct for self-preservation. What use is it if a nation achieves victory but, as a result of the sacrifices made to achieve it, dies out as a nation? I believe every woman who can share the joys and cares of her children with her beloved husband in the security of a happy marriage will show understanding and sympathy for a mother who must carry on life's struggle alone with her child.

In any case, nowadays a woman who consciously takes the decision to become and possibly remain an unmarried mother in the middle of a war with all its uncertainties—a woman who wants a child and commits herself to it—must receive no less respect. A suitable age, healthy genes, and a relationship with an equally racially highly qualified man whom she loves and knows to be so worthy that she is filled with the desire to marry him if possible—these are naturally the preconditions for her honoured status being undiminished. Such a woman has a difficult path to follow. She knows that she and her child will probably have to do without the security of a family, the protection of a husband and father. But she also knows that it is better to bring up a child in such circumstances, however difficult they may be, than not to have a child.

Nowadays it is quite natural for a wife and mother who is widowed or divorced to be able to enter another marriage. It will become equally acceptable for a woman who has a 'war child' to be able to enter a marriage with a man who is not the father of this child and who sees in the woman's motherly qualities precisely the basis for a married life.

The family is the basic cell of the state: but nevertheless a nation, particularly during a war, cannot avoid continuing and maintaining its healthy racial inheritance to the greatest possible extent. The welfare of the whole community, the life of the nation is of greater importance than all the norms, which may be the expression of recognized customs but are not the expression of morality as such, and, above all, than prejudices. The supreme service which women can perform for the community is to contribute to the continuation of the nation in the form of racially healthy children

Feel fortunate that you are granted the privilege of performing this supreme service for Germany.

Be grateful that the man you love lives on in your child.

Heil Hitler R. Hess

---

The public response to these statements was evidently such that Himmler was soon obliged to issue the following order:

**1157**　The Reichsführer SS and
　　　　Chief of the German Police　　　　　　　Berlin, 30 January 1940

*SS* Order for the whole of the *SS* and Police

You are aware of my order of 28 October 1939, in which I reminded you of your duty if possible to become fathers of children during the war.

This publication, which was conceived with a sense of decency and was received in the same sense, states and openly discusses actual problems. It has led to misconceptions and misunderstandings on the part of some people. I therefore consider it necessary for every one of you to know what doubts and misunderstandings have arisen and what there is to say about them.

1.　Objection has been taken to the clear statement that illegitimate children exist, and that some unmarried and single women and girls have always become mothers of such children outside marriage and always will. There is no point in discussing this; the best reply is the letter from the Führer's Deputy to an unmarried mother which I enclose together with my order of 28 October 1939.

2.　The worst misunderstanding concerns the paragraph which reads: 'Beyond the limits of bourgeois laws and conventions . . .' According to this, as some people misunderstand it, SS men are encouraged to approach the wives of serving soldiers. However incomprehensible to us such an idea may be, we must discuss it.

What do those who spread or repeat such opinions think of German women? Even if, in a nation of 82 million people, some man should approach a married woman from dishonourable motives or human weakness, two parties are needed for seduction: the one who wants to seduce and the one who consents to being seduced.

Quite apart from our own principle that one does not approach the wife of a comrade, we think that German women are probably the best guardians of their honour. Any other opinion should be unanimously rejected by all men as an insult to German women.

Furthermore, the question has been raised as to why the wives of the SS and police are looked after in a special way and not treated the same as all the others. The answer is very simple: because the SS through their willingness to make sacrifices and through comradeship have raised the necessary funds, through voluntary contributions from leaders and men, which have been paid for years to the *Lebensborn* [Lifespring] organization.

Following this statement all misunderstandings should have been cleared up. But it is up to you SS men, as at all times when ideological views have to be put across, to win the understanding of German men and women for this sacred issue so vital to our people and which is beyond the reach of all cheap jokes and mockery.

———

In fact, however, there were no changes to the law altering the position of illegitimate children. Evidently the regime found the issue too controversial in wartime given the conservative attitude on such matters of most Germans, a position strongly endorsed by the churches.

This was not the only aspect of its population policy on which the regime was obliged to adjust its position because of the war. Thus, while the 'euthanasia' programme, which began in 1939, was designed to purge the 'national body' of the unfit in the shape of the mentally ill and handicapped, the operation of the Sterilization Law was largely suspended as a result of a shortage of doctors and the regime was obliged to soften its anti-birth control line.[3] On 6 February, Kurt Daluege, the head of the Order Police, acting for the Reichsführer SS, issued the following instruction to the state governments:

**1158** Re: *Condom dispensers*

In view of the increased threat of the spread of venereal disease as a result of wartime circumstances, I request that for the time being you do not intervene to prevent the installation of condom dispensers in public lavatories and in the lavatories of large pubs if there is a need for them and if the dispensers are installed in an unobtrusive manner.

Such a need can be assumed in cities, especially near railway stations, in places with regular troop concentrations (training areas), as well as in places with large interchange stations etc. In medium-sized and small towns, especially in the countryside, the need to install such dispensers can only be assumed if it is justified by special circumstances.

Nevertheless, the regime did further develop its policy of subjecting marriage to eugenic criteria. Thus in 1941 all those wanting to marry were obliged to present to the Registry Office a certificate declaring there were no objections to marriage (*Eheunbedenklichkeitsbescheinigung!*). However, a medical examination was only carried out when, after the responses to a special questionnaire and to the so-called genealogical questionnaire (*Sippenfragebogen*), one of the engaged couple or their relatives had attracted the attention of the Office of Public Health as being a 'negative factor'.

As the war continued the increasing casualty figures caused growing anxiety among those members of the regime who had a particular interest in and were particularly involved with population policy, namely the SS and the Health agencies. By mid-1942, such were the losses among the German troops that Hitler felt obliged to issue an order recalling from the front the last sons of families where more than one son had been killed. Himmler issued the following order for the SS:

---

[3] On the 'euthanasia' programme see Vol. 3, Chapter 36. On the Sterilization Law of 1933 see Vol. 2, doc. 334.

**1159** The Reichsführer SS

Field Command Post
Hegewald, 15 August 1942

SS Order to the Last Sons

1. As last sons you have been withdrawn from the front line by the Führer's orders. This step has been taken because nation and state have an interest in your families not dying out.

2. It has never been the way of SS men to accept fate and not contribute anything to change it. It is your duty to ensure as quickly as possible by producing children of good blood that you are no longer last sons.

3. Endeavour to guarantee in one year the survival of your ancestors and your families so that you may be available once again to fight in the front line.

Moreover, these concerns occurred against a background of a falling birth rate and a decline in the number of marriages as is clear from the following figures:

**1160** Marriages and Births 1938–1943

| Year | Births | Marriages |
| --- | --- | --- |
| 1938 | 1,348,534 | 645,062 |
| 1939 | 1,413,230 | 774,163 |
| 1940 | 1,402,258 | 613,103 |
| 1941 | 1,308,232 | 504,200 |
| 1942 | 1,055,915 | 525,459 |
| 1943 | 1,124,718 | 514,095 |

There was also a fear that the loss of so many of the fittest males in their prime would lead not only to a fall in the birth rate but also to a qualitative decline in the population.

In response to this situation a number of ideas were put forward as to how best to rectify the deteriorating population situation. One suggestion, for example, was that all German women should be required by law to give birth to at least four children by the age of 35. Another idea which had some support from Hitler and Bormann was the introduction of a so-called national emergency marriage (*Volksnotehe*), which would permit racially and eugenically high-quality front-line soldiers to practise polygamy. Martin Bormann, the head of the Party Chancellery, had strong views on these matters. He himself had nine children and in the winter of 1943 began an affair with a woman called M. whose fiancé had been killed. His wife, Gerda, responded to the news in a letter dated 24 January 1944:

**1161**    . . . I had sensed for some time that there was something between you and M., and when you were here last I felt sure of it. I am so fond of M. myself that I cannot be angry with you, and the children too love her very much, all of them . . . It is a thousand pities that fine girls like these two should be denied children.[4] In the case of M. you will be able to alter this, but then you will have to see to it that one year M. has a child, and the next year I, so that you will always have a wife who is mobile. [WHAT A WILD IDEA].[5] Then we'll put all the children together in the house on the lake, and live together, and the wife who is not having a child will always be able to come and stay with you in Obersalzberg or Berlin. [THAT WOULD NEVER DO EVEN IF THE TWO WOMEN WERE THE MOST INTIMATE FRIENDS. EACH STAYS BEST BY HERSELF. VISITS, ALL RIGHT, BUT EVEN THAT WITHOUT EXAGGERATION.] . . . That she shouldn't have a child is something which seems to me out of the question, you being you [YOU'RE STUPENDOUS.] . . . Only in one thing, dearest, you will have to be careful with her and educate her very gently. She isn't a churchwoman, but at the same time, she is not yet quite free of the Christian faith. If you attack Christianity you will only make her stubborn, [TRUE, THAT SPIRIT IS VERY STRONGLY DEVELOPED IN HER!] Give her enlightening books, but do it discreetly, and then she is sure to come to the right conclusion in due course.

The following memorandum for the two leading officials of the Party Chancellery no doubt represents Hitler's views, but probably with Bormann's own 'spin' on them:

**1162**    Minute for Comrade Friedrichs,          Headquarters, 29 January 1944
Comrade Klopfer

1. During the night of 27/28 January the Führer discussed with us the problems of our national future. The following points can be established from this and earlier conversations and reflections:

After the war our national position will be catastrophic, for our nation is experiencing the second enormous loss of blood within a thirty-year period. We shall undoubtedly win the war militarily but lose it in national terms if we do not decisively transform all our previous views and the attitudes which have resulted from them. For the loss of blood is not a one-off event but rather its effects will go on year after year into the distant future.

How many more children would have been born in this war if it had been possible to grant our front soldiers leave or to have done so more often.

How terrible the political consequences of a war can be is demonstrated by the Thirty Years War. When it started the German nation had a population of over 18 million; at its end barely 3½ million. The consequences of this loss of blood have still not been resolved to this day. For we lost the world domination

[4] Gerda Bormann had also referred to another friend called Ilse R.
[5] Comments in brackets by Bormann.

which, at the beginning of the Thirty Years War the German nation seemed predestined to achieve. Our political divisions lasted until 1871, our national ones basically till 1933; the confessional division has still not been resolved . . .

3. The Führer pointed out that after this war we shall have 3 to 4 million women who have no husbands or cannot get them. Think how many divisions we would be lacking in twenty to forty-five years time, said the Führer.

4. The greater the number of births in a nation the more secure will its future be. The calculation made by many parents, namely that they have to limit the number of their children to secure the future of the ones who have been born is thus completely wrong; the opposite is true! Thus, if they thought about it properly, all women who have one child ought to be particularly concerned to see that not only they themselves but all other women have as many children as possible, because the more children that are born the more secure their children's future will be. That is a very sober assessment of the situation.

5. Now the women who after this tremendous war are not married to a man or do not get married cannot get their children from the Holy Ghost but only from the German men who are left. Increased procreation by individual men is of course only desirable from a national point of view in the case of some of these men. The decent, physically and psychologically healthy men of character should increase their procreation but not those who are physically and mentally deformed . . .

7. There is no point in relying on state regulations alone in this delicate area. The only thing which can convince people is a very serious campaign by the movement. This is issue is too important for stupid jokes. It really is a matter of securing the future of our people.

8. After this war we cannot order all women and girls to have children. The most sensitive—and here the over-used superlative is appropriate—education is required . . .

12. . . . At first many women will accept the general principle but—a lack of logic is after all innate in women—reject it in the personal circumstances of their particular case.

13. For obvious reasons, public, i.e. general education can only begin after the war. Let me just give one reason for this. We cannot now call on the women whose husbands will probably still get killed and we cannot begin the education campaign out of consideration for our soldiers because, beforehand, we would have to get our men who are now soldiers used to these ideas: not every soldier will necessarily want his wife or fiancée to have children by another man after he has been killed . . .

14. Right now we must remove all undesirable barriers to our goal. In particular, we must involve our poets and writers. New novels, stories, and plays which equate 'marriage drama' with 'adultery' will no longer be permitted. Nor will poems, writings or films which treat illegitimate children as inferior. The word illegitimate must be eliminated as I pointed out long ago . . .

15. Now the 'dislike' of illegitimate children undoubtedly has a reason which we too—or rather we in particular—must acknowledge. We too do not want our sisters or daughters irresponsibly to have children by some man or other or from more than one man. We must, therefore, desire that, after this war, our nation's women who cannot get married in the traditional way can join up with a man who really suits them and have children by him.

If I consider carefully how in animal breeding only those animals who suit each other are paired, then I have to observe that the rules which are valid for all mammals also apply to humans. If I want children who have a balanced character and are not inwardly torn then I must state the view that only people who are really suited to each other should have children with each other. We cannot want a woman to have children from any old man even if it is done through so-called long distance procreation [?! *Fernzeugung*]. Rather only people who are really fond of each other should have children. . . .

17. The upshot of all this is: we must hope that women who after the war do not have or get a husband will have a relationship with a man similar to marriage which produces as many children as possible. The fact that such relationships will not last a lifetime is not an argument against them but is natural. Many marriages too end in divorce after a longer or shorter period. Moreover, I believe that two people who are bound together in friendship but do not see each other so often can stay together for a whole lifetime more easily than others and even more so if children strengthen the love and friendship of this bond.

18. I have already mentioned above that any defamation of relationships which are desirable from the point of view of the nation should be prevented. Anyone who insults a woman who has children without a husband must be harshly punished. Anyone who opposes the encouragement of national needs —that will affect a number of clergy—must also be harshly punished . . . .

21. Very many women and girls would gladly have children, indeed many children, if they were sure that they would really be looked after for the whole of their lives. They don't want to have children and then, one day, because the father of these children dies, or becomes poor, or abandons them, to be left with their children dependent on the grace and mercy of some welfare institution.

22. It is clear that women who are employed and have children must be paid more and, moreover, that these women should be assigned flats appropriate to the number of people in the family. After the war I want to build such flats for Party Chancellery personnel who have children in the Sonnenwinkel . . .

24. The number of boarding schools . . . must be enormously increased so that all women who for whatever reason cannot bring up their children themselves without difficulties can send them to boarding schools. That applies to boys as well as girls. These boarding schools are also necessary

because the best and most efficient men are mostly pretty wild in their youth and can hardly be controlled by their mothers on their own . . .

25. Furthermore, these women should not only send their children away to boarding schools when they reach school age but, in accordance with the Führer's directive, the NSV should, as has been previously emphasized, set up the best maternity homes in which the children should be brought up from babyhood to school age. This upbringing in these children's homes must be far better that it generally is in the bosom of the family. That is the great future task for the NSV.

26. For the sake of the future of our nation we must encourage a cult of motherhood and no distinction must be made between women who have been married in the traditional way and women who have children with a man to whom they are bound in friendship; all these mothers are to be honoured equally (naturally this does not apply to those asocial elements who do not even know who is the father of their children) . . .

   (i) We must create for those mothers who have not been officially married in the traditional way a very similar comprehensive state of psychological and material security. Among other things: the children must be able to acquire their father's name without difficulty.

   (ii) In addition: on special request, men must be able to have a firm marriage relationship not only with one woman but with another one in which the women without further ado acquire the man's name and the children their father's name . . .

   (iv) As I mentioned above, it is necessary for us to get rid of and ban the current terms for a 'relationship' which sound more or less morally dubious. On the contrary, we must find good and friendly-sounding expressions. We must, therefore, consider what the relationship between a woman and a man to whom she has not been married in the traditional way can be called; we must consider how the children from such a bond of friendship should be termed.

   The more successful we are in finding a name, the easier it will be to remove existing inhibitions. However, these inhibitions must be removed, for otherwise all the sacrifices of the last World War and this war will have been in vain because our nation will inevitably fall victim to the next storms.

   In twenty or thirty years or forty or fifty years we shall lack the divisions which we shall definitely need if our nation is not to perish.

   (v) After this war childless marriages and bachelors must be taxed much more heavily than hitherto. The current bachelor taxes must be child's play compared with the tax burdens imposed on them in future. The income from these bachelor taxes must serve to support the mothers who have children, i.e. for the mutual support of our attempts to secure offspring.

Please give the whole problem careful thought and then let me have your views.

The following memorandum by Dr Walther Gross, the head of the Racial Political Office of the NSDAP, whose final version was dated 10 October 1944, provides an interesting analysis of these proposals, within the parameters of Nazi ideology and goals, and a relatively realistic assessment of their viability:

**1163**    Understandably, one cannot at the present time make definite pronouncements about the size of the prospective surplus of women. It is clear that, despite the substantial surplus of males of marriageable age, which existed at the beginning of the war, at the end of the war there will be a significant surplus of women. Disagreements about its prospective size are by comparison of secondary importance.

It is understandable that, in our poor situation in terms of population policy, it is a tempting notion that those women, who must inevitably remain single because of the shortage of men and because of our practice of monogamous marriage, should also be able to have children. This aspiration will become even stronger the more we observe that among those women obliged to remain single are a high percentage of particularly valuable ones . . . This principle underlies the following discussion. If there is a better way of coping with the serious problem of the female surplus than through the exclusive recognition of monogamous marriage, if there is a method which provides us with more and not less valuable children than the institution of marriage is capable of doing, then, in view of the seriousness of the situation, Germany will have to go down this path. In our eyes these values are not absolute and eternally valid but the expression of our experience of how best to organize our life. They will have to make way for a superior means if such a one is possible . . .

The majority of their proposals, however, are based on the notion of extending procreation outside the family while maintaining the family itself. All these plans have this idea in common, despite the variety of their titles and their juridical formulations. Irrespective of whether they refer to unmarried or extramarital procreation, mothers' children, state children, people's children or war children, they invariably involve the birth of children to single women whose partners simultaneously live in a marriage and a family with another wife and children. The frequently discussed proposal of liaisons [*Nebenehe*], multiple marriages etc. are basically along the same lines. It invariably involves the simultaneous relationship of a man with several women in which the only difference is whether one of them is granted precedence before the others as wife or housewife or whether they are all granted equal rights.

Numerous plans and memoranda are currently being produced in order to provide a legal basis for these various possibilities . . .

The usual argument is: if these women had only one child each then, with a female surplus of 1 million there would be 1 million more children . . .

Even if one rejects the utopian dreams of racial breeding and instead deals with the realities, we must start from the assumption that, because of their inferior value, it would be better if a not inconsiderable number of groups within the nation did not exist and from the point of view of the general good it would be better if they were to die childless. The fact of the concentration camps, the great efforts being made to fight criminality and sub-humanity, the numerous problems involved in the struggle with those who are physically and spiritually weak and therefore a burden on the community are all proof of the correctness of this opinion. On the other hand, it is equally the case that we must demand from the fit section of our nation vigorous procreation in order to maintain ourselves as a nation. The question is, therefore, whether the reform proposals referred to can produce an additional increase in the section of our nation which is generally worthy of procreation alongside monogamy. This expectation will only be fulfilled if the births occurring outside marriage do not produce a reduction in the number of births within marriage. They must not be allowed to impair the increase in procreation within marriage which may certainly be achieved in peacetime and which is so necessary from the point of view of population policy. Rather we must insist that married couples achieve and sustain a much higher birth rate . . .

There will be no difficulties from a physiological and numerical point of view. Much discussion has been devoted to the economic problems which could arise, for example, through the need for the man to look after a mother and child outside his real family. But all these problems can easily be solved if the state approves the principle of the necessity of such relationships and is prepared to provide appropriate material support. There can also be satisfactory juridical solutions to questions of inheritance, surnames, and rights over education. There may be initial difficulties as a result of all these aspects but there cannot be serious obstacles to achieving the solution which is desirable from the point of view of population policy . . .

In general the psychological situations which arise from extramarital relationships during a simultaneously existing marriage are rightly considered to be particularly problematic. It seems obvious to encourage men to concentrate their extramarital relationships and procreation in their youthful years in the period before they get married. It is suggested that this would avoid some of the feared conflicts. The preconditions and consequences of such a plan need to be carefully thought through in order to clarify the possibilities of its realization . . .

In the case of the woman who is not married, it is necessary to deal with the natural feelings of envy which inevitably will occur as a result of her suffering discrimination vis-à-vis the wife. She will have to bring up her child or children in a much looser relationship to their father and come to terms with the fact that the father of her children devotes more time and attention to the children of the other woman. Experience shows that even in the case of serious-minded women who have been clear in their own minds about the situation from the start, the emotional difficulties increase enormously after the birth of their first child which often lead to attacks on the man's family which were never previously intended or anticipated . . .

In order to deal with these difficulties, memoranda and discussions often refer to a second possibility: polygamy should be recognized as a legal institution with full rights. A scenario is sketched of a common household with the children brought up in common and the two wives living together with their common husband. It is maintained that, given appropriate education and a high level of suitability on the part of all the partners, this would be a viable option, and rejection of it is portrayed as a reactionary view stemming from faulty education in the past. A few successful cases which in the past or in the present appear to illustrate the satisfactory implementation of such polygamous marriages are used as models and as proof for the basic feasibility of this plan.

However, it must be strongly emphasized that, contrary to certain enthusiastic memoranda composed by men, women's response to the question concerning the feasibility of such polygamous unions is for the most part extremely negative . . .

If they reject this possibility, whether from instinct or from inner spiritual necessity, then all such plans are not only without foundation, but from the point of view of population policy represent a threat since, if the nation's women are deeply disturbed, then this will inevitably reduce the level of normal procreation among our married couples and thereby exacerbate a population situation which is already serious . . .

Sometimes it is suggested that the various wives of the same man and their children should each be given a separate household. But this arrangement would not solve the problems . . .

Sometimes, the idea is discussed whereby older men, whose wives have ceased to produce children, would procreate outside marriage. This assumes that the older wives would be able to tolerate their husbands having a relationship with young women of child bearing age more easily from an emotional point of view and that, in addition, in the event of serious conflicts at least no biological disadvantage need be feared since the marriage could not be expected to produce any more children.

Thus, it has sometimes been suggested that the unsatisfactory aspect of this situation and its conflict potential could be avoided through divorce after the marriage partners have passed child-bearing age. When no more children are expected from the marriage and the existing children have reached the age of 14, the husband should be granted the option of divorce and thereby the possibility of a second marriage with a younger woman from which additional children would then emerge.

This proposal is the most likely to avoid intolerable conflicts. But it too is based on the assumption that the women would accept it with the same calmness with which its proposers put it forward. Women are expected to see their role exclusively in the birth and the bringing up of children and to accept that, after fulfilling this task, they will be placed in the corner. It can be assumed that such a trend would also lead to opposition from women and the more valuable and the prouder the woman the stronger would be the opposition. There is a clear threat that such a plan would also provoke a dangerous rejection of it by women, which could then lead them to reduce the numbers of children in marriages, particularly in the case of high-quality women. In view of these possible consequences, a particular protection against divorce has been requested for those wives who have produced four or more children. But this would mean right from the start restricting the application of the whole plan to marriages with an inadequate level of procreation, in other words, effectively making it superfluous. For the whole discussion about increasing the number of births from the reservoir of surplus women has the aim of increasing the number of children above the normal level of procreation within marriage. A further serious objection is the fact that such a radical form of protection against divorce, while increasing the willingness of women to have children, would put off a significant number of men; men would tend to prevent the birth of four or more children in order not to lose the possibility of divorce for ever . . .

I must mention in this context a remarkable conceptual error which is common to all these reform proposals. The undeniable fact that even those marriages concluded after the takeover of power on average do not show a tendency to produce a large number of children, but rather have produced an inadequate number of children, despite all the efforts of our population policy, this fact has led to the assumption that it proves the inadequacy of marriage as an institution in terms of population policy and, therefore, that its replacement by other forms of procreation is desirable . . .

According to the most recent figures for 1 January 1942, there were 18,938,000 married couples. Of these, the wives were under 45 years of age in 11,267,000 marriages. (The figures relate to the territory of the old Reich, including the Alp and Danube Gaus and the Sudetenland; the true figures, therefore, are somewhat higher.) If one assumes that an additional child was born to only 2/3 of the married couples of whom the wife is under 45 years of age, this would produce an increase of 7,511,133 births and, even if only every two of these couples, which were of child bearing age, produced one more child, this would still represent an increase of 5,633,500 births . . .

Thus the result would be that an increase in the number of births per married couple of one child, which is perfectly feasible and achievable, would produce a much larger result than if all the surplus women remaining single were to become mothers.

This fact makes it doubly regrettable that the question of support for the family for reasons of population policy has a very low profile in the minds of many men of authority compared with discussions about the legal status of illegitimate children. From the point of view of the community the improvement in the economic position of the family, a solution to the housing problem geared to the needs of population policy and the removal of other obstacles which stand in the way of the fecundity of the family would be far more economical than any conceivable measure designed to facilitate procreation and births outside the family . . .

The question of what measures are feasible in appropriate cases, in the light of the surplus of women, to secure the birth and upbringing of illegitimate children of parents who are worthy of procreation and how to preserve them from being materially disadvantaged and subjected to moral insults are matters of secondary importance . . .

One must bear in mind that the pressure to discuss this second issue is in present circumstances already causing noticeable disquiet at home as well as at the front. Enemy propaganda, both on the eastern front and again and again on the home front shows that the enemy believe that they can successfully exploit this disquiet to undermine Germany's war morale. The long separation of husbands and wives often combined with the rumours about extreme measures of population policy outside the family must damage morale. Numerous queries indicate that even the enemy lies about the introduction of an official duty to produce children, to be implemented by compulsory measures, are believed by some and are causing concern. Thus, it is urgently necessary to put an end to this public concern by preventing the circulation of relevant memoranda and their more or less public discussion, by prioritizing the necessity for a family policy geared to the needs of population policy, and by limiting the examination of legal regulations for the protection of extramarital motherhood to a small group of unbiased experts without any utopian expectations about their prospective results in population policy terms . . .

The above piece was written in June–July 1944, in practice therefore before the worsening of the military and political situation which has subsequently occurred. Even if the new development once more leads to a significant increase in our war losses, the arguments developed here in my view basically retain their importance and validity.

If, however, the end of the war involves such a serious disturbance of the biological balance of our nation and such dangerous damage to its racial substance that only the most extreme radical measures can save our nation, then such a situation would of itself overcome any considerations or resistance which might be geared to conditions existing in more normal times. Thus, I believe that under present conditions the above statements retain their entire validity, while the extraordinary circumstances referred to would create a new situation without the need for theoretical discussions causing unnecessary disquiet.

━━━

In fact, far from unmarried motherhood or illegitimacy becoming an accepted status, the regime was obliged to respond to the large numbers of women whose fiancés had been killed by arranging for post mortem marriages (a step which clearly ran directly counter to its population policy), for example in the following:

**1164**   The *Oberbürgermeister* of Berlin                     30 June 1944

To the Registrar of Berlin-Kreuzberg

With the request for speedy consideration whether there is proof that a serious intention existed to enter upon matrimony and that there are no grounds for believing that the intention was given up before the death of the fiancé. In the first instance the following may be regarded as proof:

1. Permission to marry from the military unit or a report from the unit that the fiancé had requested permission to marry.
2. Recent letters from the front from the fiancé in the original or as officially endorsed copies.

3. Information from military superiors or comrades of the fiancé which indicate that without any doubt there was an intention to marry.

4. A death certificate or a report from the military unit that the fiancé was killed in action [lit. died a hero's death].

5. Statements by the nearest relatives (parents, brothers and sisters of the engaged couple) as well as from friends and near acquaintances of the fiancé who has been killed.

If the fiancée maintains her wish to marry the man who has been killed in action, she must make a statement to this effect to the Registrar.

The Registrar responsible for the district in which the applicant lives must establish on the basis of a statement which examines the circumstances of the engaged couple whether or not there were any obstacles to the marriage . . .

The Registrar must present the documents with the written statement that, according to his own investigations, there were no legal bans on the marriage. If a child has been born or is expected as a result of the relationship then this should be mentioned and, where necessary, a birth certificate enclosed.

Finally, it should be established whether the fiancé who has been killed left any property or whether a division of the property has taken place and what attitude has been adopted by the heirs to the proposed marriage in relation to the question of the inheritance. The heirs must give their reasons for any opposition.

The necessary investigations should be conducted without delay.

I look forward to receiving your report together with all the documentation. The report should state whether or not the fiancé was a professional soldier and whether a request by the fiancée for a change of her surname has been granted. The enclosed questionnaire should be returned when completed.

At the end of the notice of intended marriage prepared by the Registrar, in which the circumstances of the engaged couple have been considered he must state that, on the basis of his own investigations, there are no obstacles to the marriage.

___

## (iii) Female Sexual Behaviour

Inevitably, with large numbers of German males away at the front and an increasing influx of young male prisoners of war and foreign workers, many of whom lived and worked in close proximity to Germans, there were bound to be a considerable number of instances in which sexual relations with German women and girls occurred. This was particularly the case in rural areas where the prisoners often lived on the farm where they worked. The Nazi leadership regarded this whole matter with grave concern because of the danger of 'racial pollution', particularly in the case of the supposedly inferior Slav nations. From the start of the war any form of association with prisoners of war was punished and sexual relations were treated with especial harshness. This was particularly true where Poles and Russians were involved as is clear from the following document:

**1165**   The Special Court in Königsberg sentenced Frau Martha S. from Wirtberg in the district of Insterburg to ten years penal servitude and ten years loss of civil rights because she had sexual relations with a Polish prisoner of war. The punishment was in accordance with §4 of the Decree to supplement the Penal Regulations for the Protection of the Morale of the German Nation of 25 November 1939. Under that regulation association with prisoners of war is punished with imprisonment and in serious cases with penal servitude if it takes a form which grossly offends healthy popular feelings. The sentence of the Königsberg Special Court represents a serious warning to all those elements who forget their Germanness and injure our national pride during our people's fight for existence.

On 31 January 1940, Himmler issued the following instructions concerning the punishment of German women who had relations with prisoners of war:

**1166**   Re: *Relationships with prisoners of war:*

I. German women and girls who carry on relationships with prisoners of war in such a way that healthy popular feelings are seriously offended are, for the time being, to be taken into protective custody and assigned to a concentration camp for at least one year.

Any social intercourse (e.g. at parties, dances) and, in particular, sexual intercourse is to be regarded as a serious offence against healthy popular feelings.

II. If the women and girls of a community publicly denounce the woman concerned and cut off her hair before she is committed to a concentration camp, the police should not intervene.

Poles or Russians who had sexual relations with German women were liable to be hanged and then their bodies hanging on the gallows would be displayed to their fellow prisoners as a warning.

However, the regime was not just worried about the fact that considerable numbers of German women were having sexual relations with prisoners of war and foreign workers. As the war continued, it became increasingly concerned about what was seen as a general deterioration in the morals of the female population on the home front, a fact which had implications for the morale of the fighting front. On 13 April 1944 the SD produced the following report to the Reich Treasurer of the NSDAP:

**1167**                         *Immoral Behaviour of German Women*
                                  *Risks—Reasons—Proposals*

I. Women have been removed from their peacetime situation to a far greater extent in this war than in the First World War. They are in employment, often outside their home districts, or have been transplanted to strange surroundings and conditions as a result of evacuation from the districts threatened by air raids. Many hundreds of thousands of girls and women are separated from their parents, fiancés and husbands and can only be with them for short periods of leave.

As a result of the length of the war, these conditions have led to a *moral decline* on the part of some of these women. Although the signs of immorality are not yet as extensive as in the years 1914/18, nevertheless there are reports from all parts of the Reich which concur in stating that these are not exceptional cases, but rather that *large numbers of women* are tending to be *increasingly sexually active.* This is particularly evident in the case of *soldiers' wives.* In many places there are notorious clubs where soldiers' wives try to meet men in order to take them home with them. In the case of such behaviour the children are often left to look after themselves and are liable to go astray.

The following are a number of reported examples:

A woman lives in a basement room with her three children aged 2–8. She receives repeated visits from soldiers also at night. She opens an umbrella over the bed so that the children cannot see her promiscuous activity. The local population are very annoyed by the way this woman carries on.

A first lieutenant's wife who is deployed elsewhere goes around with other officers almost every day and receives visits from them in her flat. When the husband came home on leave, another officer had to move out in a hurry. Although the woman has no children and lives in a three bedroom flat, she refused to have a sergeant-major billeted on her . . .

Most of the cases which become known involve women from the lower classes. However, according to the reports, the morals of women from other classes are going the same way. The reason why there have been fewer examples from the upper classes so far is that these women can entertain male acquaintances without being so easily observed as someone who lives in a bedsit or a small flat in a crowded block.

According to the reports, soldiers often complain that the authorities at home remain passive in the face of this behaviour by the soldiers' wives or do not act with sufficient vigour. An NCO, who had been informed by neighbours on a number of occasions about his wife's promiscuous behaviour, contacted his [NSDAP] branch leader with the request to look into these reports. He was then informed that these accusations were unfounded, that his wife had invariably behaved impeccably and there were no grounds for the soldier's suspicion. During his leave, the NCO contracted venereal disease from his wife and only then discovered that a member of the Luftwaffe had already reported that he had been infected by his wife . . .

Apart from the soldiers' wives, who often cause annoyance by their immoral way of life, the morals of large numbers of *single women* are, in the population's view, not beyond reproach and show a strong tendency to promiscuity as can be seen from the large numbers of pregnancies and births among 14–18 year olds and of cases of venereal disease . . .

*Sexual relationships with prisoners of war and ethnic alien workers* represent a particular form of moral turpitude. In general the population strongly disapproves of such relationships. Even women and girls who have formed such relationships with ethnic aliens are generally aware that they have done wrong. Nevertheless, there is a rising curve of such cases reported from rural districts and industrial cities where close contact with the ethnic aliens is unavoidable, which must be regarded as disturbing. It is repeatedly noted that the Catholic clergy, with their references to the equality of all people in the sight of God, arouse compassion for the prisoners of war and the ethnic alien civilian workers, particularly among women in the countryside, and thereby weaken their inhibitions against relationships with these people.

II. According to the reports the following represent particularly *dangerous aspects*:

    1. The effect of the poor example being set.
    2. A continual reduction of women in men's eyes.
    3. The impact of marital infidelities on men at the front.

In view of the moral decline among some women, men, particularly soldiers, are already saying that 'nowadays any women can be had'. While, on the one hand, they welcome a more positive response from women, on the other hand, they condemn it.

A soldier (graduate) writes:

> What I find extremely upsetting about the stories of my comrades is their moral attitude. The stories of crowds and queues in certain ugly streets and of houses only for officers, but above all, the stories of the absolutely incredible behaviour of the female signals auxiliaries. All soldiers, even the most dubious ones, are agreed that they would never marry a female signals auxiliary. A man who has contacts with the authorities says that venereal disease among girls has overtaken the First World War levels and the effect of this on fertility will create serious problems for post-war population policy. But the moral attitudes of men are also shocking. I keep asking myself: what has happened to the ideal of the German man? National Socialism, i.e. the Party will have a post-war task of tremendous importance. Indeed, it will be a matter of life and death.

The effect of the marital infidelities of soldiers' wives at the front must be regarded as particularly serious. The men are very upset by news from their neighbours about their wives' behaviour. In many cases the state is then blamed for not being in a position to keep the family in order while they are at the front. Often Party offices and the police are requested to keep a watch on the wives or they ask their military superiors for help.

> The Military Court of the Section Field Post No. 38,843 has been informed by Private T. that his wife has committed adultery. T. was at the front during this period. He has been away for over a year. It is probable that he will have to go for several more months without leave. He has been severely shocked by his wife's dishonourable behaviour. The Military Court hereby informs the police of this behaviour which has weakened the front. It is

proposed that Frau T., who is not yet in employment, should be placed in a labour camp after the birth of her child which is expected in May. This is advisable, apart from anything else, in order to ensure that the adulteress cannot inflict any further damage through her promiscuous behaviour. T's children can very easily be placed with her mother, who also lives in Landsberg. Finally, the Military Court requests that the name of the adulterer should be ascertained through interrogating the wife so that proceedings can also be taken against him, since the front cannot tolerate unscrupulous elements at home destroying the marriages of front-line soldiers . . .

III. The following reasons are put forward to explain the development of immorality among women:

1. *Young women* have retained few of the things which previously interested them and provided their social pleasures before marriage (dancing, fashion, cafes, travel, books, tennis, riding etc.) In addition, there is the fact that, by contrast with their previous practice of preaching to their daughters that they should be reserved in their behaviour towards men, mothers now frequently point out to them how many more marriageable women than men there will be after the war and so encourage them to try and get a husband as early as possible. As far as young men are concerned, they regard relations with girls less in terms of the choice of a wife and much more as friendships without any commitment. For young men are no longer in a position to plan long-term. They know that they will be called up at 16 or 17 years of age as anti-aircraft auxiliaries, Labour Service men or soldiers, and that their future fate will be uncertain. Thus, they regard young girls as comrades or 'girl friends' and their aim is more to have as carefree a love affair as possible than to enter into a deeper commitment geared to the longer term.

2. In the case of the *soldiers' wives* sexual needs are often the cause of the decline in their moral behaviour, particularly when there are long intervals between brief periods of leave for their husbands. The leaders of military units report that they receive letters from wives with the urgent request for leave for their husbands with the frank declaration that, in the event of leave not being granted, the wives will be compelled to satisfy their urges elsewhere ('to go on the streets').

3. The comparatively *high level of family allowances for the wives of soldiers and war widows* is also of vital importance. These women are not dependent on gainful employment since in many cases the amount of family allowance permits them a higher standard of living than they had before the war. The time and money at their disposal encourages them to spend their afternoons and evenings in cafés and bars; they can easily afford expensive wines and spirits and, furthermore, are in a position to invite men—mainly soldiers—to join them in this.

4. The feeling that men in barracks in occupied territories etc. would not pass by the opportunity of 'having a bit on the side' leads some women to the view that they 'had equal rights and were also entitled to amuse

themselves'. *Women and girls who live in the districts threatened by air raids* often try and justify their tendency to live their lives to the full with the claim that they were just as entitled as the front soldiers to partake of the very limited joys of life while they still could. An enemy bomb could easily kill them the following night or at least destroy their homes. Such considerations often remove their last inhibitions and their sense of responsibility vis-à-vis their husbands and children.

5. The cause of the moral decline of women is seen not least in the excessive eroticization of public life, which continually finds expression in the texts of hit songs, in films, illustrated newspapers, short stories and theatrical performances.

6. *The behaviour of leading figures* has had a pernicious influence on some women. The divorces of leading local personalities as well as their notorious liaisons with artistes or secretaries set a bad example.

7. In the case of those women who have no connections through which to acquire scarce commodities a certain role is played by the possibility of securing silk stockings, cloth, shoes, cigarettes and spirits from relationships with soldiers from the occupied territories.

8. Relationships with ethnic aliens are sometimes encouraged by seduction with such desirable items (chocolate). In the case of the French, women find their flattering gallantry attractive and anticipate from them the satisfaction of a certain desire for exotic sexual experience.

IV. The population are not unaware of the fact that the immoral behaviour of German women is in part an inevitable consequence of the war (e.g. the front soldiers' rare and brief periods of leave). But they are of the opinion that these excesses must be fought and that measures must be taken so that, even if a further development in this direction and an infection of the weak-willed masses cannot be completely prevented, it will nevertheless be made more difficult.

The following proposals have been drawn up:

1. In the demand for a healthy and natural sexual morality *National Socialist racial and population policy* must be removed even more strongly than hitherto from all tendencies towards sexual excess, which demonstrate a lack of responsibility towards the community and towards people's own health and efficiency.

2. The *original values of German womanhood* should be referred to and emphasized much more strongly than hitherto in the press, radio, and film. It is not sufficient for women to be referred to as 'the guardians of morality' 'protectors of life' etc. in books which will not be read by the majority and which nowadays are unobtainable by those who are interested, whereas films, hit songs, short stories and illustrations (the entertainment section of journals, fashion journals) cultivate the type of the erotic woman, who bewitches all the men.

The eroticization of public life must be stopped. It is not necessary for every hit song to be given a more or less erotic lyric. Films should at last get round to having plots which are appropriate to the requirements of population policy and which portray women without 'a provocative image' and instead as national socialist ideology wishes German people to be both now and in the future. Comics and journals ought to start portraying bachelors as comic types instead of treating the relationship between men and women simply in terms of erotic sexual tension.

3. A further possibility is envisaged in an *appeal to men*:

(a) the national socialist *Wehrmacht* should make it a principle of its disciplinary procedures that sexual intercourse between a member of the Wehrmacht and the wife of another man in the Wehrmacht represents a very serious breach of honour and comradeship which must be rigorously punished.

(b) furthermore, this view should become a fixed principle in *the other offices and work places* (boycott of the person concerned by his workmates).

4. Soldiers' wives who, in the absence of their husbands, are guilty of particularly reprehensible behaviour through promiscuous relations with men, who sit around in bars with the clear intention of meeting men and who thereby neglect their children should:

(a) have their family allowance cut or stopped;

(b) be conscripted for work irrespective of their age and of whether or not they have children, who if necessary could be accommodated in homes.

## (iv) Homosexuality

Long before the war the Nazis had taken a tough line against male homosexuality. In an amendment to the Reich Penal Code of 28 June 1935, the notorious §175, which made 'unnatural sexual offences between persons of the male sex' a penal offence, was broadened to include not just intercourse but all sexual activity, including even embraces, engaged in by adults. On 10 October 1936 a secret order from Himmler in his role of Chief of the German Police established a special Reich Office for the Combating of Homosexuality and Abortion, which gathered information and coordinated the campaign against homosexuality. Among other things, the police carried out periodic raids on known or suspected homosexual haunts. As a result of all this increased activity the number of arrests shot up. Whereas between 1931 and 1933 a total of 2,319 people were sentenced by the courts under §175, in the years 1937–9 there were 24,450 sentences. Many offenders were consigned to concentration camps after the completion of their sentence under the preventive detention measure introduced by the regime for habitual criminals.

In a lecture delivered to a conference of medical heads of department and experts on 5–6 April 1937, the head of the new Reich Office, Dr Josef Meisinger, defined the position of his office and indeed of the SS in general on the question of homosexuality as follows:

**1168** . . . Since, as we know, homosexuals are useless for normal sexual intercourse, homosexuality also has an effect on young blood and will eventually lead to a drop in the birth rate. The result is a general weakening of the nation's strength of the kind that threatens not least a nation's military capacity. In the end, however, homosexuality is a permanent threat to order in the life of the state. Apart from being itself a punishable violation of that order, it is especially dangerous because it is often the starting point for a series of further crimes. Very often it comes as a preliminary to treason and, in numerous cases it lays the basis for blackmail . . .

If one is really to appreciate the hidden danger of homosexuality, it is no longer enough to consider it as before from a narrowly criminal viewpoint. Because it is now so enormously widespread, it has actually developed into a phenomenon of the most far-reaching consequence for the survival of the nation and state. For this reason, however, homosexuality can no longer be regarded simply from the viewpoint of criminal investigation; it has become a problem with political importance. This being so, it cannot be the task of the police to investigate homosexuality scientifically. At the most it can take account of scientific conclusions in its work. Their task is to ascertain homosexual trends and their damaging effects, so as to avert the danger that this phenomenon represents for nation and state. No one says to the police: you shouldn't arrest this thief because he might have acquired kleptomania. Similarly, once we have recognized that a homosexual is an enemy of the state, we shan't ask the police—and much less the Political Police—whether he has acquired his vice or whether he was born with it. I should mention here that experience has shown beyond doubt that only a vanishingly small number of homosexuals have a truly homosexual inclination, that most of them by far have been quite normally active at one time or another and then turned to this area simply because they were sated with life's pleasures or for various other reasons such as fear of venereal diseases. I should also say that, with firm education and order, and regulated labour, a great number of homosexuals who have come to the attention of the authorities have been taught to become useful members of the national community.

In connection with the combating of homosexuality may I here briefly dwell on a problem that has often arisen in the recent period: namely the combating of lesbianism. In our view the danger to the nation's survival is here not at all as great as in the case of homosexual men. Quite different presuppositions are involved. First, it should not be forgotten that in Germany we have always had more females than males; second, we lost 2 million men in the war; and, third, that of the available men several more million do not count because they are homosexuals. The fact that a sizeable part of the female sex is in a state of sexual crisis cannot be denied. To the best of our knowledge, however—insofar as it has been at all possible to carry out reliable and discreet investigations—most girls who are active as lesbians are far from being abnormally inclined. If such girls later have the opportunity to assume the purpose given them by nature, they will certainly not decline. Many other factors are involved in lesbian activity: e.g. a lack of male acquaintances, a stern upbringing, and so on. If we are really to speak of lesbian activity, it is crucially important to ask what was the object of mental images when sexual behaviour was taking place. There is reason to suppose that for an overwhelming majority the imagination was directed to normal intercourse. Proof of this is the onanistic devices often found among women, not least the ever popular candle.

▬▬

During the Second World War, the new harsh attitude towards homosexuality was reflected in the increase in the number of prosecutions by comparison with the First World War period. Thus, whereas in the First World War homosexual acts made up less than 5 per cent of sexual offences, in the Second World War it was over 40 per cent. With the outbreak of war, the Wehrmacht acquired a growing responsibility for dealing with the matter as more and more men were called up into the armed forces. In 1939 there were 7,614 convictions of civilian adults for homosexual offences and 690 of youths. In 1940 this had dropped to 3,773 adults and 427 youths. In 1941 there were 3,739 convictions of adults and 645 of youths. In the Wehrmacht there were 1,134 convictions in 1940 and 1,700 in 1941, a figure which then remained more or less constant for the rest of the war. By 30 July 1944, there had been a total of just under 7,000 convictions in the Wehrmacht.[6]

Basically pragmatic on this issue, Hitler now took a strong line and made his views clear at a meeting in August 1941:

**1169**    Yesterday evening the Führer spoke for a long time about the plague of homosexuality. He said that we must prosecute it with ruthless severity, because there was a time in youth when boys' sexual feelings could be easily influenced in the wrong direction; it was precisely at that age that boys were corrupted by homosexuals. More often than not, a homosexual seduces a huge number of boys, so that homosexuality is actually as infectious and as dangerous as the plague. But our youth must not be lost to us—on the contrary, it must be brought up properly. So wherever symptoms of homosexuality appear among the youth, they should be attacked with barbaric severity.

Precisely our state and our order can and must be based only on the performance principle. Any kind of favouritism is to be rejected; we want no specially protected children and so on.

A homosexual, however, does *not* judge other men by their performance; he dismisses the most capable men even though, or even because, they are not homosexual; for he prefers homosexuals. In the Röhm case and others we saw that a homosexual will fill all positions of authority with other homosexuals.[7]

---

[6] Figures in F. Seidler, *Prostitution, Homosexualität, Selbstverstümmelung. Probleme der deutschen Sanitätsführung 1939–1945* (Berlin 1952), pp. 205–06.
[7] On Röhm see Vol. 1, docs 119–29.

Especially in the Party and its various organizations, as well as in the Wehrmacht, it is necessary to act with ruthless severity against any case of homosexuality that appears in its ranks. If this is done the state apparatus will remain clean, and it must remain clean.

In *one* organization, however, any case of homosexuality must be punished with death, and that is in the Hitler Youth. If it is to be the elite of the nation, then any misconduct in its ranks must never be given any other sentence.

____

While there had been no uniform view within the regime about the nature of homosexuality (innate or socially conditioned) or its best treatment, Himmler had long been a hard-liner on the matter and in November 1941 he persuaded Hitler to agree to issue the following order, which was kept secret in order not to damage the reputation of the SS in the eyes of the public:

**1170** The Führer                                      Führer Headquarters
                                                         15 November 1941

In order to keep the SS and Police clean of vermin with homosexual inclinations, I hereby resolved:
I. For members of the SS and Police the following sentences shall apply instead of §§175 and 175a of the Reich Penal Code:
A member of the SS and Police who commits unnatural acts with another man or lets himself be abused for unnatural acts shall be punished with death.

In less serious cases penal servitude or imprisonment of not less than 6 months may be imposed.

Where a member of the SS or Police was not yet 21 years of age at the time of the offences and was seduced into it, the court may in especially minor cases refrain from punishment.
II. Imposition of the sentences threatened under I is independent of the offender's age.
III. The crimes designated under I come under the jurisdiction of special SS and Police courts in accordance with the provisions applying to them. The competence of Wehrmacht courts is not affected.
IV. The provisions necessary to enforce and supplement this decree shall be ordered by the Reichsführer SS and Chief of the German Police in the Reich Ministry of the Interior.

The Führer                                    [signed]: ADOLF HITLER
____

Meanwhile, there had been considerable discussion within the Wehrmacht about how to respond to homosexual offences, which in turn led to a renewal of the ongoing debate about the causes of homosexuality and whether or not it was an innate condition or acquired through corruption. Finally, on 19 May 1943 the head of OKW, Field-Marshal Keitel, issued the following Guidelines for the Handling of Criminal Cases of Unnatural Sexual Acts (§§175, 175a and 330a of the Reich Penal Code):

**1171**                                    A

A distinction must be made between:
I. offenders who have acted out of a predisposition of an acquired and clearly incorrigible urge;
II. offenders who have strayed on only one occasion, especially if they were seduced;
III. offenders in whom a tendency remains a matters of doubt.

On I:
The tendency must be established in the judgement. The most careful enquiries are necessary, already in the preliminary stages and not only at the main hearing. Questioning of comrades, including from the Wehrmacht reserve. Perhaps evidence going back before military service. If there are doubts the offender may be placed in the reserve. The court in the person's home area has more opportunity, in cooperation with the Reich Office for the Combating of Homosexuality and Abortion at the Reich Criminal Police Bureau, to arrive at the necessary conclusions.

In the case of serious crimes, long sentences of penal servitude are appropriate. In especially serious cases the death penalty may be imposed, in accordance with the more serious range of sentences allowed under §5a of the Special Wartime Penal Ordinance. Convicts should be discharged from military service if they are not already ineligible as a result of a verdict having the force of law. If the execution of the sentence is not directly transferred to the public authorities, the judge shall request that they take over the execution of sentence.

On II:
Once again the most careful enquiries. That the offence [was] committed under the influence of alcohol is not by itself proof that no tendency is present. Special vigilance in offences by superiors against subordinates. To conclude that no tendency is present is just as fraught with consequences as a positive conclusion.

Such convicts should be treated in accordance with the general provisions, and so are eligible for parole in the face of the enemy after completion of all or part of their sentence.

On III:
In these cases detention in a field punishment camp or completion of sentence in field penal units. Strictest supervision necessary both there and after release among the troops. If unusable for military purposes, discharge and transfer to Reich administration of justice for further serving of sentence. Treat repetition according to I.

**B**

Cases judged before these guidelines were decreed should in general also be handled in accordance with them. This applies especially to the question of whether the man may or may not remain in military service. If, contrary to I of the guidelines, the man has been kept on duty, he should be discharged even if he has proved himself as a soldier. An exception may be made only if such a soldier has behaved irreproachably over a long period of time, so that as far as anyone can judge a repetition is not be looked after [sic].

**C**

It is recommended that confirmation is still reserved for a person in higher authority.

——

After completion of a prison sentence many homosexuals were then taken into preventive detention in a concentration camp. The number of civilian homosexuals confined to a concentration camp during the war has been estimated to be at least 2,300 per year.[8] Here they were obliged to wear a pink triangle distinguishing their category of prisoners and were subjected to particularly harsh treatment surpassed only by that meted out to the Jews and some 'asocials'.

## List of Sources

1154   *Aus deutschen Urkunden,* op. cit, pp. 173–4.
1155   Bundesarchiv Berlin (BAB) ZSlg. 101/34.
1156   *Aus deutschen Urkunden,* pp. 175–7.
1157   Ibid., pp. 174–5.
1158   Hauptstaatsarchiv Stuttgart (HStAS) E 151 CII Bu 754.
1159   *Aus deutschen Urkunden,* p. 177.
1160   *Statistisches Handbuch von Deutschland 1928–1944* (Munich 1948), p. 47.
1161   H.R. Trevor-Roper ed., *The Bormann Letters* (London 1954), pp. 42–3.
1162   H.-A. Jacobsen & W. Jochmann, eds, *Ausgewählte Dokumente zur Geschichte des Nationalsozialismus,* Vol. 2 (Bielefeld 1964), n.p.
1163   *Aus deutschen Urkunden,* pp. 179–83.
1164   Landesarchiv Berlin (LAB) Rep. 57, Nr. 121.
1165   *Völkischer Beobachter* 28.12.1939.
1166   BAB R 58/272.
1167   H. Boberach, *Meldungen aus dem Reich,* Vol. 16 (Herrsching 1984), pp. 6481–8.
1168   G. Gau, *Hidden Holocaust* (London 1995), pp. 113–15.
1169   Ibid., pp. 165–6.
1170   Ibid., pp. 176–8.
1171   Ibid., pp. 193–4.

————

[8] See Seidler, op. cit., p. 215.

# CHAPTER 47

# *Youth*

## (i) Introduction

The treatment of young people, i.e. those under the age of 18, raised a number of issues for the regime. In the first place, young people represented the future of the nation and so their health, education, ideological indoctrination and moral welfare was regarded as a major priority. Concern for the health of youth was, for example, reflected in the strict regulations, issued by the Reich Labour Ministry, limiting the hours and type of work to be performed by young people. Also, the Reich Education Ministry lobbied hard for the maintenance of a full programme of school education. At the same time, however, young people, or at any rate those over the age of 10, were capable of contributing to the war effort in a variety of different ways and so constituted a significant resource which could be deployed on the home front. Policy towards and the treatment of young people was determined by these various considerations which, however, increasingly came into conflict with each other. For the growing shortage of adult males progressively compelled the regime to call on young people to perform tasks which jeopardized their education, health and ultimately their lives. Moreover, well before the end of the war teenage boys were no longer being regarded as potential or future soldiers but were actually being called upon to act as soldiers by manning anti-aircraft guns. The culmination of this process was the deployment during the last months of the war of boys in their early teens in a suicidal role as anti-tank units.

## (ii) The Hitler Youth (HJ) and League of German Girls (BdM)

Up to the age of 14 young people's lives were dominated by three authorities: parents, school and the Hitler Youth/League of German Girls in their junior forms of the German Young People (*Deutsches Jungvolk*) and the Young Girls' League (*Jungmädelbund*). At the age of 14 many young people left school to enter employment or an apprenticeship. However, until the age of 19 they were still subject to the authority of their parents and of the HJ, membership of which had been made compulsory in a decree of February 1939 which established the so-called Youth Service Duty.[1]

Even before the war the HJ had involved its members in a whole range of tasks such as collecting money for the Winter Aid programme, collecting medicinal herbs and assisting with the harvest. With the outbreak of war the range of these tasks expanded and the intensity of commitment increased and, above all, they were geared specifically to the war effort. In the case of boys the Hitler Youth focused almost entirely on preparing them for their future role as soldiers. The following two documents give some idea of the HJ's wartime role. The first contains excerpts from an article in the January 1940 issue of the official Nazi Party monthly journal (*NS Monatshefte*) with the title 'German Youth on the Domestic Front':

**1172**    The war has confronted youth only to a limited extent with completely new types of task; essentially their involvement has simply been increased. For, as is well known, in the past the Hitler Youth has always been deployed wherever it was needed: to help with the harvest, to pick berries, to collect acorns, beechnuts, chestnuts and sunflower seeds, to salvage valuable scrap, in the Winter Aid programme etc. However insignificant the actions of the HJ may at first sight appear to be, their value becomes apparent if one observes the overall effect of the work carried out by 8 million young people. The figures speak impressively for themselves: Germany's consumption of camomile blossoms, our most frequently used medicinal herb, amounts to 800,000 kilogrammes, of which in the past only 1 per cent was collected in Germany, whereas 99 per cent, with a value of 1.6 million marks, was imported. In the same way, almost all the—not exactly rare—stinging nettles were imported with the result that the chemical industry was planning to plant fields of them . . .

The shortage of agricultural labour led the HJ some years ago to place itself at the disposal of the campaign to liberate Germany from dependence on food imports. The resultant positive experiences persuaded the Reich Youth Leader to make help with the harvest one of the compulsory duties of the HJ so that, as a result, agriculture acquired an adequate labour reserve. This also had the

---

[1] See Vol. 2, doc. 300.

advantage that boys and girls were made more and more familiar with farming work and can now be regarded as trained labour . . . Help with the harvest was also the first wartime activity of the boys and girls as the peasants and agricultural workers were called up into the armed forces in large numbers: 600,000 boys and girls from the ranks of the HJ were employed in bringing in the harvest. According to an official report from the province of Brandenburg, without the boys and girls of the HJ it would have been impossible to have brought in the harvest this year . . .

. . . The plans for the development of pre-military training came into force a month after the outbreak of war and met all the Wehrmacht's requirements. The training is intended to make it easier for the Wehrmacht personnel to carry out the difficult task of training recruits. It involves all 10–18-year-old boys in the HJ. Fieldcraft lies at the core of this military training. There are schools ready to train the necessary number of fieldcraft instructors and 30,000 pass through each year. The same number will be turned out by the Wehrmacht as a result of a recent agreement between the Reich Youth Leadership and the Supreme Command of the Wehrmacht. By practising fieldcraft, which represents a kind of pre-infantry training, the boys learn how to master the territory in which they are operating, which involves disguise and camouflage, the use of every hollow in the ground, orientation in darkness and in a strange environment. These exercises, which have the character of military training and at the same time satisfy the youthful urge to play games, correspond to the tasks of military reconnaissance units. Since—unlike many foreign youth organizations—the HJ does not carry military weapons—this is all the training the HJ can carry out. But this is sufficient in order to learn movement in the field so that when it comes to the real thing it has become a matter of habit.

Everyone involved in Wehrmacht training values this preliminary practice, for the difference between a completely inexperienced recruit and a member of the HJ who has been trained in this way, is unmistakable. That is above all the view of those senior Wehrmacht officers who frequently attend the exercises of the HJ. In addition, the HJ fieldcraft plans have always been based on the infantry training manual so that all the Wehrmacht requirements are fulfilled and so neither the Wehrmacht's fieldcraft instructors nor the HJ leaders need to change their practices for the military instructor training which now takes place every Sunday. There are sufficient instructors, training grounds and shooting stands available.

An activity which is closely linked to the fieldcraft training and which has been carried out for years by the HJ is shooting practice with small-calibre weapons. More than a million good shots, some of them even top-class shots, have emerged from this training during peacetime. Recently 4000 HJ shooting certificates, only awarded after really good results, have been issued every month. That means that the HJ has been turning out the equivalent of a regiment of good average shots every month. And, although the boys do not yet learn to use a military weapon in their shooting practice, nevertheless the fact that they learn how to use and look after a small-calibre weapon is of incalculable value for their later training as recruits.

While the training plans for fieldcraft and shooting practice apply to all HJ units equally, the military training of the special formations also involves an intensification of the training in their particular branch. For the members of the motorized HJ, the Naval HJ, the Air HJ, and the Signals HJ are intended to provide the recruits for the corresponding branches of the Wehrmacht . . .

All the forty-four leadership schools of the HJ are currently deployed for the preparation of the young leaders for their war tasks. By the end of 1939 ninety-eight fortnightly war courses for the senior HJ leaders and seventy-six courses for the middle-rank leadership had been carried out involving a total of over 12,000 HJ leaders. The training of the leaders in the leadership schools is intended to instruct them in the effective deployment of the HJ formations in wartime. Thus the curriculum is as varied as the tasks carried out by the HJ. The boys are acquainted with the possible activities of the HJ in the service of the Wehrmacht, the party, the air raid and fire brigade services, hospitals, the distribution of ration cards, the collection of medicinal herbs and scrap, the pilot service during the blackout and the Winter Aid collections.

The treatment of political and ideological questions in the leadership schools is geared to the organization of the HJ evening sessions which at the present time are primarily focused on the inculcation of a military spirit in young people.

The main method for inculcating a military spirit is through the evening sessions at which the main topics to be treated are both the great soldiers of the German past and the current war situation. This education is being backed up through the programme 'Front Soldiers Speak to the HJ', which involves participants in the present war talking about their experiences to the boys at their evening sessions and also through the recently established 'War Library of German Youth', whose pamphlets—published with the cooperation of the headquarters of the three armed services—treat the war developments in an easily understood fashion.

In order to provide new opportunities for the ideological and political indoctrination of young people Reich Minister Dr Goebbels placed the cinemas at the disposal of the HJ for the showing of youth films and for holding ceremonial hours on two Sundays each month.

The success of such political education became very clearly evident in the HJ collection for the War Winter Aid programme in December. This action with the slogan 'Piratical War of the Hitler Youth' demonstrated the political wit of our boys and showed that young people have completely grasped the point of our defensive struggle against British piracy.

The girls are no less committed than the boys. In accordance with their female character and training they find employment in the auxiliary services of the Red Cross, assisting large families and peasants' wives in the household; they look after the children of working mothers, help with the distribution of ration cards, assist in kitchens and with the railway station service. The BdM leaders are being prepared for these tasks at the 44 BdM leaders' schools.

———

The following document contains excerpts from the Hitler Youth War Service Plan for 1940 issued on 3 February 1940:

**1173**    1. *Ideological and political indoctrination*

The weekly evening sessions for Hitler Youth and BdM and the afternoon sessions for the German Young People and the Young Girls' League for ideological indoctrination and character training will be retained. In the event that a fifth Wednesday or Thursday falls within the month, a further meeting will be arranged. The evening and afternoon sessions may only last two hours. In the case of the BdM section 'Faith and Beauty' the evening sessions of the various working groups will replace the regular BdM evening.

The Hitler Youth will also continue to carry out 'Youth Meetings'. These events which, in contrast to the Youth Film Hours are not ceremonial in character but rather are modelled on the 'time of struggle' [i.e. pre-1933], are intended to articulate the political and combative will of youth. Since the HJ evening session following the 'Youth Meetings' will be cancelled, an additional burden on young people will be avoided.

2. *Cultural activity*

The cultural activity of the HJ will also be continued. In the summer there will again be singing in the town and village squares. The brass and pipe bands will perform in the open air and at the Youth Meetings and the Youth Film Hours. The HJ will also continue to sing and play at parents' evenings, and in hospitals and factories. The boys and girls will be exposed to our nation's most valuable cultural heritage in the youth concerts, theatre evenings, poetry recitals and other performances of the Hitler Youth Cultural Circle organization.

3. *Physical training*

All units with the exception of the 16–18 year old Hitler Youth boys and the members of the BdM section 'Faith and Beauty' will take part in a two-hour sports session every week involving basic gymnastics. This compulsory sport can be scheduled for weekdays or Sundays depending on the local availability of gymnasia and sports fields. However, if held on Sundays it should only be on the first and third Sundays of the month. Basic gymnastics for the 14- and 15-year-old members of the special units [e.g. the Naval HJ] will take place twice a month . . . The second and fourth Sundays of the month are available for voluntary sports.

4. *Pre-military training*

The training plan of the 16–18-year-old Hitler Youth boys is extended from six to twelve months so that the final tests will be finished by 15 October 1940. The Saturday instruction will in future only take place every fortnight and the shooting and fieldcraft duties on two Sundays in the month.

5. *Leadership training*

Candidates for leadership posts will increasingly be concentrated in Leadership Training units and systematically trained. In view of the frequent change in HJ leaders as a result of their being called up, it is vitally important even for the smallest units to ensure that there is always a team of leadership candidates in training ready to take over. The district leaders of the HJ and BdM will pay particular attention to ensuring the careful selection of leaders. The HJ leadership will continue to be systematically trained in a monthly leadership session ...

### 6. *Parades*
Parades will take place every two months in winter and every month in summer and be timed to coincide with some other event. Long periods of standing around and long marches to the parade ground are to be avoided. Parades of large units are forbidden.

### 7. *General duty regulations*
As has already been laid down, the evening sessions for the German Young People and German Girls' League will end at 6 o'clock in the evening during February 1940, 7 o'clock during March and during the summer months until the end of September at 8 o'clock. In October, they will end at the latest at 7 o'clock, during November and December at 6 o'clock. The HJ and BdM evening sessions will end at 10 o'clock. Party rallies and evenings put on by the Cultural Circle (theatre performances, concerts etc.) are excluded from this regulation.

Bearing parents in mind and the heavy demands on young people made by school and job, leaders are expected to ensure that these times are strictly adhered to ... Parents will thereby be guaranteed that they can expect their boys and girls back from the Hitler Youth at specified times. Regular times also mean that parents no longer have to be continually informed about the times.

As is clear from the timetable, the Hitler Youth requires the first and third Sundays of the month for its duties. The second and fourth Sundays are free; on these days boys and girls are at the disposal of their parents in so far as they do not report for voluntary sports. In view of the extensive educational tasks which the Hitler Youth has to fulfil alongside parents and school, leave of absence on the Sundays designated for duty cannot be granted.

### 8. *Summer time duties*
Trips and camps will continue to take place during the summer months. However, only short trips and camps lasting a fortnight with a maximum number of 100 boys taking part are permitted. Trips and camps will be adjusted to the prevailing circumstances and may only be carried out in the local area or in the region. Berlin, Hamburg and Vienna are exceptions in this respect. The railways may not be used for the purpose of trips and camps. Trips and travel to and from camps will be carried out by bicycle in accordance with health regulations. The girls and boys may only be absent from their parents for a longer period at harvest time. Only one weekend trip during the summer months is permitted.

### 9. *Special actions during war time*
In addition to the war-time duties, the HJ and BdM will continue to be called upon for collections and other forms of assistance. However, if the additional duties last for a lengthy period, the regular duties will be correspondingly reduced. Those Hitler Youth boys involved in pre-military training will be absolved from extra duties.

The 13- and 14-year-old cubs and young girls will continue to be involved in air raid protection training. It will be carried out by the unit leaders in eight two hour sessions in accordance with local conditions.

The model aeroplane teams of the two oldest age groups of the German Young People will have two hours extra per week. Once a month there will be a special session to fly the models.

The 16- and 17-year-old girls will receive an additional training in First Aid for which two sessions per month will be available.

▬

Much of young people's experience of the HJ took the form of compulsory attendance at the so-called 'hostel evenings' (*Heimabende*), which took place every week. Hitler Youth leaders received instruction on how to organize these evenings with material supplied by the HJ indoctrination office. The following excerpts from the Indoctrination Service manual of the HJ for April 1942 provide a typical example of the kind of material to which HJ members were exposed:

**1174**  Comrades!

During these past months our Wehrmacht has destroyed the Bolshevik armies and thereby removed the most fearful danger which has ever threatened our nation and Europe from the east. As a result, our future is secure.

In two evening sessions we shall try to get to grips with this most tremendous event in our nation's history.

In the first evening session we shall discover that the core of our German history is a movement from west to east, i.e. our nation has always sought to find its necessary living space in the east.

The second evening session will show us that the Führer is continuing and completing this historic mission of our nation. It is only in the east that the fate and therefore the future of our people lies.

Comrades! You must work especially hard at these two evening sessions in particular. You may find it rather hard going this time. But you can easily overcome these difficulties through your idealism, your hard work and your thoroughness. So prepare the sessions with particular care so that you can give your units a lasting impression of the historic mission and task of our nation.

Through our nation's struggle against Bolshevik chaos we are now experiencing like no other generation before us the meaning and goal of our history: to open up the huge eastern spaces for the life and future of our people, to bear culture and morality [*Sitte*] to eastern barbarism and to establish the Germanic Reich of the German nation as the power to maintain order in Europe.

*Excerpt from a speech by Hitler on 6 October 1933:*

In the year 1919 this state [Poland] took over from Prussia and also from Austria provinces which had been developed through centuries of work and which were blooming. Today, twenty years later, they are in the process of gradually reverting to steppe. The Vistula, this river whose estuary was always so incredibly important to the Polish government, is already unsuitable for any serious traffic, thanks to a lack of care, and, depending on the time of year, either a wild torrent or a dried-up stream. Towns and villages are neglected. The streets, with very few exceptions, are dilapidated and run-down. Anyone who visits this country for the first time for two or three weeks will really get an idea of the meaning of the term *'polnische Wirtschaft'* (lit. 'a Polish business' = a shambles). These undeniable facts require us Germans to bring to the Slav peoples of the east the blessings of political order and the light of true culture. The more the German nation takes over the east and the further German influence reaches the happier will be the lives of the Slav peoples, the Poles, the Czechs and the Russians. History has shown clearly enough that these peoples have always been worst off when, in a fatal overestimation of their capabilities, they have believed that they can do without German leadership. National Socialism has once more given the German people the strength to fulfil its leadership task in the east.

▬▬▬

The extra burdens imposed on young people during wartime tended increasingly to interfere with their school work and family life provoking protests from both teachers and parents. The Reich Education Ministry was sensitive to this problem and, after a long period of pressure finally obliged the HJ to reach an agreement on the demarcation of young people's time between school and HJ. The agreement was published by the *Völkischer Beobachter* on 11 February 1941:

**1175** In recognition of their respective educational tasks, the Reich Minister of Education and the Youth Leader of the German Reich have reached an agreement, with the approval of the Führer's Deputy, which regulates the demands on youth. This agreement, to be carried out in a spirit of cooperation between the schools and the Hitler Youth, represents a further contribution to the unity of youth education. The difficulties in education caused by the war will now be alleviated by the fact that the educational bodies, namely the schools, together with the Hitler Youth, and with the support of parents, are erecting a barrier against the excessive demands on youth. By clarifying how much of young people's time may be taken up by school, on the one hand, and the HJ on the other, and how this time should be utilized, this demarcation—based on years of experience—will benefit their Hitler Youth and school work and the performance of young people will thereby secure significant encouragement.

The Reich Youth Leader announced the regulation implementing this agreement in Vienna. According to his announcement, the agreement concerning schools in general regulates the respective demands on youth so that the morning hours of all weekdays are at the disposal of the school whereas the afternoons are absolutely at the disposal of the HJ and the parents. However, Saturday afternoons and a further afternoon, which is to be decided locally by both sides, are to remain free of homework so that they remain completely at the disposal of the HJ. In the event that HJ duties—and, in particular, leadership duties—are scheduled for other afternoons in addition to those laid down in the plan drawn up by the Reich Youth Leadership, this will require the permission of the responsible HJ district leader [*Bannführer*], who should ensure that the young people still have sufficient time for their family and their homework and also personal free time.

---

1940 was the first year in which the so-called Youth Service Duty, introduced in February 1939, was fully implemented. In the spring of 1940 all 10-year-old boys and girls were compulsorily enrolled in the DJ and the 1923 cohort was for the first time forced to join the HJ. The regime endeavoured to lend prestige to the HJ and challenge the hegemony of the Churches through the creation of a ceremony for induction into the HJ and BdM of the age 14 cohort, which took place each spring. This would correspond to and compete with the ceremonies of confirmation (Protestant) and First Communion (Catholic) which traditionally represented an important rite of passage in German social life and were invariably marked by major family celebrations.

The following is an analysis of the significance of the ceremony in a study of Nazi education published in 1943:

**1176** The importance of the ceremony of admission into the national socialist youth movement on the Führer's birthday [20 April] is being recognized through the introduction in the middle of the war of a new national socialist ceremony in honour of the transfer of the 14-year-old boys and girls from the Young People and Young Girls' League into the HJ and BdM. The ceremony, which has the title 'Youth Dedication' took place for the first time on 22 March 1942. It has in truth the character of a celebration of a rite of passage of the young people involved. It is not only a festival of the national socialist youth movement but, in addition, is intended to include *family, school and job*. The young person's experience of *leaving school* and entering employment will also be reflected in the presence of the head teachers and future *apprentice masters* at the youth dedication ceremony. However, great emphasis will also be placed on the participation of the parents, who should help to make this day, which will bring about a transformation in the life of the boys and girls, a solemn and a festive one. They should, therefore, be present to witness these young people entering life under the leadership of the Party, whose responsibility to provide leadership for the people finds symbolic expression in the Youth Dedication ceremony. The Youth Dedication Day is also a feast day which expresses the uniform objectives of all educators in the national socialist state: family, school, career field and youth movement. The Dedication Day will already have been introduced on the previous evening by theatre and concert performances. Many boys and girls will thereby have experienced for the first time in their lives such a lofty cultural experience, something which will provide a lasting memory of this day in the lives of these young people. The fact that the participation of the 14-year-old boys and girls and their parents in such events is free of charge is also a convincing indication of the fact that cultural expression in the life of the national socialist state is a matter for the community as a whole and not for a specially privileged group or class. On the day itself, on which the responsible cadre of the NSDAP, the head teacher and the HJ leader will address the young people, each boy and girl will receive a scroll with a picture of the Führer as a memento. Insofar as wartime circumstances permit, the dedication ceremony will be followed by a small family celebration in which the festive character of this occasion in the lives of the young people will be emphasized through giving them presents. In his address on the occasion of the first Reich celebration of Youth Dedication on 22 March 1942, the Reich Youth Leader, Artur Axmann, announced on the Greater German Radio: 'Honour the great spiritual and martial heroes. Honour the heroes of this war, among whom you know that your fathers and brothers can be counted and let your hearts be fired by their incomparable deeds. Above all, be grateful to your parents for this day is their celebration day. They have given you everything in your life. Return it to them through love and decency!'

In the national socialist calendar of celebrations Youth Dedication has a particularly important place. In truth it is a revolutionary act because it does not commemorate a historic event as do the 30 January or 9 November, or, as in the case of the Führer's birthday, express love and adoration for a unique and inspired personality, but touches on people's private lives and places them at the centre of a ceremonial act. In this way people's personal lives are directly affected by the NSDAP's task of leadership and a new path is taken which may lead to new forms of truly secular importance.

The oath which is taken on transferring to the Hitler Youth is:

'I swear that I will serve the Führer Adolf Hitler faithfully and selflessly in the Hitler Youth. I swear that I will always strive for the unity and comradeship of German youth. I swear obedience to the Reich Youth Leader and to all leaders of the HJ. I swear on our holy flag that I will always be worthy of it, so help me God.'

---

It is not easy to assess the success of these ceremonies, which no doubt varied from place to place depending partly on the extent of commitment to the church of the particular local community involved and partly on the propaganda skills and resources of the local party organization. The following report of the Party Chancellery for 11–17 April 1943 based on a compilation of the Gau reports gives some indication of how these ceremonies were received and is generally rather pessimistic in its conclusions:

**1177**    Almost all the HJ induction ceremonies this year followed the suggestions put forward by the main [NSDAP] cultural office and the Reich Propaganda Headquarters.

Taking into account the difficulties both technical and in terms of personnel caused by the war, the ceremonies *undoubtedly represent a considerable improvement on last year*. Various Gaus even report extraordinarily strong participation by the parents and the population at large. However, this should not be allowed to disguise the fact that these ceremonies are still not accorded the importance which they deserve, particularly in those districts where the churches are strong.

The fact that a large number of those being inducted had already participated in a corresponding church ceremony was particularly invidious. The clergy had been working on parents and relations for months by visiting their homes in order to press upon them the importance of the church ceremonies. These induction ceremonies are like all the similar party events which are breaking new ground in that the response and the participation of the population depend not least on the ideological persuasion and enlightenment by the party as a whole, i.e. not only the local branch leader.

### 1. *Preparation and setting of the ceremonies*

The Gaus paid particular attention to the decorations as well as the musical background of the ceremonies.

The setting naturally suffered from the wartime conditions. In particular, there was a lack of suitable rooms and of appropriate musical backing. This applies in particular to the rural branches.

### 2. *Participation by the parents and population*

. . . The events went off in a very impressive fashion in Gau Düsseldorf. The participation by the parents as well as the party and its formations *was significantly greater than last year*, but was not 100 per cent as it is in the case of the Church ceremonies.

The Baden Gau headquarters also reported a markedly improved participation by the parents, *but it was not uniformly satisfactory*: 'According to the available accounts, some branches have reported full attendance, while others complained about the parents' participation which is probably mainly due to the Church'.

The Gau believes that the reason for the partial lack of participation by the parents is also to be found in the fact that frequently the school-leaving ceremonies are also carried out without parent participation and that this practice has more or less been transferred to the Party ceremonies. The Confirmation and Communion ceremonies of the church continue to be regarded by the majority of the population as the real leaving ceremony and so attendance is greater at those.

### 3. *Impression of the ceremonies on the population*

. . . In Saxony the ceremonies have in general made a deeper impact. 'It is also reported that a considerable number of young people who were to be confirmed the following Sunday at the instigation of their parents, rejected the Confirmation after having undergone the induction ceremony. In several cases even the parents thought that Confirmation was superfluous after the solemn induction ceremony'.

In Gau Baden the ceremonies were also well received by all the participants and particularly by the parents. During the ceremonies, it was already noted that the parents who were present followed the proceedings with emotion. Even the parents who were churchgoers were very impressed and did not fail to praise the way the ceremonies were conducted.

4. *Proposals and suggestions for future ceremonies*

. . . (b) Gau Düsseldorf points out that in future years there is a lot of educative work to be carried out in the careful preparation of the ceremonies. In the first place, this work will have to focus on the young people themselves. *The boys and girls had not yet grasped the deep meaning of the induction ceremony.* The ideological indoctrination carried out by the Hitler Youth as preparation for the ceremony was by no means sufficient. It was necessary to have additional preparation for the induction from the appropriate political leaders as well as through short ceremonies with speakers and appropriate reading material so that the boys and girls await this day in a mood of great awe and also have the encouragement that not only their parents but *the whole national community is taking part in the ceremony.*

(c) The population must be made aware of the importance of the induction ceremony much earlier and much more intensively. The preparations must not be restricted to propaganda for the day of the ceremony. The Gaus point out that the churches prepare their Confirmation candidates for a long time and take the instruction very seriously. The population must, therefore, be made much more aware of the idea behind the induction. Radio and the press are insufficient; the party must seek personal contact with the parents and point out to them the importance of the induction ceremonies.

(d) The commemoration certificates were very inadequate both in terms of the paper used and in terms of the design and print quality. The Gaus found these faults particularly irritating. Despite the paper shortage, the churches continue to produce beautifully designed Confirmation certificates. The small documents which were given out certainly did not reflect the dignity of the ceremony and so the young people and their relatives hardly took any notice of them.

There can be no doubt that the numerous services provided by the Hitler Youth played an important role in the war effort on the home front. In 1942, for example, 600,000 boys and 1,400,000 girls were involved in bringing in the harvest. The HJ was also responsible for organizing the huge children's evacuation programme (KLV) which is dealt with separately below.[2] However, as the new Reich Youth Leader, Artur Axmann, who replaced Baldur von Schirach in August 1940, pointed out in a speech to the press on 21 October 1940: 'During the next period, the leadership issue is the most important one for the Hitler Youth and, as a result of the big shortage of personnel, it will get even worse during the coming years.' Despite its elaborate training pro-

[2] See pp. 421ff. below for the KLV.

gramme, the HJ was unable to fill the vacancies left by the vast numbers of HJ leaders who were called up into the armed forces. The problem was that the quality of its leadership was the most decisive factor in determining the success or failure of an HJ unit. Particularly at local level almost everything depended on whether the leader could inspire his young charges and establish a good relationship with the local community. Although there were undoubtedly some HJ branches which functioned reasonably effectively until the later stages of the war, the following three documents illustrate these problems and are not untypical. The first is a report from the NSDAP district leadership in Neustadt/Aisch, a small industrial town in northern Bavaria:

**1178**    Youth: here, based on my own experience and reports from all sides, things are in a big mess. There is a lack of suitable leaders. In some branches there is no one there at all. In most of the others boys 'operate' as leaders, who are not up to the job. They are good at ensuring attendance but the activities have not the slightest value. There can be no question of their having any educative effect. On the contrary the opposite is true . . .

The second document is a letter from the Hitler Youth leader in Wiblingen in rural Württemberg to his superior dated 7 June 1944:

**1179**    During my last official visit to Schnürpflingen on 31 May 1944 extraordinary obstacles were placed in my path by the local population. I feel obliged to inform you of this and provide a detailed report.

When I appeared on the parade ground in front of the school house at 8 o'clock in the evening, there were hardly any young people there and I discovered that they were all still in church. It only remained for me to wait until the church service had finished in order for me to be able to collect them together. While doing this, I was verbally harassed by the population in the most offensive way. For example [in dialect]: 'Go home, boy. Get yourself back to Wiblingen' or 'He's only come here to get some eggs to hoard'. Since I had finally had enough of these insults, I got hold of the nearest boy to accompany me to the mayor's office. With incredible insolence the boy claimed not to know the names of any of these people and started to become tearful when threatening shouts came through the window of the mayor's office saying 'Don't say anything or you'll get it in the neck'.

The mayor even encouraged the boy in his attitude by remarking that he could not possibly know who these people were since he'd only just moved there . . . When I complained about his behaviour, he just left me standing there and, without saying a word, turned his attention to the papers on his desk. When I became convinced that I was not going to get any assistance from the mayor, I was forced to leave this rowdy village.

The local Nazi Party branch leader commented on this report in a letter to the district headquarters dated 23 July 1944:

**1180**    There can be no question of Schnürpflingen being a rowdy village. I can guarantee that any time. Why doesn't S report that he was the one who was responsible for the attitude of the people concerned: (1) through his remark about them being in church; (2) through his boasting about his achievements and his denigrating the achievements of the rural population; (3) his behaviour towards a soldier home on leave from the front. Nowadays it is very difficult to lead such a black [i.e. Catholic] local branch. I don't deny that attendance at HJ assemblies is bad, but it must be pointed out that it was all right when we had a local HJ leader. Unfortunately, at the moment we don't have a suitable boy. Attendance is very bad since the HJ is alleged to have stolen the school clock . . .

---

### (iii) The Military Involvement of Young People

During the course of the war, the paramilitary emphasis within the HJ steadily increased. In 1942 the HJ established military training camps (*W-E Lager*), where 17-year-olds were sent on three-week courses under Wehrmacht and Waffen SS instructors to prepare them for their call-up. In the case of those still at school the whole class went together; those in work were obliged to attend during their holidays. By November 1942 there were 120 such camps operating with Wehrmacht instructors and 42 with Waffen SS ones.

From January 1943 onwards, schoolboys and apprentices born in 1926 and 1927 were called up as Air Force and Naval Auxiliaries to be deployed mainly on air defence duties. School classes were conscripted en bloc and often sent to barracks far from their homes. School instruction was provided by visiting teachers. Significantly, once these teenage boys had put on Air Force and naval uniforms they came to identify with the Wehrmacht and to despise the HJ. As one of them put it after the war:

**1181**    There were a number of reasons for our rejection of the HJ. For several of us political motives certainly played a part, but the unanimous character of the rejection, from which there were virtually no exceptions, requires a more comprehensive explanation. Our self-image was collectively based on the fact that it was we who did the shooting, who fought, who were in danger, who wore a uniform which had to be taken seriously, that of the Wehrmacht, and not a toy uniform such as the youth organizations wore. In short, it was the fact that we were involved in a crisis that made it a point of honour for us not to let ourselves be bossed about by some HJ leader or other who was avoiding military service. One can say without exaggeration that the Air Force auxiliaries despised the HJ. That is meant in a purely pre-political sense, although it already contained the germs of a political assessment of the situation. As far as the Air Force auxiliaries were concerned, HJ leaders were civilians in disguise who could sleep every night in their own beds and whose mothers put out their slippers for them.

The marked bitterness with which the Air Force auxiliaries responded to the HJ had even more profound causes. The more intelligent Air Force auxiliaries at least quickly saw through the fact that the HJ armbands were intended to calm and mislead the public. The aim was to prevent the German public and even more the world outside from gaining the impression that the leadership felt itself compelled to use 15- and 16-year-olds as combat troops. This fact, it must be said, could have had a disturbing effect on morale; it would have been obvious that the German Wehrmacht had bled to death and was finished . . . If one was going to have to be sent into action in a crisis, then at least one wanted to be respected for that and not be confused with some cub collecting scrap.

Our fight against the claims of the HJ was made easy for us; it did not involve any risk. And so one must be wary of seeing it as some kind of resistance attitude. The Wehrmacht made sure that we were protected and did not allow the HJ to interfere in its sphere of responsibility and it only rarely made any serious attempts to do so . . . However, one cannot ignore the fact that an important objective of the National Socialist youth policy had failed—at least with the 1926, 1927 and 1928 cohorts: the fact that it was taken for granted that one would adjust to the National Socialist set of values.

———

Girls were also heavily involved in the war effort. In 1942, for example, there were 1.4 million girls engaged in bringing in the harvest compared with 600,000 boys. Girls knitted socks for the troops, collected herbs and beechnuts, while the older ones were employed in industry and other services. Girls' experience of the war years varied enormously. Many, particularly those from sheltered middle class or strongly religious backgrounds, found that the experience of getting away from home, taking part in new activities and generally broadening their range of experience had a liberating effect and enabled them to develop organizational and other talents, encouraging self-reliance and boosting their self-esteem. And for some the sense of community generated by the BdM and KLV camps based on order, discipline, and fitting in with the majority was attractive. But for those of a more sensitive or independent disposition the experience of being regimented and the loss of privacy was much less congenial.

The complex and ambivalent response of some young people to the war and the regime is illustrated by the following excerpts from the diary of the son of a wealthy farmer from Pomerania, a sensitive and intelligent youth who as a teenager was recruited into the naval auxiliaries and manned an anti-aircraft battery on the Baltic coast:

**1182** 22.7.1944. Today, at the end of the week (or is Sunday already the start of a new week), I have to write my weekly report so to speak. A lot has happened: an attempt was made to assassinate Hitler. But he was all right. Those responsible, senior officers in the Wehrmacht with famous names, have been executed, a number are still being sought. Now all the armed forces have been subordinated to Hitler and the Heil Hitler greeting is being introduced everywhere.

We too had long debates in our bunker and in the end a real quarrel started between Zitzewitz and Mühlhan. Mühlhan's father is apparently a high-ranking Party boss in Dramburg or Deutschkrone and so he talks a lot about the 'new Reich' and 'fate' which protected Hitler.

Zitzewitz poured scorn on the big mouth, but his sarcasm was laced with wit and humour. Marvellous stuff! Fritz isn't very bright but compared with Mühlhan he's a genius.

Fritz said something about the traditions of Prussian officers and a soldierly sense of duty, which an Austrian corporal could know nothing about. That really put the cat among the pigeons! Mühlhan babbled on about what had been on the radio, that any ordinary soldier could immediately shoot his superior if he knew that he'd been involved in the conspiracy.

Fortunately Muck saved the situation because he'd brought back the latest political joke from his leave . . .

How we laughed. But Mühlhan got even more angry. And then Muck told him: 'what's the matter with you. The jokes are spread by the Propaganda Ministry.'

'I don't believe it!'

'Yes they are. Göring gets people to tell him the latest jokes about him every day. It's only through the jokes that he's become so popular.'

The idea was too far-fetched for Mühlhan and he fell silent and disappeared in the direction of the Flak bunker.

Afterwards I discussed the assassination attempt once again with Muck and also the Zitzewitz–Mühlhan quarrel. Muck said he didn't know which of them was right. He often experienced similar quarrels at home. Although there were a lot of grumbles about Hitler, his oldest brother was a senior HJ leader, even a *Bannführer,* I think. It's his oldest brother who is missing in Russia.

17.8.1944. Then comes the all clear. Sort out the gun. An extra two hours of sleep. Quickly into our bunks with a terrific feeling: we know that we're needed. Here we can prove that we are gladly doing our duty as we have sworn to do. My leave is now not so important. What does it matter compared with tonight . . .

Today I was a runner. On parade this morning the boss read out an order from the commander: 'Naval auxiliaries deserve the highest praise.' The section is credited with shooting down six planes; our battalion with two. We saw them come down. We will certainly get the credit for them. Everyone's very excited; they say it would be great if we got the Flak badge.

1.10.1944. Nowadays, words, like many other things, are cheap. The most ordinary things are talked about in the most inflated terms. People go over the top in their use of language on even the most trivial occasions, e.g. in every little Party meeting people vow 'unswerving, unbreakable loyalty to the Führer' and constantly talk of 'eternity' and 'heroes'. And yet these words just don't fit. Everything should be used in its proper place.

After all, plain and simple words make a far greater impression than a raucous article in the *Reich* (Muck always called it Clubfoot's [Goebbels] bedtime story).

'In the beginning was the word', the saying goes. But in the end too judgment will be passed on the word. Individuals, nations and governments will be known by the word and at the end of the world the word will stand.

10.12.1944. The swearing-in ceremony! On Saturday, we spent the whole day rehearsing for the great day with the sergeant-major. It went quite well despite the excitement.

Today it all happened. And it was the very day when I was on barrack room duty. But I managed all right because the inspection was very slack, probably because it was too late to change things. Also, they probably wanted to keep us in a good mood because a lot of people had grumbled about the hard drill. Later, at the swearing-in ceremony some people wanted to point two fingers of their other hand down towards the ground behind them so that the oath would be diverted into the ground like a flash of lightning and so wouldn't count. It was meant more as a joke than anything but the instructors took it seriously and reported it . . .

The ceremony took place in the market square. A huge platform covered with a shining swastika was erected in the middle and we recruits were lined up in rows of four in front of it. The HJ and DJ of Ortrand were paraded to the left of us and to the right the recently formed home guard [*Volkssturm*] and representatives of the town.

Then the Gau band marched into the square playing a rousing march tune and took up its position beside the platform. The swearing-in flag was carried in and then four of us had to step forward in helmets and with rifles at the ready.

The major arrived and inspected us. After that he spoke about the significance of the oath and remembered the dead who had given their lives for Germany loyal to this oath. Then the band softly played 'I had a comrade'. It was very solemn; this song is very moving. The large numbers of civilians and spectators pulled out their handkerchiefs.

Then came the swearing-in. Repetition of the formula. We were all gripped by it and no longer thought of the lightning conductor. Now our hearts were really in it.

I kept having to repeat to myself and to think about it: I have now sworn loyalty to the German flag and to Adolf Hitler and have to keep my oath. Can I do it? There is so much criticism of national socialist Germany that at some point I will certainly get involved in arguments.

The most notorious example of the results of the militarization of the Hitler Youth was the formation by the Waffen SS of a special Hitler

Youth division during 1943 composed of volunteers led by former Hitler Youth leaders. Although there can be no doubt that some of these boys had been fanatasized by their indoctrination, which may partly explain the remarkable fighting quality of this division, some of the young recruits to the Waffen SS had been virtually press-ganged, as is clear from the following post-war account:

**1183**    The events happened in March 1945. All the HJ Home Guard [*Volkssturm*] members were assembled in a common room which was then locked and a guard placed outside! Our HJ district leader [*Bannführer*] made a speech in the presence of the instructors. He declared that, according to a secret order from the Führer, all offers to volunteer for active service were no longer valid except for those for the SS and for the one-man torpedo weapons. He therefore called on those present to volunteer for the SS en masse; it was, he said, a matter of honour to do so. But if this did not occur 'he had plenty of time'. The room would remain locked until evening; there would be no meals and anyone who didn't sign up for the SS would be sent straight to a 'recruitment camp' . . .

At first there was a discussion. The district leader refused demands for him to show the so-called Hitler order or at least read it out on the grounds that it was secret; in any case, he shouted, he had given his word. He also refused the further demand to summon the responsible recruitment officer so that he could confirm the statements and release the individuals from their commitment to volunteer. When he realized that he wasn't achieving anything with his surprise tactics, he then ordered 'the whole club' to stand at attention. Those who remained stayed in this position until the evening, i.e. for over eight hours. The District Leader, assisted by the instructors, then began to address each person in turn in the most aggressive tone of command spending about ten minutes with each 'case'. If he met with a rejection then insults rained down such as 'coward', 'dud', or—in the event that the refusal was based on the SS being an ideologically motivated troop—'what a pious Christian you are'. By the evening, the result of all this was that around 90 per cent of those present had 'signed up' and were released; the others were pushed together in a small room and the light was turned out. They didn't get anything to eat.

The night that followed was unforgettable. The mood alternated between a high, despair, and depressing uncertainty. There were long discussions of a hitherto unprecedented frankness and conclusiveness. Finally, everybody gave their word that they would not change their minds.

We had barely fallen asleep exhausted when the alarm was sounded. We were drilled for an hour in the darkness. And this was repeated two or three times during the night. Towards morning we were summoned individually into the office and under humiliating circumstances received our call-up to the recruitment camp. Beforehand, each of us had to sign a statement on oath that he would remain silent about the day's events because we had to go home for a short time to pack our things.

Although this was an extreme example, there are several recorded instances of the pressure put on teenagers during the last phase of the war to join the Waffen SS.

During the course of the war the age of call-up had been progressively reduced. In 1940 19-year-olds were called up; in 1941–2 18-year-olds; in 1943–44 17-year-olds. In the autumn of 1944 a major campaign was launched to persuade those born in 1928 to volunteer and allegedly 70 per cent did so. At the beginning of February 1945, the remaining 265,000 who had not yet volunteered were called up and on 5 March 1945 those born in 1929.

The final stage in the military involvement of young boys saw the conscription into the *Volksturm,* which had been created on 25 September 1944, of those aged 16 and over, who were not fit to be called up into the armed forces. They were deployed to dig anti-tank ditches and to form anti-tank units armed with bazookas [*Panzerfäuste*]. Again the response of young people varied greatly. While some committed themselves with greater or lesser enthusiasm out of a misguided loyalty, others tried to avoid becoming involved as best they could. In his final days in the Berlin bunker Hitler took comfort from the belief that he could count on 'his boys', as is clear from the following newspaper report of a reception by Hitler in his military headquarters of twenty HJ boys who had been 'tested in battle'. This incident has subsequently become familiar through the showing of the newsreel pictures taken at the time:

**1184**  The Führer received Reich Youth Leader Artur Axmann and a delegation of twenty members of the Hitler Youth in his headquarters. The youths had proved themselves in the use of the bazooka, as machine gunners, in reconnaissance, as runners, or by blowing up important installations in the defence of their homes in Pomerania, Upper and Lower Silesia.

In the shape of these twenty boys German youth as a whole was symbolically lined up in front of the Führer, a youth which at the present time is acting as the most faithful assistant of our soldiers and the Home Guard and is committed to defending German soil courageously and intrepidly wherever it is threatened. Through these twenty boys the Führer was at the same time honouring their comrades who at such a young age had already given their lives for the nation in battle as martyrs and blood witnesses of German youth.

The youngest of the retinue who were lined up was the 12-year-old Hitler Youth Alfred Czech, who rescued twelve wounded soldiers under enemy artillery and machine-gun fire and caught a Soviet spy in the district of Oppeln. Some of the 15-,16- and 17-year-old boys were surrounded for days on end. They all assisted the troops and the Home Guard wherever they could, destroyed enemy barracks with bazookas, transmitted important messages to units which had been temporarily cut off, brought in booty and prisoners, and carried German wounded out of the battle zone.

Two of them wore the Iron Cross First Class, all the others had the Iron Cross Second Class, some of them had the Infantry medal and most of them had the medal for those who have been wounded.

The Führer greeted each of the Hitler boys with a handshake and listened to the accounts of their experiences. Finally, the Führer declared: 'You have now experienced battle for yourselves and know that we are involved in a struggle for the very existence of the German nation. Despite all the difficulties which currently face us, I am convinced that we shall be victorious in this struggle above all because of German youth and, in particular, because of you, my boys.' The boys replied to the Führer's greeting as one with a 'Heil, my Führer!'

---

## (iv) Education

The war saw a number of significant reforms to the education system, of which several appear to have been prompted by Hitler himself. Hitler had strong views on education, which he expressed at length both in *Mein Kampf* and in his so-called 'table talk'. The following report came from a member of the confidential Press information service of the Propaganda Ministry and was dated 18 December 1940:

**1185**   I have already informed you briefly about my visit to SS Group Leader Heissmeyer[3], and want now to give you some details about the conversation with him and his adjutant concerning education matters, which I am sure will interest you.

The Führer is completely clear about the need to pay particular attention to questions of education because the future of the Reich entirely depends on it. That is particularly true of the period after his death for which preparations must be made in every sphere. In this connection it is interesting that recently the Führer asked to see the figures on German grammar and secondary schools and emphasized that he wants to give priority to education in the humanities. The English language is no longer so significant for us as previously since German must replace English as far as possible. Education in the humanities, even in the form of 'dead languages' gives the individual a superb grounding which really could not be improved. According to Heissmeyer, the Führer and the Reichsführer SS show great interest in and support for the National Political Educational Establishments (Napolas) and the suggestion that these institutions should be expanded stems from a direct initiative of the Führer. A total of 100 schools are envisaged. However, this figure is still confidential.[4] At the moment there are twenty-one and six are almost ready. A very important aspect is the

---

[3] August Heissmeyer, a graduate, was head of the SS Main Office 1935–1939 and from 1936 Inspector of the Napolas. On the Napolas, see Vol. 2, doc. 313.
[4] See Vol. 2, docs 313–14.

intention to establish these schools in the occupied territory and gradually draw the local elite into these schools in order to educate them in our ideas and thereby bind them closer to Germany. This aspect is considered very important for the maintenance of Germany's strength. So Napolas will be established in all the occupied territories, including Denmark and Norway, probably as soon as 1 April, and initially in Holland and Norway. In Norway it is simply a question of finding a suitable building for the Napola. They would then pick the headmaster from the ranks of Plön and, in addition, transfer two so-called teams (equivalent to classes) to Oslo so that a basis is established. Then, to start with, the Quisling youth will be integrated in these schools and then the rest of Norwegian youth so that purely German teams can be reduced, eventually leaving purely Norwegian Napolas.

A very interesting point in connection with the statements on humanities education is the fact, which by the way I will deal with in my article, that Schulpforta and Illfeld, the two oldest Napolas are based on a humanities curriculum, and that will always be the case.

Moreover, it is still worth noting that there is of course a big difference between the Napolas and the so-called Adolf Hitler Schools. It was only after the Napolas had been founded that Ley and Schirach suddenly decided to set up these Adolf Hitler Schools and for this purpose an inspector was sent to visit all the Napolas in order to see how they operated. The purpose of each institution is completely different because the Adolf Hitler Schools are designed to train the next generation of party leaders. However, they are now wondering whether the pupils should not after all be given a free choice of occupation when they leave. Although ten foundation stones were laid on a single day, not a single one has been completed. The current Adolf Hitler pupils, around 900 in all, are provisionally accommodated in the Ordensburg Sonthofen and are being taught there. The Napolas want above all to avoid the recreation in any form of the old cadet schools. For that would then increase the variety of school types still further, above all because it can then be assumed that every section of the Wehrmacht and also the SS would establish its own schools. Moreover, the Napolas already provide as many recruits for the Wehrmacht as the old cadet schools, although there is a free choice of occupation on leaving.

▬▬

In fact, by the end of the following year, only ten more Napolas had been established, all of which were either in the so-called *Altreich* (pre-1938 Germany) or in territory subsequently incorporated into Germany such as the Sudetenland, Alsace and Luxembourg.

On 31 October 1940, Martin Bormann informed Lammers that the Führer wished 'to introduce the educational institutions which have proved themselves in the Eastern March [Austria]—the Main School [*Hauptschule*] and Teacher Training Institutions [*Lehrerbildungsanstalten*]—into the Reich as well'.[5] The Main Schools were officially

---

[5] Bormann to Lammers 31.10.1940 Bundesarchiv Berlin (BAB) R 43 II/955.

initiated in the *Altreich* through a ministerial decree of 28 April 1941. They were designed to select the best third of the elementary school (*Volksschule*) children after four years of education, i.e. at the age of 10 and give them four more years in a school which would be geared to producing the middle level or technician grade in the various trades and professions. Unlike the grammar schools (*Gymnasien*), the Main Schools would concentrate more on practical than academic work. However, by teaching a foreign language they would enable pupils to move more easily to a grammar school during the course of their education if they showed exceptional promise. The reform was introduced first into the territories which had been incorporated into the Reich, e.g. Alsace and Lorraine, and seems to have been immediately prompted by Hitler's concern to establish a model education system there, which could then be introduced into the *Altreich* where such changes were more likely to be met with resistance. Bormann pressed for the rapid introduction of the Main School into the *Altreich* since he envisaged they would 'initiate the revolutionizing of the German school system'[6] The Nazi party was involved in the selection of pupils to the extent that parents could appeal to their local party district leader about the placement of their children. However, on 13 June 1942 their further introduction was postponed until the end of the war. By then, there were only fifty-three Main Schools in Württemberg and fifty-one in the Saar in addition to the 1,938 in the occupied or annexed territories.

The second major educational change initiated by Hitler was to the arrangements for training elementary school teachers. Hitherto budding elementary school teachers had required a grammar school leaving certificate (*Abitur*) or, following a decree of 18 February 1939, for bright elementary school leavers an equivalent certificate achieved after a four-year course of education. They then received two years of training at a teacher training college. Under the Weimar Republic some universities (e.g. Hamburg) had begun enabling those wishing to become elementary school teachers to study for a degree in education and it had long been the objective of most elementary school teachers and their professional organizations for them to become an all-graduate profession.

However, under the reform announced by the Reich Education Minister of 5 March 1941, this trend was put into reverse. In future, elementary school teachers would be drawn primarily from the products of the new Main Schools and, after leaving school at 14, would be trained for five years in new 'Teacher Training Institutions' (*Lehrbil-*

---

[6] Bormann circular of 27.8.1941, Nr. 105/41, BAB NS 12/694.

*dungsanstalten*). Moreover, in order to deal with the acute shortage of elementary school teachers, in good part a reflection of their low salaries and status under the Third Reich, school auxiliaries would be able to become teachers after an abbreviated period of training. These measures reflected Hitler's contempt for teachers in general and elementary school teachers in particular, a contempt which he frequently expressed in his so-called 'table talk'. Finally, Hitler ordered a change from the gothic (*Fraktur*) to the roman (*Antiqua*) script in the writing of German.

A report by Dr Kausch of the Propaganda Ministry's confidential press information service on a background briefing by the Reich Education Minister Bernhard Rust, himself a former grammar school teacher, dated 20 March 1941, provides fascinating insights into these reforms and in general represents a devastating critique of the state of German education during this period:

**1186**     On Wednesday evening I visited Reich Education Minister Rust who, together with his senior officials, wanted to inform a small group of fifteen journalists with complete frankness about the whole state of the German education system. The discussion was very productive and revealed the unusual difficulties with which the Education Minister finds himself confronted.

The Minister began by dealing with the Führer's decree on the new system of teacher training. As is well known, the demand for a graduate training for elementary school teachers is one of the most fundamental points of the party's programme. In 1932 Professor Stark published a memorandum through the [party's] Eher publishing house with Adolf Hitler's approval, which spelled out this programme in detail. As late as April 1939, the leaders of the NS Teachers' League declared that there was no question of there being anything other than a proper higher education for future elementary school teachers. Naturally that makes things difficult. The elementary school teachers wanted to acquire greater prestige through higher education and now see their justified hopes being gravely disappointed. Many teachers are at the front and believe that the greatest heritage of the struggles of their predecessors is being betrayed. Nevertheless, the Führer order was vitally necessary. The Führer has always rejected the exaggerated cult of education and qualifications and demanded that elementary school teachers should come from the large reservoir of the elementary schools in the towns and the countryside. Furthermore, in view of the low salaries of the elementary school teachers, there are practically no recruits from those who have the *Abitur* and, in order to solve the problem of teacher shortage in broad terms, we simply have to fall back on the elementary school leavers . . .

This question is connected with a second decisive problem which has been resolved by the Führer, namely the introduction of the so-called Main School throughout the whole of the Greater German Reich. The decrees concerning the introduction of the Main School may be published in about four weeks. The Reich is thereby effectively adopting the Austrian educational principle of the Main School, which consist of the following: four years in the elementary school; after four years one-third of the elementary school children will be selected who must then attend the Main School for a further four years. Compulsory school for these pupils will thus be extended from six to twelve years. On the other hand, the state will meet all the expenses for the additional two years of education. So those boys who are selected for the Main School cannot go out into the world after six years of education but only after eight. However, by learning a foreign language they will have a much better chance of getting a job in business, in the middle ranks of the administration etc . . .

The issue would not have been decided yet if the incorporation of the new eastern Gaus, Danzig and Wartheland, had not forced clarification. The new eastern Gaus are intended to be model Gaus for the future greater German Reich in every respect. As a result, the aim is to introduce the ideal type of administration and educational and cultural institutions so that one will not need to experiment any further after a few years . . .

Since the Main Schools are being set up by the state, this decision represents an extraordinary burden for the *Länder*, which still have to meet the costs of the school system. The system of financial equalization between the Reich and the *Länder* has completely broken down for years. The *Länder* and also the Reich Finance Ministry are understandably strongly opposed to the introduction of this new and general type of school for financial reasons. But the Führer command will silence their doubts as well . . .

To return to the question of teacher training, Rust hopes in future to secure the main contingent of the future elementary school teachers from the Main School leavers. They will then receive a two- or three-year boarding school type education in the seminaries or Teacher Training Establishments. The question of teachers' pay and of the combination of the tasks of an elementary school teacher with those of a Hitler Youth leader or a political leader at village level is being looked at. In addition to their professional skills, the young elementary school teachers are going to be trained as political leaders.

An additional problem that is urgent is the 'performance crisis' in the German education system. There is no question that school performance has declined dramatically, that business, the Wehrmacht and the Universities all complain bitterly about the low average quality of education. Rust, however, pointed out that the abnormal times in which we live naturally could not fail to have an effect on young people's learning abilities. So much is demanded of boys outside the school what with Hitler Youth, harvest duties, political indoctrination, evacuation, scrap collection, 'instruction of their parents', parades and, furthermore, through the incredibly increased amount of political education and ideological material so that the brains of our youth cannot keep up and all attempts to increase performance are thwarted by physical exhaustion. This is virtually a medical matter from which conclusions must be drawn if a whole generation is not to be totally messed up. The recent agreement between the Education Ministry and the Hitler Youth leadership has, for the first time, produced a reduction and a demarcation of the time which young people spend with their family, in school and with the Hitler Youth. After eight years of struggle by the Education Ministry to free young people from non-school demands, this is the first sign of progress. The new Reich Youth Leader and the

Reich Education Minister have a good relationship but it has taken a long time to achieve. In the meantime, we have seen the defamation of the teaching profession, the exploitation of youth to an intolerable extent and a reduction in performance which is without precedent. Many young people between 14 and 16 years of age are already as stressed as if they had a life's work behind them. It has been noted that 15-year-old leaders of the German Young People, who carry a certain responsibility for their groups, play with the toys of 9-year-olds when they are at home and unobserved because there has simply been a physical reaction. The Education Ministry knows very well that what young people need is *rest*. But it has frequently been unable to get its way in the face of the political authorities. In the final analysis, Rust himself may bear a heavy burden of guilt for this. But things are supposed to get better. For this reason the REM welcomes the new system of holidays under which young people get at least two months during which they can rest and so become capable of digesting the greatness of our period and the demands of school. Still, the Ministry's daily struggle continues. Gauleiter Wächtler, as leader of the NS Teachers' League, has made two demands. Every week in every German school one of the Führer's statements should be posted up in the classroom to which the teacher should refer *in every class he takes* and on which he should base his teaching. Rust rejected this as a tremendous threat to the whole school system. However, Wächtler has, for the time being, succeeded in ensuring that every week several hours are spent in every class in politically indoctrinating the children with the clear intention *that the children should lecture their parents on the political state of affairs*. The Minister has estimated the loss of useful instruction as a result of this propaganda as 90 schooldays per year He has assured us that this totally unnecessary additional burden, which also only annoys parents, will be got rid of. There is naturally a great deal of tension between Rust and Wächtler.

The introduction of the *Antiqua* script is another huge problem. As is well known, to begin with the *Antiqua* script is only going to be adopted by the newspapers. But instructions from the Führer already exist that the schools must gradually move over to using *Antiqua*. It could be that as early as the next school year only *Antiqua* will be taught. This depends on the necessary primers, arithmetic books and indeed all the textbooks being published in the meantime. Since, in recent years, all the propaganda has been in favour of the gothic script, this represents a revolutionary upheaval in the whole textbook market with the corresponding concerns about raw materials and skilled workers. But even if everything works and the boys only learn *Antiqua* for the foreseeable future (since it is *impossible to teach both scripts* in elementary school), the result of this change will be that a whole generation will not be in a position to read three quarters of German literature . . . However, the introduction of *Antiqua* is necessary so that the European empire of the German nation can make itself understood abroad. This final goal will under no circumstances be given up. The amount of book production of both old and new works can be imagined.

During the evening, we also discussed the position of the universities and of higher education in general. I had a long talk with Under Secretary *Ministerialdirektor* Holfelder, who in fact is the only man of high intellectual calibre in the Reich Education Ministry. An Austrian, a passionate heretic as far as the current educational methods are concerned, he is Rust's only influential adviser. Like the Minister, he too advocated 'freedom of thought', which has acquired such a bad reputation in Germany's institutions of higher education, above all because of the views of the Heidelberg professor Krieck, who wanted to orientate all the lecturers and students towards the notion that scholarship is only important and valuable if it serves the nation. Unfortunately, Krieck has been having official backing for many years. And, in the meantime, not only scholarship but above all scholarly method has gone for a burton. That is a very serious matter. Even if, despite all political resistance, the demand for academically respectable scholarship manages to break through and assert itself and the forces of the German intelligentsia will compel this to happen, as far as the methodology of scholarship is concerned, we shall have to start again *from scratch*—just like Jakob Böhme had to do a long time ago. If there was not so much opposition, the Ministry would probably secretly commission a single German University to bring together a group of responsibly-minded scholars to set up a new think tank [*Geisteswerkstatt*], which, while naturally taking account of the new German values and the events of our time, would at the same time provide them with an impeccable scientific foundation. There are so many issues which are crying out for scientific examination, e.g. the science of race, about which there are now only popular rather than solidly based opinions, or a conception of the world based on biology, or the European state system on a Germanic basis etc. One cannot continually live on the basis of a brilliant idea and indulge in ethnic [*völkisch*] slogans without scientific precision. This has probably been appreciated, but one knows that the idea of this 'secret Reich University' would immediately be torpedoed, either by the responsible Gauleiters who want to see their work glorified in the Gau universities, or by the NS Lecturers' League, which has a line of march but no academic goal—or, which would be even more dangerous for this idea, the intellectual opponents of National Socialism would come to the support of the secret Reich University in droves and thereby make it immediately politically suspect.

I am reporting very frankly the lines of thought which we discussed for hours with the men from the ministry in order to demonstrate that they possess many insights but in the present whirl of events have neither the power nor perhaps the right leadership. Rust has recently spoken to the Reich Marshal [Göring] and pointed out to him that, while at the moment what was going on in schools and universities was irrelevant, provided they fulfilled the most necessary technical requirements in order to achieve the necessary results demanded by the state in the sphere of armaments and the economy, in ten years' time the great vacuum would become so visible that what was irrevocably lacking in the overall military and overall economic performance of the Reich would become clearly apparent. The Reich Marshal then became very serious and expressed his agreement with Rust's views and promised him his support.

## (v) The Children's Evacuation Programme (KLV)

The measure taken by the regime which had the biggest impact on German children during the war was the so-called 'Expanded *Kinder-*

*landverschickung'* (KLV): the evacuation of some 850,000 boys and girls aged 10–14 to KLV camps, approximately the same number of 6–10 year olds to foster homes and half a million children under 6 years old with their mothers from the areas threatened by bombing, mainly the big cities of the north and west, to the countryside, mainly in the south and east.[7] The term *Kinderlandverschickung* is untranslatable as a single word. It means the sending of children from big cities to the countryside for their health and safety. The practice of KLV had a long history dating back to the previous century when the churches began organizing holidays in the countryside for young people from the poorest districts of the big cities. During the Weimar Republic the practice was then taken up by political groups, notably by the Workers' Welfare Organization of the SPD. The children either stayed in camps or with individual families. On coming to power, the Nazi welfare organization, the NSV, had immediately taken up KLV in a big way and by various mechanisms progressively squeezed out the rival agencies.

In September 1940 Hitler reacted to the first sustained bombing campaigns by the RAF on German cities, and particularly Berlin, by ordering the voluntary evacuation of all children from those areas threatened by bombing. On 26 September 1940 he instructed Baldur von Schirach, former Reich Youth Leader and, since the end of June 1940, Gauleiter of Vienna, to draw up the necessary plans. Schirach, who as 'Delegate for the Inspection of the Whole of the Hitler Youth' still retained a major interest in the Hitler Youth, seized the opportunity to expand its role at the expense of the education authorities (Reich Education Ministry and National Socialist Teachers League (NSLB)). On 27 September 1940 he made the following notes on his interview with Hitler:

**1187**  1. In reply to my question whether or not the evacuation [*Verschickung*] of young people should be compulsory or voluntary the Führer replied that the whole action should be on a voluntary basis. The number of teachers should if necessary be halved. I pointed out that in these circumstances regular instruction could not be absolutely guaranteed. The Führer said that one would have to put up with that.

2. The Führer agreed to the proposal that the expression 'evacuation' should be avoided and that instead the expression 'sending away to the country' [*Landverschickung*] or extended *Landverschickung* proposed by me should be used.[8]

---

[7] Figures in Gerhard Hock, *'Der Führer sorgt für unsere Kinder . . . 'Die Kinderlandverschickung im Zweiten Weltkrieg* (Paderborn 1996), pp. 142–3. The present section owes much to this book.

[8] Nazi propaganda had been exploiting the evacuation of children in Britain.

3. The Führer read the *exposé* proposed by me for the sending away of the school age children from Berlin and Hamburg and approved it in all particulars.

4. With reference to point 4 of the *exposé*, namely that the instructions to the Reich Transport Minster, the Reich Finance Minister, the Reich Agriculture Minister and the Reich Education Minister requested by me should be issued immediately, the Führer gave the appropriate order.

5. Teachers should not have a say in the transports. [Added in pencil]

---

On 27 September 1940, Bormann issued the following circular to the Nazi party, which was to carry out the programme, although it was financed by the state:

**1188** The Führer has ordered that young people who live in areas which are subject to repeated air raid alarms should be sent to the other areas of the Reich on a voluntary basis. This should apply in particular to children from allotment estates and those districts which do not have adequate air raid shelters. The accommodation will be organized as far as possible so that schools and classes can remain together. The teachers of the schools in the home districts will be heavily involved in organizing the move and will ensure that school lessons can be effectively resumed in the new locations.

Accommodation will be in youth hostels, inns, and other suitable accommodation. If such accommodation is currently being used as a hospital or for other purposes, it can also be used for this action unless particular reasons exist in individual cases why it should not be so used.

The Führer has appointed Reichsleiter Baldur von Schirach to implement this measure and the NSV, the Hitler Youth, and the NS Teachers' League will support him in carrying it out. The NSV will take on the responsibility for sending away the pre-school children and the children in the first four classes. The Hitler Youth will undertake the accommodation of children from the fifth school year onwards. The accommodation action will begin on Thursday 3 October 1940. The following Gaus are envisaged for the reception of the young people from the big cities: Bavarian Eastern March, Brandenburg, Upper Danube, Saxony, Silesia, Sudetenland, Thuringia, Wartheland, Ostland.

Reichsleiter Baldur von Schirach will issue further instructions for the sending away of young people from the big cities. The closest cooperation between the organizations involved is necessary during the implementation of this measure. The Gauleiters are responsible for smooth cooperation. In addition, the Gauleiters must carry out a uniform propaganda among parents to persuade them to volunteer their children for the action. The draft of a letter from the local branch leaders of the party to the parents will shortly be sent to those Gauleiters from whose districts the young people threatened by air attack will be sent for distribution in the schools. There must be no public propaganda, particularly in the press. There can be brief reports in the local papers of the reception areas when the youth transports arrive. However, in accordance with a directive from the Führer, there must be no mention of an evacuation but only of the sending of young people from the big cities to the countryside.

Further questions should be directed to Reichsleiter von Schirach.

▬▬▬

Hitler had ordered the immediate voluntary evacuation of children from Berlin and the first transport left Berlin for Saxony on 3 October. Initially, only Berlin and Hamburg were involved and within the first two months a total of 189,543 had left these two cities, half to KLV camps the remainder to stay with foster families.[9] The result was that the KLV actions had to be improvised in a great hurry, which inevitably created problems. However, within a few weeks an effective organization had been created. Schirach established a central KLV office staffed with Hitler Youth leaders who already had extensive experience of organizing transports to camps and youth hostels. It even contained former leaders of the SPD Workers' Welfare Organization who, while in principle opposed to the regime, believed that this was a worthwhile programme. District KLV officials (*Gebietsbeauftragte*) were appointed from the HJ to organize the reception in their areas and liaise with the state and local government officials who were inevitably involved. At the same time, the Gauleiters appointed Gau representatives to deal with the party side. On 5 December, the Gau representative of the KLV in Gau Württemberg (the number of Gaus receiving children had been expanded to cope with the numbers involved) wrote to all district leaders of the Party outlining the nature of the new programme:

**1189**     In accordance with the Führer's instructions children from districts which are repeatedly subject to air raid alarms will be sent to the other areas of the Reich on the basis of the voluntary approval of the responsible parent. The Führer has appointed Reichsleiter Baldur von Schirach to implement this measure.

In the districts [*Kreise*] the [NSDAP] district leaders are responsible for the smooth carrying out of the necessary measures. They will be supported by the NSV, the HJ, the NS Teachers' League, the NS Women's Organization and the Office for National Health.

The voluntary dispatch of the young people will occur in two groups:

Group I (6–10 year-olds)

Group II (10–14 year-olds)

'The NSV will accommodate the young people in Group I in families. The young people in Group II will be accommodated in:

camps

youth hostels

---

[9] Ibid., p. 136.

school country hostels
other suitable buildings (guest houses, hotels, inns etc.)
The Gau headquarters of the NSV have issued the enclosed guidelines in consultation with me . . .

Please begin *at once* with the recruitment of host families, since the children are expected to arrive in the middle of January. You should take note of the fact that the number allocated to you by the Gau Headquarters of the NSV in the enclosed letter must be adhered to without fail.

Propaganda in the press is banned in accordance with the instructions of Reichsleiter von Schirach. However, there will be no objection to trying to recruit hosts in membership meetings, public meetings, Party evenings.

I have appointed HJ district leader S of the Reich Association for German Youth Hostels to carry out the measures relating to Group II (10–14 year-olds). The district leaders will receive further instructions concerning accommodation in youth hostels, hotels, inns etc. Moreover, I shall be in personal contact with them over this matter.

The KLV district representatives set about organizing the requisitioning of hotels, guest houses, and other buildings under a Reich law (*Reichsleistungsgesetz*) of 1 September 1939. For this they received financial compensation. While some hotels welcomed the fact that they were thereby able to ensure all-the-year-round occupancy and retain their personnel, others, particularly the more expensive hotels in spa towns or fashionable resorts, were less happy.

Meanwhile, on 20 April 1940, the NSV headquarters of Gau Württemberg issued 'Guidelines for the Reception of Children in Host Families on the Basis of the Special Action (Extended *Kinderlandverschickung*)', from which the following excerpts have been taken:

**1190** *Preamble*
. . . It is a fundamental principle that the children are being sent as the result of a free decision of the responsible parents . . .

*Recruitment*
The recruitment of free places in families will be carried out by the NSV. The [party] district leader will be responsible for carrying out the programme in his district.

The NSV will be responsible for carrying out the programme, i.e. including recruitment. However, the political leaders will give extensive support to the NSV.

*The start of the recruitment and the instructions to the political leaders will be determined directly by the Gau headquarters . . .*

Initially free places will be recruited for children from 3–10 years of age.

*Lists of children*
. . . One should note that, in order to achieve a uniform system of accommodation, the children who come from a particular background should be sent to

host parents with equivalent home circumstances. In order that the Gau sending the children can fulfil this requirement, it is necessary—in so far as this is not clear from the statement of occupation—to state in the column 'Alterations or other remarks' what the domestic circumstances are.

Since it is a special programme of a very particular character, the selection of children cannot be made on the basis of need.

Finally, the request of the host parents: boy or girl? Approximate age? should be put in the last column of the list—'Alterations or other remarks' . . .

*Financial compensation*

As a matter of principle, the children should be boarded free of charge. However, the Main Office envisages that parents who cannot be expected to make such a sacrifice should receive a daily payment of RM 1. Naturally such a payment should only be made in exceptional circumstances . . .

*Supervision*

A suitable person to look after the children should be appointed for every NSV local area. She must visit the host families regularly and form conclusions about how the children are getting on and about possible conflicts with the host parents in order to be able to take immediate steps to resolve the difficulties. Regular afternoon sessions of games and events should be arranged to take place at least two or three times a week in order to relieve the host parents. Working closely with the NSF and the JM and JV, arrangements must be made so that the children are entertained with games, outings or other events so that the host parents get a bit of a break. It is intended to come to an arrangement about this with the NSF and the HJ for the whole Gau.

The persons responsible for looking after the children must ensure that the children remain in regular contact with their parents through writing letters; children who cannot write must be given suitable help with this. In so far as the Gaus which dispatch the children have sent liaison personnel as envisaged by the Main Office, the people looking after the children in the various NSV local areas must cooperate with them as closely as possible. These liaison personnel should not, however, interfere with the local NSV offices which are looking after the children. They only have the task of helping to ensure that difficulties are resolved as quickly as possible.

*Educational Problems*

In the event that educational difficulties arise with these children, the NSV Youth Welfare Office should be involved . . .

*Bedwetters*

It has been arranged that these should only be sent by the dispatching Gau after prior agreement has been reached. Chronic bedwetters should not be sent to host families on principle. That means that the host families should be given advice and assistance in the case of those children who occasionally wet their beds as a result of their changed circumstances and in some cases a doctor should be brought in to advise on how to proceed. The Main Office envisages that host parents who suffer significant damage through bedwetters should be given replacements by the NSV. Regulations will also be issued on this by the financial administration. Cases of chronic bedwetters should be reported to the Gau NSV HQ so that alternative accommodation can be arranged.

*School*
The schoolchildren are subject to compulsory school attendance in the districts to which they are sent. The [NSDAP] district must get in touch with the district HQ of the NSLB about the provision of school textbooks. Also, on the basis of the agreements with the NSLB, the district must inform the [NSLB] district how many children are liable for compulsory school attendance in the various individual localities together with their ages and sex, so that the NSLB can get in touch with the responsible school authority concerning their allocation to the public schools and the provision of sufficient teachers.

*Kindergartens*
Children who are not compelled to attend school are to be admitted to NSV kindergartens during the day in so far as these exist.

▬

However, it quickly became apparent that the reliance on individual host families to take in small children and mothers with infants would produce insufficent accommodation, so the NSV was obliged in addition to use guest houses and small hotels with less than thirty beds, whereas the HJ sought accommodation with a minimum of thirty beds. As a result, it proved impossible to rely on families giving free board and lodging to the evacuees. The NSV was obliged to compensate the hosts. The rates were progressively increased and became more differentiated. Thus, for example, according to a letter from the Economic Group for Hotels and Restaurants headquarters in Berlin to its district representatives dated 28 March 1941, the following daily rates were to prevail from then on:

**1191**

|            | for mothers      | for infants and children |
|------------|------------------|--------------------------|
| Class I    | up to 5.50 RM    | up to 3.00 RM            |
| Class II   | up to 4.50 RM    | up to 2.50 RM            |
| Class III  | up to 3.50 RM    | up to 2.00 RM            |

▬

In the case of host families the NSV laid down a maximum of 3.50 RM for mothers and 2 RM for children.

Although evacuation was voluntary, the practice of evacuating whole classes and schools, together with their teachers, meant that parents and children were in fact subject to strong indirect pressure to go because if they remained behind the children would be without their classmates and would be obliged to transfer to other classes or schools. This was spelled out quite clearly in the appeals to parents to send their children away, as the following document makes clear:

**1192**    The Gau Representative for the Extended *Kinderlandverschickung* in Gau Hamburg of the NSDAP

*Announcement to Parents*

Hamburg, 7 November 1942

As part of the Extended KLV the school class attended by your child is soon to be sent to Bohemia/Moravia.

It is the Gauleiter's strongly held wish that as many Hamburg children as possible should be protected against risks to health this winter. As is well known, up to now over 150,000 boys and girls from our city have spent six months at a time in southern Gaus and have had many happy experiences in the KLV camps. Experience has shown that their education can best be assured if they are sent away together with their classmates. For this reason, the Führer has permitted the children to travel en bloc as schools and classes. The teachers are the people who know them best and are best qualified to perform the temporary role of father or mother. In particular, school lessons can be carried on without disturbance and most successfully when the children are all together in such KLV camps. They will come to enjoy learning in the KLV camps since they will be staying in new and beautiful surroundings with good food and arrangements geared to the needs of young people. Carefully selected efficient HJ and BdM leaders support the teachers in their work and ensure that HJ duties are performed in an exemplary manner.

The children are being sent as before on a voluntary basis. But naturally it is best if all the children in the class take part. Parents are, therefore, requested to give their permission on the reverse side of the application form. If they have important reasons for keeping their children back they should put them in writing. While the children who are sent will have the best possible education from their own teachers, those who remain behind will have to expect to be transferred to a class containing a collection of children from several classes or to another school.

The class teachers request that parents should send in their forms during the week of 9–14 November. This will then be followed by the medical examinations and the assemblies held to check on whether the children have adequate clothing and other necessities. The special trains will probably leave in the last week of November. Parents will be given all other details by the school.

Please help to ensure that the KLV is an exemplary operation for the recuperation and education of our big city youth.

HENRY MEYER
KLV Gau representative

I hereby give my permission for my son/daughter to be sent away on the programme of the Extended *Kinderlandverschickung* by the NSDAP. I agree to

him being sent away for a period of at least six months and appreciate that
he/she cannot return before this period has elapsed. I also give my consent to
him/her being vaccinated prior to departure.

Signature of father or legal guardian

In practice it was impossible for the regime to prevent parents from
removing their children from the KLV; it could only insist on their
paying for the return journey. And, from 1942, onwards, despite the
increasing numbers and seriousness of the air raids, it became more and
more difficult to persuade parents to allow their children to be sent
away. Inevitably, most parents felt torn between, on the one hand, the
realization that their children would probably be better off well away
from the threat of bombing and together with their teachers and
classmates and, on the other hand, the desire to keep their children with
them at home, particularly during such critical and uncertain times. But,
as the bombing intensified, so parents became increasingly unhappy
about sending their children away on the principle that 'if we have to
die, we would rather die as a family together'. There were also instances
of children leaving KLV camps of their own accord to seek their parents
after news of a particularly heavy raid.

Another thing which put off some parents from sending their
children away and which worried others while they were away was the
concern that their religious education and practice would suffer. This
was a very real problem since, apart from the fact that the HJ was in
charge of the children's activities outside school lessons and the HJ's
hostility to religion was notorious, there was also the problem that the
children were often evacuated to districts in which a rival denomination
was predominant. Protestant children from Hamburg, for example, were
sent to Catholic districts of Bavaria, while children from Catholic parts
of the Rhineland were sent to Protestant parts of Württemberg. The
church authorities were themselves very concerned about this problem
and encouraged parents and children to try and maintain regular church
attendance and religious instruction. However, whereas the Protestant
Church accepted the necessity for the programme, the Catholic Church
strongly opposed it from the start. In fact, the KLV authorities placed
few direct obstacles in the way of children attending church or going to
confirmation classes, since they were anxious not to alienate the parents.
However, it was largely left to the children themselves to take the
initiative, since teachers were discouraged by the NSLB from associating
themselves with the churches. In fact, there appears to have been some

variation in policy between different Gaus depending on their respective attitudes towards the relationship of Church and school. In the case of Hamburg, for example, where there was a strict separation of the two, the school authorities issued the following directive to its teachers:

**1193**    The KLV camps should be made to exercise the strictest possible reserve in confessional matters. On no account should there be any instruction by clergy, members of religious orders or church representatives. On the other hand, there should of course be the closest possible cooperation with official agencies of the NSDAP, its formations and organizations in the receiving Gau.

Nevertheless, in the case of children evacuated from the Rhineland, the Catholic Church appears to have managed to maintain quite good contact with them. In any case, however, there were the practical difficulties. For example, the problems confronting a Protestant child wishing to attend church in an overwhelmingly Catholic rural area with poor communications were clearly formidable. And finally, in the case of children boarding with host families who belonged to a different religious denomination there was the very real concern that they might be converted by them.

Tensions arising from the differences between the life style of the big cities and that of the countryside were commonplace. This was particularly true where children were boarded out with host parents. Parents complained about their children being forced to work too hard on the farms where they were based, work which was regarded as a matter of course for the farmers' own families. There were also complaints from parents about the poor quality of schooling in the village schools where there were often only one or two classes covering the whole age range. But some of the children also found it difficult to settle down and fit in. For example, a school head in Bamberg, an arch-Catholic town in northern Bavaria, reported to the authorities:

**1194**    I had a big over-mature boy from Hamburg in my 5th class [10–11 year-olds] and I said to him: 'tell our Bamberg boys and girls all about tides.' He replied: 'I've never had any interest in that.' 'What are you interested in, then?' 'A good glass of beer.' The school inspector reports: 'A 12-year-old boy was boarded with a family. He looked round the room and saw the crucifix on the wall, which is normal among Catholic families of the district. Whereupon he said: 'For as long as I'm here take that thing away.' He took the crucifix away. Girls from Hamburg were accommodated in a nice village about 18 km from Bamberg. Already on the second day of their stay we met them in the town. They had got hold of bicycles, had gone to the NSV in Bamberg and had vigorously demanded that they should be moved to the town and were now furious that their wish had not been granted. In reply to our questions they admitted that they had good host families and good food, but they found it too isolated there. They couldn't do anything and the only thing to be seen was oxen. There was probably a ringleader who stirred them up—this is the most unpleasant case: a boy from Harburg, who had already acquired a bad reputation here, was boarded with a good family. Already on the second day he was discontented with something and physically attacked his host mother. Then he went to the station with his suitcase and demanded from the ticket collector that he let him have a ticket to Harburg for 2 RM. This case has been dealt with in the appropriate way . . .

The state of the KLV programme in the autumn of 1943 was summed up by the SD in its report of 30 September as follows:

**1195**  In the case of the implementation of the measures for the evacuation [*Umquartierung*] of schoolchildren it has become apparent that the success of the parent meetings, whose purpose consisted essentially in making clear to parents the need to protect their children from the effects of enemy terror attacks and prompting them to send their children away, depended very much on the skill of the speakers. It has also become evident that this task should be given to suitable head teachers and teachers since the parents have more trust in them than in anybody else and so they are asked for their advice by parents in the case of any doubts. This demonstrates *the need for greater involvement of the schools in the evacuation measures*. The fact that at numerous parents' meetings, particularly in the capital of the Reich, the speakers—in Berlin the majority of them were provided by the Party—could give no accurate information about the future location of the school, the time when they would be setting off etc. created a very unfavourable impression.

Often parents were prompted to adopt a negative attitude by rumours of an unfriendly attitude shown towards and poor treatment of the children by the population in the reception districts, which were a long way from their homes. There were numerous requests for their children to be sent somewhere nearer (the rural hinterland of the big cities), if possible in their own Gau, since there is then the possibility for them to find out how the children are being looked after through weekend visits. However, frequently, a whole number of other factors were responsible for the parents refusal to send their children. Thus, for example, the reports note that:

> Again and again it is brought home to one through conversations with parents that many more children would be sent on the KLV if the teachers were more in evidence in this programme.

Parents and schoolchildren at secondary schools say that they have *no faith in the HJ* and only send their children because they know that the supervision is largely carried out by the teachers. Churchgoers express the view that *the whole point of the evacuation* is to separate the young people from their parents in order *to teach them to be heretics* in camps.

We won't let our children be taken from us. We still have the right to determine what is to
be done with our children.

If we must die then we all want to die together

We won't let our children be taken from us; there is no law which allows it to happen

The districts in which our children are put aren't safe either.

Further objections which are made to the evacuation stem mainly from
concerns about food, the treatment and care of the children when they are sick,
the threat to the moral well-being of the girls, the care of underwear and
clothing etc. In addition, a number of parents say they cannot do without their
children because they rely on their assistance at home or in their business.
Others believed they could not subject their children to separation from their
home because they would not be able to bear it (homesickness). The wish to
have their children with them derived in some cases from the attempt to acquire
special allocations of food and to maintain the whole family's supply of food at
the same level . . .

[Figures were then given of the numbers of children who had been sent on
the KLV programme and of those who had remained behind in the cities. For
example, on 15.9.1943, of the 260,000 children of school age, the parents of
65,000 had refused to send them, while another 6,000 were unaccounted for. In
smaller cities a higher proportion tended to be sent.]

It is clear from the examples given that a considerable number of school-age
children have remained behind in the areas affected by the air war. From our
experience so far one must assume that a large number of parents will continue
to refuse. However, teachers emphasize that through intensive propaganda and
information a considerable number of pupils could be sent away from the
threatened areas. However, care must be taken that the objections of churchgoers—particularly from the West German districts [Catholics!]—can be met by
ensuring that the *promises* made to parents about the provision of religious
instruction in the curriculum *are fulfilled*. The KLV camps which have been
established to cope with the evacuation of whole schools cannot be compared
with the previous work of the KLV which was primarily intended for the
recuperation of young people. Thus the regulations concerning education in the
KLV camps, according to which no confessional education was to be given in
the camps, must be adapted to the changed circumstances.

——

As far as life in the camps was concerned, the evidence is unclear. The
following regulations were issued governing the running of the KLV
'camps' and suggest a relatively liberal regime. Noteworthy is the ban on
corporal punishment. However, the recollections of former KLV
participants suggest that these regulations were by no means always
adhered to and that the regime was on occasions harsh, even brutal:

**1196**    . . . 5. The basic form of the KLV camp varies according to that of the
school which is housed in it. Upper, middle and Main Schools should as a
matter of principle be accommodated in large units or in large centres so that

the requirements of the various specialist subjects can be met.

6. The leadership personnel in the KLV camps are as follows:

(1) Camp head [*Lagerleiter*]
(2) Camp team leader [*Lagermannschaftsführer/Lagermädelführerin*]
(3) Deputy camp head
(4) Camp teacher
(5) Camp boys/girls section leader [*Lagerjungzugführer*]
(6) Camp boys/girls group leader [*Lagerjungenschaftsführer*]
(7) Camp matron
(8) Personnel for maternal care
(9) The domestic bursar

7. The educational task of the KLV requires a unified and clear educational leadership of the camp. In order to guarantee this the direction of the school activities and that of the camp as a whole must be concentrated in the same person. It will be exercised by the camp head. He is responsible for the overall direction of the KLV camp and is the superior of all the leadership personnel in the camp. The responsibilities of the camp head have been assigned to him by the Führer's representative for the Extended KLV. He carries out the activities of the school head and teacher in the service of the state school administration . . .

9. Despite the often considerable difference in age, a comradely relationship should be established between the camp head and the camp team leader which will find expression in a happy and responsible camp regime. The camp head has the ultimate power of command in all camp matters in every case. In the event of a difference of views his decision is binding on the camp team leader.

The camp head does not have disciplinary powers vis-à-vis the camp team leader. Here the camp rules of the Extended KLV should be applied.

12. The personnel involved in maternal care duties are employed in order to deepen the educational experience of the camp and to maintain the spiritual bond with the family. One of their practical duties is to look after clothing and equipment. The camp head will determine their other activities.

I   All members of the camp community are subject to the camp rules.

II   Punishments can be imposed on those who fail to fulfill the duties imposed on them by membership of the camp community.

III   Educational punishments consist of
1. A reprimand face to face in private.
2. A reprimand in front of the class or school.
3. Special additional duties. They should not exceed one hour per week, in the event of several breaches of duty three hours per week.
4. A ban on going out of the camp for a week.
5. Confinement to a room for up to a week; during free time in a locked single room with full board.
6. Transfer to another camp.
7. Expulsion from the camps of the KLV.

IV   The following are banned:

1. The imposition of heavy work which is calculated to damage young people's health.
2. Corporal punishment.
3. Unnecessary denigration in the eyes of other young people or insult to their sense of honour.
4. Punishment exercises.
5. Removal of food . . .

XI   The camp rules and the penal code of the Hitler Youth. Minor transgressions which, according to the HJ's penal code would only lead to a reprimand or a warning are to be replaced by the list of punishments contained in the camp rules. An action under the HJ's penal code should only be initiated in serious cases.

Minor transgressions are bound to occur more frequently in the context of a camp community than in normal HJ activities. These kinds of transgression should, therefore, not be punished under the HJ penal code since such punishments will be recorded in the personal file of the individual concerned.

The school regulations are applicable for the maintenance of order during lessons.

The teacher should report more serious transgressions and punishments (detention for several hours, repeated amounts of extra work etc.) to the school head, who should in certain circumstances inform the camp head.

Corporal punishment is banned within the framework of the KLV educational programme.

———

While the HJ was responsible for the overall organization of the KLV, the NSLB was in charge of organizing the teaching arrangements, at least until 1944, by which time it had been closed down under Bormann's party rationalization scheme and was replaced in this function by the Reich Education Ministry. Within the 'camps' the teachers were responsible for the school lessons, whereas the HJ Camp Team Leader and his subordinates organized the children's activities during the rest of the day. Thus, the division of responsibilities within the organization of the KLV provided opportunities for conflict between the HJ and the teachers and tension was indeed endemic, particularly in the early days. For example, according to a letter from a Hamburg teacher to the liaison staff in Bayreuth dated 25 October 1940:

**1197**   We already noticed the opposition of the BdM to the teachers at the preliminary meeting before the departure of the transport. In response to a remark of district leader Marx [of the NSLB] concerning our responsibility for the dispatch of the children, one of the [BdM] leaders declared that they were not teachers' skivvies and that they received their instructions from the BdM alone. This negative attitude led to various tensions during the journey. For example, our instructions were criticized and revoked in front of the children. Also, with the exception of the one accompanying me, a former pupil of our school, none of the BdM girls found it necessary to introduce herself to the respective teachers. The tension increased towards the end of the journey to such an extent that it finally led to a discussion. At this point the BdM girls announced that they had the decisive authority in the KLV programme and the teachers were responsible for school work. We naturally rejected this claim since we must be responsible for the children entrusted to us.

Schirach had seized the opportunity of securing the responsibility for setting up the KLV programme in the hope of realizing a long-standing goal of establishing for the HJ the dominant role in German education and, in the process, transforming it in accordance with its own particular version of Nazi educational principles. The HJ was indeed successful in marginalizing the NSLB and, at least until the last phase, virtually excluding the state authorities (Reich Education Ministry) altogether. However, it appears that the teachers were increasingly able to assert their authority within the 'camps'. This was partly because the camp heads were teachers. However, at any rate in the case of the HJ, as if not more important was the fact that the HJ Camp Team Leaders, who were responsible for supervising the boys' outside school activities, became younger and younger as the older ones were called up into the armed forces. As a result, those who remained lacked the experience, maturity and self confidence to assert themselves.

In theory the KLV 'camps' provided a golden opportunity for the indoctrination of the children with Nazi ideas and values since they were away from their families and other potentially distracting influences and this was the assumption which underlay the HJ's direction of the programme. In practice, however, any such programme was faced with serious problems. Most important was concern for the attitude of the parents. For if the programme was to succeed it had to retain their approval and support, which an ideologically hardline and harsh regime would be liable to jeopardize. Indeed, at the end of 1943, the Party Chancellery felt obliged to issue the following directive:

**1198**   Rumours have been spread in various Gaus in the Reich that the sending away of young people of school age is not purely a war-time measure but intended to remove from parents the education of their children and to place the boys and girls under the exclusive influence of the state and the party. These rumours must be vigorously refuted. They are spread by enemy propaganda to disturb parents and are gladly passed on by negative elements among our people. The extended *Kinderlandverschickung* is of course a measure designed purely for the protection of the lives of German youth as a result of the air war. After the war the *Kinderlandverschickung* will be returned to its original purpose and will have the sole task of providing children with impaired health with the opportunity to recover.

▬▬

Another problem was that the programme was increasingly forced to rely on teachers of the older generation and those recalled from retirement, since most of the younger ones had been called up into the armed forces. This older generation, while generally strongly national-istic, tended to be more traditional and conservative in its views and pedagogical practice. One participant, who attended KLV 'camps', has described his teachers as follows:

**1199**   We came after all from a humanities grammar school and the majority of our teachers had already retired and now, during the war, had been reactivated. Certainly two or three were convinced Party members, but the majority were so old that they regarded Hitler, National Socialism and the war with a certain, in some cases considerable, reserve. I can still remember how we rolled through the room in our bedding bawling our heads off during the broadcast of a Hitler speech which we were supposed to listen to. The peaceful old gentlemen also provided completely normal, traditional lessons. They taught Latin and Greek just like they'd been used to doing for decades. Nowadays, one can laugh about it, even find it absurd. In those days this durability was a positive force, less vulnerable and not so easily manipulable. One shouldn't forget what a short time this all took place in. One shouldn't compare it with other periods. Adenauer governed for ten years, Hitler only for twelve, the war lasted for only six years.

▬▬

In general, there appears not to have been significantly more political indoctrination of young people in the 'camps' than already existed through compulsory membership of the HJ and normal school lessons, though this undoubtedly varied from 'camp' to 'camp'. The following is a typical plan of the day's events:

**1200**

| | |
|---|---|
| 7.00 | Getting-up time |
| 7.05–7.15 | Early morning PE |
| 7.15–8.00 | Washing and cleaning the room |
| 8.00 | Morning parade |
| 8.15 | First Breakfast |
| 8.45–10.20 | Lessons |
| 10.30 | Second Breakfast |
| 10.40–12.15 | Lessons |

| 12.20–15.00 | Lunch+Free time |
| 15.00–16.00 | Sports |
| 16.00 | Teatime |
| 16.30–18.30 | Homework |
| 19.00 | Supper |
| 19.30–20.45 | Time for writing letters, mending, cleaning, singing |
| 20.00 | Evening news on the radio |
| 20.45 | Bedtime |
| 21.00 | Lights out |

In addition, the HJ held its usual regular 'hostel evenings'.

In fact the situation in the 'camps' appears to have been extremely diverse. Although, inevitably, given the degree of improvisation necessary and the problems of wartime, the physical conditions were often by no means ideal, in general they seem to have been adequate and in some cases were better than those at home. For example, an assessment of the quality and quantity of food provided at the camps based on 500 post-war statements by former evacuees concluded that 2 per cent were very bad, 16 per cent bad, 40 per cent satisfactory and 42 per cent very good.

Other aspects of camp life were even more varied. The standard of education appears to have been quite high, particularly in those areas such as art, crafts, drama and music which benefited most from the opportunity for intensive practice. In the case of the more specialized academic subjects, particularly the sciences, which required books and equipment, it was clearly more difficult to maintain standards. Outside the school lessons great emphasis was placed on keeping the children occupied with various kinds of games, crafts and sports. Teachers and HJ leaders were given crash courses to equip them with the necessary skills. Much depended on the quality and attitude of the teachers few of whom had any experience of boarding school life beyond the occasional class trip. Some 'camps' were run with a relatively harsh regime and some teachers were hardline Nazis, while others allowed their pupils quite a lot of free time and operated in a fairly relaxed way. The celebration of Christmas, for example, differed considerably from 'camp' to 'camp'. In some it followed the official Nazi line of being a festival of light with virtually all the Christian elements removed; in others it was much more traditional. However, the regulations laid down for punishment in the 'camps', with the specific exclusion of corporal punishment, demonstrate the authorities' concern not to alienate parents by operating too harsh a regime and the general emphasis seems to have been in that direction. As a result of this variety and also of the different characters of the children involved, inevitably people's experiences of the 'camps' were very diverse. For some it was one of the happiest periods of their lives, for others it was a traumatic period which they were anxious to forget. The following documents reflect these different experiences. First there are two extreme examples of differing physical conditions:

**1201** (*a*) We had enough free time. On hot days we used it to bathe in one of the fountains in the inner park of the palace. Some of us were allowed to use the pony trap. In the autumn we used to roast potatoes on an open fire and in winter we went sledging. We had brought our own skis and skates. There were cosy theatrical performances and numerous sports competitions in the outer courtyard.

(*b*) In Berchtesgaden I received marching orders for myself and my 67 girls in the direction of Regensburg. It was only on the train that we learnt where we were going. After changing trains four times we arrived around 23.15 in Arrach in the district of Cham. A soldier then led us uphill through thick forest. After two hours we arrived at our destination with our completely exhausted children. It was an isolated farm 900 metres above sea level. It was a two-hour walk to the nearest house. There was an inn in the farm house. Nobody knew we were coming. We were accommodated in an annexe and lay in unmade beds. Mice and rats ran round the rooms. During the following weeks our bedding and clothing was continually being nibbled by mice. To fetch our post four of our girls had to walk for hours down to the valley along the bed of a stream. The farm does have a marvellous situation. There is also enough food. In the meantime, three stoves have been brought up; the water freezes in winter and there is a weekly contact with the outside world by using skis. The district representative [of the NSV] from Cham, who is living in his own warm flat, is quite optimistic that we can make it through the winter. We are determined to defend our position until the very last moment. Nobody is going to accuse us of cowardice. All 67 of our girls have lost their homes in Hamburg; two girls have lost their mothers. I have just had news that my parents are homeless, their house is completely burned out.

The following documents represent contrasting accounts of the way in which the camps were run:

**1202** (*c*) We had enough free time because the main emphasis as far as our lot was concerned was on school work. Once our homework was done and everything in order we could do sports or at certain specified times go out on our own.

(*d*) With a total complement of 180 in the Pump Rooms at Bad Peterstal I think there was too little free time. The camp was controlled by the HJ. After the morning lessons the boys were continually occupied by the HJ leaders with marches, competitions, and fieldcraft exercises. When I became the person who made the rules at the next camps I always ensured that there was enough free time. Apparently they had seen what nonsense it was to have camps that were too large and set up units which could be more easily overseen.

(*e*) We did not have an exceptional amount of political indoctrination. Herr Birth even taught us sailors' songs in English, which we sang with gusto. We performed plays at Christmas for the local inhabitants or, for those who were lucky, for our parents who came to visit us from Berlin when it was possible. In March 1944 it was time for Class 8 to leave. We were to begin our apprentice-ships in Berlin and no one was ashamed of his tears when we said goodbye to the boys who were staying behind and to Frau and Herr Doll. When we arrived next day in the bombed-out Anhalt station and saw the houses burning to left and right, we realized what was awaiting us and that a marvellous time was over which could never return.

(*f*) The daily routine was the same as in Bad Kissingen, though the duties were stricter, almost military. The drill or the bull was like in a barracks so that the neighbours often complained to the camp leader. But one thing I learnt there has stuck, namely correctness, punctuality, readiness to help, a concern for cleanliness bordering on the fussy. A tremendous emphasis was placed on cleanliness whether in terms of keeping the room tidy, or bed making, or bodily hygiene, above all finger nails and teeth were inspected before every meal. Otherwise it was a time which one is glad to forget and had little to do with youthful freedoms.

▬▬

In a boarding-school situation it is of course not just the regime imposed from above which is important but also the atmosphere which exists among the pupils themselves, though clearly the first has an important effect on the second. One participant described the atmos-phere in his 'camp', based in a sanatorium, as follows:

**1203**    At that time [1940] we knew little about the effects of bombing and so fear, despair and mourning were in this phase not so evident. They probably only expressed themselves indirectly: the number of bedwetters was incredibly high and also we children were subject to strange outbursts which are difficult to explain but possibly derived from repressed anxiety states. In the sanatorium there were often real battles, the flower pots flew out of the windows . . . We behaved altogether very badly . . . We slept sixteen to a room. Sometimes a boy would wake up and cry at night. We didn't behave in a very friendly way towards these chaps. Sometimes, it ended quite harmlessly with a pillow fight but sometimes also with a beating up for the person concerned. Yes, unfortunately one has to admit that we were pretty merciless. But we had a Camp Team Leader who, although he played a secondary role during the daytime was a good friend to us. He intervened during one of these beatings-up and told us that we shouldn't treat each other like this. He was later killed in action.

▬▬

Dahrendorf's 'camp' was located in Poland and many of the other 'camps' were based in the occupied territories. He later described the relations between the German boys and the local inhabitants as follows:

**1204**    We behaved very badly altogether during this period, also towards the Poles. One is ashamed to admit it today, but it was true. We were the occupiers, or rather the children of the occupiers. And we behaved accordingly. Some of us stole things. At first of course the children stole with a bad conscience. But the Polish shopkeepers didn't dare go to the police. When the children noticed that nothing happened, more and more went to the shops and stole. Our sanatorium was often put under quarantine, which was rather strange, allegedly because of scarlet fever. But now I'm not sure whether it wasn't something else. Perhaps what we were up to even became too much for the German authorities.

---

### (vi) Morale and Morals

One of the major concerns of the German authorities was what was seen as the serious threat of young people 'running wild' under wartime conditions. To some extent this reflected the experience of the First World War, which largely shaped expectations for the next war. But it was also a reaction to an increase in various forms of juvenile delinquency during the pre-war years. In part this was no doubt a response by young people to the norms of the new regime, which encouraged a contempt for civility and humane behaviour and glorified force and the ruthless assertion of will.

Even before the war the regime had responded to this development by establishing, on 24 May 1939, a Reich Headquarters for the Combating of Juvenile Delinquency in the Reich Criminal Police Office. Then, on 4 October 1939, a Decree for the Protection against Hardened Criminals was issued permitting the application of adult penal law to young people over the age of 16, so that they could be subject to penal servitude and the death penalty. The issue received an even higher profile when 'The Supervision of Youth' formed the subject of a meeting of the Ministerial Council for the Defence of the Reich held on 1 February 1940. It was attended by most of the top government and party leaders and Göring gave the opening address:

**1205**    The Field Marshal expressed the view that during the war youth needed to be looked after particularly well in every respect. In addition, Germany, like every belligerent country, must take steps in good time to ensure that its young people did not go off the rails. The blackout and the lack of supervision under wartime conditions facilitate a lack of discipline and the commission of criminal offences on the part of young people, but do not generally explain them. Extensive measures must, therefore, be introduced; they should not be restricted to superficialities.

▬▬▬

The main measure of youth supervision agreed at the meeting was a series of lectures by leading Nazis through which young people would be 'informed of their everyday duties in wartime'. They would be broadcast, with teachers and employers obliging the young people to listen to them. These broadcasts were to be organized by Reichsleiter Alfred Rosenberg in his capacity as 'the Führer's representative for the comprehensive intellectual and ideological indoctrination of the NSDAP'. After an introduction by him, the first lecture would be given by Göring. The lectures were to be accompanied by weekly slogans and to be elucidated further by the teachers in school and by the Hitler Youth leaders in the regular Hitler Youth evenings. They were to be supported by further speeches at Gau level. In his guidelines for the lecture series, dated 16 February 1940, Rosenberg laid down that:

**1206**    On the negative side one should avoid dealing with problems that are controversial. So talks should not refer to the confessional struggle; the whole issue of Church policy must, therefore, be excluded from the campaign. Moreover, difficult problems of an economic nature should not be discussed in a theoretical way since young people are not sufficiently prepared for this.

The lectures must appeal above all to the character and feelings of German youth and continually arouse their sense of duty. In this connection it is necessary to portray courage in the struggle of life as decisive and to explain why their fathers are at the front and what this involves or why they are serving on the home front and are having to exert their energies to the limit. The same applies to the work of their mothers.

Furthermore, it is necessary to refer to the connection between the external freedom of a nation and its ability to work and develop independent productive energy at home. Examples from German history, particularly from the period 1918–33, should be used to explain the necessity for the present struggle. Since the lectures will often coincide with the commemoration days of great personalities, these should be incorporated in the reflections.

In addition to these lectures concerned with the general attitude of youth, there are the crucial particular issues which in general should provide the immediate and concrete topic of the lectures. Social justice should be demonstrated in terms of the Party and the Labour Front and the necessary rationing of foodstuffs shown to be a sometimes tough but necessary means for the just provision for all. The honour of labour and the concept of the soldierly qualities of labour will continually recur through references to the German Labour Service.

In connection with the Four-Year Plan, young people will need to be reminded of the need to conserve used materials, to assist with sowing and harvesting and of many other facts of life. They will be instructed to see in this assistance an important part of their duty as young people and to regard work in these areas not as something unpleasant to be rejected but as help for their fathers who have been called up and for their working mothers and given as a matter of course.

The Reich Women's leadership will speak to the boys and girls on behalf of the mothers . . .

However, judging by the following report on the April–June 1940 lecture series, organized by Rosenberg with Hess, Rust, Ley et al. as speakers, the scheme was a total failure. It is from the head teacher of the St Mary's State Secondary School for Boys in Oldenburg to the Oldenburg state Ministry for Churches and Schools, dated 30 September 1940:

**1207** Re: *Decree of 9 August 1940 on School radio broadcasts*

We have all become convinced that the intended effect is not always achieved. As is the case with every broadcast listened to en masse, the same was true on this occasion, namely that even a not particularly good speaker, who appears in person in front of the pupils, sometimes has more impact than the best speaker on the radio. They were held at 8 o'clock in the morning. A large number of pupils fall asleep on such occasions, namely the younger children, particularly when they happen too often. In our view they should be restricted to special events.

There have also been occasions when young people's delight in sarcasm has made itself felt when a speech appears to have been given off the cuff. We have learnt that the boys often joked about the intellectual coherence, the formulations and the definitions in the speeches (e.g. the concept of freedom) [in the margin in pencil: Ley]. 'People are free when, in the first place, they have something to eat and drink, clothes to wear and somewhere to live, as they need it and want it; secondly, they are free when they can go out into the world as and when they want; and thirdly, they are free when the rest of the nation respects and values their work and performance. Then they are free; that is the point of freedom.'

As far as I could gather the whole thing has caused great disappointment among all types of schools. I consider it my duty as a responsible educator to bring this to your attention. Other head teachers reported the broadcasts had been disturbed by the smaller children or by poor radio reception and many did not have radios.

Understandably, therefore, the authorities were not prepared to rely solely on lectures by Nazi leaders to ensure that young people remained on the straight and narrow. And, less than a month later, on 9 March

1940, the following Police Decree for the Protection of Youth was issued, which standardized for the Reich as a whole a number of regulations which had already been issued by several regional authorities:

**1208** § 1. *Exclusion from public streets and squares during the hours of darkness*
Young people under 18 years of age are not permitted to hang around in public streets and squares or in other public places during the hours of darkness.

§ 2. *Exclusion from public houses*
(i) Young people under 18, who are not accompanied by the responsible parent or guardian or an adult designated by him, are forbidden to frequent places of refreshment of all kinds after 9 o'clock at night.
(ii) Young people under 16 unaccompanied by the responsible parent or guardian or an adult designated by him are not permitted to frequent places of refreshment.

§ 3. *Exclusion from public cinemas and variety and cabaret performances*
Young people under 18 unaccompanied by the responsible parent or an adult designated by him are forbidden to visit public cinemas and variety and cabaret performances after 9 o'clock at night.

§ 4. *Ban on alcohol consumption*
Young people under 18 are forbidden to consume spirits or beverages consisting mainly of spirits; young people under 16 in the absence of the responsible parent or an adult designated by him are also forbidden to consume other alcoholic beverages.

§ 5. *Ban on smoking in public*
Young people under 18 are forbidden to smoke tobacco products in public.

§ 6. *Exclusion from public dances*
§ 1 clause 1 of the Police Decree Concerning the Exclusion of Young People from Dances of 29 November 1939 is revised as follows:
(i) Young people under 18 are only permitted to be present in rooms in which public dances are taking place or at dances held in the open air when accompanied by the responsible parent or guardian or an adult designated by him and then only until 11 o'clock at night.

§ 7. *Exclusion from public shooting and gaming establishments*
The exclusion from public shooting and gaming establishments is regulated in accordance with the Police decree of 24 October 1939.

§ 8. *Exceptions*
(i) The regulations of this decree do not apply to members of the armed forces and of the Reich Labour Service.
(ii) The regulation contained in § 2 does not apply to events organised by the Party or to young people who are in transit.
(iii) Exceptions from the bans in §§ 2–3 can be made by the district police authority.

§ 9. *Penalties*

I Young people.

1. Young people who wilfully contravene §§ 1–5 of this decree will be punished with imprisonment for up to three weeks or a fine of up to RM 50.

II Adults.

2. The following will be punished with a fine of RM 150, in particularly serious cases with imprisonment for up to six weeks.

(a) Responsible *parents and persons designated* by them who, through the wilful or negligent neglect of their duty of supervision, enable young people to offend against § 1–5 of this decree.

(b) Proprietors of the establishments and organizers of the events referred to in § 2–3, who wilfully or negligently enable young people to offend against the §§ 2 and 3 of this decree.

——

The Nazi party's welfare organization, the NSV, had been seeking for some time to expand its role in the field of youth welfare where, hitherto, the main responsibility had lain with the state Youth Offices (*Jugendämter*) often assisted by the Protestant and Catholic Church welfare organizations. In the summer of 1939, the NSV had established a special department for youth welfare (*Jugendhilfe*). This now leapt to exploit the opportunities opened up by this new decree, as is clear from the following circular issued by the Gau Württemberg NSV headquarters to its district branches on 26 March 1940:

**1209**    With reference to the workplan for March sent to the districts with the letter of 5 March 1940, it was established that initially, independently of the further development of cooperation with the Youth Offices, the fight against the particular threat to youth posed by the war would be at the forefront of the work of the NSV Youth Service (see point 3 of this circular).

Meanwhile, the enclosed Police Decree for the Protection of Youth has appeared which covers all the aspects which posed a threat. From now onwards this decree is authoritative for the development of the programme for the prevention of juvenile delinquency; it requires cooperation and support from the Youth Service for the police measures in all those cases in which, going beyond the individual young person involved, the whole family as the unit responsible for his or her upbringing must be dealt with through the provision of advice or in order to provide a substitute for it. This special task derives from the new regulation concerning the legal responsibility of the parents or guardians as well as those to whom they delegate the responsibility (§ 9, 2a). As a result, the entire preventive work of our Youth Service will now receive a degree of support from the police authorities which it has not hitherto possessed. That implies, however, a duty for us to work that much harder. For the point of such a police decree is to be seen not only in the prevention of individual young people from being damaged in their health or morals or being punished, but rather the aim is at the same time to exercise a positive educative influence on neglectful or ignorant parents and to recognize inadequate parents before it is too late. For this reason it is intended that, in addition to police bans, warnings or punishments, all those agencies which deal with orphaned, vulnerable and delinquent young people should become involved.

In view of this and *in conjunction with the HJ* please initiate the systematic involvement of all the relevant agencies either (a) in the form of an immediate meeting with the police [*Landrat*] *with the participation of the HJ* or (b), in the event that no delay occurs as a result, you can use the opportunity to have the *Landrat* summon the new Youth Office Advisory Council.

The representative and assistants of the NSV Youth Service will in any case be involved:

1. through participation in the police and HJ patrols;
2. in the continuous clandestine observation by our male and female local branch youth assistants of those places and pubs which, on the basis of previous experience, require watching and the passing on to the local police station of the information gleaned by such observation;
3. through the receipt of police reports in all those cases in which, on the basis of police investigations, it is assumed that family upbringing has been flawed (father's absence, mother's outside employment, marriage breakdown, alcoholism, poor parental example etc.) and the establishment of appropriate guardianship arrangements for the protection of the individual child, of siblings etc. (use the enclosed form which should be duplicated and placed at the disposal of the police);
4. through the establishment of cooperation between the family under supervision and the local HJ (BdM) leader;
5. through the involvement of the Youth Office in those cases in which, on the basis of the family situation, guardianship measures appear necessary (legally imposed custody orders, the removal of custody, remand school education etc.)

I expect a report on what has been initiated by April.

———

Thus, on the basis of the Police Decree of 9 March 1940, the NSV sought to establish its right to exercise a supervisory role over the family in all those cases where children stepped out of line. This would then enable it to subject the process of parental upbringing to its own ideologically determined criteria of what was 'good' as opposed to 'poor' parental example. By establishing a close association with the police in their operation of the decree, it would be enabled to enforce its will.

The main principle behind the NSV's youth work was set out in an article to mark the first decade of the NSV 'Mother and Child' organization as follows:

**1210**   The National Socialist Youth Welfare [NSV] organizes its welfare measures according to the young person's value to the national community. Thus, welfare is directed in the first instance at morally vulnerable young people who are worthy of support and educable, whereas young people who are ineducable and incapable of fitting into the community [*gemeinschaftsunfähig*] are only supervised in order to ensure that they do not pose a threat to morally healthy young people.

▬▬▬

The thrust of the NSV to take over the responsibilities of the official Youth Offices was partially parried by the state authorities, who successfully played off the HJ, which had similar ambitions, against the NSV. In any case the NSV lacked the trained personnel fully to take over the responsibilities of the Youth Offices. A compromise was reached in an edict of the Reich Interior Ministry dated 24 October 1941. However, the result of all this bureaucratic warfare so typical of the Third Reich was a deterioration of the service, as was pointed out by the city of Görlitz in a report to the Reich Interior Ministry dated 21 January 1944:

**1211**    The Youth Office has always had the municipal social workers at its disposal to investigate family circumstances. In the old days the reports of the social workers were regarded as quite satisfactory, since they are professionals and are often already familiar with the cases involved through their welfare work. Now, however, because of the agreement [of 24.10.1941], the NSV has to be consulted and, in addition, the HJ and BdM are required to comment on the individual cases. Also the schools, the employers etc. are expected to give their opinion about the young people involved. These investigations take far too long and often weeks go by before all the results of the enquiries reach the Youth Office. This procedure complicates the carrying out of our duties. In urgent cases social workers can report in a matter of hours, whereas that is quite impossible for the other agencies because the chain of command is far too long. In the case of the NSV the NSV Youth Welfare Office, the local branch leader, the youth desk officer and possibly the cell and block leaders are all involved.

▬▬▬

On 4 October 1940, the regime endeavoured to strengthen its hand in dealing with young offenders by introducing the Decree to supplement the Youth Penal Code:

**1212**    The Ministerial Council for the Defence of the Reich has ordained for the territory of the Greater German Reich by law:

§ 1 *Youth Detention*
1. If a young person has committed a punishable act the judge may impose youth detention in place of imprisonment or custody.
2. The maximum period of youth detention which may be imposed is one month, the minimum is a week or a weekend. Youth detention will be measured in full days, weeks, or a period of a month, or as weekend detention for a period of between at least one and at most four weekends.

The judge in the Juvenile Court is entitled to impose youth detention and it will be imposed under his supervision in rooms of the Reich judicial administration.

§ 2 *Accelerated Procedure*
1. If a sentence of youth detention is anticipated then the accelerated procedure contained in . . . of the decree of 21 February 1940 is applicable.
2. On the application of the public prosecutor the judge can order the immediate imposition of youth detention either in his judgment or subsequently. The judgment cannot be appealed. The appeal court can order a postponement or an interruption of the sentence.
. . .
1. Anyone who fails to ensure adequate supervision for a person under 18 years of age, for whom he has the responsibility for supervision will be punished with imprisonment of up to six months or with custody or with a fine if the person being supervised commits a punishable offence which the person responsible for supervision could have prevented by adequate supervision. This does not apply where other provisions impose another punishment.
2. A person is considered responsible for supervision within the meaning of this provision who has the care of the young person concerned or who has been entirely or mainly entrusted with their education and with looking after them.
3. Criminal proceedings will only be instituted on the application of the responsible agency [Public Prosecutor].

▬▬▬

The Reich Youth Leader Artur Axmann, explained the purpose of the new decree in a speech to the Academy for German Law in Berlin on 6 November 1940:

**1213** The only reforming measures recognized by the Juvenile Court Law [of 16.2.1923], apart from warnings and the imposition of particular obligations, were a supervision order or borstal. The practice of handing over the juvenile to the discipline of parents or school was little used. What was lacking was a means of discipline which fell between custodial punishments and these educative measures. For this reason penal practice tended to move in the direction of not implementing custodial sentences but suspending them. We believe, however, that the educative effect of a suspended sentence is more than suspect. In our view a more healthy approach and one more appropriate for young people is to punish a misdemeanour on the spot harshly and strictly and thereby to deal with the matter once and for all. Youth detention, which has been introduced, is intended to replace short custodial sentences and at the same time to eliminate the imposition of suspended sentences. It is the last call to young people: Up to here, but no further! We hope that educative measures will be favourably influenced by this new disciplinary procedure.

▬▬▬

There were, however, mixed views among those who were involved in dealing with juvenile delinquency. For example, on 3 March 1942 the

President of the Higher *Land* Court in Düsseldorf reported to the Reich Ministry of Justice as follows:

**1214** On the basis of the available information, most of which comes from juvenile court judges, it could be assumed that youth detention had generally had a favourable impact on the young people involved and in this sense had proved beneficial. However, a somewhat different picture has emerged from a lengthy circular of the Reich Trustee of Labour for the Economic District of Westphalia, whose area also covers the district of the Higher *Land* Court in Hamm, dated 23 December 1941, which was based on excerpts from the reports of all the Labour Offices. The majority of these reports dealing with young people upon whom youth detention has been imposed for breaches of the obligation to work (labour discipline) state that there was no evidence that the imposition of youth detention had any noticeable effect let alone that of a shock. This is, however, mostly attributed to the fact that the measures taken came too late or were too mild. While it was recognized that, although to start with the punishment had not been imposed and carried out with sufficient speed, later on significant improvements had occurred. Nevertheless, the opinion was expressed that the weekend detention did not have a lasting impact on those involved. Indeed, there were even frequent reports that weekend detention was a measure which many young people experienced as a badge of honour; remarks had even been made to the effect that 'every decent German boy should have been in weekend detention at least once'.

In general, it was said that breaches by young people of their work contracts had not been reduced since the introduction of youth detention; in some reports it was mentioned that those affected had repeated the offence. The imposition of protective custody, a spell at a labour re-education camp [*Arbeitserziehungslager*] and in general mercilessly compelling them to work hard had proved much more effective than the weekend detention which was usually imposed.

The President of the Higher *Land* Court in Darmstadt produced a shrewd and relatively balanced assessment of the development of juvenile delinquency during the war in his report to the Reich Ministry of Justice on 21 May 1943:

**1215** The following reflections may be of interest as a contribution to the assessment of juvenile delinquency:

One cannot speak of a general decline in the morality of youth. In response to the frequent complaint that young people often lack the requisite reticence, are arrogant and much less disciplined than was previously the case, one must, in my view, point out that these facts are to some extent simply manifestations of what otherwise should be regarded as a very positive development. Whereas previously young people acquired responsibility too late, nowadays, above all under the pressure of war, young people are faced with demands which in normal times only adults are confronted with. The lively, more valuable and more active sections of youth have shown themselves to be very much equal to these demands and have demonstrated an exemplary commitment and willingness to work hard both at the workplace as well as in other spheres (above all during and after air raids). Probably as a result of this young people's desire for independence has grown. They are less prepared to acknowledge authoritarian relationships and demonstrate a greater ruthlessness in the assertion of their desires.

However, there are in addition certain excesses which certainly represent the negative effects of wartime conditions. It is becoming regrettably apparent that young people earn comparatively high wages and that at the same time their labour is urgently needed. In fact, in many cases they are the only support of their masters. Their awareness of their indispensability tends to lead them to overestimate themselves. On the other hand, they are aware that they can get away with more than they could otherwise do, while their employers, since they are absolutely dependent on their apprentices as workers, are often loath to deal with them with the appropriate strictness. One keeps seeing employers who not only do not report them when they slack off, but if a young person is sentenced to youth detention because of a misdemeanour, take all available steps to postpone its implementation until he is called up into the Wehrmacht or the Reich Labour Service (RAD). Another problem is the absence of the younger and middle-aged members of the retinue in the individual plants who used to ensure that the apprentices in their factories respected authority and maintained discipline. Those who are still working there are too few in number, to some extent too old, and are too busy themselves to generate the necessary respect or to make a perceptible contribution to the training of the apprentices and youngest workers.

As far as the commission of punishable offences is concerned, the expectation of an impending call-up into the Wehrmacht plays a certain role. There have been repeated instances where, in the event that young people are about to be called to account for misdemeanours, they straight away volunteer for the Wehrmacht, the Waffen SS, O[rganization] T[odt] or the RAD on the assumption that in this way they can escape the unpleasant results of an offence. If they succeed in their intention, it is then quite difficult to institute proceedings or execute the sentence. In the case of minor transgressions this outcome may be acceptable. More serious is the fact that, as a result of such events, some young people may form the opinion that one can risk doing something just before being called up without having to bear the consequences.

More serious in my view are certain manifestations in the sphere of morality. Above all, according to the unanimous reports of the judges concerned with youth matters, among wide circles of female youth there is a disappearance of the natural sense of modesty, which manifests itself in the relationship between young girls and much older men, in the contact with prisoners of war and foreign workers, and in the frequent visits to bars and places of public entertainment by such adolescent girls in the company of males. Sometimes, one also gets the impression that the struggle waged by National Socialism against a religious morality which is alien to the people is wrongly interpreted by a section of youth as a removal of previous bonds and barriers and not as a call to an increased sense of personal responsibility and a clear moral stance.

Thus, verdicts show that criminal offences are increasing in particular in the area of sexual offences . . .

In addition to sexual offences, property offences are particularly frequent in the sphere of juvenile delinquency, of which a number of serious ones were dealt with by the courts. Also, cases of refusal to work on the part of young people have been very frequent.

According to the reports of the enforcement director of juvenile prisons, the imposition of sentences without a fixed duration has proved itself. Where really criminal tendencies have revealed themselves, the juvenile courts have made systematic use of this sentence.

———

The following report by the Reich Ministry of Justice on the emergence and combating of youth gangs, produced at the beginning of 1944, provides a comprehensive account of the problem as it was seen by the authorities. It is interesting as much for the insight it provides into their thinking as for the details of the phenomenon itself:

**1216**　The problem of the threat to youth and juvenile criminality manifests itself in particular in the formation of youth gangs. For, since the beginning of the war, and above all since the start of the terror air raids, there has been an increasing number of reports about combinations of young people who are pursuing partly criminal, but also to some extent political and ideological goals . . .

In Gelsenkirchen a gang of approximately fifty young people were involved in thefts and robberies. They called themselves 'Edelweiss Pirates', met together every evening and were opposed to the HJ. Similar observations have been made in Essen, Bochum and Wattenscheid. In Cologne the Edelweiss Pirates have also made an appearance. They carried out propaganda for the *bündisch* (see below) youth and printed leaflets.

Düsseldorf has also reported Edelweiss Pirates who, in addition to harmless ringing of doorbells, have beaten up pedestrians. In some cases they have smeared human excrement on the faces of other national comrades. There was a particular increase in attacks on HJ members.

The same conditions are prevalent in Leipzig, for example; there a large number of young people set up a party-like organization in order to oppose state measures of youth education and to beat up members of the HJ.

In Wismar/Mecklenburg young people set up the Ring bands with the same aim. In addition, they aimed to disrupt law and order in the state and were prepared to mount armed attacks on the police. In the event of revolution they intended to string up the HJ patrols and the HJ leadership from trees. Their attitude was deliberately anti-German. In Düsseldorf the gang 'Club of the Golden Horde' printed pamphlets with the heading 'Down with Hitler—we want freedom'. In Duisburg the Edelweiss or Kittelsbach Pirates became active in opposition to the HJ.

Finally, there are several reports of illegal youth associations which are essentially liberal with a clear tendency towards an 'easy-going English life style'.

The main representatives are the so-called 'Swing gangs', who were particularly evident in Hamburg, but also in other parts of the Reich, e.g. Dresden and Vienna.

This section alone suffices to show that we are dealing with three different sorts of gangs:

(a) The politically hostile gangs.
(b) The liberal-individualistic gangs.
(c) The criminal-anti-social gangs.

Their development has clearly shown that they initially emerged in big cities but then spread to the countryside (possibly through the evacuation measures). In order to combat this problem effectively it is necessary to examine how these gangs came about, what makes them tick, and whether they pose a threat, and what sort of threat, to the state and youth education.

### (a) Politically hostile gangs

These associations derive from the so-called *bündisch* youth. It is, therefore, necessary to look briefly at the earlier youth movements. Around the turn of the century, a youth movement emerged from the desire to resist the bourgeois superficiality of the Wilhelmine period and to provide youth with a real experience through nature. As time went on, this basically good idea was overlaid by a desire for an autonomous youth, which soon separated youth off from the nation as a whole. A large number of organizations were established, each of which wanted to continue to operate as a league [*Bund*] and pursue its own ideas into adult life. While the HJ educates boys and girls to be efficient national comrades and members of the community, the leagues wanted precisely to pursue a distinct life outside the national community. Their league was their life and gave their life its meaning. They advocated male friendship and thereby encouraged homosexuality among the naive to a horrific extent. Instead of community education they chose the principle of selection and favoured a distinct life style and the notion of a group bound by fate. The boys themselves had— and this explains the considerable attraction—the satisfying feeling of having their own world view, which in fact was extremely unclear. In addition, the experience of the *bündisch* young people remained stuck in a false Romanticism which in part descended into a wild criminality or finally into male prostitution. After the change of regime, the *bündisch*—confessional and politically hostile— youth organizations were dissolved or integrated [into the HJ]. But soon a considerable number of groups re-established themselves, which must be regarded as illegal successors to the *bündisch* groups.

The Reich Youth Leadership established a special 'West' central office to combat these groups with its HQ in Düsseldorf, which was in operation from 1937–8. With the outbreak of war the groups revived. The politically hostile groups organized mostly *bündisch* or Marxist elements and mainly included young people who had not yet belonged to the HJ or had left it. This partly explains their hostile attitude to the HJ.

The best-known politically hostile group are the Edelweiss Pirates. They organized in the West, namely in Cologne and Düsseldorf, but have subsequently spread over wide areas of the Reich. The Cologne juvenile court judge has recently described their external characteristics in a report. They wear the Edelweiss badge on or under the left lapel or coloured pins in the colour of Edelweiss or in black, red and yellow. In so far as they belong to the HJ these badges are worn either openly or secretly on the uniform. One often sees the skull badge. The regulation uniform of the Edelweiss Pirates is short trousers, white socks, a check shirt, a white pullover and scarf and a windcheater. In addition, they have very long hair. A comb is worn in the left sock and a knife in the right one. In so far as girls belong to the gangs they wear white socks, a white pullover or waistcoat. In the warmer months they leave town in their hundreds on foot, by bicycle or train. They distinguish between gatherings and trips. Normally, they meet at night on street corners, in doorways or in parks. They sing their own songs which mostly come from the *bündisch* movement or reflect Russian culture; they exchange experiences from their trips and report on criminal acts they have committed. There is little homosexuality. Instead, they practise sexual intercourse with the female members. The boys belong mostly to the 14–18-year-old age group. But there are also some pre-teens and adults. The leaders, in particular, who are mostly tough and intelligent, come from previous leagues or from political parties. The members have often not learned a trade or are constantly changing their jobs. There are often absentee workers among them. The organization is divided into groups which are named after streets, squares, parks or bunkers, It is astonishing that groups are marked by common external characteristics. This suggests that an umbrella organization or at least a uniform leadership exists which issues directives. However, this is not certain.

The characteristics described here are also manifest, though sometimes in a slightly different form, in the structure of other groups, which appear under a variety of names, e.g. *Mob, Blasé, Mete, Platte,* or *Schlurf.* They base themselves largely on *bündisch* ideas without being conscious of it and have links with other groups of either a friendly or a hostile nature.

As is demonstrated by the examples referred to above, most have an anti-HJ attitude, hate all discipline and thereby place themselves in opposition to the community. However, they are not only politically hostile (recently their attitude has reached the point of being hostile to the state), but, as a result of their composition, they are also criminal and antisocial, so that one often cannot make a distinction between the two types of group.

*(b) Liberal-individualistic gangs*

They originated in north Germany, namely in Hamburg. The most striking example among these groups is the so-called Swing Youth, on whom there have been reports from various parts of the Reich. They began in Hamburg. These groups are motivated by the desire to have a good time and have increasingly assumed a character bordering on the criminal-antisocial. Even before the war boys and girls in Hamburg from the socially privileged classes joined groups wearing strikingly casual clothing and became fans of English [US] music and dance. At the turn of the year 1939/40, the Flottbeck group organized dances which were attended by 5–600 young people and which were marked by an uninhibited indulgence in swing. After the ban on public dances they organized dances at home, which were marked above all by sexual promiscuity. The whole life style of these members cost a considerable amount of money which they endeavoured to procure through criminal acts and, in particular, through theft. The hunger for English dance music and for their own dance bands led to break-ins in shops selling musical instruments. The greed to participate in what appeared to them to be a stylish life in clubs, bars, cafés and house balls suppressed any positive attitude towards responding to the needs of the time. They were unimpressed by the performance of our Wehrmacht; those killed in action were sometimes held up to ridicule. An attitude of hostility to the war is clearly apparent.

The members dress in clothes which imitate English fashions. Thus, they often wear pleated jackets in tartan designs and carry umbrellas. As a badge they wear a coloured dress-shirt button in their lapels. They regard Englishmen as the highest form of human development. A false conception of freedom leads them into opposition to the HJ.

Partly as a result of the evacuation measures, these gangs have spread to other areas. Thus, for example, there was the Harlem Club in Frankfurt am Main, which held house balls of the worst kind. Even the youngest female members indulged in sexual intercourse with several partners consecutively. These parties were marked by alcoholic excesses at which people 'swung' and 'hotted'.

*(c) Criminal-anti-social gangs*
These groups have no peculiarities. They are a sign of typical degradation to some extent determined by the war. Their members are almost entirely recruited from the offspring of genetically inferior, antisocial family clans. Their personal characteristics normally show the same traits: no criminal convictions, weak-willed or very dynamic (the leaders), with an underdeveloped emotional side, in some cases mentally deficient or psychopathic. There are hardly any young people with talent from the socially privileged classes among them. They have no commitment to ideological goals. They follow a leader uncritically to whom they sometimes submit themselves totally.

*Reasons for the increase in gang activity*
The appeal of the criminal/anti-social groups is primarily due to the fact, as has been mentioned already, that the war has resulted in a reduction in the supervision of young people who are especially liable to indulge in criminal acts and the fact that they are that much more exposed to infection from their environment.

The appeal of the politically hostile and liberal-individualistic groups has other causes in addition:

(*a*) The young people who lack keenness are left to themselves a great deal. They avoid HJ duties as far as possible. Favoured by the blackout, they meet in the streets or in the parks, bring along a musical instrument and soon form a group with each person making a contribution to its further development. It represents an urge to enjoy a group experience, something which can be regarded as a manifestation of puberty and which is not satisfied by the HJ. In addition, there is the fact that the HJ cannot involve people to the extent it did before the war. Most of its leaders are in the Wehrmacht. The units are often led by young people who are of the same age and do not always possess leadership qualities. The duties themselves offer little that is new. The romantic urge which exists in every boy finds no outlet, particularly since, as a result of wartime necessity, the HJ has ceased its trips. For this reason older, more experienced comrades who had a *bündisch* attitude to life were easily able to attract the young people. At first, there were only small gatherings, but then these turned into trips which gripped the young people to such an extent that they rejected the HJ.

(*b*) The urge to independence, which is naturally present in certain age groups, cannot be sensibly channelled by the parents, since the fathers are mostly away at the front and the mothers have either been conscripted for war work or are too weak firmly to oppose these activities.

(*c*) The importance of the work problem cannot be underestimated. The deployment of young people in workplaces which they find uncongenial, in addition to the heavy demands being made upon them, produces signs of a lack of enthusiasm or tiredness, which leads to absenteeism. They thereby come into contact with groups which have a bad influence on them. Contact with foreign workers at the workplace contributes towards producing liberal dreams which he endeavours to fulfil in the company of like-minded comrades.

(*d*) As is emphasized by the Cologne Juvenile Court judge, the hostility to the HJ is increased by one fact in particular. As long as it is the police who are enforcing state measures and, in particular, the Police Decree for Youth Protection, incidents generally do not occur. But the HJ patrols and the Youth Duty of Service introduced a new factor. For those who were demanding the maintenance of discipline and order and wanted to stop the trips were now people of the same age. And so punch-ups soon developed between the gang members and the HJ patrols, which led to the destruction of and damage to HJ hostels and finally to the harassment of individual Hitler youths. This is one reason for the hostile attitude to the HJ and thereby to the state. In some cases, however, there are also Bolshevik notions, which, when spread by a leader, soon find fertile soil.

(*e*) In so far as sexual promiscuity manifests itself, this is mainly the result of a lack of supervision by the parents and thus is the result of the free association of the young people with each other.

(*f*) The terror air raids have exacerbated the illegal formation of gangs. Apart from the military duties of the HJ, there are few activities in which they can take part in their spare time. There are no cinema performances, sporting events or sport in those cities which have been badly damaged. When the young people come home in the evenings tired from work, they find a damaged flat or accommodation which has been severely restricted by the need to take in relatives who have lost their homes. In these circumstances the young person seeks company which he enjoys, which provides fun and makes a change. In so far as they are still carrying out HJ duties, these too have changed. The HJ hostels have been destroyed and the activities transferred to the streets or the exercise yard.

As far as the asocial and criminal young people are concerned, they are driven even more to crime by the terror air raids. If their workplace has been destroyed, then they stop working for a while, often live on their own without relatives, hang around in bunkers and so inevitably join up with similar kinds of people of the same age. This produces a negative selection which gradually forms the core of these groups.

*Combating the gangs*
The gang problem prompted the Reich Youth Leadership and the local headquarters of the HJ to initiate major actions against the gangs in cooperation with the Security Police and the judicial authorities . . .

As far as the choice of judicial measures is concerned, briefly it must be said that a distinction should be made between leaders, active participants and finally passive followers. In minor cases a warning can be issued or youth custody may be sufficient. But one must avoid condemning a large group of young people to youth custody. This simply strengthens their sense of solidarity and binds the young people even more strongly together.

Consignment to a work re-education camp for a period of up to three months will be an appropriate measure in the case of those young people who have not yet committed a criminal act if there are signs of remorse. In the case of more deeply rooted wildness but without criminal tendencies assignment to borstal will be required. However, it must be emphasized that the leadership of the gangs and the prominent active members can only be educated and prevented from continuing their gang activity by the toughest punishments. Inappropriate mildness is out of place here. In the case of criminal gangs an indeterminate sentence will be an appropriate measure. As a last resort there is consignment to a youth detention centre.

——

The extent to which the activities of the Edelweiss Pirates can be regarded as 'resistance' has been a matter of some controversy. To the extent that they opposed and even physically attacked the HJ and tried to avoid service in the Wehrmacht there are clearly some grounds for using the term. However, the motives for their 'resistance' appear to have been primarily a desire to assert personal and group autonomy and avoidance of the various restrictions imposed on young people rather than an ideologically inspired critique of the regime based on ethical values or an alternative political agenda. Their attitude was shaped rather by a mixture of *bündisch* notions and a youthful desire for independence and could and in some cases did degenerate into pure juvenile delinquency.

There were, however, groups within the so-called 'politically hostile' category, as defined by the Reich Justice Ministry, whose resistance was entirely motivated by political ideas and ethical values. On the Left there were groups of young people associated more or less closely with the KPD and SPD such as those round Hanno Günther and Herbert Baum; there were also survivors of the *bündisch* movement in a purer form than the Edelweiss Pirates such as the followers of Eberhard Koebel (Tusk). There were in addition survivors of the Catholic youth movement. But perhaps the most remarkable of these resistance groups was the so-called White Rose. Based mainly in Munich, it had a few offshoots elsewhere, notably in Hamburg. It was led by five students at Munich University: Hans and Sophie Scholl, Alexander Schmorell, Christoph Probst and Willi Graf together with a Professor of Musicology and Philosophy, Kurt Huber. The group took its name from a novel popular in the 1930s with a Mexican setting by the pseudonymous writer B. Traven. Its members were influenced by a mixture of *bündisch* ideas and values derived from Christianity and from the tradition of German idealism developed at the end of the eighteenth century by writers and philosophers such as Kant, Schiller and Goethe. They stressed above all the significance of individual moral development and personal freedom, particularly freedom of thought. Their political ideas were vague and somewhat utopian.

During 1942–3, the White Rose group produced six typed and cyclostyled broadsheets. The first four, which were strongly influenced by the Catholic publicist Carl Muth and the Catholic theologian and humanist Theodor Haecker, with whom Hans Scholl was closely associated, were composed by Scholl and Schmorell, and about one hundred of each were distributed between 27 June and 12 July 1942. The main target audience was the educated middle class in Munich, with the aim of reminding them of their moral and political obligations. The fifth broadsheet was also composed by Scholl and Schmorell but with additions from Professor Huber. This time the target was 'all Germans' and several thousand were distributed in the southern German cities of Augsburg, Stuttgart and Frankfurt am Main, and also in Vienna, Salzburg and Linz. It was assumed by the authors that the south had a more liberal mentality.

The sixth and final broadsheet was written by Professor Huber with corrections by Hans Scholl. It was triggered by news of the defeat at ˚Stalingrad and was targeted at their fellow students, who were seen as having revolutionary potential following their negative response to Gauleiter Greiser's offensive references to female students in a speech on 13 January 1943. The following document is the fifth broadsheet produced on 18 February, 1943:

**1217** *Broadsheet of the Resistance Movement in Germany*

CALL TO ALL GERMANS

The war is approaching its certain end. As in 1918 the German government is trying to divert all attention on to the growing U-boat threat, while in the East the armies are constantly flooding back and in the West the invasion is expected. American rearmament has not yet reached its peak but already surpasses anything known in history. One can say with mathematical certainty that Hitler is leading Germany over the precipice. *Hitler cannot win the war but only extend it.* His guilt and those of his aides is beyond measure. His just punishment is coming ever closer!

But what are the German people doing? They do not see and they do not listen. They are following their seducers to disaster. They have adopted the motto: victory at any price. I shall fight to the last man says Hitler—but the war is already lost.

Germans! Do you want your children to suffer the same fate as the Jews? Do you want to be judged in the same category as your seducers. Are we to be forever the nation that is hated and spurned by the rest of the world? No! So break with the national socialist subhumans. Show, through your deeds that you think differently! A new war of liberation is about to start. The better part of the German nation is fighting on our side. Tear off the cloak of indifference with which you have covered your hearts. Decide *before it is too late.*

Don't believe the national socialist propaganda which has scared you with the fear of Bolshevism. Don't believe that Germany's well being is indissolubly linked to the victory of national socialism! A German victory cannot be achieved by criminals. Break with everything associated with national socialism before it is too late. Afterwards a terrible but just court will preside over those who have taken cover in such a cowardly and indecisive way.

What does the outcome of this war, which was never a national one, teach us? The imperialist concept of power from whatever side it may come must be eliminated for all time. A bigoted Prussian militarism must never again come to power. Only through the generous cooperation of the European nations can the ground be laid on which a new start can be made. Every form of centralized power, such as the Prussian state tried to exercise in Germany and Europe must be smothered at birth. The future Germany can only be federalist. Only a healthy federalist state structure can now fill a weakened Europe with new life. The workers must be liberated from their condition of debased slavery by a sensible Socialism. The chimera of an autarkic economy must disappear from Europe. Every nation, every individual has a right to the goods of this world.

Freedom of speech, freedom of confession, protection of the citizen from arbitrary criminal power states—those are the foundations of the new Europe. Support the resistance movement, distribute the leaflets.

An important motive for the resistance of the White Rose was their horror and disgust at the treatment of the Jews and the Poles and Russians. The second of the broadsheets distributed by the White Rose group, composed by Hans Scholl, contains a searing indictment of his fellow citizens and reveals the extent to which ordinary Germans were in fact aware that major crimes were being committed in their name against Jews and others. For Hans Scholl was an ordinary middle-class young man without special connections within the regime:

**1218**  . . . It is not up to us to pass final judgment on the meaning of our history. But if we are to benefit from this catastrophe then it can happen only by our being cleansed by sorrow, through longing for the light in darkest night, by arousing ourselves and at last helping to throw off the yoke which is oppressing the world. We do not intend to say anything about the Jewish question in this broadsheet; nor do we want to enter a plea in their defence. No, we simply want to cite as an example the fact that since the conquest of Poland 300,000 Jews have been murdered in that country in the most bestial fashion. In this we see the most fearful crime against human dignity, a crime with which no other in the whole history of mankind can be compared. For whatever one thinks of the Jewish question, the Jews too are human beings and this has been done to human beings. Perhaps someone may say the Jews deserved such a fate; this statement would be an incredible presumption. But assuming somebody did say this, how would he deal with the fact that the whole of the younger generation of the Polish nobility has been annihilated. (Please God let it not yet be true!) You may say: How did this happen? All male offspring of Polish noble families between the ages of 15 and 20 were transferred to concentration camps in Germany for forced labour; all girls of the same age were dragged off to SS brothels in Norway! Why do we tell you all this since you yourselves know of it already—and if not of these then of other serious crimes committed by these fearful subhumans. Because this touches on a question which deeply concerns us all and must give us a lot to think about: why are the German people so apathetic in the face of all these terrible crimes which are so unworthy of humanity? Hardly anybody gives any thought to them. The fact is simply accepted and then filed away. And the German people go on sleeping their dull and stupid sleep and give these fascist criminals the courage and opportunity to go on wreaking havoc—and they do.

Is this a sign that the Germans' most basic human feelings have been brutalized, that they have no chord to be touched by such deeds, no voice that cries out inside them, that they are sunk in a deadly torpor from which there is to be no awakening, never, ever? It appears so and will certainly be the case if the Germans do not at last rise up out of their lethargy, if they do not protest wherever they can against this gang of criminals, if they do not share the suffering of these hundreds of thousands of victims. And it is not only compassion that they must feel; no, it's much more: a shared guilt. For it's only through their apathy that they give these men of darknesss the opportunity to act in this way; they tolerate this 'government' which has brought upon itself such immeasurable guilt; indeed they are themselves guilty that it could come to power in the first place!

Everybody wants to acquit themselves of such shared guilt; they all do it and then go to sleep again with a quiet and good conscience. But they cannot acquit themselves; everyone is guilty, guilty, guilty! But it is not yet too late to get rid of this most repulsive of all freaks of a government in order not to take even more guilt upon oneself. Now that in recent years our eyes have been fully opened; now that we know with whom we are dealing; now it is high time to exterminate this brown horde. Until the outbreak of war the majority of the German people were dazzled; national socialism did not show itself in its true colours. But now that we have recognized it for what it is, it must be the sole and highest, indeed the sacred, duty of every German to eradicate these beasts.

In February 1943 the White Rose group became increasingly daring, painting 'Freedom', 'Down with Hitler' and 'Hitler Mass Murderer' on various Munich buildings, including the main University entrance. The end came on 18 February when Hans and Sophie Scholl scattered copies of the sixth broadsheet in the University courtyard and were caught by the porter, who handed them over to the Gestapo. Despite the brave refusal of the Scholls to reveal the names of their accomplices under torture, they were soon rounded up and all six were found guilty of treason and beheaded. Hans Scholl died with the word 'Freedom' on his lips. On 25 February the Gau student leader gave an address in the University in which he dissociated the German students from the activities of the White Rose. The students stamped their feet in applause for the porter, who received the ovation standing up with his arms outstretched.

The main group in the Reich Justice Ministry's 'liberal-individualist' category of youth gangs was the 'Swing Youth' largely based in Hamburg. They were mainly upper middle-class sixth-formers and students who imitated Anglo-Saxon cultural forms and styles. The regime did not take kindly to them, as the following newspaper article indicates:

**1219** *Get Lost, You Creeps!*

We don't want to see any more of them. With their umbrellas, '*ready-rolled*', and their hats, *made by Bloody*, and their jackets, the latest *city* fashion—and all the bits and pieces of being a *gentleman*.

The details needn't bother us. Anyone who needs an umbrella should carry one. A hat is a hat and a jacket a jacket. That's not the point. It's the fact that people imitate the '*English style*', the stupid, phoney magic, the yid-glamour typical of the island, which upsets us.

They like to hang out in a seaside resort right next to Hamburg. Don't get us wrong: we like seeing pretty things swanning along the beach. But we're not prepared to put up with these yid-Eton style girls and boys behaving as if there wasn't a war on and the whole thing had nothing to do with them. Soldiers coming from the front and looking for recuperation have very little time for this sort of thing. It's hard to believe but it really is the case that there are smoothies and also 'ladies' who make it very clear that they don't like seeing military grey uniforms among the colourful beach costumes.

Ladies and gentlemen, bear in mind things could be different. You are tolerated where you hang out. You tiny band—if you were to get your way we would have to doubt our victory.

It's not a question of hats and jackets. Its the attitude—your appearance and your manner which we don't like. We don't want to see you fancy lot around any more. Not like that. Please take note.

---

Himmler, in particular, found the 'Swing Youth' intolerable, challenging as they did all his most sacred notions of the ideal German young man and woman. He expressed his revulsion in the following letter to Heydrich of 26 January 1942:

**1220** I enclose a report which the Reich Youth Leader Axmann has sent to me about the 'Swing Youth' in Hamburg.

I know that the Secret State Police has already acted. But in my view the whole problem must now be radically eliminated. I am against half measures here.

All the leaders and that means both male and female and those teachers who are hostile and support the Swing Youth are to be sent to a concentration camp. There the young people should first receive a beating and then be subjected to a tough regime of drill and then be made to work. I consider that a work camp or youth camp is the wrong thing for these boys and these useless girls. The girls are to be made to work at weaving and in the summer on the land.

These young people must remain in the concentration camp for a long time, 2–3 years. it must be made clear that they will never be able to study. Their parents must be investigated to see how far they supported them. If they have, then they too must be sent to a concentration camp and their property must be confiscated.

Only if we act brutally will we be able to avoid a dangerous spreading of these Anglophile tendencies at a time when Germany is fighting for its existence. Please send me further reports.

Please carry out this action in association with the Gauleiter and the Higher SS and Police Leader.

---

In fact the Swing Youth were not intending to pose a political threat to the regime. It was just that their very existence challenged its youth norms and as such was seen as a political threat. As one former participant later put it: 'the main problem was not that we were against the Nazis but that the Nazis were against us'.[10]

---

[10] See M. Grüttner, ' "Ein stetes Sorgenkind fur Partei und Staat." Die Student-enschaft 1930 bis 1945' in E. Krause et al. eds, *Hochschulalltag im 'Dritten Reich Die Hamburger Universität 1933–1945* (Berlin–Hamburg 1991) p. 228.

The Youth Detention camp to which male members of the 'Swing Youth' and other youths who were regarded as seriously delinquent were sent was set up in a former female concentration camp in Moringen near Hanover in 1940. The following description of the camp by the President of the Regional Court [*Landesgericht*] in Essen to the President of the Supreme Regional Court [*Oberlandesgericht*] in Hamm in Westphalia, dated 31 July 1944, indicates the extent to which German penal practice had been invaded by the pseudoscience of 'criminal biology', originally developed during Weimar, which now flourished in the fertile soil provided by the Third Reich.

**1221** . . . The measures and arrangements which struck us when visiting the camp are designed to serve the purpose of the Youth Detention Camp, namely to sort out the pupils [*Zöglinge*] in accordance with the principles of criminal biology, assisting those who are capable of fitting into the community [*Gemeinschaftsfähig*] so that they can take their place in the national community and to confine the ineducable until their final transfer elsewhere, while in the meantime exploiting their labour.

The camp is routinely visited by members of the Criminal Biological Institute of the Reich Security Main Office whose director, Professor Dr Ritter, frequently visits the camp and has seconded a desk officer there on a permanent basis (currently the Principal [*Regierungsrat*] Dr Abshagen. The camp is a goldmine for this research institute, which submits the camp pupils to a criminal biological examination and divides them into categories in accordance with these principles and in association with the camp director. Every pupil is given a criminal biological examination before his admission. On his admission he is assigned to the Entry Block (*Beobachtung* = observation) and examined there for a considerable time. The process of examination and sorting out leads to assignment to another block. The pupils are divided between various blocks which are distinct from one another. Inadequates (mental defectives and the mentally ill), who are not fit for camp life, are sent to the U Block (*Untaugliche* = inadequates) with the aim of transferring them initially to a mental hospital (in so far as medical supervision is required) or later to a lunatic asylum. This block contains 5–10 per cent of the pupils.

Pupils who are difficult, those with depraved characters, those with emotional problems, those who are easily aroused, the congenitally discontented, incorrigible pests, ruthless rogues, in other words pupils who are in continual conflict with the community are clear cases for detention. According to the practice of the Institute for Criminal Biology and the camp these pupils are termed 'nuisances' [*Störer*] and, as soon as they are assessed as such, they are consigned to Block S. The 5–10 per cent of the pupils who are in this block are sent to a concentration camp as soon as they have reached the right age or, when the Community Aliens Law has been passed, they will be transferred to the corresponding institution of the Regional Welfare Agency.

Pupils with weaknesses of character, those who are fickle, lack motivation and who cannot cope with any stress, and those who have a tendency to go off the straight and narrow are also cases for detention. They are sent to D Block (*Block der Dauerversager* = permanent failures) and later will be placed in a concentration camp or in a semi-closed or closed institution. D Block contains 10–15 per cent of the pupils.

Those who are mainly insecure, lacking in independence, thoughtless, who are highly vulnerable and continually reoffend go to G Block (*Block der Gelegenheitsversager* = occasional failures); 10–15 per cent of the pupils go to this block. Some of them will later be able to be released; others will have to be kept in detention. Roughly 20–25 per cent of the pupils are assigned to F Block (*Block der fraglich Erziehungsfähigen* = the possibly educable). In this Block the main work of the camp is carried out with those who have gone astray, who are running wild, who may be late developers and who are still educable. Those in this block who prove uneducable are assigned to one of the blocks referred to above or are transferred to a concentration camp on reaching adulthood. Sometimes in special cases this is postponed to the age of 25 because the sifting process in this block is intended to be long-term. If the pupil turns out to be educable then he is assigned to E Block. E Block (*Block der Erziehungsfähigen* = the educable) contains pupils who have been transferred directly from B Block or, after further weeding out, from F Block. These are pupils who appear educable, i.e those running wild, pubescents with an unsatisfactory upbringing. Up to now 6–8 per cent of the pupils have fallen into this category. Pupils are continually being transferred from this Block to the Reich Labour Service or to military service.

The above description of the weeding out process, which is carried out in the Youth Detention Camp, shows the strong influence exercised by the concepts of criminal biology on the work of the camp. The representative of the Institute of Criminal Biology is involved in the assignment of every single pupil to the blocks referred to above. The percentages given might lead to the assumption that the work carried out by the camp is pointless or at least of little use. It must, however, be borne in mind that the Youth Detention Camp receives a negative selection of young people. The biological assessment and sifting process demonstrates that the degeneracy of very many pupils is biologically determined. Apart from the use of the data for research purposes and the rendering harmless of obvious community aliens through the use of detention, the biological sifting of the pupils is designed to separate out those who are still educable and to encourage them as much as possible. If one looks at the figures of the successful cases then the educative function, which the police emphasized fairly strongly when the camp was set up, has been less significant. But it must not be forgotten that even relatively few cases of successful re-education represent a marked achievement with this kind of human material and that the work of education is particularly difficult in this camp. Furthermore, the work of education represents, in addition to the biological sifting process, a further safety mechanism to weed out those who have been mistakenly assigned to the camp.

# List of Sources

1172 Herbert Schierer, 'Deutschlands Jugend an der inneren Front', *NS Monatshefte,* January 1940.

1173 K.-H. Jahnke & M. Buddrus, *Deutsche Jugend 1933–1945. Eine Dokumentation* (Hamburg 1989), pp. 318ff.

1174 *Schulungsdienst der Hitler-Jugend,* 4 (1942), pp. 2 and 22–23, in H.-J. Gamm, *Führung und Verführung. Pädagogik des Nationalsozialismus.* (Munich 1964), pp. 354–5.

1175 *Völkischer Beobachter,* 11.2.1941.

1176 G. Kaufmann, *Das kommende Deutschland. Die Erziehung der Jugend im Reich Adolf Hitlers* (Berlin 1943), pp. 68–71, in Gamm, op. cit., pp. 334–5.

1177 Bundesarchiv Berlin (BAB) NS 6/786.

1178 A. Klönne, *Jugend im Dritten Reich. Die Hitler-Jugend und ihre Gegner* (Düsseldorf 1982), p. 136.

1179 Staatsarchiv Ludwigsburg (StAL) PL 502/32/1921.

1180 R. Schörken, *Luftwaffenhelfer und Drittes Reich. Die Enstehung eines politischen Bewußtseins* (Stuttgart 1984), pp. 118–19.

1181 (a) K. Granzow, *Tagebuch eines Hitlerjungen 1943–1945* (Bremen 1965), pp. 96–7
     (b) pp. 102–3
     (c) pp. 117–18
     (d) pp. 137–8.

1182 A. Klönne, *Gegen den Strom* (Hanover/Frankfurt 1958), pp. 143–4.

1183 Jahnke & Buddrus, op. cit., pp. 405–6.

1184 BAB Z.Slg. 101/37.

1185 Ibid.

1186 G. Kock, *'Der Führer sorgt für unsere Kinder . . .' Die Kinderlandverschickung im Zweiten Weltkrieg* (Paderborn 1996), pp. 351–2.

1187 Ibid., pp. 353–4.

1188 Hauptstaatsarchiv Stuttgart (HStASt) E 151 cII Bü 748.

1189 Ibid.

1190 Ibid.

1191 Ibid.

1192 G. Dabel, *KLV. Die erweiterte Kinder-Land-Verschickung. KLV Lager 1940–1945,* Eine Dokumentation zusammengestellt und bearbeitet von Gerhard Dabel im Auftrag der Dokumentation-Arbeitsgemeinschaft KLV e.V. (Freiburg 1981), p. 32.

1193 Claus Larass, *Der Zug der Kinder. KLV-Die Evakuierung 5 Millionen deutscher Kinder im 2. Weltkrieg* (Munich 1983), p. 102.

1194 Larass, op. cit., pp. 75–6.

1195 H. Boberach, ed., *Meldungen aus dem Reich. Die geheimen Lageberichte des Sicherheitsdienstes der SS,* Vol. 15. (Herrsching 1984), pp. 5828ff.

1196 Dabel, op. cit., pp. 122–23.

1197 Larass, op. cit., pp. 74–5.

1198 Kock, op. cit., p. 308.

1199   Larass, op. cit., p. 212.
1200   Dabel op. cit., p. 127.
1201   Larass op. cit., pp. 93–4.
1202   Dabel, op. cit., p. 132ff.
1203   Larass, op. cit., pp. 211–13.
1204   Ibid.
1205   BAB R 43 II/512.
1206   Niedersächsiches Staatsarchiv Hanover, Hann 80 Hann IIe, Nr. 480.
1207   Niedersächisches Staatsarchiv Oldenburg 134/248.
1208   Reichsgesetzblatt (RGBl) I 1940, p. 499.
1209   StAL PL 502/32/Bü 49.
1210   H. Bernsee, 'Zehn Jahre Hilfswerk 'Mutter und Kind'' in NSVD 1943, p.
       170, quoted in H. Vorländer, *Die NSV. Darstellung und Dokumentation
       einer nationalsozialistischen Organisation* (Boppard am Rhein 1988),
       p. 80.
1211   BAB R 18/3427, quoted in E. Hansen, *Wohlfahrtspolitik im NS Staat.
       Motivationen, Konflikte und Machtstrukturen im 'Sozialismus det Tat' des
       Dritten Reiches* (Augsburg 1991), p. 268.
1212   RGBl. I 1940, p. 1052.
1213   *Das Junge Deutschland* 34 (1940), p. 278f.
1214   BAB R 22 Nr. 3365.
1215   Ibid.
1216   Jahnke & Buddrus, op. cit., 463ff.
1217   Inge Scholl, *Die weisse Rose* (Frankfurt am Main 1953), pp. 127–9.
1218   Ibid., pp. 109–112.
1219   W. Breyvogel, ed., *Piraten, Swings und Junge Garde. Jugendwiderstand im
       Nationalsozialismus* (Bonn 1991), pp. 250–1.
1220   Jahnke & Buddrus, op. cit., p. 345.
1221   D. Peukert, *Die Edelweisspiraten. Protestbewegungen jugendlicher Arbeiter
       im Dritten Reich* (Cologne 1983) pp. 139–41.

# CHAPTER 48

# *Propaganda*

## (i) Introduction

At the beginning of September 1939, the Nazi regime faced the challenge for which it had been preparing since its takeover of power in 1933—a major war. Nowhere was this more true than in the field of propaganda on the home front. Hitler's own political career had begun in direct response to the national humiliation of defeat in the First World War. He and the German Right in general attributed that defeat not to Germany's exhaustion in the face of Allied military superiority, but rather to the collapse of morale on the home front brought about by 'Jewish-Marxist' agitators, which had culminated in the revolution of early November 1918, in short to a 'stab in the back'. A constant refrain of Nazi wartime propaganda in general and of Hitler's speeches in particular, which was hammered into the German people through the media and poster propaganda, was the slogan 'Never again will there be a November 1918'.

Much of the responsibility for ensuring this lay with the Reich Ministry for Popular Enlightenment and Propaganda under its minister, Dr Joseph Goebbels. Shortly after his appointment, Goebbels defined the task of his new ministry in a speech to radio officials on 25 March 1933 as 'achieving a mobilization of mind and spirit in Germany. It is, therefore, in the sphere of the mind what the Defence Ministry is in the sphere of defence.' He claimed that 'the mobilization of the mind is as necessary, perhaps even more necessary than the material mobilization of the nation'. And he concluded: 'We did not lose the war because our artillery gave out but because the weapons of our minds did not fire.'[1]

---

[1] See Vol. 2, doc. 267.

However, although much of pre-war German propaganda had been devoted to instilling a 'military spirit' into the population, the German people's behaviour in the pre-war period—for example its obvious relief at the peaceful outcome of the Czech crisis of September 1938—had demonstrated only too clearly to the Nazi leadership how limited their success had been.

The main functions of propaganda on the German home front during the Second World War were to mobilize the energy and commitment of the population for the war effort and to sustain its morale. To achieve these goals the propaganda apparatus was faced with two main tasks. The first was to persuade the nation that the war needed to be fought. Essentially, Goebbels and the Propaganda Ministry adopted three main strategies for this purpose. Between 1939 and 1941, while Germany was on the offensive, they tried to persuade the population that Germany's military actions were a pre-emptive response to the aggressive intentions of her enemies—in short, they were in fact defensive. Then, during 1942–5, when Germany was faced with increasing setbacks and the growing threat of defeat, the propaganda emphasized the threat posed by the barbarous Bolshevik hordes from the East and portrayed Germany as the defender of European civilization. A constant theme throughout was 'encirclement'. It was claimed that Germany was the victim of a conspiracy between a Bolshevik Russia and a 'plutocratic' Britain, a conspiracy orchestrated by the Jews who dominated both states. It was a conspiracy designed to destroy the nation and state which posed the greatest threat to Jewish world domination and to rob Germany of its claim to more living space and natural resources, a claim based both on its vigorous physical health and on its cultural distinction. As the war situation deteriorated so propaganda increasingly emphasized the terrible fate that would await the German people if the Bolsheviks were victorious.

The third strategy to convince the German people of the need to fight the war was to offer them the prospect of national expansion. As far as actual war aims were concerned, the propaganda remained intentionally vague, following specific instructions from both Hitler and Goebbels. They were anxious to avoid tying their hands and causing possible diplomatic complications by making specific commitments. Instead, a vague impression was created that victory would ensure both greatness for Germany as a nation and state and prosperity for the ordinary citizen, since, as the dominant state in Europe, the country would be able to tap almost unlimited resources.

The second major task of propaganda was to persuade the German people that the war could and would be won. This mainly involved creating a picture of German strength and success and of Allied weakness and failure. Initially, from September 1939 to December 1941, this proved relatively easy in the wake of a succession of stunning German victories. From 1942 to 1945, it became progressively more difficult. In fact, compared with Britain, German propaganda suffered a disadvantage in that in Britain in 1940 there was no disguising the crisis and from then on things could hardly get worse apart from actual defeat. But in the case of Germany its propaganda had to cope with stunning initial victories followed by a progressive decline in its fortunes. This faced German propagandists with the problem of deciding how far they should admit to the deteriorating situation. If they painted too black a picture they risked damaging morale; on the other hand, if they concealed the true picture they risked losing credibility with the people. During this period of 1943–5, a crucial role in sustaining morale was played by the notion of 'retaliation', which was systematically encouraged by German propaganda, namely the idea that Germany was developing secret weapons of such destructive power that when deployed they would transform the war situation to Germany's advantage.

Then, in addition to these two major tasks, propaganda had the function of giving detailed practical advice and instructions on day-to-day matters of wartime life—about air raid precautions, dietary matters, the need to economize in the use of food and materials, the need to avoid revealing military information through careless gossip etc. Last but by no means least, propaganda had the task of sustaining morale by alleviating the stresses of war through the provision of entertainment of various kinds to suit different tastes—radio programmes, films, concerts, variety shows etc.

Direct preparations for wartime propaganda had begun in the spring of 1938 in the build-up of the Czech crisis and so there was a smooth transition from peace to war. From the beginning Goebbels concentrated the direction of German propaganda as much as possible in his own hands. Almost every day a meeting was held at 11 o'clock in the Propaganda Ministry attended by the top officials of the Ministry, senior figures from the various branches of the media and liaison staff from other ministries, the Party Chancellery and the Wehrmacht. Initially, there were some twenty in attendance gradually increasing after the invasion of Russia to fifty to sixty persons. Here Goebbels gave out guidelines and detailed instructions for the conduct and direction of German propaganda covering every conceivable aspect.

However, for a number of reasons Goebbels' domination of German propaganda was far from total. As far as the home front was concerned, there were two major limitations on his authority. First, he had little influence over military reporting which was under the control of the Wehrmacht's propaganda department and included censorship powers over the media. It prepared the daily Wehrmacht communiqué, which contained a summary of the military situation and was subject to final approval and frequent alterations by Hitler. The main problems for Goebbels arising out of this arrangement were, first, Hitler's tendency to use the Wehrmacht communiqués for foreign policy purposes. This exacerbated the second problem, which was the Wehrmacht's tendency to put an excessively optimistic gloss on the military situation, which then led to popular disappointment and consequent disillusionment with the media.

Secondly, the so-called Reich Press Chief, Otto Dietrich, although theoretically subordinate to Goebbels as a State Secretary in the Propaganda Ministry, as a member of Hitler's immediate entourage was in practice autonomous. Dietrich issued the 'Daily Directives of the Reich Press Chief', which contained Hitler's detailed directives to the newspaper editors. The institutional and personal rivalries between Goebbels as Reich Propaganda Minister and Dietrich as Reich Press Chief were typical of the Nazi political system. They were described as follows by a senior aide of Goebbels, Rudolf Semmler, in his diary entry for 28 November 1943:

**1222**  Although Dietrich is State Secretary in the Propaganda Ministry he refuses to take orders or advice from Goebbels. He shelters himself safely behind Hitler, whose chief press officer he is.

The press section of the Ministry, which took over the functions of the former press department of the Reich Government, is formally not under Goebbels at all, but under Dietrich as Press Director of the Reich Government. The headquarters of this department is the famous Room 24, which is staffed day and night. From here are issued all political directives to the German press; all requests passed down from above, from Hitler, from Goebbels, from the Foreign Office and from the Chancellery have to go through this office. I myself pass to Room 24 the press instructions which I receive, dictated by Goebbels, so that they can be passed from there to the newspapers.

Now, if there is some important news material, like a speech by Churchill, it can happen—or rather it is the rule—that at least three or four different pages of policy directives are produced. These are supposed to assist our editors in their work. But it is obvious to me that they deprive writers of their intellectual independence. These directives often contradict one another, sometimes only on a few points but more often completely and utterly. In such cases there are only two courses of action open to the wretched official in Room 24, who is almost continually talking on two telephones at once. Either he can forbid any mention or discussion of the Churchill speech for twenty-four hours—in which case the

British newspapers say the speech has given the Germans such a shock that they don't know what to say—or he will take directive points from the Hitler–Dietrich document and ignore the suggestions of Goebbels and Ribbentrop.

Then on the next day Goebbels is furious when he reads the newspapers and finds that no attention has been paid to his instructions. Often I am suspected of having not passed them on, and I can only save myself by producing the original copy of the directives.

Oddly enough, Dietrich's authority extends only to the press, while Goebbels has exclusive control over the radio and news services. So it often happens that a speech by Churchill is commented on quite differently by the press and by the radio. Generally the differences are slight but an expert can spot them at once.

---

## (ii) The War in Poland and the West 1939–1940

Even before the outbreak of war, German propaganda had come to focus on Britain as the main enemy and to attack it as a 'plutocratic' power ruled by a selfish, corrupt, Jewish-dominated elite greedily hanging on to its empire, trying to prevent younger dynamic nations like Germany from gaining a place in the world appropriate to their qualities and—just as before the First World War—encouraging other powers, in this case Poland and France, to 'encircle' Germany.

With the outbreak of war with Poland, this line was continued and embellished only by the portrayal of the attack on Poland as a response to and pre-emptive strike against Polish aggression. On 1 September 1939 the Propaganda Ministry issued a press directive from which the following excerpt is taken:

**1223**   Britain is the true aggressor in the world. Poland is its willing henchman, governed by irresponsible military leaders and megalomaniacal gang leaders. For months the Greater German Reich has been suffering provocation from these vassals of British warmongering. The Führer has observed this activity with a patience which is barely comprehensible. Despite the intolerable Polish demands and the ever-increasing threat on the Polish–German border, the Führer accepted the last British offer and waited for several days for the promised Polish negotiator to come to negotiate. Now it is clear that the British mediation was merely hypocritical and that the British government never intended to produce a settlement.

---

In the middle of the Polish campaign but when a German victory was already certain, Goebbels returned to this theme in the following directive to all Party speakers dated 17 September 1939:

**1224**     General theme: Show complete confidence but at the same time avoid becoming jingoistic.

Make clear that we are engaged in the fateful struggle of the German people which was imposed upon it by the English plutocracy. In your treatment of the Jewish world powers make quite sure that you do not include the Catholic Church in your attacks and also do not refer to international Marxism, but rather represent the international powers as Jewish plutocracy and the clique of war profiteers. The English warmongering aims to destroy the German Reich. According to the remarks of King Hall[2] and the responsible spokesmen of the English government, Germany is destined to face a dictated peace compared with which Versailles was child's play. But there will never be another Versailles. In the course of German history there will only be one November 1918. That is guaranteed by the whole German nation. We must prove ourselves equal to the struggle. The clique of international capitalists has imposed this struggle on Germany; it used the Poles for such a long time that it was no longer compatible with the honour and prestige of the Reich to stand idly by. It is essential to represent the English plutocracy as the true warmongers and to incite the whole nation to a holy rage against those who have invariably repressed other nations and have never tolerated another nation becoming strong and powerful alongside England. For years the Führer has spoken of peace and has made the English government proposal after proposal (e.g. the Naval Agreement.[3] But England has always threatened us with war—at the time of the reintroduction of conscription,[4] the occupation of the Rhineland,[5] the reintegration of Austria,[6] and the solution of the Sudeten question.[7] The English-Jewish international war clique, which claims the sole domination of the world, has always claimed it aims to prevent the expansion of the German nation.

The German people are taking on this fateful struggle which has been forced upon them. Germany is fighting for its freedom, for its honour, for its future. For this reason compatriots must be called upon to engage all their energies: women to work in the Women's Labour Service, in the Red Cross etc. Germany is fighting for the coming generations and this obligates the current younger generation to join in as well. Moreover, it should be pointed out that the families of the soldiers who have been called up are being looked after. Compatriots are to be called upon to have unshakeable faith in the Führer and his mission, which he has been given by fate, to be ready to participate and to show unity, to express firm and unshakeable confidence, to be always prepared to be actively involved wherever they are called upon. Speakers must strictly avoid any polemics against France. There must be no statements about the possible duration of the war.

---

[2] Stephen King Hall, an English military journalist.
[3] The Anglo-German Naval Agreement of June 1935, see Vol. 3, doc. 495.
[4] 16 March 1935, see Vol. 3, doc. 495.
[5] March 1936, see Vol. 3, doc. 497.
[6] March 1938, see Vol. 3, docs 510–515.
[7] September 1938, See Vol. 3, docs 517–528.

Apart from the media—press, radio and film—the main burden of propaganda fell on the Nazi Party, which had its own propaganda apparatus down to the level of the local Party cell, and which received its instructions from Goebbels in his role as Reich Propaganda Chief of the NSDAP. In his 'Guidelines for the Execution of NSDAP Propaganda', issued on the outbreak of war, Goebbels indicated the propaganda methods to be used by the Party, which included the press and radio, mass meetings, illustrated lectures, films, posters, brochures, badges, and the spreading of rumours and the pushing of a particular line through person-to-person propaganda.

On 1 October 1939, for example, the propaganda department of Gau Koblenz-Trier issued the following circular to its subordinate district, local branch, and cell propaganda sections:

**1225** In honour of the impending entry of German troops into Warsaw there will be a general display of flags for the first time during this war. The exact time will be announced on the radio. The district propaganda leaders will ensure at once that there will be a unique display of flags. No house and no window must be without its swastika flag. Preparations must be made at once to ensure that all the public decorations are everywhere in place (flagpoles, street banners etc.). Pictures of the Führer and swastika flags should be displayed in all shops in a dignified fashion. Trams and vehicles should carry pennants. The whole political leadership must be involved at once in the preparations.

However, clearly not everybody in this deeply Catholic region felt quite so keen to show their enthusiasm publicly, as is clear from the following circular of the Trier district propaganda department to its subordinate local branch and cell propaganda sections dated 3 October 1939:

**1226** It has been noted that the display of flags in celebration of the victorious conduct of the war in Poland and the entry of German troops into the former capital of that country has been extremely poor. Care must, therefore, be taken at once to ensure that flags are displayed extensively on all houses in the district. The display will last until Monday 9 October inclusive. Since, at the present time, there are compatriots from every Gau in our district as soldiers, for this reason alone we must ensure that there is a model display of flags as a public indication of the inward participation of the population in the great events which are currently taking place.

The rapid defeat of Poland raised hopes that the war would soon be over. These hopes were soon disappointed by the Allies' rejection of

Hitler's October peace offer.[8] German propaganda was obliged to cope with the problems of the 'phoney war' period (October 1939–March 1940). On 4 March 1940 Goebbels issued the following press directive:

**1227**    The German government has the impression that the people believe that after the conquest of Poland the war is over. Steps must be taken to make absolutely sure that the nation's willingness to fight, which has been gradually achieved, is not dissipated.

With the defeat of France sealed by the armistice on 22 June 1940 the focus of German propaganda switched back to Britain. At the same time, there was the problem raised by the German public's disgust at Italy's late entry into the war, which gave them the image of scavengers. The continuing dislike and contempt felt by the German population towards their Italian allies, which lasted to a greater or lesser extent throughout the war, is an indication of the limitations of German propaganda. On 23 June, Goebbels gave the following instructions at his daily conference:

**1228**    The Minister states that the topic of England must now come to the fore without in the process a peace mood towards France being allowed to develop too precipitately during the next few days.

Although it is not yet clear in what form the struggle against England will be continued, and we must avoid the impression being created that the occupation of England will be starting tomorrow, on the other hand, there can be no doubt that England will have to face the same punishment as France if it fails to see sense.

The anti-English polemics can latch onto the Churchill broadcast and the comments of *The Times* to the effect that England is allegedly the last defender of European freedom. We should explain that we are now the leaders in the conflict between continental Europe and the plutocratic island nation of Britons. The foreign language services must quite consciously and systematically operate with slogans along the lines of 'Nations of Europe—England is organizing a campaign of hunger against you!'

There is the danger that the anti-Italian mood in Germany may take on undesirable dimensions and that, because of the sensitive reaction of the Italians to such currents of opinion, this could lead to the alienation of Italians from Germans…it is vitally necessary for the press tactfully to head off the mood of fury and hatred against Italy and direct it into safer channels.

---

[8] See Vol. 3, doc. 553.

The defeat of France aroused great hopes in the German population that a general peace would soon be secured. However, the refusal of Britain to 'see sense' and the problems of launching an invasion prompted Goebbels, at his daily conference on 23 August 1940, to order his propagandists to prepare the population for the war to continue into the following year. His decision to dampen down optimism at such an early stage indicates his generally cautious approach, which was to be demonstrated in the later phases of the war and was not always shown by his fellow leaders:

**1229**    The Minister emphasizes the need adequately to prepare the nation for the possibility that the war may drag on beyond the winter. He stresses that at present it is by no means certain that the war can be expected to last beyond the winter and that it is quite possible that the war may end this year and that there is every chance that this will happen. But he emphasizes that it is better to prepare the nation for a long war, which then may not happen, than to encourage people to hope for an early peace and then to disappoint these hopes. At any rate, no further encouragement should be given to the belief that the war may be over by this autumn; on the other hand, there should not be a lot of talk about the likelihood of a long war. Furthermore, one should emphasize the toughness of the English commitment to the war and only report the absurdities of English daily life in exceptional cases.

▬▬

### (iii) The War in the East and the Campaign against Bolshevism

The question of the Soviet Union posed a particular problem for German propaganda between August 1939 and June 1941. The Nazi-Soviet Pact of 23 August 1939[9] represented a complete contradiction of the previous Nazi policy of attacking the Soviet Union as the centre of 'Jewish Bolshevism' and the arch-enemy of civilization. German propaganda was obliged to drop the anti-Soviet line and adopt at least a lukewarm attitude towards the Soviet Union. However, the combination of Soviet neutrality during the conflict with the Western powers during 1939–40, together with the main Nazi propaganda line of projecting Britain as a 'plutocratic' state, risked the danger of creating the impression of a close association between National Socialism and Soviet Communism. This danger was pointed out to the German press at the daily press conference on 2 February 1940:

---

[9] See Vol. 3, doc. 543.

**1230**    You are reminded once more that accounts of visits to the Soviet Union are highly undesirable and in all cases must be submitted. Germany's relations with the Soviet Union are restricted to the diplomatic and economic spheres. The agreement [between Germany and the Soviet Union of 23 August 1939] was reached in order to break through the encirclement front of the Western European powers and, therefore, represented a major coup for German foreign policy. However, the German public must not now be given the impression, through a description of Russian domestic life, that we want to achieve an ideological merger and that we are more or less adopting and imitating Bolshevik terminology. There is an undoubted danger that such a merger will occur because our struggle against England and France is, after all, also directed against the plutocratic system and, as a result, certain Socialist conceptions have to be discussed quite often. But one must distinguish this propaganda and keep it clearly separate from the Bolshevik ideology. The reference in some newspapers to the German state as the workers', peasants', and soldiers' state must not be repeated. This must on no account become the epitome of the German concept of the state.

With the German invasion of the Soviet Union on 22 June 1941, the gap between the Nazi regime's pretended and real views and intentions towards the Soviet Union disappeared and, at his 11 o'clock conference on that day, Goebbels gave the following instructions to his subordinates to make the necessary adjustment to their propaganda coverage of events:

**1231**    The criminal double crossing policy of the Bolsheviks, which provoked the overwhelming deployment of the million-strong German army from the North Cape to the Black Sea must be made the subject of comprehensive coverage by the German press during the next few days, through which the meaning and the historical importance of this struggle will be clearly outlined to the German people on the basis of the Führer's proclamation, the particular points made by the Reich Press Chief and other material.

We are clear about what the outcome of the struggle will be. It can only end with a victory for German arms. The press now has the decisive task of guiding the hearts and feelings of the homeland in such a way that those at the front can once more rely on those at home. This work of the German press is of decisive importance because until now for military operational reasons the German people has not been mentally prepared for this change of course.

At the moment the German people have two things on their minds:

(a) How can the war with the Soviet Union be reconciled with the hopes for a speedy end to the war?

(b) After years of struggle against Bolshevism we made a pact with the Soviet Union. How could it come to this second change of course?

(a) The most important argument in this connection is to emphasize the fact that the German armed forces could not be fully committed in the West so long as there was a power which was a treacherous unknown quantity in the East. The way this argument is handled will be decisive for the psychological attitude of the whole German nation in this struggle and it must, therefore, be well articulated.

(b) In this connection it must be made clear that this is not just a simple shift in policy. National Socialism began as a movement against Bolshevism. Under this banner it conquered the Reich and re-founded it. After the fulfilment of these tasks for the Reich the struggle against Bolshevism was postponed for two years through an apparent truce. As a result of the treachery of the Bolshevik leaders, which has been uncovered by the Führer, National Socialism, and therefore the German nation, is returning to the principle on the basis of which it began, namely the struggle against plutocracy and Bolshevism.

The Minister stated, and these were his actual words: The Führer says it will only last for four months. But I say to you now: it will only last eight weeks. For to the extent that the inner content of National Socialism is far superior to Communism to the same extent it must prove its superiority on the field of battle in the shortest possible time.

▬

Then, at his ministerial conference on 5 July, Goebbels stated:

**1232** Through Germany's settling of accounts with Moscow the biggest Jewish swindle of all time is being uncovered and exposed. The 'workers' paradise' is shown up before the whole world as a gigantic swindle, a system of exploitation in which the producers are forced by the most brutal terror to endure a miserable existence in inhuman conditions. In this system, in which Jews, capitalists and Bolsheviks work hand in hand, there is an unimaginable degree of human degradation. What the millions of German soldiers are now seeing there is a vision of the lowest possible living standards, from miserable housing and lice-ridden dwellings, neglected roads and filthy villages to the brutish dullness of the people's whole existence. The Jews have driven the peoples of the Soviet Union into this unspeakable situation through their devilish system of Bolshevism. The mask has now been torn from the face of this the biggest international swindle of all time. The struggle in the East represents the liberation of mankind from this crime.

It will now be the task of German propaganda in a hard-hitting campaign of enlightenment to spell out the above points in a dramatic way through reports and by acquiring evidence in the form of written and pictorial material. A particularly impressive way of doing this will be to contrast the inhuman conditions in the Soviet Union with the social progress, the high cultural level and the healthy joy in life of the working people in national socialist Germany. It will be particularly important to produce a good selection of pictures in which the brutish Bolshevik types are contrasted with the frank and open faces of German workers, the filthy Soviet barracks are compared with German workers' housing estates, the muddy tracks with German roads... etc. In addition, there are the pictures of the crimes of the GPU such as those which are already available from Lemberg and which the newspapers should not shrink from printing.

▬

The following documents give the text of two wall posters put out by the Propaganda Ministry containing 'weekly slogans', which illustrate the above themes. The first was issued for the week of 30 July–5 August 1941:

**1233** THAT is the Jewish Bolshevism with which Churchill and the British plutocratic clique are jointly waging war against Germany

*The German people thank the Führer for protecting them against the threat of Bolshevism*

——

The second is for the week of 17–23 September 1941:

**1234** 'Onward Christian Soldiers!'

That's what the hypocrites, Roosevelt and Churchill, sang with a pious look on their faces when they met in the Atlantic.[10] At the same time, they were giving Stalin and his Bolshevik hordes new promises of aid in their fight against Germany and a reborn Europe

That's what they look like—the 'Christian Soldiers'!

Their bestial murderous acts in Lemberg, Riga, Vilna and Dubno have filled the world with horror and disgust!

But the German Wehrmacht is smashing the Bolshevik enemy of the world with hard and ruthless blows. Hypocritical songs and pharisaical piety will not be any use, Mister Roosevelt and Mister Churchill. For, in the end, Germany will be victorious!

——

After striking initial successes, by August the German advance was becoming increasingly slowed by a combination of the difficulty of the terrain and consequent heavy wear and tear on vehicles and equipment and the stiffening resistance of the Soviet forces as they recovered from the shock of the surprise invasion, resistance which produced heavy German casualties. This situation produced a growing sense of disillusionment on the part of the German population, which in turn put pressure on the leadership to demonstrate progress. They had calculated on a period of eight to ten weeks for the campaign and Hitler had gambled on the success of this last blitzkrieg. He was well aware of the appalling risks of Germany becoming involved in a long-drawn-out war

---

[10] This refers to the meeting between President Roosevelt and Prime Minister Churchill on a battleship in the Atlantic at which they agreed and signed the Atlantic Charter, on 14 August 1941, which laid down a set of democratic values as the basis for the post-war world.

on two fronts. Moreover, Hitler was anxious to persuade the Japanese government to join in the war against the Soviet Union and remain firm in its stance towards the United States. Finally, at the beginning of October, Hitler seems to have been genuinely optimistic about the prospects on the Russian front. Thus he told his audience at the opening of the 1941 Winter Aid Programme in the Berlin Sports Palace on 3 October that 'our opponent has already been broken and will never rise again!'.[11]

All these factors help to explain why, on 8 October, a few days after the launch of the final offensive against Moscow, Hitler summoned the Reich Press Chief to receive an important announcement. Dietrich recorded the event in his memoirs as follows:

**1235**    When I arrived, together with my secretary, he received me in his study in the bunker in a very good mood. Pacing vigorously up and down the room, he told me word for word, with my secretary taking down every syllable in shorthand, what I was to announce to the press in Berlin the following day and what was to cause such a big stir. Hitler told me—to give the gist of it once again—that, after all that had happened so far, with the last two great battles of annihilation [Kiev and Vyasma] he had weakened the enemy to such an extent in terms of the numbers of its army and its war materiel that it no longer had the strength to resist the victorious German panzer armies with any hope of success. Although a number of more or less serious battles lay ahead before the enemy was completely conquered, nevertheless, the German armies were over the worst and the decision in the Eastern campaign had in practice been achieved. Our enemies' dream of a war on two fronts was over.

At this moment Hitler was firmly of the opinion that the whole war had now been won and he expressed this conviction to me in an emotional outburst without the experience of which I would not have gone so far as I did in my press conference. But I had no reason to doubt what the Supreme Commander had so spontaneously told about the events in the East for the purpose of their publication. But, to be quite sure, I handed a copy of the shorthand dictation, which I intended to use, to General Jodl, the Chief of the Wehrmacht Staff, for it to be checked and confirmed.

▬▬▬

The American correspondent in Berlin, Howard K. Smith, described the press conference of 9 October 1941 in his account of his time in Berlin published in 1942:

**1236**    When the telephone rang, I was lying in bed with a miserable cold and a skull-splitting headache. It was the secretary of Dr Fröhlich, the Propaganda

---

[11] *Völkischer Beobachter,* 4.10.1941.

Ministry's liaison officer for the American press and radio. She was excited, and told me I should come to an important special press conference at noon sharp; something of extremely great importance. No she did not know what it was about, but be there on time, for at five minutes after twelve the doors would be barred and guarded . . .

The red plush Theatre Hall of the Propaganda Ministry was filled with reporters from everywhere, guessing in a dozen different languages what it was about. My head throbbed. Before the audience was a long conference table, and around the table in little clots stood a bevy of gorgeous uniforms—green, brown, grey and two shades of blue, well stuffed with Prussian officers, party officials and just bureaucrats of the Ministry, beaming with joy at an opportunity to appear before their daily *Publikum* in costumes which lent glamour to waistlines and limbs made for mufti.

As on all Nazi 'historic' occasions—except those in which Hitler is the leading man, for he can afford to risk non-conformity—the central show-piece was impressively and precisely late. At 12.30 on the dot, a few officers rushed through the door into the room, indicating the coming of the Leader's emissary. The clots dissolved into one fine phalanx and in walked Dr Dietrich, flapping his right palm back over his shoulder in imitation of his Führer's salute and grinning as if fair to bursting with the tidings he bore. There was profuse handshaking sandwiched each time between stiff-armed salutes. Cameras snapped and flashlight bulbs flashed. On the great stage behind the central figure, Dietrich, the red velvet curtains were drawn apart to reveal a monstrous map of European Russia thrice as high as the speaker. The effect was impressive.

Dietrich was introduced briefly and oilily by Dr Brauweiler, a musty old Nazi Party wheel-horse who had been appointed leader of the foreign press section of the Ministry after the arrest of Boehmer, and given a natty blue uniform for having kept his mouth and head shut for eight years. Then the little doctor rose and held forth. I regret I cannot quote him directly. But it is a strange feature of this grand occasion that the text of what Dietrich said has never been published. Unlike most other important utterances of Nazi leaders his words were never re-broadcast to the German people—a feature which caused inquisitive whisperings in German and foreign circles alike . . .

For Dietrich said bold words and cast moderating and conditional phrases to the four winds. In the vernacular of the diplomatic correspondent, Dietrich put himself away, away out on a mighty high limb. With an air of finality, Dietrich announced the very last *remnants* of the Red Army were locked in two steel German pockets before Moscow and were undergoing swift, merciless annihilation. This was sensational. To understand how big the story was one must remember the circumstances. This was the first substantial news about the mighty new offensive. It came directly from Adolf Hitler himself and could not be doubted. Dietrich continued: behind the two pockets there stood between the German armies and Moscow just so much space and nothing more. As one correspondent later put it, Dietrich indicated that between Germany and the complete conquest of the untold riches of Russia there remained only 'the time it takes man and machine to cover the given distance'. After seven short days, the Führer's offensive had smashed the Red Army to splinters, the decision was reached and the eastern continent lay like a limp virgin, in the mighty arms of the lustful, hungry German Mars. 'And on that, gentleman, I stake my whole journalistic reputation . . .'

When Dietrich finished tense excitement prevailed. The uniforms gathered round him and pumped his hand as a sort of mutual congratulation on the German victory. The agency men had burst through the doorway and were giving short, hot bulletins over the phones to their offices. Axis and Balkan correspondents applauded and cheered, then stood and raised their arms in salute to Dietrich who sped out of the room to return to the Führer's headquarters and be on hand for the last terrible blows, the *coup de grace*, the Grand Finale.

Although neither the exact words used by Hitler nor those used by Dietrich were ever published or broadcast, the following morning the German press reflected their sentiments. Thus the official party newspaper, the *Völkischer Beobachter,* reported that 'Stalin's armies have disappeared from the face of the earth'.

According to his young aide at the Propaganda Ministry, Rudolf Semmler, Goebbels was furious about the Dietrich press conference:

**1237** Can Dietrich's rash statement be justified as an effort to bring the Japanese into the war? Goebbels says firmly No! He is of course less worried about the effects of it abroad. He feels himself responsible for morale at home and among the troops and the mood there is uncertain. At the front soldiers who heard of Dietrich's statement laid down their weapons in masses. There were rejoicings all over Germany. Yesterday people were opening the last bottle of champagne kept for the great day. To the ordinary man Dietrich's statement, 'The war has been won!' simply meant: 'the war is over. We have won. Sieg heil!'

The disillusionment which will come in the next few days will be terrible. Goebbels has protested to Hitler about such a reckless news policy. He was told in reply that this was only a tactical move to rouse the Japanese from their apathy. We will see whether this frivolous trick will pay.

Nevertheless, the mood of this period is captured in the following statement made by Hans Fritzsche, the head of the press division of the Propaganda Ministry, to the Berlin Foreign Press Association on 13 October 1941. In its language and sentiments it is a highly revealing expression of Nazi imperialism and undoubtedly reflected the views of Fritzsche's masters:

**1238** Militarily speaking the war has been decided. What remains to be done is primarily a matter for domestic and foreign policy. At some point the German armies in the East will call a halt and we shall then establish a border which will shield from the East the greater Europe and the European interest bloc under German leadership. It is possible that military tensions and even military conflicts on a small scale may *last for eight or ten years*. However, this situation does not in any way alter the will of the German political leadership to construct the European continent and order it in accordance with its own laws dictated by Germany. It is true that this is a '*Europe behind barbed wire*' but this Europe will be economically, industrially and agriculturally autarkic and effectively militarily *impregnable*.

The German political leadership does not intend to pursue England and America into distant regions and challenge them there. As far as Europe is concerned, there is nothing to be gained by doing that; the expenditure of men and materiel would bear no relationship to what could be achieved. The area of the British Isles is a different matter. The very strong denial by Germany of alleged peace feelers made by the Reich to England and the USA has already demonstrated the political line which is now being taken. After the decision in the east there is no question of our making an offer of a settlement to England. Rather the most that can be expected is that, at the time of its total military defeat, the British will approach us in order to be assigned a place in the new Europe as an island on the periphery. The question of whether the British Isles will be militarily attacked and occupied very soon, or in the spring of next year, or whenever is of no importance. Such a military operation will only need to be carried out and concluded by a small section of our total armed forces. Germany will now construct the European continent well-protected and secured albeit behind barbed wire and always ready to defend itself. We do not want to chase after far-off lands but to concentrate on the huge European tasks of the future. If we are disturbed in this by enemy air raids or attacks on the eastern frontier or in other border areas we shall retaliate with fearful force until such enemy operations cease. The language we shall use vis-à-vis the nations dominated by us will be much franker and colder. Naturally, it is not on for a piddling little state [*kleiner Miststaat*] to buck against the European peace by coming with special wishes and special requests; it will be strictly reminded of its European duty. This is linked to the fact that, in future, when the state of a peaceful Europe has been declared, the German press will be much freer in its treatment of the European nations and small states. There will then no longer be the need for censorship since the imperialist instinct should be sufficient to ensure that the German standpoint is asserted on every occasion.

If military activity is reduced—since the war as a chain of military engagements is essentially over—then politics will move that much more into the foreground. Here newspapers are of enormous importance and basically the decisive means for guiding the nation. The German people is to be led to think in terms of European empire, to the awareness that the state of tension may remain for many years and that this represents the natural world order as far as our European future is concerned. Just as the English in India continually have skirmishes on the north-east frontier so in the same way Germany may have to fight on some frontier. This will strengthen the fighting spirit and assist the training of the youth of the Reich.

■■■

In fact in the second week of October the rains came and the German advance bogged down. The rain was then followed by snow and the extreme cold of the Russian winter which set in early that year. In the first week in December the Russians launched a massive counter attack, driving the German forces back from Moscow.[12]

Meanwhile, Goebbels had been carrying out an agonizing reappraisal of German propaganda insisting that it adopt a more 'realistic' line. Already, on 9 November 1941, he had published an article in *Das Reich,* the popular up-market weekly modelled on the British *Observer*, which had been introduced in May 1940, with the title '*When or How?*', in which he advised against speculating on when victory might come, concluding: 'Let us not ask when it will come; let us see to it that it comes.' He summed up his views in his address to the Propaganda Ministry conference on 7 December 1941 as follows:

**1239**    Hitherto, our propaganda has made the following basic error, namely by protecting the German population from any unpleasant news it has made it oversensitive to any temporary setbacks. The population itself generally knows more about the overall situation than can be gained from the press and it can cope with and demands to be informed about unpleasant truths as well. Churchill did the right thing when, shortly after the beginning of the war, he promised the English 'Blood, sweat and tears'. German propaganda, which naturally must make justified optimism about the outcome of the war the basis of its attitude should in all its branches be more realistic in future. As examples, the Minister suggested that the population could be told that, in view of the overall situation, Christmas presents were superfluous and that the reductions in travel were not just going to be for a few days but for a lengthy period.

The assumption that the German forces would defeat the Soviet Union before the onset of winter had led the Wehrmacht authorities to neglect to provide sufficient winter clothing for their troops. Goebbels had already raised this matter with the Wehrmacht in August, when the German advance was visibly slowing, suggesting that he should organize a 'wool collection' among the civilian population and he returned to the issue again in October. However, on both occasions he was fobbed off by the military who were convinced that they would be able to withdraw most of the troops before the onset of winter and were anxious not to alarm the home front. Now Goebbels determined to use the crisis of December 1941 on the eastern front as an example of the new 'realistic' propaganda line and as a way of reinforcing the links between the

---

[12] See Vol. 3, docs 593–594.

fighting front and the home front and diverting people's attention away
from the crisis by giving them a practical task, one which would clearly
benefit their menfolk at the front. On 20 December 1941, therefore,
Goebbels broadcast an appeal to the German people:

**1240**    Today I look to you to give our soldiers additional help from the
German homeland, a present from all German compatriots to the Front!

. . . This year, in the vast territories of the east and the south-east, in Norway
and in Finland winter has set in early and with a severity uncommon in normal
years. The competent branches of our Armed Forces have done everything to
equip the Front adequately for winter conditions. As we all know, they are now
about to use their last transport facilities to send the enormous amounts of
winter equipment for our soldiers to the front line. Yet in spite of these
preparations, carried out with the greatest exertion of materiel and energy, our
soldiers still need many things for the winter. Our armed forces at the front
today count so many million men that it is extremely difficult to supply them
with all that each individual man needs from one quarter alone. But for this very
reason the homeland would not deserve one single peaceful hour if even one
single soldier—in particular in the east, in the south-east, in Norway, let alone in
Arctic Finland—remained exposed to the hardships of the climate without
sufficient winter equipment.

I know that at the last clothing collection the German population gave
everything it could spare in view of the strained textile supply situation. But
there are still countless items of winter equipment in the homeland, which the
civilian population can certainly hardly spare, but which the front certainly
needs more urgently than the homeland. It is quite true that in the third year of
war we at home must also put up with great restrictions. Yet we would not be
doing justice to the front if we were to compare these with the sacrifices which
our soldiers have to make—particularly in this War winter. At home we all have
a roof over our heads and a bed to sleep in. Though food is restricted, it is
certainly still sufficient compared to almost all the other European countries,
and our people at home can obtain—through newspapers, theatres, concerts,
films or wireless—that relaxation which they so urgently need owing to the
extraordinary efforts they have to make for their strenuous work

Our soldiers on the eastern front lack nearly all these things. That cannot be
changed. But the homeland can help by giving its sons and fathers protection
against the hardships of the winter weather! As long as there is still a serviceable
object of winter equipment in the homeland, it must be sent to the Front. I know
that even at home many people can hardly do without such equipment. At
present there is no chance of replacing it. Yet, our soldiers need it a thousand
times more urgently than they do. I should be exaggerating were I to refer to
sacrifices in this connection. Whatever discomforts the homeland has endured up
to now in the course of the war are but small privations in comparison to what
our front has been taking upon itself for more than two years, hourly and daily.

Thanks to the readiness of our soldiers, the Reich still enjoys life in security.
Yet the front must stake life and health. Today it is mounting guard over nearly

the whole of Europe, for the whole of Europe, and thus specially for us. Just as our soldiers carried on their victorious advance unwaveringly in summertime, through burning heat or cloudbursts, through dust or mud, accomplishing superhuman feats of marching, they are today ready to protect the homeland along the defensive fronts of the winter, in snow, ice, rain, frost and cold. They must endure the hardships of weather in all seasons, while we at home can avoid them almost entirely. Even against the heat the front can hardly protect itself, yet the homeland alone can help it against the cold. Who at home would refuse to answer the call to this communal aid?

The following objects are needed at the front particularly urgently; the following objects must therefore be put at its disposal:

[There follows a lengthy list of clothing.]

The Party with all its affiliated and branch organizations, has been instructed to be ready to collect during the time fixed all these winter garments urgently needed at the front. The collection will begin on 27 December and ends on the evening of 4 January 1942; it will be carried out by the Party from house to house and from flat to flat. Every compatriot will greatly facilitate the work of the collectors and will be of the utmost help in speeding up the collection if they deliver the winter garments which they are going to give personally at centres which will be made known in local newspapers. Arrangements have been made with the competent military and transport authorities to send the objects collected as soon as possible to the foremost front lines. Our fighting soldiers shall benefit by them at the earliest possible moment.

In spite of all the air raids, Germany has so far noticed comparatively little of the effects of war, yet this is a war deciding the existence or non-existence of the German nation. Our soldiers who are fighting at the front have by their heroic efforts taken from us the greater share of the burden of this war. They have had to bear doubly hard all that which we have been spared. I think that the homeland, now at this third wartime Christmas in particular, has the urgent desire to prove to the front, which is doing its duty silently, its gratitude in a way more tangible than mere words.

The festive season known all over the world as the most German festival is close upon us. For the third time in this war our soldiers are denied home leave for Christmas or even any home leave on a larger scale. What is more obvious than that the homeland, beyond mere words of thanks should show solidarity with the front and express its deep gratitude to our soldiers by National Socialist communal help of the most generous order? . . .

The Führer himself has asked me to make this appeal to the homeland. He supports this collection by words designed to prove to the homeland the great result he expects. Let us show him the response which his appeal awakens in the German people's hearts.

The Führer's message to you is: 'German nation! While, apart from air attacks, the German homeland is not threatened by the enemy, millions of our soldiers, after a year [*sic*!] of the most severe fighting, are at the front up against an enemy vastly superior in number and materiel. Thanks to their leadership and gallantry, officers and men have won victories unequalled so far in world history. Thus the largest front of all times is now holding out and fighting from the Polar regions to the Black Sea, from the snow fields of Finland to the Balkan mountains, until the hour of the final annihilation of the most dangerous enemy arrives. If the German nation wishes to give a Christmas present to its soldiers it should renounce all that there is in the way of the warmest articles of clothing, which can be spared during the war, and which later on, in peacetime, can in any case be replaced. For, whatever the leadership of the armed forces and the individual armed services have provided in winter equipment, every soldier deserves far more! This is where the homeland is able to help! The soldier of the eastern front will gather from this that the national community he is fighting for is not an empty phrase in National Socialist Germany.

[Signed] ADOLF HITLER

And now, compatriots, do your duty loyally in accordance with the Führer's words: This collection must be the most generous which we have ever made and must be completed in a very short time. Let everybody do his utmost. I appeal to you all for the great collection of winter clothes for the eastern front. The German nation's answer must be worthy of the victories which the eastern front has won for the whole German nation and for the future of the Reich.

On 23 December, Hitler issued a decree imposing the death penalty for anyone who misappropriated articles of clothing from the collection for the front.

The collection was extended by one week to 11 January because of the size of the response. On 14 January 1942 Goebbels proudly announced that the collection had produced 67,232,686 articles of clothing which were transported to the Wehrmacht in 4,003 railway wagons. There were, among other things, 8,686,647 pairs of socks and stockings, 6,756,138 scarves, 5,611,393 cardigans, pullovers and waistcoats, and 3,889,747 pieces of fur.

Hitler referred to the collection in his Reichstag speech of 30 January 1942 to commemorate the ninth anniversary of his take-over of power as follows:

**1241**    Behind this front there is now a homeland which is worthy of it. Recently, recognizing that what had been prepared for protection against the frost was completely insufficient, I made an appeal to the German people. I want now to express my thanks to this people. This appeal was also a vote. The others speak of democracy; this was true democracy! It has proved itself in these days. And I know that so many ordinary people have given, and this time, very many who found it difficult and who previously would have considered it impossible to part with a valuable fur. They have now given it in the knowledge that the most insignificant musketeer is more valuable than the most expensive fur. And I have ensured that things didn't happen like in the First World War when the homeland gave up copper and a copper distribution company paid out a 2,260% dividend, when the homeland had to give up other things, like leather or couldn't get any leather and then the leather processing industry paid out a 2,700% dividend. Anyone in the German Reich who enriches himself on the proceeds will die. Because I don't know whether out there there isn't an ordinary, poor musketeer whose hand can be saved with a woollen glove or who could be protected from freezing to death by a warm waistcoat, which he is being robbed of by someone at home. I shall represent the interests of the soldiers here and I know that the whole of the German nation stands behind me in this.[13]

Meanwhile, German propaganda had been faced with the need to respond to the situation created by Hitler's declaration of war on the United States. Initially, the line taken was to play down its significance on the grounds that the United States had already been virtually at war with Germany and that it would take a long time for America to mobilize its resources in order to have any impact on the war in Europe. However, on 16 December 1941, Goebbels issued the following instructions at his daily conference:

**1242**       The Minister requests the following propaganda measures against the USA:

1. The production of publications which are targeted at the German intelligentsia and which objectively demonstrate that the USA possesses virtually no culture of its own, that, on the contrary, its cultural products stem essentially from European achievements. The issue of American films should be dealt with in this connection.

2. In addition, publications should be produced in a popular style aimed at the masses and, in particular, at young people, and should demonstrate that the uncritical adoption of certain American activities, such as Jazz music etc. shows a lack of culture. Reference should be made to the grotesque distortions which occur, for example, in the transposition of Bach's music into jazz.

3. This internal German propaganda should be prepared now. It should not, however, be deployed at the present moment because currently there is a considerable wave of inner rejection of the USA. However, in view of the German tendency to objectivity, the Minister stated that we must assume that this wave will ebb after a certain time and be replaced by a more friendly assessment of the Americans as has sometimes occurred in the relationship with England during the course of this war. The material must be ready for the moment when this change of mood occurs.

By the spring of 1942, the German forces in the East had stabilized the front and were preparing to launch another major summer offensive. However, at home the mood had been severely damaged by cuts in the

---

[13] For the popular response to this action see below pp. 537ff.

food rations.[14] It was probably in response to this crisis of morale that, on 31 May 1942, Goebbels wrote the following lead article in *Das Reich* with the title 'What's it all for?' It was part of a new emphasis in German propaganda aimed at reassuring the German people not only by spelling out in public the imperialist goals of the war in crude material terms, but also by stressing the importance of Germany's possession of the vast food and raw material resources of the Ukraine:

**1243** ... today, every German soldier, worker and peasant knows what we are fighting and working for. This isn't a war for throne and altar; it's a war for wheat and bread, for a well-stocked breakfast, lunch, and supper table, a war to secure the material preconditions for the solution of the social question, the housing question and the question of roads, the construction of a navy, a merchant marine and a fleet of cruise liners, the production of people's cars [*Volkswagen*]. And its a war for tractors, for theatres and cinemas for the whole nation right down to the smallest village, a war for raw materials and rubber, for iron and ores, in short it is a war for a national life worth living, which, up to now, we as poor people have not been able to enjoy.

It may confer a good reputation on a nation to say that it knows how make do with little and has developed the Spartan lifestyle into something which appears natural. But this must not become something done for its own sake and national poverty must not be pushed so far that it no longer permits the full development of the nation's abilities and strengths. And that has been the case with us. It may be that, as a result of this, other energies were mobilized in our people, which, to a considerable extent are responsible for our current position of power. But at some point a nation must be able to expect to see the realization of its national aspirations. One can't always be fighting for ideals and, in the long run, to act as cultural fertilizer for the world is more a sign of the good-naturedness of a nation than of its intelligence and political vision. We as a nation want at last to cash in [*einkassieren*]. It is our dearest wish at the end of this war to enjoy the fruits of our endless working and fighting, of all our efforts and our patience.

Apart from everything else which motivates us as a nation in this gigantic struggle, it is the longing for peace and happiness, for prosperity and a secure existence which is one of the main driving forces in our will to victory and our tough persistence in following this goal. Each of us in his most secret thoughts dreams of a future life which is at any rate better than the one he left when he took up his rifle or stood at his lathe or behind his plough so that with redoubled efforts he could produce the daily bread for our people and the weapons and ammunition for our soldiers. We dream of a happy people in a beautiful land, traversed by broad roads like bands of silver which are also open to the modest car of the ordinary man. Beside them lie pretty villages and well laid-out cities with clean and roomy houses inhabited by large families for whom they provide sufficient space. In the limitless fields of the east yellow corn is waving, enough and more than enough to feed our people and the whole of

---

[14] See below, pp. 518ff.

Europe. Work will once more be a pleasure and it will be marked by a joy in life which will find expression in glittering parties and contemplative peace. The theatres and music halls, the cinemas and community halls will fill up every evening with happy people. Art will go to the people and the people will go to art. We don't want this nicer life to be only something for our children to enjoy; we want to conquer it for ourselves and to find in the happiness which it brings our historic reward for over a quarter of a century of struggle, care, work and trouble.

We can only smile pityingly when the imperialist plutocrats like Churchill and Roosevelt accuse the Führer of wanting to conquer the world in order to satisfy his demonic ambition. No! He has called upon the nation to fight and to work so that the most elementary conditions of our life, which are threatened by its enemies, can be defended and, in addition, in order to secure the preconditions for a national prosperity which will give our people the amount of earthly happiness they deserve. That is our war aim. It affects us all. The only thing we can lose is the restrictive quality of our lives which is the cause of our national and ethnic [*völkisch*] crisis.

Thus, if one asks what are we fighting for, then we don't have to beat about the bush. We say clearly and bluntly and without prevarication: for a life that is worthy of a hundred million people.

---

## (iv) 'Total War'

After initial striking successes, the German summer campaign became bogged down in the siege of Stalingrad. On 19 November 1942 the Russians began a major offensive and by November 22 their two pincers north and south of Stalingrad had locked together surrounding the German Sixth Army.[15] The increasingly grave situation developing in the winter of 1942 prompted Goebbels to press for the introduction of 'total war' on the home front. It also caused him to reflect on the weaknesses of German propaganda. At his ministerial conference on 4 January 1943 he reviewed the situation as follows:

**1244** The Minister made a number of fundamental statements about the war situation and emphasized the seriousness of the position and the necessity of doing everything to mobilize the last reserves for the war effort. At the beginning of the new year it was necessary to report on the work done hitherto and to draw the conclusions from it for the future. He was glad that this demand for a more total conduct of the war was now slowly being realized. He has repeatedly emphasized in the ministerial conferences that a more radical conduct of the war was alone capable of producing military victories. Every day brings further proof of the fact that in the East we are facing a brutal opponent whom

---

[15] See Vol. 3, doc. 603.

one can overcome with the most brutal means and for this purpose there must be a total commitment of the whole of our forces and reserves. This will then put German propaganda on the rails again and the contradiction between theory and practice will disappear. If the nation felt that total war is not simply a matter of propaganda but that the necessary conclusions were being drawn then propaganda would prove really substantial and effective. It is now time to act and one should not wait for the spring. If we do not mobilize all the reserves now then one shouldn't imagine that that would happen in the spring or summer when in any case optimism tends to develop. One must exploit the opportunity to go over to total war now when the difficulties are so great.

On the question of war propaganda itself the Minister said that one must reduce it to a number of key sentences. In view of the length of the war, it was unavoidable that our propaganda had become disjointed as a result of having to deal with the day to day events and that in the process the basic principles of this war had slipped into the background. The history of national socialist propaganda proves that the basic principles are always decisive and a true propagandist seizes every opportunity to bring these basic principles of the war once more to the fore by applying them to particular current events. It was necessary continually and repeatedly to emphasize a number of fixed principles at every opportunity and to hammer them into the nation's conscience.

As such he put forward amongst others:

1. The war had been forced on the German people.
2. In this war it was a matter of life or death.
3. There must be total war.

The Minister compared these principles with the leitmotivs of a Wagner opera and considered that these sentences must continually appear in a variety of forms. Every day there was an opportunity to remind the people of these basic themes.

———

Two days later, Goebbels provided the audience at his ministerial conference with a devastating assessment of German propaganda's failings hitherto, in the process contradicting an instruction given in the previous document:

**1245**    With reference to his comments yesterday about the measures for implementing the total war measures, the Minister stated that our propaganda must naturally avoid producing a defensive attitude on the part of the German people. Under no circumstances should slogans be used such as 'life or death' and 'Fortress Europe', which produced undesirable notions. Since the beginning of the war our propaganda had followed the following erroneous path:

First year of the war: we have won.
Second year of the war: we shall win.
Third year of the war: we must win.
Fourth year of the war: we cannot be defeated.

Such a development is catastrophic and cannot be allowed to continue under any circumstances. Instead, it must be brought home to the German public that we not only want to and must win, but also and above all that we can win because the preconditions are there as soon as the work and effort at home have been placed fully at the service of the war.

━━━

In January 1943 Hitler responded to Goebbels' promptings to introduce total war measures, but not to the latter's satisfaction, and Goebbels decided to try and increase the pressure on Hitler by trying to mobilize public opinion. These developments are illuminated by the following entries in the diary of Goebbels' aide, Rudolf Semmler:

**1246** 18 January 1943

On Hitler's orders Goebbels proposals are to be carried out by a Committee of Three consisting of Lammers, Bormann and Keitel.[16] Goebbels will be called in to advise. He is bitterly disappointed at the subordinate place he is to occupy. He did all the work of planning and now he is to have nothing to say about its execution. He complains to the Führer.

20 January 1943

Today the first meeting of the Committee of Three for Total War took place in the Reich Chancellery. Goebbels spoke for an hour and proposed the following measures: conscription of women for work; all luxury shops and businesses to be closed down—including stores and luxury cafés.

After the meeting Goebbels says he had to fight like a tiger to get his proposals through. Lammers he called a wet blanket. But there was some hope that this winter would not go by with the same illusions as last winter.

26 January 1943

Goebbels is disappointed at the slow progress that is being made with the plans for total war. Everything is going too slowly for his impulsive nature. He is still furious at the total powers being given to someone else. He had hoped to be head of the Committee of Three. He is merely their adviser.

29 January 1943

. . . Goebbels is brooding over a daring plan. He will try and bring pressure to bear on Hitler by putting forward radical demands in a speech at the Sports Palace. The crowd will applaud wildly. In this way he may be able to force Hitler to put an end to half-measures. If his demands are not met then the Government will be compromised. The Führer could not afford that at the moment.

━━━

On 18 February 1943 Goebbels made a lengthy speech in the Berlin Sports Palace before an audience which had been carefully selected to

---

[16] See above pp. 26ff.

make it representative of every section of the German people. This speech contained the main themes of Nazi propaganda during the last phase of the war: anti-Bolshevism, antisemitism and the demand for the waging of total war. The following excerpts are taken from a transcript of the radio broadcast of Goebbels' speech, which began at 8.15 pm and was carried on all German radio stations:

**1247**    To begin with, I address my reflections to world opinion and put forward three propositions concerning our struggle against the Bolshevik danger in the East.

The first of these propositions is this: if the German armed forces were unable to break the danger from the East, Germany, and soon afterwards the whole of Europe, would fall victim to Bolshevism

The second of these basic propositions is as follows: the German Armed Forces and the German nation, together with their Allies, represent the sole force capable of delivering Europe completely from this menace. [*Shouts*]

The third of these propositions is: delay involves danger. Swift and thorough action is required, otherwise it will be too late [*Prolonged applause*] . . .

The German people and their leaders at any rate are not willing even tentatively to abandon themselves to this danger. [*Prolonged applause and cries of 'Perish Judah!'*]. Behind the onrushing Soviet divisions we can see the Jewish liquidation squads—behind which looms terror, the spectre of mass starvation and unbridled anarchy in Europe. Here once more international Jewry has been the diabolical ferment of decomposition, cynically gratified at the idea of throwing the world into the deepest disorder and thus engineering the ruin of cultures thousands of years old, cultures with which it never felt anything in common. Thus we know the historic task confronting us. The constructive work achieved by Western man in 2,000 years is jeopardized. One cannot exaggerate the gravity of this danger; but it is rather significant that as soon as this danger is shown up in its true colours international Jewry in all countries will make noisy representations in protest. This is the pass to which we have come in Europe—that one must no longer call a danger dangerous, if it happens to originate in Jewry. This shall not prevent us from a plain statement of the facts. [*Shouts*] We have never been afraid of the Jews and today we are less afraid of them than ever. [*Applause and shouts*] We have unmasked Jewry's aims and infamous manoeuvres to deceive the world in fourteen years of struggle before the accession to power and in ten year's struggle afterwards. The aim of Bolshevism is the world revolution of the Jews. They want to bring chaos upon Germany and Europe and to exploit the ensuing hopelessness and desperation of the people for the establishment of their international capitalist tyranny under the guise of Bolshevism . . .

It is now possible to understand—I only mention it here—our consistent policy against the Jews; even though today the Jews in Berlin are sending out their cards asking for sympathy. We see in Jewry an immediate danger for any country. We do not care how other nations defend themselves against this danger. On the other hand, it is our own affair how we defend ourselves and we cannot brook any interference in this. [*Applause*] Jewry represents an infectious phenomenon which is contagious. If our enemies abroad sanctimoniously protest against our anti-Jewish policy and shed crocodile tears over our measures against Jewry, this cannot prevent us from doing what is necessary. Germany in any case has no intention of bowing to this threat, but means to counter it in time and if necessary with the most complete and radical exterm—[*correcting himself*]—elimination (*Ausrott–Ausschaltung*) of Jewry. [*Applause. Shouts of 'Out with the Jews'. Laughter*] All these considerations have determined the military strain which the Reich has to bear in the East. The war of the mechanized robots against Germany and against Europe has reached its climax. The German people, together with its Axis partners, is fulfilling a European mission in the truest sense of the word by countering this immediate and serious vital threat by force of arms. We shall not be deterred from the courageous and upright prosecution of the gigantic struggle against this world plague by the shrieks of international Jewry throughout the world. [*Shouts*] It is a struggle which cannot, must not, have any end except victory. [*Applause and shouts of 'out with the Jews'*]

The broad working masses of our people do not blame the government for acting too ruthlessly, but rather for being too considerate. [*Loud applause*] One could ask people up and down the country, and one would get but one answer: The most radical methods are today just about radical enough and the most total ones just about total enough to lead to victory . . .

Of course the prerequisite for all this is that the burdens will be justly distributed. [*Shouts of 'Bravo' and applause*] The leaders of the State cannot tolerate that by far the largest section of the people should bear the whole burden of the war and a small passive section should attempt to shirk its burdens and responsibilities. [*Shouts of 'Hang them' and applause*] The measures which we have already taken and which we must still take will, therefore, be animated by the spirit of National Socialist justice. [*Shouts*] We respect neither station in life nor occupation. [*Prolonged applause*] Poor and rich, exalted and lowly must be made use of in equal measure. Every man will in this serious phase of our fateful struggle be induced to fulfil his duty to the nation; if necessary he will be compelled to do so. [*Applause*] . . .

The normal aspect [*Optik*] of the war, that is the outward appearance of the conduct of the war, has a decisive political importance in the fourth year of the war . . . The home front must remain clean and intact as a whole. Nothing can be allowed to disturb its warlike appearance. Therefore a number of measures have been taken which take into account this new visual aspect of the war . . .

[After describing a crackdown on clubs and restaurants Goebbels continued:]

Even trifles at times fire public indignation. It is, for instance, irritating today if young men and women ride through the Tiergarten at 9 am. [*Indignation and applause*] I imagine they sometimes meet a working woman after her ten-hour night shift, and who perhaps has to look after four or five children at home. The picture of a cavalcade galloping by as in peacetime can only rouse bitterness in the soul of this good working woman. [*Applause*]

For this reason, for the duration of the war, I have proclaimed a ban on riding on horseback through the streets and squares of the Reich capital. [*Applause*] In this way too I believe I take into account the psychological demands and at the same time the consideration demanded by the front. The soldier, for instance, who is home on leave for a few days from the eastern front, and stays a day in Berlin, will get quite the wrong impression of our Reich capital if he happens to see such a spectacle. [*Shouts of approval*] For he does not see the hundreds of thousands of industrious and decent working men and women who toil for twelve, fourteen or even sixteen hours a day in our war factories; he sees only that gay and idle party on horseback. What will be the impression of the homeland that he is going to pass on to his comrades at the front? In fact everyone must regard it at this time as a self-evident imperative of war morale to pay the greatest attention to the justified demands of the working and fighting people. [*Shouts*] We are no spoilsports but we won't have our sports spoilt either! . . .

The Government, on the other hand, does everything to preserve for the people the badly needed opportunities for relaxation. Theatres, cinemas, concert halls will continue to be open without restriction. The radio will further endeavour to extend and perfect its programmes. It is by no means our intention to create a grey, wintry atmosphere for our people. That which serves the people, that which preserves and hardens its power and fighting and working capabilities, that is good and important for the war effort. That which does not has to be abolished. Thus, mental and spiritual recuperation are—in cooperation with our Party comrade, Dr Ley—not to be reduced but further increased. [*Cheers and applause*] The same applies to sport. Sport is today not an affair of privileged circles . . .

We know now what we have got to do. The German people wants a Spartan way of life for everybody. For high and low, for poor and rich. Just as the Führer sets an example to the whole nation, so the whole nation, people of every rank, must take his example as a model. If he knows only work and cares, then we don't want to leave work and cares to him alone, but want to take on our shoulders that part which we can take off him. The time through which we are living today has for every true National Socialist a striking likeness to the time of our struggle for power. Then and ever since we have acted in this way. We always went with the people through thick and thin and therefore the people have followed us everywhere. We have always shared all burdens with the people and, therefore, these burdens seemed to us not heavy but light. The people want to be led. Never in history have the people in a critical hour of the nation's life refused to follow a brave and determined leadership . . .

I am coming to the end. Recently the Anglo-American press has commented in great detail about the attitude of the German people in the present crisis . . . To find out what the truth is, fellow Germans, let me ask you a number of questions, which you must answer to the best of your knowledge and convictions. When my audience indicated their spontaneous approval of my demands of 30 January, the next day the British press claimed that it had been a propaganda spectacle and did not represent the true mood of the German people. Well, I invited to this meeting today a cross-section, in the truest sense of that word, of the German people. In front of me sit row upon row, wounded soldiers from the eastern front, men with scarred bodies, with legs or arms amputated, men blinded in action who have come here with their Red Cross nurses, men in the prime of life whose crutches are standing in front of them. In between them I count as many as fifty wearers of the Oak Leaf Cluster of the Knight's Cross,[17] a splendid delegation from our fighting front. Behind them is a block of armament workers from the armoured car factory in Berlin. Behind them sit men from the various Party organizations, soldiers from our fighting forces, doctors, scientists, artists, engineers, architects, teachers, officials, civil servants from their offices and studies, proud representatives of our intellectual life at all levels, to whom the country in this time of war owes miracles of inventiveness and human genius. I see thousands of German women distributed throughout the entire auditorium of the Sports Palace. Youth is represented and so is venerable age. No estate, no profession, no age group was overlooked when our invitations went out. So I can say with justification that facing me is a cross-section of the whole German nation, at the front and at home. Am I right? [*Loud shouts of 'Yes'. Lengthy applause*] But Jews are not represented here![18] [*Wild applause, shouts*] Then you my audience are at this moment representative of the nation. And it is to you that I want to put ten questions which you are to answer with the German people before the whole world, particularly before our enemies who are also now listening to their radios. Do you want to do that? [*Loud shouts of 'Yes' and applause*]

First: The English allege that the German people have lost their belief in victory [*Frenzied shouts of 'No!' 'Never!'*] I ask you: Do you believe with the Führer and with us in the final total victory of German arms? [*Wild shouts of 'Yes!' Loud applause. Cries of 'Sieg Heil! Sieg Heil!'*] I ask you: Are you determined to follow the Führer through thick and thin in the struggle for victory and to put up even with the heaviest personal burdens? [*Wild shouts of 'Yes!' Loud applause. Chants of 'Sieg Heil!' 'We greet our Führer'*]

Second: The English allege that the German people are tired of fighting. [*Shouts of 'No!' 'Shame!'*] I ask you: Are you ready together with the Führer, and as a phalanx of the home front standing behind the fighting armed forces, to continue this struggle with a fierce determination and impervious to all twists of fate until victory is in our hands? [*Frenzied shouts of 'Yes!' and loud applause*]

Third: The English allege that the German people are no longer in a mood to shoulder the ever-increasing war work demanded by the Government. [*Shouts of 'Shame!'*] I ask you: Are you and the German people determined, if the Führer orders it, to work ten, twelve and, if necessary fourteen and sixteen hours a day and to give your utmost for victory? [*Loud shouts of 'Yes!' and lengthy applause*]

Fourth: The English allege that the German people are resisting the total war measures of the Government. [*Cries of 'Never!'*] They don't want total war, they want to surrender, say the English [*Loud shouts of 'No! Shame!'*] I ask you: Do you want total war? [*Loud cries of 'Yes!' Loud applause*] Do you want it, if necessary, more total and more radical than we can even imagine it today? [*Loud cries of 'Yes!' Applause*]

---

[17] Germany's highest military decoration.
[18] This sentence was deleted from the published version of the speech.

Fifth: The English allege that the German people have lost their confidence in the Führer [*Loud shouts of anger and cries of 'Shame!' A lengthy period of noise*] I ask you. [*Chants of: 'Führer command us. We will follow you'*] I ask you: Do you trust the Führer? [*Shouts of 'Yes!'*] Are you absolutely and unconditionally willing to follow the Führer down all the paths he is following and to do everything necessary to bring the war to a successful conclusion? [*Loud shouts of 'Yes!'*]

I ask you my sixth question: Are you prepared from now onwards to devote all your strength to providing the eastern front with the men and materiel it needs to defeat Bolshevism? Are you ready to do that? [*Cries of 'Yes!' Loud applause*]

I ask you my seventh question: Do you swear a solemn oath to the fighting front that the country is behind it, with its morale high, and that it will give everything necessary to achieve victory? [*Cries of 'Yes!' Loud applause*]

I ask you my eighth question: Do you, especially even you, the women, want the government to ensure that German women too will devote all their energies to carrying on the war? [*Female shouts of 'Yes!*] And that they will fill jobs wherever possible to free men for action and so to help their men at the front? Do you want to do that? [*Loud shouts, particularly female voices: 'Yes!' Loud applause*]

I ask you my ninth question: Do you approve, if necessary, the most radical measures against a small group of people who dodge the call-up and operate the black market [*Loud cries of 'Yes!' and loud applause*], who in the midst of war play peace, and who intend to exploit people's sufferings for their own selfish ends? [Cries of 'String them up!'], that anyone who exploits the war should lose his head? [*Loud cries of 'Yes!' Loud applause*]

And for my tenth and last question I ask you: Is it your wish that even in wartime, as the Party programme requires, equal rights and equal duties shall prevail [*Cries of 'Yes!'*], that the home front shall give evidence of its solidarity and take the same heavy burdens of war upon its shoulders, and that the burdens be distributed equitably, whether a person be great or small, poor or rich? Is that what you want? [*Loud cries of 'Yes!' Loud applause*]

I have asked you; you have given me your answers. You are part of the nation, so your voices have demonstrated the attitude of Germany. You have told our enemies what they must know to prevent them from indulging in spurious fantasies . . . If ever we have faithfully and irrevocably believed in victory, then at this moment of national reflection and inner renewal we can see it within our grasp—we need only seize it. We must simply develop the determination to subordinate everything to its requirements; That is what is needed now! And so from now onwards the motto is: now let the nation arise let the storm break![19] [*Loud shouts of 'Heil!' and applause. Cries of 'Our Gauleiter—Sieg Heil! Sieg Heil!' The national anthem is played*]

---

[19] A slight variation on a famous 1814 quote from the patriotic poet Theodor Körner, at the time of the war of liberation against Napoleon: 'Das Volk steht auf, der Sturm bricht los'.

Meanwhile, at his ministerial conference on 12 February, Goebbels had defined Bolshevism as the number one propaganda target from then on:

**1248**    The Minister states that we now have a unique opportunity to put out a powerful propaganda slogan. The fight against Bolshevism and the threat of the Bolshevization of Europe is now preoccupying friend and foe in the same way. Our struggle against Bolshevism must dominate all the propaganda instruments as the great and all-pervading propaganda theme. From this point of view, the insignificant current issues of the day must take a back seat. With the approach of the Bolshevik threat the fear of the neutral states was increasing and the sense of belonging on the part of those states which are friendly towards us or allied with us was growing. The theme of Bolshevism made an impact on everyone. In England too there were certainly circles which were conscious of the threat of Bolshevism. The Minister says he cannot imagine that the Bolshevik-eater Churchill has overnight become a philobolshevik. For the English policy vis-à-vis Russia was an alliance of convenience. The English were hoping that the Bolsheviks and National Socialists would beat each other to death so that, at the decisive moment, England would secure its political goals and dominance . . .

In our propaganda it was essential to adopt a systematic line and he would ensure that, from now on, for weeks and months on end anti-Bolshevism would dominate our propaganda. He was having brochures prepared, of which millions of copies would be printed. It was true that such propaganda had certain disadvantages because of its uniformity, but one had to accept these in view of the success which such a systematic line would achieve.

From now onwards, every radio talk, every report, every speech and every weekly slogan must end with the stereotypical comment that the struggle against Bolshevism is our great task. The Minister referred to Cato who succeeded in his demand for the destruction of Carthage . . .

The Minister instructs the head of the press department always to mention Bolshevism when dealing with the daily slogan. In this connection, the Minister emphasizes that we should always say Bolshevism and not Communism because the word Communism has a different resonance to it and may remind certain people of past times.

The Minister gives instructions for the creation of a propaganda committee under the leadership of the Reich Propaganda headquarters [of the NSDAP], which will direct and lead this propaganda. From now onwards, until the end of the war, Bolshevism will be bashed and in every meeting the struggle against Bolshevism will be the number one issue.

Between now and the end of the war this theme of anti-Bolshevism was increasingly used in an attempt, on the one hand, to frighten the German people with the prospect of a Soviet invasion and so galvanize them for the war effort and, on the other hand, to frighten the Western Allies with the aim of driving a wedge between them and the Soviet

Union. The discovery by German forces, in April 1943, of a mass grave with some 4,000 Polish officers at Katyn near Smolensk, who had been murdered by the Soviet secret police [GPU], was grist to the mill of Goebbels' anti-Bolshevist campaign and heavily exploited by German propaganda.

With the Soviet invasion of East Prussia in the summer of 1944, German propaganda exploited the atrocities committed by the Russian troops against German civilians. To facilitate this and other propaganda Goebbels introduced a new concept of 'poetic truth, as Rudolf Semmler recorded in his diary:

**1249**   2 November 1944

Goebbels has introduced a new expression into the vocabulary of propaganda. It is only for internal use! He is now using the phrase 'poetic truth' in contrast to—or rather in amplification of—the 'concrete truth'. Whenever we only know a little about some event or plan or operation of the enemy's then—so Goebbels says—we shall not be violating the truth if we add something to the story to fill in the gaps. We should describe things as they might well have happened or as they probably did happen. To put it in Goebbels' own words: 'We are only helping the public when we call imagination to our aid in certain cases where the record of the facts is for some reason incomplete!' Many events in international politics, he said, could not be understood unless one embroidered them a little with the 'poetic truth' and so made them understandable to the German public.

Goebbels illustrated his idea by pointing out how inadequate were the details we were getting about atrocities and cruelties perpetrated in the East on German women and children. It must be the task of German propaganda to make powerful indictments out of these stories by embroidering them with suitable details. What happened in reality would be much worse than anything we could imagine; so what we added would be 'poetic truth', which would generally be reasonably accurate.

This was a tempting piece of sophistry for any propagandist and, ironically, in the particular case referred to it was true.

### (v) The Anti-Jewish Campaign

Goebbels had always been one of the most hardline antisemites within the Nazi leadership and antisemitism had formed part of German propaganda ever since the beginning of the war. However, it was with the outbreak of the war with the Soviet Union and, above all, with the defeat of Stalingrad that the anti-Jewish campaign became—together with anti-Bolshevism, with which of course it was closely related—a dominant theme in German propaganda until the end of the war. The following documents illustrate very clearly how this campaign was orchestrated and its ferocity:

**1250**    Reich Propaganda Office Berlin                        3 May 1943
          Secret!

Press Circular No. II/5/43

Re: *Confidential information.*
(For information only, not intended for publication)

1. Further to the previous instructions on the Jewish question, journals are requested to devote more attention to this question in the future and to make the Jewish question a permanent issue in their work. It is clear that one cannot produce antisemitism in a vacuum and that one must have some basis, a topic through which one can develop it. The newspapers are now getting a daily Jewish topic which the journals need not leap onto; it should rather be regarded as a stimulus. The journals have a wide field and can choose the topics that they need themselves. For example, there are the countless sensational stories in which the Jew is the villain [*Urheber*], which can be used. Above all, American domestic politics offers an inexhaustible reservoir. If those journals, in particular, which are geared to commenting on current affairs apply their staff to this issue, they will be able to show the true face, the true attitude and the true aims of the Jews in a varied manner. Apart from that, of course the Jews must now be used in the German press as a political target: the Jews are to blame; the Jews wanted the war; the Jews are making the war worse; and, again and again, the Jews are to blame.

Reports which, on the face of it, do not offer the possibility for an antisemitic message must be turned into such an antisemitic propaganda action. For example, if, after their air force have lost twenty planes following an attack on a German town, the Jewish-English newspapers write in typical Jewish fashion that the defence of this town was poor, then one can comment that it is the Jews who are writing like that and that they aren't the ones sitting in the bombers' cockpits.

The possibilities for exposing the true character of the Jews are endless. In fact, there really is not any section of the press where it is impossible to do so. For example, the Jewish-Bolshevist murder at Katyn is a model example for the German press of how one can use such a topic to bring out the Jews' initiating role and their guilt.

It is the duty of the whole of the German press to join in the antisemitic action outlined here . . .

**1251**    Reich Propaganda Office Berlin                       25 May 1943
          Secret!

Press Circular No. II/15/43

Re: *Confidential information*
(For information only, not intended for publication)

1. It is now time once again, independently from current events, to put force-fully to our readers particular arguments about the meaning and purpose of the war. The following points should inform the line taken by individual press organs:

(a) The war guilt of international Jewry, which through its Bolshevist-plutocratic satellites has imposed this struggle on the nations in order to destroy the vigorous nations and so establish its international hegemony.

(b) The decisive struggle which, with the full commitment of the front and the homeland, will certainly be victorious and which is being fought to preserve the highest human cultural values which are the creation of Europe.

(c) The great war aim of the Axis powers: the pacification of the European continent and the restructuring of the world's resources which, after the collapse of the decrepit international powers, offers the creative nations the opportunity for a new and undreamt of development.

You are recommended to cover these and similar themes during the next weeks in accordance with an internal editorial plan.

**1252**    Reich Propaganda Office Berlin                    1 June 1943
          Secret!

Press Circular II/16/43 1.6.43

Re: *Confidential Information*
(For information only, not intended for publication)

1. None of the German journals is there for its own sake; particularly at the present time; their sole justification is as servants of the national community and as educative organs of the state. Thus, no journal can opt out of the anti-Jewish front. In this connexion it is not intended that the specialist journals should carry contributions which are alien to their particular field, but rather should attack Jews.

For example: If a specialist journal mentions 'the increase in the production of synthetic rubber in the USA' and refers to a committee set up to study the matter and says: 'the committee consists of the financier Bernard Baruch . . .' that is not satisfactory, for one should include the fact that he is a Jew.

## (vi) Air Raids

A crucial issue facing German propaganda, particularly from 1942–3 onwards, was the problem of dealing with the effects of air raids on popular morale.[20] Goebbels drew attention to this in his ministerial conference on 10 March 1943:

**1253**    The issue of the air war was currently a matter of great concern. The minister is afraid that the German people could succumb to a certain

---

[20] See also below pp. 552ff.

resignation. Such resignation was quite possible because no one knew when the debilitating air war would end. We must do everything to resist this threat and bear this in mind when carrying out measures. In future, he no longer wishes to hear the word 'mood' [*Stimmung*] because one could not speak of mood when houses were being burnt down and cities were being devastated. He wants people to speak only of a good bearing [*Haltung*]. One could not expect that, in the aftermath of an air raid, the people would start shouting 'Hurray!' The English propaganda, which was carried out in the autumn of 1940 to counteract the air attacks, was not viable for us. In Germany any propagandist who asked: where are the next bombs going to fall? as the English did in autumn 1940, would be hounded out. The Minister believes that the air war can only be ended if a major counterattack is launched against England . . .

The Minister requests that caution should be exercised in the treatment of the issue by our propaganda. It is completely wrong for our propaganda now to make big promises of revenge. The only reply which can be made is a counter-attack. The sole task of propaganda is to strengthen the will to resist, but on no account to antagonize the population.

The Minister warns against making the mistake of suddenly, after not mincing words in our news policy, going to the other extreme and painting things blacker than they are. We don't know how many deaths our last raid on London caused, whereas we continue truthfully to report the Berlin casualties. We shouldn't wallow in the love of truth in the way that we previously went over-board in keeping everything secret. All publications should be judged on the basis of expediency. Figures such as, for example, air raid casualties should only be published when the need arises. Similarly, he ordered that the publication of sentences for plunder should cease in order not to create the impression that there was a lot of plundering going on in Berlin.

The Minister reports that the Führer was full of praise for the anti-Bolshevik propaganda and, in particular, described the Minister's Sports Palace speech [of 18 February] as a psychological masterpiece. We should continue with this propaganda and continually beat the same drum. A 150-year-old oak will only fall if one keeps striking it at the same point and doesn't simply strike an occasional blow. The successes which we have achieved with our anti-Bolshevik propaganda should, however, on no account be commented upon. It is equally wrong to rub one's hands because the enemy propaganda finds itself to some extent in a dilemma on account of our anti-Bolshevik campaign.

——

## (vii) Retaliation

Despite Goebbels' condemnation of 'big promises of revenge', the theme of retaliation became a major, indeed crucial, component of German propaganda during the last two years of the war. It was launched at a mass NSDAP rally on 5 June 1943, which was broadcast, and at which both the Armaments Minister, Speer, and Goebbels spoke in reassuring terms about the strength of Germany's economic/ armament position. Having explained the need for a cut in the meat ration, Goebbels continued:

**1254**    So if we at home have to make sacrifices in *this* war, at least we know *what they're for*. In so far as food is concerned, however, it seems to me that they are bearable in comparison with the sacrifices which the population in the areas hit by air raids have had to make almost *night after night* for the past *weeks* and *months*. [*Applause*] Our enemies are attacking their goods and belongings and their lives with *brutal cynicism* in an attempt to wear down their morale. They even *admit it quite openly*. It will be to their *eternal shame* that in this attempt they have destroyed German cultural treasures. But they want to do more. They are waging war against the *morale* of our nation; they are killing civilians, *old people, women and children*, and are barely trying any longer to cover their infamous bloody terror with a cloak of humanity. A few days ago, the Church of England stated hypocritically that English bombs no longer discriminate between men, women and children. [*Booing*]

This statement seems, however, almost too meek when compared with the infernal outbursts of *hatred and triumph* which can be found in the London *Jew* papers. We present-day Germans are not the kind of people who seek indulgence from an enemy who is out to destroy us. We know that against British-US bomb terror there is only one effective *remedy: counter-terror.* [*Applause*]

Today there is but one thought in the minds of the whole of the German people: *to repay the enemy in his own kind*. [*Applause*] Far be it from us to boast or threaten. We merely take note. *Every English comment today* which considers the bombing of German women, old people and children an entirely humane or even Christian method of conquering the German nation *will one day be a welcome argument in our reply to these villainies.* [*Applause*] The British people have no cause to triumph. They will have to pay for the bill marked up by its leaders by order of those Jews who instigated and spurred them into their bloody crimes. Until then we must try to put up with the consequences of the British-American air terror which are at times very hard . . . The enemy can make dust and ashes of our houses; but this makes the hearts of our population burn with *hatred*, but not to burn to ashes. *One day the hour of retribution* [*Vergeltung*] *will come.*

The population's hopes were sustained by further hints of retaliation in various speeches and press articles, culminating in a piece in *Das Reich* by Schwarz van den Berk, the official overseeing the campaign, who, on the basis of information supplied him by Speer, claimed that Germany already possessed new weapons of exceptional power and was merely waiting for the right moment to use them. This produced a further wave of intense speculation among the public obliging Goebbels to issue a directive temporarily banning the further use of the term 'retaliation' by the media.

When the first flying bombs were finally launched on 14 June 1944, there was a low-key announcement by the Wehrmacht, which nevertheless re-ignited hope and speculation. Schwarz van den Berk suggested that the bomb should be named the *V[ergeltung] 1*, thereby intimating a series of further weapons and so helping to sustain morale. The retaliation propaganda was probably the most important single campaign of the war in terms of sustaining morale.

—

## (viii) Radio and Film

Radio and film played a particularly important part in German wartime propaganda. During the war, radio became even more centralized than before under the control of the radio department of the Propaganda Ministry. Goebbels himself maintained a detailed supervision of programme planning, deciding which artists should perform, which composers' music should be played, even determining what Christmas carols should be broadcast and that they should be played and not sung.

German wartime radio contained a great variety of programmes. In addition to the regular news broadcasts every day, between 19.00 and 19.30, and at the end of the 22.00 news, there were reports of events from the front produced by the Wehrmacht 'propaganda companies'. A compilation was then broadcast at the weekend for those who worked in the evenings. There were instructive talks on various aspects of the strategic and military situation given by officials of the Propaganda Ministry, notably Hans Fritzsche, and by senior Wehrmacht officers, of which the latter were particularly popular; from time to time there were major speeches by Nazi leaders; and there were frequent concerts of classical music.

But there was also much lighter fare. Even before the war the Nazis had shown themselves acutely conscious of the importance of entertainment as a crucial element in propaganda. Soon after his appointment as Reich Propaganda Minister, Goebbels had told the Controllers of German radio: 'First principle: at all costs avoid being boring. I put that before everything.'[21] He continued with this approach in his wartime propaganda. For he was aware of the people's need to relax and unwind under the appalling stresses of wartime life. The Wehrmacht repeatedly complained that the 'catchy' music put out by the British radio stations was tempting members of the armed forces to switch to their programmes, particularly in the evening. Goebbels responded to

---

[21] See Vol. 2, doc. 270.

these complaints, as is clear from the minutes of his ministerial conference on 21 May 1941:

**1255**    The Minister gives instructions that, from today, after 20.15, only light music should be broadcast.[22] He delegates Herr Fischer to draft a circular to the Reich Propaganda Offices [of the NSDAP], the Party and its formations based on the following principles:

In response to urgent requests from all military agencies from OKW down to our air force squadrons, but also from broad circles of our working population whose nerves are stressed by their daily toil, German Radio has now decided to redesign its evening programme for the summer months to produce comedy, light entertainment and relaxation. We know that there are a number of grumblers who can't bear that idea and believe that one would survive the war better in sackcloth and ashes than with entertainment, cheerfulness and inner calm. These things have been carefully thought out and considered from all sides. We also know that these people tend to be more frequent letter writers than those who request more light entertainment. The arguments for and against are well known. We request that such letters should no longer be passed on. They will not alter our decision to introduce this change. Rather we request that these letter writers should be informed of the arguments which were decisive for this change. According to Herr Glasmeier,[23] the light entertainment channel can be started up as soon as the word is given. The Minister will determine the type of music which is to be broadcast.

The Minister delegates Herr Tiessler[24] to discuss the matter with Herr Bormann and to tell him that the aim is to prevent severe damage [to morale]. The population had once again been listening to more English broadcasts in connection with the Hess affair; it must now be cured of that. Nobody's soul will be damaged if he listens to Lehar or Paul Linecke of an evening or even Mackeben or Kollo, but it will be if he listens to English broadcasts which he will do not so much for the news but because of the lively music—such as, for example, airmen. After all, one can't place a policeman or a party official beside every holder of the Knight's Cross.[25]

———

The most popular radio programme of all was a request show of songs, music and words, compered by Heinz Gödecke and designed to link the home and fighting fronts—*Wunschkonzert*. Beginning on 1 October 1940, the programme was initially broadcast twice a week and then, after a break in summer 1940, every Sunday afternoon until the seventy-

[22] In fact one of the two major radio stations was devoted to light music in the evenings.
[23] Dr Heinrich Glasmeier, the head of the Greater German Reich Broadcasting Service.
[24] Walter Tiessler, the Party Chancellery's liaison officer in the Propaganda Ministry.
[25] The Knight's Cross [Ritterkreuz] was Germany's highest military award for valour.

fifth performance on 25 May 1941. The series began again on 1 March 1942. The programme was tightly controlled by the Propaganda Ministry and the Wehrmacht, with Goebbels insisting on vetting the programme three days before it went out. It employed Germany's best actors, soloists, choirs, orchestras and bands, who were obliged to perform without a fee as part of their war effort. A sign of the programme's popularity is that it gave the title and a key element of the plot to one of the most popular films of the war.

Towards the end of the war Goebbels evidently felt obliged to justify the reduced level, range and quality of programming imposed by wartime exigencies and did so in an article in *Das Reich* dated 12 November 1944:

**1256** During the first years of the war, whole radio stations had to be closed down in order to release personnel and transmitters for foreign broadcasts. Many performers, organisation and technical personnel went into the Wehrmacht. Some of them established the front line reporting carried out by the propaganda companies; others were transferred to armaments production.

It might appear to an outsider as if the reduction of the varied and multi-faceted programmes put out by numerous Reich radio stations before the war with broadcasts which reflected the variety of German Gaus and provinces to a single programme which is broadcast for only a few hours a day on two wave lengths represents a diminution in cultural quality. But that is not the case. Even before the war, the individual Reich radio stations did not only broadcast their own programmes, they swapped and made joint programmes. It is only possible to produce a programme which has been prepared a long time in advance and of which every detail has, therefore, been artistically polished if the broadcasting schedule has been fixed a long time ahead and does not have to keep being renegotiated and changed at the last minute because one of the participating stations has overrun its time. That is the real and unavoidable compulsion to have a Reich programme.

A programming schedule has been worked out to which we want to stick and which produces roughly the following balance between different types of programme. Of the 190 broadcasting hours in a week 32 are made up of regular political talks, 3 of cultural talks; there are 5 in which words and music are combined, 24 hours of highbrow music which listeners have sometimes called 'difficult',15 of folk music, and 55 hours of light entertainment combining music and talking. There are only 56 hours left for the really light music which used to make up a large part of the programme and which is now restricted to a few hours in the morning and at night.

134 hours of broadcasting per week are, therefore, conceived with great love and care and are artistically prepared before they go on the air. In the case of all these broadcasts a principle has emerged: not only have the programmes which are rich in content become ever more popular, but the popular ones have become ever more rich in content.

Apart from radio, film arguably had the most important role as a propaganda medium on the German home front during the Second World War, though probably more in terms of its function as a relief from tension than its effectiveness as a vehicle for ideological indoctrination. Great efforts were made to take the cinema to the widest possible audience with the Nazi Party, for example, establishing mobile cinemas to cover rural areas, which were very well attended.

Before the main film a lengthy newsreel was shown incorporating footage from the front line, which was provided by mobile 'propaganda companies' first established in 1938, and operating with the various armed forces. By the outbreak of war there were only five of them, with some 150 personnel, but by mid-1943 there were twenty-three attached to the army alone, with some 3,000 men. Each of the companies had film, radio and press units staffed with specialists and equipped to produce material ready for broadcasting/publishing. Control over them was shared between the Wehrmacht, which had censorship powers, and Goebbels, who appointed the heads and issued 'propaganda directives'. The weekly newsreel was sent to Goebbels on Saturdays and then passed on to the Führer's headquarters, where he viewed it on Monday evening making whatever corrections or additions he saw fit, though by late autumn 1944 he was no longer seeing it on a regular basis. Initially, the newsreels were popular with audiences. But as the war continued and turned against Germany Goebbels was obliged to compel audiences to watch the newsreel if they wanted to see the main film.

The German Newsreel Company also produced short information films, which were shown before the newsreel. One series which achieved considerable popularity was 'Tran and Helle' produced by Johannes Guter and designed to educate the German population in proper wartime behaviour. It involved two characters played by Rhineland comedians. One, Ludwig Schmitz, was an amiable rogue; the other, his friend, Jupp Hussels, set him to rights on how to behave. In their conversations they discussed things like hoarding scarce commodities, foolish gossip, English propaganda leaflets, and the proper behaviour towards prisoners of war. In spring 1940 they acquired a wife and a fiancée respectively. The series came to an end in September 1940. A similar series, 'Liese and Miese', aimed specifically at women, ran during 1943–4.

A number of so-called cultural films, basically documentaries, were also produced; but it was the feature films which were by far the most popular. By summer 1940 almost all the American films had been withdrawn by the Propaganda Ministry and so Germany was largely dependent on its own production. The following document gives some figures on German feature film production and attendance during the war:

**1257**

*German Film during the Second World War*

|  | 1939 | 1942 | 1943 |
|---|---|---|---|
| Visits to the cinema in millions | 624 |  | 1117 |
| Visits per capita of the total population | 10.5 |  | 12.4 |
| Visits per capita of the communities with cinemas | 12.2 |  | 20.2 |
| Total number of long feature films shown: |  |  |  |
| produced in Germany | 111 | 57 | 78 |
| produced abroad | 33 | 29 | 23 |

▬

Throughout the period of the Third Reich 1,094 feature films were produced of which 48 per cent were comedies, 27 per cent melodramas, 14 per cent propaganda films and 11 per cent action films.

The first major success was *Request Concert* (*Wunschkonzert*), premièred on 30 December 1940, about two lovers who meet at the Olympic Games in 1936, lose touch, and are then reunited through the radio request show. It shows them experiencing the frustrations and vicissitudes of war and its main themes are an affirmation of the national community and self-sacrifice. However, it was surpassed in popularity by another wartime love story, *The Great Love* (*Die grosse Liebe*), which, like *Request Concert* showed love overcoming the problems of war, self-sacrifice and a reaffirmation of the national community. It was notable for its female star, the Swedish actress Zarah Leander, and two big hit songs of the war—'I know there'll be a miracle one day' (*Ich weiss es wird einmal ein Wunder geschehen*) and 'The world won't come to an end because of that' (*Davon geht die Welt nicht unter*). Premièred on 12 June 1942, this film was seen by some 27 million people, more than a quarter of the German population.

After an initial burst in 1933, blatant propaganda films had gone out of fashion. But the outbreak of war saw a revival. They fall into three main categories: first, the military documentaries designed to show the German people how strong their armed forces were and to intimidate enemies, allies and neutrals. These include *Campaign in Poland* (1940) and *Victory in the West* (1940). Secondly, there were films designed to encourage hatred for a particular enemy. These included: the anti-British films *Ohm Kruger* (1941) about the Boer War and *Carl Peters* (1941) about German/British colonial rivalry; the anti-Jewish films *The Jew Süss* (*Jud Süss*; 1940) and *The Eternal Jew* (*Der ewige Jude;* 1940*)*; and a film which combined both anti-British and anti-Jewish feeling, *The Rothschilds* (1940). Whereas *Jud Süss,* about the Court Jew of the eighteenth century Duke Karl-Eugen of Württemberg, made a big impression according to the Security Service reports and was seen by over 20 million people, the crudity of *The Eternal Jew* put many people off.

The final category of propaganda film was more indirect and involved films about historic individuals and events which were designed to carry a message about the current situation. A classic example was the film *The Great King* (*Der grosse König*) about Frederick the Great of Prussia, showing how against all the odds and through his grim, steadfast determination he had finally triumphed in the Seven Years War.

But the most remarkable film of this kind was the last major feature film of the Third Reich, *Kolberg*, about the siege of the East Prussian town of Kolberg by Napoleon's forces in 1807. On 1 June 1943 Goebbels wrote to the leading film director Veit Harlan as follows:

**1258**    I hereby instruct you to produce a major film 'Kolberg'. The aim of the film is to demonstrate on the basis of the example of the town which gives the film its title that a nation which is united at home and at the front can overcome any enemy. I authorize you to request assistance and support from all agencies of the Wehrmacht, the State and the Party wherever necessary on the grounds that the film ordered by me is designed to strengthen morale.

Goebbels threw massive resources into this film, including thousands of soldiers who were diverted from the front to act as extras. He clearly saw this film as a work that future generations of Germans would go to see and regard as an expression of the spirit of him and the regime. The following dialogue from the film between the mayor of Kolberg (Nettelbeck) and the garrison commander (Gneisenau) gives an impression of the flavour of the film and of the *Götterdämmerung* mood of Goebbels and other fanatical Nazis in 1945:

**1259**    *Gneisenau*: 35,000 men, Nettelbeck, and at least 500 guns and all aimed at our town. Can you imagine what that means. By comparison with that everything which we've experienced up to now is child's play.

*Nettelbeck*: Herr Kommandant, tell me frankly, what are you trying to say?
*Gneisenau*: It's all over Nettlebeck; there's no point in it any more. We can't hold the town.
*Nettelbeck*: And so?
*Gneisenau*: Surrender, Nettelbeck.
Nettelbeck: Ah, like in Magdeburg, Erfurt, Stettin, Spandau. It has all been in vain? The end—disgrace?
*Gneisenau*: It's not a disgrace if soldiers have fired their last bullet. Even Blücher had to capitulate.
*Nettelbeck*: But we haven't fired our last bullet, Herr Kommandant. And, what's more Blücher didn't have to surrender the town in which he was born. You weren't born in Kolberg, Gneisenau. You were ordered to go to Kolberg. But we have grown up here. We know every stick and stone, every spot, every house. No, we're not going to give up now. And even if we have to dig our nails into the ground of our town, we're not going to give up. No, no. They'll have to cut off our hands one by one or brain us one after the other. Gneisenau, you can't inflict such a disgrace on an old man and give up our town to Napoleon. I promised our king: I'd rather be buried in the ruins than surrender. Gneisenau, I have never bent my knee before anybody. But I'm doing it now, Gneisenau. Kolberg must not be surrendered, Gneisenau!
*Gneisenau*: That's what I wanted to hear from you, Nettelbeck. Now we can die together.

▬

The film was premiered on 30 January 1945 when Goebbels had it flown into the fortress of La Rochelle under siege by the Allies. As a gesture it summed up only too well the total loss of contact with reality which was the most marked feature of the Nazi leadership in general and Hitler and Goebbels in particular during the last phase of the war. However, the ultimate test for German propaganda was how far it succeeded in sustaining the morale of the people.

## List of Sources

1222   Rudolf Semmler, *Goebbels: The Man next to Hitler* (London 1947), pp. 111–13.
1223   Vertrauliche Information (VI) Bundesarchiv Berlin (BAB) ZSlg. 109/3.
1224   Franz-Josef Heyen, *Nationalsozialismus im Alltag. Quellen zur Geschichte des Nationalsozialismus vornehmlich im Raum Mainz-Koblenz-Trier* (Boppard 1967), pp. 299–300.
1225   Ibid., p. 300.
1226   Ibid., p. 301.
1227   BAB ZSlg.101/14.
1228   W.A. Boelcke ed., *Wollt ihr den totalen Krieg? Die geheimen Goebbels-Konferenzen 1939–1943* (Munich 1969), pp. 92–3.

1229   Ibid., pp. 120–1.
1230   BAB ZSlg. 101/15.
1231   BAB ZSlg. 101/17.
1232   Boelcke, op. cit., p. 238.
1233   J. Heyen, ed., *Parole der Woche. Eine Wandzeitung im Dritten Reich 1936–1943* (Munich 1983), p. 91.
1234   Ibid., p. 93.
1235   Otto Dietrich, *12 Jahre mit Hitler* (Cologne n.d.), p. 102.
1236   Howard K. Smith, *Last Train From Berlin* (London 1942), pp. 61–4.
1237   Rudolf Semmler, op. cit., pp. 55–6.
1238   Boelcke, op. cit., pp. 246–8.
1239   Ibid., p. 256.
1240   Imperial War Museum (IWM), BBC Monitoring Service Report.
1241   M. Domarus, *Hitler. Reden und Proklamationen 1932–1945*, Vol. 2 (Wiesbaden 1973), pp. 1832–3.
1242   Boelcke, op. cit., pp. 259–60.
1243   *Das Reich* No. 22, 31.5.1942.
1244   Boelcke, op. cit., pp. 414–15.
1245   Ibid., pp. 417–18.
1246   Semmler, op. cit., pp. 66–8.
1247   IWM, BBC Monitoring Report.
1248   Boelcke, op. cit., pp. 439–41.
1249   Semmler, op. cit., pp. 163–4.
1250   Landesarchiv Berlin (LAB) R 055/001389.
1251   Ibid.
1252   Ibid.
1253   Boelcke, op. cit., pp. 452–3.
1254   H. Heiber, ed., *Goebbels Reden, Vol. 2: 1939–1945* (Düsseldorf 1972), pp. 225–8.
1255   Boelcke, op. cit., pp. 225–6.
1256   J. Wulf, *Presse und Funk im Dritten Reich. Eine Dokumentation* (Gütersloh 1964), pp. 384–385.
1257   B. Drewniak, *Der deutsche Film 1938–1945. Ein Gesamtüberblick* (Düsseldorf 1987), pp. 37, 819.
1258   E. Leiser, *'Deutschland erwache!' Propaganda im Film des Dritten Reiches* (Hamburg 1989), pp. 110–11.
1259   Ibid., p. 119.

# CHAPTER 49

# *Morale*[1]

## (i) Introduction

The mood of the German people on the outbreak of war has been summed up by two German historians, one of whom (Helmut Krausnick) had personally witnessed it, as 'reluctant loyalty'.[2] The great foreign policy successes of the preceding years—the Rhineland, the *Anschluss* with Austria, Munich, Prague etc.—had been extremely popular. But the most popular thing about them had been that they had been achieved without war. Only a few fanatical Nazis and naive Hitler Youth members actually wanted a major war. This had represented a significant failure of Nazi indoctrination.[3] However, although the German people entered the war reluctantly, their loyalty to the regime was not in question. For, by 1939, the Nazi regime had acquired a very large reservoir of support which it could draw on when the going got tough. The overcoming of the crisis of the early 1930s and the restoration of Germany's international prestige, and the fact that these achievements were associated with an individual, Adolf Hitler, who had come to embody not only the regime but, as far as many Germans were concerned, the nation itself—these facts provided a great reserve of strength. By 1939, most people trusted the Führer to know and to do what was best for Germany even if it might not always seem so. It would take a considerable time and a series of major defeats before this confidence was seriously eroded.

---

[1] For a discussion of the problem of assessing German popular opinion during the Third Reich and the question of sources see Vol. 2, docs 435–36.

[2] Helmuth Krausnick and Hermann Graml, 'Der deutsche Widerstand und die Allierten', *in Vollmacht des Gewissens,* Vol. 2 (Frankfurt 1965), p. 482.

[3] See Vol. 2, docs 464–66.

On 3 September 1939, the American journalist William Shirer commented on the mood in Berlin after Britain and France had declared war on Germany in fulfilment of their obligations under the guarantee to Poland of 31 March 1939:

**1260**   It has been a lovely September day, the sun shining, the air balmy, the sort of day the Berliner loves to spend in the woods or on the lakes near by. I walked in the streets. On the faces of the people astonishment, depression. Until today they have been going about their business pretty much as usual. There were food cards and soap cards and you couldn't get any petrol and at night it was difficult stumbling around in the black-out. But the war in the east has seemed a bit far away to them—two moonlit nights and not a single Polish plane over Berlin to bring destruction—and the papers saying that German troops have been advancing all along the line, that the Polish air force has been destroyed. Last night I heard Germans talking of the 'Polish thing' lasting but a few weeks, or months at the most. Few believed that Britain and France would move. Ribbentrop was sure they wouldn't and told the Führer, who believed him. The British and French had been accommodating before. Another Munich, why not? Yesterday, when it seemed that London and Paris were hesitating, everyone, including those in the Wilhelmstrasse, was optimistic. Why not?

In 1914 I believe, the excitement in Berlin on the first day of the world war was tremendous. Today, no excitement, no hurrahs, no cheering, no throwing of flowers, no war fever, no war hysteria. There is not even any hate for the French and British—despite Hitler's various proclamations to the people, the Party, the east Army, the West Army, accusing the 'English warmongers and capitalistic Jews' of starting this war. When I passed the French and British embassies this afternoon, the sidewalk in front of each of them was deserted. A lone *Schupo* [policeman] paced up and down before each.

---

## (ii) The Rationing System, Shortages and their Impact on Morale

Shirer's mention of food cards and soap cards points to a crucial factor in sustaining morale on the German home front during the Second World War. One of the main reasons for the poor morale in Germany during the First World War had been the inadequacies of the rationing system, the perceived unfairness of the allocation and distribution of the necessities of life, and the consequent flourishing black market. The Nazi regime was determined to avoid repeating those mistakes, and so preparations had been made to introduce an effective rationing system from the start of the war. For, contrary to Nazi propaganda, German food supplies were not in fact substantial and, in the case of fats and proteins, were inadequate. Thus, as early as 27 August 1939 a series of decrees were issued establishing a rationing system for specified foodstuffs and other vital commodities, and rationing began the following day. Pink ID cards for the purchase of foodstuffs had already been printed in 1937 in preparation for a war and were stored locally; they were distributed on Sunday, 27 August. During the first four weeks, the detailed rationing arrangements were provisional and were then replaced by a permanent system whose regulations were issued on 7 September. The following document shows the food items which were subject to rationing in comparison with the First World War:

**1261**
*Foodstuffs rationed in Germany
during and after the First and Second World Wars*

| Foodstuffs | First World War | Second World War |
|---|---|---|
| Bread | 7.3.1915 to 17.11.1923 | 25.9.1939 to 31.1.1950 |
| Cereal products [4] | 15.7.1916 to 15.8.1920 | 28.9.1939 to 31.10.1949 |
| Potatoes | 1.3.1916 to 15.2.1920 | 6.4.1942 to 30.9.1948 |
| Meat | 23.4.1916 to 1.10.1920 | 28.8.1939 to 31.12.1949 |
| Fats | 1.1.1916 to 1.8. 1920 | 28.8.1939 to 31.1.1950 |
| Butter | 16.1.1916 to 1.6. 1921 | 28.8.1939 to 31.1.1950 |
| Cheese | 15.1.1916 to 1.6.1921 | 28.8.1939 to 31.10.1949 |
| Full cream milk | 1.12.1915 to 1.6.1921 | 28.8.1939 to 31.1.1950 |
| Sugar | 23.4.1916 to 1.10.1921 | 28.8.1939 to 28.2.1950 |
| Bread spreads | 15.1.1917 to 15.5.1920 | 28.8.1939 to 30.9.1949 |
| Eggs | 1.11.1916 to 1.4.1919 | 28.8.1939 to 30.6.1949 |

Consumers were issued with colour-coded ration cards for each food item (e.g. red for bread), which were valid for a period of twenty-eight days, enabling the authorities to alter the amounts allocated at short notice depending on supplies. Initially, fruit and vegetables were not rationed. However, rationing was introduced for fruit in mid-1941 and vegetables from the beginning of 1942, and potatoes were rationed from 6 April 1942, although all these items had already been subject to ad hoc local controls via customer lists from 1941. By the end of 1942, non-rationed foodstuffs made up only 0.3 per cent of the total food supplies of an average working-class household compared with 18.4 per cent in 1939/40 and 20.6 per cent in 1940/41.[5] There were chronic shortages of

---

[4] e.g. oatmeal, rice, pulses, flour. But the German term *Nährmittel* also included tea and coffee (substitutes).

[5] See W.F. Werner, *'Bleib übrig'. Deutsche Arbeiter in der nationalsozialistischen Kriegswirtschaft* (Düsseldorf 1983), p. 201.

fruit and vegetables, including potatoes, for which rice and pulses sometimes had to be substituted.

The food rationing system introduced criteria for allocation based on age and on how strenuous an individual's work was deemed to be. The age categories varied from item to item and over time. But, generally, a distinction was made between five age groups: adult over 20 or 18; youth from 10 to 20 or 18; child from 6 to 10; small child from 3 to 6; very small child under 3.

Initially, there were three categories based on work: a *normal consumer,* who received 2,400 Calories per day; a *heavy worker,* who received 3,600 Calories per day; and a *very heavy worker,* who received 4,200 Calories per day. The assignment of the various jobs to the three categories, which took place during the first four-week allocation period through negotiation between the employers and the health and safety inspectorate (*Gewerbeaufsichtsämter*), proved problematic. For while in the case of some jobs, e.g., office worker = normal consumer, miner = very heavy worker, it was easy, others were much more difficult. In fact, it inevitably produced discontent among those who felt they had been unfairly assigned to the wrong category. Under pressure from employers, the DAF and the Party, on 1 November 1939 the Government was obliged to create a new fourth category, between the normal consumer and the heavy worker, for workers who worked very long hours—at least a ten-hour shift (women and youths nine hours) involving 9¼ hours of actual work or at least eleven hours away from home—and for night workers, despite the fact that their calorie consumption was in fact identical to that of day workers. However, the calorie allocation to this category was clearly below that which was physically required for the work performed. Supplement ration cards were distributed by their employers to those workers entitled to them, which helped to bind the workers to their plants. Approximately 40 per cent of the German people were estimated to be in the category of 'normal consumers'; the remainder were either in one of the other three categories, in the Wehrmacht, or were so-called self-providers, i.e. farmers and their families. It was estimated that Wehrmacht personnel needed approximately three times the rations of normal consumers.[6] On 18 May 1942 Reich government figures showed that there were 584,000 very heavy workers, 3,381,000 heavy workers, and 5,050,000 long hours/night

---

[6] See Württemberg State Ministry, Minute re: the meeting of the State Food Offices at the Reich Agriculture Ministry on 17.2.43 in Hauptstaatsarchiv Stuttgart (HStAS) E 597 Bü 71.

workers and that 2½ million workers were being fed in works canteens for which they had to provide coupons from their allocation.[7]

Finally, there were special allocations of specific foods for a few exceptional categories, such as expectant and nursing mothers, who received extra milk, and the sick, who received no more than three of the following items of food per week: 500g of meat, 270g of fats, of which no more than 160g could be butter, 1,800g of bread and flour, 750g of cereals, 5.25l of full-cream milk, 3 later 7 eggs.[8] Jews received much reduced rations, soon being forced to subsist largely on a diet of potatoes.

**1262**

*Food rations of an adult not eligible for supplements,*
*by four-week distribution periods*
(grams; eggs in numbers)

| | Date | Bread | Cereals | Coffee subst. | Meat | Fat | Cheese* | Quark/Sour milk cheese† | Eggs | Sugar | Potatoes | Fish |
|---|---|---|---|---|---|---|---|---|---|---|---|---|
| 1 | 28.8–24.9.1939 | ** | 600 | 325 | 2400 | 1400 | 320 | ** | ** | 2840 | ** | ** |
| 2 | 25.9–22.10.1939 | 9600 | 600 | 400 | 2000 | 1080 | 250 | ** | 4 | 1160 | ** | ** |
| 3 | 23.10–19.11.1939 | 9600 | 600 | 400 | 2000 | 1075 | 250 | ** | 4 | 1160 | ** | ** |
| 4 | 20.11–17.12.1939 | 9600 | 600 | 400 | 2120 | 1200 | 250 | ** | 4 | 1160 | ** | ** |
| 5 | 18.12–14.1.1940 | 9600 | 975 | 400 | 2120 | 1200 | 250 | ** | 3 | 1160 | ** | ** |
| 6 | 15.1–11.2.1940 | 11100 | 850 | 400 | 2120 | 1075 | 198.5 | ** | 4 | 1160 | ** | ** |
| 7 | 12.2–10.3.1940 | 11100 | 850 | 400 | 2120 | 1075 | 187.5 | ** | 2 | 1160 | ** | ** |
| 8 | 11.3–7.4.1940 | 9600 | 600 | 400 | 2000 | 1075 | 187.5 | ** | 7 | 1160 | ** | 500 |
| 9 | 8.4–5.5.1940 | 9600 | 600 | 400 | 2000 | 1075 | 187.5 | ** | 11 | 1160 | ** | 375 |
| 10 | 6.5–2.6.1940 | 9600 | 600 | 400 | 2000 | 1075 | 250 | ** | 11 | 1350 | ** | 250 |
| 11 | 3.6–30.6.1940 | 9600 | 600 | 400 | 2000 | 1077.5 | 250 | ** | 14 | 1350 | ** | – |
| 12 | 1.7–28.7.1940 | 9600 | 850 | 400 | 2000 | 1077.5 | 312.5 | ** | | 1350 | ** | 125 |
| 13 | 29.7–25.8.1940 | 9000 | 600 | 400 | 2000 | 1077.5 | 312.5 | ** | 7 | 1350 | ** | – |
| 14 | 26.8–22.9.1940 | 9600 | 600 | 400 | 2000 | 1077.5 | 312.5 | ** | 4 | 1350 | ** | – |
| 15 | 23.9–20.10.1940 | 9000 | 600 | 400 | 2000 | 1077.5 | 250 | ** | 5 | 1350 | ** | – |
| 16 | 21.10–17.11.1940 | 9000 | 600 | 400 | 2000 | 1077.5 | 250 | ** | 5 | 1350 | ** | – |
| 17 | 18.11–15.12.1940 | 9000 | 600 | 400 | 2000 | 1077.5 | 187.5 | 125 | 7 | 1350 | ** | – |
| 18 | 16.12–12.1.1941 | 9000 | 600 | 400 | 2000 | 1077.5 | 187.5 | 125 | 2 | 1850 | ** | 250 |
| 19 | 13.1–9.2.1941 | 9000 | 975 | 400 | 2000 | 1077.5 | 187.5 | 125 | 2 | 1350 | ** | – |
| 20 | 10.2–9.3.1941 | 9000 | 975 | 400 | 2000 | 1077.5 | 187.5 | 125 | 3 | 1350 | ** | – |

[7] Reich Chancellery minute 18 May 1942, Bundesarchiv Berlin (BAB) R 43 II/614, p. 39.

[8] See H. Schmitz, *Die Bewirtschaftung der Nahrungsmitteln und Verbrauchsgüter 1939–1950* (Essen 1956), p. 471. This section owes much to this extremely informative book.

| | Date | Bread | Cereals | Coffee subst. | Meat | Fat | Cheese* | Quark/Sour milk cheese† | Eggs | Sugar | Potatoes | Fish |
|---|---|---|---|---|---|---|---|---|---|---|---|---|
| 21 | 10.3–6.4.1940 | 9000 | 725 | 400 | 2000 | 1077.5 | 250 | 125 | 4 | 1350 | ** | 250 |
| 22 | 7.4–4.5.1941 | 9000 | 725 | 400 | 2000 | 1077.5 | 250 | 125 | 13 | 1350 | ** | – |
| 23 | 5.5–1.6.1941 | 9000 | 600 | 400 | 2000 | 1077.5 | 250 | 125 | 8 | 1350 | ** | – |
| 24 | 2.6–29.6.1941 | 9000 | 850 | 400 | 1600 | 1077.5 | 250 | 125 | 8 | 1350 | 7000 | – |
| 25 | 30.6–27.7.1941 | 9000 | 1225 | 400 | 1600 | 1077.5 | 187.5 | 250 | 6 | 1850 | 3000 | – |
| 26 | 28.7–24.8.1941 | 9000 | 850 | 400 | 1600 | 1077.5 | 187.5 | 125 | 4 | 1350 | 7000 | 125 |
| 27 | 25.8–21.9.1941 | 9000 | 1225 | 400 | 1600 | 1077.5 | 187.5 | 125 | 2 | 1350 | 8000 | – |
| 28 | 22.9.19.10.1941 | 9000 | 600 | 400 | 1600 | 1077.5 | 125 | 125 | 3 | 1350 | 10000 | – |
| 29 | 20.10–16.11.1941 | 9000 | 600 | 400 | 1600 | 1077.5 | 125 | 125 | 2 | 1350 | 10000 | – |
| 30 | 17.11–14.12.1941 | 9000 | 600 | 400 | 1600 | 1077.5 | 125 | 125 | 2 | 1350 | 10000 | – |
| 31 | 15.12–11.1.1942 | 9000 | 850 | 400 | 1850 | 1077.5 | 125 | 125 | 5 | 1350 | 10000 | 250 |
| 32 | 12.1–8.2.1942 | 9000 | 850 | 400 | 1600 | 1077.5 | 125 | 125 | – | 1350 | 10000 | 175 |
| 33 | 9.2–8.3.1942 | 9000 | 600 | 400 | 1600 | 1077.5 | 125 | 125 | 2 | 1350 | 10000 | 250 |
| 34 | 9.3–5.4.1942 | 10750 | 700 | 400 | 1600 | 1077.5 | 125 | 125 | 3 | 1350 | 6000 | – |
| 35 | 6.4–3.5.1942 | 8000 | 600 | 312.5 | 1200 | 825 | 187.5 | 125 | 6 | 1250 | 10000 | 600 |
| 36 | 4.5–31.5.1942 | 8000 | 600 | 312.5 | 1200 | 825 | 187.5 | 125 | 7 | 1250 | 10000 | 250 |
| 37 | 1.6–28.6.1942 | 8000 | 600 | 312.5 | 1200 | 825 | 187.5 | 125 | 5 | 1250 | 10000 | 250 |
| 38 | 29.6–26.7.1942 | 8000 | 600 | 312.5 | 1200 | 825 | 187.5 | 125 | 3 | 1250 | 10000 | 500 |
| 39 | 27.7–23.8.1942 | 8000 | 600 | 312.5 | 1200 | 825 | 125 | 125 | 3 | 1250 | 10500 | – |
| 40 | 24.8–20.9.1942 | 8000 | 600 | 212.5 | 1200 | 825 | 312.5 | 125 | 3 | 1250 | 12000 | 625 |
| 41 | 21.9–18.10.1942 | 8000 | 600 | 250 | 1200 | 825 | 187.5 | 125 | 1 | 1250 | 12000 | 500 |
| 42 | 19.10–15.11.1942 | 9000 | 600 | 250 | 1650 | 825 | 187.5 | 125 | 3 | 1250 | 10000 | – |
| 43 | 16.11–13.12.1942 | 9000 | 600 | 250 | 1800 | 825 | 187.5 | 125 | 2 | 1250 | 10000 | – |
| 44 | 14.12–10.1.1943 | 9000 | 600 | 250 | 1850 | 950 | 187.5 | 125 | 4 | 1500 | 10000 | – |
| 45 | 11.1–7.2.1943 | 9000 | 975 | 250 | 1600 | 825 | 125 | 125 | – | 1250 | 10000 | 500 |
| 46 | 8.2–7.3.1943 | 9000 | 600 | 250 | 1600 | 825 | 125 | 125 | – | 1250 | 16000 | – |
| 47 | 8.3–4.4.1943 | 9950 | 600 | 250 | 1750 | 890 | 312.5 | 125 | 5 | 1250 | 14000 | 250 |
| 48 | 5.4–2.5.1943 | 9950 | 600 | 250 | 2000 | 890 | 250 | 125 | 6 | 1250 | 14000 | 500 |
| 49 | 3.5–30.5.1943 | 9650 | 600 | 250 | 1700 | 860 | 250 | 250 | 5 | 1250 | 14000 | – |
| 50 | 31.5–27.6.1943 | 10550 | 850 | 250 | 1350 | 890 | 250 | 125 | 3 | 1250 | 14000 | 625 |
| 51 | 28.6–25.7.1943 | 10200 | 850 | 250 | 1400 | 900 | 187.5 | 250 | 4 | 1250 | 14000 | 850 |
| 52 | 26.7–22.8.1943 | 10505 | 850 | 250 | 1350 | 990 | 250 | 125 | 2 | 1250 | 14000 | 125 |
| 53 | 23.8–19.9.1943 | 9900 | 725 | 250 | 1200 | 875 | 312.5 | 125 | 1 | 1250 | 12000 | – |
| 54 | 20.9–17.10.1943 | 9900 | 600 | 250 | 1200 | 875 | 187.5 | 125 | 1 | 1250 | 12000 | – |
| 55 | 18.10–14.11.1943 | 10700 | 600 | 250 | 1200 | 876 | 125 | 125 | 2 | 1250 | 12000 | 250 |
| 56 | 15.11–12.12.1943 | 10300 | 600 | 250 | 1200 | 875 | 125 | 125 | 2 | 1250 | 12000 | – |
| 57 | 13.12–9.1.1944 | 11500 | 1100 | 250 | 1200 | 1000 | 125 | 125 | 2 | 1500 | 10000 | – |
| 58 | 10.1–6.2.1944 | 11500 | 600 | 250 | 1450 | 875 | 125 | 125 | 2 | 1250 | 10000 | – |
| 59 | 7.2–5.3.1944 | 11500 | 600 | 250 | 1450 | 875 | 125 | 125 | 2 | 1250 | 10000 | – |
| 60 | 6.3–2.4.1944 | 11500 | 725 | 250 | 1450 | 875 | 125 | 125 | 6 | 1250 | 8000 | 500 |
| 61 | 3.4–30.4.1944 | 12450 | 1375 | 250 | 1450 | 942 | 125 | 125 | 8 | 1250 | 8000 | 500 |
| 62 | 1.5–28.5.1944 | 12450 | 2025 | 250 | 1500 | 927.5 | 187.5 | 125 | 7 | 1250 | 8000 | 250 |
| 63 | 29.5–25.6.1944 | 10900 | 1225 | 250 | 1200 | 875 | 187.5 | 125 | 7 | 1250 | 8000 | 500 |

| | Date | Bread | Cereals | Coffee subst. | Meat | Fat | Cheese* | Quark/Sour milk cheese† | Eggs | Sugar | Potatoes | Fish |
|---|---|---|---|---|---|---|---|---|---|---|---|---|
| 64 | 26.6–23.7.1944 | 10300 | 975 | 250 | 1200 | 875 | 187.5 | 125 | 4 | 1750 | 10000 | 500 |
| 65 | 24.7–20.8.1944 | 9700 | 600 | 250 | 1200 | 875 | 250 | 125 | – | 1250 | 10000 | 250 |
| 66 | 21.8–17.9.1944 | 9700 | 60 | 250 | 1400 | 875 | 125 | 94 | 4 | 1250 | 12000 | 250 |
| 67 | 18.9–15.10.1944 | 9700 | 600 | 250 | 1400 | 750 | 62.5 | 94 | – | 1250 | 10000 | 250 |
| 68 | 16.10–12.11.1944 | 10500 | 600 | 150 | 1650 | 900 | 62.5 | 94 | – | 1250 | 10000 | 125 |
| 69 | 12.11–10.12.1944 | 8900 | 550 | 150 | 1700 | 625 | 62.5 | 94 | – | 1250 | 10000 | – |
| 70 | 11.12–7.1.1945 | 10500 | 550 | 150 | 1900 | 875 | 62.5 | 62.5 | 2 | 1250 | 10000 | – |
| 71 | 8.1–4.2.1945 | 8750 | 800 | 250 | 1450 | 625 | 62.5 | 62.5 | – | 1250 | 10000 | 250 |
| 72 | 5.2–4.3.1945 | 8900 | 899 | 125 | 1450 | 625 | 62.5 | – | – | 1250 | 10000 | 250 |
| 73 | 5.3–1.4.1945 | 9900 | 550 | 125 | 1250 | 760 | 62.5 | – | 1 | 1250 | 10000 | – |
| 74 | 9.4–29.4.1945 | 3600 | 225 | 100 | 550 | 300 | 62.5 | – | – | 375 | 10000 | – |
| 75 | 30.4–27.5.1945 | 6800 | 300 | 100 | 150 | 325 | 62.5 | – | – | 500 | 10000 | 250 |

* Periods 61–5: includes 94g sour milk cheese instead of 62.5g cheese.
† Period 66–73: includes 125g quark in addition.
** Unrationed.
‡ Periods 73 and 74: the rations had to last for 9 instead of 8 weeks.

**1263**

*Supplements allocated to the different categories*
*of workers per distribution periods*
(grams)

| Distribution period | Bread | | | Meat | | | Fats | | |
|---|---|---|---|---|---|---|---|---|---|
| | Very heavy | Heavy | Long hours night worker | Very heavy | Heavy | Long hours night worker | Very heavy | Heavy | Long hours night worker |
| 1 | – | – | – | 2000 | 2000 | – | 200 | 200 | – |
| 2–3 | 9600 | 5600 | – | 2400 | 2000 | – | 1885 | 490 | 80 |
| 4–23 | 9600 | 5600 | 2400 | 2800 | 2000 | 400 | 1875 | 500 | 80 |
| 24–34 | 9600 | 5600 | 2400 | 2400 | 1600 | 800 | 1875 | 500 | 80 |
| 35–41 | 9600 | 5600 | 3200 | 2200 | 1200 | 600 | 1475 | 400 | 80 |
| 42–54 | 9600 | 5600 | 2400 | 2400 | 1400 | 800 | 1475 | 400 | 80 |
| 55–67 | 9600 | 5600 | 2800 | 2400 | 1400 | 800 | 1475 | 400 | 80 |
| 68–73 | 9200 | 5600 | 3600 | 2400 | 1400 | 800 | 1475 | 400 | 80 |
| 74 (3 weeks) | 4800 | 3300 | – | 1800 | 1050 | – | 620 | 170 | – |

The government was concerned that some poorer workers whose allocation of rations went beyond their normal peacetime consumption might demand a wage rise, so on 15 September 1939 the Reich Labour

Ministry produced the following figures comparing the annual consumption of workers' families in 1937 with the rations they had been allocated on the outbreak of war, in order to be able to rebut any such claims:

**1264**        *Actual annual consumption in workers' families in 1937*
                *compared with allocated amounts of rationed foodstuffs in 1939*

| | Childless couple | | Married couple | | | | | | | |
|---|---|---|---|---|---|---|---|---|---|---|
| | | | With 1 child under 6 yrs | | With 1 child under 6 + 1 over 6 yrs | | With 1 child under 6 + 2 over 6 yrs | | With 2 children under 6 + 2 over 6 yrs | |
| | 1937 | Ration | 1937 | Ration | 1937 | Ration | 1937 | Ration | 1937 | Ration |
| Meat or meat products* | 71.3 | 72.8 | 93.8 | 109.2 | 116.3 | 145.6 | 138.8 | 182.0 | 161.3 | 218.4 |
| Milk products, oils or fats* | 49.0 | 43.8 | 64.5 | 65.7 | 80.0 | 87.6 | 95.5 | 109.5 | 111.0 | 131.4 |
| Sugar | 28.9 | 32.2 | 37.9 | 48.3 | 46.9 | 64.4 | 55.9 | 80.5 | 64.9 | 96.6 |
| Jam | 6.7 | 11.4 | 8.8 | 17.1 | 10.9 | 22.8 | 13.0 | 28.5 | 15.1 | 34.2 |
| Barley, groats, semolina, sago or similar foodstuffs | 12.4 | 15.6 | 16.3 | 23.4 | 20.2 | 31.2 | 24.1 | 39.0 | 28.0 | 46.8 |
| Coffee or coffee substitutes | 8.0 | 6.6 | 10.5 | 9.9 | 13.0 | 13.2 | 15.5 | 16.5 | 18.0 | 19.8 |
| Tea | 0.2 | 0.4 | 0.2 | 0.6 | 0.3 | 0.8 | 0.3 | 1.0 | 0.4 | 1.2 |
| Milk (litres) | 214.9 | 146.0 | 282.7 | 401.5 | 350.5 | 475.0 | 418.3 | 547.5 | 486.1 | 803.0 |

*Heavy and very heavy workers receive in addition 25.5 kg meat and meat products as well as 18.3 kg milk products, oils or fats.

The following document is an assessment of the development of food allocation in Germany during the Second World War in terms of calories. According to two different estimates from the 1930s, the actual normal daily consumption of calories at the time was between 2,900 and 3,072, composed of 114.8–130g of fats, 84–5g of protein, and 400–434.6g of carbohydrates.[9]

---

[9] See Schmitz, op. cit., p. 296.

**1265**

The development of food allocation in Germany
during the Second World War in Calories

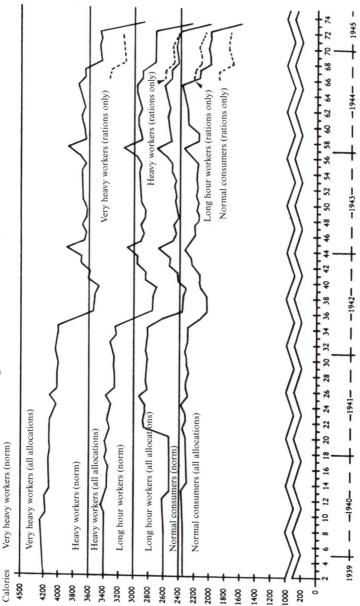

Very heavy workers (norm)

Very heavy workers (all allocations)

Heavy workers (norm)

Heavy workers (all allocations)

Long hour workers (norm)

Long hour workers (all allocations)

Normal consumers (norm)

Normal consumers (all allocations)

Very heavy workers (rations only)

Heavy workers (rations only)

Long hour workers (rations only)

Normal consumers (rations only)

Popular morale was acutely sensitive to the issue of the supply of necessities and particularly foodstuffs. The most serious cut in food rations was introduced on 6 April 1942. From the 34th to the 35th distribution period there was a reduction of *c*.200 kilocalories per day and, with the beginning of the 36th period, another one of about 50, so that, between the 34th and the 36th periods, normal consumers got 250 less, night and long workers, heavy and very heavy workers around 500 kilocalories less. The significance of food supplies for the maintenance of morale and the damage that could be caused by cuts is clear from the following report from the Security Service (SD) on the effect of the severe cuts introduced in April 1942. The disillusionment was even greater because, a few months earlier, Göring had publicly boasted that, with the capture of the Ukraine, Germany's food supplies were now secure:

**1266**    According to unanimous reports from all parts of the Reich, the announcement of the reduction in food rations has caused great disappointment and, in particular among working people, considerable disquiet.

Several reports state that the announcement of the 'deep cuts' in food supplies has had a really devastating effect on a large section of the population to a degree which is virtually unparalleled by any other incident during the war. Although people are generally aware of the fact that, in order to achieve final victory, the German people will have to adjust to this new situation, relatively few people have been prepared to show the requisite understanding for the new cut in food rations. In particular, the workers in the big cities and industrial areas, who often considered the previous supplies pretty limited, are apparently adopting an attitude which shows no understanding whatsoever for this new measure. The mood amongst these sections of the population has reached the lowest point ever in the course of the war. Numerous compatriots have expressed their disappointment in ironical remarks about the allegedly secure German supply situation and in frank hints about a future deterioration in their work performance. The new restrictions are felt particularly acutely by housewives who find it impossible to feed their families adequately . . .

In the context of the announcement of a cut in food rations the population is once more becoming increasingly preoccupied with the fairness of the allocation of food and other goods in short supply. People, particularly workers, mention with great bitterness the fact that a large section of the so-called better-off circles can get hold of things in short supply in addition to their food rations through their social connections and their bigger purses. There is widespread concern that, after the implementation of the new food allocations, bartering on the black market will become even more widespread than hitherto.

The cuts were partially restored in the autumn of 1942, which improved morale. There were also special allocations at Christmas of food, spirits, coffee, chocolates and sweets. However, food shortages and also a decline in quality—for example, the introduction of 10–20 per cent of barley flour into bread, which gave it a bitter taste, and heavy milling of the flour to make it go further, which spoiled the texture and made it less digestible—were a major source of complaint for the rest of the war. Moreover, transport and distribution problems often meant that people did not get the full rations to which they were entitled or they had to make do with substitutes. Housewives had problems adjusting their recipes to what was available and persuading their families to alter their eating habits.

Nevertheless, despite problems, food supplies and their allocation and distribution remained markedly superior to those of the First World War, as is clear from the following figures:

**1267**  *Rations of an adult living in Essen in the First and Second World Wars (kilograms per capita) per year*

| Year | Bread | Cereals | Coffee subst. | Meat | Fats | Cheese | Eggs (no.) | Sugar | Potatoes | Fish |
|------|-------|---------|---------------|------|------|--------|------------|-------|----------|------|
| 1916 | 108.5 | 1.9  | –   | 18.2 | 6.8  | –   | –  | –    | 180.0 | –    |
| 1917 | 107.3 | 5.6  | –   | 18.6 | 3.3  | –   | 30 | 12.8 | 127.5 | –    |
| 1918 | 98.3  | 8.0  | –   | 12.8 | 3.2  | –   | 19 | 17.7 | 195.0 | –    |
| 1919 | 120.2 | 14.4 | –   | 11.5 | 6.1  | –   | –  | 11.4 | 187.8 | –    |
|      |       |      |     |      |      |     |    |      |       |      |
| 1940 | 124.2 | 8.6  | 5.2 | 26.2 | 14.0 | 3.1 | 89 | 17.3 | **    | 1.5  |
| 1941 | 117.0 | 10.8 | 5.2 | 23.0 | 14.0 | 2.5 | 62 | 18.1 | –     | 0.8  |
| 1942 | 111.8 | 8.2  | 4.1 | 18.5 | 11.6 | 2.3 | 42 | 16.8 | 130.5 | 3.2  |
| 1943 | 131.2 | 9.6  | 3.3 | 18.8 | 11.6 | 2.6 | 33 | 16.5 | 168.0 | 3.1  |
| 1944 | 139.6 | 11.0 | 3.0 | 18.9 | 11.1 | 1.7 | 42 | 17.6 | 124.0 | 3.1  |
| 1945 | 113.5 | 14.0 | 1.8 | 8.1  | 5.6  | 0.7 | 1  | 9.5  | 99.5  | 2.2  |
| 1946 | 109.3 | 12.8 | 1.8 | 7.1  | 4.1  | 1.4 | 7  | 9.1  | 60.0  | 8.3  |
| 1947 | 123.3 | 16.9 | 1.6 | 5.2  | 2.2  | 1.4 | 7  | 7.3  | 37.0  | 6.9  |
| 1948 | 123.6 | 22.0 | 1.6 | 2.7  | 5.4  | 7.6 | –  | 21.8 | –     | 10.2 |
| 1949 | 120.0 | 18.2 | **  | 9.1  | 11.1 | –   | ** | 18.0 | **    | –    |

– Figures not available.
** Unrationed.

The following assessment is based on the results of a survey of 1937, which established a daily requirement for adult physical health of 76.1g of protein, 103.2g of fats and 400g of carbohydrates:

**1268**   *Nutritional content of food rations in Essen during the*
*First and Second World Wars*

| Period (half-year and distribution period) | Daily Calories | Daily amounts (grams) | | | Percentage of requirements | | |
|---|---|---|---|---|---|---|---|
| | | Protein | Fats | Carbohydrates | Protein | Fats | Carbohydrates |
| Summer 1916 | 1326 | 19 | 19 | 241 | 25.0 | 18.4 | 60.3 |
| Winter 1916/17 | 1010 | 35 | 13 | 290 | 46.0 | 12.6 | 72.5 |
| Summer 1917 | 1176 | 32 | 12 | 227 | 42.1 | 11.6 | 56.8 |
| Winter 1917/18 | 1370 | 57 | 16 | 401 | 74.9 | 15.5 | 100.3 |
| Summer 1918 | 1353 | 30 | 11 | 294 | 39.4 | 10.7 | 73.5 |
| Winter 1918/19 | 1337 | 30 | 10 | 284 | 39.4 | 9.7 | 71.0 |
| Summer 1919 | 1883 | 44 | 28 | 373 | 57.8 | 27.1 | 93.3 |
| Winter 1919/20 | 1194 | 24 | 26 | 234 | 31.5 | 25.2 | 58.5 |
| Early 1940 = 10 | 1552 | 52 | 42 | 235 | 68.3 | 40.7 | 58.8 |
| Early 1941 = 22 | 1515 | 49 | 42 | 227 | 64.4 | 40.7 | 56.8 |
| Early 1942 = 34 | 1751 | 52 | 39 | 291 | 68.3 | 37.8 | 72.8 |
| Early 1943 = 48 | 1895 | 67 | 37 | 318 | 88.0 | 35.9 | 79.5 |
| Early 1944 = 62 | 2103 | 68 | 37 | 367 | 89.4 | 35.9 | 91.8 |
| Early 1945 = 75 | 663 | 27 | 12 | 153 | 35.5 | 11.6 | 38.3 |
| Early 1946 = 88 | 997 | 42 | 18 | 185 | 55.2 | 17.4 | 46.3 |
| Early 1947 = 101 | 893 | 35 | 9 | 191 | 46.0 | 8.7 | 47.8 |
| Early 1947 = 110 | 1297 | 46 | 7 | 283 | 60.5 | 6.8 | 70.8 |
| Early 1948 = 114 | 1676 | 42 | 15 | 334 | 55.2 | 14.5 | 83.5 |
| Early 1948 = 121 | 1906 | 49 | 23 | 356 | 64.4 | 22.3 | 89.0 |
| Early 1949 = 126 | 1850 | 56 | 29 | 329 | 73.6 | 28.1 | 82.3 |

One reason for the improved food supply situation in the Second World
War was the fact that Germany produced more food than in the First
World War, as the following figures indicate:

**1269**

Germany's grain and potato harvests in the
First and Second World Wars
(columns 1 and 3: millions of tons; columns 2 and 4: 1914 = 100

|      | 1    | 2     | 3    | 4     |      |
|------|------|-------|------|-------|------|
|      |      | Grains |     |       |      |
| 1914 | 27.1 = 120 | | 27.2 = 100 | | 1939 |
| 1915 | 22.0 =  81 | | 23.7 =  87 | | 1940 |
| 1916 | 22.0 =  81 | | 22.0 =  81 | | 1941 |
| 1917 | 14.6 =  54 | | 22.6 =  83 | | 1942 |
| 1918 | 17.3 =  64 | | 24.0 =  89 | | 1943 |
|      |      | Potatoes |   |       |      |
| 1914 | 45.6 = 100 | | 56.3 = 124 | | 1939 |
| 1915 | 54.0 = 118 | | 57.4 = 126 | | 1940 |
| 1916 | 25.1 =  55 | | 47.5 = 104 | | 1941 |
| 1917 | 34.4 =  76 | | 54.4 = 119 | | 1942 |
| 1918 | 29.5 =  65 | | 40.2 =  88 | | 1943 |

However, this was by no means the whole story. An important reason for the difference between the food supply situation in Germany in the two world wars was its ability to exploit its empire during the Second World War, thereby ensuring supplies for its own population at the expense of those of its occupied territories as is clear from the following figures:

**1270**

Imports of food and fodder from abroad (millions of tons)

|         | Bread grains | Fodder grains | Meat and fat |
|---------|--------------|---------------|--------------|
| 1938/9  | 1.2          | 1.7           | 1.1          |
| 1939/40 | 1.5          | 0.9           | 0.9          |
| 1940/1  | 1.4          | 2.1           | 0.9          |
| 1941/2  | 3.0          | 1.3           | 0.9          |
| 1942/3  | 3.6          | 2.8           | 1.1          |
| 1943/4  | 3.5          | 1.9           | 0.9          |

**1271**

*Food supply in Germany and the occupied areas during the Second World War (calorific values of standard rations)*

|  | 1941 | 1942 | 1943 | 1944 |
|---|---|---|---|---|
| Germany (G) | 2,445 | 1,928 | 2,078 | 1,981 |
| Occupied areas (O) (excluding Poland and the Soviet Union) | 1,617 | 1,495 | 1,503 | 1,494 |
| Poland (P) | 845 | 1,070 | 855 | 1,200 |
| O expressed as a % of G | 66 | 78 | 72 | 75 |
| P expressed as a % of G | 35 | 56 | 41 | 61 |

In June 1942 the German government produced figures comparing the rations in Germany with those in Britain:

**1272**

*Weekly rations in Germany and Britain for a normal consumer, June 1942 (grams)*

|  | Germany | Britain |
|---|---|---|
| Bread | 2,000 | Unrationed |
| Meat | 300 | 300–400 depending on quality + 113 bacon |
| Fats | 206 | 226 |
| Sugar | 225 | 226 |
| Jam or | 175 | 113 |
| bottling sugar | 87.5 | 13 |
| Coffee/coffee substitute | 78 | unrationed |
| Tea | – | 56 |
| Cereals, i.e. oats, rice etc. | 150 | varying quantities |
| Cheese | 78 | 113 |
| Potatoes | 2,500 | unrationed |

Unlike with foodstuffs, no elaborate system had been prepared for clothes rationing. Initially consumers were obliged to apply for permits (*Bezugscheine*) to purchase clothing. But this produced a flood of applications and a spate of panic buying ensued. To restore the situation, on 16 November 1939, a clothing card (*Reichskleiderkarte*) was introduced, of which there were five issues before the end of the war:

**1273** *The Reich Clothing Card*

| No | Issued | Valid from/to |
|---|---|---|
| 1 | 29.11–08.12.39 | 01.11.39–31.03.41 |
| 2 | 05.09–11.09.40 | 11.11.40–31.08.43 |
| 3 | 30.10–05.11.41 | 01.09.41–31.12.44 |
| 4 | 04.01–09.01.43 | 01.01.43–15.12.45 |
| 5 | 18.09–06.10.44 | 01.09.44–15.12.45 |

**1274** *The allocation of points on the Reich Clothing Card*

| Type | Age | Colour | Reich Clothing Card | | | | |
|---|---|---|---|---|---|---|---|
| | | | 1 | 2 | 3 | 4 | 5 |
| *Reich cards* | | | | | | | |
| Men | from 15 | Yellow | 100 | 150 | 120 | 100 | |
| Women | from 15 | Brick red | 100 | 150 | 120 | 100 | |
| Teenagers(M) | 15–18 | Brown | | | | | 100 |
| Teenagers(F) | 15–18 | Red | | | | | 100 |
| Boys | 3–15 | Green | 100 | 150 | 120 | 120 | 100 |
| Girls | 3–15 | Light blue | 100 | 150 | 120 | 120 | 100 |
| Small children | 1–3 | Pink | 70 | 150 | 120 | 120 | 100 |
| Babies | | | | | | | |
| *Additional cards* | | | | | | | |
| Teenagers | 5–18 | Grey | 60 | | | 30 | |
| Boys | 3–15 | White | | 50 | 30 | | |
| Girls | 3–15 | White | | 40 | 20 | | |
| Pregnant women | | Grey | | | | 50 | |
| Mourning | | Grey | | | | 40 | |
| Bombed out | | Green | | | | 50 | |

**1275**    *List of points allocated to each piece of clothing*
*by the Reich Clothing Card (25 August 1940)*

I     Men's and teenagers' clothing
II    Women's and teenagers' clothing
III   Boy's clothing
V     Girls' clothing
V     Clothing for small children
VI    Baby clothes
VII   House and table linen, bed linen

| Article of clothing | I | II | III | IV | V | Baby clothes | VI |
|---|---|---|---|---|---|---|---|
| Suits | 80 | – | 40 | – | 18 | Vests | 1 |
| Jackets | 42 | – | 26 | – | 6 | Jackets | 1 |
| Trousers | 28 | – | 14 | – | 9 | Trousers | 4 |
| Boiler suits | 56 | – | – | – | – | Sleeping bags | 5 |
| Winter coats | 120 | 75 | 50 | 37 | 20 | Pyjamas | 6 |
| Macintosh | 25 | 25 | 18 | 18 | 10 | Over jacket | 5 |
| Other coats | 65 | 50 | 50 | 37 | 17 | Coats | 5 |
| Pullovers | 21 | 19 | 14 | 14 | 11 | Scarves | 1 |
| Knitted waistcoats | 28 | 23 | 14 | 14 | 11 | Mittens | 1 |
| Track suits | 38 | 38 | 20 | 20 | 12 | Nappies | 1 |
| Hankerchiefs | 1 | 1 | 1 | 1 | 1 | Cotton paddings | 2 |
| Shirts | 24 | 12 | 20 | 10 | 5 | Bath towels | 7 |
| Polo shirts | 11 | – | 7 | – | 5 | 2 bibs | 1 |
| Night shirts | 30 | 22 | 17 | 17 | 11 | Pram blanket | 22 |
| Pyjamas | 45 | 30 | 25 | 25 | 18 | Sheets | 16 |
| Gloves | 5 | 3 | 2 | 2 | 1 | Quilt | 34 |
| Socks | 6 | 3 | 2 | 2 | 2 | Pillow case | 4 |
| Stockings | 5 | 4 | 8 | 8 | 3 | Socks | 1 |
| Vests | 14 | – | 6 | – | – | Dresses | 8 |
| Underpants, long | 14 | – | 6 | – | – | Leggings | 4 |
| Underpants, short | 10 | – | 6 | – | – | Pullovers | 4 |
| Bathing trunks | 9 | 15 | 8 | 8 | 5 | Duvet | 18 |
| Bath robe | 30 | 30 | 15 | 15 | – | Pillow | 4 |
| Gym shirt | 6 | 6 | 5 | 5 | – |  |  |
| Gym shorts | – | 8 | 8 | 8 | – |  |  |
| Dresses | – | 42 | – | 24 | 15 |  |  |
| Suits | – | 56 | – | 44 | – |  | VII |
| Skirts | – | 18 | – | 16 | 6 | Sheets | 35 |
| Jackets | – | 38 | – | 33 | 3 | Pillow cases | 14 |
| Windcheater | 25 | 25 | 15 | 15 | – | Duvet covers |  |
| Dressing gowns | – | 60 | – | – | – | Bed spread | 44 |
| Blouses | – | 20 | – | 9 | 4 | Pillows | 18 |

| Article of clothing | I | II | III | IV | V | Baby clothes | VI |
|---|---|---|---|---|---|---|---|
| Smocks | – | 42 | – | – | – | Duvets | 73 |
| Aprons | – | 10 | 5 | 10 | 4 | Woolen blankets | 75 |
| Bed jackets | – | 18 | – | – | – | Tablecloths | 22 |
| Hairdressing capes | – | 6 | – | – | – | Hand towels | 5 |
| Brassieres | – | 3 | – | – | – | Bath towels | 22 |
| Corsets | – | 10 | – | – | – | Tea towels | 3 |
| Knickers | – | 12 | – | 10 | – | Mattress covers | 20 |
| Petticoats | – | 14 | – | 10 | 6 | Flannels | 4 |
| Scarves | 6 | 6 | 6 | 5 | 3 | | |
| Vest | – | – | – | 3 | 3 | | |
| Spats | – | – | 16 | 16 | 11 | | |
| Shorts | – | – | 8 | 8 | 8 | | |

Although the second Reich Clothing Card increased the points to 150, reflecting the improvement in the supply situation due to plunder, some clothes now required more points, there were substantial price increases, and the quality of the cheaper ranges was often poor. With the third clothing card (1941/2) work clothes, which had previously been available through special permits, were now included. On 1 August 1943, the fourth clothing card was suspended in order to give priority to the victims of bomb damage. The only exemptions were for children under 15, and for those whose health was threatened, or who could otherwise no longer carry out their job. With the mass air raids beginning in spring 1943 special permits had to be issued to those whose clothing had been destroyed. In Essen, for example, these special permits envisaged the following wardrobes for men and women:

**1276**  *Men*: 1 suit, hat or cap, shirt, tie, collar, vest, pair of underpants, nightshirt or pair of pyjamas, pair of socks, and 3 handkerchiefs.

*Women*: 1 dress, petticoat, shirt, pair of knickers, brassiere, nightgown or pair of pyjamas, pair of stockings, and 3 handkerchiefs.

Shoes could be purchased only with a special permit. Consumers were entitled only to two pairs of shoes, one pair of house shoes, one pair of gym shoes (until October 1943) and one pair of work shoes if their employment required them. A permit for a new pair was only issued after the applicant had declared that he/she only had two pairs, one of which was worn out. Random checks were sometimes made. A shortage of shoes—in 1938/9 nearly half of German leather was imported—was one of the major grumbles of the winter of 1939/40, particularly on the part of miners and outdoor workers, and a shortage of shoes remained a problem throughout the war. Even if one could get them, good shoes were expensive and cheaper shoes of poor quality were still relatively expensive. Another area of short supply, which was important for hygiene and morale was soap and washing powder. Initially one piece of 'standard' soap (80g) or 75g of quality soap and 250g of washing powder or equivalent was issued per month. Permits were introduced for furniture on 1 August 1942 and household goods were rationed from 30 January 1943, with priority given in both cases to those who had been bombed out. As a result of the massive air raids, a chronic shortage developed during 1943–5.

Food prices were controlled by a Price Commissioner and, in the case of major items such as bread, were enforced by the police, with shopkeepers who overcharged or gave short weight being subject to fines. Despite this, prices did increase, particularly for semi-luxury foodstuffs. In its report of 12 May 1942 the Stuttgart SD reported that the 'price commissioner was now regarded as a joke'. But the items referred to in the report were things like chocolates, nuts, wine, geese, with cauliflowers and Bismarck herrings being the only more necessary items.[10] More serious were the price rises for clothing and household goods such as china, glass, furniture, kitchen utensils etc. and shortages meant plenty of scope for the black market. Nevertheless, by comparison with the First World War, until the last few months, inflation seems to have been kept under control relatively successfully.

___

### (iii)  The Period of Victories 1939–1941

The period of the 'phoney war' from the end of the defeat of Poland in October 1939 to the spring offensive of 1940 was marked, as far as German popular opinion was concerned, in the first place by the hope that the war would soon be over and by strong hostility to Britain, which was seen as the main cause of the war through its previous support for Poland and now its failure to come to terms after Poland's defeat. This hostility was in part a product of a propaganda campaign specifically targeted against Britain, a campaign which could exploit latent feelings of resentment which went back to the naval rivalry and

___

[10] See excerpt from an SD report of 12.5.42 in HStAS E 398 Bü 48.

fears of encirclement which had so exercised Germans before the First World War and had then been stoked up again by the Treaty of Versailles. This anti-British feeling reached a high point after the courageous carpenter, Georg Elser, tried unsuccessfully to assassinate Hitler in Munich during his speech, on 8 November, to commemorate the anniversary of the failed Beer Hall putsch of 1923.[11] German propaganda blamed the British secret service for the attempt. The SD reported on 10 November 1939 as follows:

**1277**  Yesterday, the whole German nation was concerned about the attempted assassination of the Führer. The event was the subject of intense and emotional discussion by all sections of the population. The hymn 'Now let us give thanks to God . . .' was sung in many schools. Various employers informed their employees of the assassination attempt in factory meetings. People were particularly concerned during the morning before details of the effects of the assassination attempt became known. Everywhere rumours spread—for example, that the Führer had been severely wounded and that various leading men of the Party and State had been killed. When, in the course of the day, further information on the assassination attempt became known, the problems arising from it were discussed. The English and the Jews, who were generally seen as the instigators of the assassination attempt, were the object of bitter comments. In some places there were demonstrations against the Jews. In general the hope is that in future the Führer will not subject himself to such dangers as he has recently. It is further anticipated that various retaliatory measures will be taken against all enemies of the state and, abroad, a sudden attack will be made on Great Britain. There are numerous reports of conversations—particularly among workers—in which it was said that 'not a stone should be left standing in England' or that Göring should use the German air force to 'turn London into dust and ashes'. The joy which was expressed about the failure of the assassination attempt demonstrated a clear and unifying sense of gratitude towards fate and the strength of faith in the Führer which exists everywhere, even in the circles of previously Marxist workers.

The winter of 1939/40 was exceptionally severe and its effects were made worse by a serious coal shortage exacerbated by a partial breakdown of the railways system as a result of years of maintenance neglect. Many schools and factories had to be temporarily closed and the population shivered at home, while morale plummeted.

But, with the victories in the west between April and June 1940, the situation was transformed. The German population, which had begun the war with little enthusiasm, was delighted at the speedy and, compared

---

[11] See below, pp. 592–94.

with the First World War, painless successes which their Führer had brought them. The SD report of 24 June 1940 stated:

**1278**    *Victories and Activity of the Opposition*

With regard to this question, reports from the whole Reich are unanimous in presenting the following picture:

Under the impression of the great political events and under the spell of military success, the whole German nation is displaying an inner unity and a close bond between the front and the homeland which is unprecedented. The soil is no longer fertile for opposition groups. Everyone looks up to the Führer in trust and gratitude and to his armed forces pressing forward from victory to victory. Hostile activities meet everywhere with sharp rejection.

Again the German people hoped for peace and again Britain's refusal to deal with Hitler stoked up the hostility towards her. On 25 July 1940 the Oschatz branch of the Leipzig SD reported as follows:

**1279**    The effect of the Führer's speech is making itself felt among all sections of the population.[12] In general the opinion was that the Führer would not appeal again to England to see reason but rather people thought that the British world empire would be destroyed at once. But now the general view is that the Führer can now face world opinion free from criticism and will not suffer any reproach for this struggle which is pointless for England.

The fact that England has responded with a strict 'no', as is clear from the press and radio reports and, above all from Halifax's speech,[13] and the fact that it wants 'a fight at any price' is treated with disgust here. Everywhere people spontaneously demand England's total destruction. Judging by the mood which has existed since the beginning of the war, people do not 'want' England to accept peace terms. The propaganda which has been directed against England since September 1989 has had such an effect that the nation is burning to destroy the arch enemy.

People greet the fact that it is now happening or will happen in the foreseeable future with fanatical glee. If at this point in the final phase of the struggle one bears in mind the simple worker here who publicly declared his intention to give the whole of his weekly wages to the German Red Cross as soon as German troops set foot on British soil, then that says all that needs to be said about England. A worker is here acting as an interpreter, expressing in his own words the mood of the great mass of the people. The barometer of the public mood has reached its highest point and the recent reports on England's air raids on the civilian population and on non-military targets in Germany have made even the most die-hard optimist see sense. Everyone here is ready and waiting for the great moment which will begin the total destruction of England.

---

[12] On 19 July Hitler spoke in the Reichstag offering Britain a peace settlement. See Vol. 3, doc. 571.

[13] Lord Halifax, the British Foreign Secretary.

By September 1940, the euphoria had subsided. It was now clear that Britain was not going to sue for peace and people were impatient for the promised invasion. The fact that Britain even dared to launch small-scale air raids increased the sense of frustration. It was partly in order to deal with this domestic pressure that Hitler issued a warning to Britain on 4 September. The speech illustrates the mood in which he made the fatal decision at this time to switch the German bomber offensive from British air fields to London and other cities, thereby removing any chance of a German victory in the Battle of Britain:

**1280**      . . . If people in England are at the moment highly inquisitive and ask: Well, why doesn't he come? I say to them: 'Don't worry, he's coming!' One shouldn't go on being so inquisitive.

This world will be set free. Once and for all this nonsense must be stopped by which one nation is able to blockade a continent at will. It must be made impossible in future for a pirate state to follow a whim from time to time and expose 450 million people more or less to poverty and misery. We Germans are fed up with always being told by England to do this or not to do that, perhaps even being told whether Germans may or may not drink coffee. If it does not please England the import of coffee will be stopped. It does not concern me personally: I do not drink coffee. But I am annoyed that others should not be allowed to drink it.

In any case I find it intolerable that a nation of 83 million people should be punished physically and mentally by another nation whenever it pleases some plutocrat in London. I have held out my hand to the English so often with the offer of an agreement. You yourselves know that it was my foreign policy programme. Recently I repeated it for the very last time. Now I prefer to fight until at last a clear decision has been reached. This clear decision can only be that this regime of mean and pathetic warmongers shall be eliminated and that a state of affairs shall be established which will make it impossible in future for one nation to be able to tyrannize the whole of Europe . . .

It is wonderful to see our people in war, with their discipline. This is particularly true now when Mr Churchill is demonstrating his invention of night air raids. He does not do this because these air raids are particularly effective but because his air force cannot fly over German territory during the day. Whereas German pilots and German planes are over British territory day after day, no Englishman comes over during the day; they hardly even get across the North Sea. So they come during the night and, as you know, drop their bombs at random (without any aim or plan) on civilian residential areas, farms and villages. Where they see a light they drop a bomb.

For three months I have not reacted to this in the belief that they would stop this nonsense. Mr Churchill saw in that a sign of weakness. You will understand that we are now increasingly responding night after night. And if the British air force drops two, three, or four thousand kilograms of bombs, we will drop a hundred and fifty thousand, a million kilograms in one night. If they announce that they will attack our cities on a large scale—we shall wipe out their cities! We shall put these night pirates out of business, so help us God. The hour will come when one of us will crack, and it will not be National Socialist Germany. Once before in my life I have carried out such a fight to the finish; and then my opponent [i.e. democracy], who now sits in England on a last island in Europe, was also smashed.

▬▬

However, by the autumn of 1940 the German population was becoming increasingly frustrated about the failure to defeat Britain and increasingly disillusioned with the forecasts of German propaganda, as the following SD report of 7 October 1940 indicates:

**1281**    It is clear from the Gau reports of the past week that large sections of the population are adopting a completely unappreciative and thoroughly uncooperative attitude which expresses itself, in particular, in comments about the press and radio.

1. There are many reports that the excitement after the conclusion of the Tripartite Pact[14] has already been dissipated. Only a few people appreciate that the press dealt with the importance of the event in a thorough and exhaustive fashion. Impatience with the fact that the 'big blow' against Britain has not yet occurred predominates (e.g. Allenstein[15]) People are already switching their attention to other topics (e.g. Dresden). Even interest in military developments has declined most regrettably. Grudgingly and reluctantly the population is getting used to the thought of a second winter of war, and daily worries, particularly about fuel, have come to the surface. The thought frequently comes up that the Tripartite Pact shows that the war has been enormously extended . . .

2 . . . The pictures of the destruction of England are still thought to be making a considerable impact, particularly those published by the *VB*[16] (e.g. Innsbruck, Berlin). The close-ups of bombed streets, individual blocks, etc., were what the masses wanted to see.

An extraordinarily large number of people, however, have complained about the 'sameness' of the daily reports. People have got used to hearing that the recent attacks were heavier than the previous ones and that they had again had a devastating effect (e.g. Dessau, Bielefeld, Koblenz, Augsburg, Königsberg). People have been asking themselves impatiently how long this situation of daily attacks is going to last (e.g. Karlsruhe). After the Führer's remark, 'Don't worry, he's coming',[17] people were expecting the final operation against Britain to begin soon. In fact, the struggle against England was being fought mainly by the press and with a great use of tough talk. But it was obvious that the press was laying it on thick. One only had to think of headlines like: 'Whole of London in Flames',

---

[14] The Tripartite Pact signed between Germany, Italy and Japan on 27 September 1940.

[15] The names of places inserted in brackets in SD reports refer to the origin of those reports.

[16] *The Völkischer Beobachter*, the official Nazi Party newspaper.

[17] See above, p. 529.

'London Air Force Bleeding to Death', 'Death and Destruction in London', 'Life in London Unbearable'. People are surprised that the Londoners are nonetheless withstanding it. Apparently things were not as the German press had heard from foreign reports—that things were already worse than those in Warsaw and Rotterdam (e.g. Frankfurt am Main). A few people interpreted the report that the English had already moved their airfields inland as an important success and an indication of the progress of planned destruction. More often people comment that, according to the press reports, there ought not to be much left of the English air force (e.g. Breslau). People are frequently cynical about the ratio of planes shot down on either side . . .

3 . . . Like the reports on the evacuation of children, the oral and written reports on the effects of English bomb attacks have generated a psychosis which has an extremely adverse effect on our propaganda. For example, the guests at the Spa in Baden-Baden who were 'convalescing after the effects of night air raids' continually described their 'war experiences' with the result that the reports in the press and on the radio now meet with considerable mistrust . . .

---

In this situation Hitler's role as a morale-booster was vital, as is clear from the following SD report dated 14 November 1940:

**1282**    The Führer's speech on November 8 continues to be discussed among all sections of the population with great approval. It was 'the right thing to say at the right time' (Liegnitz) and had lifted the spirits of large numbers of people once more who have recently been disgruntled and sceptical as a result of personal or economic worries prompted by the proximity of a second winter at war, and it has cleared the atmosphere of numerous rumours which were having a negative effect on morale.

---

In the spring of 1941 the regime suffered the most severe blow to its prestige—the flight, on 10 May, of the Führer's Deputy for Party Affairs and Reich Minister without portfolio, Rudolf Hess, to Scotland. On 17 May 1941 the Leipzig branch of the SD reported on the response of the population:

**1283**    The whole population in this area is still—one can almost say more than in the first few days—affected by the events involving the Führer's deputy, Rudolf Hess. All other military and political developments have been very much pushed into the background by this affair and arouse little interest at the moment. The German press and radio reports on the affair are described by everyone from the workers to the intelligentsia as very crude and even to some extent stupid. It is these very reports which have prompted people to become particularly interested in the Hess case and which have so shaken people's trust in German propaganda (the truthful reporting of the press and the radio) that, during the next period, the whole of the press and radio reporting will be regarded as untrue from the very start.

As was to be expected, opponents and reactionary circles have used this opportunity to campaign against National Socialism and the national socialist world view. In particular, spokesmen of the former German nationalist camp have kept stressing 'what about these old fighters? What sort of people are these so-called leaders? Not a single general has run off yet!' In addition, people say that the official party explanation is rubbish because, if Hess had been mad, then that would be particularly serious because the responsible government department and leaders must have known about it and not done anything to prevent it. However, a substantial section is convinced that the Führer would never tolerate a madman in the government.

Increasingly, the opinion is being expressed that, as a result of the behaviour of Party comrade Hess, the war will be considerably prolonged. The press report, or rather the official Party statement, that it was a shame about his 'idealism' meets with no sympathy at all, rather people—and in particular intellectuals—raise the question: since when are traitors or those who commit high treason—and that is what party comrade Hess is being called—'idealists'? . . .

*Business circles.* Party comrade Hess's deed is unreservedly condemned as treason against the Führer and nation. Press and radio are rejected as a Party swindle. People are generally sorry for the Führer and a particular point was made of the fact that it is always his old colleagues who keep disappointing him. Some people from these circles see in the disappearance of Party comrade Hess a sign that Germany has once again killed itself with victories and that presumably National Socialism is finished.

People are definitely expecting a major attack on Britain to begin shortly. In this connection it is being said that, if nothing happens, then it really will soon be all up with Germany's power. The German people could not bear or cope with a third winter at war, but in view of the situation one must increasingly anticipate open and concealed sabotage attempts etc. Furthermore, it would not be surprising if activists now started their agitation and staged another November 1918 for us . . .

*Intelligentsia, academics etc.* These circles also unreservedly condemn the behaviour of Party comrade Hess. There are one or two accusations against the Führer himself for choosing such a mentally unstable personality as his possible successor. However, the majority of these people are convinced that the Führer is absolutely unaware of the real mood and situation in the Reich and that most things are kept from him . . .

*Party circles.* Party circles are totally shocked about the Hess affair and describe it in terms of a lost battle. Party comrades of long standing are almost exclusively of the opinion that the blow which the Party has received from this event will be at least twice as bad and serious in its effects as the SA affair (1934).[18]

---

Meanwhile, a few days earlier, on 5 May, the SD had commented on people's growing concern about a possible war with Russia:

---

[18] On the 1934 SA affair see Vol. 1, docs 115–36.

**1284** *Münster* notes people's comments which express the fear that an *expansion of the war* will gradually weaken Germany. 'We shall have to call up everybody because we're occupying all these countries. But the men and women in their sixties cannot keep the home front going.' 'We can easily find that we are occupying ourselves to death like Napoleon, who was destroyed by this division of his forces.' 'We want to get our colonies back, but we can't occupy the whole of Africa. People can no longer see where we're going; the occupation of England has once more receded into the distant future. The war is going to go on for years. *It's harder than we thought it would be . . . '*

*Halle* notes that *all political and military reports are considered in the light of whether they could have the effect of shortening or lengthening the war . . .*

*Oppeln* notes similar phenomena among the rural population. Above all, farmers' wives, who are quite heavily burdened by the absence of their husbands, by the drafting of the male workers, by bad weather etc., often remark: 'If only it was all over' . . . If only the damned war was over . . . '

Reaction to the news of the German invasion of the Soviet Union on 22 June 1941 was mixed and uncertain, as is shown by an SD report of 26 June:

**1285** The reports on the war with Russia, which have been received in the meantime, unanimously confirm that the initial nervousness and shock, which was particularly noticeable among women, lasted only a few hours and, as a result of the comprehensive campaign of enlightenment, has given place to a general attitude of calm and confidence. The mood of the population has swung round to such an extent that most people now tend to have a very low opinion of Russia as a military opponent. In some reports there are warnings of 'an obvious underestimation of the opponent' . . .

While throughout the Reich there are no doubts about the military situation, here and there fears are emerging that it will be extremely difficult to administer and maintain security in the Russian sphere. In this connection people continually refer to the lack of manpower everywhere. References to the fate of Napoleon, who was defeated by the expanse of Russia, have been comparatively rare so far.

By the end of July 1941, when relatives at the eastern front had begun to report on the toughness of the fighting and as the numbers of casualties continued to rise, concern on the home front deepened and there was a mood of disgruntlement which derived from a multitude of discontents. This situation was reflected in two SD reports. The first was from the Stuttgart SD dated 29 July 1941:

**1286** In domestic politics *the mood and bearing of the population* is still depressed, worried, full of mistrust, annoyance and frustration, although the *food supply situation* has improved somewhat. There is also no lack of loud *expressions of indignation* and bitter complaints from the population. These continue to be about *illicit trading, hoarding, 'good contacts', the behaviour of the better-off and of Party comrades, the idleness of the vacation visitors, the disadvantaging of women in employment in the allocation of food and fruit, the lack of tobacco products* and the queues in front of tobacconists.

There is great discontent among families with children and wives in employment about the *lack of home helps*, while by contrast they can observe that married couples without children and 'women of the upper classes', who are not employed, still have servants, who have to take the dog for a walk, while the lady of the house sits in a café or is playing tennis.

Everywhere people are saying that 'in this war too once again it's *the little people who are the dummies'*. They have to work, to do without and keep their mouths shut, while the others can get anything they want with money, contacts, selfishness, and ruthlessness. '*It's just like in the old days*: on the one side, the fat cats, plutocrats, class pride, war profiteers and, on the other, the good-natured, stupid working people. How can one still talk about a national community?' 'The idealists are now as always the stupid ones. *Money rules the world*. These remarks are quite typical and are not made in a spiteful way but with an air of disappointment and bitterness.

▬▬

The other SD report was from Leipzig dated 6 August 1941:

**1287**    1. The events in the east are causing people a great deal of concern. Whilst nobody doubts that the Soviets will be defeated, they had not reckoned with such a tough opponent. People are anticipating heavy losses, including on our side, and expecting the exhaustion of our reserves of human material, which for months will make it impossible to achieve our real war aim of finishing off England. There is concern about a new wartime winter involving very hard work with minimum food . . .
6. The huge numbers of prisoners are a cause of concern. People consider that these sub-humans infected with Bolshevism can hardly be deployed in our industry and agriculture without endangering our own people. So they will have to be fed without doing any work at the expense of our own population, who are in any case already poorly provided for.

▬▬

The announcement by the Reich Press Chief, Otto Dietrich, on 9 November 1941 that the Soviet military strength had been broken and that the war in the east had been decided, and the subsequent press coverage which followed this line, induced a temporary mood of optimism.[19] However, the SD noted that there were no public outbursts of joy and a certain caution in people's response and, when weeks passed and there

---

[19] See above, pp. 477ff.

was still no sign of an end to the fighting, there was disillusionment. It
was in this mood that the German people faced the first major crisis of
the war.

## (iv) The Crisis of Winter 1941–1942

It took some time for the home front to become fully aware of the
significance of the German reverse before Moscow in the first week of
December 1941. Indeed, before that happened, they were confronted by
two other major developments—the entry of Japan into the war and the
German declaration of war on the United States announced by Hitler
on 11 December 1941 in a speech to the Reichstag.[20] The SD commented on the population's reaction to these events in its report of 15
December 1942:

**1288**　The Führer's speech has met with *a great response* and has left everywhere a sense of security and an awareness of the strength of the Reich.

The declaration of war on the USA came as no surprise and was considered
by many to be simply official confirmation of a situation which in reality already
existed. Only among the peasantry were there a few who reacted with surprise
and with a certain anxiety about the addition of another opponent. The creation
of *clear battle lines,* as one section of the population described the new situation,
has, according to the majority of the reports, had the effect of releasing tension,
particularly after the surprising successes of our Japanese allies. Many people
expressed satisfaction that, in contrast to the Great War, Germany has seized the
initiative this time and has therefore convincingly proved to the outside world its
strength and confidence in victory.

In the discussions about the Führer's speech there was an emphasis on the
Führer's *objective and self-confident language*, which provided the ordinary man
in the street with a clear picture of the present situation, of the absolute
necessity for the declaration of war on the USA, and of the present war as a
whole.

. . . The *Führer's detailed statement on German–American relations* convinced
the population of the necessity for declaring war on the USA as the only
possible answer to Roosevelt's attempts at interference in Europe. In the discussions on this it was repeatedly stressed that Germany had never obstructed
the USA in the slightest way and that therefore the war guilt rested on America
alone, which had continually infringed international law and in this way had
started the war.

The parts of the Führer's speech which dealt with the war and with the danger
to Germany represented by America also did not fail to make an impact. In
particular, the disclosure by the Führer that *completely impregnable U-boat bases*
had been established from Kirkenes to the Spanish frontier had a generally

---

[20] See Vol. 3, docs 596–97.

calming effect and also led to speculation that the great U-boat action forecast on previous occasions by the Führer would now begin. For the time being, the population has no clear idea of what effect the war with America will have for Germany. They expect a predominantly defensive strategy with a long-drawn-out overseas war. In this context there are rumours that the Führer's headquarters has already been transferred and that the emphasis of the war is being shifted from east to west.

The way the Führer dealt with Roosevelt received particular attention and approval and there was surprise in some quarters that former World Enemy No. 1, Churchill, had been replaced by Roosevelt. The contrasting of the Führer's personal background as a worker and soldier until his takeover of power with that of Roosevelt, who from birth had been predestined to high office in the State, met with a response of deep satisfaction and pride.

▬

The first real sign that something was seriously wrong came with Field Marshal von Brauchitsch's resignation as Commander-in-Chief of the army, on 19 December 1941, and Goebbels' broadcast appeal to the nation to collect winter clothing for the soldiers on the eastern front.[21] The SD described the population's response to these events in its report of 5 January 1942:

**1289**    The announcement of the collection of winter things has produced a great response among all sections of the population and is still at the forefront of people's concern. It is unanimously reported that the announcement aroused great astonishment in view of the fact that recently the good and adequate provision of winter clothing for our soldiers has been repeatedly reported in the press and in various newsreels. The announcement was clear confirmation of the fact that the accounts of men on leave from the front about the lack of equipment capable of coping with the Russian cold were accurate and were not, as one would have assumed from the propaganda to the contrary, long out of date. In this connection, many people expressed their surprise that the collection had not already been carried out in the late summer. The present time for the collection of winter things was considered far too late by all compatriots and they deduced from that that the soldiers must be poorly equipped for the winter.

The takeover of the command of the army by the Führer has caused great surprise according to unanimous reports from all parts of the Reich. There was astonishment, in many cases bordering on consternation, among large sections of the population that the change in the command in the army came just at the time of the toughest struggles on all fronts and just before the Christmas holidays. Many considered this proved that the Führer could only have been prompted to take this step for very important reasons with major implications. The heart condition, which was given as the reason for the resignation of the previous Supreme Commander, was not generally regarded as plausible. People

---

[21] See above, pp. 483ff.

consider that this assumption is confirmed by the lack of any mention of Field Marshal von Brauchitsch's name in the Führer's announcement and in the lack of any words of recognition for the services which he has performed hitherto

Many people assume that the announcement of the collection of winter things was intended to prepare the population for the existing difficulties in the East in order to then announce the change in the army command, and that Field Marshal von Brauchitsch underestimated the armament potential and the powers of resistance of the Soviets and, in misinterpreting the situation, failed to prepare for a winter campaign in time . . .

Faith in the Führer is so unshakeable that the initial consternation about the resignation of the previous Commander-in-Chief of the army was soon replaced by a more confident assessment of the situation and this event has now largely receded into the background.

It is clear that the woollens collection did provide a valuable diversion from the shocks of December and gave people a positive sense of active participation in assisting their menfolk. Nevertheless, despite the optimistic concluding sentence of its report, less than three weeks later, on 22 January 1942, the SD was forced to admit that these events had had a very damaging effect on morale and, above all, on the reputation of the official media:

**1290** It is clear from a number of reports *that the impact of the public media of guidance is at the moment greatly impaired.* Of the various explanations usually given the following are the most frequent:

People had the feeling that, when things were going badly, the public media of guidance always preserved an 'official face'. As a result, in such situations large sections of the population no longer regard the press as the best source of information but construct 'their own picture' from rumours, stories told by soldiers and people with 'political connections', letters from the front and suchlike, often accepting the craziest rumours with an astonishing lack of discrimination.

Also, as regards the reasons for and implications of the wool collection, the event which has affected the population in the civilian sector more than any other since the beginning of the war, the public media of guidance had preserved their 'official face' in the sense of not giving any answers to the questions about the alleged organizational deficiencies of winter planning and the late timing of the collection, questions that were being asked by everybody. People had seen in the dismissal of Field Marshal von Brauchitsch an indirect reply to the many important questions as to who was responsible for the inadequate winter equipment on the eastern front . . . People argue that even if the winter had begun at the normal time, the preparations would not have been sufficient.

Furthermore, word had got round through numerous rumours that Field Marshal von Rundstedt was being replaced by Field Marshal von Reichenau and that moreover Field Marshal von Bock was no longer at his post. The report of von Brauchitsch's operation, therefore, and the cordial wishes of the Führer for his speedy recovery had been extremely surprising. The allusion to the convalescence now needed for Field Marshal von Brauchitsch seemed to leave open the possibility for his return some day. The same was true of the report that Field Marshal von Rundstedt represented the Führer at Field Marshal von Reichenau's state funeral, when von Reichenau, according to numerous rumours, was supposed to have only just taken over command from von Rundstedt. Finally, the surprise was completed by the new picture which showed Field Marshal von Bock after a short convalescence together with the Führer. Now the population could not 'make head or tail' of the wool and winter clothing collection and the reasons for it. Above all, the question again came up of who was to be held responsible for the situation our soldiers were in, and people speculated on why Field Marshals who, according to the rumours, had just been 'sacked' were suddenly treated kindly again or brought back, as in the case of Bock. People said that they could no longer find their way about in the confusion between what they 'heard' and what was in the papers.

In connection with the reports, during and after the winter- and woollen clothing collection, the letters from the front and reports from soldiers play a great part according to many statements. Many soldiers reported home absolutely hair-raising accounts of hardships endured, cold, bad nourishment, clothing etc.

The popular mood was summed up by the President of the Hanseatic State Court in Hamburg in his March 1942 report to the Reich Justice Minister, which contained a devastating critique of German propaganda methods:

**1291** I . . . In general it is recognized that, in view of the present military situation, there will not be an early end to the war. People are beginning to come to terms with that. The question of how long the war will go on is hardly discussed now that people have recognized that the optimism which was initially shown in this connection was without foundation . . .

II 1. There are frequent comments from my retinue that in Germany the effect of our own propaganda is exaggerated and, at the same time, the ability of the people to form judgments is underestimated. There is general criticism that the reports are painting a rose-tinted picture and that it would be better not to present things as if victory was just round the corner. People are well aware that, in the case of such a world war, one cannot always count on quick, immediate military and political successes, and that occasional setbacks are only too natural. It would seem appropriate to create an awareness of this where it does not exist. There are frequent references to Japan, which made an official announcement directly following its great victories to the effect that they were well aware of the seriousness of the situation and of the difficulties and possible setbacks which could be expected in the future, particularly since the war could under certain circumstances last for 5–10 years. This is seen as an expression of the conviction that, ultimately, success depends not so much on burning enthusiasm and continued shouts of hurrah, but much more on a quiet and stubborn determination to hold on come what may. For example, it is being said quite openly that it was a serious mistake to create the impression among the people already in 1941 that Russia was in a process of disintegration and was in its death throes.

2. In general people are asking for much more openness. As an example, people cite the case of Brauchitsch.[22] The only reason why this contributed to the rumours about a serious split between the Führer and the Party on the one hand and the generals and the officer corps on the other was that there was a complete lack of a sensible explanation. People believe that an open admission of faults and mistakes is calculated to strengthen their trust. There are even some people who refer in this connection to our English enemies who, as is clear from our newspapers, openly discuss mistakes.

People often express the opinion that our propaganda shouldn't make the enemy appear too ridiculous, not always portray them as inferior and not always adopt a sarcastic attitude towards them. Soldiers and men on leave, in particular, are continually pointing out that they experience this denigration and ridiculing of the enemy as a denigration of the Wehrmacht's efforts. Many compatriots are equally unhappy about the continual mocking and lampooning of Churchill, Roosevelt, Roosevelt's wife etc. People say that one should moderate the tone here and that exaggerations and too frequent repetition have an exactly contrary effect on ordinary compatriots.

▬

## (v) The Response to Ideological Indoctrination

One important aspect of the gradual discrediting of German propaganda was the way in which the population came to compare Nazi ideological stereotypes with the reality as they saw it. In addition to the remarkable defensive performance of the Soviet armies, this was strikingly evident in the response to the influx of large numbers of allegedly 'subhuman' Russian POWs and slave labourers, many of whom came to work and, in the case of agricultural workers, live in close proximity to Germans. The SD drew attention to this problem in its report of 17 August 1942:

**1292**    Recently there have been numerous reports from various parts of the Reich and from all sections of the population which indicate that the population is increasingly endeavouring to form *a coherent picture of the Soviet Union*, of the country, its internal situation, and the internal and external conditions of its people. In the process it is pointed out that, during the course of the war against

---

[22] See above, p. 536.

the Soviet Union, all the *previous notions have changed* and that there are a series of contradictions for which there is no satisfactory explanation.

1. Our previous propaganda against the Soviet Union emphasized that the Communist-Bolshevist system had been established by the Jews as a system which involved the overwhelming oppression and impoverishment of the whole Russian population . . .

2. The picture was one of great chaos. People recall the impressive reports of the disorganization of agriculture and transport, for example, of the failure of the Five-Year Plans in the industrial sphere etc., which have been written over the years. Already during the first months of the war against the Soviet Union, the feeling grew that in this connection we had been the victims of a certain *misconception*. The great mass of weaponry, its technical quality, the vast industrialization were the first surprising impression which contradicted the basic arguments which represented the previous image of the Soviet Union.

3. The people of the Soviet Union have been portrayed as animals, as bestial. The commissar and the politruk are regarded as the epitome of subhumanity. The reports about atrocities in the first months of the eastern campaign confirmed the opinion that the members of the enemy army were beasts. People were concerned about what could be done with these animals in the future. Many compatriots thought they should be ruthlessly exterminated. In view of the reports about atrocities committed by escaped Russian POWs, there was some concern that these types could come to the Reich in large numbers and even be employed as labour. But now, many compatriots contrast this view with the qualities of intellect and character of the *thousands of eastern workers*. Workers in particular note that these Russians are quite intelligent, fit in easily, are quick to understand even quite complicated mechanical processes. Many learn German quickly and are often by no means badly educated. These experiences have undermined their previous image of the people from the East . . .

5. In particular, compatriots note the fighting strength of the Red Army which, in addition to the extent and quality of its astonishing armaments, represents the second big surprise. Up till now, this fighting grit has been explained in terms of fear of the commissars' and politruks' pistols . . . But the idea keeps cropping up that simple compulsion is not an adequate explanation for such fighting qualities which show a contempt for death . . . At any rate, Bolshevism by whatever means has penetrated large sections of the Russian population with ruthless results. Soldiers, in particular, remark that such organized determination on the part of the Russians was never encountered during the [First] World War. It was clear that the people in the East were very different from us on racial and ethnic grounds, but behind the enemy's fighting strength there still lay a form of affection for the Fatherland, a kind of courage and comradeship and contempt for life, which, *as with the Japanese, seems strange but must be acknowledged.*

▬▬▬

Another example of resistance to ideological indoctrination was the popular response to the press reporting of the RAF's 'dambuster raid,' as recorded in the report of Gau Brandenburg to the Party Chancellery for the week of 23–9 May 1943:

**1293**     It is mentioned in the press reports about the English air raid on the dams that a Jew was responsible for the idea of these raids. The population is sharply critical of this report. It takes the view that dams, locks and other such installations naturally count as military targets and, if attacks on such targets in England have not yet occurred, because we needed to wait for the inspired idea of a Jew, then the men responsible should demand their money back from those who taught them their profession. Thus the population is strongly critical of two things in particular:
1. The destruction of the dams is an extraordinary success for the English and it does not accept the transformation of a justified attack into a purely terror attack.
2. The emphasis on the role of a Jew in connection with the above is completely incomprehensible.

▬▬▬

Gau Halle-Merseburg's report took a similar line.

As the war progressed the limits of Nazi ideological penetration became evident in another sphere, namely the persistent loyalty of a large section of the population to the Christian churches, despite a decade or so of anti-church propaganda. This was particularly, but by no means exclusively, true of rural areas. In a report of 31 May 1941,the County official (*Landrat*) of Ebermannstadt, a rural district in northern Bavaria, noted:

**1294**     The vast majority of the rural population still cling faithfully to their particular religious community. All attempts to shake their faith meet with an icy rejection; in some cases they produce disgruntlement and hatred. The celebration of Corpus Christi [whose status as a public holiday had been officially cancelled] by the Protestant as well as the Catholic population was a clear and united demonstration against the state ban. The abolition of Corpus Christi, as well as the ban on the rogation processions and pilgrimages on workdays, is regarded as simply a pretext for a gradual and systematic removal of the religious holidays altogether in the context of the complete annihilation of the Christian religious communities. This opinion will receive additional confirmation when the decision of the Bavarian State Minister to remove the crucifixes from schools in the near future leaks out to the public

▬▬▬

In fact, the removal of the crucifixes from schools by the Interior Minister and Gauleiter of Munich-Upper Bavaria, Adolf Wagner, caused such a storm of popular protest that Hitler ordered their reinstatement in order not to jeopardize morale. The growing influence of the churches was a constant refrain in the reports of the Party and the SD. For example, referring in his report of 9 April 1943 to the fact that, on the matter of ceremonial, the churches had a significant advantage over the Party, the head of indoctrination in the Nazi Party branch in the village of Maxfeld near Nuremberg continued:

**1295** In this connection one must mention the fact that, with the increasing toughness of the war, the churches have a following like never before. It is now the case that it is no longer the pastor who runs after the people but the other way round: the people run after the pastor. The overwhelming majority of young people are confirmed, in almost all the newspaper notices for those killed in action there is a reference to a memorial service, even in the case of those in the Waffen SS, and even those in the Bodyguard [*Leibstandarte*—the elite SS military unit] . . . There is no point in denying these facts. We shall have to get used to even more of this in the future, for the newly awakened interest in the churches has penetrated so deeply into the circles of our supporters that we cannot disregard it.

## (vi) The Crisis Winter of 1942–1943

Already by the autumn of 1942 the German population was becoming exhausted by the war. The monthly report of the district officer [*Landrat*] of Ebermannstadt, dated 2 November 1942, noted:

**1296** The longing for the war to come to an end at last manifested itself recently in particular in the eagerness with which people seized on the rumours of armistice negotiations with the Russians. The fact that for a long time the eastern front has been at a standstill, that Stalingrad has still not been taken, that news of deaths at the front never stops coming in, that the cancellations of the reserved status positions of young farmers are increasing at an alarming rate, and that the youngest cohorts are already being called up are interpreted as signs of exhaustion. Speeches by the Führer, the Reich Marshal, the Foreign Minister, the Reich Propaganda Minister and the other propaganda measures and local propaganda campaigns no longer have a lasting effect. Tiredness with the war is already so strong that all appeals to do more have no effect.

However, despite the fact that the German Sixth Army had been surrounded since 22 November 1942, it was only on 16 January 1943 that the Wehrmacht communiqué admitted that the German forces were involved in a defensive battle against an enemy 'attacking from all sides'.[23] In its report of 28 January 1943 the SD commented on the population's response to this disaster:

---

[23] On the siege of Stalingrad see Vol. 3, docs 602–03.

**1297** At the moment *the whole nation is deeply shaken* by the impression that the fate of the sixth Army is already sealed and by concern about the further development of the war situation. Among the many questions arising from the changed situation, people ask above all why Stalingrad was not evacuated or relieved, and how it was possible, only a few months ago, to describe the military situation as secure and as not unfavourable. In particular, people discuss, with a marked undertone of criticism, the underestimate of the Russian combat forces through which now for the second time a severe crisis has been triggered. Apart from this, our compatriots are once more concerned about various developments in the domestic situation which were partly responsible for this blow hitting us so extremely hard. Despite their readiness to subject themselves to the introduction of total war, many compatriots, particularly those who are politically reliable, say that this step was taken very late. Even if every individual was willing to exclude everything from his private and professional life that was not absolutely necessary for achieving victory, it may be questioned whether the great complexity of life could be reduced to the necessary level with the speed and intensity needed, but also without going too far. Above all, our compatriots doubt whether it will be possible to distribute the burden of war equally between everybody without distinction. Thus, people fear that with the coming use of female labour the upper classes will know how to escape it. *It was regrettable that the Führer had not found time by now to deal intensively with the situation at home. According to all the reports the nation is urgently waiting for a speech by the Führer* on 30 January and hoping it will provide an answer to all these questions.

Fearing that an unfavourable end to the war is now possible, *many compatriots are seriously thinking about the consequences of defeat. While some people say that* 'perhaps it would not be so bad', most people are convinced that losing the war will amount to extinction. Although, on the one hand, this alarming thought strengthens the will to keep going, it causes many people, on the other hand, to be thinking already of the possibilities of a way out in the last resort and to be talking of the final bullet that would still be left when everything was over.

*Despite the widespread ill-temper* and acute symptoms of depression in some circles, the *attitude of our compatriots is strengthening*, according to all parts of the Reich. There is every chance, these reports state, that the inner resources of the people, now mobilized, will prove themselves during the crucial tests to come.

There was also widespread criticism of the role of the press and propaganda in general. This was reflected in the reports of the SD and the Nazi Party. The summary of the reports from the Party Gaus to the Party Chancellery for the week of 24–31 January 1943 did not mince words:

**1298** The general approach of the German press during the war years has hitherto been decidedly optimistic. The Gaus have frequently requested that it should not present a rosy picture but simply tell the people the truth; they are mature enough to bear it. The press articles which ridiculed the enemy, repeatedly underestimated them and questioned their strength and power were a particular object of criticism.

Reports from the Gaus which have arrived here in the last few days only show that the editors of many newspapers and to some extent the radio have turned the toughening propaganda into a definitely pessimistic propaganda.[24] If one wants to develop a tough attitude in people then one should not remove all hope from them, otherwise one will destroy their faith. One must also not describe the sufferings of the Stalingrad fighters to their hundreds of thousands of relatives in too stark terms because that will not produce toughness but horror and despair.

*Report from Gau Hanover-East.* The unvarnished reporting by the press and propaganda apparatus has produced very grave disquiet in the population. The population notes with a certain bitterness the striking contrast between the reporting hitherto and the current approach. The press and propaganda media are accused of previously having seen things in much too rosy a light. Not only was the opponent in the East underestimated but a completely false picture was given of his powers of resistance and his armament potential. Now things have swung to the opposite extreme and everything is seen in the blackest terms. This has produced a considerable crisis of trust in the people's relationship to the press and the propaganda media.

As a result of the pessimistic tone of the reporting, there is the danger that this crisis of trust will develop into a much more serious crisis in the relationship with the military and political leadership. Even earlier on, the disparagement of the enemy was very often treated with great scepticism since the reporting of the soldiers coming from the front indicated the opposite.

The gloomy situation at the moment probably derives above all from the fact that the propaganda media do not give any reason for this development and also that there is no attempt to raise hopes of a change in the situation. The whole German people are sharing the fateful hours of the German soldiers on the eastern front. But they will experience a feeling of hopelessness if there is no sign of any assistance or of a way out. Already, a few people are saying that this is the beginning of the end and in some cases spontaneous parallels are being drawn with the development in the First World War where similarly we kept winning until 1918 and then lost the war after all.

The press and propaganda media bear the sole responsibility for this current mood. The German people wanted and want to hear the truth and to have clarity. They know that their existence is at stake and that everyone is fighting for their lives. They don't want to be given a rosy picture, but they also want to know how the struggle can be continued and want to be sure that one can rely on a continuation of the struggle leading to success.

---

[24] On the new line of 'toughening' propaganda see above, pp. 487ff.

The attempt by the Reich Propaganda Minister, Joseph Goebbels, to respond to and mobilize the desire for total war in his Sports Palace speech of 18 February 1943[25] had a rather mixed reception, which was summed up in the SD report of 22 February:

**1299**  According to the reports we have received, a large section of the population listened to the speech of Dr Goebbels, despite the fact that the announcement of it came late and as a surprise. Furthermore, through the repeat of the broadcast, through its publication in the press and through the lively discussion of its content, it has penetrated into the furthest corners of the country. Its effect—and the reports were unanimous on this—was unusually great and on the whole very favourable. The morale of the population had reached a low point on account of the most recent developments on the eastern front, particularly the evacuation of Kharkov, and they were longing for a clear explanation of the situation. Dr Goebbels' speech, despite its frank description of the seriousness of the situation, had the effect of easing tensions and strengthening confidence and trust in the war leadership. Dr Goebbels understood how to develop an enthusiasm and a spirit like that in the 'time of struggle' [i.e. before 1933] which communicated itself through the radio.

The theme of 'imminent danger' confirmed the fear of many people that as yet there was no question of stabilizing the eastern front, that the series of setbacks was not yet at an end, and that the war could still take a serious turn. To some extent, people had only now become aware of the terrible seriousness of the situation. But, though they were shaken, they were not despairing. The population was grateful to the leadership for speaking frankly at last and for telling the plain unvarnished truth. But many people had expressed the wish to hear more concrete details about military developments, in so far as it was compatible with military security. One or two people commented that Dr Goebbels had 'painted the situation blacker than it was' in order to give emphasis to the measures for total war. In his treatment of these measures Dr Goebbels 'had spoken the mind' of the population, although various people pointed out that his comments did not go beyond the measures and points already known and, as before, people said that total war was being introduced 'very late'. The announcement that the measures would be carried out in the most radical fashion was hailed everywhere. The doubts as to whether they will be carried out in a just manner, applying to all classes, have decreased though they have not yet ceased . . .

The last section of the speech had a mixed reception. While the force of the ten questions was universally emphasized, nevertheless, compatriots and Party comrades from all sections of the population pointed out that the propaganda objective of the questions and answers was all too apparent to listeners and readers.

The population continued very seriously to discuss the question of *where the front would be stabilized, why there had to be a Stalingrad* and what the with-

---

[25] See above, pp. 489ff.

drawals would cost in terms *of losses* of men, weapons, materiel, and territories necessary to supply important areas and *what success the spring offensive* would have.

▃▃▃

However, Goebbels' 'class-war tendencies' evoked criticism from some sections of the Party as is clear from the following Party Chancellery summary of the Gau reports dated 15 March:

**1300**    Various press comments as well as the remarks of leading Party comrades—to some extent the sharp attacks by Party comrade Dr Goebbels on certain propertied circles—have now, as was indicated in the last report, mobilised those destructive elements who are using this opportunity to act out their proletarian instincts and infect the nation with their class-war tendencies. It is clear that every sensible compatriot endeavours to oppose such a development

The report from Gau Halle-Merseburg, dated 11 March, is very significant in this connection:

In well-meaning national socialist circles, which are open to just criticism, a real antipathy to the so-called Goebbels method is becoming apparent. *People have become mistrustful of the national socialist propaganda* because, within a matter of a few weeks, it has been possible to go from one extreme to another, and so they have become mistrustful of every new regulation. Every comment by the Minister is taken apart and criticized whenever there is an opportunity to do so. The contradiction which often exists between the realities of people's attitudes and mood and the front presented by our propaganda in the press and on the radio—clearly intended for the outside world—is sometimes so obvious and crass that people are often alienated. In particular, the confusion of decrees and edicts, where one often cancels out another, does not exactly increase people's trust in the departments of state.

▃▃▃

The winter of 1942–3 saw a crisis for the German military not only on the eastern front but also in North Africa with the defeat at El Alemain and the retreat of the Afrika Korps which followed. This added to the sense of depression which was further exacerbated by worries among certain sections of the population about the effects of the total war measures introduced early in 1943. These fears were referred to by the SD in its report of 5 April 1943:

**1301**    Many comments by individuals suggest that a large section of the nation cannot imagine how the war will end. Even if the Soviet Union was decisively defeated this year and even if England too was finished, there would still be a long war with America. In the light of the question, 'how will Germany stand when the war is over?' people discuss future prospects with a good deal of concern. Those belonging to the professions, such as lawyers and doctors, fear they will be turned into civil servants; the civil servants, on the other hand, are concerned about the contempt for them which is spreading among the population and from which they do not feel adequately protected from above. In the circles of medium- and small-scale industry there is the belief that large concerns and the 'State capitalist concentrations of power' put their whole future in question. Small shopkeepers and craftsmen are worried about the closure operation,[26] and in many cases fear the 'end of the middle class [*Mittelstand*]'. People were also frequently concerned about the possible loss of their property through the expected tax increases but also through rumoured capital levies. The rise in prices and the general lower valuation given to money were seen by many people as indicating an inflation.

One suggestion for improving morale was for the Führer to be given a higher profile in German propaganda. For, since the euphoric days of 1940, and particularly since the crisis on the eastern front, Hitler had drastically reduced his public appearances, burying himself in his headquarters. In its report of 19 April 1943 the SD commented:

**1302** It has been emphasized in some reports that the whole population has appreciated the fact that recently they have heard more of the Führer. Judicious and positive-minded citizens have remarked that it is not a good idea for the Führer to remain 'out of sight' for too long. The nation wants to have its close personal relationship with the Führer confirmed by frequently receiving news of him. But in the course of the war it has become rare for a picture of the Führer to appear in the newspapers or in the newsreels; the same is true of speeches by the Führer. A picture of the Führer in which one could see that his hair had not gone completely white, as rumour once had it, would have a more positive effect on the population than many fighting slogans. In order to keep alive the contact between leader and nation, it was frequently suggested that the Führer should be shown not only at highly official occasions and at military conferences, but more often in his personal life, as was done before, at the field kitchen or while having a walk, and that there should be reports on his daily routine, and his remarks and comments should be published.

However, the Führer myth had already begun to decline as a result of the crisis of 1941–2 and this decline had been markedly accelerated by Stalingrad. The Party Chancellery summary of the Gau reports for 7–20 March 1943 commented on this development:

**1303** The rumour-mongers are still, or rather more than ever, at work. The rumours of an impending devaluation remain persistent. There is talk of 'taxing

---

[26] On 30 January 1943 the Reich Economics Minister issued a decree for the closure and amalgamation of some small businesses. The intention was to save manpower for drafting to the front and to save fuel etc. See above, pp. 239ff.

away savings accounts' etc. The following rumours and political jokes have been reported from the following Gaus: Pomerania, Kurhessen, Westphalia South and North, Moselland, Berlin, Saxony etc.

1 . . . .

2. The clock goes tick tack and the hand goes forward; Rommel goes backwards and that is described as tactic[s].

3. One can now get the book of the Germans, *Mein Kampf,* on points—on the clothing ration book [*Spinnstoffkarte. Spinnen* means 'to spin', but used colloquially to fantasise or talk rubbish].

4. The *Führer* is mentally disturbed and is tearing down the pictures and curtains in his headquarters.

5. The current successes on the eastern front were only achievable because Halder[27] and Brauchitsch had been summoned back by the Führer.

6. We needn't have any fear of the Bolsheviks because only the British and Americans will come to the Moselland.

7. The reason why there are so few anti-aircraft guns in the Rhineland is that the majority of Catholics live there and the state has little interest in them.

*What is particularly dangerous about these things is the fact that people are now daring openly to criticize the Führer and to attack him in the most mean and spiteful manner.* These rumours and political jokes are all too readily listened to by a certain group of compatriots. *Unfortunately, inspired by a certain sensationalism, boastfulness or indifference many compatriots repeat everything which they are told without* contradiction and without bearing in mind that in doing so they are becoming channels of enemy propaganda. *It is a regrettable fact, which one is continually being made aware of, that our party comrades frequently display an incredible doziness and thoughtlessness since they no doubt witness such demoralizing enemy propaganda and yet rarely show the courage needed to crack down on this!* If one tries to ask one of these 'badge wearers', who 'indignantly' relates what he has just heard, how he responded in this situation, one very rarely gets the reply which one ought to expect, simply because of a lack of civil courage, one could also say of cowardice, but often because of laziness or fear of hassles with the police.

▬▬▬

Four weeks later the Party Chancellery report for 11–17 April returned to this theme:

**1304**    There are unanimous reports from many Gau headquarters that, in particular recently, the number of political jokes *which involve the Führer have increased sharply.* The following are examples of the large number of such jokes which are on file here:

What's the difference between the sun and Hitler? The sun rises in the East, Hitler goes down in the East

What's the difference between India and Germany? In India one person starves for everybody [Gandhi], in Germany everyone starves for one person.

---

[27] General Franz Halder, formerly Chief of the General Staff.

Zarah Leander is summoned to the Führer's headquarters. Why? She has to sing 'I know there'll be a miracle one day' every day.[28]

Morale continued to deteriorate throughout the summer. By the end of May 1943, it was becoming clear that the U-boat war on which many Germans had now pinned their hopes was no longer going Germany's way. On 8 July the SD reported:

**1305** The telling of vulgar jokes detrimental to the state, even about the Führer himself, has increased considerably since Stalingrad. In conversations in cafés, factories and other meeting places people tell each other the 'latest' political jokes and in many cases make no distinction between those with a harmless content and those which are clearly in opposition to the state. Even people who hardly know each other exchange jokes. They clearly assume that any joke can now be told without fear of a sharp rebuff, let alone of being reported to the police. Large sections of the population and even a section of the Party membership have clearly lost the feeling that listening to and passing on political jokes of a certain type is something which a decent German simply does not do.

This was clearly potentially very serious and the situation was made even worse by the fall of Mussolini on 27 July 1943. A week later, on 2 August, the SD reported on the response of the population:

**1306** *The idea that the form of government in the Reich, which was considered immutable, could also suddenly change in Germany as well is very widespread.* In this connection there are more frequent references to individual cases of corrupt behaviour by party comrades in leadership positions in the Party, the state and the economy and there is often talk of a totally 'corrupt system'. At the same time, the rumours which have been around for some time about the alleged flight of the Reich Marshal, the Reich Foreign Minister, or Reichsleiter von Schirach have once again become current. There are also some reports of old spiteful jokes such as the one about the Führer's having withdrawn to write a book with the title 'My Mistake' or that the Führer and Reich Minister Dr Goebbels had capsized in a U-boat and that it wasn't the two of them who had been saved but the German people.

An important factor in the decline in popular morale was the growing contempt of the German population for much of its leadership. This

---

[28] Zarah Leander was a Swedish actress whose song 'I know there'll be a miracle one day ' (Ich weiss es wird einmal ein Wunder geschehen) from the popular film *The Great Love* (*Die grosse Liebe*) became a big hit of the war. See p. 505 above.

point was the subject of a special report by the SD to the Party
Chancellery with the title 'Basic issues concerning the mood and
behaviour of the German people: trust in the leadership' and was dated
29 November 1943:

**1307**    The first serious shocks occurred with the reverses of the last two winters
of the war in Russia. It was then that for the first time doubts emerged about
whether the leadership was fully capable of grasping the enormous problems
created by the war and of mastering them. In the course of this year's
developments the question has been raised more frequently as to whether the
leadership really 'made the right decisions' both in terms of military operations
and as far as measures at home were concerned.

In such deliberations the population makes a clear *distinction between the
Führer and the other leading figures.* Whereas a loss of trust in individual leading
personalities or leading agencies occurs comparatively frequently, faith in the
Führer is virtually unshaken. While it has certainly been subjected to various
serious stresses, above all after the fall of Stalingrad, nevertheless recent months
have seen a strengthening of trust in the Führer despite the setbacks on all
fronts. Recently it reached a high point with the *freeing of Mussolini* and the
*Führer speech* on the night before 9 November. 'Here the German people
believed they were seeing the Führer once more in all his greatness.' Faith in him
has been so steeled by the painful crises of the fourth year of the war that it can
now hardly be shaken even by unfavourable political or military developments.
Many people see in the Führer the only guarantee of a successful conclusion of
the war. For our compatriots the idea that anything could happen to the Führer
is unthinkable.

Thus, while the Führer is the only person who is considered capable of
mastering the present situation and future problems, the remaining leadership of
the Reich is no longer trusted unconditionally. In particular, the failure of
promises and prophecies to be fulfilled has seriously undermined trust in
individual leaders as far as many compatriots are concerned . . .

Above all, there is a marked reduction in trust in the media. The attempt from
time to time to disguise the true picture when the situation was serious or to play
down ominous military developments, for example 'by portraying withdrawal as
a success' or 'portraying territory which previously was described as valuable as
now being not so important after all' or 'thinking that periods of delay or quiet
have to be filled up with flannel-type reports about events in India or plutocratic
excesses in England or America' , have largely undermined trust in the press and
radio which previously existed.

Thus, in their desire for objectivity and openness and their dislike of attempts
to portray things as better than they are the population has gradually begun to
read between the lines and, in particular, increasingly to turn to the news from
neutral and enemy states.

A further factor leading to expressions of mistrust in the leadership is the
behaviour of individual local leading figures in the state and Party at the lower
and middle levels. Although the measures of the Reich Government are basically

approved of, much of what they see being done by the executive organs of the state and Party gives compatriots cause for thought. Thus, for example, the population note that barter and illicit trading keep spreading or that the total war propagated by the leadership is not being fairly implemented (e.g. in the case of the deployment of women, the question of housemaids, the allocation of housing and, above all, in the granting of reserved worker status) and that some of the leading figures of the state and Party are not being fully affected by the restrictions which are imposed on everybody else. The observation that leading personalities are buying up agricultural land during the war or were able to *expand* their villas and country houses despite the shortage of building materials, as well as providing themselves with private air raid shelters and, finally, the sparing of members of the middle ranks or top leadership who have committed offences, through the dismissal of court cases or their postponement for several months, which has allegedly occurred in individual cases, have led many to believe that the leadership does not always take its share of the nation's sacrifices. There are 'double standards' and 'they preach water but drink wine'. Poor behaviour by individual persons in authority in public life often damaged trust in the top leadership at the local level.

Workers' trust in the leadership of their plants, in the DAF and other organizations and authorities is also often subject to particular strain. Many workers are once more beginning to *think in terms of classes* and talk of classes [*Schichten und Ständen*] who would 'exploit' them.

As far as the Wehrmacht is concerned, the population is convinced of the professional and personal qualities of the German military leadership . . . However, the excesses in the bases and to some extent in the home garrisons have been the subject of growing criticism. This culminates in the statement that the First World War conditions are being surpassed by the present situation. Reference is made, in particular, to the alleged growing gap between the officers and men among the troops behind the front and at home (special provisions for the messes, use of spirits, shopping trips to the occupied territories, the inappropriate use of soldiers who are capable of front-line service in messes, offices etc.).

To sum up, the reports reveal the following:

1. The population makes *a distinction between the Führer and the rest of the leadership* in its assessment of professional performance and personal behaviour.
2. The criticism of individual leading figures and of measures ordered by leading agencies, which in some cases comes not just from opponents or the usual grumblers, but from wide circles of the population, indicates a certain reduction in trust in the leadership.
3. *Fairness and the equal distribution of the burdens of war will determine the degree of trust in the leadership.* This trust is shaken above all if measures are not applied equally or totally and when exceptions are made and when there are 'back doors' and when action is not taken irrespective of the person affected.

———

By the late autumn of 1943, however, the situation had stabilized. This was partly because the position in Italy appeared to have improved as a result of the ruthless action taken against the Italians. More important, however, was the fact that the regime had cracked down on 'defeatists' and had made this public with death sentences which were widely reported. The President of the Higher State Court in Bamberg commented on this change in his report to the Reich Justice Ministry of 27 November 1943:

**1308**     Apart from that, in the last few weeks and months a marked change has occurred, perhaps less in the mood itself than in the way it is expressed. While a short while ago it was noticeable that there was a great lack of inhibition in the way rumours were passed on and political and military events were discussed in public, particularly in pubs, railway compartments, shops etc., now, probably under the impression of the increasing number of death sentences against defeatists, this has been replaced by the greatest caution in all matters affecting the war and politics. Since no one is prepared any longer to say what they think and, on the contrary, everywhere there is a real unwillingness to engage in conversations about anything other than the most mundane matters, it is hardly possible any longer to gauge the real mood of the people, particularly its variations. Evidently people discuss what really concerns them only in the most intimate circle in which they feel free from denunciations.

The provision of food supplies is satisfactory. People recognize that the rations to which they are entitled are available on a regular basis and without problems and that to this extent the provisioning of the population is considerably better than in the [First] World War.

---

### (vii) Air Raids, the Government's Response and the Impact on Morale

A key factor influencing morale on the home front, particularly from the spring of 1942 onwards, was the air war; but its impact though large was also complex and is not easy to assess. Some 305,000 Germans were killed and 780,000 injured in air raids and nearly two million homes were destroyed.[29] However, the initial response seems to have evoked a degree of solidarity among the affected population and a determination to try and get back to normal as soon as possible. The first major raid in the campaign of mass bombing of civilian targets by the RAF, designed by Air Marshal Arthur Harris, the chief of Bomber Command, to break the morale of the German population, took place on the night of 28–9 March 1942. The target, a test case, was Lübeck, a small, historic and beautiful city near the Baltic coast in north-west Germany. It was

[29] See Overy, *The Penguin Historical Atlas of the Third Reich* (Harmondsworth 1996), p. 102.

selected because its narrow mediaeval streets and half-timbered buildings lent themselves well to the use of incendiaries intended to create a firestorm. Around 8,000 incendiaries were dropped as well as 'liquid bombs' made of petrol and rubber with high explosives. On 9 April the SD filed the following report on the raid:

**1309** According to a final report from Lübeck summarizing the effects of the heavy British air raid which took place on the night of 28/9 March 1942, the population of Lübeck showed a really remarkable composure, despite the extreme destruction and loss of life This was mainly the result of the readiness to assist those compatriots who suffered damage shown by all sections of the population during the several waves of bombing and, in addition, of the work of the Wehrmacht, the Reich Railways and similar units, as also of the immediate deployment of craftsmen from outside. The HJ, BdM, and NSV have been particularly praised by the population for their tireless commitment free from any petty bureaucracy, and for providing the first practical help through the provision of food, clothing and care for the injured and homeless. Never before has the sense of community and sense of belonging been so clearly demonstrated as during that night.

The rescue operations during the attack benefited from the fact that many members of the Wehrmacht were on weekend leave and made themselves available without waiting for orders from above and gave active assistance. During the raid, the population remained calm and disciplined in an exemplary manner, although it was the first major raid they had experienced. It was only this fact that enabled the rescue organizations to save numerous compatriots by getting them out of the cellars of the burning houses which soon afterwards collapsed. However, the fight against incendiaries was hampered by the fact that numerous occupants were not at home on a Saturday evening and that many occupants, because of their lack of experience, had failed to search their houses for incendiaries. Moreover, the lack of hoses, water, sand, pickaxes and crowbars etc. for breaking through into cellars proved disadvantageous because otherwise numerous losses could have been avoided.

There was a mixed response on the part of the population to the performance of the local Security and Aid Service.[30] It was reported that the SHD Lübeck had hitherto had no previous experience and was largely composed of elderly men. However, the SHD from Hamburg, which was brought in later, performed exceptionally well on account of its previous experience; the help provided by outside fire engines was also praised.

The provision of vital necessities in the immediate aftermath of the raid proved particularly difficult because a large number of the grocers and butchers, restaurants etc. had been destroyed. However, these problems were soon dealt

---

[30] The Security and Aid Service (*Sicherheits und Hilfsdienst* = SHD*)* was the organization responsible for dealing with air raids—rescuing people from collapsed buildings etc.

with through the acquisition of food supplies from Hamburg, Kiel, Stettin etc. and through the setting up of canteens.

It was a sign of the calm, determined attitude and the unbroken spirit of the people of Lübeck that on the very next day numerous tradespeople demonstrated their unbroken spirit by opening their shops, despite the damage, with placards saying things like 'Here life goes on as usual' and 'We are selling air raid butter'. It should also be mentioned that, already on the Monday, 70 per cent of the employees turned up for work in most Lübeck plants, despite having to clear up in their damaged flats.

The flak defences were generally not criticized by the population, particularly as it was known that Lübeck was only sparsely protected by flak . . .

The population was more annoyed by the report in the OKW communiqué on Sunday which stated among other things that Lübeck had been attacked by British bombers and that the civilian population had suffered 'some losses'. This minimizing formulation of the Wehrmacht communiqué had the effect of undermining the credibility of the Wehrmacht communiqués among the Lübeck population. Many compatriots used more or less strong language in their comments on this kind of reporting, particularly since the Lübeck newspaper, the *Lübecker Volksbote,* which appeared the following day, printed in Hamburg, reported in great detail the sports events of the week but restricted its account of the Lübeck raid to the Wehrmacht communiqué. Since the radio was out of action because of a power cut, people literally tore the newspapers out of the newsvendors' hands in order to get news and so their disappointment was very great. However, this critical attitude was reduced by the appearance of additional information in the press during the following days.

————

The most appalling examples of firestorms created by Allied air raids occurred in the cities of Hamburg on the night of 27–8 July 1943, which killed some 35,000–40,000 people, and Dresden on 13–14 February 1945, which killed a similar number. In the seven raids on Hamburg between 25 July and 3 August, which involved around 3,000 British and US aircraft, at least 42,000 people were killed and over 100,000 injured; more than 40,000 blocks of flats with around 225,000 flats, 24 hospitals, 277 schools, 580 industrial plants and some 3,000 other businesses were destroyed. The following document contains excerpts from the report of the Police President of Hamburg on the these raids:

**1310** The impression created by viewing a burnt-out city pales beside the fire itself: the howling of the firestorm, the cries and moans of the dying and the crashes of the falling bombs.

The reason for the damage being so serious and, above all, for the unusual number of deaths compared with previous raids is the fact that firestorms developed. They, and in particular the one during the second major attack on the night of 27/8 July, created a situation which must be described as novel and hitherto inconceivable in every respect . . .

Firestorms and their characteristics are established phenomena well known in the history of urban fires. The physical explanation for them is simple. As a result of a combination of a number of fires the air overhead becomes heated to such an extent that, because of its reduced specific gravity, it develops a tremendous upward pressure which creates a very strong suction effect on the surrounding air masses pulling them towards the centre of the fire in a radial direction. As a result of the firestorm and, in particular, the tremendous suction effect, winds are produced which are even stronger than the well-known wind strengths [1–12]. As in the case of meteorology so also in the case of firestorms the air movement is produced by a rebalancing of differences of temperature. But, while in the case of meteorology these temperatures are generally of the order of 20–30 degrees Celsius, in the case of firestorms there are temperature differences of 600 or even 1,000 degrees. This explains the huge force generated by the firestorms which cannot be compared with normal meteorological processes . . .

The development of a firestorm is encouraged or hampered by the architectural conditions of an affected area in the same way as by the type, extent and size of the original fires. In Hamburg the firestorms originated in areas in which the buildings were close together and densely populated and in which, therefore, the type and density of the buildings affected already provided favourable preconditions for the development of a firestorm. The affected areas in Hamburg were characterized by narrow streets with big blocks of flats with large numbers of courtyards, terraces etc. In these yards fireballs could develop very rapidly which became, in the truest sense of the word, mantraps. The narrow streets formed fire channels through which the long flames were whipped.

As a result of the concentric enemy attacks and the heavy concentration of incendiaries a huge number of fires developed in such areas in a very short time. It should be noted in particular that there were not only roof fires but, as a result of phosphor bombs and liquid [petrol and rubber] bombs, in many areas large blocks of flats were suddenly set alight from the bottom floor. The fires could develop with incredible speed since roofs had been torn off, walls had caved in, windows and doors had been torn out of their frames or smashed by concentrated attacks with high-explosive bombs and mines and on these the fires could feed without any hindrance. For these reasons, the intermediate stage of the fire's development, which in the case of previous raids it was possible to combat and which produced some of the biggest successes of the Hamburg civil defence forces, did not occur. For in many places extensive fires developed in a very short time. And because of the laws of physics, which have been outlined above, a firestorm developed in every one of these districts where there was an extensive fire. The suction effect of the firestorm in the larger or largest of these extensive fire areas had the effect of pulling in the already superheated air of the smaller fire areas. So the cores of the most ferocious fire areas sucked the fires from the smaller fire areas towards them. As a result of this phenomenon, fires in the smaller fire areas were pumped up as if by bellows, since the central suction effect of the largest and strongest extensive fires had the effect of pulling in the surrounding masses of fresh air. In consequence, all the fires grew into a single huge conflagration . . .

In order to form an impression of this massive firestorm which was created from countless smaller fires, one must bear in mind that, for example, the area affected by the major raids on 28 July was some 5.5km long and 4km wide, i.e. 22 sq. km in extent . . .

The speed with which the fires and firestorm developed negated all plans and every attempt by the population to fight them. Houses which in the previous raids had been able to be saved by the brave actions of the civil defence and other forces, fell victim to the flames. In many cases escape routes were cut off before the need to escape became apparent.

After the alarm was sounded, the civil defence forces waited in their shelter, the firefighters in the extended civil defence and factory defence units were at their posts awaiting the start and progress of the raid. Sticks of high-explosive bombs shattered the houses down to their foundations. Already a short time after the first explosive bombs had fallen, a huge number of fires had started as a result of a massive amount of incendiaries mixed with high-explosive bombs. People who now wanted to leave their shelters in order to see what was happening or to fight the fire were met by a sea of flames. Everything around them was on fire. There was no water and, in view of the huge number of fires and their extent, any attempt to put out the fire was useless from the start . . .

The fact that even now on some days up to a hundred or more corpses are being found and removed provides only a feeble impression of what happened. Overall, the destruction is so devastating that, in the case of many people, there is literally nothing left of them. On the basis of a layer of ashes in a large air raid shelter, doctors could only provide a rough estimate of the number of people who died there, a figure of 250–300. It will only be possible to produce an exact figure when all the people who were living in Hamburg at that time who are still alive have once more registered with the authorities.

The horrific scenes which occurred in the area of the firestorm are indescribable. Children were torn from the hands of their parents by the tornado and whirled into the flames. People who thought they had saved themselves collapsed in a few minutes in the overwhelmingly destructive force of the heat. People who were fleeing had to make their way through the dead and the dying. The sick and frail had to be left behind by the rescuers since they themselves were in danger of burning . . .

And each one of these nights of fire and flames was followed by a day which revealed the horror in the pale and unreal light of a smoke-covered sky. The heat of high summer, increased to an intolerable degree by the embers of the firestorm, the finest of dust particles from the churned-up earth and the ruins and rubble of the destroyed city which penetrated everywhere, soot and ashes raining down, and again heat and dust, and over everything a pestilential smell of decomposing bodies and smouldering fires bore down on the population.

And these days were followed by new nights with new horrors, even more smoke and soot, heat and dust, with still more death and destruction. People were given no time to rest or to plan the rescue of their belongings or to look for their relatives. The enemy drove on with ceaseless attacks until the work of destruction had been completed. His hatred revelled in the firestorms which mercilessly destroyed people and things with equal force.

The seemingly utopian [*sic!*] vision of a major city in rapid disintegration without gas, water, light and transport, with formerly flourishing residential districts turned into deserts of stone, had become reality.

The streets were covered with hundreds of corpses. Mothers with their children, men, old people, burnt, charred, unscathed and clothed, naked and pale like wax dummies in a shop window, they lay in every position, quiet and peaceful, or tense with their death throes written in the expressions on their faces. The situation in the air raid shelters was the same and made an even more gruesome impression because, in some cases, it showed the last desperate struggle which had taken place against a merciless fate. Whereas in one place the occupants were sitting quietly on their chairs, peaceful and unscathed as if they were sleeping and had unsuspectingly been killed by carbon monoxide gas, elsewhere the existence of the fragments of bones and skulls showed how the occupants had sought to flee and find refuge from their prison tomb.

It will be impossible for anybody ever to imagine or conceive the horrific and gruesome scenes which must have occurred in numerous air raid shelters which were buried. Posterity will only be able to maintain a respectful silence in the face of the fate of these innocents who fell victim to the bloodthirstiness of a sadistic enemy.

The behaviour of the population which at no time and nowhere displayed signs of panic and was worthy of the greatness of this sacrifice showed its commitment. It befitted the Hanseatic spirit and character which, during the raids, found its finest expression in comradeship and assistance and solidarity and, after the raid, demonstrated through its deeds an unshakeable determination to rebuild the city.

▬▬▬

The reality was rather different than suggested in the final paragraph, as Mathilde Wolff-Mönckeberg, a middle-class woman living in Hamburg, recorded in a letter to her children:

**1311**  The following morning Maria reported that all women and children had to be evacuated from the city within six hours. There was no gas, no electricity, not a drop of water, neither the lift nor the telephone was working. It is hard to imagine the panic and chaos. Each one for himself, only one idea: flight. We too—W. raced to the police station for our exit permits. There were endless queues , but our permits were issued because we had a place to go to. But how could we travel? No trains could leave from Hamburg because all the stations had been gutted, and so Harburg was the nearest. There were no trams, no underground, no rail-traffic to the suburbs. Most people loaded some belongings on carts, bicycles, prams or carried things on their backs and started on foot just to get away, to escape. A long stream of human beings flooded along the Sierichstrasse, thousands were prepared to camp out, anything rather than stay in this catastrophic inferno in the city. During the night, the suburbs of Hamm, Hammerbrock, Rothenburgsort and Barmbeck had been almost razed to the ground. People who had fled from collapsing bunkers and had got stuck in huge crowds in the streets had burning phosphorus poured over them, rushed into the next air raid shelter and were shot in order not to spread the flames. In the midst of the fire and the attempts to quench it, women had their babies in the streets. Parents and children were separated and torn apart in this frightful upheaval of surging humanity and never found each other again. It must have been indescribably gruesome. Everyone had just one thought: to get away. W. tried vainly for some kind of vehicle. Most people in our house made hasty impromptu arrangements, carrying bits and pieces into the cellar, and we also towed away a few things. Since nobody could cook, communal kitchens were organized. But wherever people gathered together, more unrest ensued. People wearing party badges had them torn off their coats and there were screams of 'Let's get that murderer.' The police did nothing.

The NSV tried to revive morale by providing lorry-loads of food and drink, including items in short supply such as chocolate and real coffee. This was already part of the regime's strategy for dealing with air raids, as the following letter from the Reich Minister for Food and Agriculture to the Gauleiters dated 24 September 1942 indicates:

**1312**     Following the meeting with the Gauleiters of the districts vulnerable to air attack on 16 and 17 September 1942, I hereby give the following instructions:

I. The population of those cities and places which, in addition to a large number of air raid warnings, are subject to serious raids or, with a smaller number of air raid warnings, are subject to repeated and serious raids may be granted a supplementary meat ration of 50g per head per week . . .

The Gauleiters determine on the basis of their own conscientious assessment and within the parameters of their allocation to which cities and places and the periods for which the special ration cards will be allotted. They will utilize the Food Offices to implement this allocation.

II. In the event of catastrophes [i.e. heavy raids] in which the water, gas, or electricity supplies are seriously disrupted, the Gauleiters will be empowered to grant special allocations of fats, meat and bread for up to three days on a pro rata basis linked to the allocation for a normal consumer. The special allocations can be granted to a whole city or, depending on the circumstances, be restricted to particular districts of the city. The special allocations will be delivered through the issuing of special food cards . . .

III. The previous practice whereby, with my permission, in individual cases, after serious raids, special grants of items on the margins of the food-rationing system, such as, for example, real coffee, sweets, spirits etc. can be made depending on the available supplies will not be affected by these regulations. I will endeavour to ensure speedy delivery as far as I can. Thus, for example, there are already certain amounts of raw coffee stored with major distributors in vulnerable areas which can be roasted at once if need be.

IV. In addition I shall continue priority deliveries of vegetables, fruit, fish and fish products, spirits etc. to those Gaus which are particularly vulnerable and expand them as much as possible . . .

_____

After major raids in Essen, for example, the local Gauleiter would distribute 50g of proper coffee and half a bottle of brandy to each adult, which came to be popularly known as 'shiver coffee/brandy' (Zitterkaffee/Cognac), and 125g of sweets to children. Also, those bombed out received free meals from mobile canteens for the first three days after the raid.

However, extra food supplies did not go far in solving the problems facing those who had been bombed out and lost their homes and/or possessions. Two factors were crucial to the maintenance of morale in the aftermath of air raids: the provision of alternative accommodation for those who had been bombed out and adequate compensation for the damage to personal property, personal injury, and disruption to family life produced by the air raids. By spring 1943,[31] the following standard instructions were being issued on what to do in the event of being made homeless in an air raid:

**1313**        *Instructions for the Care of the Population after Air Raids*

1. Compatriots who become *homeless* as a result of air raids should go to the nearest *assembly point* indicated through a house notice or in some other way. There they will be fed and if necessary be given the necessary articles of clothing etc. If they do not wish to stay in the place where they are, or in the surrounding area (Gau), or in the designated reception districts; they will be assigned accommodation by the assembly point.

*for —— the following Gaus have been designated: ——* [32]

2. It is permitted to secure *accommodation with relatives* throughout the Reich (Relatives' Aid).* To secure *accommodation with relatives* it is necessary to fill out a '*Relatives' Registration Card*' (available from the NSV).[33]
3. *People should not leave the area before having registered with the assembly point* so that those who have gone off without registering are not counted as missing persons.

_____

[31] I have not been able to establish when these instructions were first introduced. This form was part of a document dated 19 April 1943.
[32] e.g. for Hamburg, Schleswig-Holstein, Bayreuth, Hanover-East, Mark Brandenburg and Danzig were the designated 'Reception Gaus'.
[33] This was introduced to prevent people with Polish relatives staying with them in the mixed German-Polish districts in eastern Germany. The relatives would be inspected by the local NSV.

4. *People should only move to the designated reception Gau*, otherwise they will be refused accommodation and will subsequently have to be transferred to the reception Gau (those securing accommodation with relatives are exempt).

5. After settling in their accommodation people should *in all cases immediately register their arrival and departure with the police.*

6. Those people being rehoused outside their home district will receive a *written confirmation of their move* at the assembly point (essential proof for acquiring food ration books, coupons, maintenance payments etc.).

7. People who have suffered air raid damage who are staying in their home district will receive an *Air Raid Damaged Person's card.*

8. *Food ration cards, coupons, advance cash payments, maintenance payments etc.* will be handed out at the assembly points.

9. For those staying in their home districts the following agencies will later be responsible for

the *replacement of food ration cards*—the Food Office; *the issuing of coupons* for destroyed or lost household items—the Economic Office; claims for compensation for *damage to property* and *loss of use*—the Assessment Office; for *personal injury claims*—the local council (also the Welfare Office: *Versorgungsamt*).

10. *Further information* will in all cases be provided by the local council (town hall, mayor, district office of the (Lord) Mayor, also the District Office of the Government: *Landratsamt*).

11. *Those rehoused outside their home districts* will be accommodated by the NSV at their place of reception. They will go with their Confirmation of Departure Certificate to the Food and Economic Offices to be issued with the requisite food ration cards, coupons etc. They will apply for *family maintenance payments* to the mayor or District Officer (information will be provided by the local council).

12. To prevent unnecessary burdens on the transport system every return journey which is not absolutely necessary should be avoided.

*Only valid for Evacuation Gaus and those cities to which the rehousing of sections of the population is permitted.

▬▬

The issue of accommodation was particularly problematic because, even before the war, Germany had been suffering from a serious housing shortage. Building had come to a virtual standstill during the depression of 1929–33 and then the Nazi regime had given priority to rearmament during the 1930s. At the beginning of 1939 there was an estimated shortage of 1.5 million dwellings. With the Allied bombing campaign of 1942–5, the housing situation became progressively worse, putting even more strain on the housing market. As a result, there was growing pressure from those responsible for providing accommodation, including local Party officials, for state controls on housing and, in particular, powers to sequestrate empty flats, houses or rooms which were not being fully utilized. However, housing controls had been imposed during and after the First World War and had been very unpopular, and Hitler was highly sensitive about anything which might generate unpopularity as well as being unsympathetic to bureaucratic controls. He therefore resisted the imposition of such measures as is clear from the following correspondence, which additionally provides an interesting example of Hitler's intervention on a domestic issue during the war. On 8 May 1941 the Reich Labour Ministry, largely responsible for housing matters, wrote to all the top regional governmental authorities as follows:

**1314** As a result of the housing shortage, I have been frequently approached with suggestions for measures of various kinds to provide accommodation for those seeking it—for example, through official intervention in the rental sector to assign accommodation or other measures to take over rooms which have become vacant and are not being re-let or are insufficiently utilized. These suggestions propose in effect the reintroduction of the previous system of housing controls. In view of the great political significance of such measures, I have been in contact with the Führer's Deputy. He has told me in a letter of 23 April of a decision by the Führer and a circular to all Gauleiters of 26 March 1941 of which I enclose a copy.

The Führer's Deputy                                        26 April 1941
Chief of Staff

*Circular to all Gauleiters*

Various suggestions have been made to utilize housing which is not being used or fully used in order to provide for those seeking accommodation and to do so by means of sequestration.

For your information, the Führer has strongly objected to a proposal to issue legal regulations along those lines, although it concerns a district which was very badly affected by the housing shortage. The Führer gave as his reason the fact that such measures could not produce a really noticeable improvement in the housing crisis. On the other hand, according to all experience hitherto, such sequestration usually led to an unpleasant situation The Führer is of the opinion that, after the war, really comprehensive measures must be taken to resolve the housing crisis. It is, therefore, inadvisable to initiate stopgap measures now which will necessarily prove inadequate.

However, as the air raids intensified and the damage to the housing stock and the numbers of homeless increased, it proved impossible to resist pressure for introduction of housing controls. On 21 June 1943 the Government introduced the Decree for the Provision of Accommodation for the People Affected by Air Raids, of which Section C provided for the sequestration of under-used dwellings and rooms. Landlords were soon receiving the following standard form, which was issued on 7 July 1943:

**1315**    In the recent survey of accommodation for bombed-out homeless people or those who require to be rehoused for safety reasons carried out by the NSV in Gau —— you kindly agreed to place —— rooms at our disposal/ —— rooms suitable for accommodation were noted in your house/flat.

These rooms can continue to be used for your own purposes until they are taken by homeless people etc.; however, they are to be kept ready in the event of their being needed for accommodation.

In order to secure these rooms for the purposes of accommodation, I am obliged—on behalf of the District Officer [*Landrat*] in accordance with §25 together with §5 of the Reich Services Law [*Reichsleistungsgesetz*] of 1.9.1939[34] to sequestrate them. As already mentioned, this sequestration does not prevent the temporary use of these rooms for your own purposes. It does, however, have the effect that, without my permission any legal actions taken in connection with these rooms will be null and void in so far as they would prevent their use for accommodation as indicated. Also, any building alterations which might have a deleterious effect on their use for accommodation as indicated may not be carried out without my permission.

Appeals against this sequestration may be made to me or to the District Officer District Governor [*Regierungspräsident*] in ——.

As the raids grew in intensity, the German Government produced an elaborate system of compensation payments. This was regulated above all by two decrees issued in November 1940: the Personal Injury Decree [*Personenschädenverordnung*] of 10 November 1940 and the War Damage Decree [*Kriegsschädenverordnung*] of 30 November 1940. According to the instructions for implementing the War Damage Decree the procedure was as follows:

**1316**    *Initial Measure*

Arrangements have been made so that, following air raids in which bombs have been dropped [i.e. not propaganda leaflets], aid centres will be set up involving the collaboration of the local Party officials, the Economic and Food Offices, the city police, and the local Welfare Administration [*Verwaltung Volkspflege*]. The action units set up by the Welfare Administration have the task of paying sums in advance as compensation for personal injury and material damage in accordance with specific directives. Those who have suffered material damage will, at the same time as the advance payment, be issued with a printed 'Application for Compensation in accordance with the War Damage Decree of 30.11.1940' together with a list to fill in of the items damaged. They will be instructed to hand the filled-in form to the War Damage Office. In the event of a loss of

---

[34] This was a very important law which enabled the Government to sequestrate any form of property or demand the use of it for war purposes in return for compensation.

income and additional expenditure the relevant form should also be handed out. Advance payments will in general not be made for this type of damage.

This measure will ensure that those who have suffered damage will receive adequate and immediate assistance.

———

Standard forms were printed for people to claim compensation as follows:

**1317**   To Frau ——

In ——

Re: your compensation claim on account of the war damage to your flat, No. —— Street caused by the air raid on —— I am issuing the following preliminary

*Notification*

in accordance with §§19 & 20 of the War Damage Decree of 30.11.1940:

1. The German Reich recognizes your claim for compensation for damage, destruction or other form of loss of household goods. We reserve the right to make a final assessment of the amount of compensation to be granted.
2. We have assessed that, on the basis of pre-war prices, your damage amounts to at least RM —— .

On the basis of this assessment you will be granted compensation of this amount. Any advance payments will be based on this amount.

3. On presentation of this preliminary notification you may receive advance payments for the immediate repair or replacement of household goods.

*Grounds*

In accordance with the War Damage Decree the German Reich will provide full compensation for compatriots who have suffered damage to property caused by enemy action. It thus recognizes in principle your compensation claim for damage, destruction or other forms of loss to your property.

Since armaments production must now have priority over every other form of production, only a small amount of household equipment can be currently produced. The full replacement of household equipment which has been lost will normally only be possible after the war. The decision on the final amount of your compensation will thus be left until the full replacement or repair of your household goods occurs.

In order to provide you with the means to pay for repairs or replacements which may currently be possible, your damage has been provisionally assessed on the basis of pre-war prices. The following is the detailed assessment.

*[Reverse side]*

This provides the basis for the compensation sum referred to above. You may receive advance payments from the Assessment Office at any time up to the amount of this sum after the deduction of any previous advance payments so that you may immediately replace or repair your household goods.

The compensation promised to you provides an indication of the sum of money which you will later have to cover your replacement purchases. This is intended above all to restrain you from purchasing less important and more expensive items before you have replaced the more urgently needed furniture, clothing, linen and utensils. You must provide proof of the use of an advance payment by presenting receipts before you may receive any further advance payments.

*Appeal procedure*

You may appeal against the notification within two weeks of its receipt. This procedure is also open to the representative of the Reich's interests. The appeal should be made in writing to the Compensation Office referred to above, mentioning the reference number.

▬

The extent of the compensation available to those who had suffered bomb damage is clear from the following statement, which appeared in the press at the beginning of December 1944:

**1318**   *Compensation for Resettlement Costs*

In order to clear up any doubts the President of the Reich War Damage Office has announced details of the circumstances in which the Reich will provide compensation for the travelling and rehousing expenses which those who have been bombed out may incur. According to this statement, the costs incurred by a bombed out person for the purpose of renting alternative accommodation, in particular travel expenses, will count as additional expenses, in accordance with the regulations governing damages for current expenses.

The Compensation Authority will examine each individual case to see whether and how far these expenses should be compensated. Expenses incurred by aimless travelling around or through journeys to Reich Gaus which are not reception Gaus will, on principle, not be compensated. Compensation for expenses incurred by a bombed-out person in order to visit his family who have been accommodated elsewhere cannot be granted under the Damage Law. Grants will be given for this purpose from the budget of the Evacuated Families Maintenance Fund.

A similar situation exists in the case of the additional expenses incurred by bombed-out persons in travelling to their place of work. If a bombed-out person resides together with his rehoused family away from his previous domicile and travels from there daily to his place of work, then he too will receive a grant from the Evacuated Families Maintenance Fund. Furthermore, the increased cost of board which rehoused families incur can be compensated at an appropriate level on the grounds that it represents additional expenditure in those cases where meals need to be taken in restaurants.

The Evacuated Families Maintenance Fund can also provide refunds for bombed-out persons who have remained behind while their families have been rehoused elsewhere by assessing the amount which they have to pay in maintenance for their family members who have been settled elsewhere. The extra amount involved will be met by the Evacuated Families Maintenance Fund. Even the expenses of bombed-out persons for services of all kinds, in particular tips to expedite the removal of furniture, will be refunded by the Reich at an appropriate level.

Naturally, so-called bribes [*Schmiergelder*] will not be refunded. Expenses incurred by bombed-out persons for putting up family members who have been called up and who have to be accommodated elsewhere while on leave may be refunded. Finally, the increased costs incurred by parents who have to pay increased travel expenses for their children to go to school after their flat has been destroyed may receive grants from the Evacuated Families Maintenance Fund.

The bombing could generate feelings of defiance towards the enemy which tended to reinforce ties of solidarity. This attitude is exemplified by the young Prussian noblewoman, Ursula von Kardorff, who was unsympathetic to the regime, but who wrote in her diary after a major raid on Berlin on 30 January 1944:

**1319**    3 February 1944

I feel a growing sense of vitality within me mixed with defiance, the opposite of resignation. Is that what the English are trying to achieve with their attacks on the civilian population? At any rate, they are not softening us up in the process. Everyone is preoccupied with their own affairs. Is my block of flats still standing? Where can I get roof slates, cardboard for windows? Where is the best air raid shelter? The catastrophes which are hitting the Nazis and the anti-Nazis equally are binding the nation together. After every raid special rations are issued: cigarettes, real coffee, meat. 'Give them bread and they will go along with you.' That's what Dostoevsky's Grand Inquisitor said. But if the British think they are going to undermine our morale they are barking up the wrong tree.

Nevertheless, it is clear that the anxiety and disruption to everyday life caused by the air raids, and not least by the air raid warnings, forcing people into air raid shelters, often for hours at a time night after night, had a generally demoralizing effect. In 1944, for example, the city of Cologne had an air raid warning once a day and an air raid twice a week. In a post-war survey of morale 91 per cent of those interviewed said that bombing was the worst hardship to bear followed a long way after by food shortages with 10 per cent.[35]

The increasing amount of time spent in air raid shelters could cause problems other than stress and loss of sleep, problems which revealed

---

[35] See Overy, op. cit., p. 103.

themselves early on in the war as the President of the Higher State Court in the Westphalian industrial city of Hamm noted in his report to the Reich Justice Ministry dated 7 November 1940:

**1320** Unfortunately, there has been a large increase in the number of private court actions . . . The disputes often derive from the time spent together in the air raid shelters. A judge responsible for private court actions in a large district court reports on this as follows:

A review of the individual cases reveals that unsuitable compatriots, including above all women, have frequently been appointed as civil defence house wardens. The police or rather the civil defence organization is not really to blame for this. Unfortunately, many suitable compatriots have previously declined to take up such a post. Compatriots who live in individual houses and who are regarded as outsiders in the neighbourhood and as not easy to get on with have often been appointed. The inevitable result is that there are tensions from the start.

It has become apparent that the civil defence house wardens and also to some extent the block wardens often misconceive the office to which they have been appointed. This happens, on the one hand, because they give out instructions, which are essentially correct, in an inappropriate manner, often even in an offensive, peremptory tone of voice. But there are an even greater number of cases in which they issue orders when they are not entitled to do so. Quite often, existing personal differences are the cause of further quarrels. The functions of the office and personal affairs are not kept separated from each other.

On the other hand, there are also numerous compatriots who impertinently criticize the legitimate sensible measures of the air raid wardens. In the case of incorrect measures they do not contact the superior office in order to reach an understanding. Disputes and personal attacks occur which are not restricted to the initial cause. Often other compatriots join in. There are quarrels which expand to such an extent that, finally, the air raid house warden, the Block Warden, the occupants of the block of flats, the neighbours, and even the owner of the block of flats become involved. There are enough issues to dispute about. Those which have been particularly evident are: inadequate fulfilment of the blackout regulations, not going to the air raid shelter in time, the furnishing and equipping of the air raid shelter as well as the distribution of the costs for it.; topics of conversation of a political nature (the war, night-time air raids); conversations about the distribution of ration points, the allocation of shoes and clothing, the issuing of cards granting priority in shops. In general, it can be said that the close contact of compatriots often provides a welcome opportunity for denigrating others, particularly those who are not there. This particular compatriot is in the view of others in the air raid shelter unsuitably or inadequately dressed when the alarm goes. Another leaves the air raid shelter and has a smoke on the stairs. Another takes somebody's usual place or the place where one can sit. A fourth according to the others is drinking alcohol when it is not permitted. A fifth isn't quiet enough. Children are playing and making a noise so that a sixth won't come into the air raid shelter at all. All these points are endlessly discussed. Harmless discussions between people whose sleep has been disturbed and who are, therefore, in any case irritable too often end in shouting matches or even punch-ups.

———

Air raid shelters were notorious centres for the exchange of rumours, a fact that was sometimes exploited by the Propaganda Ministry to plant rumours which they wanted the population to believe.

As the air raids continued so they began to have an increasingly debilitating effect on the population, leading to a loss of sympathy and support for the regime. With an attack on Essen on the night of the 5/6 March 1943, a series of major raids on Western Germany began, of which there were forty-three between then and the end of July. On 17 June 1943 the SD reported on the effects of these raids on morale:

**1321**    The reports which have come in from all over the Reich are unanimous in the view that the urban and rural populations are increasingly concerned about the state of the air war and the effects of the latest terror raids by the British–American air force on the west German cities and by the questions they raise. Almost all the reports state that in those areas which are not affected, in particular in central, south, and east Germany, exaggerated descriptions and, in particular, figures of those killed are circulating and being believed and, as a result, the fear of air raids is spreading to even the most remote villages. There has been widespread fellow feeling expressed for the compatriots from West Germany who have been affected after details of the raids on Wuppertal-Barmen and Düsseldorf, some of them correct and some highly distorted, had been recounted by evacuees and eyewitnesses in all parts of the Reich. This has once again intensified the hatred against England and increased the demands for speedy retaliation for these raids, which, following the declaration by Reich Minister Dr Goebbels in his most recent speech in the Berlin Sports Palace, must now definitely be anticipated . . .

Despite the comparatively rapid response of the emergency services, help for the homeless was made very difficult by the effects of the catastrophe and by the fact that the number of homeless went into the hundreds of thousands, in particular since many of the assembly points had been destroyed by bombs and the compatriots sought and found accommodation with acquaintances.

The special allocation of provisions, which was immediately announced, had a beneficial effect; however, the wish was frequently expressed that these special allocations *should be given out to those who had been bombed out straightaway in the emergency aid centres,* since because of the lack of documentation many feared that they would be unable to claim them.

After the attacks the population appeared completely exhausted and apathetic. Most of the compatriots who had been totally bombed out were, however, *cheerful and glad to have got away with their lives.* The number of individual tragedies initially overshadowed all other considerations.

While the population of the affected areas *in general demonstrated* an *exemplary attitude* and calmly accepted the fate which had befallen them, there were *on a small scale signs of a pragmatic attitude*. A few opponents who emerged made hostile remarks about the State, the Party and the leadership. There were frequent cases in which it was observed that inquisitive people who frequented the bomb sites tried to incite those who had suffered bomb damage. There were also numerous cases in which compatriots *who have lost their nerve* on account of the catastrophe *make negative comments* and allow themselves to be led into making remarks hostile to the state. A typical case is the remark of a compatriot from Düsseldorf, who said, in the presence of an SS man: 'The Führer's to blame for this'. When the SS man forcibly took him to task, he explained that his nerves were in such a state that he no longer knew how he came to make such a remark. In Barmen there was the case of a mother who was found standing in front of her ruined house in which the bodies of her son, her daughter-in-law, and her two-year-old grandchild were lying and was weeping in a state of shock. Two SA men went to comfort her, but the woman shouted out loud: 'The brown cadets are to blame for this war. They should have gone to the front and made sure that the English were unable to come here.' It is also striking that the German greeting is used only very rarely in those cities which have been hit; instead people greet each other ostentatiously with 'good morning' . . . Typical of this attitude is the following joke that has been told in many parts of the Reich for some time:

A Berliner and an Essener are comparing the extent of destruction in each of their two cities. The Berliner says that the bombing in Berlin was so bad that even five hours after the raid the windows were still falling out of the houses. The Essener replies that that was nothing, for in Essen fourteen days after the last air raid the pictures of the Führer were flying out of the windows.

As a result of such accounts, many compatriots will be inclined to generalize these things. Remarkably, however, those who had lost everything grumbled less than those who had only suffered slight damage or none at all.

To summarize, the reports state that, apart from such individual instances, the population of the air raid districts' behaviour is impeccable and there is just a sense of defencelessness and helplessness vis-à-vis the air raids, which will, however, disappear as soon as the counter-attacks, which have been announced, take place.

■■■

The cities most affected by these raids tended to be in the Rhineland and Westphalia, among them Cologne and Aachen. On 22 July 1943 the SD produced the following 'Report on the terror raids on Cologne and Aachen and their impact on the public mood':

**1322**    The raid on Cologne on 8/9 July was the third and felt to be the worst because it disrupted the attempts to get back to normal after the devastation caused by the first two. Nevertheless, the reports emphasize that the population's behaviour continued to be good. Compatriots maintained their composure and clearly tried to show guts and to cope with this new blow of fate as well. This attitude could be observed not only in the case of Party comrades but also in the case of the rest of the population, even among arch-Catholic circles which were hostile to National Socialism.

According to reports from Aachen, there too the sorely tried population had put up with the raid with remarkable composure. However, here, as in the case of Cologne, there were a lot of complaints. For example, above all, one kept hearing that the Rhineland had evidently been written off by Berlin. Based on the reports in the press and on the radio, people reckoned that the population in the other parts of the Reich were not informed about the true situation in west Germany. One could see this best from the way the evacuees were treated in the reception Gaus. It was necessary to give the whole nation an idea of what conditions the population in the bombed cities had to live under for weeks on end. The necessity—because of the suspension of public transport—of having to go to work over piles of rubble and through clouds of dust; the impossibility of washing oneself properly or of cooking at home because there was no water, gas or electricity; the sudden value acquired by a spoon or a plate which had been rescued; the difficulty of shopping for food because most of the shops had been destroyed or had closed of their own accord; the continual explosions of delayed action bombs or duds or the blowing-up of parts of buildings which were in danger of collapsing; the delay in postal deliveries, the stopping of newspapers; the impossibility of listening to the radio because the electricity had been cut off; the disappearance of every means of relaxation such as the cinema, the theatre, concerts etc.—these were aspects of a life which was being lived as if on the front line and of which people in the rest of the Reich had no idea.

The population of these cities consider the emphasis in the Wehrmacht report and in propaganda on the damage to Cologne cathedral or on the completely insignificant 'scratch' on the roof of Aachen cathedral represents a playing down of the serious damage to residential areas and above all of the loss of life. One frequently hears the comment that such incidents enable one to test the accuracy of the Wehrmacht report. Apart from that, the conversations and remarks of compatriots basically consist of people saying with a deep sigh: 'when will these raids come to an end?' There is still a lot of talk of retaliation but a large number of compatriots cannot really believe in it. At least many comment that the *retaliation will come too late for west Germany* given the fact that the largest and most important cities have already been almost completely destroyed. Also many compatriots who had been totally or severely bombed out could no longer really believe that the war would have a positive outcome. Specifically anti-State or anti-Party comments are fairly rare but such remarks are made in public without inhibition . . .

The most vital problem for the population of the bombed cities is rehousing [*Umquartierung*].[36] The idea of a 'compulsory evacuation' is very unpopular with compatriots. A large number initially find accommodation with relatives or acquaintances in the city itself or in the immediately surrounding area. From there they seek a place to stay with relatives or acquaintances elsewhere in the

---

[36] The Nazis used the term rehousing [*Umquartierung*] rather than evacuation [*Evakuierung*] because they had already mocked the British evacuation programmes in 1939–40 in their propaganda.

Reich. They insist that people who know each other or are relatives can get on better in closely confined conditions than people who are total strangers and who were brought together in accordance with some schematic evacuation plan. The compatriots would, so the reports indicate, resist being removed from areas in which they have found a place to stay with relatives or acquaintances *because these areas are not the 'official' reception Gaus for them.*

▬▬

The references to 'retaliation' and 'counter-blows' in the SD report of 17 June 1943 point up the absolutely crucial role played by the notion of retaliation in sustaining morale on the German home front during 1943 and 1944. This was spelled out in a special SD report with the title 'What does the population expect from retaliation?', dated 18 October 1943:

**1323**    Since the spring 'retaliation' has played a major role in the thoughts and conversations of all compatriots. In the SD report of 4.10.1943 it was shown how much the population is preoccupied with alleged technical details of the weapons of retaliation and their effects, purely on the basis of rumours. The following account will elucidate how the concept of retaliation has developed in the last few months and what notions are now associated with it.

At the time it was launched the slogan of retaliation was taken up by the whole German people with unanimous approval in a way comparable to hardly any other political or military goal. After it had become apparent that, for the time being, the flak and the night fighters were not capable of defending the homeland from the enemy air terror, retaliation appeared the only means of forcing the enemy to cease these attacks. Only counter-blows which would put the effects of the enemy air raids completely in the shade could—that was the opinion of our compatriots—finally break this terror. Initially, the importance of retaliation in the overall context of the war was considered great but not decisive. However, during the past few months, the significance of retaliation has changed in this respect. Under the impression of the overall development of the war since Stalingrad, compatriots have come to feel that the ring around Germany and the occupied territories is getting ever tighter and the development is moving inexorably towards a crisis from which the only way out appears to be through a miracle. And the *majority of compatriots*—in the areas affected by the air war—even the totality—expect this miracle, the *decisive change in the course of the war, to come from the retaliation.* Even, indeed in particular in the case of those compatriots whose confidence in victory has a positive effect on those around them and who stiffen the backbone of a number of gloomy and wavering people, their faith in victory is primarily based on the hopes which they invest in the future deployment of new weapons and military means. These hopes go much further than envisaging an end to the terror raids. That is the least that they expect from the retaliation. Rather the counter blow is intended to lead to England being 'knocked out' of the war within a few days or weeks. It is envisaged that immense destruction in England's major cities will create the conditions for the occupation of the island, which will then lead to an armistice with England. America would then, so the argument goes, have little interest in continuing the war. The whole strength of the German Wehrmacht could then be directed against Russia which would then be bound to lead to a speedy collapse of Russia's offensive capability. The extent to which the bearing of large sections of the population is influenced by such a line of thought is shown by the numerous comments which have been recorded such as:

'If the retaliation doesn't happen, or doesn't happen as I imagine it, then I see no more chance of our winning the war.'

The doubts about whether the 'talk of retaliation is simply a propaganda manoeuvre to intimidate the enemy or to pacify the population' falls outside the issues discussed here. Anyone who does not believe in retaliation—and there are only a few of them—no longer believes in victory anyway. Moreover, the doubts about the retaliation, which emerged mainly because it did not occur for months, have been reduced since the Führer's declaration that its technical and organizational preconditions are being created. Indeed, since the timing of the counter-blow is being postponed, the expectations associated with it have become even greater. Now people are saying that the preparations are lasting so long because they must be so comprehensive in order to ensure that the retaliation is 100 per cent successful and to exclude the possibility of failure completely.

The fact that the *retaliation* has become for very many compatriots *the most crucial element* in their hopes of victory is shown above all by the reports from the districts affected by air raids. It is significant that the attempt of the Catholic Church to oppose the retaliation propaganda by referring to the 'un-Christian' character of this notion has been decisively rejected even by the arch-Catholic parts of the population in the Rhineland and Westphalia. People have no sympathy with this attitude of the clergy and demand revenge and retaliation more vigorously than ever. But once again the decisive point is that the notion of retaliation *means more than the word itself; it means the decisive chance of victory,* without which, in many cases, people cannot conceive a successful outcome of the war.

▬

## (viii) Various Forms of Demoralization

Using the term loosely to describe a relaxation of traditional norms and codes of good citizenship within the terms of the regime, the war saw an increasing process of demoralization among substantial sections of the population. In part, this was a consequence of the extreme situation created by the air raids, which led to a desire to cast aside all inhibitions and to live for the day, leaving tomorrow to take care of itself.[37] Ursula von Kardorff captured this mood in her diary:

---

[37] See also the section on female immorality above, pp. 385ff.

**1324**    13 December 1943

Life is strange. Up and down, bad and then once again good. But always colourful. Yesterday, an evening in Zehlendorf[38] at which people drank in an uninhibited almost dogged fashion. Everyone flirted with everyone else and I too succumbed to the general dissolution. A shimmering swamp.

17 December

After every air raid I get the same feeling of an irrepressible vitality. One could embrace the world that has been given back to one. Presumably that's the reason why we so greedily grab every opportunity to have a party.

The combination of shortages of the necessities of life and a widespread sense that there was some unfairness in the distribution of scarce commodities, with the rich and those with connections having access to additional supplies, and the feeling that the authorities were failing to deal with the situation created a climate which was conducive to widespread illicit trading and the black market. According to a Nazi Party district leader, the population demanded 'above all absolute fairness [*Gerechtigkeit*]' and resented the fact that, for example, there were coupons for (cheap) horse meat, whereas poultry was not rationed and could be had at exorbitant prices.[39] He continued:

**1325**    Anyone who is not a regular customer of long standing with a grocer or with market stalls, anyone who does not have time to wait and queue, anyone who is too decent to push himself forward everywhere has to put up with getting the worst that's on offer. One should not be surprised that, in these circumstances, hoarding and uncontrolled purchasing—under the counter, round the back, on the black market and through barter, inevitably with excessive prices—is continually on the increase as is, at the same time, the bitterness of all those groups who lack 'connections' or time and opportunity for illegal purchases, or whose conscience forbids them to break the law.

These practices proved very difficult to combat, as was pointed out by the General State Prosecutor in Bamberg in his report to the Reich Justice Ministry of 4 February 1941:

**1326**    The development of the prices of various goods and services also makes the population concerned that the public administration is not mastering the

---

[38] A posh suburb in the south-west of Berlin.
[39] W. Domarus, *Nationalsozialismus, Krieg und Bevölkerung. Untersuchungen zur Lage, Volksstimmung und Struktur in Augsburg während des Dritten Reiches* (Munich 1977), pp. 86–87.

situation and that things could go the same way as in the [First] World War. The occasional harsh punishments of individuals often meet with the response that these are more or less arbitrary actions dealing with individual cases through which the general development cannot really be seriously affected. The practical impossibility of effective measures against the, in some cases, enormous price increases of poultry before Christmas was considered particularly annoying. But, as in the case of black market slaughtering, intervention by the authorities is made particularly difficult by the fact that those immediately involved remain silent; apart from anything else, the village community keeps quiet because generally most farmers do similar things. The local authorities (mayor, local peasant leader etc.) obviously do not pursue these matters with the requisite energy, so that the ground is not particularly fertile for the investigations by other authorities.

▬

The result was that, by 1944, various forms of barter and illicit trading had become virtually the norm, as was pointed out in a special SD report on 'the spread of illicit trading and barter and its effects on the population', dated 20 January 1944:

**1327**    I. The length of the war has led to a general relaxation in the strict views about the reprehensiveness of compatriots acquiring additional provisions. Whereas during the first years of the war barter and illicit trading in any form was frowned upon by the majority of compatriots and was often rejected as sabotage of the provisioning of the German people, the population has gradually taken to using every conceivable means of avoiding the wartime economic regulations on a small scale without, in the majority of cases, being conscious of having committed any offence. Wide circles who previously adopted a strict view on these matters now take the position that there is no point in considering whether this or that action is in accordance with the law, given the fact that every day they see hundreds of cases in which 'everyone sees what they can get'. Nowadays everybody follows the mottoes 'anyone who has got one thing has got everything' or 'everyone barters with everyone else' to the extent that those who fail on principle to take advantage of the opportunity to improve their standard of living, as determined by rationing, are regarded as stupid.

Basically, three forms of acquiring provisions outside the official allocations have emerged. In the first place, there is the exchange among compatriots of goods which are in short supply and which have been acquired legally for other similar goods (e.g. a smokers' ration card for bread coupons). On the other hand, there is the exchange of goods in short supply which are rationed among certain groups of tradesmen (butchers and the owners of clothing stores, or purveyors of spirits and tobacconists). Thirdly, there is the granting of priority in the provision of services in return for goods which are in short supply or rationed, occurring above all in the relations between craftsmen and their private customers.

Compatriots speak quite openly nowadays of the 'black market' where things are to be had, which outsiders and, in particular, anyone who has not got anything to offer in exchange only rarely get to see. Many tradesmen, for example, exchange goods with each other without using coupons or points and peasants exchange agricultural produce for goods they desire. It can often be observed that the owners of butchers' shops have extremely good-quality clothing and numerous pieces of it and, on the other hand, the owners of clothes shops are well supplied with foodstuffs. The same thing occurs among the peasant population . . . Tobacco products are considered to be 'new money' in exchange for which a lot can be acquired in the countryside but also in the towns. According to a report from a Gau in the Alpine/Danube region, there half a kilo of bacon or half a kilo of butter can be had for a packet of pipe tobacco and an egg for a cigarette, . . .

According to several reports, it has become customary among craftsmen to give priority to those customers who can provide goods in short supply instead of money. Even old and honourable master craftsmen are quite blunt about the fact that they will do the repairs required more speedily in return for tobacco, spirits, foodstuffs etc. A chemist, for example, could not get any windows to replace those blown out in an air raid in his pharmacy. It was only when his wife took two packets of glucose to a glazier that the windows were fixed. Anyone who has nothing to exchange often finds it impossible to get a craftsman to carry out urgent work.

Even those items most vital for daily life often cannot be acquired without connections. A female compatriot who had been bombed out tried in vain for weeks to get a coat and a suit for her son with coupons. It was only through a relative's 'connection' with a sales assistant in a department store that she got access to a room where there were large supplies of what she was looking for. As with craftsmen, a certain number of officials are also exposed to offers for priority or privileged treatment. A headmaster from Hamburg reports that various parents brought parcels for his teachers in order to get their children admitted into the school . . .

II. It should be noted that one of the most important reasons for the increase in barter and illicit trading is the fact that large numbers of people no longer have the feeling that they are committing an offence when they 'shop around' or 'organize something'. For many illicit trading with small quantities has become such a customary part of life that any queries are usually met with the comment: 'Anyone who doesn't look after himself will never gain an advantage.'

The feeling that in doing so one is removing something from the community hardly exists any more. Rather, the point is made that in the present hard times everyone has to see how they can best get by and that it is up to every individual to tap the sources which are open to him. With regard to the illicit trading in fruit which was particularly prevalent last summer and autumn, compatriots took the view that in this area 'self-help' was the only way of getting anything at all. It was, therefore, only sensible to try and get hold of fruit under the counter. It was frequently argued that the allegedly inadequate supply and distribution of fruit by the official agencies had the effect of forcing people into illicit trading.

However, the tolerant attitude is clearly restricted to those forms which serve to increase the food supplies of individuals and which remain within certain limits. Nobody, for example, considers it an offence to get some butter or meat products 'under the counter' for one's own household. Black marketeering on a large scale, which is carried out purely for profit is, however, strongly condemned. The population's attitude is well summed up in the following report:

'Illicit trading for the sake of profit is certainly strongly condemned by compatriots. But nobody finds anything wrong with getting small amounts of butter or a few eggs or 2 or 3 kilos of flour for one's own use in return for money or through barter. The view on this is that one would be really stupid if one didn't get hold of something illegally.'

The Reich Marshal's comment is often quoted in this connection, namely that a generous line should be taken, since our situation was not so bad that everyone had to look into each other's cooking pots and feel they had to keep an eye on each other.

The compatriots conclude from all this, therefore, that although there are rules, within certain limits they can be broken. The rationing of food and goods is working well and guarantees to everyone that they get the minimum necessary, but that is all. The powers that be silently tolerate people getting something extra for their personal needs. There is no sharp line dividing what is officially permitted and what is punishable but rather a more or less broad strip on which people have to use their wits to move about on. While this is not actually allowed 'everyone does it, everyone knows that everyone does it'; as far as the leadership is concerned—so the argument goes—the illegal bartering forms part of the overall plan for supplying the population.

Furthermore, the population claims the right partially to ignore the wartime economic regulations on the basis that numerous leading figures in the state and Party have an above average standard of life as far as their provisions go.

The population's attitude to these issues can be summed up as follows:

The general view is that the only barter and illicit trading which really needs prosecuting is the clandestine sale of large amounts of rationed goods for individual profit and that the small-scale 'social exchange' which is based on links between relatives or close acquaintances should not be punished. This view has become increasingly strongly held as the war has continued. The sentences passed by the courts for economic offences are judged accordingly. The increasingly tough sentencing policy which has emerged during the course of the war has met with the population's approval. The death sentences passed by the Special Courts in serious cases as well as the harsh sentences imposed on typical war black marketeers are generally approved of.

▬▬

Mathilde Wolff-Mönckeberg wrote to her children how she too had succumbed to the general practice of bartering, but then went on to refer to another aspect of the home front which helped to sustain morale: a kind of cultural/spiritual engagement at a level which had been unknown in peacetime. Like Ursula von Kardorff's partying, this reflected the heightened state in which people lived in the extreme situation of the home front:

**1328**    Believe it or not, even I have taken to bartering, as everybody else does, and it really has its fascination . . . Down below in the cellar is our large dining room table, which we cannot house here any more. It is getting damp and warped, poor old thing. For many years the Wolff family gathered round it to eat big wholesome meals . . . I am quite upset about this table, but we cannot afford sentimentality now. I have exchanged the table for fat and meat and quite a number of other delicatessen, which the new owner will bring from her canteen. But what else can one do these days? The stomach demands its due and money does not buy a thing. Everyone has oodles of money. Our clothing coupons are supposed to last until the end of the war. When will that be? So there is no temptation in that direction as so often in the old days, and one cannot be extravagant. You can only persuade workmen into your house if you press cigarettes into their hands or treat them to a glass of brandy. The man from the gas board, whom I tried to inveigle into letting us have a new cooker, had to be softened with a can of beer, two sausage sandwiches and finally a cigar.

Yet our life is not completely materialistic, concentrated solely on business deals. Never before have I listened to such beautiful music as during this fifth war winter. We treated ourselves to season tickets for various music cycles and trudged through rain and storm, and even when it snowed like fury, to the 4 p.m. concerts in the Musikhalle . . . More than ever people need to restore themselves with spiritual and artistic gratfications. W.'s public lectures on Shakespeare are packed. The biggest University auditorium is stuffed to capacity with all sorts of people who, in the old days, would never have dreamed of coming.

---

There were even more serious signs of demoralization as reported by the General State Prosecutor in Celle to the Reich Justice Ministry on 29 January 1944:

**1329**    Following the air raids on Hanover, there was a large amount of looting. According to the observations of the Gau HQ, it can be assumed that every third, or at least every fourth bomb site was looted. Regrettably, by contrast very few looters have been arrested. The immediate, energetic and tough intervention by the Special Court has, therefore, in my opinion not had a powerful deterrent effect, despite the fact that care was taken to give full publicity to the death sentences and executions which resulted.

---

## (ix)  The Last Phase 1944–1945[40]

By the spring of 1944 the mood on the home front had darkened still further and was probably well summed up by the SD in its report of 30 March 1944:

---

[40] See also the final chapter.

**1330**     The news of the deterioration on the eastern front, the unchanged situation in the air war, the lack of any sign of a counter blow from us or of an enemy invasion, which would release the general tension, together with the day-to-day problems caused by the war—all these sustain a downbeat mood among the population. At the moment, large sections of the population are intimidated by the military situation. People do not know 'what they should believe'. *Even compatriots who have hitherto been loyal are finding that 'the situation is gradually getting worrying'.* The invasion of Hungary by our troops showed that things were 'not right' in the Balkans, although we acted at the right moment. The 'inexorable advance' of the Bolsheviks, the lack of any prospect of a foreseeable end to the air war, the noticeable increase in tension because of the numerous air raid warnings by day and night, and the thought that, *almost like in the First World War, we are being forced to fight against a group of powerful enemies,* together with the devastation caused by the air terror and the deaths in many families reduce the belief that a change for the better can occur, which will bring about final victory, and instead concentrates people's thoughts on the question—what is the point of it all? (Berlin, Munich, Stuttgart, Stettin)

     The majority of compatriots hold to the belief that whatever happens they have to keep going and *'grit their teeth'.* One does it simply because one has to and *because there is no alternative left.* But there is a feeling of impatience that 'something has got *to happen soon'* , either a counter-blow against the Soviets or the invasion and the 'settling of accounts' with England. It really is *no longer easy 'to stick at it.'*

—

Attempts to mobilize the Party and use it to galvanize the population proved abortive, as was pointed out by the President of the Higher State Court in Karlsruhe in his report to the Reich Justice Ministry of 30 March 1944:

**1331**     One district reports a certain weariness with the Party, which manifests itself in a reduction in the wearing of the Party badge, a failure to give the Hitler salute etc. Although during the period after Stalingrad and the apparent demise of Mussolini there was no lack of people scenting a change in the air, this mood has much reduced in the meantime, which is explicable, on the one hand, in terms of the Führer's brilliant mastering of the situation in Italy and, on the other hand, by the poor performance of the Allies in Italy. The Party, as is well known, is trying to influence Party comrades through branch and cell evenings without as a rule achieving the intended goal or making any significant progress towards it. Many of the cell leaders, and to some extent the branch leaders as well and their wartime substitutes, are poor speakers and not in a position to organize the evenings in such a way that they are really stimulating and encouraging. This is only the case where, on occasion, an inspiring speaker can be found, as for example in recent cases provided by the Wehrmacht.

—

Up until the summer of 1944, the hope of defeating the expected invasion in the west held out by German propaganda and of 'retaliation' helped to sustain spirits to some extent. But, by August, it had become clear that the Allies were making rapid progress in France and that the weapons of retaliation (V1s) were proving far from decisive. The Stuttgart SD summed up the current mood in its report of 8 August 1944:

**1332**    It is significant that, at the moment, the issue being discussed is not whether we can win the war—the vast majority are convinced the enemy powers will win—but rather how long this war will go on and whether we shall come under an Anglo-American or Russian protectorate. At the moment, nobody in our Gau believes in victory apart from a very small number of compatriots and Party comrades, unless a miracle happens and people no longer believe in miracles . . .

The most serious aspect of the whole thing is probably the fact that most compatriots, even those whose belief has hitherto been unshakeable, have lost all faith in the Führer. Previous reports from here have been very cautious in making such comments because they were not yet entirely confirmed by our observations; but now it must be clearly stated.

However, despite this reported loss of faith in Hitler, he was still able to command the loyalty of many Germans, as is clear from their response to the attempt on his life, which had taken place on 20 July 1944, only three weeks before this report was written.[41]

## List of Sources

1260    W. Shirer, *Berlin Diary* (New York 1942), pp. 162–3.

1261    H. Schmitz, *Die Bewirtschaftung der Nahrungsmittel und Verbrauchsgüter 1939–1950* (Essen 1956), p. 2.

1262    Ibid., pp. 466–7.

1263    Ibid., p. 484.

1264    Bundesarchiv Berlin (BAB) R 41/59.

1265    F. Werner, *'Bleib übrig'. Deutsche Arbeiter in der nationalsozialistischen Kriegswirtschaft* (Düsseldorf 1983), p. 50.

1266    H. Boberach, ed., *Meldungen aus dem Reich. Die geheimen Lageberichte des Sicherheitsdienstes der SS 1938–1945,* Vol. 2 (Herrsching 1984), Vol. 9, pp. 3504–5.

1267    H. Schmitz, op. cit., p. 464.

---

[41] See below, pp. 630ff.

1268  Ibid., p. 482.
1269  L. Burchardt, 'The impact of the War Economy on the Civilian Population of Germany during the First and Second World Wars', in W. Deist, *The German Military in the Age of Total War* (Leamington Spa 1985), p. 47.
1270  Ibid., p. 51.
1271  Ibid., p. 53.
1272  BAB R 43 II/614, p. 137.
1273  H. Schmitz, op. cit., p. 188.
1274  Ibid., p. 189.
1275  Ibid., p. 190.
1276  Ibid., p. 185.
1277  Boberach, op. cit., Vol. 2, pp. 441–2.
1278  Ibid., Vol. 4, p. 1305.
1279  *Aus deutschen Urkunden 1935–1945* (n.d.), pp. 225–6.
1280  M. Domarus, ed., *Hitler: Reden und Proklamationen 1932–1945*, Vol. 2, pp. 1576–7.
1281  Boberach, op. cit., Vol. 5, pp. 1645–7.
1282  Ibid., p. 1763.
1283  *Aus deutschen Urkunden,* op. cit., pp. 243–5.
1284  Boberach, op. cit., Vol. 7, pp. 2260–1.
1285  Ibid., pp. 2440–1.
1286  Staatsarchiv Ludwigsburg (StAL) K110 Bü 48.
1287  *Aus deutschen Urkunden,* op. cit., p. 247.
1288  Boberach, op. cit., Vol. 8, pp. 3089–90.
1289  Ibid., Vol. 9, pp. 3120–1.
1290  Ibid., pp. 3195–6.
1291  BAB R 22/ 3366.
1292  Boberach, op. cit, Vol. 11, pp. 4084–5.
1293  BAB NS 6/414.
1294  M. Broszat et al., *Bayern in der NS-Zeit. Soziale Lage und politisches Verhalten der Bevölkerung im Spiegel vertraulichen Berichte* (Munich 1977), p. 148.
1295  Ibid., p. 576.
1296  Ibid., p. 162.
1297  Boberach, op. cit., Vol. 12, pp. 4720–1.
1298  BAB NS 6/414.
1299  Boberach, op. cit., Vol. 12, pp. 4831–2.
1300  BAB NS 6/414.
1301  Boberach, op. cit., Vol. 13, p. 5063.
1302  Ibid., p. 5145.
1303  BAB NS 6/414.
1304  Ibid.
1305  Boberach, op. cit., Vol. 14, pp. 5445–6.
1306  Ibid., pp. 5551–2.
1307  Ibid., Vol. 15, pp. 6064–5.
1308  BAB R 22/3355.

1309 Boberach, op. cit., Vol. 10, pp. 3597–8.
1310 E. Klöss, ed., *Der Luftkrieg über Deutschland. Nach den Dokumenten deutscher Kriegsschäden, herausgegeben vom Bundesministerium für Vertriebene, Flüchtlinge und Kriegsgeschädigte* (Munich 1963), pp. 35ff.
1311 M. Wolff-Mönckeberg, *On the Other Side: To my Children from Germany 1940–1945* (London 1979), pp. 78–9.
1312 BAB R 43 II/614 Nr. 169–170.
1313 BAB R 18/1531 Nr. 44–5.
1314 Landesarchiv Berlin (LAB) Rep. 57/1168.
1315 Hauptstaatsarchiv Stuttgart (HStAS) E 151c/II Bü 255.
1316 Dienstanweisung des Amts für Kriegsschäden in 'Tagesfragen der Wohlfahrtspflege. Mitteilungen des Deutschen Gemeindetages, Reichsgaudienststelle Danzig-Westpreussen' Januar/März 1944 LAB Rep. 142 O.5.50.
1317 MBliV 1944 Nr.30 LAB Rep. 142 0.5.50.
1318 'Ersatzleistung für Umquartierungskosten,' *Deutsche Allgemeine Zeitung*, 6.12.1944.
1319 U. von Kardorff, *Berliner Aufzeichnungen aus den Jahren 1942–1945* (Munich 1962), p. 117.
1320 BAB R22/3367.
1321 Boberach op. cit., Vol. 14, pp. 5354–7.
1322 Ibid., pp. 5515–6.
1323 Boberach, op. cit., Vol. 15, pp. 5885–7.
1324 Kardorff, op. cit., pp. 95, 97.
1325 W. Domarus, *Nationalsozialismus, Krieg und Bevölkerung. Untersuchungen zur Lage, Volksstimmung und Struktur in Augsburg während des Dritten Reiches* (Munich 1977), pp. 86–87.
1326 BAB R 22/3355.
1327 Boberach, op. cit., Vol. 16., pp. 6260–3.
1328 M. Wolff-Mönckeberg, op. cit., pp. 96–7.
1329 BAB R 22/3356.
1330 Boberach op. cit., Vol. 16, p. 6455.
1331 BAB R 22/3366.
1332 *Aus deutschen Urkunden*, op. cit., p. 264.

# *Resistance*[1]

## (i) Introduction

During the war, resistance—in the sense of principled and active opposition to the regime[2]—was very limited in size. In the case of the leftist-proletarian milieu, the socialist ideals had already suffered serious erosion during the 1920s through growing disillusionment with the performance of the Social Democratic party (SPD) and the divisions within the labour movement. Above all, the existence of a latent nationalism and social resentments within the milieu had facilitated the integration of the working class into the 'national community' with its promises of 'work and bread', a classless society, and the reward of individual advancement for those who worked hard and obeyed the rules. Resistance within the Protestant and Catholic milieus was focused above all on the defence of church autonomy. The church authorities avoided conflict with the regime wherever possible and had considerable sympathy for its professed role as a bastion against godless Bolshevism and the defender of the national interest. This found expression in the churches' support for the war effort, particularly after the attack on the Soviet Union in 1941.

In the case of the Conservatives, in particular, the outbreak of war had created a new context for the German Resistance. For, whereas in the occupied territories resistance to the German rulers was regarded as a patriotic act, which could count on the moral and in some cases the practical support of large sections of the community, in Germany resistance to the regime could be, and indeed overwhelmingly was, seen as not just unpatriotic but treasonable. This was not such a problem for the Communist Resistance because, ideologically, their primary loyalty

---

[1] The 'White Rose' resistance group is dealt with in Chapter 47, see pp. 456ff.
[2] For a brief discussion of the problem of definitions of resistance, opposition etc. see Vol. 2, Chapter 24, (iii).

was not to the nation but to the international working class. Moreover, they had no sympathies whatever for Nazism, its goals and values, and had been oppressed since the Nazi takeover in 1933. For them, therefore, the Nazis appeared as an occupying force and the Soviet forces were seen as liberators. For the elite resisters, however, the new wartime context was of particular significance, since they ranked the power and prestige of the nation and the nation-state extremely high in their hierarchy of values. For them to engage in actions which would risk contributing to the defeat of their country in a major war against enemies whom they feared and despised required an agonizing reappraisal of their whole value system. This reappraisal was made more difficult by the temptations created by initial Nazi foreign policy and military successes, which had restored Germany's power and prestige in the world and by the inhibitions caused by the emphasis on second-order virtues such as 'duty' and 'loyalty', which had characterized the socialization of the German elites in this period, and which was particularly prevalent within the military and the civil service from whom effective resistance alone could come. For some, unwillingness to break their personal oath of loyalty to Hitler as Head of State was not merely a rationalization of their unwillingness to act but a genuinely felt inhibition.

Although the German Resistance was very limited in size, it came from a wide range of groups and individuals: from army officers (though not, with the important exceptions of, Admiral Canaris, Berthold von Stauffenberg, a naval judge, and Lieutenant-Commander Alfred Kranzfelder of Naval Headquarters, Berlin, from naval or air force ones), from diplomats and civil servants, from clergy, academics and students, from workers and peasants, but not, with few exceptions, from businessmen[3]. While among the elite resistance groups women on the whole played a supportive role in the background, Communist women were in the front line. Many women had the task of sustaining their families following the arrest of their menfolk. Ideologically, resisters came from all directions. There were Conservatives, Liberals, Socialists, committed Christians, and Communists. This made co-operation among them difficult, but, given their common hostility to the regime, not impossible. By 1944 there were even links emerging between the elite resisters and the Communists.

Given the problems of clandestine organization under Nazi terror, typically resisters formed small groups round particular individuals, some of which were linked together in loose networks. These groups

---

[3] Robert Bosch, the electrical products manufacturer from Stuttgart is the most striking exception.

were formed and held together through ties of family and friendship, in many cases going back before the war, as well as shared values and a common purpose. Several of the aristocratic resisters were related to one another and several were members of the same elite Infantry Regiment No. 9 based in Potsdam, whose officers retained a traditional Prussian noble ethos which made them regard the Nazis with contempt. These close ties helped to shield the resisters from infiltration and betrayal. Among workers, groups were formed from those who worked in the same factory and/or lived in the same neighbourhood. In the case of the Communists links between the groups were maintained by party functionaries striving, largely unsuccessfully, to create formal networks. In the case of the elite resisters the circles were linked by duplicate membership and ties of friendship among individuals.

## (ii) The Communist Resistance

During the autumn of 1939, the German Communist Party (KPD) was forced to confront the repercussions from two developments which had transformed its situation: the Nazi–Soviet Pact of 23 August and the outbreak of war. Its initial response to the first of these was contained in a statement issued by the Secretariat of the Central Committee based in Paris on 25 August, which called for 'an intensified struggle against the Nazi dictatorship'. It also called for a fight to ensure that similar peace pacts were made with other states 'which have reason to feel themselves threatened by Hitler's policy of aggression', demanded an end to German occupation of Austria and Czechoslovakia and national self-determination for those countries. In the event of a war breaking out it called on its members to work for the Nazis' defeat, echoing Karl Liebknecht's words of 1915: 'The main enemy is at home.'[4] Four months later, in its 'Political Platform' of 30 December 1939, the party toned down its attack on the regime, hinting at possible collaboration and adopting a sharp tone towards Britain and France, portraying the war as an imperialist struggle. However, it continued to demand 'the organization of the struggle against the deprivation of the political rights of the working masses' and 'the organization of the struggle against the national suppression and for the self determination of the Austrian, Czech, Slovakian and Polish peoples'.[5]

---

[4] See A. Merson, *Communist Resistance in Nazi Germany* (London 1985), p. 215. The present section owes much to this book.
[5] See W. Ruge and W. Schumann, eds, *Dokumente zur deutschen Geschichte 1939–1942* (Berlin 1973), p. 31.

Meanwhile, the outbreak of war had massively disrupted what remained of the Party's organization. Before the war, this had consisted of leaders attached to the Comintern in Moscow with operational control in the hands of a Party secretariat in Paris. This worked via sector leaders in countries adjacent to Germany who supervised geographical sectors within Germany through Instructors who in turn kept in touch with the clandestine groups through occasional visits. With the outbreak of war the members of Paris secretariat were either interned or forced to flee, while the Instructors found it increasingly difficult to operate, particularly after the German occupation of Denmark, Holland, Belgium and France.

In fact, a decision had already been taken in principle at the Party's Bern conference in January 1939 to pursue the unrealistic course of establishing a national leadership (*Landesleitung*) in Berlin and a new network of district leaderships. Under a plan adopted in December 1939 an attempt was now made to implement this. A new external leadership of young experienced Central Committee members was established in Stockholm under Herbert Wehner, and five Instructors were then sent to Germany in the course of 1940 to re-establish contact with the clandestine groups and link them into networks, only one of whom (Arthur Emmerich) succeeded in evading arrest for any length of time.

The most important of the KPD groups were the factory cells in Berlin, which had been coordinated by Robert Uhrig, a toolmaker and long-serving Communist. By June 1941, there were eighty-nine Communist-led cells in Berlin plants. For a time, Uhrig's organization effectively became the new KPD leadership in Berlin. He worked together with Beppo Römer, a former Free Corps leader, and during 1940–1 they together produced a regular pamphlet, *Informationsdienst* (Information Service), which encouraged acts of sabotage and reported on the economic and military situation in an attempt to provide an alternative to the Goebbels propaganda machine. In general, however, between 1939 and 1941 Communists limited their activity to sustaining contacts with comrades. Thus, the number of Communist leaflets registered by the Gestapo every month, which had remained at around 1,000 during 1938, fell to 277 in December 1939 and 82 in April 1940, remaining at around this level until after June 1941. Similarly the number of Communists arrested fell from over 950 in January 1937 to just over 500 in January 1939 and to 70 in April 1940, remaining at around that level.[6]

---

[6] See D. Peukert, *Die KPD im Widerstand. Verfolgung und Untergrundarbeit an Rhein und Ruhr 1933 bis 1945* (Wuppertal 1980), p. 333, n. 20.

The German invasion of the Soviet Union in June 1941 galvanized the KPD Resistance to even greater efforts. During the first half of 1941, the monthly total of various propaganda leaflets found by the police fluctuated between 62 and 519, but it rose to 3,787 in July and remained at approximately that level until October when it rose to a peak of 10,227.[7] The following is an example of such a leaflet from the Uhrig group with the title 'Germans' and composed by the Communist Willy Sachse. It shows the new 'patriotic', i.e. above-class, emphasis which marked Communist Resistance propaganda after the German invasion of the Soviet Union:

**1333**  Middle-class citizens [Bürger], Peasants, Workers—in a word Patriots! Germany is in peril! It is in peril from within. If a ship is in distress, people throw everything overboard which can threaten them. So everything which can harm the nation must now be removed from its midst . . . Hitler is not the State, we are the State, we the people! The people must now form themselves into battalions. On this side, the workers—peasants, on the other the middle class. But they must march together as a national front for a free and independent Germany. And this Germany must be fought for.

Although Berlin had the largest number of Communist cells, there were cells in other industrial centres, for example in Hamburg (Bästlein–Jacob–Abshagen group), Central Germany (Robert Büchner) and Mannheim under Georg Lechleiter, a former Communist editor and member of the Baden state parliament. The Mannheim group produced its own paper, *Der Vorbote* (The Herald), which appeared from October 1941 until February 1942, when the Gestapo arrested the group as it was preparing the fifth issue for publication. The November 1941 issue contained the following basic guidelines for conspiratorial activity, which were standard for all Communist groups:

**1334**  It is true that our work at the present time of Nazi terror is not easy. But revolutionary activity has always been associated with dangers and difficulties. And anyone who is aware of the dangers and difficulties must and will know how to confront them unless he is willing right from the start timidly to capitulate before them and in the process, unintentionally, recognize the present ignominious situation as unalterable. The most important principles for our illegal activity must be reliability, punctuality and caution. Anyone who sins against these three commandments not only jeopardizes himself but all our work. Appointments which have been arranged must be kept punctually and an exact description of the meeting place must be given and it must be chosen so that it will be easy to

---

[7] See Merson, op. cit., p. 235.

find and safe from being spied on. Meetings in comrades' flats should be avoided if possible since experience has shown that the blocks are often under surveillance. One should not go straight from home to the meeting place but take a roundabout route in order to spot and avoid anyone who may be following.

Our organization will only be based on factory cells which should not contain more than three people. Only workers who have proved reliable should be admitted to these cells. Gossips and those partial to alcohol are to be excluded from party work on principle. Inquisitiveness and boastfulness have no place in the party.

The links between the cells do not occur from cell to cell but exclusively from the group headquarters to the cell, i.e. no vertical, only horizontal links. Thus in larger plants the cells should be combined into groups as required, which should have a leadership of three men who will maintain links with the cells. The groups in a plant will be controlled and supervised by the factory cell leadership, in order to ensure that the work in the plant proceeds in accordance with the common interest, that uniformity of aims is ensured, and that coherent action is facilitated.

———

Following the arrival in Berlin in January 1942 of the Central Committee member, Wilhelm Knöchel, to take over the operational leadership, the KPD appeared to have implemented the organization plan worked out in 1939. There was now a national leadership which controlled district party organizations in Berlin, Hamburg, Saxony, Thuringia and the Ruhr, which had been re-established by functionaries recently released from long periods of imprisonment. From February 1942 he published a monthly paper, *Der Friedenskämpfer* (The Freedom Fighter) in which he propagated a new line.

Following the German reverse before Moscow in December 1941, Knöchel was convinced that Germany would lose the war and was concerned that it would face a 'national catastrophe' if Germans did not take the liberation of the country from Nazism into their own hands. By a 'national catastrophe' he meant a vengeful peace imposed by those whom Germany had so brutally oppressed. He was also concerned that *German* Communists should retain a large say in the future direction of their country despite the debt they would owe to the Soviet Union. As a result, following his arrival in Berlin, in a series of pamphlets and other publications, Knöchel pressed for a more determined and active resistance, as in this pamphlet from late May 1942:

**1335**  Despite the fact that the great majority of our people doubt that Hitler will achieve victory and consider defeat to be unavoidable, and despite the fact that our people are full of a longing for peace, that more and more people are becoming aware that the Hitler war is a war of Hitler against Germany, and that our nation is caught up in the middle of a catastrophe which is getting bigger with every day that the war continues and that the sole beneficiaries of the Hitler war are the Nazi parvenus and our plutocrats—despite all this, the aroused national consciousness of our people is primarily negative in character in terms of its assessment of the path which must be taken in order to save the nation. Although the great majority of our people would prefer to see Hitler's government disappear today rather than tomorrow, nevertheless, confronted with the horrifying prospect of a military defeat, Hitler appears the lesser evil and they hope for a victory even though they seriously doubt whether it is possible.

This situation requires the Party to take on the urgent task of continually enlightening our people about the fact that military defeat is inevitable and the national existence of our people can only be secured by achieving an immediate and just peace. However, peace which alone can save the nation and will bring about the liberation of the German people from the fascist yoke can only be achieved by overthrowing the Hitler regime.

Thus, the Hitler gang and their root, the monopoly capitalist mob, who bear the sole guilt for and are the beneficiaries of this war, must be overthrown by a true popular revolution, expropriated and rendered harmless for ever so that our people cannot be plunged into war for a third time, but rather that the preconditions can be created for building a new, free Germany.

The sooner our people carry out this deed the lesser will be the national catastrophe; the nations which have been attacked and subjugated by Hitler will, thereby, recognize that the German people are not identical with Hitler and his crimes and, instead of exacting revenge, they will extend to us the hand of brotherhood, grant us a just peace and treat us as a nation with equal rights. But woe betide our nation if it does not take part in the destruction of the Hitler beast. For what is being said by many miners in the Ruhr area, 'If only our workers' state—the Soviet Union—doesn't lose the war, for then we will be enslaved for decades', is the expression of a true national consciousness which articulates a great concern about the national existence of our people and the future of Germany. For Hitler-fascism is war without end and the victory of the Red Army over Hitler's Wehrmacht will bring the German people an immediate and just peace. Thus the military defeat of Hitler and his fall are vital for Germany. And it is the duty of every German to help energetically to achieve this goal without delay.

---

Despite their precautions, the Communist organizations were highly vulnerable to infiltration by the Gestapo, partly because much of the activity was carried on by Communist activists who had been released from prison and concentration camps during 1939–40 and were therefore, known and in some cases still kept under observation. Also, the Gestapo was successful in 'turning' a number of Communists through various kinds of pressure and persuading them to betray their comrades. In the spring of 1942 the Uhrig organization was destroyed and by the spring of the following year virtually all the major networks had been 'rolled up'; Knöchel himself had been arrested in January 1943.

The arrests of 1942–3 devastated the KPD Resistance but did not entirely destroy it. For example, of the 89 Berlin factory cells only 22 were destroyed, although the others were weakened and left largely uncoordinated. Moreover, in Berlin two former Hamburg KPD officials, Anton Saefkow and Franz Jacob, who had escaped to the capital, managed to knit together one or two networks, particularly in the Berlin armaments works, and establish links with central Germany, where there were particularly active groups in Thuringia (Neubauer–Poser), Saxony (Georg Schumann) and Magdeburg (Hermann Danz). These pursued an independent line stressing the idea of a 'dictatorship of the proletariat' and a Socialist Germany rather than the popular front approach hitherto characteristic of Communist propaganda. However, in the Ruhr and in many other parts of Germany Communists largely restricted themselves to sustaining personal contacts in plants and neighbourhoods on a social basis. Finally, in the summer of 1944, Saefkow and Jacob made contact with the Social Democrats of the Kreisau Circle (Julius Leber and Adolf Reichwein), at which point the Gestapo stepped in once more and arrested virtually all the leading members of the KPD Resistance.

In the course of the war several thousand Communists were arrested, and for a Communist arrest almost invariably meant a death sentence or a long period of imprisonment. The following farewell letter from the Communist, Walter Husemann, to his father, written prior to his execution on 13 May 1943, indicates the spirit which helped to sustain them:

**1336**    My dear Father,
Be strong! I am dying as I lived; as a fighter in the class war! It is easy to call yourself a Communist as long as you don't have to shed blood for it. You only show whether you really are one when the hour comes when you have to prove yourself. I am one, father . . .

The war won't last much longer and then your hour will have come!

Think of all those who have already travelled down this road that I must go down today and will still have to travel down it and learn one thing from the Nazis: every weakness will have to be paid for with hecatombs of blood. So be merciless! Remain hard!

I would have gladly experienced the new era. The fact that I will never now experience it has sometimes made me bitter. But Lenin, Liebknecht[8], Luxemburg[9]

---

[8] Karl Liebknecht, a leader of the Spartakus League, the forerunner of the KPD, was murdered by members of the right-wing Free Corps during the Spartakus uprising in Berlin in January 1919.

[9] Rosa Luxemburg, another leader of the Spartakus League, was murdered at the same time as Liebknecht.

weren't able to harvest the fruits of their labours and they deserved to a thousand times more than I do. We are merely the fertilizer which has to be in the earth for a new and finer seed to grow for the sake of humanity . . .

Oh father, father you dear and good man! If only I did not have to fear that you will collapse under the shock of my death.

Be tough, tough, tough!

Prove that you have been a whole-hearted life-long fighter in the class struggle!

Help him Frieda, raise his spirits. He must not be allowed to succumb. His life does not belong to him but to the movement! Now, a thousand times more than before!

___

### (iii) The *Innere Front* Group, the Red Orchestra and the Herbert Baum Group

While the KPD resistance groups were overwhelmingly proletarian in their social basis, there were two important groups linked to the Party composed mainly of middle-class intellectuals and professionals. One was the *Innere Front* (Home Front) group, which was made up of former Communist editors and Marxist intellectuals and took its name from the newspaper it published from June 1941 to autumn 1942. Its leaders, Wilhelm Guddorf, John Sieg, Martin Weise and Jon Graudenz, had worked for the KPD daily, *Die Rote Fahne* (The Red Flag) before 1933 and then, after years of imprisonment, had been released during 1939–40. They concentrated on disseminating news and views based on Soviet and BBC broadcasts designed to neutralize Nazi propaganda. Some of their pamphlets were in foreign languages and designed to reach the foreign workers.

For the second non-proletarian group, which was, however, more loosely linked to the Party, the Gestapo coined the name 'The Red Orchestra'. It originated before the war in the form of circles of family, friends and professional acquaintances who were hostile to Nazism and, like many young members of the European middle-class intelligentsia in the 1930s, were interested in Marxism and impressed by the achievements of the Soviet Union. They formed two main groups, one around Arvid Harnack, an Assistant Secretary in the Reich Economics Ministry, and his wife Mildred, and the other round Harro Schulze-Boysen, a flight lieutenant in the Air Ministry. The groups came together in 1940 and subsequently established contact with Soviet Intelligence, supplying limited amounts of secret information gleaned from their professional activity via radio contact with Soviet agents in Belgium and elsewhere. They also carried out conventional propaganda work through leaflets. One can capture something of the flavour of their propaganda and political outlook from the following pamphlet by Harro Schulze-Boysen, which was sent to several hundred addresses throughout Germany in February 1942:

**1337**    *'Concern about Germany's Future fills the Nation'*

*. . .What should happen?*
. . .The German people need a Socialist government of the workers, the soldiers and the working intelligentsia. Only through the decisive cooperation of the forces in the Wehrmacht, who are close to the people, with the best sections of the working class and the intelligentsia can one seize control from the dominant party . . .

Even now a satisfactory answer could be provided to the question about the country's future. But for that Germany needs a government which bases itself on those sections of the nation which have the ability and the power to present to the nation and to the world a new policy for Germany. Those are naturally not the people who brought Hitler to power . . .

As soon as the nation has given itself a new government it must look for new friends and allies in the world. These are not to be found among those who have an interest in the restoration of the European conditions of 1918–39 and in the more or less overt humiliation of the German people, i.e. not among the reactionary circles in Europe.

The policy of certain German feudal lords, diplomats, bankers etc. who dream of providing the country with a new political basis after carrying out a coup and a bloody persecution of all those who have hitherto been in power, and who then want to secure a reconciliation with the 'Plutocrats' on the basis of a Germany restored at the expense of Russia, such a policy has no basis in reality and will not bring about peace. A future cannot be built with hatred, demagogy and reactionary attitudes. The friends of our nation are rather to be found among the progressive forces in Europe and in the USSR . . .

What can the individual do in order to make an impact? Everybody must make sure that wherever he can he does the opposite of what the present state demands of him . . .

The people must be told the truth about the real situation. So do not let any opportunity go by in which you do not contradict the propaganda. Read old Führer speeches! Remember old newspapers and compare the promises which the people were being made a year ago with the grim facts of the present time. Pass on the letters from the eastern front; they expose the mendacious reports of Nazi propaganda; they show how the war is really going. Write to your soldiers at the front about what is going on at home. People are being increasingly open about saying that we are no longer prepared to put up with the rule of the Party bosses. We demand the restoration of freedom of opinion, a people's court for those who have driven us into the Russian campaign and so into a two-front war and who are responsible for the completely inadequate preparations. They are guilty of the senseless deaths of hundreds of thousands in ice and snow.

Oppose the continuation of a war which at most will turn not just the Reich but the whole continent into a heap of ruins.

It is not enough to grumble or to make stupid jokes. Every individual must decide on a clear YES or NO.

Read the newspapers and look at the newsreels with a critical eye! Remember that they are doing everything to paint a distorted picture of the situation. Protest more and more loudly if you have to keep standing in queues everywhere! Stop putting up with everything! Don't let yourselves be intimidated any more.

Oppose the general fear! One keeps hearing the phrase: 'We've got to get through it!' If we don't win now then we'll all be for it because we shall have to pay for the crimes of the Nazis. This is the kind of talk which the current power holders are spreading in order to strengthen their rule. Naturally, this whole approach is wrong . . . We shall only save ourselves and the country if we find the courage to join the battle front against Hitler and thereby prove that fascism and warmongering are not peculiarly German but the consequences of an unhealthy system for which the whole world shares the blame and that therefore must be overcome by the constructive forces of the whole world including Germany. So when the NSDAP shouts that the victorious Americans or Bolsheviks would sterilize all Germans then it is, as always, spreading lies. The gentlemen are scared for their own skins and it is quite true that those responsible will be called to account. But those who honestly express their desire for a new policy won't be touched at all.

Treat the SS with contempt! Let it feel that the people despise murderers and spies from the depths of their hearts. Stop this nonsense of collecting Winter Aid badges! Every penny, all help for the ruling regime prolongs the war and only leads us deeper into misery! Put an end to thoughtlessness and sentimentality.

Everything which needs to be said is summed up in the demand to get serious at last.

Send this letter to all and sundry as often as you can. Pass it on to friends and workmates! You're not alone! Fight at first off your own bat and then in groups. TOMORROW GERMANY BELONGS TO US.

---

One of the most remarkable actions of the Red Orchestra group was to distribute stickers at the anti-Soviet exhibition 'The Soviet Paradise' organized by the Propaganda Ministry in the Lustgarten park in Berlin in May 1942, which read 'The NAZI PARADISE. War, Hunger, Lies, Gestapo. How much longer?'

This same exhibition was also the target of the most striking action by the third group loosely linked to the Communist Resistance, which was based in Berlin and led by a young Jewish electrician, Herbert Baum, and his old schoolfriend Martin Kochmann, a salesman, and their wives Sala and Marianne. The group was made up of around 100 young Jewish workers, many of them women, most of whom came from the Zionist youth movement. Baum and Kochmann and their wives had been involved in the Communist youth movement but because of their Jewish backgrounds now operated largely independently of the Party. Their activities focused on attacking the regime with leaflets and by painting slogans and, after September 1941, in trying to avoid deportation for themselves and others. Their activities culminated in an arson attack on Goebbels' 'Soviet Paradise' exhibition on 18 May 1942. The Gestapo was quickly on their trail and over twenty members of the group were sentenced to death, while Baum himself died in prison after severe torture, possibly from suicide.

### (iv) The Resistance by Individuals

There were numerous cases of individual Germans who resisted the regime in various ways, for example by refusing to serve in the armed forces on moral grounds, and who paid for their courageous actions with their lives or with long terms of imprisonment. Perhaps the most remarkable individual act of resistance during the war was the assassination attempt carried out by Georg Elser, a simple joiner from Württemberg. After a year of careful planning and preparations and acting entirely on his own, Elser succeeded in installing a bomb in a pillar in the Bürgerbräu beer cellar in Munich where Hitler was due to speak on the evening of 8 November to commemorate his Munich putsch, launched in the same hall on the same day in 1923. Unfortunately, bad weather prevented Hitler's plane from taking off and he was therefore forced to leave early to catch the train to Berlin and so escaped more or less certain death when the bomb duly went off. Elser was arrested crossing the Swiss frontier and during his subsequent interrogation by the Gestapo explained his motives as follows:

**1338**   Recently I have often gone into a Catholic church on weekdays, if there wasn't a Protestant church available, to say the Lord's Prayer. In my view it doesn't matter if one does this in a Protestant or a Catholic church. I agree that these frequent church visits and this frequent praying has to do with my act, which was very much on my mind, in that I certainly would not have prayed so often if I had not prepared or planned the act. It is the case that after a prayer I was always somewhat comforted

If I'm asked whether I consider the deed I have done as a sin within the meaning of Protestant doctrine then I would like to say no! . . . After all, through my deed I wanted to prevent more blood being spilled.

Personally I have never been politically active. After reaching voting age I always voted for the KPD list because I thought that is a workers' party which certainly supports the workers. But I never became a member of this party because I thought it was enough if I voted for it. I never took part in any actions such as distributing leaflets, demonstrations or graffiti . . . I have never been interested in the programme of the KPD . . .

I didn't know that there are no longer any churches or clergy in Russia. I have never read and don't believe it. But I believe that the German Government wants to get rid of the existing churches in Germany. As far as I know or have heard all Germans are now supposed to believe in only one faith. They are supposed to become German Christians. If I'm asked whether that is a good thing or a bad thing I can't say because I don't know the doctrine of the German Christians . . .

In my opinion the conditions of the workers have deteriorated in various respects since the national revolution. For example, I have noticed that wages have been getting lower and deductions getting higher. While in 1929 in the watch factory in Konstanz I earned on average RM 50 per week and the deductions for tax, health insurance, unemployment insurance and invalidity benefit were only about RM 5, now the deductions are still as high even with a weekly wage of RM 25. The hourly rate for a joiner in 1929 was RM 1, now it is only 68 pfennigs. Through conversations with other workers I discovered that in other occupations after the national uprising [i.e. spring 1933] wages were reduced and the deductions increased. Furthermore, in my view, since the national revolution the workers are under a certain amount of restraint. For example, workers can no longer change their jobs when they want and now-adays, as a result of the HJ, they are no longer in charge of their children And in the religious sphere too they are no longer as free as they were. I am thinking here in particular of the activities of the German Christians. I noticed these facts in the period up to 1938 and subsequently. During this period, I noticed that, as a result, the workers were getting fed up with the Government . . .

In the autumn of 1938 I noticed that among the workers generally the view was that there would be a war . . . As a result there was great concern among the workers. I too thought that 'things would go wrong' because of the Sudeten question. After the Munich Conference things quietened down among the workers; people thought there wouldn't be a war.

The year before last I already thought that it wouldn't stop with the Munich Conference, that Germany would make further demands on other countries and would annex more countries so that a war would be unavoidable, i.e. I thought it would come to this. That was my own view.

The discontent among the workers which I had observed since 1933 and the war that I thought was unavoidable since autumn 1938 preoccupied my thoughts. Whether this was before or after the September crisis I cannot now remember. I simply started thinking about how one could improve the conditions of the workers and avoid a war. I was not prompted to do this by anybody and was not influenced by anybody along these lines . . .

The result of my deliberations was that conditions in Germany could only be altered by removing the current leadership. Under leadership I meant the 'top people', I mean Hitler, Göring and Goebbels As a result of my deliberations I became convinced that, through the removal of these three men, other men would come into the Government who would not make impossible demands of foreign countries, 'who would not want to annex foreign territory' and who would ensure an improvement in the social conditions of the workers. Neither then nor later did I think of any particular persons who should take over the Government . . .

At that time I could not stop thinking about my idea of removing the Government and already in autumn 1938—it was before November 1938—I took the decision on the basis of my observations to set about removing the Government myself.

Although he had voted Communist during Weimar, Elser was basically an unpolitical individual, but one with a strong sense of social justice and loyalty to his fellow workers and a simple but strong moral sense.

If Elser drew his strength to act from simple moral principles, the following case is of someone who reached the same decision on the basis of deep and sophisticated religious and ethical considerations—the Protestant theologian and pastor Dietrich Bonhoeffer. In fact, Bonhoeffer was involved in the Resistance movement which eventually led to the July 1944 plot to assassinate Hitler and so strictly speaking does not count as an 'individual resister'. However, he represents a larger group of individual churchmen. While the Christian churches as institutions, generally speaking, failed lamentably in bearing witness to the spiritual and ethical values of their Christian faith, they were partially redeemed by the considerable number of individual priests and pastors who, often with little or no support from their superiors, in various ways challenged the regime and in some cases paid for this with their lives. Among these none was more impressive than Bonhoeffer, who was executed in April 1945. At Christmas 1942, a few months before his arrest by the Gestapo, Bonhoeffer spelled out to his friends the lessons he had drawn from the experience of Nazism in a piece entitled 'After Ten Years', from which the following extracts are taken:

**1339**  *Who can resist temptation?*

The great masquerade of evil has confused all ethical concepts. The fact that evil can take on the appearance of light, benevolence, historical necessity and social justice is simply bewildering to someone who comes from our traditional ethical world; for the Christian, whose life is guided by the Bible, it is very much a confirmation of the profound evilness of evil.

The failure of those who claim to be 'followers of reason', the people who, with the best of intentions, and in their naive blindness to reality think they can put the collapsing edifice together again with a bit of reason is patently obvious.

Their dim vision leads them to want to be fair to all sides and, as a result, they are ripped apart by the contradictions between the opposing forces without having achieved anything. Disappointed by the irrational nature of the world, they see themselves condemned to sterility, step resignedly aside or yield themselves up completely to the stronger party.

The failure of all ethical *fanaticism* is even more shocking. The fanatic thinks that he can oppose the power of evil with the purity of principle. But like a bull he charges at the red rag instead of at the person holding it, tires and then succumbs. He gets tied up in insignificant details and falls into the trap set by his cleverer opponent.

The man of *conscience* fights a lonely struggle against the overwhelming pressure of dilemmas requiring a decision. But the extent of the conflicts within which he has to choose—with no one to advise and support him but conscience—tears him apart. The countless honourable and seductive disguises in which evil approaches him make his conscience anxious and uncertain until he finally contents himself with salving his conscience rather than keeping it clear, until, in order not to despair, he lies to his own conscience; for the man for whom his conscience is his only support cannot understand that a bad conscience can be healthier and stronger than a deceived conscience.

*Duty* seems to point the certain way out of the confusing mass of all the possible decisions that are available. In this case what has been ordered is taken as the most reliable thing to do, for the person who gives the order takes the responsibility and not the person carrying it out. But by restricting oneself to doing one's duty, one can never dare to act on one's own responsibility, yet only that kind of action can strike at the heart of evil and so overcome it. In the end, the man of duty will have to do his duty even towards the devil.

But anyone who tries to hold his own in the world by exercising his personal *freedom*, anyone who values the necessary deed higher than the purity of his own conscience and reputation, anyone who is prepared to sacrifice a sterile principle to a fruitful compromise or even a sterile notion of the happy medium to a fruitful radicalism should watch out that his freedom does not bring him down. He will accept the bad in order to avoid something worse and in the process he will no longer be able to recognize that it is precisely that something worse, which he is trying to avoid, that may prove preferable. This is the very stuff of tragedies.

In their flight from public conflict this or that person may find sanctuary in a private *virtuousness*. But he must close his eyes and shut his mouth in the face of the injustice around him. It is only at the cost of self-deception that he can avoid dirtying his hands with responsible action. In everything he does he will be continually haunted by what he has left undone. He will either die destroyed by this disquiet or become the most hypocritical of Pharisees.

Who can resist temptation? Only he for whom neither reason nor his principles, nor his conscience, nor his freedom, nor his virtue is the final measure of all things, but who is prepared to sacrifice all these when, in faith and bound solely to God, he is called to responsible action, and who in his life seeks nothing more than to respond to God's question and his call. Where are these responsible people?

*Civil courage*

What really lies behind the complaint about the lack of civil courage? During these years we have come across much courage and self-sacrifice but very little civil courage even in ourselves. It would be psychologically too naive to explain this lack in terms of personal cowardice. What lies behind it is very different. In our long history we Germans have had to learn the need for and acquire the strength of obedience. We saw the meaning and greatness of our lives in the subordination of all our personal wishes and thoughts to the task assigned to us. Our eyes were directed upwards not in slavish fear but in voluntary trust which regarded an assigned task as a profession and a profession as a calling. The readiness to follow an order from 'above' rather than act at one's own discretion represents a legitimate mistrust of one's own heart. Who would dispute the fact that, as far as obedience and fulfilling tasks are concerned, in their professional lives Germans have repeatedly demonstrated the utmost courage and commitment. However, the Germans preserved their freedom—and where in the world has there been more passionate talk about freedom than in Germany from Luther to the idealist philosophers—by trying to liberate themselves from self-will in service to all. Their profession and their freedom seemed to them to be two sides of the same coin. But in thinking this they misunderstood the world; they did not reckon with the fact that their readiness to subordinate themselves, to commit themselves fully to their assigned tasks could be misused for evil. When this happened the practice of their professions itself became dubious, and then the whole basis of German moral concepts was inevitably shaken. It could not but become apparent that the Germans lacked a crucial fundamental insight, namely the need voluntarily to take responsibility for an action which runs counter to one's professional code or to the task which one has been assigned. In its place came, on the one hand, an irresponsible lack of scruple and, on the other, a self-tormenting scrupulousness which never led to action. However, civil courage can only grow from free men taking responsibility for their own actions. The Germans are only now beginning to discover what individual responsibility means. It depends on a God who demands the free leap of faith involved in responsible action and who promises forgiveness and consolation to those who become sinners as a result of making that leap of faith.

---

## (v) The Conservative and Military Resistance

In the pre-war years a number of senior army officers, diplomats and officials had become increasingly concerned about various aspects of the regime. This disillusionment had come to a head in 1938. It had partly reflected a shift in the balance of power within the regime as a result of a virtual purge of Conservatives from a number of important positions (Schacht, Fritsch, Neurath et al.), with the result that the relationship between the Nazis and the Conservative elites had ceased to be an entente between more or less equal partners and had become the clear subordination of one to the other. It also reflected the growing concern that Hitler's increasingly aggressive foreign policy was leading to a war with the Western powers which Germany would lose. This had already produced a resistance movement in the autumn of 1938 which aimed to remove Hitler, but which had been pre-empted by the Munich Agreement, although doubts must remain about whether it would have been successful even had Munich not intervened.

Despite the easy victory over Poland, the Conservative-military resistance remained deeply concerned about the prospect of an offensive against France, which at that time Hitler was still planning for the autumn. They were also horrified by the behaviour of the SS in Poland. These concerns were recorded in his diary by the former German ambassador to Italy, Ulrich von Hassell, a Conservative and nationalist, who had been dismissed as part of the 1938 'purge':

**1340** *19 October 1939* . . . Among well-informed people in Berlin I noticed a good deal of despair. In wide circles there is still rejoicing over the 'inspired chess move of the pact with Russia', over the victories in Poland, over the performance of the submarines and the Air Corps against England. But among informed people there is a growing awareness of our impending disaster.

The principal sentiments are: the conviction that the war cannot be won militarily; a realization of the highly dangerous economic situation; the feeling of being led by criminal adventurers; and the disgrace that has sullied the German name through the conduct of the war in Poland; namely the brutal use of air power and the shocking bestialities of the SS, especially towards the Jews. The cruelties of the Poles against the German minority are a fact too, but somehow excusable psychologically. When people use their revolvers to shoot down a group of Jews herded into a synagogue one is filled with shame. A light court martial sentence pronounced against some of these criminals was set aside by Brauchitsch;[10] a second sentence, likewise light, was voided by the disgraceful general amnesty for such deeds. And all this time a man like Niemöller[11] has been sitting for years in a concentration camp!

I hear that Blaskowitz,[12] as commander of the Army, wanted to prosecute two SS leaders—including that rowdy Sepp Dietrich—for looting and murder. But in vain. Those who saw Warsaw, with its devastation and the many thousands of dead bodies lying around, came away with horrible impressions. Of course the commander of the city should not have permitted this to happen, but the Nazi determination to bring the war to a quick end was primarily responsible . . .

---

[10] Field Marshal Walter von Brauchitsch, Commander-in-Chief of the Army.
[11] Martin Niemöller, the pastor of the Protestant parish church of the wealthy suburb of Dahlem in south-west Berlin, had been imprisoned since 1937 for opposition to the regime's attempt to control the Protestant Church.
[12] On General Blaskowitz see Vol. 3, docs 655–56.

The situation of the majority of politically clear-headed and reasonably well-informed people today, while Germany is in the midst of a great war, is truly tragic. They love their country. They think patriotically as well as socially. They cannot wish for victory, even less for a severe defeat. They fear a long war, and they see no feasible way out: the latter because there is no confidence that the military leadership possesses enough insight and willpower to assert itself at the decisive moment.

---

In this situation the autumn 1938 movement to remove Hitler revived. Hassell reviewed the difficulties in his diary:

**1341**      *30 October* . . . In the morning I took a walk with Goerdeler.[13] According to his information this is the situation:

. . . (3) POLITICALLY: the situation being what it is, every effort for peace must be made. Under the present leadership, however, peace negotiations could neither be initiated nor entertained. Our goal must be to go into action the minute the order for invasion is given. If Hitler should decide against this solution, we would have some more time. If it should prove impossible to organize resistance against the order, the show would simply have to go on and the first setback would have to be exploited. Of course the chances to get a decent peace would then be considerably smaller, although the domestic situation would be riper.

(4) PROSPECTS: Goerdeler does not believe that Brauchitsch can be persuaded to act. At best there was a possibility that, with the help of Halder,[14] he could be persuaded to 'tolerate action'. Everything else was easy to arrange; the necessary number of determined generals is ready to proceed quickly and energetically if the order comes from the top. Herein lies the whole problem. Goerdeler said he maintained constant contact with key people of the High Command of the Wehrmacht. A memorandum presenting the case against the invasion and for seeking an early peace had already been prepared by groups within the Army and the Foreign Office (Etzdorf[15]) and presented to Brauchitsch.

I asked Goerdeler whether anything ever came of the mission planned for Krupp-Bohlen.[16] Goerdeler said Krupp had declined to take action (I never expected anything else), making an irrelevant reference to the flight of Thyssen,[17] which had compromised the industrialists.[18]

---

[13] Carl Goerdeler, Lord Mayor of Leipzig 1930–7, Reich Price Commissioner 1934–5.

[14] General Franz Halder, Chief of the General Staff 1938–42.

[15] Hasso von Etzdorf, Liaison Officer between the German Foreign Office and the General Staff.

[16] Gustav Krupp von Bohlen und Halbach, the Essen coal and steel magnate and arms manufacturer.

[17] Fritz Thyssen, the Duisburg coal and steel magnate, initially a Nazi sympathizer, had fled to Britain in 1939.

[18] The absence of major business figures with one or two exceptions was a notable feature of the German Resistance.

My final impression: Goerdeler bases everything on Morgenstern's phrase 'that which may not be cannot be'.[19] He views matters with great optimism, gives credence to everything unfavourable to the Nazis, especially in economic matters, and rejects everything that is favourable. He also has many illusions about the generals. I expressed my doubts on this score, and warned him further against the assumption that after the invasion of Belgium it would still be possible to get a decent peace. I agreed with him fully that every effort must be made to induce the army to refuse to carry out the invasion . . .

. . .The principal factor, however, is still lacking: a soldier in a position of decisive authority willing to take the initiative. Halder is not equal to the situation either in calibre or in authority.

In one of the numerous contacts that were taking place between the British Government and members of the Resistance at this time, on 22–3 April 1940 Ulrich von Hassell met an Englishman by the name of J. Lonsdale Bryans in Arosa. Lonsdale Bryans was acting with the approval but not on behalf of the British Foreign Secretary, Lord Halifax. Hassell presented him with the following statement on the conditions for peace which would be acceptable to the Conservative Resistance with the hope that they would meet with British approval. Understandably, they did not. However, they provide a good insight into the foreign policy goals of the Conservatives at that particular juncture:

**1342**                                                                *22 February 1940*

CONFIDENTIAL

I. All serious-minded people in Germany consider it as of utmost importance to stop this mad war as soon as possible.

II. We consider this because the danger of a complete destruction and particularly a Bolshevization of Europe is rapidly growing.

III. Europe does not mean for us a chessboard of political or military action or a base of power but it has 'la valeur d'une patrie' in the frame of which a healthy Germany in sound conditions of life is an indispensable factor.

IV. The purpose of a peace treaty ought to be a permanent pacification and re-establishment of Europe on a solid base and a security against a renewal of warlike tendencies.

V. Condition, necessary for this result, is to leave the union of Austria and the Sudeten with the Reich out of any discussion. In the same way there would be excluded a renewed discussion of occidental frontier questions for the Reich. On the other hand, the German–Polish frontier will have to be more or less identical with the German frontier of 1914.

VI. The treaty of peace and the reconstruction of Europe ought to be based on certain principles which will have to be universally accepted.

---

[19] Christian Morgenstern, the nineteenth-century poet.

VII. Such principles are the following:

1. The principle of nationality with certain modifications deriving from history. Therefore,

a. The principles of Christian ethics.

b. Justice and law as fundamental elements of public life.

c. Social welfare as leitmotiv.

d. Effective control of the executive power of state by the people, adapted to the special character of every nation.

e. Liberty of thought, conscience and intellectual activity.

——

The first major programmatic statement of the Conservative Resistance movement was contained in the memorandum with the title 'The Goal' (*Das Ziel*), which was composed at the beginning of 1941 at the height of German power. Its main author was Carl Goerdeler, but it also contained input from the former Chief of the General Staff, General Ludwig Beck, and others. It contained a general framework for a reform of the political system and emphasized in particular the importance of the re-establishment of the rule of law. But its main focus was on the foreign policy goals of a future non-Nazi German government:

**1343**   . . . II. *The foreign policy goal*

. . . *Thus a sensible and favourable development can only be achieved if we succeed in combining the idea of nation states with the need for large areas [Grossraum].* Recognition of this fact provides the *political goal* for our German fatherland. This goal is all the more fruitful in view of the fact that Germany, lying in the centre of Europe, has been placed by nature between the cold and the heat, between the sea and the continent and therefore could develop, comparatively speaking, the best qualities for the struggle in and with nature, i.e. the best qualities for securing and developing its life. It is not by chance that Germany has developed so many poets, philosophers and musicians. This too has to do with the fact that a particularly effective nation has been compelled by nature to undertake an eternal but propitious struggle for life and, in the course of this struggle, has not neglected its spiritual energies . . .

1. *All Germans who live together belong in a nation-state*; it does not weaken Germany's prestige if substantial numbers of Germans live outside the boundaries of the German Reich. These elements can, however, only remain bearers of German culture [*Deutschtum*] if they integrate into the foreign nation state. Only then do they and the German Reich have the opportunity of ensuring that they can maintain and cultivate German ways.

2. The nature of human beings and Germany's central position in a group of other nation-states compels the German Reich to maintain a sufficiently strong Wehrmacht. This must also be secured on the diplomatic front. Whether it will later provide the core of European military forces depends on future developments. The possibility and the aim of achieving this should be kept in sight. *The maintenance of the German Wehrmacht is so important that this factor should be*

*placed in the foreground when considering the timing and the form of the conclusion of peace.* The Wehrmacht is also essential as a domestic political bond and as a school for the nation; however, to secure this role it requires the restoration of and respect for soldierly values. It can only possess and maintain these on morally sound foundations.

3. The development of technology requires larger economic spheres than those created during the nineteenth century. Almost all members of the white and yellow races recognise this fact. Before this war, Europe was ready for such a union and outside Germany has already taken various steps in this direction (Oslo Group, Balkan League). The greater economic area which is appropriate for Germany is certainly *Europe.* But, apart from the fact that, in view of Russia's backwardness, for the next two decades it will not be large enough, it would be a feeble abdication if we were not to exploit our capabilities in the other parts of the world as well. So let us deploy them round the world aggressively in all directions; but let us not assume that this kind of aggression has anything to do with military aggression.

If it is to have any hope of lasting the *European economic sphere* can only be achieved through the organic union [*Zusammenfassung*] of independent European nation-states and not by forcing them together [*Zusammenraffung*]. Here too, the intellectual, economic and spiritual forces will have to be deployed in the first instance as happened a century ago in the case of Prussia within Germany. Its central position, its demographic strength and its high level of capability will guarantee *the German people the leadership* of the European block *if* it does not destroy its chance through a lack of moderation or through a bullying manner. It is stupid and arrogant to talk of Germans as a master race. It is foolish to demand respect for one's own national honour and independence and to deny them to others. The nation which respects the small nations and which tries to guide their fortunes with wise counsel and a wise hand and not with brutal force will grow into the leadership of Europe. The objective correctness of particular viewpoints must be decisive. Legitimate interests must be mediated in an intelligent and far-sighted manner. If one does everything one can to conceal the leadership role, if one allows others to take the lead on peripheral matters then one can easily lead the European states to their mutual benefit. In this event— and only in this event—one will succeed in a comparatively short time in also uniting the military forces of the European nation-states.

As was said before, Europe was ready for this before the war. As a result of this war, it has come no nearer to this goal; on the contrary, it has moved away from it. The current superficial coordination is irrelevant here. In reality, it is a coordination based on a system of compulsion, the destruction of currencies and, in the final analysis, hunger. The spiritual and intellectual leaders of other nations are more alienated from us than in the First World War. As a result, the achievement of this goal is only possible if Germany dispenses with the wrong political means *at the right time and of its own free will* and decides to adopt a comprehensible political goal and tolerable means to achieve it.

The union of Europe must not occur crudely and ruthlessly through coordination but can only happen if is based on the wisdom which Bismarck embodied in the case of the unification of Germany. *The nation-states of Europe must have complete freedom to order their internal affairs in a way which they consider appropriate to their own particular characters and needs;* this naturally includes complete freedom in all intellectual and spiritual spheres. Initially, the only thing necessary is a community whose members agree on common rules for the balancing of their budgets, thereby securing their currencies, the gradual reduction of all tariffs and travel restrictions, regular discussions with the aim of aligning their economies, aligning their transport systems etc. etc. Based on this community, in a few years one can move to tariff agreements, to mergers, to currency arrangements etc. From there one will move to a confederation with military agreements etc. It is not too bold a statement to say that if action is taken at the right time, i.e. *by ending the war in favour of a sensible political system*, the European Confederation under German leadership will have come about within a matter of ten to twenty years. *If the right moment is missed then there can be no question of German leadership for a long period . . .*

In the east a fruitful economic and political cooperation cannot develop with a Bolshevik Russia. It can be readily observed the Bolshevik system of collectivism, soullessness, mechanistic organization, godlessness has not developed the economic capabilities of the Russian people to the extent that would be feasible for a country so rich in raw materials . . . It is advisable in all circumstances to maintain permanent contact with England, the USA, China and Japan. The aim must be gradually to integrate Russia in a European union; for within its wide spaces lie the raw materials and potential foodstuffs which would considerably improve the situation of a united Europe vis-à-vis all other parts of the world.

4. It is useful for the German Reich to possess colonies . . . A concentrated block of colonial territory in Africa is generally preferable to one that is scattered far and wide . . .

6. On the basis of points 1–5 it will be possible to come to a lasting agreement with the English empire as well as the United States. This understanding will ripen quite organically from the European community. Moreover, the English empire—having rearranged its colonial possessions to Germany's benefit—will, just like the United States, have complete freedom to pursue policies appropriate to its needs. There will be no lack of opportunities for peaceful understanding. For the time being, they will be guaranteed by armaments in view of the fact that mutual trust has been shaken for the past twenty years. Any discussion of disarmament can and must initially be rejected. But the exhaustion of economic resources compels every major state to make cuts and in the end to seek an agreement on a sensible degree of disarmament. This search must emerge organically from a need and be capable of being realized as a result of a restoration of trust. *Such a peaceful policy is to be preferred to any war policy* because it is precisely in times of peace that these two great empires will find themselves confronted with the problems which are peculiar to them . . .

11. A rearrangement of the position of the Jews appears necessary throughout the world., for everywhere movements are in progress which cannot be halted without an organic order and which without such an order will only lead to injustices and inhumanity or at least to an unsatisfactory disorder. The fact that the Jewish people belong to another race is a commonplace. Among the Jewish

people there is disagreement as to whether they should seek to form an independent state or not. The Zionists have been demanding and preparing for their own Jewish state for a long time. Up until 1933 they did not play an important role. However, the world will only find peace if the Jewish people acquire a really effective opportunity to found and maintain their own state. Such a territory, providing quite reasonable living conditions, could easily be found either in parts of Canada or South America . . .

▬▬▬▬

By the end of 1941, Ulrich von Hassell was becoming increasingly disillusioned about the flaws in the various Resistance leaders and the ideological differences between its members. A major problem was how to reconcile the views of the older Conservatives, like Beck and Goerdeler, with those of younger members of the Resistance, and the need to win mass support through sympathetic Trade Union leaders like the Social Democrat, Wilhelm Leuschner, and the Catholic, Jacob Kaiser:

**1344** *21 December 1941.* What has engrossed and disquieted me most during the past weeks has been the numerous conferences on questions concerning a change of the regime. One major difficulty is Goerdeler. He is too sanguine, always sees things as he wishes to see them, and in many ways is a real reactionary, though otherwise he has splendid qualities. Nevertheless, we finally agreed on the main issues. We also agreed, despite all doubts about his position, that the Crown Prince must come to the fore. Beck[20] assented, although through past connections he knows the Crown Prince well.

The principal difficulty with Beck is that he is very theoretical. As Popitz[21] says, a man of tactics but little will power, whereas Goerdeler has great will-power but not tact(ics). Popitz himself often displays a slightly professorial manner, the somewhat abstract views of an administrator. Nevertheless, all three are capital men.

I have always feared that we have too little contact with younger circles. This fear has now been demonstrated, but only to reveal new and formidable difficulties. First of all, I had a long talk with Trott,[22] during which he passionately contended for the avoidance, within as well as outside the country, of any semblance of 'reaction', of a 'gentlemen's club', or of 'militarism'. Therefore, though he is also a monarchist, we must under no circumstances have a monarchy now, for a monarchy would not win the support of the people or win confidence abroad. 'Converted' Social Democrats, that is Christian Social Democrats, one of whom (a former Reichstag deputy) he named, would never go along with us on the monarchy and would wait for the next group.

---

[20] Colonel-General Ludwig Beck, Chief of the General Staff 1935–8.
[21] Johannes Popitz, a Conservative, was Prussian Finance Minister.
[22] Adam von Trott zu Solz, a former Rhodes Scholar at Oxford, was attached to the Information Department of the German Foreign Office.

To these negative points he added the single positive thought, that Niemöller should be made Chancellor of the Reich. He was, on the one hand, the strongest internationally recognized exponent of anti-Hitlerism, and, on the other hand, the most popular reformer here and the one most likely to appeal to the Anglo-Saxon world.

Afterwards I met the alert, cultured Peter Yorck,[23] a true scion of a family of high intellect, though sometimes too inclined to theorising. He expressed similar sentiments. Finally, at Yorck's request, I went to see him again. There I met Moltke,[24] Trott and Gutenberg.[25] All four, under the leadership of Trott, set to work on me furiously.

On the day of my departure, at Popitz's, Fritzi Schulenburg[26] hammered away at the same theme. Of the five young men he was easily the most sober-minded, the most politically conscious but, on the other hand, the most prejudiced against the Crown Prince, since his father had absolutely enjoined him to oppose any such possibility because of the stand taken by the Crown Prince in the crisis of 1918. So far as Prince Louis Ferdinand is concerned, he apparently considers himself the man of the hour, though he lacks many essential qualities. He seems to have got along without them by insisting that they are part of his inheritance.

Goerdeler takes an almost completely unsympathetic attitude towards the ideas of these young men, who for their part disapprove of him. He maintains that he himself has good relations with the Social Democrats In the matter of the Crown Prince his views are less positive.

Beck firmly supports Goerdeler in this as in most questions. Popitz, more than anyone, favours the Crown Prince as an immediate solution. All three emphasize that we should not permit ourselves to be unduly influenced by the passing moods of the populace; but Goerdeler, of course, overestimates the degree to which people in general resent the present system and long for a move towards liberation.

I am trying to find some sort of a connecting link with the younger men by arguing somewhat as follows: The premise 'No reaction, but attempt to get popular support' was correct. Therefore it is most earnestly to be desired that we find, to head the government, a man whose name will stand both for liberation and for a policy. This is important also, even if only to a limited degree, in the interest of foreign policy. This interest is necessary because the national character of this change, rising out of the peculiar will and needs of our people,

---

[23] Count Peter Yorck von Wartenburg, scion of a distinguished Prussian noble family, was a member of the staff of the Reich Price Commissioner.

[24] Count Helmut James von Moltke, a member of a distinguished Silesian noble family, worked in the prisoner-of-war division of the High Command of the Wehrmacht.

[25] Baron Karl Ludwig von Gutenberg was a Bavarian nobleman who served with Military Intelligence and was editor of a clandestine Bavarian monarchist newspaper, the *Weisse Blätter*.

[26] Count Fritz-Dietlof von der Schulenberg, a Pomeranian Junker, had initially sympathized with the Nazis and was now deputy Police President of Berlin. See Vol. 2, docs 153–155.

can be maintained only if we do not look over our shoulder at other countries: also because the Christian-pacifist circles among the Anglo-Saxon peoples, on whom Trott counts most heavily, are entirely useless as a dependable political factor.

In general I am against Trott's theoretical and visionary outlook. Unfortunately, the kind of person we are hoping for is not to be found. I am convinced that the man whom Trott has proposed (Niemöller) has some unsuitable characteristics. He is somewhat unbending, non-political, and not a good strategist. Aside from all this, I think that after the first effect has worn off he would not be a successful symbol. On the contrary, he might even create opposition.

In this state of affairs there is nothing left but to act without such a popular personality—for act we must, and that very soon. It is clear that the situation has reached such a pitch that the role of any new government will be an utterly thankless one, taken on in the middle of a mess—indeed the role of a kind of liquidator.

We must bear in mind that we may be used only to clean up and will then be replaced by others, or that we may fail altogether. The task is to manage this as well as humanly possible. Moreover, we shall have to assemble a government as free as possible of any whiff of reaction, militarism or the like. Action is now, however, the main thing.

So far as the Hohenzollern family[27] is concerned, the situation is serious enough. Nevertheless, in spite of all doubts, this is the one way which still offers the greatest hope of coordinated action. The decision will have to be made according to the situation of the moment; and the one who swings into action first will have the most to say . . .

▬▬

The variety of different elements contained in the wartime Resistance movement is well brought out in the following report by Bishop Bell of Chichester, who had contacts with Protestant resisters and was trying unsuccessfully to persuade the British Government to take the German Resistance seriously and negotiate with them. In the spring of 1942, Dietrich Bonhoeffer and Hans Schönfeld from the foreign relations office of the Protestant churches both seized the opportunity of a visit by Bell to Stockholm. They travelled independently and apparently without coordinating their trips. Schönfeld, who was representing members of the Kreisau circle, met Bell on 26 and 29 May and on 31 May Bell prepared the following report on the interview—the 'Statement by a German Pastor at Stockholm'.

The points made by Schönfeld reflect the views of a number of different members of the Resistance from the Kreisau circle to Goerdeler and others and appear to have been an attempt to cover a broad spectrum of

---

[27] The Prussian-German royal family.

Resistance thinking. Bonhoeffer, who arrived later, then injected a theological element into the discussion by saying that his 'Christian conscience was not quite at ease with Schönfeld's ideas' and that 'there must be punishment by God. We would not be worthy of such a solution. We do not want to escape repentance. Our action must be understood as an act of repentance.'[28] Impressed, particularly by Bonhoeffer's attitude, on his return to Britain Bell tried to convince the Foreign Secretary, Anthony Eden, of the importance of the message from the two pastors—to no avail. Quoting 'national interest' Eden refused to permit any response to be made.

**1345**  I. Towards the end of May 1942 two German pastors came from Berlin to Stockholm in order to meet the Bishop of Chichester there. They arrived independently of one another and one of them only stayed for forty-eight hours. The bishop spoke to them separately as well as together on four different days. Both men are well known to the bishop and have worked together with him for many years in connection with the ecumenical movement and the World Council of Churches and at various stages in the German church struggle [against the regime's interference in church life]. One of them lives in Switzerland but visits Germany frequently. The other lives in Berlin and is one of the leaders of the Confessional Church; he has been banned from speaking and preaching by the Gestapo. Their intention was:

A. To give information about a strong organized resistance movement within Germany which had prepared plans for the destruction of the whole Hitler regime (including that of Himmler, Göring, Goebbels and the chief leaders of the Gestapo, SS and SA) and for the formation of a new German Government, consisting of:
1. Representatives of strongly anti-National Socialist forces in the Army and central State administration.
2. Former trade-union leaders.
3. Representatives of the Protestant and Catholic Churches.
They commit themselves to the following policy:
(a) the abandonment of offensive operations;
(b) the immediate suspension of the Nuremberg Laws,[29]
(c) the gradual withdrawal of German troops from countries which have been occupied and attacked;
(d) the withdrawal of support from Japan, and the supporting of the Allies in order to end the war in the Far East;
(e) collaboration with the Allies in order to rebuild the areas destroyed or damaged by the war.
B. To ask whether the Allies would be prepared, provided the whole Hitler

---

[28] See K. von Klemperer, *German Resistance against Hitler: The Search for Allies Abroad 1938–1945* (Oxford 1992), p. 286.
[29] See Vol. 2, docs 403–406.

regime had been destroyed, to negotiate with such a new German Government a peace settlement which would provide for the following:

1. the institution of a system of law and social justice in Germany combined with a far-reaching distribution of tasks to single states;

2. the creation of mutual economic dependence between the various nations of Europe which would be justified in itself as well as the most efficient guarantee against militarism;

3. the foundation of a representative federation of free nations or states which would include a free Polish and a free Czech nation;

4. the setting up of a European army for the control of Europe under central direction in which the German army could participate.

## II. *Structure of the opposition*

The opposition had been developing for some time and was already in existence before the war. The war now gives it a chance which is only waiting to be seized. The opposition crystallized in the autumn of 1941 and could have seized an opportunity when many officers refused to continue fighting in Russia. But nobody took on the leadership. Hitler's most recent speech in which he claimed quite openly to stand above the law has shown the German people more clearly than ever the complete lawlessness of the regime.[30] The opposition has complete confidence in the struggle of the German army and is prepared to fight the war to the bitter end if the Allies should refuse to negotiate with the new Government of a Germany freed from Hitler after the overthrow of the whole Hitler regime, but it also believes that the continuation of the war on its present or even on a bigger scale would condemn further millions to destruction especially in the occupied countries. It also believes that to fight until a decision had been reached would be suicidal for Europe. From this springs the wish to destroy Hitler and his regime first and then reach a peace settlement by which all European nations are to become economically interdependent, are to be defended against aggression through the possession of adequate European military forces, and are in some way to be allied with one another. Although the opposition has some doubts with regard to Russia, none the less, relying on impressions made on German officers by some of the higher Russian officers, it hopes that it may be possible to reach an agreement.

## III. *Organization of the opposition*

The opposition is based on members of the state administration, the state police, former trade union leaders and high-ranking officers of the army. It has contacts in every ministry, military officials in all the big cities, commanding generals in all armies. It has contact men in the wireless stations, in the big factories, in the main offices of the army depots and in the gas distribution network. It is impossible to give the numbers of the opposition. The main thing is that key

---

[30] For the speech referred to see above, p. 14.

positions everywhere are in the hands of the opposition and that key positions are of the greatest importance in Germany.

The following names were given of men thought to be closely connected with the resistance movement:

| | |
|---|---|
| Colonel-General Beck | Chief of the General Staff before the Czechoslovakian crisis in 1938, 60 years old. |
| Colonel-General von Hammerstein | Chief of the General Staff before Beck.[31] |
| Goerdeler | Formerly Price Commissar, Lord Mayor of Leipzig, director of the Civil Front. |
| Leuschner | Former President of the United Trade Union.[32] |
| Kaiser | Head of the Catholic Trade Union.[33] |

All those mentioned above are said to be convinced Christians; the most important of them are Beck and Goerdeler.

Certain other people of less pronounced Christian character would be available such as Schacht, for example. Most of the Field Marshals can be relied on, especially von Kluge, von Bock, Küchler and possibly Witzleben. The question was whether England would recommend a monarchy in Germany, in which case Prince Louis Ferdinand was eligible. But it was not stated whether he was a member of the opposition or not. He had been brought back from the United States by Hitler after the heroic death of the Crown Prince's eldest son. He had had a job as a worker in the Ford factory and now lives on an estate in east Prussia. He is a Christian, shows a genuine social conscience and is known to one of the two German pastors. The leaders of the Protestant and Catholic churches also are closely connected with the whole resistance movement, especially Bishop Wurm of Württemberg (Protestant) and Bishop von Preysing, who acts as spokesman of the Catholic bishops. At the same time it should be mentioned that many members of the opposition are not only filled with deep remorse for the crimes committed in the name of Germany but even say: 'Christians do not want to shirk any penance or disaster if God's will places it upon us.'

## IV. Course of action by the opposition

The opposition knows of the rebellion against Hitler by Himmler and his associates which is threatening within the Nazi Party;[34] but while a successful

---

[31] Kurt von Hammerstein-Equord, Chief of the Army High Command 1930–4.

[32] Wilhelm Leuschner, Deputy Chairman of the German Trade Union Association in 1932 and SPD Interior Minister in Hesse 1929–33.

[33] Jacob Kaiser was on the board of the Christian Trade Unions of Germany 1924–33.

[34] There was in fact no such rebellion brewing; it was only in the last phase of the war that Himmler began to distance himself from the regime and seek contacts with the Allies.

*coup d'etat* by Himmler could be useful to the opposition, the complete extermination of Hitler, Himmler and the whole regime is indispensable. The plan of the opposition consists of a cleansing action which would have to be carried out as simultaneously as possible in the fatherland and in the occupied countries. After that a new government would be set up. The opposition is aware of the necessity for an effective police control everywhere, in Germany and in the countries which have been occupied and attacked, in order to secure the new Government, and it seems as if the help of the Allied army as a means of maintaining order would be necessary and welcome, the more so if it was possible to combine the army of a neutral power with the Allied army to maintain order.

## V. *Questions put by the opposition to the Government of the Allies*

After the course of action and plans of the opposition have been explained, the question arises of what support can be given their leaders to start the operation, and to meet all the dangers connected with it. The following questions are put as examples of means for promoting it:

1. Would the Allied Governments be prepared to enter bona fide negotiations with a new German Government constructed according to the guidelines of paragraph I. A, for a peace settlement as described in Paragraph I. B.

(The reply to this could be sent privately to a representative of the opposition through a neutral country.)

2. Could the Allies announce to the world now and in the clearest terms that, if Hitler and the whole regime were overthrown, they would be ready to negotiate with a new Government with regard to a peace settlement of the kind described in paragraph I. B, which renounced all aggression and committed itself to a course of action as described in paragraph I. A?

▬▬▬

Meanwhile, during 1942–3 Goerdeler had been making desperate attempts to win over one or more of the senior army commanders for a move against Hitler and the regime. The most promising appeared to be the commander of Army Group Centre on the eastern front, Field Marshal Hans von Kluge. His chief of staff, Major-General Henning von Tresckow, had been involved in the Resistance since before the war and was trying to win him over, and for this purpose he arranged for Goerdeler to visit the headquarters of Army Group Centre in Smolensk in the autumn of 1942. Goerdeler impressed Kluge and his staff but the Field Marshal remained true to his nickname, 'clever Hans' (*der kluge Hans*) by refusing to commit himself. In the following summer, becoming increasingly desperate, particularly after the loss of his son in what he regarded as a senseless war for an immoral regime, Goerdeler appealed once more to Kluge in a letter dated 25 July 1943, which was, however, never sent. It expresses both Goerdeler's moral disgust with the

regime and his burning commitment for action but also reflects the
illusions which he held about the potential support for action within the
German population and among senior members of the regime:

**1346**     At the moment all moral ties have been torn; what remains is merely
convention. Anyone who like me travels around sees how corruption is rife, for
example in the big hotels. He sees figures in the shape of officers who have
nothing more in common with our good old officer corps; he sees young lads,
wearing Party badges who win victories with their mouths but have no intention
of doing their military service. Even within the Wehrmacht the foundations of
morality must have been seriously shaken because the religious basis has been
abandoned and because comrades can report each other behind their backs
without being treated with contempt. The establishment of the Special Court at
the Reich Military Court, the infiltration of the army with spies says it all! A
week ago, I heard the report of an 18-year-old SS soldier who used to be a
decent boy and now calmly told how 'it wasn't exactly pleasant to machine-gun
graves full of thousands of Jews and then throw earth on the bodies which were
still twitching'. What have they done to the proud army of the Wars of
Liberation [against Napoleon] and of Kaiser William I? But the people know
and feel this with an admirable and instinctive certainty which, thank God is still
there. For God's sake, do not be deceived, Herr Field Marshal, when people tell
you that the people believe the lies that are imposed on them. The nation
despises these lies and hates those who spread them. That is the truth. It will
break through with all the more elemental force the more one tries to suppress
it. But it will then turn against all those who bear a share of the responsibility
for all this . . . In view of the national disaster which is evidently developing and
into which we have been plunged by a crazed leadership, which despises all
divine and human law, I am taking the liberty of addressing a final request to
you, Herr Field Marshal. You may be certain that it will be the last. The time
has now come for us to reach a final decision on our personal fates. The path to
which our consciences direct us leads in one direction; the other, the easier one
points in another direction. The one involves dangers but is honourable; the
other will lead to the bitter end and fearful remorse. Given the increasing
destruction of German cities, do you know, Herr Field Marshal, of a way of
securing a victory, which (1) enables us to keep Russia away from Europe for
good; (2) compels the USA and the English world empire to give up these
attacks and formally to make peace? *That* is, after all, from a political and a
military point of view the issue that is facing us. If such a victory is possible then
one must explain to the German people how it can be achieved and not with lies
but with the truth which must really exist. But if a victory is not possible then
the continuation of the war is nothing but a crime, for a nation never
experiences a heroic end but instead invariably has to keep on living.

I have once more established and take the responsibility for saying that there
is still a possibility of securing a favourable peace for us if we Germans once
again transform ourselves into people with whom it is feasible to negotiate. It is
obvious that no statesman in the world will be prepared to negotiate with

criminals and fools because he will not foolishly place the fate of his people in the hands of fools. Naturally, the possibilities of realizing this are fewer than a year ago. And they can only be exploited if the politician involved has a certain period for manoeuvre, in other words if he is not suddenly confronted with the military assessment: 'We can't go on!' as happened in 1918. If this second precondition, which is dependent on the military, is fulfilled then we can calmly and sensibly reduce the level of fighting straight away in the air and gradually on land as well. Whoever can announce to the German people that the air war is over will have the people behind him and no one will dare to complain or lift a finger against him. That's the situation and no mistake.

I am ready to make such a move in which one would simply call a spade a spade and grab the criminals whatever the danger involved. I could even become an officer again if that would ensure systematic and rapid action. I can say to you now that I can provide you, Herr Field Marshal, or any other general who is determined to act with the support of the overwhelming majority of the working class, of the German officials and of German business. I can even, if you want, make Herr Goebbels or Herr Himmler into your allies; for these two men have also long realized that with Hitler they are lost. So it is really only a question of making the decision, of cool calculation and of taking the right action. The most dangerous thing which in the end becomes intolerable is, day after day, to close one's ears to one's conscience. I am convinced Herr Field Marshal that you will agree with me on this . . .

We must stop permitting fools to impose their illusions and lies on the German people, to claim that a war of conquest born out of a desire to dominate is really a necessary defensive war. We have no need at all to fear Bolshevism or the Anglo-Saxons. At bottom they're no different from anybody else and we have a lot going for us. They too are dependent on our strength and our abilities. But it must once more be decent Germans who are representing German interests with energy and intelligence.

I shall no longer trouble you, Herr Field Marshal. There is only one reply that I have to request from you and I know what it will mean if you deny me that answer. I ask of you only one thing: do not deny it to me because you are worried. I know what I owe to those men whom I trust. But if at least three or four men in Germany can no longer trust one another then we can pack it all in.

> With best wishes,
> Your obedient servant,

> [signed] GOERDELER

---

## (vi) The Kreisau Circle

The term 'Kreisau Circle' was first used by the Reich Security Main Office to describe a group of resisters which held three important meetings during 1942–3 at the estate of one of their two leaders, Count Helmut von Moltke, in Kreisau, Lower Silesia. Before the war, and independently from one another, two groups of friends and acquaintances who were hostile to Nazism had formed round Moltke and another scion of a distinguished Prussian noble family, Count Peter Yorck von Wartenburg. The members of the group (around twenty active ones with a similar number of sympathizers) came from very diverse backgrounds. Among others, there were Protestant theologians, Jesuit priests, former SPD politicians, as well as several noblemen with legal training. They were influenced by Christianity and various forms of socialism, while many had come from the German youth movement. Many had foreign contacts and experience and a breadth of outlook uncharacteristic of most Germans. Several had posts within the regime, particularly in the Foreign Ministry and Wehrmacht agencies, notably its military intelligence branch (*Abwehr*).

One can gauge something of the character of Moltke and of the values and principles which underlay his resistance to the Nazis in the following letter written to an English friend, Lionel Curtis, in 1942:

**1347**      I will try to get this letter through to you, giving you a picture of the state of affairs on our side.

Things are worse and better than anybody outside Germany can believe them to be. They are worse, because the tyranny, the terror, the loss of values of all kinds, is greater than I could have believed a short time ago. The number of Germans killed by legal process in November was 25 a day through judgements of the civil courts and at least 75 a day by judgements of the courts martial, numbers running into hundreds are killed daily in concentration camps and by simple shooting without any pretence of a trial. The constant danger in which we live is formidable. At the same time the greater part of the population has been uprooted and has been conscripted to forced labour of some kind and spread all over the continent untying all bonds of nature and surroundings and thereby loosening the beast in man which is reigning. The few really good people who try to stem the tide are isolated as far as they have to work in these unnatural surroundings, because they cannot trust their comrades and they are in danger from the hatred of the oppressed people even when they succeed in saving some from the worst. Thousands of Germans who will survive will be dead mentally, will be useless for normal work.

But things are also better than you can believe, and that in many ways. The most important is the spiritual awakening, which is starting up, coupled as it is with the preparedness to be killed if need be. The backbone of this movement is to be found in both the Christian confessions, Protestant as well as Catholic. The Catholic churches are crowded every Sunday, the Protestant churches not yet, but the movement is discernible. We are trying to build on this foundation. And I hope that in a few months more tangible proof of this will be apparent outside. Many hundreds of our people will have to die before this will be strong enough, but today they are prepared to do so. This is also true of the young generation . . .But today it is beginning to dawn on a not too numerous but active part of the population not that they have been misled, not that they are in for a hard time, not that they might lose the war, but that what is done is sinful, and that they are personally responsible for every savage act that has been done, not of course in a mortal way, but as Christians. Perhaps you will remember that, in discussions before the war, I maintained that belief in God was not essential for coming to the results you arrive at. Today I know I was wrong. You know that I have fought the Nazis from the first day, but the amount of risk and readiness for sacrifice which is asked from us now, and that which may be asked from us tomorrow, require more than right ethical principles, especially as we know that the success of our fight will probably mean a total collapse as a national unit. But we are ready to face this.

The second great asset which we are slowly but steadily acquiring is this; the great dangers which confront us as soon as we get rid of the NS force us to visualize Europe after the war. We can only expect to get our people to overthrow this reign of terror and horror if we are able to show a picture beyond the terrifying and hopeless immediate future. A picture which will make it worth while for the disillusioned people to strive for, to work for, to start again and to believe in. For us Europe after the war is a question of how the picture of man can be re-established in the breasts of our fellow citizens. This is a question of religion and education, of ties to work and family, of the proper relation of responsibility and rights. I must say that under the incredible pressure under which we have to labour we have made progress, which will be visible one day. Can you imagine what it means to work as a group when you cannot use the telephone, when you are unable to post letters, when you cannot tell the names of your closest friends to your other friends for fear that one of them might be caught and might divulge the names under the pressure?

We are after considerable difficulties, in communication with the Christian groups in the various occupied territories . . . These people are simply splendid and are a great accession of strength to us, giving trust to many others. Of course their position is easier than ours: moral and national duties are congruous even to the simple-minded, while with us there is an apparent clash of duties.

Happily I have been able to follow the activities of my English friends, and I hope they all keep their spirits up. The hardest bit of the way is still to come, but nothing is worse than to slack on the way. Please do not forget that we trust that you will stand it through without flinching as we are prepared to do our bit, and don't forget that for us a very bitter end is in sight when you have seen matters through. We hope that you will realize that we are ready to help you win war and peace.

Yours ever,

JAMES

___

In its meetings the Kreisau Circle discussed how a just and humane political and social order could be established in Germany after the fall of Nazism and how Germany could be integrated into a new peaceful European order. While the Kreisauer advocated a democratic system, they shared a traditional German suspicion of liberal democracy on the

Western model with its political parties, a suspicion greatly reinforced by their experience of Weimar. They opposed what they saw as the modern atomized mass society in which they believed all human bonds had been dissolved and for which they blamed both the weaknesses of Weimar and the tyranny of Nazism. They were concerned about what they considered the political immaturity of the German people, which in their view had been demonstrated by the experience of Weimar, and which had now been exacerbated by the period of Nazi tyranny. They emphasized the importance of encouraging personal freedom and responsibility and wanted to build democracy from the grass roots upwards through 'small communities', with strong self-government in the tradition of Freiherr vom Stein,[35] and then up through district and state governments and parliaments to the national level. The state and national parliaments were to be elected indirectly by the district and state parliaments respectively. They disliked unbridled capitalism and believed the State should play an important role in the economy with key industries nationalized. Finally, they were hostile to the traditional international order of rival nation states with its concomitant encouragement of nationalism and they advocated the integration of the European-nation states into a European federal order. They summed up their main goals in their 'Basic Principles for a New Order in Germany' of 9 August 1943:

**1348** The Government of the German Reich sees in Christianity the basis for the moral and religious revival of our people, for the overcoming of hatred and lies, for the reconstruction of the European community of nations.

The starting point is man's commitment to the divine order on which his inner and outer existence depends. Only when one has succeeded in making this order the criterion for relations between people and nations can the disorder of our time be overcome and a genuine state of peace be created. The internal reorganization of the Reich is the basis for the achievement of a just and lasting peace.

In view of the collapse of a power structure which no longer feels any obligations and which is based solely on its command of technology, European humanity is faced above all with this task. The way to its solution lies in the determined and active realization of Christian values. The Reich Government is therefore determined to realize the following indispensable requirements, which cannot be renounced inwardly or outwardly, with all available means:

---

[35] Freiherr vom Stein played a key role in the Prussian reforms which followed Prussia's defeat by Napoleon in 1806. He introduced a measure of municipal self-government, partially emancipating Prussian towns from the tutelage of central government with the aim of encouraging the development of a responsible citizenry.

1. Justice which has been trampled underfoot must be raised again and made predominant over all areas of human life. Under the protection of conscientious, independent judges free from the fear of men, it is the foundation for all future plans for peace.

2. Freedom of faith and of conscience will be safeguarded. Existing laws and regulations which violate these principles will be repealed at once.

3. Totalitarian moral constraint must be broken and the inviolable dignity of the human person must be recognized as the basis for the order of justice and peace which is to be striven for. Everybody will partake in the responsibility for the various social, political and international spheres of life. The right to work and to hold property will be under public protection, irrespective of race, nationality or faith.

4. The basic unit of peaceful social life is the family. It will be under public protection which, apart from education, will also secure its material needs: food, clothing, a dwelling, garden and health.

5. Work must be organized in such a way that it promotes personal responsibility and does not let it wither. Apart from creating the material conditions of work and further professional training this requires everyone's effective co-responsibility in the factory and further in the general economic context to which his work contributes. Through this he will contribute to the growth of a healthy and durable structure of life in which the individual, his family, and the community can achieve organic development in a balanced economic system. Those who manage the economy must safeguard these basic requirements.

6. The political responsibility of every individual demands his cooperation in the self-government of small communities which are to be revived. Rooted and tested in these, his co-determination in the state and in the community of nations must be secured by elected representatives and in this way he must be convinced of his co-responsibility for political events.

7. The special responsibility and loyalty due from every individual to his national origin, to his language and to the intellectual and historical traditions of his people must be guarded and respected. But it must not be misused for the concentration of political power or for the degrading persecution, or suppression of foreign races. The free and peaceful development of national culture can no longer be reconciled with the claim to absolute sovereignty of individual states. Peace requires the creation of an arrangement comprising individual states. As soon as the free agreement of all nations concerned is guaranteed, those responsible for this arrangement must have the right to demand obedience, reverence, if necessary even the risking of life and property for the highest political authority of the community of nations . . .

The Reich will remain the supreme leading authority of the German nation. Its political constitution should be supported by the true authority, cooperation and co-responsibility of the nation. It is based on the natural subdivisions of the nation: family, local community and province [Land]. The Reich will be structured on the principle of self-administration. It will combine freedom and personal responsibility with the requirements of order and leadership.

This structure is intended to facilitate the unity and the combined leadership of the Reich and its integration in the community of the European nations.

The political activity of the nation will occur within a context which is easily comprehensible for the individual. Provinces which are geographically, economically and culturally homogeneous will be formed on the basis of the natural subdivisions of local communities and districts. In order to achieve effective self-administration the provinces should contain between and 3 and 5 million inhabitants.

The distribution of tasks will be based on the principle that every corporate body is responsible for carrying out all those tasks which it makes sense for it to carry out itself . . .

## IV. *The Reich*

The Reich parliament will be elected by the provincial parliaments. Every male Reich citizen who has reached the age of 27 is entitled to be elected. Political officials and members of the armed forces are electable. The electoral law will ensure that, for the time being, at least half of those elected do not belong to one of the corporate bodies involved in the election . . .

Following the arrest of the conspirators in the Military Intelligence section of OKW in the autumn of 1943, among whom were several members of the Kreisau Circle, Moltke was himself arrested in January 1944 and hanged a year later. Many other members, including Peter Yorck von Wartenburg, shared his fate, while a few survived the war.

## (vii)   The Plot of 20 July 1944

The arrests of the *Abwehr* conspirators and of Moltke gave added urgency to the plans of the other conspirators to remove Hitler and this urgency was increased by the deteriorating war situation, which meant that if Germany was to achieve an acceptable peace they would have to act sooner rather than later. The Resistance was still hoping to achieve what in their eyes would be reasonable peace terms until quite a late stage. This was partly because of their sense of national pride and partly because of their understandable desire to legitimize the new government in the eyes of the German people as far as possible.

This view was shared in particular by the man who, in the autumn of 1943, had become the most dynamic figure in the conspiracy, a Bavarian nobleman, Colonel Claus Schenck von Stauffenberg. A Romantic conservative, Stauffenberg, like many of the military Resisters, had initially been sympathetic to the regime but had turned against it because of its conduct of the war on the eastern front—the mass murder of Jews and the maltreatment of Soviet prisoners of war. The following document, part of the record of the Gestapo interrogations following the failure of the July coup, contains Stauffenberg's proposal submitted to a British agent in Stockholm by his fellow conspirator, Adam von Trott zu Solz. The demands are more modest than those of Goerdeler in the past but are still remarkably ambitious given Germany's military situation:

**1349** The recent interrogation of Captain Kaiser has produced several indications that Stauffenberg had two channels to the English via middlemen. The details are currently being investigated. Already on 25 May, Kaiser produced a note for Stauffenberg to serve as the basis for negotiations with the enemy:

1. To cease the air war immediately.
2. To give up plans for invasion.
3. To avoid further sacrifice of blood.
4. To maintain a permanent defence capability in the east, withdraw from all occupied territories in the north, west and south.
5. To avoid any occupation.
6. A freely elected government as part of an independently formulated constitution.
7. Total participation in the implementation of the armistice conditions and in the preparation of peace.
8. The Reich frontiers of 1914 in the east. Austria and the Sudetenland to remain with the Reich. Autonomy for Alsace-Lorraine. The acquisition of South Tyrol down to Bolzano, Merano.
9. Energetic reconstruction with participation in the reconstruction of Europe.
10. The right to deal with the enemies of the people ourselves.
11. The reacquisition of honour, self-respect and the respect of others.

At the end of June 1944 Kaiser learned from Goerdeler that inquiries were being made at the highest level in England about the clique of conspirators. Stauffenberg sent over a list of the men who would be the future negotiation partners, expressing the wish that Austria should remain with the Reich and that the settlement of accounts with the war criminals should be left to the future German government.

▬▬▬

The Allied invasion of France on 6 June 1944 finally put an end to such hopes. A young officer on Tresckow's staff, Fabian von Schlabrendorff, recorded after the war what happened:

**1350** Lehndorff[36] had just arrived from Stauffenberg with the job of asking Tresckow whether, after the invasion, there was any point in continuing with our

---

[36] Count Heinrich Lehndorff, an East Prussian nobleman and lieutenant on von Tresckow's staff.

plan since there no longer appeared to be any practical purpose to it. Tresckow replied as follows: 'The assassination attempt must take place *coûte que coute*. Even if it does not succeed we must still act. For it is no longer a question of whether it has a practical purpose; what counts is the fact that in the eyes of the world and of history the German Resistance dared to act. Compared with that nothing else is important.'

Stauffenberg was convinced and, on 4 July, agreed with a friend that what mattered now was 'internal purification' and the question of honour.[37] The conspirators were aware that, in the event of failure, they would be vilified as traitors by most of their fellow countrymen. After the war, Schlabrendorff recalled taking his leave of Tresckow shortly after the failure of the coup:

**1351**    On the following day, on 21 July 1944, Tresckow and I said goodbye to each other. Tresckow was completely calm and relaxed. The whole world will vilify us now. But I am still firmly convinced that we did the right thing. I consider Hitler to be the arch enemy not only of Germany but of the world. When, in a few hours, I appear before the judgment seat of God, in order to give an account of what I have done and left undone, I believe I can with a good conscience justify what I did in the fight against Hitler. If God promised Abraham that he would not destroy Sodom if only ten righteous men could be found there, then I hope that for our sakes God will not destroy Germany. None of us can complain about our own deaths. Everyone who joined our circle put on the robe of Nessus. A person's moral integrity only begins at the point where he is prepared to die for his convictions.

Several attempts had been made to assassinate Hitler since March 1943, all of which had failed for one reason or another. Already in the summer of 1943, Tresckow had drawn up the following proclamation which was to be issued under Beck's name to the German people in the aftermath of a successful coup:

**1352**    Germans!
Hitler's dictatorship has been destroyed.
    In the last few years monstrous things have been going on before our eyes. Hitler, who was not summoned by the German people but arrived at the pinnacle of government through the worst sort of intrigues, through *demonic arts and lies*, through the *incredible wastage of resources*, which appeared to bring advantages to everybody but in reality plunged us into debt and shortages, confused the minds and spirits of our people and even produced fatal illusions

---

[37] See K. von Klemperer, op. cit., p. 384.

*outside Germany*. In order to maintain himself in power he established a reign of terror. Our nation could once be proud of its honesty and its system of justice. But Hitler mocked God's commandments, *destroyed the law, condemned decency* and ruined the happiness of millions. He considered *honour and dignity, the freedom and the lives of others* to be of no value. Numerous Germans but also members of other nations have been languishing in *concentration camps* for years, exposed to the worst forms of torture and often subjected to terrible torturers. Many of them have died. Our good name has been besmirched by cruel mass murder. With his hands steeped in blood, Hitler has followed his tortuous path *leaving tears, suffering and misery in his wake.*

His insane contempt for all human feelings has with deadly certainty plunged our nation into ruin, *his claim to military genius* has led our brave soldiers to disaster. Lust for power, arrogance and the insane drive for conquest have found their ultimate expression in this war. The bravery and devotion of our soldiers have been shamefully misused, the *huge sacrifices of our people senselessly wasted.*

In his thirst for glory and in his lust for power, against the advice of the experts Hitler has sacrificed whole armies under the blasphemous delusion that he is *the chosen and blessed instrument of fate.*

We shall present to the public the evidence for the tremendous betrayal of the German people and its spiritual values, for the total subversion of the law, for the mockery of the noble precept that the interests of the community should have priority over self-interest, for shameless corruption. Anyone who continues to doubt these fearful truths because, as a decent person, he considers it impossible that high-flown rhetoric could conceal such dastardliness will be convinced by the facts.

*Things could not go on like that!* We would not have been worthy of our fathers. We would have been despised by our children if we had not had the courage to do everything, absolutely everything in order to avert the fearful danger that threatened us and to regain our self-respect.

Hitler has broken the oath which he gave the nation ten years ago countless times through breaches of divine and human law. Thus, no soldier, no official, no citizen of any kind is any longer bound to him by an oath.

In this exceptional emergency I have acted together with men from all walks of life and from all parts of the Fatherland. I have taken over the provisional leadership of the Reich and ordered the establishment of a government under the leadership of the Reich Chancellor.[38] It has started work. [General von Witzleben] has taken over the supreme command of the Wehrmacht to whom the supreme commanders on all fronts have subordinated themselves. *These men have joined me in order to prevent a collapse . . .*

The basic principles and aims of the government will be announced. They are binding until it becomes possible to let *the German people decide.* Our aim is to achieve *the community of the people based on respect, helpfulness and social justice.* We want the fear of God to replace self-idolization, the *rule of law and freedom* to replace force and terror, *truth and probity* to replace lies and selfish-

---

[38] Goerdeler was envisaged as the new Reich Chancellor.

ness. We want to restore our honour and thus our respect in the community of nations. We want to do our best to contribute towards healing the wounds which this war has inflicted on all nations and to restore the trust between them.

The guilty ones who have ruined the good reputation of our nation and have caused such a disaster for us and other nations will be punished. We want to put an end to the sense of hopelessness that this war has to go on for ever. We seek *a just peace* which, instead of the nations fighting and destroying each other will ensure peaceful cooperation. Such a peace can only be based on respect for the freedom and equal rights of all nations . . .

Have courage and put your trust in us! The task is enormously difficult. *I cannot and will not make you empty promises*. We shall have to work hard in order once again slowly to make progress. But we shall take this path as free and decent men and once more with a good conscience. Let everyone do their duty!

▬▬▬

The final plot, which came to fruition on 20 July 1944, involved, on the one hand, an attempt to assassinate Hitler and, on the other, a military coup by senior army officers using the cover of an official plan, code-named 'Operation Valkyrie', designed to suppress any attempt at internal revolt. On 20 July Stauffenberg, who as chief of staff to General Fromm, the head of the Reserve Army, had access to the Führer's headquarters in Rastenburg, East Prussia, placed a bomb hidden in his briefcase under the table in the room where Hitler was holding a military conference and then excused himself. The meeting was held in a wooden hut instead of the usual concrete bunker and this, together with the fact that someone moved the briefcase behind a table leg and that Stauffenberg was unable fully to prime the bomb because of his injured hand, ensured that the effects of the bomb were reduced. The bomb went off just after 12.40 p.m. While several of those inside the hut were killed and injured, Hitler escaped with only minor grazes and burns. Seeing the explosion, Stauffenberg assumed that Hitler had been killed and flew to join his fellow conspirators at the War Ministry in Berlin.

Meanwhile, the Berlin conspirators had been told by their contact at the Führer's headquarters, the chief of communications, General Fellgiebel, that Hitler had not been killed but that Valkyrie should be put into operation. However, uncertain what was happening and whether or not Stauffenberg had been arrested, the conspirators delayed launching the coup until shortly before 4 p.m. They were finally prompted to act by a misleading message from Rastenburg and by Stauffenberg's return to Berlin when he informed them that Hitler was dead.

The following teleprinter message was issued by the military conspirators in the War Ministry to all military districts, but since it was given the highest secrecy rating it took over three hours to transmit because there were only four typists available who were cleared to send top secret teleprinter messages: Otherwise, it could have been sent out over more than twenty machines at much greater speed.

**1353** – FRR-HOKW 02150 20.7.44 16.45

The Führer Adolf Hitler is dead.

I. An unscrupulous clique of party leaders without frontline service have exploited this situation to stab the fighting front in the back and to seize power for their own selfish ends.

II. In order to maintain law and order in this situation of acute danger the Reich Government has declared a state of martial law and has transferred the executive power to me together with the supreme command of the Wehrmacht.

III. I hereby transfer executive power with the right of delegation to the territorial commanders, in the home territory to the Commander of the Reserve Army, while simultaneously appointing him Supreme Commander in the home territory . . .

[*There follow details of the various appointments to the military districts*]

2. The following are subordinated to the holders of executive power:

A. All Wehrmacht offices and units in their area of command, including the Waffen SS, the RAD, and the OT.

B. All public authorities (of the Reich, the states, and local government), in particular the entire order police, security police, and administrative police.

C. All officials and formations of the NSDAP and its associated leagues.

3. The whole of the Waffen SS is to be integrated in the army with immediate effect.

4. The holders of executive power are responsible for the maintenance of law and order. They are to ensure in particular:

A. The security of the communications networks.

B. The neutralization of the SD.

Any resistance against the military authorities is to be ruthlessly suppressed. In this hour of the greatest peril for the Fatherland the unity of the Wehrmacht and the maintenance of discipline is the most important requirement. I therefore make it the duty of all army, navy, and air force commanders to support the holders of executive power with all means at their disposal and to ensure that their directives are obeyed by the agencies subordinate to them.

The German soldier is faced with an historic task. It will depend on his energy and behaviour whether or not Germany will be saved.

The same thing [is true?[39]] for all territorial commanders, the supreme commanders of the sections of the Wehrmacht and the subordinate commanders of the army, navy and air force.

The Commander-in-Chief of the Wehrmacht Field Marshal von Witzleben

[signed] COUNT STAUFFENBERG

---

[39] There is something missing in the German here.

However, by now Hitler knew that Stauffenberg was responsible for planting the bomb. Moreover, and due to a switching error, messages from the War Ministry were also arriving at the Führer headquarters so that he now knew that a coup was in progress centred on the Reserve Army. Around 4.00 p.m. he appointed Himmler to replace General Fromm as head of the Reserve Army and put him in charge of suppressing the coup. Unfortunately, the conspirators had failed to take over the radio station/transmitters and, from 5.42 p.m. onwards, a series of announcements were made over the radio such as the following timed at 6.28 p.m.:

**1354**    18.28 *German Home Service*

An attempt was made to assassinate the Führer using explosives.
The following colleagues of his suffered serious injuries from this attempt: Lieutenant-General Schmundt, Colonel Brandt, colleague Berger.[40] Colonel-General Jodl, Generals Korten, Buhle, Bodenschatz, Heusinger, Scherff, Admirals Voss, v. Puttkamer, Naval Captain Assmann and Lieutenant-Colonel Borgmann were less seriously injured.[41]

The Führer himself has not been injured apart from slight burns and bruises. He has immediately continued his work and—as envisaged—received the Duce for lengthy discussions.

Soon after the attack the Reich Marshal arrived to see the Führer.

The War Ministry responded by sending the following message:

**1355**    – FRR-HOKW 756851 20.7.44 19.47

The communiqué issued on the radio is incorrect. The Führer is dead. The measures which have been ordered are to be implemented with maximum speed.

Since the commander of the Reserve Army, General Fromm, was refusing to sign orders, because he had heard that Hitler was not dead, the conspirators issued the following order:

**1356**    – FRR-HOKW 75866 20.7.44 20.08

I appoint General Hoeppner Commander of the Reserve Army and Supreme Commander in the home territory.

[signed] V. WITZLEBEN
GENERAL OF THE INFANTRY OLBRICHT

---

[40] These three died from their injuries. Berger was a stenographer.
[41] General Günter Korten, Chief of Staff of the Luftwaffe, also died of his injuries.

This elicited the following response from the Führer's headquarters:

**1357** FHQ 20.35

The Führer has appointed the Reichsführer SS Himmler Commander of the Reserve Army and transferred to him all the relevant powers over the members of the Reserve Army. Only orders from the Reichsführer SS and from me are to be carried out.
Any orders from Fromm, von Witzleben or Hoeppner are invalid.

CHIEF OF THE OKW, FIELD MARSHAL KEITEL

---

Meanwhile Bormann had issued the following order:

**1358** Führer Headquarters, 20 July 1944, 20.30
Reichsleiter Bormann to all Gauleiters

*Circular No. 1*

EXTREMELY URGENT! FOR IMMEDIATE ATTENTION!
Simultaneously with the attempt to murder Führer, army generals have attempted a putsch which must be and will be suppressed with all means.

It is necessary for you to draw all the conclusions arising from this situation and that you are extremely careful.

Only orders from the Führer or his men are valid and not the orders of disloyal reactionary generals.

The Führer has transferred all necessary powers to the Reichsführer SS. Establish immediate contact, therefore, with the responsible police chiefs in your area.

You are responsible for ensuring that you maintain the leadership in your Gau firmly in your hands in all circumstances.

Heil Hitler!

M. BORMANN

---

The response from the various military districts had varied. Most were confused by the conflicting reports and awaited developments. In Vienna and Paris the military arrested the Party, Gestapo and SS leadership, whereas in Breslau the military commander took an early decision not to join the coup and in Hamburg the SS and military leaderships toasted each other in vermouth and sherry. However, the most critical district was Berlin. And the fact that Goebbels and Hitler managed to persuade the commander of the troops deployed in the Government district, Major Otto Remer, to ignore his orders and assist in crushing the coup proved fatal to it.

In the meantime, the radio was continuing to report on the coup attempt:

**1359**    22.00 *German Home Service*

Murderous attempt on the Führer's life. For the second time in this war started by Jewry, a foul and murderous attempt has been made on our Führer's life and again, as on that 9 November 1939,[42] Providence protected the man who holds in his hands the destiny of the German people. The Führer remained unhurt. For us, this attempt is a sign not only of the enemy's knavish mentality, but reveals also that the enemy, whose propaganda pretends that he has already won the war, does not in reality reckon with victory on the battlefields. Nearly five years of our soldiers' heroic struggle and of a selfless effort by the German homeland have taught the enemy that he will never be able to force this people to its knees. The fact that the Führer is alive is most important for us. The feeling of gratitude for his salvation is the supreme, the overpowering emotion of all Germans. It finds its expression in the demonstrations of loyalty to and love for the Führer, which have already poured in from all over Germany. They bear the stamp of unconquerable determination. The German people will answer the cowardly attack on the Führer's life with a renewed profession of its allegiance to its National Socialist ideals, virtues and duties, and with the solemn promise to fight even more fanatically and to work even harder. 'With the Führer—to Victory'. That is the slogan of the German people, and now all the more so.

———

At twenty-seven minutes past midnight the German Home Service announced that Hitler would 'shortly' address the German nation. The announcement was repeated at five-minute intervals, during which martial music was played, until one minute before one o'clock in the morning when Hitler spoke as follows:

**1360**    My fellow German men and women!

I don't know how many attempts to assassinate me have been planned and carried out. But I am speaking to you today for two reasons, in particular: first, so that you can hear my voice and know that I am unhurt and in good health; secondly, so that you can hear the details of a crime for which there can be few comparisons in German history.

A tiny clique of ambitious, unscrupulous and at the same time criminally stupid officers hatched a plot to remove me, and together with me virtually to exterminate the staff of the German High Command. The bomb, which was placed by a Colonel Count von Stauffenberg, exploded two metres to the right of me. It very seriously injured a number of loyal colleagues of whom one has died. I myself am completely unhurt, apart from a few very minor grazes,

---

[42] See above, p. 592.

bruises and burns. I consider that to be a confirmation of the task given me by Providence to continue in the pursuit of my life's goal as I have done hitherto. For I can solemnly confess to the whole nation that since the day when I moved into the Wilhelmstrasse I have had but one thought namely to do my duty to the best of my ability and according to my conscience. Also, since the time when it became clear to me that war was unavoidable and could no longer be postponed I have known nothing but worry and work and, through countless days and sleepless nights, have lived only for my people.

At a time when the German armies are engaged in a very tough struggle, a very small group, as in Italy, thought they could stab us in the back just like in November 1918. But this time they have made a very big mistake. These usurpers' claim that I am no longer alive is at this very moment being refuted by the fact that I am now speaking to you, my dear compatriots. The circle represented by these usurpers is extremely small. It has nothing to do with the German Wehrmacht and, above all, nothing to do with the German army. It is a very small clique of criminal elements, which will now be mercilessly exterminated.

Thus, I now order that no civilian authority must follow any orders from offices which these usurpers claim to hold. Secondly, that no military authority, no troop commander and no soldier should obey any order from these usurpers; that, on the contrary, everyone is in duty bound to arrest the person bearing or issuing such an order or, in the event of resistance, to kill [*niedermachen*[43]] him at once.

To restore order at last I have appointed Reich Minister Himmler as Commander of the Army at home. I have appointed Colonel-General Guderian[44] to the General Staff to replace the Chief of the General Staff, who had to retire on health grounds, and I have appointed another proven leader from the eastern front as his assistant. There are no other changes to Reich offices. I am convinced that by crushing this tiny clique of traitors and conspirators we shall at last create that atmosphere in the rear at home which the fighting front needs. For it is an impossible situation if hundreds of thousands and millions of brave men are doing their utmost, while at home a tiny clique of ambitious and miserable types are continually trying to sabotage this. This time we shall settle accounts in our accustomed manner as National Socialists. I am convinced that every decent officer, every brave soldier will understand that at this time.

Probably very few people can imagine the fate that would have befallen Germany if today's attack had been successful. I myself give thanks to Providence and to my Creator, not because I have been spared—my life is merely care and work for my people—but rather I thank them simply for giving me the opportunity to continue to bear this burden and to continue my work as I have to answer for it before my conscience.

Every German, whoever he may be, has the duty [shouting] of ruthlessly opposing these elements and either immediately arresting them or, if they

---

[43] This word has a crude and brutal ring to it inappropriate to the public vocabulary of a head of state.

[44] General Heinz Guderian, currently Inspector General of Panzer troops.

attempt to resist—to kill [*niedermachen*] them without further ado. Appropriate orders have been given to all the troops. They are being carried out blindly with the obedience typical of the German army.

I would like to give you, my old comrades in arms, a special greeting, glad that I have once more been spared a fate which had no terrors for me personally but which would have brought terror to the German people. But I read into that the finger of fate pointing me towards the continuation of my work and so I shall carry on with it.

▬▬

This was followed by speeches by Admiral Dönitz for the navy, who said: 'We will get even with these traitors', and by Göring for the air force. At 19.15 the following day Field Marshal von Kluge issued an order of the day in which he announced that 'it was with indignation and bitterness that we soldiers learnt of this conspiracy. For us there will be no repetition of 1918 or of that of Italy . . . long live the Führer! Long live Germany!'

On the morning of the 22 July, Robert Ley's speech to workers in a Berlin factory was broadcast. Significantly, the 'class war' aspects were toned down in the press release of the speech:

**1361**    *Announcer*: 'Long live the Führer!'—this slogan is stretched out over banners and iron-grey machinery. One thought inspires and fills the great hall; it is reflected in the determined faces of German workers. The workers are leaving their work benches and surging towards the centre of the hall. Reich Organization Chief Dr Ley is standing in their midst on an improvised platform and about to address all German armament workers. Today, as ever, Dr Ley is the link man between the German workers and the Führer. [Loud applause].
*Ley:* My German compatriots! Workers! Women! You have lived through last night and the day before sharing the same feelings as the rest of us. You had the same experience as I and millions of other Germans when we heard that there had been an attempt on the life of Adolf Hitler. We held our breath. I was travelling in a German Gau and an icy shudder ran down my spine. I realized within a second what would have become of Germany if this murderous attempt had had the consequences intended by the murderers, if Adolf Hitler were no more. It is too terrible to comprehend, too difficult to imagine. At one stroke all our efforts destroyed! At one stroke all prospects of victory shattered! Above all, however, millions of Germans cast into indescribable misery, slavery, destruction, poverty, starvation, quite apart from the fact that the sacrifices of all those thousands and millions of soldiers who have given their life's blood would have been in vain. Our nation would have been helpless. We were all the more grateful when we heard the next sentence: 'The Führer is unharmed. The Führer lives!' [Prolonged cheers] We took in that sentence, we drank it in: 'The Führer— unharmed!', as if by a miracle. All the others were either severely or slightly injured, but he escaped unharmed, despite being the nearest to it.

Fellow Germans! I am, God knows, no mystic and do not believe in miracles, but in this case I would really like to say that the Lord God had something to do with it, and struck the murderer's bomb from his hand. We stand full of reverence in the face of such happenings. (I have received precise reports of how it happened. It wasn't a small thing but a bomb of the heaviest kind, imported from England [cries of 'shame'], not a German bomb. The Jew of Moscow gave the order and England and her lords supplied the bomb. And German counts and noblemen, conspirators [cries of 'shame']—they threw it. Dirty dogs, that is the only name for them, dirty dogs with blue blood. Fools and idiots, criminals and murderers, reactionaries! Here, Germans, you see Reaction and Bolshevism walking arm in arm; Stalin and German counts arm in arm! That shows you where this Bolshevism would like to lead you. Back into that slavery from which we have freed Germany! Back into the same bondage![45]) The fact that they have lost all their influence does not suit these gentlemen ['certain reactionary gentlemen' in the press release]. And yet how has the Führer treated them? He gave them everything to which they might have been justly entitled. He gave them back their uniforms [i.e. expanded the army]; in giving Germany might and glory he gave it to them too. And now they repay him with bombs and murder and ingratitude.

A worker said to me yesterday: 'Thank God it wasn't a worker'. Yes, all Germans in every walk of life are ashamed to be connected with such a murderer. (Bolshevism and Reaction arm in arm, paid by the Jews, traitors and cowardly dogs. And international ties. His wife was born in Poland, his sister-in-law is a Russian Bolshevik. There is the international plot. There are the 'liberators' of Germany.[46]) No we demand today that the revolution should now make up for what it failed to do before. [Prolonged applause] These creatures must be destroyed [applause]. Every German must know that if he betrays Germany his blood will be exterminated; every German must know that. Germans, I believe that I am speaking in the name of all of you: first of all in saying that we are possessed by a sacred anger, which rises from the depths of the nation. While the German worker, decent, industrious, indefatigable, works and toils on and on, 10, 11, 12–16 hours, without Sunday, without holidays, without anything, we must not allow some idling, idiotic, (criminal members of the nobility[47]) to attack Germany and threaten to deprive it of its Führer. That must not happen. Adolf Hitler is everything to us. He inspires Germany. We belong to him and he belongs to us. The good thing this deed has revealed is the close ties between the broad masses and this unique man, Adolf Hitler—that is not only a battle won, it is the war won; believe me that is our victory. [Loud applause]

And I thank you, my German men and women, for your decent and sound bearing, and I believe I am speaking in the name of all the thousands assembled

---

[45] The sections in parentheses were excluded from the press release of Ley's speech.

[46] The press release read: ' The murderers possessed those international connections with which we are familiar in their circles'.

[47] In the press release this read 'criminals'.

in this great hall, when I pray to God: preserve Adolf Hitler for us, as You preserved him hitherto. Protect him, help him, hold Your strong hand over him, preserve him for us. Send us whatever you will, O destiny—work, burdens, and struggle, bombs and shells—we shall bear it all, however hard it may be; we shall bear it. But we ask You for one thing: preserve Adolf Hitler for us. O Destiny, that is what we pray for from You. Sieg Heil! [Loud applause]

*Announcer*: German workers, take up again the swastika flag. Raise the flag: we greet the Führer, Adolf Hitler—Sieg Heil! [The crowd repeats three times: 'Sieg Heil!'; 'Deutschland, Deutschland über alles'; Horst Wessel song.]

On 23 July, the Home Service broadcast the following:

**1362**     *German Home Service* 14.00 23.7.44

*Announcer*: Before the news, the Chief of the General Staff of the Army, Colonel-General Guderian, will read the Order of the Day issued to the army by the Führer on 21 July.

*Guderian*: The Führer in his capacity as C.-in-C. of the Army, has issued the following Order of the Day: 'Soldiers of the Army! A small group of unscrupulous officers committed a murderous assault on me and the staff of the High Command of the Wehrmacht in order to seize power in the state. Providence caused this crime to miscarry. Through the immediate intervention of loyal officers and soldiers of the army at home, the clique of traitors was wiped out or arrested within a few hours. I did not expect it to happen any differently. I know you are fighting with courage, as in the past, and with exemplary obedience and in loyal fulfilment of your duty until victory is ours, despite everything. The Führer's HQ, 21 July 1944. The Führer, Adolf Hitler.

In making public the Führer's Order of the Day to his army, I would like to add the following on behalf of the German army: A few officers, some of them on the retired list, had lost courage, and out of cowardice and weakness preferred the path of disgrace to the only path befitting an honest soldier—the path of duty and honour. The army has cleansed itself and cast out the dishonest elements on all the fighting fronts and in the homeland feverish work and sacrifice for victory continue. The people and the army stand firmly united behind the Führer. The enemy was mistaken when he believed that he could count on a split to his advantage among the generals in the army. I guarantee to the Führer and the German people the close unity of the generals, the officer corps, and the men of the army with the sole aim of fighting for victory and with the motto so often impressed upon us by the venerable Field Marshal von Hindenburg: 'Loyalty is the mark of honour'. Long live Germany and our Führer, Adolf Hitler! And now: Nation to arms!

Meanwhile, on 23 July, the Reich Propaganda Ministry had sent the following instruction to its propaganda offices:

**1363** *Highly Confidential*

Over the next few days a wave of demonstrations of loyalty to the Führer must be organized in all Gaus and districts of the Reich as a spontaneous reaction of our people to the nefarious assassination attempt on the Führer. Full participation of local military units must be secured through collaboration with the appropriate military headquarters. Apart from these demonstrations of loyalty, factory meetings must be held with the cooperation of the Gau leaders of the German Labour Front, at which the workpeople will express their National Socialist loyalty in congratulatory addresses to the Führer . . .

The German press will receive daily instructions to provide effective publicity for the demonstrations and factory meetings as well as for the handing over and sending off of the congratulatory addresses in the various Gaus. The speakers at the demonstrations must emphasise the following points in particular . . .

1. Only a small group of reactionary traitors are behind the assassination attempt and putsch . . .

3. It was this camarilla which from hatred of the movement and snobbish class spirit has always tried to prevent the conversion of the army to National Socialism; the same clique always opposed the appointment of convinced National Socialists who had distinguished themselves at the front to leading posts in the army. It opposed the giving of the highest awards such as the Knight's Cross to NCOs and men from the ranks and it opposed giving commissions to soldiers from the ranks.

4. The army, tested again and again in the most difficult situation at the front, emerges without a blemish from the attempted putsch.

The most experienced speakers must be employed so as to guarantee the decisive success of the wave of demonstrations which have been ordered. Press and pictorial reports of the most impressive events must be sent without delay to the Propaganda Department of the Ministry for Enlightenment and Propaganda for evaluation.

———

The following document was first sent by Bormann to the Reichsleiters and Gauleiters on 24 July 1944 and then from Lammers to the Government authorities on 27 July and passed on to the Wehrmacht on 3 August 1944:

**1364** Re: *Treatment of the events of 20 July in the public arena*

The Führer wishes that in treating the events of the 20.7.44 no one should let themselves get carried away into attacking or insulting the officer corps, the generals, the nobility or sections of the Wehrmacht en bloc. Rather it should always be emphasized that the participants in the putsch were a very *particular*, fairly small clique of officers. The investigation being carried out by the Reichsführer SS is proceeding according to plan and its results will be communicated at the appropriate time. The fact that the Wehrmacht orders for the arrest of the Gauleiters and district leaders which had been issued by this gang of traitors were not carried out in any Gaus is indicative of the impeccable stance of the German army. On the contrary, they established contact with the Gauleiters and emphasized the necessity for close cooperation between the NSDAP and Wehrmacht. Thus, if the behaviour of the clique of traitors is referred to then the impeccable stance of the army, indeed the impeccable stance of the whole Wehrmacht should be emphasized at the same time. (In the meantime, the Führer has emphasized and made clear that, in particular at a time of emergency, within the Gaus, the executive power may not be transferred to the Wehrmacht or to any individual generals but rather, especially in crises, in national emergencies, must be held more firmly than ever in the hands of the Gauleiters.[48])

On 20 August 1944 the SD produced the following report on the population's response to the abortive coup and subsequent trial:

**1365**      There is hardly any recent event which has aroused so much interest among the population and had such a big impact on morale as the trial of the assassins of the 20.7.1944 at the People's Court in Berlin. Since some of those involved were high-ranking people who had important positions in the Wehrmacht and the Party, the population was generally *intrigued* as to whether the accused's offences would be tried in public or whether the attempt would be made to hush up or keep quiet about the crimes of those involved. So the population was all the more satisfied on noting that that they were receiving a detailed picture of the events of the 20.7 as a result of the comprehensive coverage of the course of the trial. In particular, it was considered right and proper that the accused were not tried in a Wehrmacht court but sent before the People's Court like any common criminal. The *speed of the legal proceedings and the immediate carrying out of the sentence* were particularly welcomed.

There was *no doubt* in the minds of the whole population that the *accused should have been sentenced to death*. Even in officers' circles and among the intelligentsia nobody has doubted this necessary conclusion of the proceedings.

The conduct of the trial by the presiding judge of the People's Court made a strong impression on the majority of the population. A large section of the working class responded with pleasure to the biting, occasionally ironic and extremely quick-witted manner of the judge . The criticisms which the presiding judge directed at the criminal objectives of the accused reflected exactly the population's disgust at the horrible crime. Details of the preparations, for example, above all, the traitors' plan to carry out the assassination on the occasion of a demonstration elicited particular disgust. The fact that the traitors planned to place the bomb in the knapsack of soldiers with frontline experience, who were to be presented to the Führer for him to inspect a new uniform. Every section of the nation is equally angry that German brains should have been capable of thinking up such a dirty trick (Weimar).

---

[48] This section was added by Bormann in his instruction to the Gauleiters, dated 31 July.

The trial proceedings have also provided *proof* and convinced the population of the fact that those involved really were incapable of governing and that had the putsch been *successful it would have been incredibly disastrous* for Germany.

It is true that there are also those who criticize the way the presiding judge handled the proceedings. Thus, in legal circles and among the intelligentsia it is pointed out that the way in which the trial was organized and commented on extensively in public (the description of the location, the presiding individuals, and their robes, when contrasted with the accused who had been divested of all marks of outward distinction, was reminiscent of earlier Soviet *show trials*. The 'cheap manner' in which the presiding judge—this is how it is put—criticized and ridiculed the accused, who had already been pronounced guilty, was not really appropriate to the dignity of the highest German court. A number of complaints were noted, in particular about the way in which the chairman entered into a discussion with the accused Hoeppner,[49] about whether 'donkey' or 'swine' was the more appropriate epithet for him.

Other compatriots point out that some of the accused are individuals who, because of their services and their efficiency, have reached a high rank and received honours within the National Socialist state. It was *strange* that these men, who not so long ago were being promoted by the Führer himself and whose deeds were being celebrated in the press as acts of heroism, were now being portrayed as foolish, stupid and indecisive. If the population was informed in this way that a field marshal and a colonel-general, who were able to decide on the deployment of tens of thousands of soldiers, had revealed themselves to be such criminals and incompetent creatures, then trust in the Wehrmacht must, as a result, receive a serious blow. This must also raise doubts about the personnel policy at the highest level since these men had been left in high and important positions for many years. Was it not conceivable that there were also such incompetent and criminal elements among those high-ranking officers who were still active?

Certain concerns were also derived from the fact that the conduct of the trial had evidently prevented voluntary confessions by the accused concerning their *true motives*. Despite the details contained in the official press reports, they still left many unresolved questions. These were undoubtedly men who were in a position to have an overview of Germany's military and political possibilities and of whom one could hardly assume that they would have carried out such a contemptible crime without any reason or reflection. Finally, some individuals have expressed their surprise that the criminal group could prepare their assassination plan for months on end.

*Despite these doubts expressed by individuals,* the general effect of the reporting of the trial may be assessed as in every respect a positive one. The population's anger at the crime and the contemptible way it was committed is so great that the *carrying out of the sentence by hanging is considered to be far too mild.*

'Such swine as these should have been drowned in a river like cats' (officers).

'These blackguards and swine shouldn't have been hanged; they should have been beaten to death and then cut to pieces' (a soldier).

---

[49] General Erich Hoeppner was one of the leading military conspirators.

There are frequent comments that one should have employed the traitors for a time clearing dud bombs.

'Such swine should have been subjected to medieval tortures' is another comment. Whereas in the case of soldiers and young officers, hanging is regarded as a thoroughly appropriate punishment for their crime, comments by older officers have been recorded which suggest that the officers should have been granted a bullet. 'It is a terrible thought that an officer has been condemned to death by hanging and not by shooting' (a colonel). 'The idea that such high-ranking officers have gone to the gallows is terrible' (a lieutenant-colonel). *'It is a disgrace for the Wehrmacht and the whole officer corps which will be difficult to remove from the minds of the population.'* According to the reports, there is a *tendency* to generalize the criminal behaviour of the small clique of officers and to mistrust the officers and generals as a group. Could it not be the case that the failures and losses at the front were the fault of other such treacherous officers?

The population's interest is now turning above all to the *traitors' further contacts*. The reverses on the central sector of the eastern front are now frequently linked to the assassination plan. In general, people are demanding that *absolutely every opposition nest should be rooted out and destroyed.* One ought to hang one too many rather than one too few. Trust in the Führer himself has, according to the reports, once more considerably increased among the population as a result of the assassination attempt. The vast majority of the population takes the view that *only the Führer is in a position to master the difficult situation* and to keep all the threads in his hands. The mood of the soldiers has also received a considerable boost. The *commitment* and *combat readiness* of the troops has been strengthened. Satisfaction has been expressed that *this blow* did not come from the fighting troops but from a small clique in the home army.

---

Despite the caution with which they should be regarded given the circumstances, the interrogations by the Gestapo, reports of which were sent by the head of the Reich Security Main Office, Ernst Kaltenbrunner, to Bormann, provide important insights into the ideas and motives of the resisters. One such report on the 'attitude of the conspirators towards National Socialism and the NSDAP', dated 16 October 1944, dealt with their attitude towards the 'racial question':

**1366** *Attitude towards the racial question*

. . . A lot of criticism was directed at the implementation of racial theory as it was carried out during the pre-war period. The opinion was that the expropriation of the Jews should have been undertaken in a way which was more 'worthy' of Germany.

Popitz said : 'As somebody who was very familiar with conditions in the system period [i.e. Weimar], my view of the Jewish question was that the Jews ought to disappear from the life of the state and the economy. However as far as the *methods* were concerned I repeatedly advocated a somewhat more gradual approach, particularly in the light of diplomatic considerations.'

At another point in the interrogation, referring to the same issue, he said: 'The Jewish question had to be dealt with, their removal from state and economy was unavoidable. But the use of force which led to the destruction of property, to arbitrary arrests and to the destruction of life could not be reconciled with law and morality and, in addition, seemed to me to have dangerous implications for people's attitudes to property and human life. At the same time, I saw in the treatment of the Jewish question a great danger of increasing international hostility to Germany and its regime.

A number of other persons who were interrogated expressed similar views. Thus Count Yorck von Wartenburg, for example, said that the extermination measures against the Jews, which went beyond the law and justice, caused him to break with National Socialism.

Count Lehndorff declared 'that, although he was hostile to the Jews, nevertheless he had never quite approved of the National Socialist view of race, in particular *its practical implementation'*.

Count Alexander von Stauffenberg[50] said he 'took the view that the Jewish question should have been dealt with *in a less extreme manner* because then it would have produced less disturbance among the population'.

Count Berthold von Stauffenberg took a similar line: 'He and his brother had basically approved of the racial principle of National Socialism but considered it to be *exaggerated* and *excessive.'*

As evidence for the contradictions within the National Socialist approach to racial policy, Count Berthold Stauffenberg pointed to the alliance with Japan, the war against England and the importation of foreign workers. The statement reads as follows: 'The racial idea has been grossly betrayed in this war in that the best German blood is being irrevocably sacrificed while simultaneously Germany is being populated by millions of foreign workers, who certainly cannot be described as of high racial quality.'

[The Goerdeler memo 'The Goal'—see pp. 602–03 above—is then referred to:]

Goerdeler's government declaration then adopts virtually a pro-Jewish standpoint. It reads: 'The *Jewish persecution,* which has taken the *most inhuman, merciless* and deeply shaming forms, for which no recompense can be adequate, is to be halted immediately. Anyone who believed that he could enrich himself with Jewish property will discover that it is a disgrace for any German to seek such dishonestly acquired property. The German people truly want nothing to do with marauders and hyenas among God's creatures.'

Thus, although in some statements the National Socialist racial idea is approved in theory, in practice the clique of conspirators would have implemented a Jewish policy which, at least in the economic sphere, would have reinstated the Jews in their previous legal position and allowed them the free pursuit of their activities.

----

[50] Alexander and Berthold von Stauffenberg were brothers of Claus.

However, despite the ambivalence in some of the attitudes of some resisters and despite the partial identification of some of their views with some Nazi ideas, a fact which goes a long way towards explaining why a number of them were initially attracted to and then prepared to go along with the regime for so long, it would be wrong to end this chapter on such a negative note. For, in the final analysis, the fact remains that they were prepared to risk their lives and in many cases to pay that price in order to try and overthrow a regime which they had come to see as a monstrous tyranny. The following document, a letter from Count Peter Yorck von Wartenburg, provides an insight not simply into the motives—in this case a sense of *noblesse oblige* and patriotism— but above all into the human tragedy of the Resistance:

**1367**    Mother
Countess Yorck von Wartenburg
Klein-Oels/Ohlau Land

Dearest Mummy,
This is my farewell letter; when you receive it I shall probably no longer be alive.

At the end of a life blest with so much love and friendship I feel only a sense of gratitude to God and of humble acceptance of his will. I feel a great sorrow that I am causing you this grief. On top of all the sad things which you have had to go through. I beg you from the bottom of my heart to forgive me. I have had over two weeks to place myself and my actions before God and am convinced that I shall find in him a merciful judge. The amount of inward distress which people like me have had to live through in the last few years cannot be felt by those who are borne up by their faith, something which I cannot share. I can assure you that it was not ambition or lust for power which determined my actions. My actions were influenced solely by my patriotic feeling, my concern for my Germany as it has grown over the past two thousand years, the attempt to shape its internal and external development. And so I can stand tall before my ancestors, before my father and brothers. Perhaps a time will come when my stance will be judged differently, when I will not be considered a rogue but an admonisher and a patriot. My most urgent prayer is that this wonderful calling may be the cause of people paying their respects to God.

Thank you dear Mummy for a life full of motherly love, and the only thing that saddens me is that I have not repaid you sufficiently for it. But you should know that throughout my life it has always been a source of strength to me. My final prayer will be for God to grant you his grace, friendship and compassion, and my last request to you is to look after Maria with motherly love. Things will in any case be very difficult because of the anticipated sequestration of our property. I rely on you and particularly on your Doris. You know what a sensitive person Maria is and how close we were. Please help her as much as you can and ease her path into a lonely life. Perhaps later she may find another loving man; then help her to reach a decision of which I would certainly approve. The time left to me is so short that I cannot write to my sisters. You must pass on to them, to all my loved ones my thanks, my best wishes for them, their husbands and children. Also to T. Give Doris my love and your sisters. I have made my peace with . . . I hope you make things up and that my death will form the basis for a new harmony. He too needs that badly.

Now let God's will be done, my dearest beloved Mummy. Daddy and my brothers will receive me and I go without hatred and with only love in my heart. And let your loving son who puts his trust in God kiss your hand very gently for the last time.

## List of Sources

1333 W. Runge and W. Schumann, eds, *Dokumente zur deutschen Geschichte 1939–1942* (Berlin 1973), p. 102.

1334 Ibid., pp. 94–5.

1335 Runge and Schumann, op. cit., pp. 116–17.

1336 W. Runge and W. Schumann, eds, *Dokumente zur deutschen Geschichte 1943–1945* (Berlin 1973), p. 35.

1337 P. Steinbach and J. Tuchel, eds, *Widerstand in Deutschland. Ein historisches Lesebuch* (Munich 1994), pp. 271–3.

1338 A. Hoch and L. Gruchmann, *Georg Elser, der Attentäter aus dem Volke. Der Anschag auf Hitler in Münchener Bürgerbrau 1939* (Frankfurt am Main 1980), pp. 75–84.

1339 D. Bonhoeffer, *Widerstand und Ergebung* (Gutersloh 1983), pp. 10–12.

1340 *Von Hassell Diaries 1938–1945* (London 1948), pp. 76–7.

1341 Ibid., pp. 80–1.

1342 Ibid., pp. 109–11.

1343 Steinbach and Tuchel, op. cit., pp. 295–304.

1344 *Von Hassell Diaries 1938–1945*, pp. 209–11.

1345 E. Bethge, ed., *Dietrich Bonhoeffer: Gesammelte Schriften* (Munich 1958), pp. 488–93.

1346 G. Ritter, *Carl Goerdeler und die deutsche Widerstandsbewegung* (Stuttgart 1954), pp. 597–600.

1347 *A German of the Resistance. The Last Letters of Count Helmuth James von Moltke* (Oxford 1947), pp. 26–9.

1348 W. Hofer, ed., *Der Nationalsozialismus. Dokumente 1933–1945* (Frankfurt am Main 1957), pp. 333–5.

1349 G. Ritter, op. cit., p. 609.

1350 F. Von Schlabrendorff, *Offiziere gegen Hitler* (Frankfurt am Main 1959), p. 138.

1351 Ibid., p. 154.

1352 W. Michalka, ed., *Das Dritte Reich.* Vol. 2: *Weltmachtanspruch und nationaler Zusammenbruch 1939–1945* (Munich 1985), pp. 367–9.

1353 H.-A. Jacobsen, *Opposition gegen Hitler und der Staatsstreich vom 20. Juli 1944. Geheime Dokumente aus dem ehemaligen Reichssicherheitshauptamt,* (Stuttgart 1989), Vol. 2, p. 597; Vol. 1, p. 63.

1354 Imperial War Museum (IWM) BBC Monitoring Service Report 1,830.

1355  Jacobsen, op. cit., p. 70.
1356  Ibid., p. 69.
1357  Ibid., p. 75.
1358  Ibid., p. 591.
1359  IWM BBC Monitoring Report 1,830.
1360  Ibid with modified translation. German text in Michalka op. cit., pp. 365–7.
1361  IWM BBC Monitoring Report 1,832 with modified translation. German text in Michaelis et. al. eds, *Ursachen und Folgen. Vom deutschen Zusammenbruch 1918 und 1945 bis zur staatlichen Neugründung Deutschlands in der Gegenwart,* Vol. 21 (Berlin undated), pp. 453–4.
1362  IWM BBC Monitoring Report 1,833 with modified translation. German text in H. Michaelis, op. cit., p. 460.
1363  *Aus deutschen Urkunden 1933–1945* (Allied publication undated), pp. 289–90.
1364  Jacobsen, op. cit., Vol. 2, p. 597.
1365  Ibid., pp. 275–8.
1366  Ibid., pp. 449–50.
1367  Ibid., Vol. 2, p. 794.

# CHAPTER 51

# *Defeat*

## (i) Introduction

Despite the increasing disillusionment with the regime, and despite the growing burdens of the war, the German people did not revolt in 1945; there was no equivalent to November 1918. And this was despite the fact that the relative improvement in material circumstances by comparison with the First World War, which had helped to sustain morale, particularly when the going got tough during 1943–4, was replaced in the last few months by a marked deterioration in the supplies of food and other necessities and a partial collapse of vital services such as electricity, gas, and transport. To this extent the regime had succeeded in one of its major goals.

However, if there was little popular resistance to the regime, there was also, at least as far as the home front was concerned, little support for it. Thus, there was little popular resistance to the Allied advance, except for pockets, particularly in the east such as Breslau; and what there was was largely the product of intimidation by fanatical individual Nazi leaders such as the Gauleiters Karl Hanke in Breslau or Karl Holz in Nuremberg, or lower-level Nazi district leaders or SS officers. Instead of support for the regime, or much active resistance, such as occurred, for example, in Italy, more typical was a kind of resignation to the inevitable, a desire to see an end to the war as soon as possible. Why was this?

As far as lack of support for the regime was concerned, we have seen in the chapter on morale how disillusionment with the Nazi Party and its officials had grown during the course of the war so that, while a residual loyalty to Hitler continued to exist among some Germans, by 1944 the Party had forfeited any respect it had ever had. But, as will become clear from the following pages, it was the Party to which Hitler delegated direct responsibility for organizing civilian resistance between

September 1944 and May 1945. Understandably, therefore, there was little enthusiasm to follow such discredited leaders.

As far as the relative lack of resistance to the regime was concerned, one important factor was the machinery and processes of terror, which had experienced a tremendous expansion during the war and now, during the last phase, reached a new level of ruthlessness as, conscious of their looming defeat, Nazi true believers lashed out at those who they believed would welcome the collapse of the regime and settled old scores. In this atmosphere of terror there were powerful reasons for people not to draw attention to themselves. As one worker put it: 'Rather than let them string me up I'll be glad to believe in victory.'[1] Added to this was the fact that the regime's virtual monopoly of organization combined with its control of the media ensured that, over the previous decade, the German people had been atomized and deprived of access to alternative sources of information apart from their immediate contacts among family, work colleagues, and friends. They had thus been seriously hampered in developing an effective critique of, let alone mobilizing a challenge to, the regime of the kind that developed between 1916 and 1918.

This process of atomization was aided by the progressive dilution of the workforce through waves of conscription of German workers from plants and their replacement by foreign workers, women or very young workers. Older male German workers, who were potentially more capable of independent and critical judgment than their younger colleagues, often suddenly found themselves in positions of authority within new racial and gender hierarchies, which no doubt increased their already ambivalent feelings about the regime. Women and young workers were notoriously ill-disciplined, but it was the indiscipline of individuals and posed no threat to the regime.

But it would be a mistake to attribute the lack of a November 1918 solely to the effects of terror, or to portray the Germans as a cowed population. It is highly significant, for example, that the response of the German public to the July 1944 plot against Hitler was not one of approval and disappointment at its failure, but rather of disapproval and relief. There was a widespread feeling that these officers had rocked the national boat at a time when it was going through very choppy waters. By that time (July 1944), most people had come to feel that, whether they liked it or not—and as has been shown, many had by then become disillusioned with the regime and even with the Führer—they were bound together to the bitter end.

---

[1] Quoted in Werner, *"Bleib übrig" Deutsche Arbeiter in der nationalsozialistische Kriegswirtschaft* (Düsseldorf 1983), p. 341.

This sense of national solidarity was generated not so much by a residual patriotism, though this may well have existed, but more by a fear of the future, in particular of the Red Army (and to this extent German propaganda had had some success).

This fear was reinforced by two other factors. The first was a growing sense of unease about the presence of some 7–8 million foreign workers who now lived and worked in Germany. Apart from the fact that Germans were unused to the close proximity of large numbers of foreigners, their unease was increased by the awareness of the hostility of these, largely conscripted, labourers, a hostility which was becoming more and more openly expressed as Germany's situation deteriorated in the form of what was seen by many Germans as 'uppityness'. This concern may well have encouraged a solidarity with the existing order or at least a concern not to undermine it. One captures a sense of these feelings from the diary entry by the young Prussian noblewoman Ursula von Kardorff, living and working in Berlin:

**1368**   30 November 1944

Friedrichstrasse station with its broad staircases which lead into a kind of underworld is considered to be secure against air raids. There it is like I imagine Shanghai to be. Ragged, colourful characters in padded jackets with the high cheek-bones of the Slavs among them, blond Danes and Norwegians, coquettishly dressed French women, Poles with hatred in their eyes, pale shivering Italians—an international mixture hitherto unique in a German city. They're almost all foreigners down there. One hardly hears any German spoken. The majority have been conscripted into armaments firms. Nevertheless, they don't give a dejected impression. Many are loud and happy, laugh, sing, barter, trade and live according to their own laws . . . In the big beerhalls in the Friedrichstrasse station too there are almost no Germans. Anyone who doesn't belong there is stared at mistrustfully. Here everybody knows everybody else. Girls go from table to table, young men with bright scarves and long hair stroll around. The foreign workers are supposed to be superbly organized. It is said that there are spies among them, officers, agents of the various underground organizations, who are well armed with weapons and radio transmitters . . . Twelve million foreign workers in Germany.[2] An army in itself. Some call them the Trojan horse of this war.

These fears were reinforced by a sense of guilt for the German conduct of the war in the east and the treatment of the Jews. The ambivalence and variety of Germans' attitudes to the foreigners in their midst

---

[2] In fact, at this stage there were just over 7m, but the exaggeration is suggestive.

emerges from the following report of the 'Special Project Berlin' [*Sondereinsatz Berlin*] for the week of 20–6 November 1944. This was a secret operation in which a Wehrmacht unit in civilian clothes sounded out public opinion in Berlin between November 1944 and January 1945:

**1369**    . . . 9. *Day-time cinema 'Biograph', Münzstr. 9.* On 23.11 once again a large number of young men, mostly healthy-looking foreigners, was observed standing at the ticket office. The programme began with the newsreel, which was completely ignored. Most of the audience chatted together as if they were in a pub, others went out and then a new lot came in. When it was pointed out that the newsreel was a serious matter they just laughed. It was pointed out that one was not allowed to come in during the newsreel. In other daytime cinemas it was noted that the majority of the audience consisted of foreigners, whereas if Germans, such as soldiers on leave or people passing through, arrived just before the show was due to begin, they could not get in and had to go away again.

10. *Foreigners.* It crops up again and again in conversations with Berliners that we are treating the foreigners too well. Also, people often come across foreigners at night in blocks where they don't belong. It is assumed that they are looking for suitable burglary targets. Nobody dares say anything, since (particularly in the light of recent newspaper reports) one has to reckon on being gunned down.

In a tram an Italian was reminded that it was good manners to give up his seat to an elderly lady. In response to his remark that he'd paid his fare too, other German women took the Italian's side. It was not his fault that he was here; he'd had to go to war just like the German men. One had to be humane because we already had enough guilt on our shoulders through our treatment of the Jews and the Poles which would rebound on us.

In the Leipziger Strasse a German worker complained that Polish women and girls were having to lay paving stones.

Some, perhaps many, Germans had come to feel complicity with the regime and so to some extent bound to it. This sense of partial complicity, together with a deep physical and emotional exhaustion after five years of war, helped to produce a paralysing belief that there was no alternative, an impression reinforced but not created by the Allied doctrine of 'unconditional surrender'. This situation was vigorously exploited by Nazi propaganda in its attempt to persuade the German people that they were indeed bound to the regime in a *Schicksalsgemeinschaft,* a 'community of fate'. There was thus a widespread feeling that there was no real alternative to staying on board and going over the waterfall together.

Underpinning this national solidarity was the local solidarity at the workplace and in local communities. It was this solidarity that the Allied bombing campaign had been designed to break However, despite their demoralizing impact described above, like the much less extensive raids in Britain, ultimately they failed in their main objective. Workers continued to return to work after the raids. Even foreign workers cooperated voluntarily in the firefighting and clearing up afterwards. Only a few took the opportunity to flee. Why was this?

One factor was undoubtedly fear, fear of losing their status as re- served workers and being sent to the eastern front. This need not even be an individual punishment. For, if a plant was unable to keep pro- ducing after a raid, all the workers would inevitably be liable to conscription. However, there were also material benefits to be gained from continuing work. In order to secure their supplementary rations as heavy workers etc. they had to sign on in their plant. In fact some firms provided useful help in dealing with the authorities by bulk-buying various scarce commodities such as bedding. Employers were anxious to keep their workers to avoid being shut down.

Last, but by no means least, there were the psychological benefits from carrying on as before. The ordered routine of work provided a point of stability in a world of increasing chaos and a distraction from having to think about the future. The miner who commented: 'I look forward to the evening with horror. As long as I am at work I don't remember, but when I get home I'm afraid' was a case in point.[3]

Thus, while the extreme situation created by heavy bombing certainly helped to undermine confidence in the regime, as it had been intended to do by the Allied strategists of area bombing, at the same time it created an atmosphere in which people became dominated by the priority of the need to survive from day to day. A new form of greeting emerged, some- times scrawled on walls—BU (*'Bleib übrig'*) 'stay alive', 'be a survivor'.[4]

This priority of survival through a catastrophe, and increasingly one whose end could be foreseen in the not too distant future, reinforced the tendency for people to keep their heads down for fear of the Gestapo and through sheer exhaustion. As the wielder of power the Nazi regime benefited from this mood. As will become clear in the following section, those who tried to opt out of the 'community of fate' by desertion or premature surrender were summarily dealt with by the remaining hardline supporters of the regime. For the Nazis were determined to prevent another November 1918 and to ensure that their fellow Germans went over the waterfall with them.

---

[3] See above, p. 365.
[4] See Werner, op. cit., for illuminating comments on this.

## (ii) The Increased Role of the Party

On 12 September 1944, Allied troops reached the German frontier in the west and crossed it south of Aachen, while the Russians were rapidly approaching East Prussia in the east. The regime responded to this threat with a number of measures all of which had the effect of strengthening the position of the Nazi Party on the home front. Thus on 10 September 1944, in his role as Reich Interior Minister, Himmler issued the following orders to prepare for the defence of the Reich:

**1370**   Secret!

1. The Party is responsible for ensuring that all sections of the population on the home front are in the highest state of readiness for action appropriate to the war situation. The agencies of the state must support the Party in this. The supreme Reich authorities will set the main guidelines for the state sphere on principle. The initiatives of the agencies at Gau level must take place within the framework of these guidelines. The Reich Defence Commissioners are to ensure a uniform implementation of the state defence matters in their areas and will coordinate them in the closest cooperation with all agencies of the Party, the State, local government and the Wehrmacht. The individual measures are to be prepared with the aid of the responsible authorities and agencies in order to prevent duplication and to maximize the utilisation of existing experience.

2. The following guidelines are to be followed:

(a)   In the event of the construction of fortifications being ordered in a Reich defence area, the Gauleiter is responsible for those tasks which are not purely connected to the military construction project. The state agencies must support the Gauleiters in the carrying out of the construction projects, in the allocation of workers through emergency conscription, and through the provision of food and temporary accommodation for the workers . . .

(b)   The Party is responsible for the evacuation of the population. This also applies to the ethnic alien population. It should prevent the population from flooding back in an unregulated and precipitate fashion.

Ten days later Hitler issued the 'second edict concerning the exercise of command in areas where military operations are taking place'. Among the extensive powers it granted to the Reich Defence Commissioners, i.e. Gauleiters, the most remarkable was in IVc:

**1371**   I hereby cancel my edict on the command structure in an area of operations within the Reich of 13 July 1944 and decree the following in the event of an advance into Reich territory by enemy forces:

I. The civil administration will remain fully intact within the area of operations. State and local authorities will continue to carry out their duties.

II. I shall appoint the Reich Defence Commissioner for the area of operations.

III. 1. The Reich Defence Commissioner will exercise executive power within the area of operations. The Reichsführer SS Heinrich Himmler, is responsible for the uniform execution throughout the Reich of all the measures to be taken by the Reich Defence Commissioner in accordance with this edict, subject to my general guidelines.

2. The military commander will direct his requests for measures in the civilian sphere arising out of military requirements to the Reich Defence Commissioner in the area of operations.

3. The supreme military authorities are empowered to give any instructions which may be required for the carrying out of their military tasks in the immediate combat zones directly to the civilian agencies of the state and local authorities. The boundaries of these zones will be determined by the military commander in agreement with the Reich Defence Commissioner . . .

IV. 1. In exercising executive power within the area of operations the Reich Defence Commissioner may:

(a) implement all measures required by the enemy threat.

(b) issue directives to all state and local authorities.

(c) issue regulations with the force of law.

___

Finally, the growing desperation of the regime during September 1944 became most apparent in the creation of the German Volkssturm, a kind of Home Guard. However, once more, significantly, it was the Party which was given the leading role in its organization, although Himmler was responsible for its deployment. Hitler issued the following Decree concerning the Establishment of the German Volkssturm on 25 September 1944:

**1372**    As a result of the failure of all our European allies, after five years of the toughest fighting, on some fronts the enemy is near or on the German borders. He is building up his forces to smash our Reich and to destroy the German nation and its social order. His final goal is to exterminate the German people.

As in the autumn of 1939, once again we stand alone confronting our enemies. At that time, through the first major deployment of the strength of the German nation, we succeeded within the space of a few years in solving the most important military problems and in securing the existence of the Reich and, therefore, of Europe for years ahead. While the enemy now believes that he is about to strike the final blow, we are determined to carry out the second major engagement of our nation. Building only on our own strength, we must and we shall succeed, as in the years 1939–41, not only in breaking the enemy's drive to destroy us but in turning them back again and keeping them from the Reich for long enough to ensure that a peace can be achieved that will secure the future of Germany, of its allies, and therefore of Europe.

We shall confront the well-known determination of our Jewish-international enemies to destroy us with the total commitment of all Germans.

I hereby order:

1. The German Volkssturm is to be established in all the Gaus of the Greater German Reich from all men aged between 16 and 60 who are capable of bearing arms. It will defend the homeland with all weapons and all means that seem appropriate.

2. The establishment and leadership of the German Volkssturm will be undertaken in their Gaus by the Gauleiters. For this purpose they will use above all the ablest organisers and leaders of the proven organizations of the Party, the SA, SS, the NSKK,[5] and the HJ.

3. I appoint the Chief of Staff of the SA, Schepmann, as inspector for the training of the Volkssturm in shooting and the corps leader of the NSKK as inspector for training in the skills involved in motorized warfare.

4. During their deployment members of the German Volkssturm will be soldiers within the meaning of the Defence Law.

5. Membership of the members of the Volkssturm in non-professional organizations remains unaffected. However, service in the Volkssturm takes precedence over service in other organizations.

6. As Commander of the Reserve Army, the Reichsführer SS is responsible for the military organization, the training, the arming, and the equipment of the German Volkssturm.

7. The military deployment of the German Volkssturm will occur in accordance with my instructions under the Reichsführer SS as Commander of the Reserve Army.

8. The military regulations governing the implementation of this decree will be issued by Reichsführer SS Himmler as Commander of the Reserve Army. The political and organizational regulations will be issued by Reichsleiter Bormann in my name.

9. The National Socialist Party will fulfil its highest honourable duty to the German people in giving priority to the deployment of its own organizations to bear the main responsibility for this struggle.

———

On the following day, Bormann issued regulations for the implementation of the Führer decree concerning the creation of the German Volkssturm:

**1373**  I  *Organization*

1. The Gauleiters should immediately register all compatriots of between 16 and 60 years of age who are capable of bearing arms for the establishment of the German Volkssturm. In recruiting for the German Volkssturm account

---

[5] The NSKK = Nationalszialistische Kraftfahrer Korps (The Nazi Motor Corps).

should be taken of the need to maintain functions vital to the war effort, namely armaments, food supplies, transport and communications.

2. The German Volkssturm will be established by the political cadres at district and local level. It will be divided into companies and battalions.

3. The Gauleiters must appoint an aide to deal with all the questions to do with the establishment of the German Volkssturm in the Gaus and with the selection of battalion and company commanders even if they carry out these tasks themselves. As a loyal, fanatical and therefore committed National Socialist with experience as a military leader and a real organizer, he must be in a position to establish the units and select the suitable leader personalities as rapidly as possible in accordance with his Gauleiter's instructions. I am to be informed of the names of these aides, together with their Party and military records, by teleprinter by 30 September 1944.

4. The political cadres will hand over the leadership and training to political leaders,[6] members of formations, police officers or other suitable compatriots with front-line military experience. The selection is to be made according to the following principles:

Loyalty to the Führer, steadfastness and military competence.

II  *Equipment and training*

1. The subordinate offices of the Reichsführer SS, as Commander of the Reserve Army, will carry out the arming of the German Volkssturm in cooperation with the Gauleiters.

2. The German Volkssturm will be trained, in particular, in combating tanks and in infantry warfare. In the border Gaus training will take place in the fortified area. The members of the Volkssturm will train at least once a week. If possible this should not interfere with work commitments.

III . . .

1. The members of the German Volkssturm count as combatants within the definition of the Hague Convention on land warfare . . .

▬

The second set of regulations implementing the Führer decree concerning the establishment of the German Volkssturm was dated 12 October 1944:

**1374**    The Gauleiters and district leaders [of the NSDAP] are responsible for the leadership, the recruitment and the organization of the German Volkssturm . . .

---

[6] i.e. office holders within local and district branches of the Party.

1. The German Volkssturm comprises four sections. This division is only significant for the internal organization; it does not manifest itself to outside observers.

2. The first contingent of the German Volkssturm comprises—in so far as not otherwise stated—all members of the age cohorts from 1928 to 1884 who are capable of combat and whose deployment is possible without damaging vital functions on the home front.

3. The second contingent of the German Volkssturm comprises—in so far as not otherwise stated—all members of the age cohorts 1928 to 1884 capable of combat who are employed in vital plants, in the communications or transport sectors or other vital functions on the home front and, therefore do not belong to the first section. Consideration must be given to the vital tasks of the various sectors in the organization of the second contingent and in the arrangement of its duties. A flexible organization should be ensured for the second contingent in consultation with the economic agencies and the middle levels of the special administrative agencies.

4. The third contingent of the German Volkssturm comprises all members of the age cohorts 1928 to 1925 in so far as they have not yet been called up for active service.

5. The fourth contingent of the German Volkssturm comprises all those who are not capable of combat and who can be used for guard and security duties . . .

*Structure*

In the Volkssturm there will be no large staffs or a back-up organization [*Etappe*] . . .

3. The group commanders will be appointed by the company commander, the platoon commanders by the battalion commander, the company commander by the district leader [of the NSDAP] and the battalion commander by the Gauleiter. The appointments will be provisional and confirmation is dependent on performance . . .

4. The structure of the German Volkssturm corresponds to the territorial organisation of the NSDAP. The coherence of the local branch should be maintained as far as possible . . .

*Uniforms and equipment*

1. All Volkssturm soldiers irrespective of rank will provide their own uniforms and equipment . . .

The speech by the Reichsführer SS Heinrich Himmler, at its first parade, on 18 October 1944, in which he tried to draw a parallel between the Volkssturm and the role of the Landsturm in the defeat of Napoleon through a highly coloured account of the Landsturm, illuminates the mentality behind the formation of the Volkssturm. The speech, which was widely reported, was held appropriately in an East Prussian town:

**1375**     Today 131 years ago, on the evening of 18 October 1813, after bloody and highly uncertain fighting, the Battle of the Nations came to a victorious conclusion near Leipzig. As a result of this success Germany's soil was swept clean of Napoleon's apparently invincible armies. From the standpoint of military theory, the war, which was begun in the spring of 1813 by brave freedom fighters from all the German tribes and by bold revolutionary officers and generals of the Prussian army like Blücher, Scharnhorst, Gneisenau and Clausewitz, was a hopeless one. Many German states were allied to the Corsican; Prussian fortresses were occupied by French garrisons; Prussia's army was a small, insignificant rump army.

Although he had already suffered a serious defeat in Russia in 1812, an attack on Napoleon was, from a rational point of view, impossible and, for the allegedly 'sensible' politicians and military leaders, irresponsible. But the freedom fighters, who successfully asserted their will against the timid, calculating, too clever by half people and compelled the vacillating king to found the Landsturm, had faith in their hearts and made the decision to fight and put it into effect, a decision which history proved the right one. The Prussian Landsturm formed itself from peasants and townsmen who had never served in the army. But their determination to establish the organization was uncompromising. They refused to recognise any obstacles as insuperable.

In the Decree on the Landsturm it says in §43:

The weapons will be all kinds of flintlocks with and without bayonets, pikes, hay forks, sabres, flails, scythes etc.

Out of the rabble emerged battalions, out of poorly armed people fanatical freedom fighters. With the words fatherland, fatherland on their lips the Landwehr and Landsturm attacked the better-armed, highly trained and militarily experienced enemy in every province and drove the French opponent out of Prussian territory in month-long battles involving numerous reverses.

The culmination came with the famous Battle of Leipzig fought in the first instance by the Prussian and Austrian soldiers. In six months the Landsturm had created from an apparently hopeless situation the preconditions for the Army to achieve the important strategic victory at Leipzig which, in turn, was the basis for the liberation of the Fatherland and for winning the whole war.

Now, on 18 October 1944, the anniversary of the Battle of the Nations at Leipzig, our Führer and Supreme War Lord Adolf Hitler, has called upon all German men between 16 and 60 years of age who are at home and capable of bearing arms to fight in the German Volkssturm to defend the homeland.

———

Most of the Volkssturm units served locally in their village or urban district constructing tank traps or guarding installations. Some First Contingents were, however, drafted to the front. The Volkssturm turned out to be more of a 'Dad's Army' operation than a serious fighting force. Its members often lacked military experience, were poorly trained and badly equipped, while morale was generally low, except among some of the Hitler Youth in the Third Contingent, who were excited and flattered by the idea of defending the fatherland. Many men tried to get placed in the Second Contingent, where they were less likely to have to go into action, on the grounds of the importance of their job to the war effort. Despite the instruction to the contrary, the Volkssturm leadership acquired elaborate staffs and what it lacked in effective military action was made up for by a frenzied issuing of memos and instructions and the holding of parades with rousing speeches by the local Party bosses. The 'Dad's Army' quality of the Volkssturm comes out in the following post-war account of a Volkssturm man from the rural district of Fürth in northern Bavaria:

**1376**  I was never a soldier and so hadn't a clue about anything and when they gave out the 'uniforms' in Neustadt they wanted to give me an SA coat as well as a Labour Service uniform. I didn't accept the coat with the excuse that it was too big. In reality I didn't like the lots of Party badges on it. I myself wasn't a Party member. Then they gave me another coat, this time a Labour Service one; but this was too small. But I took it anyway and cut all the buttons off. I got ticked off for that at our first parade. A mate of mine who was also involved sewed the buttons back on the outside edges, otherwise I couldn't have worn the coat. If I held my breath I could even button it up. After three hours' instruction from a holder of the Knight's Cross we were 'ready for action' to use a bazooka. Our platoon had twenty-three members and for these twenty-three we even got given twelve weapons. I didn't get one and didn't make any effort to. I didn't understand how they worked in any case.

The growth in power of the Party at the expense of the state and local government administration was in part a reflection of the growing extremism of the Nazi leadership. As the war situation became more and more critical, so they tended increasingly only to trust the true believers and to assume that only they had the commitment and will-power to restore the situation. However, this development was also in part the result of the growing regionalization and localization of German government resulting from the progressive breakdown of the infrastructure of communications and administration as a result of the air war, evacuations and invasion. In this situation the Party cadres seized the initiative, an initiative left to them by government authorities who felt uncertain within a chaotic situation in which they received little or no support from their superiors. However, the lines of responsibility between the Party, state, and military authorities were so confused and the response of the population so uncooperative that, in practice, the power of Party officials and agencies to operate effectively was often much less than is suggested by official decrees and directives. Thus the

SS Obergruppenführer and General of the Waffen SS Gottlob Berger, head of the SS Main Office, complained to Himmler on 17 November 1944 about 'unclear lines of responsibility between the organs of the Reich Defence Commissioner and the military agencies as well as a lack of drive', and stressed 'the need to secure smooth and positive cooperation between the Reich Defence Commissioners and the military agencies. It does not matter so much who implements a necessary measure, what matters is that it is carried out'.[7]

## (iii) The Development of Morale: September 1944–March 1945

The months September–December 1944 saw a stiffening of German resistance, particularly on the western and Italian fronts, and this helped to improve morale somewhat, an improvement that was assisted by the announcement, on 8 November 1944, of the launching of V2 rockets against London, although in fact they had already been in operation for eight weeks. Such actions encouraged people to feel that all was not lost and gave supporters of the regime some ammunition against the increasingly numerous sceptics. This partial restoration of morale reached its height with the initial success of the German Ardennes offensive in December. However, with the smashing of that offensive by the end of December and with the launching of a major Soviet offensive in the middle of January, which rapidly engulfed East Prussia, during February–March 1945 morale sagged alarmingly. The following report is by 'Special Project Berlin':

**1377**  23 February 1945

*General.* The mood and attitude have not significantly changed from last week. The hope that it won't come to a real fight for Berlin has increased. In general, one can note a certain fatalism, a certain indifference and gloominess. 'We'll just have to put up with what happens. We can't alter it.' Everything which seems like propaganda or is referred to as such is openly rejected. People want to hear positive facts. Every report of a success, even only a small one, has a beneficial effect. Although many people still talk as if the war can no longer be won, people generally still hope for a change for the better. People are also clear about the terrible consequences which a German defeat would have. The same topics crop up at the forefront of every conversation: the eastern front, the terror bombing, new weapons, the food situation, the coal shortage, and the armaments industry. Since the large plants can only work a few days in the week,

---

[7] Bundesarchiv Potsdam Film No. 3975.

there are already thousands of unemployed in the Reich capital . . . A particular worry is, as before, the enemy air offensive. How can Germany stand it in the long run? How can it go on? What does the leadership think?

There is talk of treason and sabotage in connection with the reverse on the eastern front. It is said that many have been caught and sentenced. The shootings are carried out in Ruhleben and high-ranking officers are also involved.

Many Berliners take the view that it is not right for the press to carry so many reports of atrocities by the Bolsheviks. People were already very upset and frightened. Furthermore, people are asking why the Wehrmacht report kept quiet about the loss of Budapest for three days although the facts themselves were already known (enemy broadcasts). Similarly, the results of the Yalta conference were not published at once. Despite this, there was a lot of talk about them including details which could only have come from foreign broadcasts. The view was expressed that this 'tactic of silence' simply encouraged people to show weakness of character by listening to foreign broadcasts.

Despite the in general good attitude of the great mass of Berliners, doubts and concerns were generally and ever more openly expressed and, in the case of certain individuals, defeatist remarks. Two examples: People standing in the queue of the food section of Karstadt department store on 14.2 were discussing when the war might end. An elderly man said: 'Not for a long time.' For the Führer was so stubborn that he'd rather let everything collapse than make even an attempt to give way. The ones who suffered were the people who now, in addition to the bomb attacks, were certainly going to have to suffer hunger. Any sensible person must recognize that it was all up. Only the Führer seemed to believe in a miracle. On 13.2 a bombed-out businessman was complaining in the Lenaustrasse Ration Card office in Neukölln in the presence of many people who were waiting that it was madness to continue the war; people shouldn't tell him that the food supply was worse in 1917/18 than it was now.

——

On 27 March 1945, the Stuttgart SD reported as follows:

**1378** The Wehrmacht reports of 25 and 26 March 1945 have shocked the population and, in so far as they are concerned with the *western front,* are the focus of every conversation. The general view is that for us in Württemberg the war will soon be over. Some compatriots are shocked by the Anglo-American advance on the western front, but the majority of the population here are 'almost glad that for them this war is at last coming to an end'. Nobody is afraid of the Americans and English—they are convinced that our area will be occupied by the Americans. As a result, the compatriots are determined to stay here. It is not as if the Russians are coming but a cultured nation and they know from the areas that have already been occupied that the population are doing well under the Allied occupation . . .

Nobody believes any more in a change in the fortunes of war. Who can stop the enemy, who after all has already been able to come so far, from rolling even further into German territory? People believe that the enemy armies are now charging ahead and that one can no more stop them here than one could stop them in France. If one or two people believe—and this is, as I said, very rarely the case—that the enemy can still be beaten with new weapons which will come into use in 5–6 weeks' time, then they simply meet with pitying smiles. It is no more possible to deploy new weapons now than it was before because they don't exist, as industrialists above all point out. Where could the weapons have been produced? And, above all, what could they have been produced with? There was no transport available for the raw materials or for the individual finished parts which were made in other plants. Furthermore, there was the question when could the new weapons have been produced since there were air raid warnings the whole day. But the main point was the shortage of raw materials and the transport situation . . .

In view of the very serious situation compatriots are also again concerned about the Party people who are still home and who do not even go out with the Volkssturm. They argue that this is the final proof that with them it was all just talk because now is the time for them to put their love of Germany to the test and put it into effect if they are not going to miss their last chance to do it. For example the population of Stuttgart-Uhlbach is very annoyed about the fact that the representative of the deputy local branch leader, Party comrade Baumgärtner (the brother of the Gau official, Baumgärtner), who is the representative of the head of the Gau Staff Office, Baumert, received his call-up papers on three occasions and was also released by his factory and yet still has not gone off. If a compatriot asks Frau Baumgärtner why her husband once again did not have to obey his call-up, she replies that after all they have contacts.

'And then people wonder why we have lost the war. Could we ever have won the war with these people?' (War invalid white-collar worker.)

———

On 31 March 1945 the 'Special Project Berlin' reported:

**1379**    In three windows of the KdW [Kaufhaus des Westens, a big department store], Tauentzienstrasse, there are posters with the words: 'Berlin is working, fighting, and standing'. Three ordinary, decently dressed women going past made the following remarks: Nothing but propaganda! 'Berlin is standing' is a boast. A few more attacks [like those] of yesterday [18.3] and the only thing standing will be ruins. Also, there's not much work in Berlin, otherwise we wouldn't have been released from conscription. We didn't see much evidence of Berlin fighting last Sunday. The Americans dropped their bombs wherever they wanted. They flew all over the sky without any opposition, without any fighting.

———

## (iv)  The Regime's Response to Declining Morale

Essentially, the regime adopted three different approaches to the problem of trying to sustain morale on the home front, none of which proved very effective.

## (a) Atrocity propaganda

The first method was to emphasize the threat posed by invasion not only to the future of the German nation, but more concretely and specifically to individual Germans' lives and property. In particular, the 'Bolshevik' threat was continually stressed in slogans and newspaper reports which depicted in lurid detail the atrocities committed by the advancing Russian troops. This undoubtedly had some effect in stiffening military resistance in the east, but, as far as the home front was concerned, it contributed to the flood of refugees which fled from east to west. Finally, it had the unanticipated effect of prompting many Germans to reflect on German behaviour in the occupied territories, towards the Jews, and on the regime's behaviour towards some Germans, as was pointed out in the report of the Stuttgart SD of 6 November 1944:

**1380**    The examples [of Soviet atrocities] from Nemmersdorf in East Prussia have in many cases achieved exactly the opposite of what was intended. Compatriots say it is shameless to make so much of them in the German press . . .

'What does the leadership intend by the publication of such pictures as those in the *NS-Kurier* on Saturday? They should realise that the sight of these victims will remind every thinking person of the atrocities we have committed in enemy territory, even in Germany itself. Have we not murdered thousands of Jews? Don't soldiers again and again report that Jews in Poland have had to dig their own graves? And how did we treat the Jews in the concentration camp in Alsace [Natzweiler/Stutthof]? Jews are human beings too. By doing all this we have shown the enemy what they can do to us if they win.' (The opinion of numerous people from all classes of the population.)

'Our leaders should be ashamed of publishing such pictures. How did our people deal with their own German compatriots who were put into concentration camps because they had different political viewpoints? Weren't our SS people frequently even more cruel towards Germans, their own fellow citizens, than the Russians have been towards the East Prussians? We have shown the others how to deal with political enemies. One cannot reproach the Russians for being as cruel towards other nations as our people are towards Germans.' (A secretary, Party member; similar views held by compatriots of all classes and professions.)

The fact that these views were widely held is confirmed by the following report by the Special Project Berlin for the week of 23–9 March 1945:

**1381**    . . . 16. On 19.3 two workers are chatting in Spandau-West, Moltkestr. They are in agreement that we ourselves are to blame for this war because we treated the Jews so badly. We needn't be surprised if they now do the same to us. Similar remarks can often be heard.

## (b) Exhortation

The second method of trying to sustain morale on the home front was through exhortation. This was directed in particular at the Nazi Party cadres and membership in an attempt to recreate the atmosphere of the 'time of struggle' before 1933 and to revive the will and determination shown by the Party in its drive for power. Although, of course, these exhortations reflected the growing military and industrial impotence of the Nazi leadership, nevertheless, the emphasis placed upon and the rhetoric used in these appeals with which the German population was bombarded during the last few months of the war also reflected the leadership's genuine belief in the invincible power of the will to achieve any goal, a marked feature of the ideology and mentality of the Third Reich. The following appeal by Bormann to the Party in association with the twenty-fifth anniversary of the announcement of the Party programme on 20 February 1920 is one such exhortation:

**1382**     Now everybody, soldiers and civilians, men and women, young and old are joined together as fighters in the front line. Now, as in the time of struggle for power within Germany, the wheat will be separated from the chaff. Now it will become clear whether we are calculating fellow-travellers or selfless confessors . . . Now nothing less than our lives are at stake and this decision no longer leaves room for scruples about the choice of means or for any attempt to modify the notion of self-sacrifice. Anyone who still thinks of himself, anyone who still toys with the idea of retreat or withdrawal is a traitor to his nation and a murderer of our women and children. Anyone who never gives up fighting and would rather die among the ruins than retreat a single step is invincible and before this immutable law of nature all calculations, all seemingly clever attempts to weigh things up for and against totally fail. For at all times it was the strong and not the cowardly, the unshakeable and not the vacillating, the fighter and not the anxious calculator who in the end proved to be in the right and secured victory. The Führer demands and the nation expects from every Party leader that he will hold on to the end and never think of his own salvation. Party comrades must prove themselves to be an unshakeable rock in the war's breakers, for now, instead of supposed privileges, there is the uncompromising demand for them to do their duty. Every man who can bear arms must hurl his body against the enemy for the sake of the homeland and to protect the women and children. Every woman must submit to the needs of the hour and courageously accept every hardship, every separation from home and husband, every demand on her spiritual and physical strength, if necessary danger and the threat of death as well. Party comrades! Our lives and those of our children are at stake. There is no sacrifice of which this goal is not worthy. Now the fate of Germany is in the hands of every individual. He who wants victory must know how to make sacrifices ruthlessly and to die decently. He who tries to save his life is certain of death if only through the sentence of the people. There is only one possibility of staying alive: the willingness to die fighting and thereby to secure victory.

___

### (c) Terror

However, the regime by no means confined itself to exhortation in trying to keep the German population in line. As the Allies entered German territory it became increasingly concerned about people's response. Already on November 1944, SS Obergruppenführer Gottlob Berger was reporting to Himmler from the Rhineland that 'in many cases' the attitude of the population was giving 'cause for concern. This manifests itself in the refusal to accept the evacuation measures and in people's intention of letting the war "roll over them".'[8] On 8 March 1945 a Party Chancellery minute noted the following:

**1383** According to a phone call from Gauleiter Stöhr at 18.10, the following sentence occurs in the situation report from Army Group Gustav: 'The hostile attitude of the population in the Moselland is complicating the self-sacrificing struggle of our troops.' The army has made the same point to me today through its representative. In one place in Gau Moselland the population prevented their own troops from shooting. In another place the peasants attacked soldiers who were trying to detonate charges with pitchforks. A troop of soldiers who had struggled to our lines after escaping from the Americans was received with shouts of 'You're prolonging the war.'

___

In the middle of January 1945 Himmler issued the following proclamation:

**1384** I request my German compatriots, and particularly the women, not to show inappropriate sympathy for shirkers who attach themselves to refugee treks or otherwise move from east to west. Men who absent themselves from the front do not deserve a single piece of bread from the homeland. German women, girls in particular, are well placed to appeal to these men's sense of honour, to remind them of their duty and, instead of sympathy, to show them contempt and to drive incorrigible cowards to the front with their floor cloths.

Everybody should do their duty. After tough weeks of being tested, the day will come on which we shall move out from the position which we are now securing and liberate the German Gaus once again. We have the sacred conviction and the knowledge that God, who has imposed such burdens upon us, yet at the same time, when Bolshevism was preparing to storm Europe, sent us the one man who could avert the threat, our leader Adolf Hitler, will in the end give the victory to our brave heroic people, and thus to the true Europe.

___

[8] Ibid.

Soon, however, words were followed by deeds. On 14 February, the Reich Justice Ministry sent the following telegram to the Public Prosecutor at the Special Court in Hirschberg:

**1385** *Re: Death sentence on town council official Otto S. from Dombrowa on 6.2.45 (Special Court).*

Publication in the press will be organized here. You should publish it on posters with the following text:

'The Special Court in Hirschberg has sentenced town council official Otto S. from Dombrowa to death. S. left his official post near the front line at a time of danger without sufficient reason and without the knowledge of his superiors. The sentence has been carried out by firing squad.'

Furthermore, please send the documentation and a copy of the sentence without delay.

On the very next day, the Reich Justice Minister, Dr Thierack, regulated the procedure for dealing with those who attempted to avoid their 'duties to the community' from 'cowardice or selfishness' with the following decree on the establishment of drum-head courts martial dated 15 February 1945:

**1386** The toughness of the struggle for the continued existence of the Reich requires from every German the utmost determination and commitment. Anyone who attempts to avoid his duties to the community, in particular, anyone who does so from cowardice or selfishness, must at once be brought to account with the requisite harshness so that the Reich does not suffer damage from the failure of one individual. Thus, the following is decreed on the orders of the Führer in agreement with the Reich Minister and Head of the Reich Chancellery, the Interior Minister and the Head of the Party Chancellery:

I. Drum-head courts martial will be established in Reich defence districts threatened by the enemy.

II. 1. The court martial will consist of a judge as chairman as well as a political leader[9] or leader of a formation of the NSDAP[10] and an officer of the Wehrmacht, the Waffen SS or the police as assessors.

2. The Reich Defence Commissioners will nominate the members of the court and designate a public prosecutor as prosecuting counsel.

III. 1. The courts martial are competent to try all those offences which jeopardize German combat strength or determination.

2. The procedure will be governed by the Reich Code of Criminal Procedure.

IV. 1. The courts martial will impose a death sentence, grant an acquittal, or transfer the case to the ordinary courts. The sentence will require confirmation

---

[9] e.g. a cell leader.
[10] e.g. the SA, SS, HJ.

by the Reich Defence Commissioner who will determine the place, the time and the form in which it is to be carried out [i.e. hanging or shooting].

2. If the Reich Defence Commissioner cannot be reached and the sentence needs to be carried out immediately then the prosecutor will carry out this function.

V. The Reich Justice Minister, in association with the Reich Interior Minister and the Head of the Party Chancellery, will issue the regulations to supplement, alter and implement this decree.

VI.   The decree will come into effect on being broadcast on the radio.

Bormann wrote to the Gauleiters in the west that this would be a 'weapon with which to destroy all national pests' and 'in the Führer's view' should be used 'ruthlessly and without consideration for persons or offices'.[11]

In the meantime, a new organization had been established with the aim of waging a secret war against both the occupying forces and those who collaborated with them—the *Werwolf*. In practice it never amounted to much, although it did murder the mayor of Aachen for collaborating with the Americans:

**1387**    *Order of the Deputy Chief of the Army General Staff, Lieutenant-General Walther Wenck to all Army Groups, 6.2.45*

1.   The organization *Werwolf* (shortened to W-Organization) has been established under the leadership of the General Inspector for 'Special Defence' (SS Obergruppenführer Prützmann) to carry out special tasks behind enemy lines.

2.   This organization will be deployed in small groups ('W' Groups) and only on German soil. As a result of the movement of the fronts towards Reich territory, these groups will come under the operational areas of the Wehrmacht.

3.   The 'Special Staff Prützmann' has appointed special 'W' liaison officers to keep the Ics[12] of the Army Groups and Armies informed about the presence and deployment of 'W' Groups. They will be deployed by the 'Special Staff Prützmann' in consultation with the Wehrmacht commands. They will co-ordinate their activities with other units deployed behind enemy lines (SS Pursuit Units, Front Reconnaissance and Patrol Commandos.)

However, by March at the latest, the vast majority of the German population had concluded that defeat was inevitable and had no desire

---

[11] See K.-D. Henke, *Die amerikanische Besetzung Deutschlands* (Munich 1995), p. 845. This section owes much to this excellent book.

[12] The Ics were the Intelligence officers.

for a fight to the death, which would see the destruction of their homes and livelihoods. Thus, they tried as best they could to thwart the regime's self-destructive policies by sabotaging the defensive measures taken in their localities and surrendering their towns and villages without a fight. In this they often had the cooperation of the local Wehrmacht commanders and even on occasion of the local Party leaders whose loyalty to the community of which they were a part finally overrode their Party loyalty in a situation in which resistance was obviously futile. In most cases, however, the local Nazi leaders simply fled.

However, attempts to sabotage the defences or to surrender were fraught with danger because some military commanders, above all the Waffen SS units, were much more hardline in their attitude.[13] One example was the XIII SS Army Corps under Lieutenant-General Max Simon which terrorized south-west Germany during March–April 1945. There were also so-called 'mobile courts martial' which roved around the countryside summarily executing alleged defeatists. One such was led by a brutal army officer, Major Erwin Helm, who travelled around in a grey Mercedes with a notice 'Mobile Court Martial' on it. Several hundred brave German citizens fell victim to this terror during the last weeks of the war. These courts martial acted completely arbitrarily without even the minimal legal safeguards laid down in Thierack's February decree. At the same time, in a spasm of paranoia and brutal vindictiveness Gestapo units were murdering in total probably several thousand foreign workers, mainly Russians and Poles, for alleged subversion.

The following three documents give some insight into this period. The first is an order of Field Marshal Walter Model, Commander of Army Group B, to the commander of the Wehrmacht military police, dated 18 March 1945:

**1388**    Cases have come to light in which inferior elements among the civilian population have adopted a defeatist, in individual cases a hostile attitude. Thus, it has been reported that at one place an explosive charge was removed from a bridge by German civilians. In other cases soldiers have been asked to change into civilian clothes and give up the struggle.

For a soldier there is only one way of dealing with such cases and that is to use the harshest measures to continue the struggle and to get one's way in any situation in accordance with the task one has been given. I am, therefore, giving the following orders:

---

[13] On this see Henke, op. cit., pp. 844ff.

Those who carry out subversive actions or try acts of sabotage on the battle-field, whether they are soldiers or civilians, are to be shot. Where the military situation permits the offenders should be brought before a drum-head court martial. Civilians should only be sentenced by the head of the court martial.

———

The second is a radio message from the commander of the order police to the Governor [*Regierungspräsident*] of Lower Bavaria, dated 3 April 1945:

**1389**      The Reichsführer SS has issued the following instructions:

1. At the present moment in the war everything depends on maintaining a stubborn, uncompromising determination to carry on.
2. The toughest measures should be taken against the hanging out of white flags and the opening up of tank barriers which have already been closed.
3. Where a white flag appears all the male persons of the house concerned are to be shot. There must be no hesitation in carrying out these measures.

———

The third is the correspondence between the Gauleiter of Franconia, Karl Holz, and Hitler about the defence of Nuremberg in April 1945:

**1390**      15 April 1945

My Führer, the final struggle for the city of the Reich Party rallies is beginning. The soldiers are fighting bravely and the population is proud and steadfast. I will stay, fight and die in this most German of all cities. In these hours my heart beats more than ever in love and loyalty to the magnificent German Reich and nation. The national socialist idea will win and overcome all devils.
The National Socialists of Gau Franconia greet you with German loyalty.

16 April 1945
I thank you for your exemplary behaviour. You thereby inspire not only the compatriots from your own Gau who all know you, but many millions of other Germans.
    That fanatical struggle is beginning which reminds us of our own struggle for power. However great the superiority of our enemies may be at the present time, in the end—just as happened before—it will collapse.
    With heartfelt gratitude I am rewarding your heroic actions by conferring on you the golden cross of the German Order.

[Signed] ADOLF HITLER

———

## (v) Hitler's 'Destruction Order' of 19 March 1945

Ever since the summer of 1944, when German forces began withdrawing from France, Hitler had favoured a 'scorched earth' approach. However, this had met with much scepticism from German government departments. On 24 September 1944 one official in the Economics Ministry noted: 'Ten days ago Führer statement reported by Bormann 'create scorched earth'. Reference to Gneisenau. One should look that up. All departments agree that this line of policy can't be implemented . . . In practice one won't be able to find the people to carry it out. No peasant will destroy his farm and his cattle, no worker will destroy his factory.'[14] In fact, the the Armaments Minister, Albert Speer, persuaded Hitler to adopt a policy of 'crippling' plant and installations by removing key components rather than destroying them with the argument that Germany would need them when it reoccupied the territory having driven the enemy back again. Speer continued to apply this argument when German territory began to be invaded in the autumn–winter of 1944. At this stage, it appears that Speer genuinely believed that Germany had a reasonable chance of reversing the course of the war and did everything possible to achieve that. However, the collapse of the Ardennes offensive at the end of December 1944 and the Russian offensive in January 1945 convinced him that the game was up. From February 1945 onwards, Speer's determination to thwart the destruction of German industry was motivated partly by genuine concern for the future of the German people and partly no doubt by an attempt to rehabilitate himself in the eyes of Germany's conquerors. However, at his night-time conference on 19 March, Hitler responded to news of the defeatism of the Saar population by ordering their immediate evacuation and went on to issue his notorious 'destruction order' which reversed the 'crippling strategy'. At the same time, Speer was stripped of his authority in this sphere:

**1391** The fight for the existence of our nation compels us to exploit all means, even within the Reich, which can weaken the enemy's fighting capacity and impede his further progress. Every possibility of doing lasting damage to the striking power of the enemy must be taken advantage of. It is an error to believe that after the recapture of lost areas it will be possible to use undamaged or only temporarily paralyzed transport, communications, industrial and supply installations again for one's own purposes. During his retreat the enemy will leave only scorched earth behind him and will abandon all concern for the population.

I therefore give the following instructions:

1. All military, transport, communication, industrial and supply installations as well as equipment within the Reich which the enemy might use for the continuation of his struggle now or in the future must be destroyed.

---

[14] Quoted in Henke, op. cit., p. 424.

2. The destruction of all military objects, including transport and communication installations, is the responsibility of the military command posts; that of all industrial and supply installations as well as other material is the responsibility of the Gauleiters and Reich Defence Commissioners. The troops must give Gauleiters and Reich Defence Commissioners the necessary assistance for the execution of their task.

3. This order must be made known to all commanders as quickly as possible. Orders to the contrary are invalid.

Speer responded to this order by, in effect, defying Hitler. After a tense interview on 29 March, on the same night Speer wrote him a letter containing the following extracts:

**1392** . . . When I gave you my memorandum on 18 March, I was convinced that the conclusions which I was drawing from the present situation for the maintenance of our national energy would definitely meet with your approval. For you yourself had already on one occasion determined that, in the event of a lost war, it was the task of the leadership to preserve it from a heroic end.

However, that evening you made statements to me from which—unless I have misunderstood you—it is clear and evident that if the war is lost the nation will also be lost. This fate is unavoidable. It is not necessary to show any consideration for the bases, which the people will need for their very primitive further existence; on the contrary, it is better to destroy even these things. For the nation has showed itself to be the weaker one and the future belongs exclusively to the stronger eastern nation. Those remaining after the struggle are in any case the less valuable ones because the good ones have been killed.

On hearing these words I was deeply shocked. And when, a day later, I read your destruction order and shortly afterwards the tough evacuation order, I interpreted these as the first steps in the implementation of these intentions.

Until then, I had believed with all my heart in a successful conclusion to this war. However, I can no longer believe in the success of our good cause if, during these decisive months, we simultaneously and systematically destroy the foundations of our national life. That is such a great injustice towards our people that fate could no longer favour us . . . I therefore beg you not to carry out a step so destructive of the nation.

If you could decide to do this in some form then I would regain the faith and courage with which to continue working with the greatest energy.

You will be able to understand my inner conflict. I cannot work to my full capacity and generate the necessary confidence if, at the same time as I am demanding from the workers their fullest commitment, I am preparing to destroy the foundations of their lives.

In a second interview on the following day, 30 March, Speer managed to persuade Hitler to restore his authority and to issue the following directive, which effectively countermanded the destruction order:

**1393**  To ensure the uniform implementation of my decree of 19 March 1945, I hereby issue the following instructions:

1. The orders issued for destroying industrial installations are aimed exclusively at preventing the enemy from utilizing those installations and facilities to supplement their combat strength.

2. No measures may be taken which would impair our own combat strength. Production must be continued until the last possible moment even at the risk that a plant may fall into enemy hands before it can be destroyed. Industrial installations of all kinds, including food production plants, may not be destroyed until they are directly threatened by the enemy.

3. Although bridges and other transportation installations must be destroyed in order to deny the enemy their use for a prolonged period, the same result can be achieved with industrial installations by crippling them.

The total destruction of especially important plants will be ordered on my instructions by the Reich Minister of Armaments and War Production (e.g. munitions plants, essential chemical plants etc.).

4. The signal for crippling or destroying industrial complexes and other plants will be given by the Gauleiter and Reich Defence Commissioner.

5. Implementation will be undertaken solely by the agencies and organs of the Reich Minister for Armaments and War Production. All the agencies of the Party, the state, and the Wehrmacht are to assist them as required. The Reich Minister of Armaments and War Production may, on my authorization, give instructions for implementation. He may issue detailed regulations on procedures to the Reich Defence Commissioners.

6. These guidelines apply to plants and installations in the immediate war zone.

[Signed] ADOLF HITLER

Speer used this order to block attempts by fanatical Party officials to destroy industrial plant and vital infrastructure. However, given the fact that both employers and workers had a strong vested interest in saving their plants and took vigorous steps to protect them, Speer's role as the 'saviour of the German economy' appears to have been somewhat exaggerated—not least by himself!

## (vi)  The Allied Invasions—West and East

There were no 'typical' experiences for Germans in the Allied invasions in the sense that there was such a variety of different individual experiences depending on so many factors, not least sheer luck. However, the following two accounts are not untypical of the very different experiences shared by west and east Germans. The first is a post-war account by the mayor of the village of Frankenbach in northern Württemberg:

**1394** [15]    1. Frankenbach, 3km north-west of Heilbronn, on the state road which links Heilbronn with Heidelberg and Frankfurt was involved in the wartime events affecting the metropolis of the *Unterland* [i.e. Heilbronn], but got off quite lightly, although initially things looked very threatening.

2. The disintegration and collapse of the front in France was already visible some weeks beforehand. Columns of vehicles and individual ones—some of them lorries, some cars—full of officers and often piled with 'booty' came through here.

3. For many weeks our area had been visited by 'The Merry Eight'—fast enemy bombers—once, twice, sometimes three times a day. There was no sign of any German defences. They could seek out their targets unhindered and 'at their leisure' and drop their bombs. One could follow their path from Kl. Feldle or from Hipper and observe their often fearful effect. Hardly had the siren sounded and the enemy was there.

4. 'We are the merry eight, we come early or late, greet us with tears or a smile, we have a date.'[16] That was written on a note that they dropped in the neighbourhood.

5. One could tell how bad things were for the German troops in terms of their lack of reinforcements, apart from anything else, by the fact that troops never once came through *here* on the way to the front.

6. On one of the last days in March a small unit of about 80 men arrived. On the following day they marched on in the direction of Mergentheim. Their leader, a first lieutenant, was still absolutely convinced of our final victory to be brought about by the new secret weapon for whose deployment so many gullible people here were also hoping . . .

8. The many wounded German soldiers who came through here were completely unarmed and mostly without baggage, indeed often hobbling on crutches. They had been sent off from hospitals and dressing stations in the west in order to seek medical treatment in Heilbronn or further south. The population did what it could for these unfortunates. One was painfully reminded of the pictures by Artur Kampf of the Grande Armée retreating from Russia in 1812 . . .

On 27 March, a large number of high-ranking Party functionaries came through here on foot. They came from Baden and the Palatinate. According to their statements, they wanted to try and link up with some troops.

9. On 27.3 a troop of German prisoners—soldiers and officers—came through under heavy German guard. This sad procession made a particularly disturbing impression on the inhabitants here.

10. The general disintegration was also shown by the fact that on 29.3 the concentration camp Neckargartsch opened the doors to freedom for its in-

---

[15] I am grateful to Dr Jill Stephenson for providing me with this document.
[16] 'Wir sind die lustigen acht. Wir kommen bei Tag und bei Nacht, ob ihr weint oder lacht.'

mates.[17] Various small groups, presumably organized on the basis of nationality, came through the village.

11. Apart from great stress, one saw in the faces of the inhabitants during these days worry and concern and great uncertainty about what to do. Should one obey the orders issued in the last few days by the 'butcher of Heilbronn', the notorious [NSDAP] district leader, [Michael] Drauz? Should one blow up the mill, the pumping station, the reservoir and other important buildings? Or should the peasants even carry out Drauz's orders to pack bag and baggage on to their horse carriages and ox carts and head for the Löwenstein hills and from there even further east or south-eastwards? None of the people left house and home. Indeed, during the last two days—Easter Sunday and Monday—many people had suddenly been overcome by a kind of sensation-seeking, particularly since reliable reports suggested that the Americans had treated the civilian population humanely wherever they had been.

12. On Good Friday, the Volkssturm people put up tank traps in the Frankfurter Strasse, as well as in the Grossgartacher Strasse between Hoffmann and Hagele. Also a pear tree was felled at the exit of the Hohle near Kirchhausen. It too was intended to block the entry of the enemy tanks. After four days these 'traps', which were completely useless, had to be removed again by the inhabitants on the orders of the Americans.

And so Easter Monday arrived, 2 April. The author was on the northern wall of the cemetery to look out for 'friends and enemies'. Between 15.00 and 16.00 the sound of machine gun fire could be heard coming closer from the direction of Kirchhausen, at first isolated bursts and then soon more concentrated fire. A single German artillery piece went through our village before 15.30 in the direction of Heilbronn.

A few German soldiers came across the fields from the direction of Hipfelhof. Tense from battle, some of them exhausted having given their all. They withdrew hurriedly in the direction of Heilbronn. One heard the occasional salvo of enemy artillery from the direction of Schlupf. A big shell screamed overhead and landed in Knöllberg. A huge mushroom cloud shot up. That was the Americans' warning shot. A second enemy shell hit the roof of the Crown and caused not inconsiderable damage. Nobody was injured.

People had made sure that the Volkssturm's bazookas had no detonators. That may have saved our village from disaster.

The deputy branch leader left the village on a motorbike, together with the First Volkssturm leader, shortly before the Americans arrived. A second Volkssturm leader, who the day before had been full of how he was going to destroy every American tank, had suddenly lost his heroic heart and stayed at home.

Large numbers of enemy tanks drove over the fields between Kirchhausener Strasse and Rotbach and came to the Wilhelmstrasse. And before one knew it there was tank after tank on the Frankfurter and Neckargartacher Strasse. But a huge white flag was waving from the church tower.

---

[17] Clearly a branch camp of one of the major camps.

An officer climbed out of the first enemy tank in front of the town hall. He went up to a citizen standing in front of his house and spoke to him in [the local] pure Swabian dialect. In earlier years this soldier had often visited his father's homeland for lengthy periods. And his father came from Nörtingen.

The American tanks pushed forward towards Böckingen. But there they encountered resistance and so they returned here.

It was a great piece of luck for our village that the Hipperg was not occupied by German troops. Otherwise our nice village would presumably within a short time have become a heap of ruins.

———

The second is a post-war account by a teenage girl of her experiences moving from the far east of East Prussia to the West as part of a huge migration in which at least a million Germans died.

**1395**     On 21 January 1945 Lyck had to be evacuated. With a heavy heart my mother, my sister and I parted from my father, who had been conscripted into the Volkssturm, and from my grandparents. My grandfather intended to take as much of our movable property as possible and join a trek going in the direction of Arys.

With the last trains that were running we reached Rastenburg, where we stayed the night with relatives. Radio reports which we heard indicated that East Prussia was in a hopeless position. In the meantime, the bad news had reached us that trains to the Reich had stopped running. Now we had only one thought: to leave Rastenburg as quickly as possible. My grandmother stayed behind with her maid because she was determined to wait for her husband. We were never to see her or my grandfather again.

At the goods depot in Rastenburg we three found refuge in a goods wagon which was carrying soldiers in the direction of Königsberg. We had to leave the train at Korschen but had the good fortune to get another goods train which was full of refugees. Babies died of hunger on the way.

On 26 January 1945 we reached Bartenstein. In their fear of falling into the hands of the Russians many refugees had managed, despite the extreme cold, to attach themselves to the transport in open coal wagons. On arrival in Bartenstein many had already frozen to death.

We stayed the night in our wagon. At first light, we left the goods train and looked for lodgings in Bartenstein. A female acquaintance from Lyck joined us with her son, who had been caught out by the flight in the middle of his convalescence. It was minus 25 degrees centigrade. While we were going along we heard the dull grumble of artillery fire in the distance.

We found lodgings and rested for two days. But then the approaching artillery fire drove us out of the town of Bartenstein. With the sound of endless explosions as our own troops blew up the Wehrmacht installations in Bartenstein, we found our way out of the town amidst a headless mass of fleeing people. We soon realized that we could not make any progress along the roads. We went back to the goods depot and again had the incredible luck of finding a wagon which was only partly full. Our acquaintance got hold of a railwayman who, after much persuasion, agreed to couple this wagon onto a hospital train which was going to Braunsberg. The railwaymen looked after the refugees in a very touching way and provided them with food and drink.

On 1 February the transport arrived at Braunsberg. Here we received the latest bad news. Allenstein had fallen. Elbing was occupied by the Russians. We were in a huge trap!

The Russian planes endlessly attacked Braunsberg with bombs and gunfire. A friend of my mother's took us in. Many refugees had to camp in cellars. We stayed in Braunsberg until 10 February 1945. Every day we had to queue for food and coal. The drone of the Stalin organs [Katyusha rockets] was getting nearer and nearer. Electricity and gas had packed up. There were ten of us living in a single room. We decided to leave the town. We left our domicile in the dark with a few other fellow-sufferers and groped our way forward in a pitch black night along a road covered with human and animal corpses. Behind us was Braunsberg in flames; to the left of us—around Frauenburg—bitter fighting was going on.

Around midnight—completely filthy and muddy—we reached the little town of Passarge on the Frische Haff. We awaited the new day in a barn. Hein P., our convalescent soldier, could go no further. We had to leave them behind as we continued on foot to the Frische Haff. In the meantime, the icy cold had been replaced by constant rain. We reached the banks of the Frische Haff, paused for a few minutes and then began the walk to the opposite spit of land.

The ice was brittle and in places we had to wade through water 25cm deep. We kept testing the surface in front of us with sticks. Numerous bomb craters forced us to make detours. Often one slipped and thought one had had it. Our clothes, which were soaked through, only allowed us to move clumsily. But fear of death made us forget the shivering which shook our bodies.

I saw women performing superhuman feats. As leaders of the treks they instinctively found the safest paths for their wagons. Household goods were strewn all over the ice; wounded people crept up to us with pleading gestures, hobbling on sticks; others were carried on small sledges by their comrades.

Our journey through this valley of death took us six hours. We reached the Frische Haffe. We sank into a fitful sleep in a tiny chicken coop. Our stomachs grumbled with hunger.

On the next day we walked on in the direction of Danzig. On the way we saw gruesome scenes. Mothers in a fit of madness threw their children into the sea. People hanged themselves; others fell upon dead horses, cutting out bits of flesh and roasting them on open fires. Women gave birth in the wagons. Everyone thought only of himself—no one could help the sick and the weak.

In Kahlberg we placed ourselves at the disposal of the Red Cross and cared for the wounded in the Beach Hall. On 13 February 1945 we went on board a ship as nursing personnel. On the next day we reached Danzig-Neufahrwasser and disembarked.

On 15 February 1945 we were assigned accommodation in Zoppot. My mother, sister and I could barely keep upright. Nevertheless, we dragged ourselves to the goods depot in Gotenhafen where, for the third time, by a stroke of luck we managed to get a military postal wagon to take us to Stolp

(Pomerania). On 19 February as nursing personnel on a hospital train we arrived via Hanover in Gera in Thuringia, where we were put up by relatives. It was 28 February 1945. On that day our flight from East Prussia was over.

━━━━

## (vii)  The Last Throes of the Nazi Leadership

While other Nazi leaders—Göring and Himmler, for example—had clearly begun to think about their future position in a post-Nazi world, Hitler and Goebbels remained locked into the world which they had created. For both, Frederick the Great of Prussia had become the historical model against whom they measured their own situation, and it was his experience in the Seven Years War, of being saved by the transformation in the diplomatic situation caused by the death of Catherine the Great, which they hoped would be repeated in the form of the disintegration of the Allied coalition. When news of the death of President Roosevelt reached Goebbels on 12 April he had told Hitler excitedly that this was their equivalent to the death of Catherine. The detachment of Goebbels from reality is apparent from the fact that, a week later, he was still ruminating on Frederick. One of Goebbels' closest colleagues in the Propaganda Ministry, Hans Fritzsche, recorded the following encounter with Goebbels on 20 April 1945:

**1396**     . . . On this day, Hitler's last birthday, Goebbels suddenly quoted from memory a piece from Carlyle's *History of Frederick the Great*. It's the place where Carlyle describes Frederick's worries before the last decisive turn in the Seven Years War, before the death of the Tsarina and the resultant exit of Russia from the coalition against Prussia. At that point, Carlyle steps out of the role of historian and becomes so to speak himself an actor in the drama. He urges the hero of his story to have courage, reassures him and tells him that fate has just decided in his favour—he just does not know it yet. Goebbels then added to this quotation, such an impressive one in this situation, the comment that certain negotiations were about to be concluded.

━━━━

On the following day, Goebbels revealed more of his thoughts to Fritzsche. His remarks provide an exceptional insight into Goebbels' character and his involvement with the Nazi project. At the same time, however distorted his views, it is arguable that he had a point in his argument that men like Fritzsche and even, to an extent, the German people had signed up for a gamble which hadn't come off and now had to take the consequences:

**1397** . . . His comments represented a total attack on the old officer corps and 'Reaction'. He accused them of treason, treason which they had been committing for years . . .

I objected to these ideas, this cheap excuse . . .: 'Even if there may have been instances of treason, are they not more than compensated for by the loyalty, the self-sacrifice, the courage and the faith of the German people, who have shown more good will towards their government than any other nation has ever done.'

My interjection had an unexpected effect. Dr Goebbels abandoned the topic of the alleged treason of the officer corps and turned, initially full of cynicism and then of anger, against the German people. He accused them of cowardice. He began his reply to my objections with the words: 'What can I do with a nation whose men don't even fight any more when their women are being raped.' Then, he poured out justifications for his and Hitler's policies. It was no longer the old virtuoso performance of cold, calculating eloquence. It was an outburst in which for the first time ideas poured out with elemental force, which hitherto have been most carefully hidden, even denied.

For then he suddenly announced: the German people had failed. In the east they were fleeing, in the west they were preventing the soldiers from fighting and receiving the enemy with white flags.

His pale face became red with anger, his veins and his eyes bulged as he shouted that the German people deserved the fate that awaited them. And then, suddenly, calming down, he remarked cynically that the German people had after all chosen this fate themselves. In the referendum on Germany's quitting the League of Nations they chose in a free vote to reject a policy of subordination and in favour of a bold gamble. Well, the gamble hadn't come off.

I sprang up and wanted to interrupt him. I wanted to say that he himself and Hitler had never interpreted that referendum in terms of a choice between peace and an adventure. On the contrary, both had always insisted that they only wanted to use peaceful means in Germany's fight for existence.

Dr Goebbels saw my gesture but didn't let me speak. He too got up and continued to speak: 'Yes, that may surprise some people, including my colleagues. But have no illusions. I never compelled anybody to work for me, just as we didn't compel the German people. They themselves gave us the job to do. Why did you work with me? Now, you'll have your little throat cut.'

Striding towards the door, he turned round once more and shouted: 'but the earth will shake when we leave the scene . . .'.

---

Finally, on 29 April, during the night before his death the following afternoon and having just married Eva Braun, Hitler dictated the following testaments:

**1398** *ADOLF HITLER*
*My private Will and Testament*

As I did not consider that, during the years of struggle, I could take the responsibility of contracting a marriage, I have now decided, before the closing of my earthly career, to take as my wife the girl who, after many years of loyal friendship, of her own free will, in order to share her destiny with mine, entered this city when it was almost completely besieged. At her own wish she is going to die with me as my wife. It will compensate us for what we have both lost through my work in the service of my people.

What I possess belongs, in so far as it has any value, to the Party; should that no longer exist, to the state; should the state also be destroyed, no further decision of mine is necessary.

My pictures, in the collections which I have bought over the years, have never been collected for private purposes, but only for the extension of a gallery in my home town of Linz on the Danube.

It is my most sincere wish that this bequest be duly executed.

I nominate as my Executor my most faithful party comrade, Martin Bormann.

He is given full legal authority to make all decisions. He is permitted to take away everything that has sentimental value or is necessary for the maintenance of a modest simple life, for my brothers and sisters, also above all for the mother of my wife and my faithful co-workers who are all well known to him, principally my old secretaries, Frau Winter etc., who have for many years aided me by their work.

I myself and my wife, in order to escape the disgrace of deportation or capitulation, choose death. It is our wish to be burnt immediately on the spot where I have carried out the greatest part of my daily work in the course of twelve years' service to my people.

Berlin 29 April 1945, 4 a.m.                    [Signed] A. HITLER

As Witness: [Signed] NICOLAUS VON BELOW[18]
As Witnesses: [Signed] MARTIN BORMANN
          [Signed] DR FUHR

### *ADOLF HITLER*
*My political Testament*

More than thirty years have now passed since in 1914 I made my modest contribution as a volunteer in the First World War that was forced upon the Reich. In those three decades I have been actuated solely by love and loyalty to my people in all my thoughts, acts and life. They gave me the strength to make the most difficult decisions which have ever confronted mortal man. In these three decades I have spent my time, my working strength and my health.

It is untrue that I or anyone else in Germany wanted the war in 1939. It was desired and instigated by those international statesmen who were either of Jewish descent or worked for Jewish interests. I have made too many offers for the control and limitation of armaments, which posterity will not for all time be able to disregard, for the responsibility for the outbreak of this war to be laid on me. I have, moreover, never wished that after the first fatal world war a second

---

[18] Nicholas von Below was the Luftwaffe adjutant in Hitler's headquarters and a confidant of Speer.

against England, or even against America, should break out. Centuries will pass away, but out of the ruins of our towns and monuments hatred will grow for those finally responsible whom we have to thank for everything, International Jewry and its accomplices.

Three days before the outbreak of the German–Polish war I proposed once more to the British ambassador in Berlin a solution to the German–Polish problem, similar to that in the case of the Saar district, under international control. Nor can this offer be denied. It was rejected only because the leading circles in English politics wanted war, partly on account of the business they hoped to gain by it and partly under the influence of propaganda organized by International Jewry.

I also made it quite plain that, if the nations of Europe are again to be regarded as mere shares to be bought and sold by these international conspirators in money and finance, then Jewry, the race which is the real criminal in this murderous struggle, will be saddled with the responsibility. I further left no one in doubt that this time millions of children of Europe's Aryan peoples would not die of hunger, millions of grown men would not suffer death, nor would hundreds of thousands of women and children be burnt and bombed to death in the towns, without the real criminal having to atone for this guilt, even if by more humane means.

After six years of war, which despite all setbacks will one day go down in history as the most glorious and valiant demonstration of the purpose of a nation's life, I cannot forsake the city which is the capital of this Reich. As our forces are too small to make any further stand against the enemy attack on this place and our resistance is gradually being weakened by men who are as deluded as they are lacking in initiative, it is my wish, by remaining in this city, to share my fate with those millions of others who have taken upon themselves to do the same. Moreover, I do not wish to fall into the hands of the enemy, who is looking for a new spectacle organized by the Jews for the amusement of their hysterical masses.

I have decided, therefore, to remain in Berlin and there of my own free will to choose death at the moment when I believe the position of the Führer and Chancellor can itself no longer be held. I die with a happy heart, conscious of the immeasurable deeds and achievements of our soldiers at the front, our women at home, the achievements of our farmers and workers, and the work unique in history, of our youth who bear my name.

That from the bottom of my heart I express my thanks to you all is just as self-evident as my wish that you should, because of that, on no account give up the struggle, but rather continue it against the enemies of the Fatherland, no matter where, true to the creed of the great Clausewitz. From the sacrifice of our soldiers and from my own unity with them unto death will in any event spring up in the history of Germany the seed of a radiant renaissance of the National Socialist movement and thus of a true community of nations.

Many of the most courageous men and women have decided to unite their lives with mine unto the very last. I have begged and finally ordered them not to do this, but to take part in the future battle of the nation. I beg the heads of the Army, the Navy and the Air Force to strengthen by all possible means the spirit of resistance of our soldiers in the National Socialist sense, especially bearing in mind that I myself also, as founder and creator of the movement, have preferred death to cowardly abdication or even capitulation.

May it become, at some future time, part of the code of honour of the German officer, as it is already in our Navy, that the surrender of a district or of a town is impossible, and that the leaders here, above all, must march ahead as shining examples, faithfully fulfilling their duty unto death.

*Second part of the political Testament*

Before my death I expel the former Reich Marshal Hermann Göring from the Party and deprive him of all rights which he may enjoy by virtue of the decree of 29 June 1941 and also by virtue of my statement in the Reichstag on 1 September 1939.[19] I appoint in his place Grand Admiral Dönitz, President of the Reich and Supreme Commander of the Armed Forces.

Before my death I expel the former Reichsführer SS and Minister of the Interior, Heinrich Himmler, from the Party and from all offices of State. In his stead I appoint Gauleiter Karl Hanke as Reichsführer SS and Chief of the German Police,[20] and Gauleiter Paul Giesler as Reich Minister of the Interior.[21]

Göring and Himmler, quite apart from their disloyalty to my person, have done immeasurable harm to the country and the whole nation by secret negotiations with the enemy, which they conducted without my knowledge and against my wishes, and by illegally attempting to seize power in the state for themselves.

In order to give the German people a government composed of honourable men, a government which will fulfil its pledge to continue the war by every means, I appoint the following members of the new cabinet as leaders of the nation:

| | |
|---|---|
| Reich President: Dönitz | Economics: Funk |
| Reich Chancellor: Dr Goebbels | Agriculture: Backe |
| Party Minister: Bormann | Justice: Thierack |
| Foreign Minister: Seyss-Inquart | Education and Public Worship: |
| Interior Minister: Gauleiter Giesler | Dr Scheel |
| War Minister: Dönitz | Propaganda: Dr Naumann |
| C.-in-C. of the Army: Schörner | Finance: Schwerin-Krosigk |
| C.-in-C. of the Navy: Dönitz | Labour: Dr Hupfauer |

---

[19] Hitler had appointed Göring as his deputy to succeed him in the event of his death in his Reichstag speech on the outbreak of war. Hess had been appointed second in line. After Hess's flight to Scotland in 1941 Hitler had issued a decree confirming Göring's position as his deputy and successor.

[20] Karl Hanke was Gauleiter of Lower Silesia and had been instrumental in organizing the remarkable defence of Breslau, which was besieged by Russian troops for several weeks.

[21] Paul Giesler had replaced Adolf Wagner as Gauleiter of Munich-Upper Bavaria after the latter's death in 1944. He was a fanatical Nazi.

Reichsführer SS and Chief of the       Munitions: Saur
German Police: Gauleiter Hanke        Leader of the German Labour Front
                                                          and Member of the Reich Cabinet:
                                                          Reich Minister Dr Ley

Although a number of these men, such as Martin Bormann, Dr Goebbels etc., together with their wives, have joined me of their own free will and did not wish to leave the Reich capital under any circumstances, but were willing to perish with me here, I must nevertheless ask them to obey my request, and in this case set the interests of the nation above their own feelings. By their work and loyalty as comrades they will be just as close to me after death, as I hope that my spirit will linger among them. Let them be hard, but never unjust, above all let them never allow fear to influence their actions, and let them set the honour of the nation above everything in the world. Finally, let them be conscious of the fact that our task, that of continuing the building of a National Socialist state, represents the work of the coming centuries, which places every single person under an obligation always to serve the common interest and to subordinate his own advantage to this end. I demand of all Germans, all National Socialists, men, women, and all the men of the armed forces, that they be faithful and obedient unto death to the new government and its president.                    ·

Above all I adjure the leaders of the nation and those under them to scrupulous observance of the laws of race and to merciless opposition to the universal poisoner of all peoples, International Jewry.

Given in Berlin, this 29th day of April 1945, 4 a.m.

[Signed] ADOLF HITLER

Witnessed by:
DR JOSEF FUHR        WILHELM BURGDORF[22]
MARTIN BORMANN     HANS KREBS[23]

▬

Goebbels then appended the following addendum to Hitler's testament, rhetorical to the last:

**1399**   In the event of the collapse of the defence of the Reich capital, the Führer has ordered me to leave Berlin and participate as its leading member in a government nominated by him. For the first time in my life I must categorically decline to obey an order of the Führer. My wife and children join with me in this refusal. In the first place, on the grounds of humanity and personal loyalty we could never bring ourselves to abandon the Führer in his darkest hour; secondly, for the rest of my life I would consider myself a dishonourable renegade and a blackguard who, having lost his respect for himself would also lose the respect of his people.

---

[22] General Wilhelm Burgdorf was head of the personnel department at OKW and the Wedrmacht adjutant at the Führer Headquarters.
[23] General Hans Krebs who had recently succeeded Guderian as Chief of the General Staff.

I believe that, in doing this I am performing the best service for the German people for, in the difficult times ahead, good examples are more important than men. For this reason, I am expressing, together with my wife, my irrevocable decision not to leave the Reich capital and rather to end, at my Führer's side, a life which for me personally has no more value if I cannot use it in the service of the Führer and at his side.

---

## List of Sources

1368 Ursula von Kardorff, *Berliner Aufzeichnungen aus den Jahren 1942–1945* (Munich 1962 ), pp. 214–15.

1369 V. Berghahn, 'Meinungsforschung im 'Dritten Reich'. Die Mundpropaganda-Aktion der Wehrmacht im letzten Kriegsjahr', *Militärgeschichtliche Mitteilungen*, (1967), p. 100.

1370 H. Michaelis et al., *Ursachen und Folgen. Vom deutschen Zusammenbruch 1918 und 1945 bis zur staatlichen Neuordnung Deutschlands in der Gegenwart,* Vol. 20, (Berlin n.d.), p. 555.

1371 W. Hubatsch, *Hitlers Weisungen für die Kriegführung. Dokumente des Oberkommandos der Wehrmacht 1939–1945* (Munich 1965), pp. 339–40.

1372 *Reichsgesetzblatt,* I (1944), pp. 253–4.

1373 Michaelis, op. cit., pp. 568–9.

1374 Ibid., p. 570–2.

1375 Ibid., p. 572–4.

1376 M. Broszat, E. Fröhlich and A. Grossmann, eds., *Bayern in der NS-Zeit,* Vol. 4, (Munich 1981), pp. 648–9.

1377 Berghahn, op. cit., pp. 104–5.

1378 Staatsarchiv Ludwigsburg (StAL) K 110 Bü 58.

1379 Berghahn, op. cit., pp. 104–5.

1380 *Aus deutschen Urkunden* (Allied publication n.d.), pp. 275–6.

1381 Berghahn, op. cit., p. 119.

1382 K.-D. Henke, *Die amerikanische Besetzung Deutschlands* (Munich 1995), p. 828.

1383 Bundesarchiv Berlin (BAB) NS 6/135.

1384 W. Hofer, ed., *Der Nationalsozialismus. Dokumente* (Frankfurt/M 1957), p. 255.

1385 BA Potsdam Reichsjustizministerium Gen. Nr. 980/1, p. 125.

1386 Hofer, op. cit., p. 254.

1387 Michaelis, op. cit., Vol. 22, p. 21.

1388 W. Runge and W. Schumann, eds, Dokumente zur deutschen Geschichte 1943–1945 (Berlin 1973), p. 108.

1389 Ibid., p. 110.

1390 Michaelis, op. cit., Vol. 23, pp. 73–4.

1391 Nuremberg Document (ND) Speer 25.

1392 Michaelis, op. cit.,Vol. 23, pp. 534–7.

1393 Ibid., p. 538.

1394 Hauptstaatsarchiv Stuttgart (HStAS) J 170 Bü 8.

1395  Michaelis, op. cit., Vol. 22, pp. 388–90.
1396  Hildegard Springer, ed., *Hier spricht Hans Fritzsche. Nach Gesprächen, Briefen und Dokumenten* (Stuttgart 1949), pp. 23–4.
1397  Ibid., pp. 28–9.
1398  Nuremberg Document 3569–PS.
1399  M. Domarus, *Hitlers Reden und Proklamationen 1932–1945,* Vol. 2, (Munich 1965), p. 2241 n. 213.

# Bibliography

R. Andreas-Friedrich, *Berlin Underground* (New York 1947).

M. Balfour, *Withstanding Hitler* (London 1988).

M. Balfour and J. Frisby, *Helmuth von Moltke: A Leader against Hitler* (London 1972).

J.W. Baird, *The Mythical World of Nazi Propaganda 1939–1945* (Minneapolis 1974).

E.R. Beck, *Under the Bombs: The German Home Front 1942–1945* (Lexington, Ky. 1986).

E. Bethge, *Dietrich Bonhoeffer: Theologian, Christian, Contemporary* (London 1970).

C. Bielenberg, *The Past is Myself* (London 1970).

M. Broszat, 'The Concentration Camps', in H. Krausnick et al., *Anatomy of the SS State* (London 1968).

M. Broszat, *The Hitler State* (London 1981).

L. Burchardt, 'The Impact of the War Economy on the Civilian Population of Germany during the First and Second World Wars' in W. Deist, ed., *The German Military in the Age of Total War* (Leamington Spa 1985), pp. 40–70.

M. Burleigh, ed., *Confronting the Nazi Past: New Debates on Modern German History* (London 1996).

M. Burleigh and W. Wippermann, *The Racial State: Germany 1933–1945* (Cambridge 1991).

T. Charman, *The German Home Front 1939–1945* (New York 1989).

D. Crew, Ed., *Nazism and German Society 1933–1945* (London 1994).

H.C. Deutsch, *The Conspiracy against Hitler in the Twilight War* (Minneapolis 1968).

R.J. Evans, *Rituals of Retribution. Capital Punishment in Germany 1600–1987* (Oxford 1996).

J. Fest, *Plotting Hitler's Death: The Story of the German Resistance* (New York 1996).

H.W. Flannery, *Assignment to Berlin* (London 1942).

A. Fredborg, *Behind the Steel Wall: A Swedish Journalist in Berlin* (New York 1944).

N. Frei, *National Socialist Rule in Germany: The Führer State 1933–1945* (Oxford 1993).

M. Geyer, 'Restorative elites, German society and the Nazi pursuit of war' in R. Bessel, ed., *Fascist Italy and Nazi Germany—comparisons and contrasts* (Cambridge 1996)

M. Geyer and J.W. Boyer, eds, *Resistance against the Third Reich 1933–1990* (Chicago 1992).

J.R. Gillingham, *Industry and Politics in the Third Reich* (London 1985).

H. Graml et al., *The German Resistance to Hitler* (London 1970).

G. Grau, *Hidden Holocaust? Gay and Lesbian Persecution in Germany 1933–1945* (London 1995).

N. Gregor, 'Big Business and the 'Blitzkriegwirtschaft': Daimler-Benz AG and the Mobilisation of the German War Economy 1932–42', *Contemporary European History,* 6:2 (1997).

N. Gregor, *Daimler-Benz in the Third Reich* (New Haven and London 1987).

D.A. Hackett, ed., *The Buchenwald Report* (Boulder, Colo. 1995).

T.S. Hamerow, *On the Road to the Wolf's Lair: German Resistance to Hitler* (Cambridge, Mass. 1997).

E. Hancock, *National Socialist Leadership and Total War 1941–1945* (New York 1991).

M. Harrison, 'Resource Mobilization for World War II: The USA, UK, USSR, and Germany, 1938–1945', *Economic History Review* (May 1988), pp. 171–82.

U. von Hassell, *The Von Hassell Diaries 1938–1945* (London 1948).

U. Herbert, *A History of Foreign Labour in Germany 1880–1980: Seasonal Workers/Forced Laborers/Guest Workers* (Ann Arbor, Mich. 1990).

P. Hoffmann, *The History of the German Resistance 1933–1945* (London 1977).

P. Hoffmann, *Stauffenberg: A Family History 1905–1944* (Cambridge 1995).

E.L. Homze, *Foreign Labor in Nazi Germany* (Princeton 1967).

I. Kershaw, *Popular Opinion and Political Dissent in the Third Reich: Bavaria 1933–1945* (Oxford 1983).

I. Kershaw, *The 'Hitler Myth'. Image and Reality in the Third Reich* (Oxford 1987).

G. Kirwin, 'Allied Bombing and Nazi Domestic Propaganda', *European History Quarterly,* 15 (1985), pp. 341–62.

K. von Klemperer, *German Resistance against Hitler: The Search for Allies Abroad 1938–1945* (Oxford 1992).

M. Kitchen, *Nazi Germany at War* (London 1995).

D.C. Large, ed., *Contending with Hitler: Varieties of German Resistance in the Third Reich* (Cambridge 1991).

L. Lochner, ed., *The Goebbels Diaries* (London 1948).

T.W. Mason, *Social Policy in the Third Reich: The Working Classes and the National Community* (Providence/Oxford 1993).

A. Merson, *Communist Resistance in Nazi Germany* (London 1985).

M. Middlebrook, *The Battle of Hamburg: The Firestorm Raid* (London 1980).

A.C. Mierzejewski, *The Collapse of the German Economy, 1944–1945: Allied Air Power and the German National Railway* (Chapel Hill, NC 1988).

A.S. Milward, *The German Economy at War* (London 1965).

F.R. Nicosia and L. D. Stokes, eds, *Germans against Nazism* (Oxford 1992).

J. Noakes, 'German Conservatives and the Third Reich: An Ambiguous Relationship' in M. Blinkhorn, ed., *Fascists and Conservatives* (London 1990).

D. Orlow, *The History of the Nazi Party*, vol. 2 (Newton Abbot 1973).

R.J. Overy, *Goering: The Iron Man* (London 1984).

R.J. Overy, *War and Economy in the Third Reich* (Oxford 1994).

R.J. Overy, ed., *The Penguin Historical Atlas of the Third Reich* (Harmondsworth 1996).

A. Owings, *Frauen: German Women Recall the Third Reich* (London 1993).

D. Peukert, *Inside Nazi Germany: Conformity, Opposition and Racism in Everyday Life* (London 1987).

M. Roseman, 'World War II and Social Change in Germany', in C. Emsley et al., *War, Peace and Social Change in Twentieth-Century Europe* (Open University Press 1989).

M. Roseman, 'War and the People: The Social Impact of Total War', in C. Townshend, *The Oxford Illustrated History of Warfare* (Oxford 1997).

H. Rothfels, *The German Opposition to Hitler* (London 1948).

L.J. Rupp, *Mobilizing Women for War: German and American Propaganda 1939–1945* (Princeton 1978).

S. Salter, 'The Mobilisation of German Labour 1939–1945', D.Phil thesis (Oxford 1983).

G. Schöllgen, *A Conservative against Hitler. Ulrich von Hassell: Diplomat in Imperial Germany, the Weimar Republic and the Third Reich* (London 1991).

R. Semmler, *Goebbels: the Man Next to Hitler* (London 1947).

M. Seydewitz, *Civil Life in Wartime Germany: The Story of the Home Front* (New York 1945).

W. L. Shirer, *Berlin Diary* (New York 1941).

R. Smelser, *Robert Ley: Hitler's Labour Front Leader* (Oxford 1988).

H.K. Smith, *Last Train from Berlin* (London 1942).

A. Speer, *Inside the Third Reich* (London 1970).

J. Stephenson, *The Nazi Organisation of Women* (London 1981).

J. Stephenson, 'Emancipation' and its Problems: War and Society in Württemberg 1930–1945', *European History Quarterly,* 17 (1987).

J. Stephenson, 'Triangle: Foreign Workers, German Civilians, and the Nazi Regime. War and Society in Württemberg 1939–1945', *German Studies Review,* 15:2 (May 1992), pp. 340–59.

J. Stephenson, 'Nazism, Modern War and Rural Society in Württemberg 1939–1945', *Journal of Contemporary History,* 32:3 (July 1997).

M.G. Steinert, *Hitler's War and the Germans: Public Mood and Attitude during the Second World War* (Athens, Ohio 1977).

F. Taylor, ed., *The Goebbels Diaries 1939–1941* (London 1982).

F. Taylor, *The Berlin Diaries of Marie 'Missie' Vassilitchikov, 1940–1945* (London 1985).

H. Trevor-Roper, ed., *The Goebbels Diaries: The Last Days* (London 1978).

G. Van Roon, *German Resistance to Hitler: Count von Moltke and the Kreisau Circle* (London 1971).

D. Welch, *Propaganda and the German Cinema* (Oxford 1983).

D. Welch, ed., *Nazi Propaganda* (London 1983).

M. Wolff-Mönckeberg, *On the Other Side: To My Children from Germany* (London 1979).

# Index

There are three levels of entry in this index. The main entries are in alphabetical order, while second and third level entries are in page number order. Main entries are repeated at the top of a column when the associated sub-entries continue into that column.